CRIMINALITY IN CONTEXT

PSYCHOLOGY, CRIME, AND JUSTICE SERIES

Cop Watch: Spectators, Social Media, and Police Reform
Hans Toch

Criminality in Context: The Psychological Foundations of Criminal Justice Reform
Craig Haney

Effects of Parental Incarceration on Children: Cross-National Comparative Studies
Joseph Murray, Catrien C. J. H. Bijleveld, David P. Farrington, and Rolf Loeber

Rehabilitating Sexual Offenders: A Strength-Based Approach
William L. Marshall, Liam E. Marshall, Geris A. Serran, and Matt D. O'Brien

Violent Men: An Inquiry Into the Psychology of Violence, 25th Anniversary Edition
Hans Toch

CRIMINALITY IN CONTEXT

The Psychological Foundations of Criminal Justice Reform

CRAIG HANEY

AMERICAN PSYCHOLOGICAL ASSOCIATION
Washington, DC

Published by
American Psychological Association
750 First Street, NE
Washington, DC 20002
https://www.apa.org

Order Department
https://www.apa.org/pubs/books
order@apa.org

In the U.K., Europe, Africa, and the Middle East, copies may be ordered from Eurospan
https://www.eurospanbookstore.com/apa
info@eurospangroup.com

Typeset in Meridien and Ortodoxa by Circle Graphics, Inc., Reisterstown, MD

Printer: Sheridan Books, Chelsea, MI
Cover Designer: Beth Schlenoff, Bethesda, MD
Cover Image: "Gravity" (charcoal and collage on wood) by Jimmy Peña, reprinted with permission.

Library of Congress Cataloging-in-Publication Data

Names: Haney, Craig, author.
Title: Criminality in context : the psychological foundations of criminal justice reform / by Craig Haney.
Description: Washington, DC : American Psychological Association, [2020] | Series: Psychology, crime, and justice series | Includes bibliographical references and index.
Identifiers: LCCN 2019033085 (print) | LCCN 2019033086 (ebook) | ISBN 9781433831423 (paperback) | ISBN 9781433832130 (ebook)
Subjects: LCSH: Criminal psychology. | Criminal justice, Administration of. | Crime prevention.
Classification: LCC HV6080 .H3135 2020 (print) | LCC HV6080 (ebook) | DDC 364.3—dc23
LC record available at https://lccn.loc.gov/2019033085
LC ebook record available at https://lccn.loc.gov/2019033086

http://dx.doi.org/10.1037/0000172-000

Printed in the United States of America

10 9 8 7 6 5 4 3 2 1

To my extraordinary, loving family, without whose unqualified support I would accomplish very little and, most of all, to my wife, Aida, who makes all of the good things in my life so much better.

CONTENTS

SERIES FOREWORD

It is difficult to convey what an honor and a privilege it is to have this title included in American Psychological Association (APA) Books' Psychology, Crime, and Justice series. I began editing this series in 2011 with very specific goals in mind—both overt and covert. The explicit goal was to provide a showcase of how outstanding psychological research is contributing to the study of crime and criminal justice. Haney's encyclopedic synthesis of scholarship across dozens of subfields and drawing on five decades of his own original research and practice certainly achieves this standard.

Behind this, I have another, unspoken ambition for the series as well. As a psychologist working in the field of criminology, I wanted to disprove the absurd stereotype of the "headshrinker" that many of my colleagues have about those of us trained in psychology. We all know this caricature well: psychologists, apparently, are reductionists who love to pathologize, locating all of the problems of the world not on economics, politics, history, or culture but in the space between the ears. If ever there was a psychologist who defies—actually, obliterates—this gross misrepresentation, it is Craig Haney.

Since long before contemporary concerns about adverse childhood experiences (ACEs), trauma-informed practice, or intersectionality, Haney has been at the forefront of researching the situational, environmental, and structural influences on behavior. As an undergraduate, he worked in a mental hospital and talked his way into a graduate seminar taught by Erving Goffman, before studying at Stanford with Walter Mischel, Albert Bandura and, of course, Philip Zimbardo. He was one of the research assistants for David Rosenhan when Rosenhan was doing his renowned research for *On Being Sane in Insane*

Places,[1] and as if that were not enough, as a PhD student, Haney famously conducted and coauthored the authoritative account of the Stanford Prison Experiment with Zimbardo and Curtis Banks.[2]

Such a remarkable background begs the question of whether Haney is the product of all of these experiences or whether something about his own disposition led him to each of these encounters. (Of course, there is little question about which side of this debate Haney supports!) Regardless of how he got there, in the years since these legendary origins, Haney has become a world-leading expert on the impact of solitary confinement, death penalty mitigation, the psychology of imprisonment, racial biases in sentencing, and far beyond.

In this magnum opus, he brings all of this research together in what is surely the most persuasive and elegant articulation of the environmental argument from a psychological perspective written to date. The timing for this work could not be more fortuitous, as trauma has become a hugely popular topic in the field of criminal justice over the past decade—as if it were somehow a new finding that the overwhelming number of people in the justice system have had tragic lives of abuse, neglect, exclusion, and disadvantage. Even prisons have become aware of the need to provide trauma-informed care for those in custody, and this work will provide support for such efforts. Importantly, though, Haney's message here is much more radical than this. Haney is calling not just for trauma-informed therapy but for a trauma-informed system of *justice*. This book develops the trauma argument to its logical conclusion—from the initial stage of acknowledging trauma to developing a framework for proactively preventing the social causes of crime—that fundamentally challenges how we deal with crime in society.

A common criticism of such arguments goes something like this: "Ah, these social structural problems probably do cause crime, but there is not anything that we in criminal justice can do about structural poverty or inequality, so what is the point?" In some of the most powerful sections in the book, Haney gives the lie to this view, demonstrating how the criminal justice system itself systematically contributes to and indeed exacerbates the inequalities experienced by society's most disadvantaged. As Jim Jacobs wrote, "The criminal justice system feeds on itself. The more people who are arrested, prosecuted, convicted, and especially incarcerated, the larger is the criminally stigmatized underclass screened out of legitimate opportunities."[3]

Psychology has played a role, however limited, in this self-fulfilling cycle of stigmatization, exclusion and criminality, and it is essential that psychology play a lead in imagining a way forward. With this remarkable new work, Craig Haney is leading this charge, and I am honored to include it in this series.

Shadd Maruna, PhD, Series Editor
Professor, School of Social Sciences, Education and Social Work
Queen's University Belfast, Belfast, United Kingdom

NOTES

1. Haney, C., Banks, C., and Zimbardo, P. (1973). Interpersonal dynamics in a simulated prison. *International Journal of Criminology and Penology, 1*, 69–97.
2. Jacobs, J. B. (2006). Mass incarceration and the proliferation of criminal records. *University of St. Thomas Law Journal, 3*, 387–420.
3. Rosenhan, D. L. (1973). On being sane in insane places. *Science, 179*, 250–258. http://dx.doi.org/10.1126/science.179.4070.250

PREFACE

The inspiration for this book began more than 40 years ago. I was returning to my university office in Santa Cruz from San Quentin State Prison, in the middle of about a 2-hour drive that I had made many times before. I had just finished an interview with a prisoner housed on California's condemned row, a man sentenced to die for a terrible crime that he had been convicted of committing several years earlier. That day's interview was much like a number of others I had recently done, each time hoping to understand the origins of the violent acts that had brought this man and many others like him to this desolate place. As I thought about the harrowing childhood experiences I had heard about that morning and the way that the damage he suffered in those early years had been so painfully compounded during his adolescence and young adulthood, I was struck with an insight that now seems passé but, at the time, certainly did not. It was the simple realization that the story I had just heard was eerily similar to the ones I had been told by the several other death-sentenced prisoners whom I also had interviewed over the past few months. Their life stories, too, were filled with accounts of abject poverty and neglect, the trauma of severe emotional, physical, and sometimes even sexual abuse, of growing up in households and neighborhoods that were plagued by unemployment, disorganization, and despair, and frequently pervaded by crime and violence. More often than not, they also included tales of neglectful and cruel treatment at the hands of the child welfare and juvenile justice systems, where they had been sent for help, through state "interventions" that—although ostensibly done on their behalf—typically ended up doing more harm than good.

For some of these young men, crime had quickly become the only life they knew. In some cases, it was the "family business," a kind of craft or trade in which their parents, relatives, or older siblings were already deeply immersed. Others—those for whom no such obvious groundwork had been laid—had been forced to set out on their own, devising makeshift survival strategies to negotiate the turmoil and physical dangers of the mean streets on which they were being raised. The troubled behavior that eventually put them on a pathway to prison seemed at first to be little more than a temporary escape route, a way to cope with the pains and setbacks that they were suffering in so many other parts of their lives. Some were lured by the promise of closeness and camaraderie with other alienated and abandoned young boys like themselves, the satisfaction of finding something—even something illegal—that they were rewarded for, or the comfort of connecting with a group of peers who treated them with a modicum of acceptance, loyalty, and caring.

In short, they tried to manage the emotional distress, chaotic circumstances, and thwarted ambitions in whatever ways they could—to dodge beatings and even bullets, to steal in order to eat, or score drugs that gave them a temporary respite from anger, fear, or sadness. Some of their strategies were clever, some were clumsy and ill-conceived. Several of them had turned to the flawed role models that surrounded them, following in whatever footsteps they could find to help navigate the cruel realities that they repeatedly confronted. They struggled to meet these daunting challenges much as other children learn to master algebra or establish a valued friendship or deal with the disappointment of missing their high school prom. Over time, however, their short-term survival strategies turned into longer-term ways of being, ones sometimes embodied and enacted long after they were truly necessary, and that escalated to much more troubled and troubling levels along the way.

At the time I first perceived these surprisingly similar patterns in the life histories I was studying, the commonalities themselves seemed suddenly and clearly evident. Yet, as I tried to locate broader empirical support for the role they played in the development of adult criminal behavior, I found little systematic research on which to draw. To be sure, there was an intuitive sense among many scholars and practitioners that a background of abuse, trauma, and disadvantage was not only regrettable but also formative—that it compromised a young person's later chances in life, increasing their risk of engaging in subsequent criminal behavior. Admittedly, there were *some* studies supporting this reasoned speculation about the likely life-altering effects of these experiences and events. But really solid research that could definitively establish the kind of *long-term* "criminogenic" or crime-inducing patterns that I was seeing was still largely lacking. No one had yet assembled a comprehensive body of hard scientific evidence that clearly and systematically demonstrated the direct links from early childhood trauma, mistreatment, and disadvantage to serious, violent, adult criminal behavior. Moreover, the occasional, suggestive studies that did exist had not yet been well-integrated into anything resembling a coherent, overarching analysis or theoretical framework.

In the years that followed, however, a truly impressive body of research emerged to fill this void. As I continued my own professional work on these issues, carefully examining the social histories and life circumstances of people who had committed the very worst crimes that occur in our society—typically capital murder—I watched with intense scholarly interest as these significant research findings were amassed from within several interrelated disciplines—primarily psychology but also sociology and criminology. They have continued to mount, in a steady stream of methodologically diverse empirical studies that have been conducted by numerous researchers over the last four decades, yielding a highly consistent set of interconnected results. This literature directly addresses the many separate components of the all too common life-long patterns that I have seen reflected in case after case, in the backgrounds and circumstances of so many of the men and women whose lives I have studied and whom I have encountered in places like San Quentin and in numerous other prisons and jails across the country.

We now understand vastly more about these issues than we ever have. We understand—at least in general terms—why crime is more likely to be committed by persons who share certain kinds of backgrounds and social histories than others. We certainly can explain why criminality tends to be so highly concentrated in certain geographical areas, ones with particular socio-demographic and structural characteristics. And we have developed many insights into how these forces interact with one another—why certain traumatic experiences and events so often combine in ways that greatly increase the chances that someone will engage in serious forms of criminal behavior, and what kinds of immediate social circumstances can activate and exacerbate those criminogenic effects.

Notwithstanding this major shift in thinking and the remarkable advances in scientific knowledge on which it is based, there is still a curious and highly problematic disconnect between what we know as researchers and mental health practitioners and what the larger society and institutions of justice routinely—sometimes stubbornly—assume about these issues. That is, these new insights, developed over the last several decades, have created significant gaps between existing scientific knowledge about the origins of criminal behavior, on the one hand, and persistent and prevailing beliefs among members of the public about who commits crime and why, on the other. Perhaps less understandable than continued *public* misunderstandings, these new scientific insights are also clearly at odds with many of the basic operating assumptions that still govern the criminal justice system itself. Indeed, I have written this book to help close some of those important gaps, not only by summarizing and integrating much of that emerging knowledge but also by highlighting its implications for implementing a new framework with which to more justly and fairly assess legal and moral culpability, to more equitably distribute punishment, to achieve alternative and more benign criminal justice outcomes, and to develop truly effective and humane strategies of crime control.

The initial interviews that I conducted in those early years at San Quentin led me to focus systematically on the patterns I saw. As it turned out, I would go on to do these kinds of background "social history" analyses scores of times over the next several decades, often in the unique context of death penalty trials and appeals. Capital cases still represent really the only area of criminal law where this kind of knowledge can be routinely brought to bear, where a person's social history is regarded as legally relevant to the official decision-making process, and where juries and judges regularly rely on them to decide the defendant's fate.[1] That fact—the special legal relevance of the social histories of *capital* defendants—has provided me with a rare opportunity to directly witness and to conduct in-depth analyses of the way that these research findings fit together over a life course, in order to try to understand and explain the lives of many of the persons who have committed very serious violent crimes.

Yet the research I will review in the chapters that follow applies with equal force and validity to criminal behavior more generally, not just to death penalty cases. Indeed, the substantial empirical data and numerous theoretical insights can provide the basis for a major shift in the way criminal behavior is understood, judged, and addressed. I argue in the pages that follow that this new framework represents the psychological foundation for the widespread and long overdue criminal justice reform that is finally underway in the United States.

NOTE

1. See, e.g., Haney, C. (1995). The social context of capital murder: Social histories and the logic of capital mitigation. *Santa Clara Law Review, 35*, 547–609.

ACKNOWLEDGMENTS

Writing a book provides a rare opportunity—even a responsibility—to pause and reflect on where all these ideas came from. Intellectual origin stories are always subjective and, for that reason, suspect. I am sure that mine is no exception. However, especially at later stages of a career, when opportunities to publicly recognize previously unacknowledged debts may be numbered, they are increasingly important. Among my most important unacknowledged debts are those to professors Dale Noyd, Jerome Carroll, Rochelle Gelman, and especially Jane Piliavin, who were early, formative influences, modeling ways of doing psychology that were rigorous, ethical, and compassionate. With Jane's encouragement, I had the good fortune to come to the psychology department at Stanford at a truly exciting time—when many aspects of the psychological framework that I employ in the pages that follow were being developed, written about, and helping to transform the field. Contact with Albert Bandura, Eleanor Maccoby, Walter Mischel, and Lee Ross made a lasting mark. I owe a special debt to Philip Zimbardo who, for many years, was a mentor and a friend.

Stanton Wheeler and the Russell Sage Foundation funded me to go to law school, as part of an innovative program that trained young scholars to use social science (in my case, psychology) to inject new perspectives into the American legal system and challenge existing legal categories. In my very first law school class, I met another Russell Sage fellow, Michael Lowy, an anthropology professor who, like me, was now a beginning law student. We became and have remained fast friends, spending countless hours talking about the nature of legal education and whether and how social science could be used to transform law. David Rosenhan shared my interests in applying psychology to legal issues and facilitated my transition to the very different world of the Stanford Law School.

I had the opportunity to work for several years with Tony Amsterdam, who was already a legendary constitutional and criminal law scholar. He was also a remarkably generous mentor. Anyone who has been around Tony for even a short time is inspired to work harder, think better, and care more. I certainly was. Richard Danzig, Charles Halperin, and Michael Wald each gave me opportunities to work on reform-oriented projects—on policing, mental health law, and the juvenile justice system, respectively—teaching me the importance of becoming deeply immersed in the real-world context of a legal question or issue before claiming to really understand it. I took that lesson to heart when I began teaching at UC Santa Cruz, where my colleagues supported my regular forays into the criminal justice system, allowing me to work on and write about the insights that I gleaned from my involvement in actual legal cases, in challenges to unconstitutional conditions of penal confinement that took me inside countless correctional institutions throughout the United States and in numerous death penalty trials and appeals where I developed mitigating social histories for scores of capital defendants. My Santa Cruz colleagues and friends, Tom Pettigrew, Brewster Smith, Ted Sarbin, and, especially, David Marlowe and Richard Wasserstrom, were unfailingly supportive and patient sounding boards when many of the ideas that follow first began to percolate.

As important as these more traditional kinds of intellectual influences were, I am not sure they would have mattered as much in the genesis of this book had I not had the indirect collaboration of numerous other people outside academia, whom I also very gratefully acknowledge. They include the countless number of incredibly talented attorneys and investigators with whom I have worked over the last several decades. Although they are too numerous to mention by name, their dedication to advancing the cause of justice continues to be inspirational and instructive. They also facilitated my access to persons and places that would have been impossible to obtain without their assistance. Those places include the homes and neighborhoods where persons accused and convicted of serious violent crimes grew up, the schools they attended, and the criminal justice institutions in which they and many others were confined. The persons include hundreds of criminal defendants and incarcerated persons, their family members and others knowledgeable about their lives, as well as numerous criminal justice system personnel and crime survivors whom I have interviewed in the course of compiling case-related social and institutional histories. They trusted me with their personal, moving, and often painful stories and shared many insights that helped me put the framework developed in this book in a more human context. They are the people touched most directly by the social, economic, and racial injustices addressed in the pages that follow and who have such an enormous stake in meaningful criminal justice reform. I have tried to repay their trust and their contributions to these ideas in ways that I hope are always respectful and that ultimately lead to effective solutions for the range of social problems and political challenges we collectively face.

CRIMINALITY IN CONTEXT

Introduction

For two centuries, a central legal fiction has enabled our legal system to target primarily the nation's poorest, most traumatized, badly abused and, in that sense, least autonomous citizens. This legal fiction is what I term the "crime master narrative"—the widely accepted notion that crime is the simple product of equally free and autonomous "bad" choices made by persons who are acting unencumbered by their past experience and present circumstances. Yet, as I argue throughout this book, the crime master narrative is fundamentally flawed. It has produced a basically unfair apportioning of legal punishment, one in which persons with the fewest degrees of freedom are held most accountable, with a correspondingly long-term dispiriting effect. What we now understand to be a largely misguided analysis of the real causes of crime has also thwarted attempts to develop more rational, humane, and effective policies for reducing crime. Because it is largely based on an unsupported fiction, our myopic devotion to the crime master narrative has placed countless numbers of potential crime victims needlessly at risk and placed future generations in harm's way. Thus, worse than misguided and wrong, it is dangerous.

As a result of the widespread acceptance of the crime master narrative, the United States has relied nearly exclusively on imprisonment as its core strategy of crime control, especially in the unprecedented ways it has been embraced during the so-called era of mass incarceration.[1] As I note at several different points in the analysis that follows, prison itself represents a supremely

http://dx.doi.org/10.1037/0000172-001
Criminality in Context: The Psychological Foundations of Criminal Justice Reform,
by C. Haney

individualistic response to the social problem of crime. The proliferation of this institution more than a century ago was in many ways a tribute to the crime master narrative. It was also a direct outgrowth of a 19th-century model of psychological individualism—the belief that the causal locus of people's behavior resides exclusively inside them, and the corresponding notion that social problems, such as crime, can and should be addressed primarily by acting directly on those persons who engage in it.[2] Serving as the core behavioral assumption of the crime master narrative, this form of individualism still guides our nation's crime-control policies. In this sense, the intellectual justification for these policies stands or falls on the validity of these staunchly individualistic assumptions. Yet the extensive research I review and synthesize in the chapters that follow has rendered these assumptions increasingly outmoded and indefensible.

SOCIAL CONTEXT AND CRIMINAL BEHAVIOR

Over the past several decades, a quiet revolution has taken place in the way that criminal behavior is analyzed and understood by the scholars and researchers who systematically study and theorize about it. A more contemporary and sophisticated understanding of criminal behavior carefully analyzes the past social histories and immediate situations or contexts of the persons who engage in it. This new, scientifically grounded approach represents an important, definitive challenge to the antiquated, individualistic notions that have guided our thinking about crime and punishment for such a long time. As this new model of criminal behavior becomes widely recognized and accepted, its implications for legal decisionmaking and criminal justice policymaking will become clearer. I believe it will fundamentally impact our very conceptions of justice and fairness and serve as the basis for new crime-control initiatives that emphasize community-based strategies of prevention. In fact, the perspective on the origins of social and criminal behavior that I discuss and rely on in the following chapters not only raises serious questions about our nation's unrivaled dependence on imprisonment but also poses parallel and pointed questions about the continued use of capital punishment. Indeed, the death penalty is in many ways the ultimate expression of the crime master narrative, reflecting the belief that the causes of serious violent crime reside so deeply and irredeemably inside some people that they should not be allowed to continue to live.

This book systematically reviews much of the empirical research that directly addresses the developmental, institutional, immediate situational, and structural roots of criminality as the basis for a more scientifically valid and humane counternarrative. To clarify at the outset, the kind of crime or "criminality" that I address throughout this book is what is commonly referred to as "street crime"—criminal behavior that most people think about when they hear that crime rates are "on the rise," when politicians promise to "reduce crime," and the kind of crime that the overwhelming number of men and women who fill our nation's jails and prisons have been convicted of having committed. It is also the broad category of behavior to which the crime master narrative is routinely applied and also to which the numerous studies I will cite in the pages that follow pertain. I do not assume that literally every kind of crime is subject to or needs to be explained by some kind of elusive unitary theory that encompasses literally every instance of lawbreaking. Thus, I do not attempt to address very different kinds of crimes, especially acts of so-called white collar and corporate criminality.

Another important caveat is also in order. I have made a conscious decision to focus on social history and context and not on individual-level explanations of crime that entail the supposed genetic or biological differences that some have argued distinguish lawbreakers from the rest of us. There are several reasons for this decision. The first is that although biological and genetic determinism—the belief that criminal behavior is caused by the particular biological or genetic makeup of its perpetrators—is a perspective with which our society seems perennially enamored, it represents an especially extreme and potentially pernicious form of the crime master narrative. It is also one that lends itself to misuse. Indeed, genetic explanations for complex human behavior, especially for criminality, have a sordid, racially tainted history that I discuss in several later chapters.

The second reason is that the strong forms of genetic or biological determinism—that some people are born "wired" to commit crime—lack any convincing and sustained scientific support. As several sociological commentators put it: "Genetic determinism has died a quiet death. Evidence is overwhelming that human beings are never simply instructed by their genes to show a particular trait or behavior."[3] My own reading of even the more carefully worded and nuanced contemporary versions of genetic explanations suggests that what we really know about these interconnections is still entirely tentative and very much in flux.[4] In fact, the most sophisticated interpretations of what were once understood as genetic predispositions now seem to concede that, at most, they seem to reflect differences in sensitivity to those aspects of an environment or context that trigger or activate behavior, in a field that has come to be known as "epigenetics."[5] Thus, much like the earlier claims made about the genetic basis of IQ, however, there is reason to believe that whatever individual differences do exist still depend very heavily on substantial environmental influences (such as the ones I discuss in this book) for their expression.[6]

And that leads to my third reason for excluding these theories from discussion in a book about the role of social history and social context in crime causation: There are as yet no practical, positive applications for this kind of knowledge.[7] Although the challenges of addressing the criminogenic factors and forces I discuss in the chapters that follow are daunting, they are susceptible to feasible social and political interventions and remedies. Notwithstanding their questionable scientific status, the alleged biological and genetic causes of crime are not. Thus, the impact of social historical and contextual factors is far more scientifically well-documented, they have repeatedly been shown to have a far more important and powerful influence on human behavior (even in emerging epigenetic models), and they are far more within our capacity as a society to control and modify in ways that have important practical implications for meaningful criminal justice reform.

OVERVIEW OF THIS BOOK

To begin telling the story of context and criminality, Chapter 1 summarizes and critically analyzes the traditional individualistic model of criminal behavior—a crime master narrative that conceptualizes the causes of crime exclusively in terms of the blameworthy free choices made by its perpetrators. Although the crime master narrative concedes that those bad choices may stem from various and sundry internal sources—perhaps a profound selfishness, deep-seated immorality, a deranged mind, psychopathic character, fundamental "evil," or some particularly unsavory and odious combination of them all—those sources are presumed to reside entirely within the perpetrator.

However, as I show in Chapter 2, the 19th-century model of behavior that is at the core of the crime master narrative has not stood up to 21st-century science. It rarely accounts for more than a small part of the real story. Research underscoring the long-lasting influence of early "risk factors"—negative and traumatic experiences—on people's later life trajectories has radically shifted the way that criminality is empirically studied and understood. So, too, have studies of the immediate power of "criminogenic" or crime-producing life circumstances and external situations to shape adult behavior. Indeed, a massive amount of systematic research conducted over the last several decades has established the causal significance of a wide range of background factors *and* immediate situations in the analysis of delinquency, crime, and violence. For this reason, the model of psychological individualism on which the crime master narrative rests is now an anachronism; exclusively internal or dispositional explanations of crime cannot bear the weight of this new evidence.

The discussion shifts in the next four chapters to a more detailed assessment of the exact role of social history and social context in crime causation. Thus, Chapter 3 summarizes what is now known about the social historical or developmental causes of crime. An extraordinary number of studies have been done that underscore the long-term, life-altering impact of events and experiences that occur early in life, including the powerful criminogenic impact of child maltreatment in all its forms. I review at length the empirical research that clearly documents the way that childhood risks and traumas and adverse experiences can contribute to delinquency and adult criminality.

Chapter 4 continues this discussion by extending it to a set of distinct and seemingly paradoxical criminogenic influences: the potentially destructive effects of harsh institutional interventions and treatment. Among other things, this chapter examines the psychological consequences of a wide range of institutional responses to juvenile misbehavior and crime, from increasingly harsh disciplinary practices that are directed toward certain public school students, to placement in the nation's historically troubled foster care system, to confinement in what are too often badly deteriorated or seriously underfunded juvenile justice institutions in the United States. I examine the still too-common victimization of children inside institutional settings as well as the fact that many "institutional risk factors" are psychologically analogous to the kinds of traumatic family and community experiences to which they were initially exposed. That is, these are children who were confined in harsh juvenile justice settings where they experienced their institutionalization as a form of "*re*-traumatization," exposing them *again* to forms of maltreatment that are all too familiar.

In Chapter 5, I add to this discussion by integrating research conducted on another critically important component in the scientific analysis of crime causation—the role of *immediate* situational or contextual influences on criminality. Research on the relationship of context to criminality has identified a wide range of precipitating criminogenic and crime-inducing social circumstances that help to provoke and precipitate criminal behavior. Thus, we know that there are specific situational conditions and dynamics that greatly increase the probability that crimes will be committed within them, correspondingly increasing the likelihood that anyone who enters them will succumb to their pervasive and powerful pressures. Here, too, despite extensive scientific research, the implications of what we know about the situational determinants of crime have yet to be widely acknowledged in public or political discourse. These theoretical insights and empirical data about the power of social contexts and circumstances to shape behavior are essential to any comprehensive understanding of the roots of criminal behavior. Yet they not only have had little or no impact in key legal decision-making arenas where the individualistic "free choice" model still reigns, but they also have failed to inspire a more rational and effective strategies of crime control.

In Chapter 6, I examine some of the various ways in which the structural and socioeconomic variable of poverty operates as a central and especially powerful criminogenic risk factor. Among other things, it functions broadly to interconnect and compound the destructive influence of the *multiple* risk factors often associated with it. Although it is a fact so obvious that its significance is often overlooked, the nation's prisons are filled with the nation's poor. Some of the disproportionate number of poor persons who are incarcerated have been erroneously caught up in the wide net of the criminal justice system because they lacked the necessary resources with which to properly defend themselves in or extricate themselves from the legal processes that ensnared them. Many others are imprisoned because they have succumbed to the severe pressures of a life of deprivation and want, the multiple other risk factors and traumas to which such a life commonly exposes them, and the host of criminogenic disadvantages that they continuously confront well into adulthood.

Chapter 7 frankly acknowledges the criminogenic implications of the fact that the United States remains deeply divided by race and ethnicity. The overrepresentation of racial minorities—primarily African Americans—in the criminal justice system can be understood in part through the lens of racial oppression to which many such communities of Color have been historically subjected.[8] Slavery and colonization produced entrenched structural divisions that still translate into fundamental differences in the day-to-day realities of many Black and, increasingly, Latino Americans. I use the term "biographical racism" to describe the sum total of racialized experiences that accumulate over a person of Color's entire social history in ways that can and often do adversely shape and undermine their life course and can themselves be criminogenic.

In Chapter 8, I directly examine and confront the various ways in which the broad framework of social contextualism that I have developed up to this point fundamentally complicates and calls into question any simplistic "free choice" model of criminal behavior. As I repeatedly note, this free choice model still dominates virtually all criminal justice settings and legal decision-making circles. Loosening its irrational grip will require us to interrogate and confront the intellectual as well as legal sources of inertia and resistance to change. I explicitly and critically examine some of the ways that the crime master narrative is used to confuse and obfuscate the analysis of criminal behavior, impeding the development of crime control policies that are based on reason rather than emotion.

Chapter 9 shifts focus to examine the direct legal and prison policy implications of the preceding chapters. As our appreciation of the breadth and depth of the social contextual determinants of behavior increases, so too does the urgency of bringing criminal law doctrines, criminal justice practices, and prison policies into line with these more scientifically valid psychological perspectives. This chapter contains the outline of at least some of those much-needed legal reforms, ones premised on an emerging counternarrative that fully acknowledges the critically important role of social history and context. I am not naïve about the difficulty of implementing meaningful change within an overarching legal system whose fundamental assumptions and standard operating procedures are so longstanding and institutionally entrenched, no matter how useful or even seemingly necessary it may be. No student of legal history can reflect seriously on past attempts to use empirical data to transform the law without acknowledging the law's deep-seated resistance to psychologically inspired change.[9] And no one can participate in related criminal justice reform-oriented efforts for very long without being forced to concede the monumental obstacles that thwart real change. Yet I also believe that a serious dialogue about these issues is not only long overdue but inevitable. The time has come to use what is known about the social historical and immediate structural determinants of crime to make the criminal justice system's basic operating assumptions more scientifically valid and its doctrines and procedures more equitable and fair.

In that spirit, Chapter 10 develops another set of broad and badly needed context-based social reforms that stem from the quiet revolution in our understanding the causes of crime. It acknowledges that proposing a series of immediate "fixes" to outdated criminal law doctrines and criminal justice practices that have led to a destructive overdependency on imprisonment still perpetuates a largely self-limiting system. Absent a viable alternative framework, these modest fixes are ultimately counterproductive. Thus, I argue that we must take steps to develop a new and fundamentally different strategy that explicitly acknowledges and then pointedly, proactively, and preventively addresses the social contextual causes of crime that are discussed throughout this book. I suggest a number of ways in which this alternative model can end our current overreliance on prison and better address our nation's crime problem. It focuses attention and resources on meaningful and effective programs designed to *prevent* criminal behavior rather than merely reacting to it. Although here, too, I recognize the truly daunting practical difficulties and political obstacles that must be overcome in order to mount the kind of structurally oriented program of crime prevention that I describe, I also believe that, in light of what we now know about the roots of criminality, anything less than this simply will not produce substantial, lasting change.

THE POLITICS OF CRIMINAL JUSTICE REFORM

I should explicitly acknowledge that meaningful criminal law reform and significant changes in crime control policy are especially vulnerable to political resistance and obstruction. Psychiatrist Judith Herman's caution that "the study of psychological trauma is an inherently political enterprise because it calls attention to the experience of oppressed people" bears repeating here.[10] Focusing on trauma in the lives of people who have committed crime is "political" in the same sense, to be sure. But it also is a topic that is easily "politicized." The way that a society conceptualizes and responds to wrongdoing connects to core debates about the role of government in controlling citizens' behavior and the proper targets of state intervention—intervention that, as Robert Cover has reminded us, is often inherently violent in nature.[11] At no time has the politicization of these issues been clearer and more sustained than over the last several decades.[12] Unfortunately, that politicization not only became remarkably one-sided during these years but also often diverted the public's attention from many of the issues that I address in this book.

Concern over potential politicization leads to another issue that bears emphasis. I want to say at the outset and repeat at several junctures along the way that I am well aware of the ease with which a focus on criminogenic traumas and risks lends itself to a painfully stigmatizing form of deficit thinking.[13] It is my intention to avoid this. The concepts and data presented in this book are not intended to imply that adverse outcomes are inevitable, irreversible, or are caused primarily by the personal deficits or failings of the persons who succumb to or engage in them. Nor are the analyses that follow intended to depict persons who are adversely affected by the array of criminogenic influences I discuss in detail as passive victims; to the contrary, whether or not they are ultimately successful at pushing back against these influences, their lives have typically been characterized by resistance, striving, and resilience. They want and deserve meaningful opportunities far more than idle sympathy. Moreover, people who have been negatively affected by the risks and traumas that they have experienced should never be blamed for their own victimhood. Yet it is also important to acknowledge and analyze the role of mistreatment and the hurtful and often harmful actions of the larger systems of oppression as well as what we now know are the predictable consequences of these experiences.

Thus, analyzing the problematic outcomes without pathologizing those who engage in them means recognizing that criminal behavior is often an adaptive response to otherwise pathological, destructive past histories and present environments. People can engage in problematic behavior without being problematic people, and the negative consequences of exposure to risk factors and criminogenic conditions are largely learned behaviors that are highly modifiable. Because they were caused by mistreatment, deprivation, and adverse external circumstances, rather than inborn, fixed internal traits or mechanisms, they are subject to being effectively addressed with the appropriate resources and changed circumstances.

Over the years, however, the work I have done studying the lives of capital defendants also has taught me a deeply troubling lesson, one that our society has seemed at many times intent on ignoring. It is that a number of the children and adolescents who have endured the very worst forms early trauma, the most severe kinds of maltreatment, the most egregious institutional neglect and abuse, and who live in the most impoverished and criminogenic neighborhoods simply cannot and do not easily overcome these things, at least not without caring intervention of the sort that is often not forthcoming. There are many remarkable souls who do, to be sure, but they are exceptions to be admired and sometimes marveled at, perhaps precisely because of the long odds they have overcome.

Despite the odds against them, of course, not all of the children who experience even the worst kinds of trauma go on to commit crimes. Aside from those with remarkable resilience and the fortunate others who benefit from the benign intervention of a caring relative or teacher, or an effective educational or a therapeutic program designed to address some of their many unmet needs, there are many other adaptations to trauma that do not involve criminality. But tragically few children who experience the worst to which our society can subject them emerge miraculously unscathed, even if they "just try hard enough," or draw on their divinely-given inner strength, or summon the will to make it so, or whatever other fiction some commentators engage to ultimately shift blame onto the victims of severe childhood trauma and societal neglect. Instead, the effects of these experiences are often life-altering, at least when necessary resources and meaningful opportunities to rise above potentially harmful pasts fail to materialize. There are still a daunting number of children in our society who endure these traumatic life histories and confront such destructively harsh life circumstances. For them, the criminogenics of prior abuse and deprivation cannot be simply forgotten, easily transcended, or successfully set aside. This book seeks to explain the paths that some of them have traveled, and the steps that can be taken to minimize the number of lives that are affected in these harmful ways.

The criminal justice system's reliance on the crime master narrative translates the predictable consequences of these experiences into nothing more than a matter of blameworthy free choices, thereby masking the underlying causes, holding the victims of mistreatment and structural injustice accountable for the consequences of social historical events and circumstances over which they often had little or no control. It not only dehumanizes and distances them from the rest of us but also ensures that we will never effectively address these larger social ills. We can and should do better. Truly meaningful and effective criminal justice reform depends on it.

NOTES

1. See, e.g., Hinton, E. (2016). *From the war on poverty to the war on crime: The making of mass incarceration in America.* Cambridge, MA: Harvard University Press. http://dx.doi.org/10.4159/9780674969223; and Kilgore, J. (2015). *Understanding mass incarceration: A people's guide to the civil rights struggle of our time.* New York, NY: The New Press.
2. Haney, C. (1982). Criminal justice and the nineteenth-century paradigm: The triumph of psychological individualism in the "formative era." *Law and Human Behavior, 6,* 191–235. http://dx.doi.org/10.1007/BF01044295
3. Simons, R. L., Lei, M. K., Beach, S. R. H., Brody, G. H., Philibert, R. A., & Gibbons, F. X. (2011). Social environment, genes, and aggression: Evidence supporting the differential susceptibility perspective. *American Sociological Review, 76,* 883–912, p. 883. http://dx.doi.org/10.1177/0003122411427580. The eagerness to uncritically accept the many empirical and theoretical claims that have been made in the past about the alleged genetic and biological causal roots of criminality should not blind us to the lack of solid and consistent evidence establishing any clear causal link between genetic makeup and crime or confirming any meaningful level of actual biological causation.
4. The recent history of an alleged genetic basis for depression is instructive. In 2003, an influential paper was published that purported to find the elusive and long-sought-after genetic basis for depression. See Caspi, A., Sugden, K., Moffitt, T. E., Taylor, A., Craig, I. W., Harrington, H., . . . Poulton, R. (2003). Influence of life stress on depression: Moderation by a polymorphism in the *5-HTT* gene. *Science, 302,* 386–389. http://dx.doi.org/10.1126/science.1083968. In retrospect, as the press later reported, this initial report of a genetic basis for depression was greeted with much fanfare: "The excitement spread quickly. Newspapers and magazines reported the findings. Columnists, commentators and op-ed writers emphasized its importance." See Carey, B. (2009, June 17). Report on gene for depression is now faulted. *The New York Times,* pp. A1, A13, p. A13. However, a meta-analysis conducted 6 years later provided a definitive challenge to the earlier finding. The

authors of the later study concluded: "The results of this meta-analysis clearly demonstrate that stressful life events have a potent relationship with the risk of depression, an association that has been one of the most widely studied environmental factors for a range of mental disorders." Risch, N., Herrell, R., Lehner, T., Liang, K.-Y., Eaves, L., Hoh, J., . . . Merikangas, K. R. (2009). Interaction between the serotonin transporter gene (5-*HTTLPR*), stressful life events, and risk of depression: A meta-analysis. *JAMA, 301,* 2462–2471, p. 2468. http://dx.doi.org/10.1001/jama.2009.878

5. See, e.g., Radley, J. J., Kabbaj, M. Jacobson, L., Heydendael, W., Yehuda, R., & Herman, J. P. (2011). Stress risk factors and stress-related pathology: Neuroplasticity, epigenetics and endophenotypes. *Stress: The International Journal on the Biology of Stress, 14,* 481–497. http://dx.doi.org/10.3109/10253890.2011.604751; Yang, B.-Z., Zhang, H., Ge, W., Weder, N., Douglas-Palumberi, H., Perepletchikova, F., . . . Kaufman, J. (2013). Child abuse and epigenetic mechanisms of disease risk. *American Journal of Preventive Medicine, 44,* 101–107. http://dx.doi.org/10.1016/j.amepre.2012.10.012; Zannas, A. S., & West, A. E. (2014). Epigenetics and the regulation of stress vulnerability. *Neuroscience, 264,* 157–170. http://dx.doi.org/10.1016/j.neuroscience.2013.12.003
6. In addition to Simons et al. (2011), Social environment, genes, and aggression, see, e.g., Belsky, J., Bakermans-Kranenburg, M. J., & van IJzendoorn, M. H. (2007). For better *and* for worse: Differential susceptibility to environmental influences. *Current Directions in Psychological Science, 16,* 300–304. http://dx.doi.org/10.1111/j.1467-8721.2007.00525.x; Caspi, A., & Moffitt, T. E. (2006). Gene-environment interactions in psychiatry: Joining forces with neuroscience. *Nature Reviews Neuroscience, 7,* 583–590; Ehlert, U. (2013). Enduring psychobiological effects of childhood adversity. *Psychoneuroendocrinology, 38,* 1850–1857. http://dx.doi.org/10.1016/j.psyneuen.2013.06.007; Rutter, M. (2006). *Genes and behavior: Nature-nurture interplay explained.* London, England: Blackwell; and Shanahan, M. J., & Hofer, S. M. (2005). Social context in gene-environment interactions: Retrospect and prospect. *Journals of Gerontology: Series B, 60,* 65–76. http://dx.doi.org/10.1093/geronb/60.Special_Issue_1.65
7. For a slightly different perspective on this issue, see Grasso, A. (2017). Broken beyond repair: Rehabilitative penology and American political development. *Political Research Quarterly, 70,* 394–407. http://dx.doi.org/10.1177/1065912917695189
8. The *Publication Manual of the American Psychological Association* advises authors to capitalize "Black" and "White" when the terms are used to denote race. I, too, believe this is appropriate and will follow this practice. As Catherine McKinnon explained with respect to the capitalization of "Black," the word is "as much socially created as, and at least in the American context no less specifically meaningful or definitive than, any linguistic, tribal, or religious ethnicity, all of which are conventionally recognized by capitalization." McKinnon, C. A. (1982). Feminism, Marxism, method, and the state: An agenda for theory. *Signs, 7,* 515–544, p, 516. http://dx.doi.org/10.1086/493898. I believe the same logic applies to "Color" when used in this way, and it is capitalized throughout.
9. Haney, C. (1980). Psychology and legal change: On the limits of a factual jurisprudence. *Law and Human Behavior, 4,* 147–199. http://dx.doi.org/10.1007/bf01040317. See also Haney, C. (1993). Psychology and legal change: The impact of a decade. *Law and Human Behavior, 17,* 371–398. http://dx.doi.org/10.1007/bf01044374
10. Herman, J. (1997). Afterword. In J. Herman (Ed.), *Trauma and recovery* (pp. 236–247). New York, NY: Basic Books.
11. Cover, R. M. (1986). Violence and the word. *The Yale Law Journal, 95,* 1601–1629. http://dx.doi.org/10.2307/796468
12. See, e.g., Haney, C. (1998). Riding the punishment wave: On the origins of our devolving standards of decency. *Hastings Women's Law Journal, 9,* 27–78; and

Haney, C. (2012). Politicizing crime and punishment: Redefining "justice" to fight the "war on prisoners." *West Virginia Law Review, 114,* 373–414.

13. See, e.g., Valencia, R. R. (1997). Conceptualizing the notion of deficit thinking. In R. R. Valencia (Ed.), *The evolution of deficit thinking: Educational thought and practice* (pp. 1–12). Abingdon, England: RoutledgeFalmer. See also John Irwin's caution about the ease with which this problematic model has been applied in corrections:

> Since the appearance of positivism in the social sciences, there has been a persistent effort to conceptualize crime as behavior committed almost entirely by aberrants. This general approach is obviously appealing to the more powerful because it conveniently narrows the definition of crime, draws attention away from their own illegal and immoral activities, and avoids any changes in basic social and economic relations. It demands only some fine tuning of various institutional activities such as those of the "criminal justice system." Also, it supplies society's leaders with bogeymen to divert the public's attention away from pressing problems—such as unemployment—that are more likely to demand structural change.

Irwin, J. (1987). Reflections on ethnography. *Journal of Contemporary Ethnography, 16,* 41–48, p. 45.

1

Individualistic Myths and the Crime Master Narrative

[The cultural organization of criminal justice] produces a construction of reality by focusing on an incident, narrowly defined in time and place and it freezes the action there. . . . The result is that the individual then becomes separated out. He is in certain important ways isolated in respect of that incident from his environment, his friends, his family, the material substratum of his world.

—LOUK HULSMAN[1]

The prosecutor in the final stage of a capital murder trial in California rose to address the jury in his closing argument. The defendant was an African American man in his 20s named Lamar Jackson. He had been convicted of truly terrible crimes—the brutal murders of two women—and now faced the death penalty.[2] Speaking directly to the jurors who soon would decide the man's fate, the prosecutor minced few words. He characterized the defendant in unequivocal, vilifying terms as a "one man crime wave" who had "stubbornly and steadfastly refused to be anything other than an egocentric, selfish, and violent criminal." He referred briefly to expert psychiatric testimony that had been presented earlier in the case, testimony that had portrayed Jackson in perhaps the worst possible clinical terms, as "a sociopath, a psychopath, a completely anti-social personality."

Not satisfied with these already deeply pejorative labels, the prosecutor offered his own more sinister twist, lest even one juror conclude that the defendant suffered from some kind of "illness" warranting the tiniest bit of

http://dx.doi.org/10.1037/0000172-002
Criminality in Context: The Psychological Foundations of Criminal Justice Reform, by C. Haney

sympathy or compassion. He argued that rather than the product of a psychiatric condition—even one as frightening as psychopathy—Jackson's violent behavior was *entirely* under his own control and that he alone was fully responsible for the consequences of his actions. In fact, he said, Lamar Jackson's criminality was "basically a philosophy. It is a road that he *chose* to go down a long time ago." Thus, immune from the influence of any internal or external forces beyond his control, Jackson's bad acts were the result of a "lifestyle *choice*"—a series of purposeful and selfish decisions that he had made totally freely and entirely on his own. The prosecutor went on to portray the defendant as utterly ruthless and, using animalistic terms to describe him, called him an "accomplished predator," one who "preys, destroys or devours . . . those persons weaker than himself."

He ended by telling the jury that there was *nothing at all* about the defendant or his background that moderated or complicated the simple, stark, frightening portrait that he had painted of the defendant. Not only had Lamar Jackson been in total control of the terrible choices he had made in his life, but he had freely and repeatedly decided to ruthlessly and viciously harm others. His "badness" was deep *and* it was all-encompassing—it was all there was to him. Quite simply, the prosecutor said, "the bad is overwhelming and in fact the good is virtually nonexistent." He repeated the theme for emphasis: "The reasonable interpretation of all of the evidence clearly shows that the bad not only outweighs the good, using that term loosely substantially, that it dwarfs it." And yet again: "as hard as [one] may look" for any good in the defendant, it is "in fact pretty much nonexistent."

This powerful, damning account of Lamar Jackson's presumably evil character and depraved motivation was for the most part the only one that the jurors would ever hear—not just from the prosecutor but at any time in the course of his trial. Even Jackson's own lawyers—legal professionals who had taken on the awesome responsibility of trying to save their client's life—offered up no more than a halfhearted response to the prosecutor's core argument. They essentially conceded most of the prosecutor's damning description of their client, including the characterization of Lamar's despicable actions as the product of his own evil choices and his vile "nature."

Not surprisingly, with nothing else to rely on but this compelling picture of a frighteningly dangerous, utterly selfish, ruthless and depraved "predator"—someone who had freely chosen bad over good and preyed on weaker victims as part of his evil lifestyle—Lamar Jackson's jury unanimously condemned him to die.

In developing his one-sided, condemning portrait of Lamar Jackson, the prosecutor had relied on an admittedly extreme version of an otherwise seemingly "commonsense" conception of violent criminality that is still very deeply held and widely shared in our society. He could confidently assert—and confidently assume that most if not all of the jurors would implicitly agree—that the causes of terribly violent crimes like those that Mr. Jackson had been convicted of committing are located entirely inside and fully under the control of the persons who perpetrate them. It is a time-honored conception that, as I say, many of the jurors not only very likely shared but also regarded as so straightforward and commonsensical as to be nearly unassailable. They likely needed little or no convincing of its truth. Most people do not.

Put simply, most of us have been taught, repeatedly and in multiple ways, that only fundamentally bad people commit bad, violent acts. We have been taught further that their badness stems from something that resides within them, something that they *chose* to indulge in or to respond to, with little or no concern for the harm they inflict in order to obtain what they desire. In this way, the bad acts that lawbreakers commit are nearly universally portrayed as the product of personal, autonomous choices that are made "freely," unencumbered by past history or present circumstances. This narrative of free choice is why the perpetrators of crime are regarded so often and easily—intuitively, really—as fully culpable for the bad things they have done.

In addition to being a widely shared, commonsense, layperson's view of crime, the seemingly intuitive model of "free choice" serves as the basis of the legal processes by which we allocate criminal responsibility and mete out punishment in our criminal justice system. In fact, these processes are founded on the same core assumptions and operate in much the same way now as they did since the inception of our justice system centuries ago. Moreover, all other things being equal, the worse the crime someone has been found guilty of committing, the harsher the punishment he *deserves* to have imposed on him. In a death penalty case, such as Lamar Jackson's, these beliefs can lead jurors to conclude that the defendant is culpable enough to pay with his life.

Yet, as I discuss at length in the chapters that follow, this venerable formulation has become scientifically indefensible. It is fundamentally at odds with what is known about the causal origins of social behavior in general and criminal behavior in particular. The remainder of this book is devoted to exploring that disjuncture—by reviewing the empirical evidence that has mounted over the last four decades to establish an alternative psychological framework for understanding the causes of criminal behavior. This more scientifically valid framework has profound implications for the way we approach crime control and promote social justice.

The present chapter traces the roots of the anachronistic but still deeply entrenched individualistic free choice model of criminal behavior and outlines the elements of the fundamental paradigm shift in psychology and related disciplines that is helping to displace it. It is a paradigm shift that has been underway for several decades in academic circles, even though it is not yet fully embraced by the public or in political discourse and debates over crime and punishment. Regrettably, it has had little or no impact on most of the all-important decisions that are made within the criminal justice system itself.

THE DOMINANCE OF THE "CRIME MASTER NARRATIVE"

"Master narratives" are official frameworks that establish broadly accepted ways of understanding human events and behavior. Contemporary historians have described master narratives as cultural lenses that are "institutionalized, canonical, and legitimizing."[3] Because they come from authoritative, institutional sources that people look to as conferring legitimacy, master narratives are widely shared and accepted as "truth." Author Toni Morrison observed that these kinds of narratives or "official stories" assist in the "manufacture of a public truth" by "control[ling] the presumptions and postulates of the discussion" in ways that "reinforce the narrative and truncate alternative opinion."[4]

In the case of the "*crime* master narrative" that has dominated American society for several centuries, criminal behavior is understood as an individual-level phenomenon in which lawbreakers themselves are seen as the exclusive causal locus of their own criminal behavior. In media messages, political discourse, and public debate and discussion, they and they alone are viewed not only as *personally* responsible for their criminal actions but also, collectively, as the source of the overall "crime problem" in our society. Lawbreaking is near universally depicted and regularly regarded in our society as the product of decisions that are made by persons who act as they freely choose to, largely unconstrained by other social and economic forces in their life. Thus, no matter how daunting, insurmountable, or extreme, their past background and present circumstances are viewed as largely irrelevant to understanding why they acted as they did or determining how severely they should be punished for their transgressions. By definition, then, all bad choices are viewed as willful and selfish, ones pursued in presumably conscious disregard of the hurtful consequences they may have for others. As depicted in the crime master narrative, criminal behavior is a reflection of the inherent, deep-seated, and condemnable "badness" of those who engage in it. This "public truth" about crime and criminality is so dominant that it effectively truncates and preempts any alternative explanations.

There is a great deal of synergy between the culturally entrenched crime master narrative and the criminal justice system's long-standing doctrines of legal and criminal responsibility. As two legal commentators put it: "The individualism of the badness model parallels the criminal law's individualistic approach to punishment."[5] Because—under the terms of the applicable criminal law *and* through the operative lens of the crime master narrative—lawbreakers are for the most part *presumed* to be fully responsible for their bad behavior, dispensing "justice" in individual cases equates with fully punishing them for the inexcusable things they have done. This narrowly individualistic and deeply held view shapes how prosecutors approach juries, and it influences the punitive sentences frequently meted out in criminal trials. It also has important implications for crime control policy in general.[6] That is, it implies that overall crime rates can *only* be reduced by making individual perpetrators pay dearly for the bad choices that they have made.

At the extremes, of course, the crime master narrative can serve as a rationale for capital punishment—leading jurors to conclude that a defendant's bad behavior and the bad character from which it necessarily comes are so extreme that he is not fit to live. As I noted, this was one of the arguments made in Lamar Jackson's death penalty trial. That is, for some citizens, the assumption that the very worst crimes are perforce committed by the very worst people justifies the imposition of the very worst punishment—capital punishment.

The crime master narrative also pushes alternative approaches to crime control out of public and political debates over crime policies. This is especially true of alternative strategies that focus more on the underlying or broader contextual causes of criminal behavior. Programs designed to lessen the long-term impact of the kind of traumatic mistreatment that is known to be criminogenic or to address adverse social conditions that are known to promote criminal behavior—through, for example, implementing child abuse prevention programs or widespread socioeconomic reforms—are fundamentally at odds with the crime master narrative. They are difficult to pursue because they are far outside mainstream thinking about crime control. Instead, because the venerable crime master narrative is unquestioningly and reflexively embraced, it ensures that other more scientifically based contextual approaches are rarely given serious consideration.

The crime master narrative has other secondary, deleterious effects as well. Its continued prominence operates to preempt or curtail careful case-specific investigations into and in-depth analyses of the actual causes of particular crimes or of crime in general. That is, legal decisionmakers (police, prosecutors, judges, and jurors) who might otherwise have undertaken such investigation or analysis instead automatically *presume* that crime is the product of the free and autonomous choice of its perpetrators. Emblematic of this short-circuiting, a crime is thought to be "solved" when someone has been found on whom it can be blamed. As one legal scholar put it,

> The process of adjudicating guilt does not contain an inquiry as to why a particular person has engaged in proscribed behavior. It is satisfied with "proof" merely that he or she chose the wrong course of conduct and acted in furtherance of that choice.[7]

I would add only that the "why" of these wrong choices is implicitly assumed and thought to be located exclusively inside the presumably deviant and damnable persons who made them.

The news media similarly see and report on crime virtually exclusively through the lens of the crime master narrative. Thus, instead of illuminating the underlying structural causes or interpersonal dynamics that are (or might be) at the root of any particular crime, media accounts are routinely focused on little more than the identity of the perpetrators (who are assumed to be exclusively "at fault") and whatever personal characteristics they may possess that seem to account for their bad behavior. These accounts are uniformly fashioned in ways that closely follow (and seem to validate) the crime master narrative, a narrative that subsequent chapters will demonstrate is unfortunately based—at best—on partial and incomplete information.[8] Its limitations notwithstanding, the crime master narrative is rarely questioned because it appears to reflect a "commonsense" account that "everyone knows" to be true.

In addition, by essentializing and exaggerating the negative qualities of the alleged perpetrators of crime—the main protagonists in virtually all crime stories—the media also simplify the stories themselves, often through contrasting frames in which pure good is pitted against unmitigated evil.[9] Victims are described in normalizing, endearing terms that connect them emotionally to the public. Perpetrators, on the other hand, are depicted in ways that emphasize their deviance and, in turn, psychologically distance them from the audience. To be sure, these characterizations of crime victims are understandable and a perhaps entirely appropriate way to elicit identification with and empathy for persons who have innocently suffered. However, the typical characterization of perpetrators produces only alienation, fear, and anger, and negates any impulse to understand them in remotely nuanced ways. It omits and seems to stifle the impulse or need to find any broader explanatory context in which to situate the perpetrator or his actions. Thus, as Maria Grabe concluded about the crime news stories that she content-analyzed, "[b]y virtually ignoring possible structural causes for crime (such as poverty or racism) criminals are portrayed as society's irrational enemies who deserve little sympathy because they presumably act as a result of their own will."[10]

Rather than connecting crime to the larger structural forces that may have operated over the course of perpetrators' lives to influence and contribute to their criminal behavior, or linking crimes to the immediate circumstances that may have helped precipitate them, the master narrative depicts criminality in what amounts to a total social vacuum. In so doing, it fails to teach important lessons about the potential influence of criminogenic factors that are outside the control of the persons who have broken the law (e.g., child abuse and neglect, poverty and inequality, racism, institutional mistreatment). Members of the public are not only the target audiences for these distorted and one-sided media messages but also are asked as voters and jurors to weigh in on criminal justice policy and legal decisions. Yet they are rarely given the kind of in-depth descriptive information that would allow them to situate criminal defendants in a broader social historical and structural context. Instead, lawbreakers are "contextualized"—if at all—primarily in terms of their criminal records; they are measured, as the saying goes, by the worst things they have ever done in their life—and, typically, little else.

In this book, I argue that the crime master narrative overlooks and is increasingly challenged by what researchers from a wide range of disciplines now understand about the influence and effect of past experiences and present circumstances on criminal behavior.[11] Yet, despite the fact that the crime master narrative lacks empirical or scholarly support, it persists. A careful look at its history helps to explain why.

PSYCHOLOGICAL INDIVIDUALISM IN 19TH-CENTURY LAW, "SCIENCE," AND AMERICAN CULTURE

The crime master narrative is not a recent invention. Understanding its origins underscores how deeply it is embedded in our culture and consciousness. The individualistic doctrines of criminal responsibility on which it is based have a very long and well-established history that predates the birth of the nation and the creation of its legal institutions. Indeed, by the 18th century, Western European jurists had firmly placed the causal locus of criminal behavior deep inside the individuals who performed it. The very concept of criminal responsibility was intertwined with a model of human behavior that both presumed and required individual autonomy. It is illustrated in David Hume's early 18th-century discussion of legal culpability and his assertion that only those actions that emanated "from some cause in the character and disposition of the person who performed them" could be used to establish legal culpability. In the presumably rare case in which someone's actions "proceeded from nothing in him that is durable and constant," then that person could not justly "become the object of punishment or vengeance."[12] But the implicit understanding and expectation was that the "character and disposition of the person" accounted for the overwhelming majority of criminal acts.

Nineteenth-century American society enthusiastically embraced the related concept of "psychological individualism."[13] Psychological individualism implied—and 19th-century American society largely came to believe—that individuals were the causal locus of their own behavior. That is, the forces that determined what a person did, and why, resided largely, if not exclusively, inside them. This implied, of course, that social deviance arose largely from some defective traits and tendencies inside the persons who manifested or engaged in it.

To be sure, the dominant 19th- and early 20th-century perspective was never *completely* individualistic; most knowledgeable members of the general public and informed commentators conceded that external factors like poverty, family disorganization, and exposure to the vices and depredations of city life could play some role in creating or exacerbating a person's internal defects. Yet legal doctrines of responsibility and culpability were already firmly premised on a model of human behavior that attached utmost importance to individual autonomy—autonomy that was for the most part presumed rather than demonstrated, largely because it was entirely consistent with the psychological individualism of the times.

Like the amateur social scientists of the day who employed the paradigm of independent and autonomous human agency in most of their causal models and analyses, lawyers and judges went about the task of finding and applying the common law with much the same perspective. Although psychological individualism was entrenched most deeply and durably in the criminal law, it influenced other legal doctrines as well. Legal historian Morton Horwitz noted that "[i]n the two decades before the Civil War, the ideologies of laissez-faire and rugged individualism had finally established a prominent beachhead in American property doctrine."[14] Roscoe Pound's sweeping but accurate generalization captured the legal spirit of these times: "[T]he common law knows individuals only. . . . And this compels a narrow and one-sided view."[15]

Moreover, at a pragmatic level, individualistic models of blame and exclusively person-centered "solutions" were proposed for a host of 19th-century social problems, including crime.[16] The individualistic model of behavior served as the conceptual underpinning for an elaborate and extensive prison system that was under construction across the land. Historian Martin Miller has estimated that the number of prisoners incarcerated in the United States grew from a little under 7,000 in 1850 to over 80,000 by 1890. Although clearly some of this growth in the prison population was attributable to the increase in the country's overall population, the *rate* at which citizens were imprisoned also increased significantly, from approximately one person in 3,400 who were incarcerated in 1850, to one in 750 by 1890.[17] The increased use of imprisonment during the 19th century was entirely consistent with the emphasis on individualism that continued to be enshrined in the entire American legal system during exactly the same period. Penal institutions were concrete and steel embodiments of the belief that individuals alone were responsible for the crimes they committed.

If prisoners were regarded, in Hume's terms, as the appropriate "objects of punishment and vengeance," it was because the source of the social ill to which they contributed—crime—was seen as residing within them. Thus, not only did people believe that a crime had been "solved" when, as I noted earlier, some person had been found on whom it could be blamed, but also that "justice" had been done when that person had been removed from society and placed in prison to be punished.

For perhaps obvious reasons, this individualism fit nicely into the worldview of those in positions of power and was consistent with the dominant ethos of wealthier nations that were in the process of creating their own elaborate state-run criminal justice systems. As historian Herman Franke noted, "judges, scholars, members of parliament, ministers, and successful merchants could regard themselves as independent, autonomous individuals who owed their places at the top of the social pile to their own moral standing and abilities."[18]

Of course, at the other end of this hierarchy of supposed personal virtues and noble traits were those on whom punishment was most often inflicted. Individualism allowed those in power "to think about the causes of crime in terms of individual shortcomings and ill nature and to consider criminality as a social phenomenon hardly at all."[19] This was largely true of members of the fledgling behavioral science disciplines as well. To the extent that serious violent crimes conjured any particular psychological view of human nature, they typically "implied in themselves nothing more than the depths of man's undoubted depravity."[20]

Consistent with the emerging scientism that characterized the 19th century, numerous theories were advanced in attempts to explain the precise nature of this "undoubted depravity." Notwithstanding the flawed, prescientific data on which they were based, popular theories of human deviance or depravity virtually always were couched in terms of the individualistic defects of those who succumbed to predation. For example, in the 1830s, English psychiatrist James Prichard coined the term "moral insanity" to describe persons who suffered from a "diseased . . . moral constitution" that led them into a life of crime.[21] Later in the same decade, American psychiatrist Isaac Ray wrote that criminality was closely connected to mental defectiveness—that criminals were, in effect, what later would be termed "moral imbeciles."[22] Eventually, as I show, many members of American society came to believe that "moral imbecility"—like most forms of deviance and depravity—ran in families and could be passed down from generation to generation.

Francis Lieber wrote in his preface to Beaumont and de Tocqueville's 1833 treatise on American penitentiaries that "[p]risons have been called hospitals for patients laboring under moral diseases."[23] In fact, most criminal misdeeds were explained in terms of biologically based mental defects. As one early writer put it: "Crime, imbecility, and insanity are hereditary diseases of the mind . . . [All] non-organic cases of imbecility show somewhere in the family annals there has been opium-eating, immoral living, drunkenness, insanity, imbecility or actual crime."[24]

Many members of the emerging discipline of psychology continued to advance this view. In 1909, prominent psychologist Walter Fernald wrote that "[e]very imbecile . . . is a potential criminal;"[25] and, a decade later, another influential psychologist, Lewis Terman—one of the early developers of IQ tests—advocated institutionalizing the mentally retarded in large part because of "their tendencies to become delinquent or criminal."[26] H. H. Goddard, one of Fernald's and Terman's equally well-known contemporaries, estimated that "from 25 percent to 50 percent of the people in our prisons are mentally defective and incapable of managing their affairs with ordinary prudence."[27] These and other alleged individual, ingrained defects were presumed to be at the root of criminal behavior. Notably, this era was also one in which the foundations of our entire criminal justice system were established—an era entirely enamored with pseudoscientific beliefs about the inherent and insurmountable defects in lawbreakers.

INDIVIDUALISM EMBODIED: CRANIOMETRY, PHRENOLOGY, EUGENICS, AND INSTINCT THEORY

Among the clearest indications of 19th- and early 20th-century America's commitment to the model of psychological individualism on which the crime master narrative is based was the enthusiasm with which citizens, politicians, and academics alike wholeheartedly embraced claims about the supposed self-contained *biological* and *genetic* origins of personality or "character." In particular, there were several pseudoscientific theories that each, in turn, dominated mainstream thinking about human nature and, perforce, the causes of crime and other forms of deviance. They were conceptually similar variations on the same basic individualistic theme. Thus, "craniometry," "phrenology," "eugenics," and "instinct theory" all supposedly "proved" that the causes of behavior could be found—indeed, were literally physically contained—in the biology of the persons who engaged in it. This meant that the defects that allegedly caused criminal behavior not only resided in the lawbreakers themselves, but that the defects were literally *embodied* in them and almost assuredly had been since birth.

The arc of all four theories was very similar. Each rose to prominence amid claims of being a "scientific breakthrough" that was soon enthusiastically and widely accepted. Then, as facts mounted to call key claims into question, the theories were increasingly discredited and eventually abandoned by the mainstream scientific community—although not necessarily by the larger public who had so ardently supported them. Moreover, notwithstanding the disfavor and disrepute into which they eventually fell, for nearly a century, one or another of these theories not only reigned as popular fads but also as "scientific truths" that served as the legitimating basis for the creation and implementation of a wide range of social policies, laws, and criminal justice practices. Importantly, key aspects of those policies, laws, and practices have persisted, as have residues of the underlying belief in biological and genetic determinism on which they were based.

The first of these 19th-century pseudoscientific theories, *craniometry*, began with claims that people's intellectual and moral capacities and characteristics were directly related to the shape and size of their brains, which, in turn, could be estimated by measuring the shape and size of their skulls. As one commentator put it, "[l]inking personality and character traits to skull shape represented the very best thinking in nineteenth-century neuroanatomy,"[28] and it eventually "dominated nineteenth-century anthropology."[29] Prominent Italian criminologist Cesare Lombroso, who linked genetic explanations of criminality with evolutionary doctrine, argued that criminals were evolutionary throwbacks whose "atavistic traits" were embodied in their physical characteristics. He termed these "stigmata" and used them as the basis for diagnosing criminal defendants and making judgments about them for use in criminal trials.[30]

Psychologists and others in the United States were much enamored of Lombroso's ideas about the biological and evolutionary origins of criminality.[31] Some thought that the practical import of this theory was that it promised legal authorities a "scientific" way of deciding who was, in fact, a criminal. As a criminological colleague of Lombroso's, Enrico Ferri, wrote: "A study of the anthropological factors of crime provides the guardians and administrators of the law with new and more certain methods in the detection of the guilty."[32]

Craniometry gradually transformed from an initial emphasis on skull size to a seemingly more nuanced focus on its shape and was eventually replaced—at least in popularity and practical application—by something called *phrenology*. Phrenologists believed that "character and intellect . . . were simply the sum of the combined functions of the organs of the brain. Character *was* the brain."[33] From this they reasoned that the external features of the skull revealed underlying truths about the size and organization of a person's brain and, therefore, his personality.[34] Thus, one "could make a fairly accurate character analysis by studying the shape of a subject's head."[35]

Phrenology was especially influential and widely embraced in the middle of the 19th century. As one historian put it, in the 1830s, it not only had a "bright future" as a budding science, with many deeply committed devotees, but it also "claimed to be more than an esoteric science—it represented itself as a social philosophy and popular movement as well."[36] There were "traveling" phrenologists and "phrenologists of the studio" who popularized these ideas by giving "individual character readings" for a fee, "purport[ing] to explain each man to himself—his virtues and vices, his potentialities, and limitations, how he could improve himself . . ."[37]—all contained within the contours of his skull.

Phrenology also had a significant role in the treatment of "insanity," which had been previously conceptualized as something akin to spiritual or demonic possession, and was correspondingly treated with what were often barbaric methods. In contrast, phrenologists assumed that "the brain was the organ of mind, and following the analogy of natures, therefore a diseased condition of the mind, i.e., insanity, indicated a diseased brain."[38] They argued that patients suffering these maladies should be treated in much more benign and caring ways.[39] For a time, at least, "phrenology as psychiatric theory had a profound influence on the conduct of American insane asylums."[40]

Phrenologists believed that criminal behavior "resulted from a pathological imbalance in the same cerebral faculties which . . . produced law-abiding conduct in more normal persons."[41] Commentators were optimistic that advances in phrenology could shine a "flood of light upon the whole subject of crime and prison discipline."[42] Editors of the *American Journal of Insanity* commented very approvingly on the newly established *Prison Discipline Journal* and encouraged the new journal's editors not to overlook "the practical excellence" of the principles of phrenology in developing ways to improve how the nation's prisons were run.[43] Criminals were thought to be relatively easy for phrenologists to identify and classify because they "were likely to have a 'ruffian head,' with little frontal area but prominence in the posterior regions of the skull."[44] Moreover, "[b]y spotting which propensities were particularly well developed"—as manifested in the size of the protuberances on someone's skull—"one might even be able to pinpoint the exact offense a given person was likely to commit."[45]

Although phrenology was said to have eventually "died a pauper's death in the late nineteenth century,"[46] its prominence through much of that century reflected the core belief that the causes of a person's behavior resided entirely inside them. Its influence on establishing what eventually became the discipline of psychology is difficult to overestimate. Indeed, Edward Boring's definitive early history of the field suggested that "scientific psychology was born of phrenology, out of wedlock with science."[47] Similarly, one of the founders of phrenology, Franz Gall, was also called "the father of psychology," as well as "the pioneer who foreshadowed the coming of modern criminology."[48]

The next iteration of these pseudoscientific theories—*eugenics*—was by far the most socially and politically influential. Despite the prestigious and widespread scientific backing that it received, eugenics was in many ways less precise than either craniometry or phrenology and did not lend itself as easily to measurable, definitive disproof. This fact may have accounted for both its impact and longevity, which greatly exceeded its two pseudoscientific predecessors. Eugenics was first proposed in the 1880s by Francis Galton as an outgrowth of his devotion to perfecting ways of measuring individual differences between people and the near religious fervor with which he approached the goal of improving "mankind" by reproducing its "superior" members. Galton believed that human "talent and character" were not only inherited but also could be manipulated at a group or national level through reproductive control—selective breeding and sterilization.[49] By the latter part of the 19th century, eugenics was seen as a way of addressing "supposedly inherited forms of 'degeneracy' including pauperism, criminality, feeblemindedness, insanity, and homosexuality."[50] These ideas continued to influence public and legal policy well into the 20th century.

Although eugenics thinking did not gain full popularity and respectability in the United States until late in the 19th century, the groundwork for its influence on the crime master narrative was laid in the 1870s by an extremely influential study published on a supposedly "degenerate" extended family of alleged criminals—the "Jukes." Its author, Richard Dugdale, was inspired to begin his research when, while working as a "volunteer inspector" for the New York Prison Association, he encountered what he thought was an unusually large number of jail inmates who appeared to come from the same family. Despite the subjectivity of his approach, Dugdale's book was cited repeatedly as "proof" of the genetic basis of criminality.[51] Although Dugdale's own thinking was far more nuanced and gave much credence to the important role that social conditions played in producing life outcomes, by the end of the century, his book was being used to support the assertion that the criminal "breeds criminals; the taint is in the blood and there is no royal touch which can expel it."[52]

This narrow brand of genetic determinism was seemingly buttressed by an alleged "follow-up" to Dugdale's original study, conducted several decades later by eugenics worker Arthur Estabrook. Using a host of ill-defined and value-laden terms (e.g., "ignorant harlots") to describe the surviving members and offspring of the original group that Dugdale had studied, and that Estabrook claimed to have personally interviewed,[53] he reported that his findings "confirmed" the earlier eugenics conclusions that Dugdale's work had been used to support. He asserted more broadly that it would be a "great mistake" for social agencies to ever overlook "the importance of heredity" in response to socially problematic behavior.

Estabrook argued that crime in particular was rampant in certain families because of their biological makeup.[54] He also claimed that imprisonment was destined to fail because "the eradication of criminality in defective stocks depends on the elimination of mental deficiency."[55] Estabrook offered "two practical solutions" to this problem—what he called "permanent custodial care" (in essence, a lifetime of incarceration) and the "sterilization of those whose germ plasm contains the defects which society wishes to eliminate."[56]

However flawed the underlying science, Estabrook's ideas about scourge of "defective stocks" and its role in criminality were widely shared by many of the 19th- and early 20th-century's most prominent intellectuals, as well as being popular with the public at large. Among the notable intellectual proponents of these theories was Oliver Wendell Holmes Sr., a well-respected man of letters and a professor of medicine at Harvard who also was the father of U.S. Supreme Court Justice Oliver Wendell Holmes, Jr. Like many of his contemporaries, the elder Holmes subscribed to a genetic theory of criminal behavior. For example, in one article he wrote for the *Atlantic Monthly*, he asked rhetorically, "Why should not deep-rooted moral defects and obliquities show themselves, as well as other qualities, in the descendants of moral monsters?"[57]

Notwithstanding recognition in some quarters of the role that poverty and other social conditions might play in the etiology of criminal behavior, eugenics played directly into the tendency to focus entirely on individuals as responsible for wrongdoing and to ignore or discount the circumstances that contributed to their actions. Individualistic responses to crime—imprisonment was primary among them—were readily at hand. Eugenics not only provided a pseudoscientific rationale for incarcerating "defective" criminals but also provided the basis for even more drastic interventions. Concern over habitual criminals and "other degenerate classes of humanity"[58] led to the passage of a number of laws providing for the involuntary sterilization of persons regarded as "unfit."[59] One physician advocate urged the passage of sterilization laws in response to a "startling increase of crime, especially in our large centers of population, by men of inborn criminal tendencies." [60] The first of such laws was passed in Indiana in the early 1900s[61] and many other states followed suit. By the mid-1930s, some 28 states had legal provisions for the "eugenical sterilization" of criminals and others.[62]

Indeed, no less a figure than the highly respected Harvard criminologist Sheldon Glueck matter-of-factly endorsed so-called defective delinquent statutes in the 1920s. He touted the laws' capacity to facilitate the early identification of persons who suffered from what he termed "constitutionally psychopathic inferiority."[63] In the name of "public protection," he endorsed keeping them in special institutions for "a wholly indeterminate period which may amount to life incarceration."[64]

Of course, the eugenics narrative was not always advanced in such unqualified terms. In fact, there were many turn-of-the-century critics who outright rejected it as an explanation of criminal behavior. David Rothman noted that, during what was known as the "Progressive Era" in American history (i.e., the end of the 19th and the opening decades of the 20th century), "[t]here was no single all-embracing explanation that dominated professional or lay thought" with respect to the causes of criminal behavior.[65] Indeed, many Progressive reformers firmly believed that environmental influences contributed to crime and deviance. Yet most of these same reformers were committed to an individual-centered *treatment* model. That is, "all of them endorsed a case-by-case approach," in which they sought to "understand the facts of each offender's life history" so that they could use diagnosis as the basis for prescribing a cure.[66] By the late 1920s, practice had come to dominate theory. That is, "an interpretation that emphasized psychological over environmental considerations" was used to explain criminality.[67] It was one that "looked more closely to the mental state than the social circumstances of the offender."[68] And, more often than not, explaining the "mental state . . . of the offender" led to an analysis of its eugenics origins.

In fact, eugenics remained widely popular among members of the public well into the 20th century and continued to be regarded as a legitimate "science" in academic circles. Its status as supposedly settled scientific doctrine was legally acknowledged in a landmark 1927 U.S. Supreme Court case.[69] Some 50 years after his father had written approvingly of eugenics interpretations of crime, Justice Oliver Wendell Holmes penned an infamous majority opinion in what would become one of the Court's most notorious decisions, *Buck v. Bell*. In his *Buck* opinion, Justice Holmes authorized the sterilization of an allegedly genetically unfit mother, Carrie Buck. His pronouncement in the case, that "three generations of imbeciles are enough,"[70] was entirely consistent with his father's earlier views and with the eugenics-dominated spirit of the times.

At the time *Buck* was decided, the eugenics ideas on which the opinion was largely based were still widely embraced. Victoria Nourse noted that

> By 1928, over 375 American universities and colleges taught courses in eugenics, as many as 20,000 students took these courses, and 70 percent of high school biology textbooks endorsed eugenics in some form. America was not alone; eugenics was a worldwide phenomenon, stretching from Canada to Denmark, and Sweden and beyond.[71]

As late as the 1930s, eugenics continued to garner "a large and diverse political following" that included members of "Junior Leagues and school principals and the Kiwanis to prohibitionists and birth control advocates and anti-miscegenationists."[72] *Buck* was decided in 1927 and would not be repudiated by the Court until its *Oklahoma v. Skinner* decision in 1942.[73] In fact, a *Yale Law Review* article published the same year that *Skinner* was decided acknowledged that "sterilization operations under compulsory states laws have been increasing rapidly," motivated in part by the desire to advance "[e]ugenic aims" as well as "reducing public welfare costs and punishing crime."[74] This large and diverse support continued at least until the advent of World War II, when the specter of Nazism and ominous implications of the pursuit of racial purity were becoming increasingly difficult to ignore.[75]

The final variation in embodied individualism emerged near the end of the 19th century and remained influential well into the 20th. *Instinct theory* purportedly explained how the "germ stock" about which eugenicists were so concerned manifested itself in the psychological make-up of individuals—in the form of innate traits or instincts that accounted for their behavioral tendencies. Although it had been mentioned by a number of late 19th-century writers, including the most prominent figure in the emerging discipline of academic psychology, William James, instinct theory was most closely associated with early 20th-century psychologist William McDougall, through whose efforts it became wildly popular well into the 1930s.

McDougall, who was described by his contemporaries as having "made in total as great a contribution to the science as any living psychologist"[76] and in historical accounts after his death as one of the "titans in psychology,"[77] achieved his academic reputation largely on the basis of a best-selling textbook, *An Introduction to Social Psychology*.[78] First published in 1908, the book appears to have gone through more editions than any other psychology text in the first half of the 20th century. Its popularity helped account for the fact that instinct theory "spread like wildfire" after the book was published.[79] In it, McDougall defined instincts as "certain innate or inherited tendencies" that he confidently asserted served as the basis of "all thought and action, whether individual or collective and from which the character and will of individuals and nations are gradually developed."[80] In the self-congratulatory preface he wrote to the 23rd edition of the book, published in 1936, McDougall claimed that other schools of psychology were finally "converging" on his ideas. He predicted that someday instinct theory would not only serve as one of the "main pillars of psychology" but also be recognized as "the indispensable basis of all the social sciences."[81]

By that time, McDougall had tied instinct theory explicitly to eugenics and used it as the basis for a host of racially and politically controversial claims. Although the vagueness and circularity of the theory eventually led to its downfall in scientific psychology, the psychological individualism nested within eugenics and instinct theory, as well as in their precursor pseudosciences, craniometry and phrenology—the metamessage that the causes of behavior resided entirely in the internal makeup of the persons who engaged in it—was never definitively abandoned. Neither were the basic biological and genetic assumptions on which it was based.

These pseudoscientific theories and the popular representations of criminality they generated played a significant role in shaping legal doctrines and criminal justice policies and practices. The 19th century has been termed the "formative era" of American law.[82] It was also the era of laissez-faire capitalism, a flourishing Protestant ethic, and a time when the cultural ethos was dominated by the "myth of rugged individualism." As one legal historian observed, the "hero of the common law was the property-owning, liberty-loving, self-reliant, reasonable man. He was also the hero of American society, celebrated by Jefferson as the freehold farmer, by Hamilton as the town merchant, by Jackson as the frontiersman."[83] He was celebrated as well by American social scientists whose disciplines were in the midst of their own formative era. By the time professional social scientists had perceived and articulated new models of behavior—particularly ones premised on a competing paradigm of "interdependence" that acknowledged the importance of social history and context,[84] psychological individualism had been crystallized into long-lasting legal doctrines and practices. It also served as the intellectual basis for powerful legal institutions and represented the more or less intractable assumptions that the general public routinely made about crime and punishment.

PSYCHOLOGICAL INDIVIDUALISM AND THE CRIME MASTER NARRATIVE IN MODERN TIMES

This brief history of the nation's commitment to the belief that the causes of behavior reside inside the persons who engage in it underscores its deep cultural and intellectual embeddedness. It helps to explain why contemporary variations of this form of individualism continue to serve as the foundation of the persistent crime master narrative. These individualistic assumptions still pervade the general public's views on crime and punishment, and aspects of the crime master narrative are still structured into a myriad of legal and criminal justice practices and policies. As I say, the same 19th century in which this embodied individualism flourished was the era in which many basic criminal law doctrines were codified and legal institutions were established—ones that persist in recognizable form to present times. Moreover, recognizable forms of the embodied individualism that was so prominent then abound now in traditional psychological writing, in much conventional religious doctrine, appear in numerous judicial opinions and scholarly legal commentaries, and are conspicuously featured in most media representations of criminal behavior.

For example, setting aside McDougall's eugenics-based extremism and the overtly racist policies to which it led, his basic belief in "innate propensities" and overall focus on "the nature and extent of the innate basis of mental life" as a causal explanation for the full range of individual and social behavior are not far afield from what arguably served, until relatively recently, as mainstream thinking in much of scientific psychology.[85] Compare McDougall's views with what social psychologist Hazel Markus described as the operative model of behavior that dominated both academic and lay psychology—what she termed the "independent model of the person." This model held that

> The person is the primary source and center of all thought, feeling and action. Agency resides within the person; it comes from internal states, capacities,

> motivations, and dispositions. From the perspective of this "it's what's inside that counts" model, people are self-determining, self-motivating, and morally responsible for their own actions. Normatively good actions originate in an independent, bounded, autonomous self and are separate or distinct from the thoughts and feelings of others.[86]

As Markus lamented, however, because the model assumed that the individual was "the source of all thought, feeling, and action," it not only led "researchers and people alike to look deep inside individual minds for sources of thought and action" but also led them "to ignore or even deny the influences of the social world."[87]

This individualistic model that sees the person as "the primary source and center of all thought, feeling and action" not only dominated conventional psychological thinking until relatively recently but remained influential in other social science disciplines as well. For example, Lawrence Bobo and Vincent Hutchings described its sway over prevailing analyses of the causes of social and economic inequality:

> The dominant stratification ideology in the United States holds that opportunities are plentiful and that individuals succeed or fail largely on the basis of their own efforts and talents. As a result, inequality of valued social outcomes is seen as not only fair, but necessary because of differential effort and ability. . . . Accordingly, individuals obtain valued social outcomes by dint of their individual qualities.[88]

As perhaps might be expected, there are a number of religious denominations whose core teachings about good and evil are premised explicitly on a free will model of behavior and that, therefore, serve as strong affirmations of psychological individualism and, by implication, the crime master narrative. For example, as an article in the United Church of God publication, *The Good News: A Magazine of Understanding*, concisely explained, although some academics may offer "many rationalizations for why society is plagued with crime" and some tend to blame "poverty, dysfunctional families, poor parenting and the like," these social ills are *"not the fundamental cause."*[89] Instead, church doctrine teaches that *"crime is a personal choice."*[90] That is, "[w]e all have freedom to weigh courses of actions, to consider the consequences, to make and follow through on decisions."[91]

However central psychological individualism and the crime master narrative have been to certain academic disciplines and particular religious doctrines, they are positively enshrined in American law and in the operating assumptions of the nation's criminal justice institutions. Thus, numerous judicial opinions have acknowledged psychological individualism, "free will," and the crime master narrative as the bedrock of American jurisprudence. As the U.S. Supreme Court wrote in a 1952 opinion, "belief in freedom of the will and a consequent ability and duty of the normal individual to choose between good and evil" are not only widely accepted views but actually "universal and persistent in mature systems of law."[92] The Court elaborated by providing some historical context: "Crime, as a compound concept, generally constituted only from concurrence of an evil-meaning mind with an evil-doing hand, was congenial to an intense individualism and took deep and early root in American soil."[93] It remained deeply rooted there.

Thus, some 20 years later, the influential D.C. Circuit Court of Appeals, known at the time for its especially sophisticated grasp of mental health issues, explicitly acknowledged that there were broad external influences that could shape a person's decisions and actions. However, although the court was "not oblivious to deterministic components" that influence what people say and do, it nonetheless insisted that "[o]ur jurisprudence . . . ultimately rests on a premise of free will." As the judges put it, "[c]riminal responsibility is assessed when through 'free will' a man elects to do evil."[94] Although the court saw the assumption of free will more as a pragmatic concession—"a governmental fusion of ethics and necessity"—it insisted that there should be no exceptions absent "an abnormal condition of the mind."[95]

Legal commentators have acknowledged that, for better or worse, the crime master narrative and its assumption about free will continue to play a central role in judicial decision making. For example, as Richard Boldt put it, the "doctrine of free will dictates that all human behavior is produced through the intent and agency of the individual."[96] The criminal law's unquestioned assumptions about the agency of the individual essentially foreclose inquiries into the myriad of external forces that might influence criminal behavior. Meir Dan-Cohen added another dimension to this view by noting,

> Blaming—that is, ascribing moral responsibility for the negative effects of one's behavior—has come to be understood in terms of what I call the *free will paradigm*. In the free will paradigm, responsibility is grounded in the agent's capacity to choose her actions freely.[97]

Similarly, forensic psychiatrist and law professor Bernard Diamond advocated broadening traditional legal concepts of responsibility to incorporate a wide range of developmental and social contextual influences on criminal behavior. Even in the 1970s, when this was an emerging view in the behavioral and social sciences, Diamond knew what he was up against in law. He regretfully observed that, still,

> most, if not all, of the various specific mental states [used to assess level of culpability] infer, in their very definitions, the existence of free-will: the capacity to make a free choice by a rational individual acting as a free agent.[98]

Many legal scholars have bemoaned the narrowness of the crime master narrative at the same time that they recognize how influential it has continued to be in contemporary judicial opinions. They critique the strong hold that these narrow views retain on contemporary legal scholarship as well. For example, legal commentators Stephanos Bibas and Richard Bierschbach decried the persistent influence of "the individual badness model"—a model closely akin to what I have termed the crime master narrative—that not only dominates legal doctrines of criminal responsibility but also has become "symptomatic of a deeper strain of thinking in contemporary criminal law scholarship: a focus on the individual offender" to the exclusion of virtually anything else.[99] They correctly noted that "[c]riminal sentencing and punishment have long been preoccupied with individual offenders,"[100] and quoted criminal law scholar Victoria Nourse to the effect that "by the 1970s and 1980s, there was a consensus within the academy that all of the most important theoretical questions in the criminal law were about individuals: individual 'self-control,' individual dangerousness, and individual culpability."[101]

Ironically, the "consensus in the [legal] academy" was increasingly embracing a view of human nature that, as I point out in subsequent chapters, was increasingly out of step with what was being learned by colleagues in other social scientific disciplines. Of course, the narrow-gauged individualistic perspective to which legal scholars were drawn remained entirely consistent with the crime master narrative that was enthusiastically promoted by politicians and the media, especially during the so-called "era of mass incarceration" that began in the United States in the 1970s and has continued to the present time.[102] As Bibas and Bierschbach put it, "the idea of individual dispositions toward or against criminality drives much of the thinking about how best to control and respond to crime,"[103] both in public policy and much legal scholarship about the issue.

Beyond its central role in the scholarship produced by many legal academics, psychological individualism and the crime master narrative that is based on it has enjoyed unquestioned status throughout much of American corrections. Given the role that the institution of prison plays in administering punishment to individual wrongdoers who have "freely chosen" to do bad things, it is not surprising that the crime master narrative has been enthusiastically embraced by prison officers and administrators. For example, the California Correctional Peace Officers Association ("CCPOA"), the powerful and well-funded correctional officers' union in California, has sponsored political advertisements that not only supported tough-on-crime legislation (such as "Three Strikes" laws) but also issued policy statements to politicians and members of the public that explicitly promoted the crime master narrative. Thus, the CCPOA instructed Californians in the mid-1990s (when the state was increasing its prison population at unprecedented rapid rates) that "the criminal is responsible for his own choice," and that any attempt by so-called experts or others to explain criminal behavior by reference to background factors such as childhood trauma or social conditions simply "makes excuses" for criminal behavior. The correctional officers' union asserted further that prison rehabilitation—something citizens might otherwise assume was part of their job—was ultimately a waste of time because criminals were irredeemable. Indeed: "The criminal pretends to change and the system pretends to believe them but they remain predators of people, situations, and institutions. They take whatever they can, anyway they can."[104]

In another illustrative example, Burl Cain, the longtime and highly influential former warden of Louisiana's notorious Angola Prison, who was widely known for his evangelical fervor, ascribed wholeheartedly to the crime master narrative. Speaking about the prisoners under his control, Cain said: "They chose a life of crime. Every choice they made is theirs. They're crybabies crying about it. What they ought to do is look in the mirror and quit looking out."[105]

In addition to being enshrined in legal thinking and criminal justice practices, the crime master narrative remains firmly implanted in the public consciousness about crime and punishment, in part because of the way that the mass media uncritically and reflexively promotes it. Nowhere in our society is this master narrative more heartily advanced, repeated, and repeatedly sensationalized. Media depictions of the nature of criminality almost universally focus on the alleged character flaws, depredations, and pathology of perpetrators, often essentializing the causes of criminality with strong echoes of the 19th century biologism that was central to craniometry, phrenology, eugenics, and instinct theory. Next, I discuss just a few examples, all published during the era of mass incarceration, when the criminal justice system was ramping up policies of unprecedented harsh punishment directed at individual lawbreakers, even as researchers were collecting extensive evidence demonstrating that the underlying causes of crime lay elsewhere.

For example, in 1993, respected journalist and *Newsweek* staff writer David A. Kaplan penned a long article on violent crime entitled "The Incorrigibles" that in many ways typifies the crime news genre, including all of the core elements of the crime master narrative.[106] Accompanied by a color collage of mugshots depicting a recently executed prisoner and subtitled "They rape and molest. They defy treatment. How can society protect itself?" it began in an ominous, frightening tone:

> They are the ones we truly fear. When the children head out to play, when a wife or sister is overdue from the office, these are the miscreants who make us wonder whether it's safe to go outside anymore. They are random and repeat sexual predators; many are killers too.

It was a compelling, unsettling piece in which Kaplan captured the spirit of the times and advanced several damning themes. For one, he suggested that even when violent lawbreakers got arrested and incarcerated ("sometimes-though only after two or three convictions"), they were invariably released prematurely, "regardless of the dangers officials believe they pose." Indeed, "[t]hey don't fall through the proverbial cracks in the criminal justice system; they walk right out its front door." Ironically, Kaplan implied that the criminal justice system in the United States was shockingly lenient at a time when it already led the Western world in the rate at which it incarcerated its citizens. He also suggested that violent crime was rampant and uncontrollably rising at a time when the national crime rates were beginning a consistent, decades-long decline. Nonetheless, the article came out four-square in favor of two criminal justice system proposals that were not only eventually implemented but that have persisted to the present time—life without parole sentences and the postprison, indefinite civil commitment of sex offenders.

Its policy prescriptions notwithstanding, the individualistic crime master narrative was at the very heart of the piece. Indeed, Kaplan attempted to "explain" violent criminality by calling its perpetrators "incorrigibles," "predators," "miscreants," "rapacious monsters," and "reprobates," and failed to reference a single social contextual cause or societal influence. Full of misleading, partial, and vague references to questionable research on high rates of recidivism among sex offenders (when most research indicated the opposite), the article asserted, without naming anyone in specific, that "[m]ost experts say these reprobates were fully formed at a young age and cannot be reformed."

Other opinion leaders joined much the same chorus. For example, at around the same time as Kaplan's screed was published, the pernicious term "superpredator" was coined by Princeton political science professor John DiIulio, who used it in the "get *tougher* on juvenile crime" editorials he penned for *The Wall Street Journal* and other newspapers in the mid-1990s.[107] In a book-length elaboration of the supposed superpredator threat, DiIulio and two conservative pundits claimed there were "thickening ranks" of superpredator preteens and teens, whom they described as "radically impulsive, brutally remorseless," who were intent on committing heinous crimes without "fear[ing] the stigma of arrest, the pains of imprisonment, or the pangs of conscience."[108]

The superpredator terminology was so widely accepted that it made its way into the 1996 presidential campaigns of *both* major candidates. Republican candidate Bob Dole embraced it in arguing for tougher juvenile laws.[109] More surprising still, in a speech that then–first lady Hillary Clinton gave on January 28, 1996, at Keene State University, when she was campaigning in New Hampshire for her husband, President Bill Clinton, she told an audience that the nation needed to "take back our streets." Mrs. Clinton warned those in attendance that the country now faced a new threat, she said, "not just gangs of kids anymore," but now "often the kinds of kids that are called 'superpredators,' [with] no conscience, no empathy." Although she conceded that "we can talk about why they ended up that way," that was not on her agenda. Instead, before the nation could focus on the causes of their behavior, "first we have to bring them to heel." She went on to tout the appointment of General Barry McCaffrey as the nation's new "drug czar," and called on voters to support the "anti-crime, anti-gang, and anti-drug" initiatives that her husband promised to implement if voters gave him a second term.[110] They did, and he made good on his promise, presiding over an unprecedented overall increase in the number of people in prison, from approximately 850,000 when he took office in 1992 to some 1,334,000 when he left 8 years later.[111]

The marginality and stigma that were attached to the criminal class were both signaled and facilitated by increasing references to criminals as profoundly "other"—whether as another species, another "breed," or another life form.[112] Thus, in the final decades of the 20th century, lawbreakers were increasingly depicted and referred to as monsters, demons, devils, and the like. These characterizations were not limited to fiction or sensationalized news stories, but occurred also in what passed as popularized "scientific" discussions of the topic of criminality, in which alleged experts helped a frightened public come to terms with the terrifying dimensions of the "otherness" that criminals represented. Indeed, one such article—a profile of the nation's alleged "#1 psychiatrist sleuth," prominent forensic expert Park Dietz—referred to the perpetrators of serious violent crime as "devils," "misfits," and "monsters," with "killer instincts," and "twisted psyches."[113]

Even though crime rates were actually dropping over most of this period, and would continue to do so, Kaplan, DiIulio, Clinton, Dietz and numerous others were both channeling and giving legitimacy to the crime master narrative. Whatever else it accomplished, referring to the perpetrators of crime as miscreants, incorrigibles, reprobates, monsters, superpredators, devils, and demons not only dehumanized them but also obviated any real need to grapple with the underlying causes of their behavior. Indeed, the crime master narrative has been so consistently advanced as an explanation for criminal behavior even in modern times that alternative perspectives simply do not penetrate or impact political, public, and media discourse on the topic. They are rarely raised in public policy debates about how best to address and reduce crime rates and have had little or no influence in shaping criminal law doctrine.

And yet, there is now much reason to believe that all of this is beginning to change, and an empirically based counternarrative is finally emerging. As I argue throughout this book, this new counternarrative is fundamental to the meaningful and lasting reform of criminal justice doctrines, practices, and institutions that have been so persistently and unshakably dependent on the deeply flawed crime master narrative.

DECONSTRUCTING THE CRIME MASTER NARRATIVE

Although the conferred legitimacy with which master narratives are cloaked creates widely accepted public truths that are often resistant to change and crowd out other points of view, official frameworks *can* be successfully challenged by competing perspectives. Social scientific and other forms of knowledge that are based on more systematic empirical data, logic, or theory may form the basis of alternative "counternarratives" that employ very different frameworks for interpreting or understanding the same phenomena or set of events. An especially persuasive and credible counternarrative that appears to better account for the facts at hand may be used to debunk, neutralize, or even supplant the master narrative with which it is competing.[114]

For example, feminist scholars effectively critiqued the master narratives that were once routinely applied to women's lives that described them in confining, distorting, and oppressive ways. The feminist counternarrative demonstrated the many ways that these previously unquestioned sexist master narratives were deeply flawed, especially because they omitted complex facts and nuanced interpretations that contradicted or posed challenges to the prevailing male-dominated power structure.[115] Absent such a systematic and sustained critique, however, master narratives stand as the presumptive, default point of view; they are only (if ever) dislodged by a persuasive alternative framework that offers compelling reasons to reject the institutionally legitimated one.

As I suggested in passing previously, the crime master narrative is now being decisively challenged by precisely such a persuasive counternarrative that frames our understanding of criminality in a more empirically supported and scientifically valid way. Decades of mounting research and coherent underlying theory represent a compelling alternative framework with which to understand the nature of criminal behavior. Some of this research grows out of a much broader set of intellectual insights that arose in the late 1960s in which previously unquestioned assumptions about the nature of the human personality were finally subjected to careful scientific scrutiny, generating mounting questions that came to be seen as scientific "anomalies" of the sort that would soon coalesce into a genuine Kuhnian paradigm shift.[116] The view that human beings were composed of a bundle of largely fixed traits that generated highly consistent behavior across a range of very different settings could not be empirically sustained and was supplanted by a more sophisticated and nuanced view that accounted for existing data.[117] The research that I discuss in the remainder of this book elaborates on this alternative framework, a "counternarrative" to the crime master narrative, one that is far more consistent with what is now known about these issues.

In fact, the widespread tendency to attribute primary causal significance to persons alone, while discounting the important influence of past and present situations and contexts, is now recognized as a cognitive bias, a form of mistaken understanding. Albeit natural and still widespread, this "fundamental attribution error" leads laypersons and policymakers alike to reach erroneous conclusions about the causal origins of everyday behavior. Social psychologists in particular have analyzed the various ways in which fundamental error in attributing causality is produced by various forms of selective information processing, including the fact that observers tend to see people in the same or similar circumstances (so that situational constancy rather than trait stability often accounts for what is perceived as apparent consistency in behavior).[118] The discipline of psychology has really not conceptualized social behavior in the same way since.

Indeed, what has been termed the "situational revolution" in academic psychology generated an extensive amount of research on the various ways in which specific social contexts and settings influence behavior, resulting in the displacement of the dominant paradigm that Marcus termed "the independent model of the person." The impressive accumulation of data that continued to be produced by this research confirmed several basic points.

For one, social scientists now recognize that much of our behavior is shaped and determined by past experience—what I describe and discuss at length in the next two chapters as our social history. In addition, behavior is also very much influenced by the objective characteristics of the social situations in which it occurs, with more such influence obviously being exercised by more powerful, compelling situations. In addition, the way those situations are cognitively represented or subjectively perceived by the people within them is heavily influenced by their past social histories which, in turn, significantly influence their specific behavioral effects, including whether and to what degree people are inclined to engage in criminal behavior.

Thus, much of the research that was conducted on the contextual causes of crime over the last several decades challenges the crime master narrative's assertion that delinquency and adult criminal behavior are caused primarily if not exclusively by the individual-level psychological characteristics, tendencies, and traits of persons who have violated the law. The entrenched notion that actions stem directly from forces that reside entirely within the actors, manifested through the exercise of their free and autonomous will, has been replaced by a more nuanced social historical and contextual view. Instead, this new theoretical and empirically based model acknowledges that much criminal behavior occurs in response to highly criminogenic past experiences (especially trauma and maltreatment) and problematic present situations. Delinquency and crime can only be fully understood by carefully examining both the background life experiences and the present circumstances of those persons who engage in it.[119] The next several chapters elaborate on the nature of this new theoretical model and the extensive empirical data that support it.

NOTES

1. Hulsman, L. (1991). The abolitionist case: Alternative crime policies. *Israel Law Review, 25,* 681–709, p. 682. http://dx.doi.org/10.1017/S0021223700010694
2. The information in this narrative is based on sworn testimony in an actual capital trial, and the quotations in the text are taken verbatim from the Recorder's Transcript of the jury trial. However, the defendant's name has been changed.
3. Klein, K. L. (1995). In search of narrative mastery: Postmodernism and the people without history. *History and Theory, 34,* 275–298, p. 282. http://dx.doi.org/10.2307/2505403
4. Morrison, T. (1997). The official story: Dead man golfing. In T. Morrison & C. Brodsky Lacour (Eds.), *Birth of a nation 'hood: Gaze, script, and spectacle in the O. J. Simpson case* (pp. vii–xxviii). New York, NY: Pantheon.
5. Bibas, S., & Bierschbach, R. A. (2004). Integrating remorse and apology into criminal procedure. *Yale Law Journal, 114,* 85–148, p. 89. http://dx.doi.org/10.2307/4135717
6. See, e.g., Beckett, K. (1997). *Making crime pay: Law and order in contemporary American politics.* New York, NY: Oxford University Press; Boldt, R. C. (1986). Criminal law and the ideology of individuality. *Journal of Criminal Law and Criminology, 77,* 969–1022. http://dx.doi.org/10.5040/9781474201957.ch-005; and Peelo, M., & Soothill, K. (2000). The place of public narratives in reproducing social order. *Theoretical Criminology, 4,* 131–148. http://dx.doi.org/10.1177/1362480600004002001

7. Boldt, R. (1986). Restitution, criminal law, and the ideology of individuality. *Journal of Criminal Law, Criminology, 77,* 969–1022, p. 1011. http://dx.doi.org/10.5040/9781474201957.ch-005
8. For research and writing on the dimensions of the media's distorted coverage of these issues, see, e.g., Haney, C. (2008). Media criminology and the death penalty. *DePaul Law Review, 58,* 689–740; Haney, C., & Greene, S. (2004). Capital constructions: Newspaper reporting in death penalty cases. *Analyses of Social Issues and Public Policy, 4,* 129–150. http://dx.doi.org/10.1111/j.1530-2415.2004.00038.x; and Bakhshay, S., & Haney, C. (2018). The media's impact on the right to a fair trial: A content analysis of pretrial publicity in capital cases. *Psychology, Public Policy, and Law, 24,* 326–340. http://dx.doi.org/10.1037/law0000174
9. Lamb, S. (1996). *The trouble with blame: Victims, perpetrators, & responsibility.* Cambridge, MA: Harvard University Press.
10. Grabe, M. E. (1999). Television news magazine crime stories: A functionalist perspective. *Critical Studies in Mass Communication, 16,* 155–171, p. 163. http://dx.doi.org/10.1080/15295039909367084
11. See, e.g., Haney, C. (2002). Making law modern: Toward a contextual model of justice. *Psychology, Public Policy, and Law, 7,* 3–63. http://dx.doi.org/10.1037/1076-8971.8.1.3; and Haney, C. (2008). Evolving standards of decency: Advancing the nature and logic of capital mitigation. *Hofstra Law Review, 36,* 835–882.
12. Hume, D. (1975). *Enquiries concerning human understanding and concerning the principles of morals* (p. 98). Oxford, England: Oxford University Press. (Original work published 1739) http://dx.doi.org/10.1093/actrade/9780198245353.book.1
13. Historian Yehoshua Arieli suggested that "[i]ndividualism supplied the nation with a rationalization of its characteristic attitudes, behavior patterns and aspirations." Arieli, Y. (1964). *Individualism and nationalism in American ideology.* Cambridge, MA: Harvard University Press, pp. 345–346. Political scientist Louis Hartz called the atomistic social freedom on which individualism is based "the master assumption of American political thought," one that became "instinctive to the American mind, as in a sense the concept of the polis was instinctive to Platonic Athens or the concept of the church to the mind of the middle ages." Hartz, L. (1955). *The liberal tradition in America.* New York, NY: Harcourt, Brace, and World, p. 62.
14. Horwitz, M. J. (1977). *The transformation of American law: 1780–1860.* Cambridge, MA: Harvard University Press, pp. 107–108.
15. Pound, R. (1905). Do we need a philosophy of law? *Columbia Law Review, 5,* 339–353, p. 346.
16. These issues are discussed more fully in Haney, C. (1982). Criminal justice and the nineteenth-century paradigm: The triumph of psychological individualism in the "formative era." *Law and Human Behavior, 6,* 191–235. http://dx.doi.org/10.1007/BF01044295
17. Miller, M. B. (1974). At hard labor: Rediscovering the 19th century prison. *Issues in Criminology, 9,* 91–114, p. 91, Table 1. I use the term "prisoner" throughout this book. I do not intend to denote or imply anything about the essence of the persons who are imprisoned but rather the essence of the context in which they are being held.
18. Franke, H. (1992). The rise and decline of solitary confinement: Socio-historical explanations of long-term penal changes. *British Journal of Criminology, 32,* 125–143, p. 137. http://dx.doi.org/10.1093/oxfordjournals.bjc.a048186
19. Franke (1992). The rise and decline of solitary confinement, p. 137.
20. Rosenberg, C. E. (1968). *The trial of the assassin Guiteau: Psychiatry and law in the Gilded Age* (p. 65). Chicago, IL: University of Chicago Press.
21. See Prichard, J. C. (1835). *A treatise on insanity and other disorders affecting the mind.* London, England: Sherwood, Gilbert, and Piper. http://dx.doi.org/10.1037/10551-000

22. See Ray, I. (1838). *A treatise on the medical jurisprudence of insanity*. Boston, MA: Little Brown.
23. de Beaumont, G., & de Tocqueville, A. (1833). *On the penitentiary system in the United States and its application to France* (F. Lieber, Trans.). Philadelphia, PA: Lea and Blanchard, p. vii.
24. Clark, M. (1894, November). The relation of imbecility to pauperism and crime. *Arena, 10*, 789, p. 789. For an excellent review of these issues, see Ellis, J. W., & Luckasson, R. A. (1985). Mentally retarded criminal defendants. *The George Washington Law Review, 53*, 414–493.
25. Fernald, W. (1909). The imbecile with criminal instincts. In Rosen, M., Clark, G. R., & Kivitz, M. S. (Eds.). (1976). *The history of mental retardation: Collected papers* (Vol. 2). Baltimore, MD: University Park Press, p. 16. See also Report of the Massachusetts Commission (1911). *To investigate the question of the increase of criminals, mental defectives, epileptics and degenerates*. Boston, MA: Wright & Potter, State Printers.
26. Terman, L. M. (1919). *The intelligence of school children: How children differ in ability*. Boston, MA: Houghton, Mifflin, p. 132. See also California State Committee on Defectives, Terman L. M., California State Board of Charities and Corrections. (1918). *Surveys in mental deviation in prisons, public schools and orphanages in California: Under auspices of the State Joint Committee*. Sacramento, CA: State Printing Office.
27. Goddard, H. H., as cited in Schlapp, M. G., & Smith, E. H. (1928). *The new criminology*. New York, NY: Boni & Liveright, p. 148.
28. Jackson, J. P., Jr. (2010). Whatever happened to the cephalic index? The reality of race and the burden of proof. *Rhetoric Society Quarterly, 40*, 438–458, p. 446. http://dx.doi.org/10.1080/02773945.2010.517233
29. Jackson (2010), Whatever happened to the cephalic index? p. 447. Practitioners of craniometry claimed that their key measurement—the so-called cephalic index, which they defined as "a ratio of the width of the head to the length of the head"—was impervious to external influences. Jackson (2010), Whatever happened to the cephalic index? p. 448. Although this was later shown to be incorrect, the claim provided the basis for an argument that any differences between people or groups of people in the cephalic index were inherent rather than acquired; they were not, the argument went, the result of experience.
30. See, e.g., Lombroso, C. (1911). *Crime: Its causes and remedies* (Horton, H. P., Trans.). London, England: W. Heinemann; Lombroso, C., & Ferrero, W. (1895). *The female offender*. New York, NY: D. Appleton; Lombroso Ferrero, G., & Lombroso, C. (1911). *Criminal man according to the classification of Cesare Lombroso*. New York, NY: Putnam. Like many American psychologists with whom he shared a biological and genetic approach to human behavior, Lombroso was especially interested in the idea of "innate" intelligence. See Lombroso, C. (1891). *The man of genius*. London, England: C. Scribner's Sons.
31. In the late 1880s, for example, psychology professor Joseph Jastrow published a Lombrosian theory of criminality in the journal *Science* in which he touted the Italian criminologist's views. See Jastrow, J. (1886). A theory of criminality. *Science, 8*, 20–22. See also Noyes, W. (1888). The criminal type. *American Journal of Social Science, 24*, 31–42. A book published in the late 19th century by English eugenicist Havelock Ellis elaborated on Lombroso's theories about "born criminals" and became extremely popular and influential in the United States. See Ellis, H. (1890). *The criminal*. London, England: Walter Scott.
32. Ferri, E. (1897). *Criminal sociology* (p. 166). New York, NY: D. Appleton.
33. Davies, J. D. (1955). *Phrenology, fad and science: A 19th century American crusade*. New Haven, CT: Yale University Press, p. 7.

34. Colbert, C. (1998). *A measure of perfection: Phrenology and the fine arts in America.* Raleigh: University of North Carolina Press; Fancher, R. (1988). Gall, Flourens and the phrenological movement. In Benjamin, L. T., Jr. (Ed.), *A history of psychology: Original sources and contemporary research* (pp. 101–108). New York, NY: McGraw Hill.
35. Davies (1955), *Phrenology, fad and science,* p. 4. Phrenologists believed that the mind was composed of a number of "faculties" or attributes that were localized in "organs" or regions of the brain, in amounts that were reflected in "the size and contour of the cranium" (p. 4).
36. Davies (1955), *Phrenology, fad and science,* p. 11. As Davies also noted,

    > By the 1830's phrenology had given rise to some sixty-six books and pamphlets which had run through many editions, and the young science was being nourished by twelve phrenological societies, which furnished readers, authors, and audiences for the many lectures on the subject (p. 11).

    Phrenology had a host of prominent followers in the United States in the mid-19th century, especially in the field of education. Well-known social and educational reformers such as Samuel Gridley Howe and Horace Mann helped organize and sponsor lectures on the topic and strongly encouraged the application of phrenological principles in a variety of educational settings. See Davies, Chapter 6.
37. Davies (1955), *Phrenology, fad and science,* p. 31. "Theoretical" or academic phrenologists were sharply critical of these popularizers for what they regarded as the commercialization and vulgarization of their "science," and worried that the practical phrenologists' "way of proceeding did injury to phrenology in public estimation as a science." Davies (1955), p. 44, quoting George Combs, a Scottish lawyer who became one of the most respectable "scientific" spokesmen for phrenology in the United States.
38. Davies (1955), *Phrenology, fad and science,* p. 90.
39. Davies (1955) put it thus:

    > The treatment of the disease varied with the individual case. The behavior of the patient and the shape of the skull, if it was unusual, were carefully observed, and it was decided what organs were at fault. . . . But the best therapy was simply a course of following "the natural laws" the neglect of which had brought on the disease: a regimen of fresh air, physical exercise, bland diet with no liquor or tobacco, plenty of rest and sleep and morel uplift, warmth, placidity, and little intellectual effort. (*Phrenology, fad and science,* pp. 91–92)

40. Davies (1995), *Phrenology, fad and science,* p. 96. In fact, Samuel Woodward, the founder and first president of an organization that became the American Psychiatric Association, was quoted in the 1840s as saying "it was impossible to successfully treat the insane without the aid of phrenology" (Davies, 1955, *Phrenology, fad and science,* p. 94). Although the commitment to phrenology that mid-19th century psychiatrists seemed to share quickly waned, the belief that insanity resulted from physical defects or diseases did not. As historian John Burnham noted,

    > In the late 19th century, physicians who dealt with the mentally ill usually were "organicists" who adhered strictly to scientific materialism. They believed that behavior and thinking were but the expression of the functioning of the nervous system and that physical defects or diseases were at the bottom of all mental diseases.

    Burnham, J. C. (1960). Psychiatry, psychology, and the Progressive Movement. *American Quarterly, 12,* 457–465, p. 459.
41. Lewis, W. (1973). Eliza Farnham and phrenological contributions to American penology. In M. B. Sampson (Ed., with E. W. Farnham), *Rationale of crime and its appropriate treatment: Being a treatise on criminal jurisprudence considered in relation to cerebral organization* (p. xiii). Montclair, NJ: Patterson Smith. (Original work published 1846)

42. Quoted in Davies (1955), *Phrenology, fad and science,* p. 98.
43. Davies (1955), *Phrenology, fad and science,* p. 98.
44. Lewis (1846/1973), Eliza Farnham and phrenological contributions to American penology, p. xv.
45. Lewis (1846/1973), Eliza Farnham and phrenological contributions to American penology, p. xv.
46. Haller, J. S., Jr. (1970). Concepts of race inferiority in nineteenth-century anthropology. *Journal of the History of Medicine and Allied Sciences, 25,* 40–51, p. 47. http://dx.doi.org/10.1093/jhmas/XXV.1.40. Haller also observed that scientific skepticism about phrenology eventually grew in strong reaction to "those enthusiasts who sought to go behind the measurements to judge moral character, intelligence, and social tendencies" of people (p. 46). But judging those things was precisely what many adherents thought most useful.
47. Boring, E. G. (1929). *A history of experimental psychology.* New York, NY: Century, p. 55.
48. Lydston, G. F. (1904). *The diseases of society.* Philadelphia, PA: B. Lippincott, p. 154.
49. See, e.g., Buss, A. R. (1976). Galton and the birth of differential psychology and eugenics: Social, political, and economic forces. *Journal of the History of the Behavioral Sciences, 12,* 47–58. http://dx.doi.org/10.1002/1520-6696(197601)12:1<47::AID-JHBS2300120106>3.0.CO;2-V
50. Stubblefield, A. (2007). "Beyond the pale": Tainted whiteness, cognitive disability, and eugenic sterilization. *Hypatia, 22,* 162–181, p. 164.
51. See Dugdale, R. L. (1877). *"The Jukes": A study in crime, pauperism, disease and heredity; Also, further studies of criminals* (3rd ed.). New York, NY: Putnam's. In fact—notwithstanding the proposition for which his work came to stand—Dugdale himself was much more sympathetic to the notion that the Juke family actually had inherited a bad environment as much or more than bad genetics. See Carlson, E. A. (2001). *The unfit: The history of a bad idea.* Cold Spring Harbor, NY: Cold Spring Harbor Press. But the prevailing Zeitgeist turned Dugdale's position on its head. As Carlson noted, "[i]t was the unhappy fate of *The Jukes* to be largely misinterpreted as the history of a condemned, unredeemable kindred" (p. 172). The eugenics message incorrectly derived from Dugdale's work retained much currency into the early decades of the 20th century.
52. Carlson (2001), *The unfit,* p. 171.
53. See Estabrook, A. H. (1916). *The Jukes in 1915.* Washington, DC: The Carnegie Institute. For an excellent history of the interconnection between biological theories of intellectual inferiority (allegedly inborn "idiocy" and "imbecility") and moral defectiveness (as the source of criminality) in the late 19th century, see Rafter, N. H. (1997). *Creating born criminals.* Urbana: University of Illinois Press.
54. Estabrook (1916), *The Jukes,* p. iv.
55. Estabrook (1916), *The Jukes,* p. 85.
56. Estabrook (1916), *The Jukes,* p. 85.
57. Holmes, O. (1875, April). Crime and automatism, *Atlantic Monthly,* XXXV, 466–481, p. 475. The article captured the tenor of eugenics thinking during this era that served as the basis for legal policies and opinions for decades. In it, Holmes summarized the results of a study of the descendants of one particular woman from New York State, concluding that a high number of her descendants had turned out to be criminals and "a large number of the others, idiots, imbeciles, drunkards, and of otherwise degraded character." As a reflection of the times in which he wrote, however, the elder Holmes was actually considered a "progressive thinker" about crime and punishment. He was often critical of what he considered to be the "narrowness" of the criminal law and attributed criminality to "misfortune" of the criminal. However, the misfortune he had in mind was primarily in the form of a defective genetic makeup.

58. Carlson, *The unfit*, p. 247.
59. As one prison superintendent put it,

> Men who have had experience of ten or twelve years in the handling of criminals can see the necessity of something being done along this line. This law will not only prevent the procreation, but in my judgement will be one of the best preventive measures to deter crime that has ever been placed upon the statute books. Surgeons to deal with criminals. (1907, March 7). *Indianapolis Star*, p. 10.

60. The sterilization of criminals and other degenerates [Editorial]. (1910). *Indianapolis Medical Journal, 13*, 163, p. 163.
61. The Indiana law was passed in 1907, and was directed at "confirmed criminals, idiots, rapists, and imbeciles." Laws of the State of Indiana Passed at the 65th Regular Session of the General Assembly 1907. Indianapolis, IN: W. B. Burford, pp. 377–378.
62. Carlson (2001), *The unfit*, p. 221.
63. Glueck, S. (1927). Psychiatric examination of persons accused of crime. *Yale Law Journal, 36*, 632–648, pp. 636–637. http://dx.doi.org/10.2307/789774
64. Glueck (1927), Psychiatric examination, p. 637.
65. Rothman, D. J. (1980). *Conscience and convenience: The asylum and its alternatives in Progressive America* (p. 50). Boston, MA: Little, Brown. http://dx.doi.org/10.1086/ahr/89.1.227-a
66. Rothman (1980), *Conscience and convenience*, p. 50.
67. Rothman (1980), *Conscience and convenience*, p. 54.
68. Rothman (1980), *Conscience and convenience*, p. 54.
69. Buck v. Bell, 274 U.S. 200 (1927).
70. Buck v. Bell, 274 U.S. at 207. For a compelling history of the case in the larger context of the eugenics movement in the United States, see Lombardo, P. (2008). *Three generations, no imbeciles: Eugenics, the Supreme Court, and Buck v. Bell.* Baltimore, MD: Johns Hopkins University Press.
71. Nourse, V. F. (2008). *In reckless hands: Skinner v. Oklahoma and the near triumph of American eugenics*. New York, NY: W. W. Norton, p. 20.
72. Nourse (2008), *In reckless hands*, p. 21.
73. 316 U.S. 535 (1942).
74. Note (1942). Constitutionality of state laws providing sterilization for habitual criminals. *Yale Law Journal, 51*, 1380–1387, p. 1380. http://dx.doi.org/10.2307/792604
75. By then, it was also possible to quote more legitimate scientific authority for the proposition that "there is more unanimity today than ever before that criminality, per se, is not inherited, and that criminals, as criminals, should not be subjected to compulsory sterilization." Fink, A., as cited in Note (1942), Constitutionality of state laws providing sterilization for habitual criminals, p. 1383. For a discussion of the merging of eugenics and criminological thinking under Nazism, see Rafter, N. (2008). Criminology's darkest hour: Biocriminology in Nazi Germany. *Australian and New Zealand Journal of Criminology, 41*, 287–306. http://dx.doi.org/10.1375/acri.41.2.287
76. Quoted in Adams, D. K. (1939). William McDougall. *Psychological Review, 46*, 1–8, p. 1.
77. Roback, A. (1952). William McDougall and hormic psychology. In A. Roback (Ed.), *History of American psychology* (pp. 253–263). New York, NY: Library. http://dx.doi.org/10.1037/10800-021
78. McDougall, W. (1936). *An introduction to social psychology* (23rd ed.). New York, NY: Methuen.
79. Pastore, N. (1949). *The nature-nurture controversy* (p. 49). New York, NY: Garland.
80. McDougall (1936), *An introduction to social psychology*, p. 17 (emphasis added).

81. McDougall (1936). *An introduction to social psychology*, p. xxii.
82. Pound, R. (1938). *The formative era of American law*. Boston, MA: Little, Brown.
83. Levy, L. W. (1957). *The law of the Commonwealth and Chief Justice Shaw*. Cambridge, MA: Harvard University Press, p. 316.
84. Haskell, T. L. (1977). *The emergence of professional social science: The American Social Science Association and the nineteenth-century crisis of authority*. Urbana: University of Illinois Press.
85. Pastore (1944), *The nature-nurture controversy*, p. 149.
86. Markus, H. R. (2008). Pride, prejudice, and ambivalence: Toward a unified theory of race and ethnicity. *American Psychologist, 63*, 651–670, p. 655 (internal references omitted). http://dx.doi.org/10.1037/0003-066X.63.8.651
87. Markus (2008), Pride, prejudice, and ambivalence, p. 655.
88. Bobo, L., & Hutchings, V. L. (2001). Perceptions of racial group competition: Extending Blumer's theory of group position to a multiracial social context. In Hogg, M. A., & Abrams, D. (Eds.), *Intergroup relations: Essential readings* (pp. 71–90). Philadelphia, PA: Psychology Press, p. 77. Compare this view with McDougall's, that "it is roughly true to say that only the grossly incompetent, the inadaptable, and the very unfortunate, suffer serious hardship." Quoted in Pastore (1949), p. 151.
89. Aust, J. (2004, November–December). Crime: How will it be stopped? *The Good News: A Magazine of Understanding*. Retrieved from http://www.ucg.org/doctrinal-beliefs/crime-how-will-it-be-stopped/ (italics in original)
90. Aust (2004), Crime: How will it be stopped? (italics in original)
91. Aust (2004), Crime: How will it be stopped?
92. Morissette v. United States, 342 U.S. 246 (1952), p. 250.
93. Morissette v. United States, pp. 251–252.
94. United States v. Brawner, 471 F.2d 969 (D.C. Cir., 1972), p. 985.
95. United States v. Brawner, p. 995.
96. Boldt, R. C. (1992). The construction of responsibility in the criminal law. *University of Pennsylvania Law Review, 140*, 2245–2332, p. 2246.
97. Dan-Cohen, M. (1992). Responsibility and the boundaries of the self, *Harvard Law Review, 105*, 959–1003, p. 959. http://dx.doi.org/10.2307/1341517
98. Diamond, B. L. (1978). Social and cultural factors as a diminished capacity defense in criminal law, *Bulletin of the American Academy of Psychiatry and Law, 6*, 195–208, p. 199.
99. Bibas & Bierschbach (2004), Integrating remorse and apology into criminal procedure, p. 108.
100. Bibas & Bierschbach (2004), Integrating remorse and apology into criminal procedure, p. 109.
101. Nourse, V. (2003). Reconceptualizing criminal law defenses. *University of Pennsylvania Law Review, 151*, 1691–1746, p. 1700. As Nourse also observed,

    > Since the 1970s, there has been an often unstated consensus that the proper level of analysis of the criminal law is at the individualized level of mind or conduct (whether of individual defendants or the collective sum of all potential defendants). (p. 1695)

102. For additional discussions of this recent era in American criminal justice history, see Beckett, K., Reosti, A., & Knaphus, E. (2016). The end of an era? Understanding the contradictions of criminal justice reform, *The Annals Academy of Political and Social Science, 664*, 238–259. http://dx.doi.org/10.1177/0002716215598973; Clear, T. R., & Frost, N. A. (2014). *The punishment imperative: The rise and failure of mass incarceration in America*. New York: New York University Press; Haney, C. (2012). Prison effects in the age of mass incarceration. *Prison Journal*. Advance online publication. http://dx.doi.org/10.1177/0032885512448604; and Hedges, C. (2012, December). Why mass incarceration defines us as a society. *Smithsonian Magazine*. Retrieved from http://www.smithsonianmag.com/people-places/why-mass-incarceration-defines-us-as-a-society-135793245/?no-ist

103. Bibas & Bierschbach (2004), Integrating remorse and apology into criminal procedure, p. 109.
104. CCPOA. (1995, May). *Public safety: Government's first responsibility* (Position paper). Sacramento, CA: Author, p. 14.
105. Cain, B. quoted in Ridgeway, J. (2009, March 3). 36 years of solitude. *Mother Jones*. Retrieved from https://www.motherjones.com/politics/2009/03/36-years-solitude/. Cain served as Angola's warden for two decades, during which time he was dubbed "the country's best-known jailer" and achieved something of an international reputation for his "folksy mix of law-and-order toughness and a belief in the ultimate power of rehabilitation through Christ." However, Cain was forced to resign in 2015 amid allegations of scandal, corruption, and ethics violations. See Russel, G., & Lau, M. (2015, December 15). Fall of Burl Cain: How 1 last side deal led to Angola warden undoing, *New Orleans Advocate*. Retrieved from http://www.theadvocate.com/new_orleans/news/politics/article_b3f58cfe-8d69-57c3-bd53-2ab81682ab19.html
106. Kaplan, D. (1993, January 17). The incorrigibles. *Newsweek*. Retrieved from http://www.newsweek.com/incorrigibles-192390
107. In 1996, DiIulio coined (but never quite defined) the pejorative and hurtful term "superpredator" and used it to promote draconian juvenile justice policies. In "Defining Criminality Up," *Wall Street Journal* (July 3, 1996), at p. A10, he warned of "the growing threat of juvenile super-predators." Congressional representative Bill McCollum quickly borrowed DiIulio's phrase and his prediction that a violent juvenile crime wave was imminent to warn of a "coming generation of super-predators" and urge passage of a bill that would allow 14-year-olds to be prosecuted in the federal justice system as adults. McCollum, W. (1996, August 17). Super-predators [Editorial]. *The Washington Post*, p. A24. See, also, DiIulio, J. J., Jr. (1997, June 11). Jail alone won't stop juvenile super-predators. *Wall Street Journal*, p. A23. In fact, DiIulio's "get tougher on juvenile crime" bona fides were established before he coined the term "superpredators." For example, in the January 26, 1994, article "Let 'em rot" (*Wall Street Journal*, at p. A14), DiIulio argued that the tough sentencing laws that were passed in the 1980s to increase the average lengths of prison terms (that, in turn, contributed significantly to the increased incarceration rates and prison overcrowding problems that would plague the nation for decades) were nowhere near tough enough because they were "filled with get-out-of-jail loopholes," making the United States a place full of "crime without punishment." He also argued that long prison sentences were the best strategy for controlling juvenile, as well as adult, crime and that "[g]et tough politics is good crime policy." Not satisfied with the punitive turn the nation had taken, DiIulio kept up the pressure to make the criminal justice system tougher. In a July 26, 1995, article entitled "Congress Can Stop Crime With STOP," (*Wall Street Journal*, p. A13), he warned lawmakers that they were facing the legislative equivalent of "high noon" and urged them to "take aim at activist federal judges" who had entered judicial orders concerning conditions of confinement that he thought were too sympathetic to prisoners. To remedy such "judicial weakness," he urged them to support a new law that would allow for even longer prison sentences and require that a greater percentage of those sentences to be served.
108. Bennett, W. J., DiIulio, J. J., Jr., & Walters, J. P. (1996). *Body count: Moral poverty and how to win America's war against crime and drugs* (p. 27). New York, NY: Simon & Shuster.
109. See Harden, B. (1996, May 29). Criminal justice failing, Dole says, eying Clinton. *The Washington Post*, p. A8.
110. http://www.c-span.org/video/?69606-1/mrs-clinton-campaign-speech

111. Bill Clinton: Mass incarceration on my watch "put too many people in prison." (2015, April 28). *The Guardian.* Retrieved from https://www.theguardian.com/us-news/2015/apr/28/bill-clinton-calls-for-end-mass-incarceration
112. Although I have taken examples primarily from the 1990s, the demonizing of lawbreakers was widespread at the outset of the era of mass incarceration as well. For example, in an influential book published in the late 1970s, clinicians Samuel Yochelson and Stanton Samenow referred to criminal offenders as literally "a different breed." Yochelson, S., & Samenow, S. E. (1977). *The criminal personality: Volume II: The change process.* New York, NY: Jason Aronson, p. 59. They made the astounding claim that *all* criminals, no matter the nature or extent of their criminal behavior, committed the same 52 errors in their thinking. Moreover, they asserted: "[W]ithout exception, one criminal is like another with respect to (these) mental processes" (p. 100), and that the same errors "pervade all the criminal's thinking, no matter what the issue" (p. x). For a more detailed discussion of the extraordinary nature of their claims, the methodological flaws in the data on which they were based, and the significant influence they nonetheless had, see Haney, C. (2010). Demonizing the "enemy": The role of "science" in declaring the "war on prisoners." *Connecticut Public Interest Law Journal, 9,* 185–242.
113. Toufexis, A. (1999, May/June). Dancing with devils. *Psychology Today,* pp. 54–58, 78–79, 85, cover page and p. 55. This kind of thoughtlessly pejorative rhetoric and imaging was deeply embedded in the public consciousness and continues to manifest itself, sometimes in unexpected quarters. For example, the "monster" terminology was recently employed by members of the generally careful Ninth Circuit Court of Appeals. See their opinion in *Apelt v. Ryan,* 878 F.3d 800 (9th Cir. 2017) to the effect that there was not "any explanation for why [the petitioner] became a monster [that] would have changed the sentence," p. 834. As dissenting Judge Paez correctly noted, "[o]nce the panel characterized [the petitioner] as a monster, the result was inevitable"; rather than a careful analysis of his legal claim, "[t]his was judicial condemnation" (906 F.3d at 843).
114. See, e.g., Adams, J., & Gorton, D. (2004). Southern trauma: Revisiting caste and class in the Mississippi Delta. *American Anthropologist, 106,* 334–345. http://dx.doi.org/10.1525/aa.2004.106.2.334; Delgado, R. (1988). Storytelling for oppositionists and others: A plea for narrative. *Michigan Law Review, 87,* 2411–2441. http://dx.doi.org/10.2307/1289308; Fine, M., & Harris, A. (2002). *Under the covers: Theorizing the politics of counter stories.* London, England: Lawrence and Wishart; Hurtado, A. (2003). Theory in the flesh: Toward an endarkened epistemology. *International Journal of Qualitative Studies in Education, 16,* 215–225. http://dx.doi.org/10.1080/0951839032000060617; Mushaben, J. M. (2005). Memory and the Holocaust: Processing the past through a gendered lens. *History of the Human Sciences, 17,* 147–185. http://dx.doi.org/10.1177/0952695104047301; and Valenzuela, A. (2005). Voice, presence and community: Challenging the master narrative. *International Journal of Qualitative Studies in Education, 18,* 139–146.
115. Romero, M., & Stewart, A. J. (1999). *Women's untold stories: Breaking silence, talking back, voicing complexity.* New York, NY: Taylor & Frances/Routledge.
116. Kuhn, T. S. (1962). *The structure of scientific revolutions.* Chicago, IL: University of Chicago Press.
117. The "situational revolution" is generally thought to have begun in 1968, with the publication of Walter Mischel's book on the limited predictive value of static measures of personality traits: Mischel, W. (1968). *Personality and assessment.* New York, NY: Wiley. Mischel showed that what had come to be known as the "personality coefficient"—the average correlation between measured personality traits and the behavior they supposedly predict—hovered at around .30, no matter the domain in which it was calculated. This meant that typically no more than about 10% of the variance in people's actual behavior could be accounted for by specific,

identifiable and measurable differences in their personalities. Not surprisingly, with so much variance remaining to be accounted for, the causal role of particular social contexts and immediate circumstances attained much greater significance in analyses of complex social behavior.

118. Ross, L. (1977). The intuitive psychologist and his shortcomings: Distortions in the attribution process, In L. Berkowitz (Ed.), *Advances in experimental social psychology* (Vol. 10). New York, NY: Academic Press. Estimates of "cross situational consistency" in research—the degree to which people behave in similar ways across different situations—remains modest, despite attempts to study it with more sophisticated methods and more reliable measures. However, the tendency to *perceive* consistency in the actions of others appears to be caused by people's tendency to focus only on select features of stable behavior and ignore or underestimate the more prevalent variations. See the discussions in Mischel, W., & Peake, P. (1982). Beyond déjà vu in the search for cross-situational consistency. *Psychological Review, 89,* 730–755; Mischel, W., & Peake, P. (1983). Some facets of consistency: Replies to Epstein, Funder, and Bem. *Psychological Review, 90,* 394–402.
119. McCarthy, B., & Hagan, J. (1992). Mean streets: The theoretical significance of situational delinquency among homeless youths. *American Journal of Sociology, 98,* 597–627. http://dx.doi.org/10.1086/230050

2

Risks and Contexts

An Alternative Paradigm for Understanding Criminality

Human violence is a product of a complex interplay of personal characteristics, environmental influences, precipitating events, and sometimes fortuitous occurrences. Hence, prediction of violence from personal characteristics alone is disappointing because it is founded on a truncated causal model that ignores the other interacting determinants of behavior.

—ALBERT BANDURA[1]

Renowned cognitive psychologist George Miller once commented that there were two kinds of psychological research that he admired, each focusing on a different aspect of human nature. "In one, our chemistry is clearly the controlling thing. The brain is a fabulously complicated biochemical machine that ticks on in ways we won't understand in our lifetime." In the other kind of research, Miller noted, "it becomes clear that we are under the control of social institutions and the social settings in which our life situations embed us. We behave well or badly according to the constraints of our situations."[2] Although great strides have been made in understanding the way our brain "ticks on" and influences our behavior, they have yet to yield much useful information about or insights into criminal behavior that can serve as the basis for criminal justice reform.

In the next several chapters, on the other hand, I discuss the ways in which the "constraints of our situation"—past and present—play critically important, controlling roles, ones that lend themselves directly to the creation of a fairer and

http://dx.doi.org/10.1037/0000172-003
Criminality in Context: The Psychological Foundations of Criminal Justice Reform,
by C. Haney

more just legal system. The research reviewed in these chapters has made it increasingly clear that the roots of criminal behavior lie primarily in the backgrounds and social histories of those who commit it and the immediate criminogenic contexts in which it occurs. Moreover, individual social histories and immediate contexts are shaped by the larger institutional and structural environments in which they are both embedded.

As I pointed out at the end of the last chapter, there is an already vast and still growing literature on the importance of past and present social contexts in understanding human behavior and the various ways in which certain kinds of past experiences can shape and influence a person's psychological development over their entire life course.[3] Few psychologists would now disagree that behavior must be examined and understood *in context*, because "[i]ndividuals are embedded in a changing social, cultural, and economic environment, as well as being products of a life history of events, beliefs, relationships, and behavior."[4] Put simply, the past greatly affects present and future outcomes, and what happens to us as children, adolescents, and even as young adults has a significant influence on our thoughts, feelings, and actions as we mature into adulthood. No one's life course can be fully and meaningfully understood without paying careful attention to these issues.

The work of "developmental contextualists" underscores the way that social contexts influence and change patterns of individual development over the entire life-span. Behavior is now understood as being shaped largely by "a particular set of time-bound, contextual conditions."[5] Moreover, a particular human characteristic or attribute "is only given its functional meaning by virtue of its relations to a specific context."[6] In addition, the "situational revolution" that I mentioned in passing at the end of the last chapter and discuss at greater length in Chapter 5 underscores the power of *immediate* situations, contexts, and circumstances to influence and affect the behavior that transpires within them. They can elicit, precipitate, provoke, and activate a wide range of behavior—behavior that is hardly the product of unencumbered "free choices."

As I suggest in the present chapter, these two broad categories of causal influences—past history and present contexts—are not independent. They are instead highly interrelated, in the sense that our social histories help to explain the kinds of social situations and circumstances that we are likely to encounter later in life and how we react to them when we do.

THE RISK FACTORS MODEL OF PSYCHOLOGICAL DEVELOPMENT

It is standard practice in medicine for physicians to routinely obtain their patients' medical histories.[7] This is in part because even physical health and illness are best understood "in context"—through a careful examination of the antecedents and immediate circumstances that contribute to them. In a similar way, social behavior—including criminal behavior—is best understood when it is viewed through the lens of a person's background social history and present life circumstances—when it is placed in context. One of the most useful frameworks for understanding the social historical context of criminality was established more than three decades ago. In 1985, developmental psychologists Ann Masten and Norman Garmezy proposed an elegant conceptual model with which to identify and understand psychologically critical events that occur in the course of an individual life history and help to direct its path and influence its long-term trajectory.[8] The model has served as the conceptual basis for countless empirical studies of the impact that certain kinds of childhood and adolescent experiences and events have on future behavior. Indeed, since its publication in 1985, it has been used extensively to predict and explain a wide range of negative outcomes that can occur in the lives of children and adolescents whose social histories include high levels of risks and traumas.[9]

Masten and Garmezy's seminal contribution was to synthesize much of what was already known in a growing psychological literature about the harmfulness of child maltreatment.[10] Many of these insights were intuitively grasped in legal circles as well.[11] In fact, the topic of child abuse and the importance of developing a coherent legal response was first recognized decades ago. However, for the most part, and quite understandably, the focus was on developing legal policies designed to reduce the amount of abuse and neglect that was occurring. Those policies were aimed generally at imposing legal sanctions on persons responsible for engaging in child maltreatment or strengthening available procedures to remove children from the settings in which they were being subjected to abuse or neglect. As important and urgent as these responses were, what was lacking was a sustained scientific analysis of exactly why and how child abuse was damaging and the kind of long-term adverse effects it could have on the lives of its victims.

Masten and Garmezy's seminal contribution was to organize existing knowledge and place it in a meaningful developmental context. Their "risk factors" model integrated the results of a number of studies that had appeared in the academic and clinical literature establishing the psychologically harmful effects of child maltreatment, providing a coherent conceptual framework into which, eventually, the results of literally hundreds of later studies could be and were incorporated. Their framework focused broadly on events and experiences that create "a higher probability for the development of a disorder" later in life. The "disorders" Masten and Garmezy had in mind were not physical illnesses but forms of socially problematic, troubled behavior. The specific factors represent "risks" because they are traumatic events that are statistically associated with a greater likelihood that a person who has been exposed to them will subsequently suffer from or experience a range of potentially serious psychological issues and behavioral problems, including delinquency and crime.[12]

BASIC COMPONENTS OF THE MODEL

More specifically, "risk factors" are events, experiences, and forms of treatment that are harmful in some way and can adversely affect a person's life course, path, or trajectory. Exposure to risk factors early in life can lead to—place people "at risk of"—a range of negative outcomes later on. Most of us are now familiar with the concept of a risk factor in the domain of our physical health,[13] such as the fact that certain kinds of ill-advised habits or behaviors or exposures to environmental toxins place us at higher risk of certain kinds of disease (e.g., the relationship between overeating, physical inactivity, and heart disease, or between smoking and certain forms of cancer).[14] Masten and Garmezy broadened this kind of model to include risks for a range of negative *behavioral* outcomes that included depression and other psychiatric disorders, substance abuse, and criminal behavior.[15] The effects of one particular category or kind of traumatic risk—child maltreatment—have become among the most extensively and carefully studied topics in psychology. For example, in an *Annual Review of Psychology* entry published in the mid-1990s, John Knutson acknowledged that since the 1962 publication of a landmark article on what was then called "the battered child syndrome," academic, public political, and legal interest in child maltreatment had "grown dramatically." By his count, some 1,250 articles on physical and emotional abuse were published between 1972 and 1994 alone. Similarly, some 2,000 articles pertaining to child maltreatment were reviewed by the National Research Council in 1993.[16] Research on these topics has continued at a rapid pace since then.

This research underscores the fact that many of the events and experiences that place people at risk of negative outcomes in life typically are experienced as painful or traumatic at the time they occur. But this is not always the case. For example, childhood neglect—a very potent criminogenic risk factor—may not feel painful or even noticeable to the children and adolescents who experience it. Neglect may even be mistakenly interpreted as something positive—children living without the constraints of conscientious adult supervision, enjoying freedoms that other children in the neighborhood or at school do not have. Yet, at the extremes, the lack of parental engagement and supervision can be harmful and place children and adolescents significantly at risk. In any event, whether they are painful or not at the time they are experienced, risk factors operate to increase the likelihood of negative life outcomes, including delinquency and adult criminality. Masten and Garmezy identified a wide range of risk factors and traumas in their work that I discuss at length in subsequent chapters, including child abuse and neglect, poverty, a chaotic family life, exposure to violence, and so on.

The basic risk factors formulation—that certain identified risks increase the likelihood of subsequent negative outcomes—is elegant and simple. But the model also includes a number of nonobvious components that make it dynamic and robust. In addition to risk factors,[17] Masten and Garmezy used the term *stressors* to refer to "any change in the environment which typically—

in the average person—induces a high degree of continual tension and interferes with normal patterns of response."[18] Of course, exposure to some kinds of life stressors, consisting of the challenging tasks, responsibilities, and events that we all confront, in varying amounts and degrees, is inevitable throughout our lives. But the nature and number of stressors a person encounters and his or her capacity to manage or cope with them are what matter most in gauging their likely effect on a life course.

Some stressors are more obviously impactful than others. When "major life events" present themselves, they threaten to significantly change, disrupt, or undermine our well-being. For children, these events might include such things as doing poorly in school, repeating a grade, having to move to a different town, the divorce of one's parents, the loss of a close friendship, the death of a loved one, or involvement with the juvenile justice system. Other stressors are more common in adulthood, including significantly increased financial responsibilities or challenges. For example, even otherwise positive events, such as a marriage or the birth of a child, can add stress to our lives—as can, most commonly, personal or professional setbacks (e.g., the loss of a job).

Figure 2.1 depicts the results of an early study that attempted to rank order the seriousness of life stressors. Thomas Holmes and Richard Rahe developed the Social Readjustment Rating Scale to estimate the degree of stress that different life events create for persons.[19] They did so by having research participants estimate how difficult they thought it would be to recover from or "socially readjust" after experiencing some 43 potentially significant stressors. The events were ones that presumably would require some adaptive or coping behavior in order to recover from—events "indicative of or requir[ing] a significant change in the ongoing life pattern of the individual."[20]

As the list in Figure 2.1 reflects, the Holmes and Rahe stressors pertained largely to the conventional, middle-class population with which the original study was done—a group unlikely to confront the kinds of stressors that many people who engage in criminal behavior encounter over the course of their lives (e.g., chronic unemployment, homelessness, exposure to community violence, racial discrimination).[21] Notwithstanding this limitation, the scale has been used to study the way that the experience of stressors is associated with negative life outcomes, such as physical illness. Although more recent research has modified the rank ordering somewhat, at least with certain groups, it nonetheless continues to show that stressors, in the form of "undesirable life events," are associated with different negative outcomes and behaviors, including ones as extreme as suicide attempts.[22]

Although the potential negative impact of major life events is not surprising, it is notable that the *accumulation* of even minor stressors, so-called common annoyances or daily hassles that comprise the "ongoing stresses and strains of daily living" can also be problematic.[23] Indeed, depending on how many of these daily hassles occur over time and how relentlessly they impinge on someone, they may aggregate in a way that is even more problematic than typically infrequent major life events.[24]

FIGURE 2.1. Holmes and Rahe's Social Readjustment Rating Scale of Potential Life Stressors

Rank	Life event	Mean value
1	Death of spouse	100
2	Divorce	73
3	Marital separation	65
4	Jail term	63
5	Death of close family member	63
6	Personal injury or illness	53
7	Marriage	50
8	Fired at work	47
9	Marital reconciliation	45
10	Retirement	45
11	Change in health of family member	44
12	Pregnancy	40
13	Sex difficulties	39
14	Gain of new family member	39
15	Business readjustment	39
16	Change in financial state	38
17	Death of close friend	37
18	Change to different line of work	36
19	Change in number of arguments with spouse	35
20	Mortgage over $10,000	31
21	Foreclosure of mortgage or loan	30
22	Change in responsibilities at work	29
23	Son or daugther leaving home	29
24	Trouble with in-laws	29
25	Outstanding personal achievement	28
26	Wife begin or stop work	26
27	Begin or end school	26
28	Change in living conditions	25
29	Revision of personal habits	24
30	Trouble with boss	23
31	Change in work hours or conditions	20
32	Change in residence	20
33	Change in schools	20
34	Change in recreation	19
35	Change in church activities	19
36	Change in social activities	18
37	Mortgage or loan less than $10,000	17
38	Change in sleeping habits	16
39	Change in number of family get-togethers	15
40	Change in eating habits	15
41	Vacation	13
42	Christmas	12
43	Minor violations of the law	11

From "The Social Readjustment Rating Scale," by T. Holmes and R. Rahe, 1967, *Journal of Psychosomatic Research, 11*, p. 214. Copyright 1967 by Elsevier. Reprinted with permission.

Of course, modest and manageable amounts of stress are not necessarily harmful.[25] In fact, stress can activate positive reactions and motivate people to perform better. Even the kind of negative stress that comes from difficult major life events is considered tolerable and even beneficial when it can be overcome or managed without adverse consequences, such as when it is buffered by meaningful social support in its aftermath.[26] But especially high levels of stress or stress that has accumulated uncontrollably over time can exceed and overload people's ability to cope. Stress at such high levels is sometimes called "toxic stress" and can be especially harmful.[27]

For perhaps obvious reasons, exposure to extreme or toxic levels of stress can be considered a risk factor. Childhood trauma or maltreatment is both stressful *and* places children "at risk." It can be damaging when it overwhelms their ability to cope with similar stressors. Thus, absorbing and attempting to manage a great many stressors, especially at a vulnerable time in one's life, can be psychologically harmful and hence considered a risk factor. Ordinarily, however, we think of stressors as external events that require our immediate adaptation and coping, especially in later childhood, adolescence, and adulthood; in contrast, risk factors are generally understood as occurring earlier and, therefore, as having longer term adverse effects.

This leads to one of the final basic components that make up the risk factors model. "Coping mechanisms" are the strategies and skills that people develop to tolerate, manage, and overcome the stressors that they face in their lives.[28] In one classic treatment of the topic, "coping" was defined as the "constantly changing cognitive and behavioral efforts" people make "to manage specific external and/or internal demands that are appraised as taxing or exceeding [their] resources."[29] In fact, the negative effects that risk factors can have on our life often derive from the way that they damage or undermine our coping mechanisms. Thus, for example, people who have been subjected to a large number of risk factors early in life may never have had the opportunity to learn entirely positive, fully effective coping mechanisms. Children who are continually "in crisis" (i.e., feel themselves to be psychologically under assault, or are struggling to survive a physically abusive home life or dangerous neighborhood) often develop exigent or "survival mode" coping mechanisms that may be difficult to relinquish if and when they are no longer needed. These makeshift strategies for dealing with the press of multiple, seemingly life-threatening stressors can ultimately become dysfunctional and counterproductive.

Mediating Factors

The robustness of the risk factors model—it has been corroborated in a wide range of empirical studies, many of which are discussed in the next chapter—means that it is sensitive to variations in people's life experiences. It explains individual differences in life outcomes, even between people who appear to have been exposed to the same or similar risk factors and stressors. Two additional components in the model are often at play as mediators in these cases.

On the one hand, different *vulnerabilities* that children have may render them especially susceptible to certain kinds of risk factors and traumas, including such things as a chronic health problem or cognitive disorder. For example, although child maltreatment is an important risk factor for subsequent delinquency and adult criminal behavior, not all children react to this risk factor as strongly or in exactly the same way. This helps to account for why exposure to criminogenic risks sometimes leads to subsequent criminal behavior and sometimes does not.[30] Moreover, exposure to a risk factor may exacerbate or even create a vulnerability. Thus, it is not difficult to understand how experiencing a particular risk or trauma repeatedly over time, especially at a young age, may make a person especially vulnerable—highly sensitive or reactive to it—if and when it is encountered later. This acquired vulnerability would make it difficult to withstand subsequent risks or traumas reminiscent of those with which someone was bombarded at an earlier time in their life.

On the other hand, the presence of protective factors, such as a warm and supportive extended family, enriched and nurturing school programs, or the serendipitous presence of a caring teacher or coach, can have life-enhancing effects that buffer children from otherwise damaging events or experiences, helping them to avoid negative outcomes.[31] Thus, studies show that the adverse effects of high levels of direct child maltreatment, "family dysfunction" (i.e., low cohesion and high conflict in a child's immediate family), and even economic disadvantage can sometimes be compensated for or buffered by the presence of extended family or "kinship" support—positive involvement with extended family members and older siblings.[32]

Protective factors also may consist of a trait or quality or skill—natural or attained—such as athletic prowess, musical talent, or intellectual capacities that can create opportunities for respite, growth, or escape. These traits, qualities, and skills increase a person's chances of finding caring connections with others or entering supportive milieus, say, in school or groups or clubs, that may not be available at home or elsewhere in their immediate neighborhood. In this way, protective factors may provide children and adolescents with avenues of escape from abusive situations, a respite from family turmoil or conflict, or a way to garner praise or reinforcement that was otherwise lacking in their home life.[33]

It is also important to note that although protective factors are key components of the risk factor model, they do not necessarily guarantee that children can overcome all of the challenges they later confront. Few children merely succumb to even a seemingly overwhelming number of risk factors; many manage to successfully resist by using whatever personal, familial, or community resources they can draw on to survive and overcome them. But some combinations of powerful, unrelenting risk factors and stressors are so daunting and damaging that only the most resilient of children can withstand them. Many of the children who eventually do become involved in serious delinquent and criminal behavior have suffered from exposure to a toxic combination of many risk factors and traumas and few, if any, buffers or protective factors. That is, the risk factors to which they are exposed are often many in number and experienced in the virtual absence of protective factors that might have buffered them against the worst psychological effects. In some instances, in fact, what otherwise might have served as a protective factor—say, an involved extended family—may instead have the opposite effect. A criminally oriented extended family may bring them closer to criminal involvement or subject them to additional chaos, trauma, and criminal influence that can compound and amplify the effects of other damaging risks factors.

In addition to the sheer number of risk factors to which someone is exposed over their life course, the *age* at which a person experiences various risk factors can also increase their potentially damaging effects. As Masten and Garmezy noted, "[t]he capacity of the child to perceive, interpret, and deal with stressors changes with development. Consequently, there are periods of development when individuals may be more or less vulnerable to certain types of stressors."[34] Young children, especially, may be particularly susceptible to certain kinds of traumas and risks. For example, as one study found, the trauma of childhood maltreatment "has its most pervasive impact during the first decade of life."[35]

There are two commonsense explanations for this. The first is that younger children are more psychologically fragile and unformed; many lack the resilience with which to withstand mistreatment or have not yet developed effective coping skills to defend against it. In contrast, many times an older child may have "acquired cognitive and socioemotional abilities that provide for different interpretations of the stressful event as well as resources for coping with it."[36] Second, a very young child who has been harmed by his or her early mistreatment is at risk of traveling on a troubled path over a much longer period of time. In fact, in the absence of effective intervention, problems encountered at an earlier developmental stage are often compounded in subsequent ones. Masten and Garmezy described this as "developmental stress," noting that there are "more difficult phases, particularly transitional stages" that occur in the normal course of child development, when a child's functioning is "less well organized" and he or she is "more vulnerable to certain stressors." In addition, "more vulnerable children" or children harmed by early exposure to powerful risk factors "may not cope well" with the normal, new, inevitable challenges that psychological development typically entails.[37]

Thus, exposure to risk factors and traumas experienced early in life can compromise a child's ability to function in subsequent stages of development as he or she moves into adolescence and young adulthood. As I say, especially when this occurs in the absence of effective intervention—intervention of the sort that is often lacking in the lives of young people who eventually become involved in early delinquent and later adult criminal behavior—then the adverse effects of early risk exposure are likely to be compounded in later developmental stages. Another way of describing this is to say that problems and issues that are not resolved at one stage usually reappear in especially troublesome or dysfunctional ways in later stages, and the earlier this compounding process begins, the worse the overall consequences may be.

Not surprisingly, the magnitude of the harmful effects that are produced by exposure to trauma and risks also depends in part on the severity or intensity of the events or experiences themselves, as well as the *duration* of the period of time over which persons are subjected to them. There are two senses in which particular risks can be "severe." The first is that the very nature of the specific risk itself may be highly potent or especially toxic. There are discussions in the risk factors literature about whether, for example, certain kinds of risks are uniquely destructive, having especially negative effects on normal, healthy development. Most researchers agree that risk factors and traumas are not necessarily all created equal, and that specific ones—such as certain forms of child maltreatment—are known to be particularly damaging.[38] In the second, more conventional sense of "severe," risk factors can be experienced in greater or more intense "doses" or amounts. Extreme traumas or very significant levels of deprivation are expected to have more harmful effects than less extreme or significant ones. Thus, "in both children and adults, greater trauma exposure is associated with more complex symptom presentation."[39]

With respect to the duration of exposure, risk factors or traumas experienced over longer periods of time are expected to have more damaging effects. The longer a developing child or adolescent is subjected to mistreatment or neglect, the more time there is for those effects to impact or impair their psychological development, and the greater the likelihood that persons will be forced to accommodate to the adverse experience by changing how they react and, in a sense, over time, who they are. That is, in addition to the obvious way in which longer term exposure to a damaging or noxious event or experience is likely to cause more harm (because the negative effects mount over time), chronic risk factors require children and adolescents to adopt habits or ways of being to cope with or adjust to the presence of the risks that will become harder to relinquish—more routine and deep-seated—the longer they are employed. Conversely, because briefer or more transient exposure to risk factors does not require this kind of prolonged accommodation, it is expected to have a less negative impact.

Finally, there is the crucial issue of the *number* of the risks or traumas to which a child or adolescent has been exposed in the course of their young life. As the research I discuss in the next section underscores, all other things being equal, the sheer number of risk factors to which someone has been exposed is a critically important aspect of their social history, primarily because multiple risks can overwhelm coping mechanisms, in much the same way that too many stressors can prove too much for people to functionally withstand. For this reason, research on criminogenic risks—those that are significantly related to subsequent delinquency and criminality—is often focused on the number and the combinations in which risk factors occur, and the way they accumulate over someone's childhood and adolescence.

In sum, as Figure 2.2 illustrates, the different parts of the risk factors model are highly interconnected. The actual impact of risk factors on a life course can be amplified by the person's age, and the severity, duration, and number of risks to which he or she is exposed. Obviously, children who are exposed to strong doses of many potentially harmful risk factors, particularly at early ages, and those whose exposure is chronic—lasting throughout long stretches of childhood or adolescence rather than brief or episodic—are placed

FIGURE 2.2. General Risk Factors Model Depicting the Relationship Between Negative Events in a Person's Past ("Risk Factors/Traumas") and Present ("Stressors") Context on Behavior

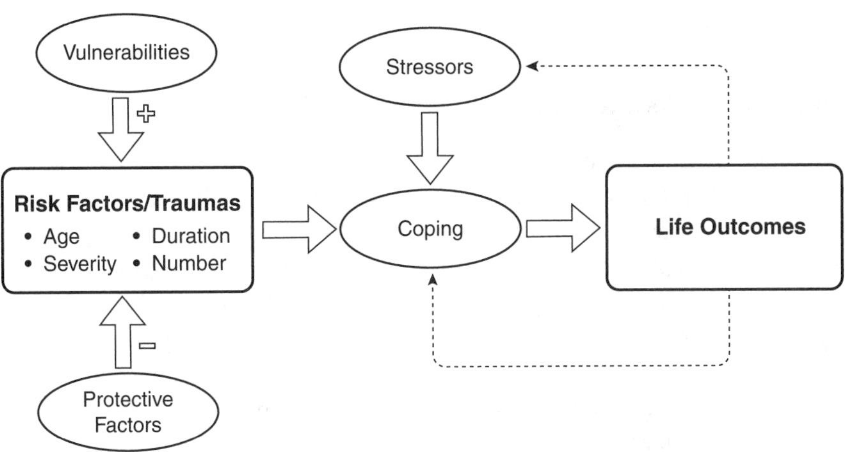

in greater jeopardy for longer term harm and negative life outcomes. This especially true if they have few protective factors to buffer them from these risks, and even more so if they have vulnerabilities that make them particularly susceptible to these adverse experiences or events.

It is important to note that exposure to early traumas and risk factors can result in very different kinds of problematic life outcomes. Although this book focuses primarily on risk factors that are associated with subsequent criminal behavior, a range of different consequences or outcomes are possible. Some of the other outcomes are themselves indirectly related to criminality, such as depression and substance abuse,[40] but others are not. For example, there is now a great deal of empirical evidence that childhood and adolescent maltreatment also serves as a risk factor for a range of negative health or medical outcomes. In fact, "stressful or traumatic childhood experiences such as abuse, neglect, or forms of household dysfunction" are so strongly related to a range of later physical maladies that include "disease, disability, and premature mortality" that are now seen as a major public health concern worldwide.[41] In addition, studies show that maltreated children and adolescents are not only more likely to suffer from depression and substance abuse later in life (both of which are indirectly related to adult criminality) but also may become especially sensitive to signs of rejection,[42] have higher numbers of attachment-related problems,[43] have difficulties regulating their emotions,[44] experience problematic interpersonal and romantic relationships,[45] suffer from anxiety disorders,[46] and manifest "poor life satisfaction" overall.[47]

Thus, exposure to risk factors and traumas can lead to a broad range of different negative life outcomes, only some of which include criminal behavior.[48] Even within a single family, whether and which negative life outcomes come to pass for any individual child as a result of exposure to many of the same risk factors will depend on a number of different variables, including the child's gender, age at the time the risk factor or trauma occurred, the presence of protective factors inside and outside the family that are unique to them, and so on.

Aggregate Risks and Toxic Combinations

Although in subsequent chapters of this book I examine a host of developmental and immediate situational risk factors separately, as if they were distinct influences, in fact, they are not actually experienced this way. In any given life, multiple risks and protective factors naturally co-occur, accumulate, and interact with each other over time. Moreover, it is especially important to keep in mind that these risk factors and traumas produce their most potent criminogenic effects when there are many of them, operating in combination to amplify the overall effects. When added up over the course of a single life, *multiple* risk factors form a whole that is much greater and potentially more harmful than its individual parts.

Thus, the greatest psychological harm—and the most criminogenic effect—is typically produced by the joint operation of many risk factors operating additively and in tandem. As one U.S. Department of Justice report that comprehensively summarized the results of past research on the criminogenic effects of aggregate risk factors concluded, persistent and serious lawbreaking is typically engaged in by persons who "have *multiple* risk factors in their backgrounds," including ones they experience with their "family, school, peers, and neighborhood characteristics" that "tend to be *cumulative* and to *interact* with one another to produce high levels of serious offending."[49]

In fact, much crime is committed by persons whose life histories have been pervaded by multiple risk factors and whose adult lives also exposed them to especially high levels of tension-producing environmental stressors. The combination of these forces inhibits the development and maintenance of prosocial and law-abiding patterns of coping behavior. Masten and Garmezy made this connection in their seminal work: "Children who pursue delinquent careers may have been exposed to very severe stresses and harmful life events, genetic disadvantage, inappropriate parental models, selective reinforcement by parents of the child's maladaptive behavior, and chronic low self-esteem."[50]

Children who are exposed to maltreatment and other risks and traumas in multiple aspects or areas of their lives, including in different settings or places, are especially susceptible to harmful effects. For example, many children who suffer abuse at the hands of family members also live in communities in which they are exposed to violence outside the home. Indeed, one study concluded that children who grew up in urban housing projects were exposed to traumatic violence comparable to children who lived in "war zones," and that many of them suffered the same kinds of psychological aftereffects and needed the same kinds of therapeutic treatment as their literally battle-scarred counterparts.[51] These children had no respite from the risk factors to which they were exposed—maltreatment inside the home was compounded by exposure to violence outside. Similarly, many African American and Latino children "still encounter expressions of racial hatred, live in racially segregated neighborhoods, and endure the suspicion widespread among many people in positions of authority."[52] This means that the effects of whatever other risk factors or traumas to which they are exposed at home or in the larger community may be exacerbated by the long-term stress to which racism subjects them.

Children and adolescents who suffer the effects of exposure to multiple traumas and risk factors may face a widening gap between their inner resources—the interpersonal skills and resilience needed to effectively plan and navigate life's challenges—and the sheer number of such challenges that they face. Because traumatic experiences can lessen people's ability to successfully negotiate the adversities that they typically confront over a lifetime, and impair their coping mechanisms, they may be more likely to encounter a higher number and a more complicated set of obstacles and stressors throughout the course of their life. When problems go unsolved or are solved poorly, they generally lead to even worse problems later. For example, as Masten and Garmezy observed, a child raised in "disadvantaging circumstances is more likely to expand his disadvantaged status" by making decisions that are conditioned by their own troubled life circumstances.[53] In this way, the patterns of coping that are adopted in order to survive an abusive, dangerous upbringing may not only prove dysfunctional later on but also ensure that subsequent challenges will be even more frequent and harder to manage or overcome.

As the several graphs included in Figure 2.3 illustrate, as the number of risk factors to which someone has been exposed increases, the greater the likelihood that they will experience negative outcomes in life, including engaging in problematic or troubled behavior such as delinquency, adult criminal behavior, and even violence. David Farrington, Rolf Loeber, and their colleagues described the pattern succinctly: "Research has uniformly showed that the larger accumulation of risk factors, the higher the probability of negative outcomes, such as juvenile delinquency."[54] Moreover, multiple risk factors have even greater impact when they interact in combination to exacerbate each other.

Subsequent chapters make clear that study after study has established that these combinations of accumulated risks and traumas form the deep roots of crime and violence in our society. As this research shows, risk factors and traumas in the backgrounds and social histories of persons who have engaged in criminal behavior are what distinguish many of them from their law-abiding counterparts. But the differences stem from their different life circumstances and the patterns of coping and adaptation those circumstances compel them to undertake, *not* in alleged differences in their inherent nature, or strength of character, or the flawed choices they supposedly "freely" make. Thus, the

FIGURE 2.3. Examples of the Increased Likelihood of Law-Breaking as a Function of Exposure to Increasing Numbers of Risk Factors

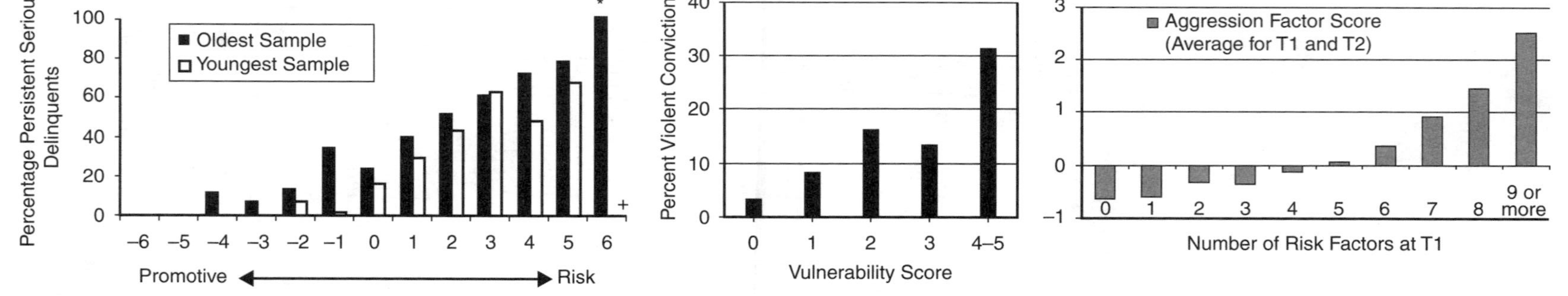

Left image is from "Risk and Promotive Effects in the Explanation of Persistent Delinquency in Boys," by R. Stouthamer-Loeber, E. Wei, D. Farrington, and P. Wikstrom, 2002, *Journal of Consulting and Clinical Psychology, 70*, p. 118. Copyright 2002 by the American Psychological Association. Middle image is from "A Review of Predictors of Youth Violence," by J. Hawkins, T. Herrenkohl, D. Farrington, D. Brewer, R. Catalano, and T. Harachi, 1998, in R. Loeber and D. Farrington (Eds.), *Serious & Violent Juvenile Offenders: Risk Factors and Successful Interventions* (p. 146), Thousand Oaks, CA: Sage. Copyright 1998 by Sage. Reprinted with permission. Right image is from "Pathways to Aggression in Children and Adolescents," by M. Watson, K. Fischer, J. Andreas, and K. Smith, 2004, *Harvard Educational Review, 74*, p. 422. Copyright 2004 by Presidents and Fellows of Harvard College. Reprinted with permission.

long-term psychological effects of cumulative social historical and structural risks, traumas, and immediate circumstances are key factors that account for a person's presence in a courtroom or a prison yard.

Risk Factors, Adverse Childhood Experiences, and Developmental Trauma

The risk factors model that I described previously and will use throughout much of the remainder of the book is closely related to several other concepts that are used in very similar ways in other areas of psychological and criminological research and writing. It is useful to clarify their relationship to the risk factors model itself. "Adverse childhood experiences" (ACEs) is a term that is essentially synonymous with the concept of risk factors. Indeed, numerous researchers who have explored primarily the public health consequences of various forms of childhood maltreatment have used the ACEs concept in ways that map directly onto what I have referred to above as risk factors and traumas.

As these researchers have noted, ACEs include but are not necessarily limited to suffering abuse (emotional, physical, sexual) and/or neglect (emotional, physical), growing up in households where domestic violence is witnessed, having family members who abuse alcohol or drugs or suffer from mental illness, experiencing relational stress (e.g., separation, divorce), or family members who engage in criminal behavior.[55] In addition to the close conceptual similarity between risk factors and ACEs, their well-documented consequences are also virtually identical. For example, as Bruce and Craig McEwen observed, "adverse childhood experiences such as sexual and physical abuse along with other events in the family and living environment increase the lifelong frequency of mental and physical health problems" from which a person is likely to suffer later in life as well as increase the chances that they will encounter levels of stress that overload their capacity to effectively cope.[56]

In addition, because the trauma of child maltreatment often produces very similar and serious negative psychological consequences, clinical researchers and practitioners such as Bessel van der Kolk and his colleagues have explored the potential value of a new diagnostic category—"developmental trauma disorder."[57] Their basic argument is that various forms of child maltreatment, broadly defined, and including many of the risk factors that I discuss in specific detail in the next chapter, produce an interrelated, common set of problematic outcomes that are not entirely captured by existing diagnostic labels. The consequences of exposure to these traumas and risk factors can be severe, chronic, co-occurring, and wide ranging, and include "problems with emotional regulation, impulse control, attention and cognition, dissociation, interpersonal relationships, and attributions."[58]

However, I share the concerns they also have expressed about "implicitly endorsing an approach to mental health that further pathologizes individuals living in toxic environments, rather than [pathologizing] the environments themselves."[59] Although final decisions both about the potential utility and possible downsides of creating this new label can be deferred to the clinicians who ultimately will decide whether or not to use it, my intention in the analyses that follow is not to diagnose but rather to explain. In that context, it is important to avoid overusing the language of symptoms, syndromes, and disorders, and to more appropriately draw attention to the nature of the "toxic environments" that have negative psychological consequences for the children and adolescents who are forced to react and adapt to them.

Whichever term is used to describe them, we know that childhood and adolescent traumas and risk factors, "as they accumulate, have powerful and lasting influences, correlating with poor physical and mental health throughout the life course."[60] Without in any way diminishing the value of the extensive data collected by ACEs researchers or the potential utility of recognizing the distinct concept of a developmental trauma disorder, the risk factors model seems to me to have several advantages in analyzing the etiology of criminal behavior. For one, it is a more variegated and complex formulation, with more component parts that lend themselves to a somewhat richer and robust life history analysis. It is also more than a diagnostic label. That is, it not only avoids implicitly pathologizing people but also represents a dynamic model that explicitly emphasizes and accounts for the way that the different component parts of someone's social history and circumstances interact over time to lead to different life outcomes.

Risk Factors as Causes or Effects

One final issue is important to address with respect to the nature of risk factors and the way the term is used in different academic contexts. There is a widespread tendency in some areas of psychology to acknowledge the role of what certain authors also term "risk factors" (sometimes termed "criminogenic needs"), but in ways that imply that the factors or needs are individualistic properties of persons. This use of the term seems to suggest that risk factors are entirely internally generated manifestations of fixed personality traits or enduring dispositions rather than the product of the experiences, events, and external influences and stressors that created them. In my opinion, either by intention or inadvertence, this different kind of risk factor formulation lends itself to demonizing and blaming the victims of the traumatic experiences to which they have been exposed.

For example, some researchers have argued that formerly incarcerated mentally ill persons tend to reoffend *not* because of their mental illness per se but because they have a higher number of what the researchers termed "risk factors."[61] But the risk factors they have in mind pertain to distinct signs of what they term an "antisocial pattern" that the recidivist mentally ill supposedly manifest in their lives. Thus, the particular group of mentally ill persons they studied was said to be "more likely to manifest early and diverse criminal behavior, a generalized pattern of trouble (e.g., financial instability, few prosocial friends), and procriminal attitudes."[62] In short, as the researchers put it, the "risk factors" consisted of "problematic personality traits" that the group under study supposedly possessed.[63] Indeed, the authors repeated the characterization for emphasis: "[a]ntisocial traits . . . are one of the most powerful predictors of violent and other criminal behavior."[64] As such, they argued, "antisocial features must be explicitly assessed, acknowledged, and targeted in correctional treatment efforts" for persons with serious mental illness and for others.[65]

Whatever the merits or pitfalls of this approach, this use of the "risk factors" concept is very clearly not what I mean by the term, either in the discussion so far or in the analyses that follow in the remainder of this book. In fact, the risk factors model I employ would treat what these authors refer to as "a generalized pattern of trouble" as an *effect* (i.e., what I believe needs to be explained) rather than a *cause* (i.e., what I argue explains these effects). From my perspective, risk factors are precisely what *lead to* the "generalized pattern of trouble" at issue and the alleged "problematic personality traits" that these authors treat as causes in themselves. Thus, problematic patterns and "traits" are merely shorthand (and, therefore, only minimally helpful) descriptions of behavior learned in response to exposure to a set of actual risk factors that the authors do not explicitly consider but on which my analysis is primarily focused.

Similarly, when another group of researchers sought to identify what they called the "well established risk factors for offending" in a study they were conducting with a group of juvenile probationers, they picked risk factors that included only the juveniles' "age at first arrest," a scale measuring the proportion of "delinquent peers" among their friends, a measure of "alcohol/drug use," and the degree to which they manifested "psychopathic personality traits."[66] Here, too, note the tendency to conflate the external risk factors to which the young persons were exposed with the criminogenic consequences of that exposure. That is, each of the "risk factors" in this study reflected behavior that was very likely the result of prior exposure to the kind of primary risk factors on which much of this book is focused. Unless one is prepared to argue and defend the proposition that certain children are born with a *propensity* to become arrested at a young age, have an *inherent* predisposition to engage in drug/alcohol use, possess an *intrinsic* desire to associate with delinquency-minded others, and are somehow *naturally* psychopathic—and I do not believe there is any reliable scientific evidence that supports any of these propositions—then these behaviors are very likely the *consequence* of prior exposure to a set of *external* risk factors, not risk factors in themselves.

Similar terminology and a similar positing of behaviors as "causes," that I would argue are better conceptualized as "effects," occur in the widely used "criminogenic needs" formulation put forward by Don Andrews and James Bonta.[67] They conceive of what they term seven primary "criminogenic needs" as "dynamic risk factors" that should be the target of rehabilitative programs. Without necessarily disputing the potential value of such an approach at certain stages in the criminal justice system (as a possible framework for providing specific programs and services), their utility as an explanatory framework is limited. Instead, the seven dynamic risk factors (procriminal attitudes, antisocial personality, "procriminal associates," low "social achievement," family/marital dysfunction, substance abuse, and "lack of prosocial pursuits") that this model identifies as characteristics of *persons* are, in fact, characteristics of, or largely produced by, prior or current social environments. From a social contextual perspective, the criminogenic needs framework lends itself far too easily to thinking about persons *as* risks, rather than risks being something *to which* persons are exposed. It also begins far too late in the causal chain; that is, it focuses attention on the symptoms of the underlying problems rather than the problems themselves.

In this regard, even the current *Diagnostic and Statistical Manual of Mental Disorders* (*DSM–5*)—hardly a distillation of social contextualist insights—concedes several important, relevant points. For example, with respect to what the *DSM–5* calls "conduct disorder"—described as a pattern of persistent and repetitive rule-breaking in childhood and adolescence and supposedly a precursor of adult criminality—the *DSM–5* lists a host of "family-level risk factors" that map very closely onto many of the social historical issues that I discuss in Chapter 3.[68] It then offers this caution:

> Conduct disorder may at times be potentially misapplied to individuals in settings where patterns of disruptive behavior are viewed as near-normative (e.g., in very threatening, high crime areas or war zones). Therefore the context in which the undesirable behaviors have occurred should be considered.[69]

More telling still, the *DSM–5*'s discussion of "antisocial personality disorder"—the diagnostic label applied to adults whose problematic behaviors are often associated with lawbreaking—goes several steps further. Setting aside the implications of the fact that the manual recognizes that this particular "mental disorder" occurs more often "in samples affected by adverse socioeconomic (i.e., poverty) or sociocultural (i.e., migration) factors,"[70] the *DSM–5* notes that the diagnosis "appears to be associated with low socioeconomic status and urban settings," and acknowledges "concerns" that the diagnostic label may be "misapplied to individuals in settings in which seemingly antisocial behavior may be part of a protective survival strategy." It further advises clinicians that it would "helpful" for them "to consider the social and economic context in which the behaviors occur."[71] Unfortunately, the fact that the *DSM–5* authors also note that the highest known prevalence rates for this diagnosis—greater than 70%—are found among persons housed in "prisons or other forensic settings" suggests that many clinicians have failed to heed their advice.[72]

Of course, no serious psychological researcher or scholar would argue that individual differences do not sometimes matter in our understanding of a wide range of behavior, including criminal behavior. However, I am more interested in issues that are typically passed over in our rush to internalize causation and attribute primary causal significance to personal or individual traits. Because of the weighty legal and societal implications of the judgments that are made about criminal behavior, this is one area where our understanding of the origins of individual differences, the extent to which they are really fixed traits or instead reflect modifiable learned behaviors, and the nature of the specific circumstances in which they manifest themselves should all greatly matter. I will argue that grappling with the social historical and social contextual origins of these individual differences—something that is regularly omitted from many forensic inquiries as well as most legal decision-making—is absolutely essential to meaningful criminal justice reform efforts that seek to make this system fundamentally more fair, effective, and humane.

Criminogenic Contexts: The Role of Immediate Situations

The second overarching component in my analysis of the relationship between social context and criminal behavior is focused less on the past than the present. Just as the risk factors model analyzes the impact of accumulated *past* contexts (i.e., the developmental factors embedded in a person's social and institutional history), it is important to acknowledge more *immediate* influences as well, in the form of the situations or settings in which criminal behavior is likely to occur. In the broadest terms, we now know that the structure of the situation in which behavior takes place can exert a powerful influence over the shape and direction of that behavior. Crime is no exception to this general rule. That is, like all social behavior, criminal behavior may be precipitated, provoked, or facilitated by the characteristics of the situation or setting where it takes place.

There are several senses in which this can be true. In some instances, the criminogenic or crime-producing context consists of microevents—immediate provocations, affronts, or inducements—that help to precipitate criminal acts. In other instances the impact of the criminogenic environment is broader, more diffuse, and long-lasting. That is, there are certain kinds of communities and neighborhoods in which the behavioral norms and expectations, available opportunity structures, and the frequency and salience of interpersonal conflicts combine to greatly increase the likelihood that residents will be provoked, pressured, or otherwise encouraged to engage in criminal behavior. Criminogenic contexts need to be understood in all of these ways—as focused, immediate, and acute as well as the broad, dispersed, and chronic dimensions of a person's social environment.

In addition, as I discuss at the end of this chapter, social history and present context are typically closely intertwined. The prevalence of criminogenic social historical risk factors is often greatest in the lives of persons who reside in those neighborhoods and communities where criminogenic contexts and influences are widespread and severe. This is in part because of the powerful role of poverty in generating risk factors in the lives of children who are exposed to it and the corresponding lack of buffers or positive interventions in many poor communities that do not have the infrastructure and resources with which to alleviate the resulting potentially negative effects.

Moreover, as I noted earlier, when a person's adaptive skills are compromised or undermined by early trauma, they may not only fail to solve current problems but create new problems of their own. Put simply, our attempts to overcome the stress in our lives are shaped by our background histories—good or bad. Thus, many people who have suffered from exposure to high numbers of risk factors earlier in life find that it is particularly difficult to cope effectively with the stressors that they later encounter. Drug use is a good example of an ill-advised but understandable attempt to manage life stress, one that frequently worsens rather than alleviates it. Although the immediate impulse is to reduce pain and lessen stress, the long-term effect is often just the opposite, including increasing the likelihood that someone will engage in subsequent criminal behavior. As I discuss in Chapter 5, in addition to drug use, gang membership is another "adaptation" to prior risk factors and stressors that frequently has long-term effects that are counterproductive and criminogenic.

Although I argue that the broad and deep contextual aspects of the model that I am advancing here are transformative and paradigm-shifting in the quest to make legal decision-making fairer and more just and to create crime control policy that is more effective and humane, it is important to note that there are forensic settings in which the importance of taking situational factors into account has already been recognized. For example, traditional models of clinical judgment have been criticized by some commentators for assuming that "behavior is largely independent of context." Thus, the most sophisticated forensic approaches to predict future violent behavior concede that the narrowly individualistic assessments that were once nearly universally used are "poorly suited" to the task. They acknowledge that "assessing risk in order to effectively manage potentially violent patients in the community"[73] requires a different, better strategy.

In fact, there is increasingly widespread recognition of the value of what has been called a "conditional" model of violence prediction. Within this model, the "enduring features of the patient's life situation" and the range of "foreseeable events or stressors" that the patient is likely to encounter are seen as contextual factors that mental health professionals should take explicitly into account.[74] This more sophisticated framework recognizes that "[t]he advantage of such an ecological approach is to increase emphasis on social and situational factors that may, in conjunction with individual characteristics, exacerbate or protect against the occurrence of violent behavior."[75] I argue in one of the closing chapters of this book that meaningful criminal justice reform must move explicitly and decisively beyond prediction to proactive prevention, using insights about the ecology of crime and violence to modify and improve people's "life situations" and to avoid their foreseeable effects. The argument is thus far more context- than trait-based in nature.

Unfortunately, despite the promising advances in knowledge derived from the social contextual perspective developed in the following chapters, the tendency to privilege models and techniques that emphasize individual-level change still predominates. Indeed, absent a dramatic shift in focus and a genuine commitment to interventions that deliver genuine situational and community change, patients and defendants are at risk of being triply blamed (and excessively surveilled and punished)—first, for their psychological profile; second, for the risk factors to which they have been exposed; and finally for the disadvantaged neighborhoods in which they live. However, at this transitional juncture, these new models of prediction at least represent the start of a new way of thinking about these issues, one that is part of a much broader set of changes that promises to modify the mechanisms by which we allocate legal responsibility and culpability and the framework we can use to devise 21st-century crime-control policies.

Connecting Past and Present

Although the two overarching categories of criminogenic influences I have discussed in this chapter—traumatic, risk-filled social histories and immediate criminogenic situations—are conceptually distinct and can be analytically separated, they often co-occur in real life. There are several obvious ways in which their interconnections can amplify their long-term effects. For one, as I noted in passing earlier, many children who experience mistreatment live in neighborhoods that also are plagued by criminogenic social conditions. If their childhood adversities have undermined or weakened their coping skills, they are more likely to be vulnerable to structural disadvantage. Moreover, their communities may lack the resources to provide helpful intervention, effective treatment, or meaningful opportunities. As I discuss in more depth in Chapter 6, structural disadvantage is a risk factor in its own right, is correlated with other risk factors (e.g., child maltreatment), and tends to trap the poor on a long-term basis inside communities where crime is more prevalent.

Thus, the consequences of early deprivation and maltreatment reverberate through the life course of many criminal defendants. Early trauma may predispose some children to socioemotional problems that can continue to plague them as adolescents and young adults. Absent positive, sustained, and nurturing interventions—access to high-quality social services, education, therapeutic resources, and economic opportunities in the communities where they live—the problems of traumatized children and adolescents tend to persist into adulthood, undermining their ability to overcome, manage, or negotiate the interpersonally complex and challenging situations that they are likely to encounter. If they also lack protective factors in their lives (e.g., are without nurturing or sustaining relationships to buffer them from the structural hardships that surround them), their ability to create healthy and competent adult identities may continue to be compromised.

In fact, exposure to trauma and risk factors can lead children and adolescents to develop patterns and styles of coping with difficult situations that, in turn, can become self-fulfilling in nature. Many of the reactions and strategies adopted to survive traumatic, hurtful, potentially harmful maltreatment counterproductively elicit the very same kind of negative treatment that originally produced them or increase the likelihood that the very outcome that the person is seeking to avoid will come to pass. For example, adolescents reacting to past mistreatment and rejection through avoidance behavior—pushing people away, becoming hostile, or acting emotionally distant—can alienate potential allies and even provoke more interpersonal rejection.[76] A cyclical pattern of mistreatment, escalating alienation, misbehavior, and rejection by others is more likely to ensue.[77] Christopher Uggen and Sara Wakefield described another kind of related, problematic, and potentially criminogenic pattern:

> Early life disadvantages such as poverty, criminal parents, and neuropsychological deficits combine to lower later educational and occupational attainment, thereby increasing the likelihood of criminal involvement. Earlier disadvantaged and delayed transitions are magnified over time resulting in problematic transitions to adulthood and increased criminal offending.[78]

The important ways that past experiences interconnect with and codetermine later life chances have been productively explored by social scientists in other contexts far removed from the analysis of criminal behavior. They are nonetheless especially useful to consider because they help to explain how and why small differences or seemingly unimportant adaptations at one point in time can lead to large and even insurmountable differences or increasingly irreversible consequences later in life. For example, Princeton economist Paul Krugman's Nobel Prize-winning research focused in part on "economic geography" and the so-called "path dependence" of industrial production on geographical location. He wrote that "[t]he long shadow cast by history over location is apparent at all scales" of industry.[79] This may seem like a remote and perhaps irrelevant insight in a discussion of criminal behavior. However, the following is how physician and writer Atul Gawande described the core implications of Krugman's kind of path dependent analysis:

> With path-dependent processes, the outcome is unpredictable at the start. Small, often random events early in the process are "remembered," continuing to have influence later. And, as you go along, the range of future possibilities gets narrower. It becomes more and more unlikely that you can simply shift from one path to another, even if you are locked in on a path that has a lower payoff than an alternative one.[80]

As applied to the world of politics, political scientist Paul Pierson has argued that path dependent processes imply that although "a wide range of social outcomes may be possible" at the start of the process, large consequences may result from relatively small events, such that particular courses of action may become "virtually impossible to reverse" once they have been set in motion.[81] Thus, there are "critical moments or junctures that shape the basic contours of social life."[82] Pierson noted that path dependence means more than the undeniable assertion that "history matters;" as he put it, once it is embarked on, "a particular path is difficult to exit."[83]

Gawande was writing about health care policy, Pierson applied these notions to political life and fields of political inquiry, and Krugman's original insights were about economics and geography, but their essential logic has as much or more to do with human psychology than with these particular issues. In fact, there are several aspects of path-dependent processes that Pierson summarized that have direct application to the study of lives in general and the unintended and unanticipated criminogenic effect of risk factors in particular. They help to explain the way in which subsequent life choices are significantly constrained by earlier ones—ones often made in response to powerful risk factors and at a time when their long-term consequences were largely unknown and *unknowable to the person who makes them.*

Specifically, Pierson wrote that the element of randomness in early events (or in initial choices) often makes later outcomes unpredictable—that is, people "cannot predict ahead of time which of [the] possible end states will be reached."[84] Furthermore, the farther into the process (or along the path) we are, "the harder it becomes to shift from one path to another." Accidental events along the way nonetheless "feed back into future choices"—they are "remembered" in the sense that they not only continue to influence the direction in which we travel but also make turning in another direction more difficult. Finally, outcomes may become "locked in" in the long run, even if they "generate lower pay-offs than a forgone alternative would have."

Children who struggle to adapt to and overcome a life filled with maltreatment, disadvantage, and trauma make many forced choices along the way, ones whose long-term consequences they cannot possibly foresee. They certainly "cannot predict ahead of time" where the path they begin to follow will lead them. Absent effective and benign interventions or the serendipitous presence of an unexpected buffer in their life, they are likely to persist on the path they have begun to travel and "the harder it becomes to shift from one path to another." In this way, early forced choices "feed back into future choices," so that many of the problematic behaviors and pathways become "locked in."

Why Does It Matter?

In real life, of course, the accumulating effects of traumas and risks and the path dependencies they create can reverberate over a life course, sometimes with tragic consequences. Children and adolescents often struggle valiantly to prevent their fates from becoming "locked in" and many succeed in doing so. But for some, the odds are simply too great. To take just one illustration, recall the closing argument in the death penalty case with which I began the last chapter—the tale of Lamar Jackson and his supposedly "freely chosen" evil lifestyle and the selfish, unencumbered choices that he made to engage in acts of extreme violence and predation. It was a disturbing and compelling narrative, one so convincing that, as I noted, even Lamar's own trial attorneys essentially conceded the prosecutor's damning assertions, treating them as if they were irrebuttable facts that lacked any real explanatory context that could possibly refute them. The defense lawyers made little effort to offer a coherent mitigating counternarrative or to attempt to meaningfully place Lamar's behavior in the larger framework of his life history. But there *was* much more to Lamar's story that the jurors never really heard, including extremely important aspects of his life that the prosecutor and defense attorneys alike either did not know or, for some reason, simply did not explain in any coherent way.

Thus, among the many things that were never fully and meaningfully explored at his trial, the jury never learned that Lamar Jackson was the seventh of 11 children, born to a young mother, Ann Butler, who, by the time she gave birth to Lamar at age 24, had already been severely traumatized and violently victimized. She had grown up in a racially divided town in Illinois, where her family had moved from Mississippi, hoping to escape racial conflict and make a better life. Unfortunately, this was not what Ann or her children ultimately found. She ended up being raised by her grandmother, and lived under troubled and tumultuous circumstances in which, among other things, her race limited the options and the resources that were available to her. Long before Lamar was born and throughout his childhood and adolescent years, Ann suffered periods of emotional and mental instability. She was hospitalized for psychiatric problems during the first year of Lamar's life and also was hospitalized on a number of occasions for various physical injuries that she suffered at the hands of several of her abusive male partners. In fact, she was once incarcerated for a violent assault that she committed while defending herself against one of her four husbands.

Ann and her children lived in dire poverty, and the family was on public assistance for much of Lamar's childhood and adolescence. Records indicated that there were many times when the children told authorities that they did not have enough to eat. Lamar and his siblings not only lived in poverty and deprivation but also suffered a chaotic and unpredictable life. The family moved frequently and often abruptly because of conflicts with neighbors or to escape from bill collectors. Like several of his siblings, Lamar did not know the identity of his biological father. Indeed, even into adulthood, he continued to wonder about his lineage and constructed several alternative scenarios that were based on no real evidence but only his own speculation about the identity of his real father. In any event, Lamar grew up fatherless and had a hard time bonding with any of the many men who passed through his home (typically in fleeting but always contentious and usually physically violent relationships with his mother).

Ann's children all attended poor, marginal schools, and their academic records were compromised by their chaotic home life and by the countless times they moved from one house, neighborhood, or school to another, often because the children's care was entrusted to others. Lamar's many siblings suffered from a range of emotional problems that were explicitly detailed by school authorities in records that described them as "unhappy and disturbed." Virtually all of the boys in the family became involved in criminal activity at young ages, struggling in the desperately poor neighborhoods where they lived. They were repeatedly incarcerated in juvenile and adult facilities, some eventually for very serious violent crimes. One of Lamar's brothers—by all accounts their mother's "favorite" (whose criminal exploits she kept news clippings of)—was stabbed to death in a motel parking lot when Lamar was still a young boy.

Lamar and his siblings were the victims of such high levels of chronic abuse and profound neglect that an Illinois hospital "sterilization committee" concluded—when Lamar was just 7 years old—that his mother should not be allowed to give birth to any more children. They ordered that she be sterilized, writing: "Following a complete review of the medical and socioeconomic indications in this case, it was the unanimous opinion of the committee that sterilization is indicated."

Of course, the pattern of abuse and neglect that the committee condemned was not the product of any "free choices" that Ann Butler had made about the kind of mother she wanted to be for her children. She was herself very much a victim of a terribly traumatic and risk factor-filled life—subjected to extreme poverty from birth, violently abused by a succession of men with whom she had troubled relationships, and compromised by the longstanding but untreated mental illness from which she suffered. Despite these many traumas, there was nothing to suggest that Ann would have rebuffed offers of meaningful help or assistance, and no reason to believe that she was somehow beyond benefitting from it, if any had been offered. Yet there was no indication in official records that authorities had made any serious efforts to assist her before making the extreme recommendation that she should be sterilized. Rather than provide her with the ongoing counseling and economic resources she needed to better care for her children, they decided instead to prevent her from having any more.

It was just a year after this "sterilization order" that Lamar began getting into trouble with the law. Eventually, a juvenile court concluded that, because his absent biological father was "not willing to take the boy and the mother is 'no good'"—literally the characterization that was used—Lamar needed to be removed from the home. Stays in a series of foster care placements, group homes, and juvenile justice facilities followed. Along with them, numerous psychological evaluations were completed and reports dutifully written, all carefully identifying a range of deep-seated emotional problems from which Lamar had begun to suffer, describing him as, among other things, "a very deprived child who has lived very much from hand to mouth for his entire life." His juvenile file was replete with recommendations for in-depth, long-term professional treatment that all of the clinical experts seemed to agree Lamar desperately needed. The recommendations were never followed.

As Lamar got older, he entered more austere and threatening juvenile facilities where his young age and small stature placed him at greater risk of victimization. He began to fight in order to protect himself. As he acknowledged to me years later, he taught himself to be

> as mean as I could be, and that's how I kept people off of me. . . . You'd see weak kids getting victimized and picked on. . . . When you are 3 feet tall you have to act like you have 2 six shooters in your hand—you have to get an attitude.

Lamar's fearsome "attitude" may have served him well when he was inside one or another juvenile institution, but much less so each time he was moved back to a regular public school classroom. He was in trouble more or less continuously in middle school and the brief period of high school he attended.

The adaptations that seemed useful—even necessary—in one context were "locked in" in another, where they doomed him. There was no benign intervention or the serendipitous introduction of an unexpected protective factor to change the direction or slow the momentum of the path he was on. Each subsequent stay in a new juvenile institution brought new recommendations for treatment and new failures by the staff to follow up on them. Finally, while still a teenager, despite his youth and small stature, Lamar was sent to the notorious Illinois maximum security prison at Stateville, where he became one of the youngest prisoners among the several thousand men who were housed there. In the succession of prison terms that followed, Lamar's anger deepened, he honed his combative survival skills, and his "bad attitude" only got worse. Over time, these consciously adopted techniques that so effectively kept others at bay became more a part of how Lamar reflexively approached the world. He had learned these lessons well, and his now intuitive reactions were difficult if not impossible for him to keep in check, even when they were no longer necessary or functional.

Eventually, Lamar learned to support himself through drug dealing, a kind of cottage industry on the mean streets where he lived. He also learned to use violence, not just for self-protection and survival but for self-esteem, to maintain status and reputation and, in a sense, to preserve a desirable identity in a world where intimidation was the way people garnered and preserved not just power but selfhood. Small adaptations—to abuse, neglect, exposure to violence, chaos and instability, racially targeted aggression, emotional problems, brutalizing juvenile institutions and adult prisons—eventually became habits that fed off themselves, making certain outcomes more likely, seemingly inevitable—as others receded into the distance. Absent meaningful interventions that exposed him to a significantly changed, more benign and therapeutic set of circumstances, these habits persisted and generated new stressors and challenges with which he was ill-prepared to cope.

The jurors in Lamar's case deserved to have these facts laid out carefully, coherently, and in great detail. They also deserved an equally careful, coherent and detailed explanation of why and how the traumas and risks that characterized Lamar's life mattered—the science of how they helped to shape and direct his life course, not to excuse his conduct but to explain and put it in a larger, more meaningful context to inform their verdict. Of course, in the final analysis it might not have mattered to the outcome of his case, although I very much think it would have. Frankly, I think the prosecutor did as well. That is likely why he labored so mightily to present such a one-sided picture of the Lamar to the jurors, lest the tiniest bit of psychological nuance or slightest glimpse of humanity creep into the crime master narrative he offered and give the jurors pause. Prosecutors in capital cases such as Lamar's have learned to argue that all that matters is that the defendant supposedly made a choice or several of them that supposedly reflected his defective essence and his inherent evil. The power and persistence of the crime master narrative ensures that they can also rely on most jurors to implicitly support this view.

In fact, until recently, this was the way most people had been taught to think about crime in our society. The rest of this book provides an in-depth discussion of the research and theory that documents and explains why and how this particular master narrative is no longer viable. It underscores how and why the details and implications of life stories like Lamar's should matter and motivate us to think differently about crime and justice. Of course, jurors, voters, and members of the public will decide for themselves whether and how to take these kinds of social historical and immediate contextual factors into account. But the days of regarding these things as unimportant or irrelevant are ending. The chapters that follow help to explain why.

NOTES

1. Bandura, A. (2016). *Moral disengagement: How people do harm and live with themselves* (p. 188). New York, NY: Worth.
2. Miller, G. A. (1980, January). Giving psychology away in the 80s (An interview with E. Hall). *Psychology Today, 13,* 38\n\n50, p. 45.
3. For key, early discussions of these now widely accepted propositions, see Caspi, A., Bem, D. J., & Elder, G. H., Jr. (1989). Continuities and consequences of interactional styles across the life course. *Journal of Personality, 57,* 375–406. http://dx.doi.org/10.1111/j.1467-6494.1989.tb00487.x; Mischel, W. (1968). *Personality and assessment.* New York, NY: Wiley; Moen, P., Elder, G. H., Jr., & Luscher, K.

(Eds.). (1995). *Examining lives in context: Perspectives on the ecology of human development.* Washington, DC: American Psychological Association; Richards, M., & Light, P. (Eds.). (1986). *Children of social worlds: Development in a social context.* Cambridge, MA: Harvard University Press; Ross, L., & Nisbett, R. E. (1991). *The person and the situation: Perspectives of social psychology.* New York, NY: McGraw-Hill; and Sroufe, L. A., Egeland, B., & Kreutzer, T. (1990). The fate of early experience following developmental change: Longitudinal approaches to individual adaptation in childhood. *Child Development, 61,* 1363–1373. http://dx.doi.org/10.2307/1130748

4. Moen, Elder, & Luscher (1995). *Examining lives in context,* p. 6.
5. Lerner, R. M., & Kauffman, M. B. (1985). The concept of development in contextualism. *Developmental Review, 5,* 309–333, p. 324. http://dx.doi.org/10.1016/0273-2297(85)90016-4
6. Lerner & Kauffman (1985), The concept of development in contextualism, pp. 324–325. See also Richards & Light (1986), *Children of social worlds.*
7. Mason, E. M. (1968). The contribution of the social history in the diagnosis of child disturbances. *British Journal of Psychiatric Social Work, 9,* 180–187.
8. Masten, A. S., & Garmezy, N. (1985). Risk, vulnerability, and protective factors in developmental psychopathology. In B. B. Lahey & A. E. Kazdin (Eds.), *Advances in clinical child psychology* (pp. 1–52). New York, NY: Plenum. http://dx.doi.org/10.1007/978-1-4613-9820-2_1
9. See, e.g., McGrath, J. J., & Murray, R. M. (2011). Environmental risk factors for schizophrenia. In D. R. Weinberger, & P. J. Harrison (Eds.), *Schizophrenia* (3rd ed., pp. 225–244). New York, NY: Wiley-Blackwell. http://dx.doi.org/10.1002/9781444327298.ch11; Nelson, C. A. (Ed.). (1994). *Threats to optimal development: Integrating biological, psychological, and social risk factors.* Hillsdale, NJ: Lawrence Erlbaum. http://dx.doi.org/10.4324/9780203773666; Rolf, J., Masten, A. S., Cicchetti, D., Nuechterlein, K. H., & Weintraub, S. (Eds.). (1990). *Risk and protective factors in the development of psychopathology.* New York, NY: Cambridge University Press; Sameroff, A. J., & Seifer, R. (1995). Accumulation of environmental risk and child mental health. In H. E. Fitzgerald, B. M. Lester, & B. Zuckerman (Eds.), *Children of poverty: Research, health, and policy issues* (pp. 233–258). New York, NY: Garland; and Shaffer, A., & Yates, T. M. (2010). Identifying and understanding risk factors and protective factors in clinical practice. In M. T. Compton (Ed.), *Clinical manual of prevention in mental health* (pp. 29–48). Washington, DC: American Psychiatric Association.
10. For example, here is a sample of articles and book chapters published on the topic of child abuse as early as the 1960s: Bennie, E. H., & Sclare, A. B. (1969). The battered child syndrome. *The American Journal of Psychiatry, 125,* 975–979, http://dx.doi.org/10.1176/ajp.125.7.975; Birrell, R. G., & Birrell, J. H. (1968). The maltreatment syndrome in children: A hospital survey. *Medical Journal of Australia, 522,* 1023–1029; Elmer, E. (1967). Abused children and community resources. *International Journal of Offender Therapy, 11,* 16–23. http://dx.doi.org/10.1177/0306624x6701100104; Fontana, V. J. (1968). Further reflections on maltreatment of children. *New York State Journal of Medicine, 68,* 2214–2215; Gil, D. G. (1969). Physical abuse of children: Findings and implications of a nationwide survey. *Pediatrics, 44* (Suppl.), 857–864; Helfer, R. E., & Kempe, C. H. (Eds.). (1968). *The battered child.* Chicago, IL: University of Chicago Press. Cf. Newberger and Bourne's 1978 observation that "[c]hild abuse has emerged in the last *fifteen* years as a visible and important social problem [emphasis added]," Newberger, E. H., & Bourne, R. (1978). The medicalization and legalization of child abuse. *American Journal of Orthopsychiatry, 48,* 593–607, p. 593. http://dx.doi.org/10.1111/j.1939-0025.1978.tb02564.x
11. For example, here is a sample of legal discussions of the issue of child abuse published by the mid-1970s: De Francis, V., & Lucht, C. L. (1974). *Child abuse*

legislation in the 1970s (Rev. ed.). Denver, CO: American Humane Association, Children's Division; Fraser, B. G. (1974). A pragmatic alternative to current legislative approaches to child abuse. *American Criminal Law Review, 12,* 103–124; Fraser, B. G. (1976). Independent representation for the abused and neglected child: The guardian ad litem. *California Western Law Review, 13,* 16–45; Goodpaster, G. S., & Angel, K. (1975). Child abuse and the law: The California system. *Hastings Law Review, 26,* 1081–1125; Katz, S. N., Howe, R.-A. W., & McGrath, M. (1975). Child neglect laws in America. *Family Law Quarterly, 9,* 1–39; Levine, R. S. (1973). Caveat parens: A demystification of the child protection system. *University of Pittsburgh Law Review, 35,* 1–52; Light, R. (1973). Abused and neglected children in America: A study of alternative policies. *Harvard Educational Review, 43,* 556–598. http://dx.doi.org//10.17763/haer.43.4.u25580361w3r843n; Newberger & Bourne (1978), The medicalization and legalization of child abuse; Paulsen, M. G. (1966). The legal framework for child protection. *Columbia Law Review, 66,* 679–717. http://dx.doi.org/10.2307/1121022; Paulsen, M. G. (1967). Child abuse reporting laws: The shape of the legislation. *Columbia Law Review, 67,* 1–49. http://dx.doi.org/10.2307/1121129; Polier, J., & McDonald, K. (1972). The family court in an urban setting. In C. H. Kempe & R. E. Helfer (Eds.), *Helping the battered child and his family* (pp. 208–224). Philadelphia, PA: Lippincott; Simons, B. & Downs, E. (1968). Medical reporting of child abuse: Patterns, problems, and accomplishments. *New York State Journal of Medicine, 68,* 2324–2330; Wald, M. (1975). State intervention on behalf of "neglected" children: A search for realistic standards. *Stanford Law Review, 27,* 985–1040. http://dx.doi.org/10.2307/1228197; Wald, M. S. (1976). State intervention on behalf of "neglected" children: Standards for removal of children from their homes, monitoring the status of children in foster care, and termination of parental rights. *Stanford Law Review, 28,* 623–706. http://dx.doi.org/10.2307/1228098

12. Masten & Garmezy (1985), Risk, vulnerability, and protective factors in the development of psychopathology, p. 3.
13. McGinnis, J. M., & Foege, W. H. (1993). Actual causes of death in the United States. *JAMA, 270,* 2207–2212. http://dx.doi.org/10.1001/jama.1993.03510180077038
14. In fact, some of the same risks that I discuss in this and subsequent chapters as increasing the likelihood of criminal behavior also have adverse effects on physical health. See, e.g., Augustin, T., Glass, T. A., James, B. D., & Schwartz, B. S. (2008). Neighborhood psychosocial hazards and cardiovascular disease: The Baltimore memory study. *American Journal of Public Health, 98,* 1664–1670. http://dx.doi.org/10.2105/AJPH.2007.125138; and Danese, A., Moffitt, T. E., Harrington, H., Milne, B. J., Polanczyk, G., Pariante, C. M., . . . Caspi, A. (2009). Adverse childhood experiences and adult risk factors for age-related disease: Depression, inflammation, and clustering of metabolic risk markers. *Archives of Pediatric and Adolescent Medicine, 163,* 1135–1143. http://dx.doi.org/10.1001/archpediatrics.2009.214
15. For example, in 1987, two authors warned in the pages of *American Psychologist* that child maltreatment was a "major threat to children's mental health." Hart, S. N., & Brassard, M. R. (1987). A major threat to children's mental health: Psychological maltreatment. *American Psychologist, 42,* 160–165, p. 160. http://dx.doi.org/10.1037/0003-066x.42.2.160. See also McCord, J., & Ensminger, M. E. (1997). Multiple risks and comorbidity in an African American population. *Criminal Behaviour and Mental Health, 7,* 339–352. http://dx.doi.org/10.1002/cbm.194
16. Knutson, J. F. (1995). Psychological characteristics of maltreated children: Putative risk factors and consequences. *Annual Review of Psychology, 46,* 401–431, pp. 401–402. http://dx.doi.org/10.1146/annurev.ps.46.020195.002153, referencing Kempe, C. H., Silverman, F. N., Steele, B. F., Droegemueller, W., & Silver, H. K. (1962). The battered-child syndrome. *JAMA, 181,* 17–24.

17. The terms "risk factors" and "trauma" are highly interrelated concepts, especially in the context in which I use them. For example, the then-editor of the journal *Traumatology*, Charles Figley, defined trauma broadly and in a way that is consistent with Masten and Garmezy's use of the risk factors concept—as "an extraordinary and potentially dangerous and life-changing event linked to human response." Figley, C. (2009). Editorial. *Traumatology: An International Journal, 15,* 1–5, p. 2. As I discuss later in this chapter, both concepts are related to what have been called "adverse childhood experiences." See, e.g., Fox, B. H., Perez, N., Cass, E., Baglivio, M. T., & Epps, N. (2015). Trauma changes everything: Examining the relationship between adverse childhood experiences and serious, violent juvenile and chronic juvenile offenders. *Child Abuse & Neglect, 46,* 163–173. http://dx.doi.org/10.1016/j.chiabu.2015.01.011
18. Masten & Garmezy (1985), Risk, vulnerability, and protective factors in the development of psychopathology, p. 6, quoting Janis, I., & Leventhal, H. (1968). Human reactions to stress. In E. F. Borgatta & W. W. Lambert (Eds.), *Handbook of personality theory and research* (pp. 1041–1085). Chicago, IL: Rand McNally. Other researchers have used a slightly different definition that includes aspects of the environment that a person experiences as "taxing or exceeding his or her resources and endangering his or her well being." Lazarus, R. S., & Folkman, S. (1984). *Stress, appraisal, and coping*. New York, NY: Springer, p. 19.
19. Holmes, T. H., & Rahe, R. H. (1967). The Social Readjustment Rating Scale. *Journal of Psychosomatic Research, 11,* 213–218. http://dx.doi.org/10.1016/0022-3999(67)90010-4. See also Holmes, T., & Masuda, M. (1974). Life changes and illness susceptibility. In B. S. Dohrenwend & B. P. Dohrenwend (Eds.), *Stressful life events: Their nature and effects* (pp. 45–72). Oxford, England: Wiley.
20. Holmes & Rahe (1967), The Social Readjustment Rating Scale, p. 217.
21. In fact, the original Holmes and Rahe sample was overwhelmingly White (only 5% of the sample was African American, and the researchers did not code for Latino origin), 82% described themselves as "middle class," and over half (54%) reported having 4 years of college. See Holmes & Rahe (1967), The Social Readjustment Rating Scale, p. 215.
22. Blasco-Fontecilla, H., Delgado-Gomez, D., Legido-Gil, T., de Leon, J., Perez-Rodriguez, M. M., & Baca-Garcia, E. (2012). Can the Holmes-Rahe Social Readjustment Rating Scale (SRRS) be used as a suicide risk scale? An exploratory study. *Archives of Suicide Research, 16,* 13–28. http://dx.doi.org/10.1080/13811118.2012.640616. See also Adams, D. M., Overholser, J. C., & Spirito, A. (1994). Stressful life events associated with adolescent suicide attempts. *Canadian Journal of Psychiatry, 39,* 43–48. http://dx.doi.org/10.1177/070674379403900109; Coyne, J. C., Thompson, R., & Pepper, C. M. (2004). The role of life events in depression in primary medical care versus psychiatric settings. *Journal of Affective Disorders, 82,* 353–361. http://dx.doi.org/10.1016/j.jad.2004.02.008; and Grimby, A., & Berg, S. (1995). Stressful life events and cognitive functioning in late life. *Aging Clinical and Experimental Research, 7,* 35–39.
23. DeLongis, A., Coyne, J. C., Dakof, G., Folkman, S., & Lazarus, R. S. (1982). Relationship of daily hassles, uplifts, and major life events to health status. *Health Psychology, 1,* 119–136, p. 121. http://dx.doi.org/10.1037/0278-6133.1.2.119
24. See DeLongis, Coyne, Dakof, Folkman, & Lazarus (1982), Relationship of daily hassles, p. 120; Kanner, A. D., Coyne, J. C., Schaefer, C., & Lazarus, R. S. (1981). Comparison of two modes of stress measurement: Daily hassles and uplifts versus major life events. *Journal of Behavioral Medicine, 4,* 1–39; and Lewinsohn, P. M., & Talkington, J. (1979). Studies of the measurement of unpleasant events and relations with depression. *Applied Psychological Measurement, 3,* 83–101 (1979). http://dx.doi.org/10.1177/014662167900300110

25. See, e.g., Kagan, J. (2016). An overly permissive extension. *Perspectives on Psychological Science, 11,* 442–450. http://dx.doi.org/10.1177/1745691616635593; Koolhaas, J. M., Bartolomucci, A., Buwalda, B., de Boer, S. F., Flügge, G., Korte, S. M., . . . Fuchs, E. (2011). Stress revisited: A critical evaluation of the stress concept. *Neuroscience and Biobehavioral Reviews, 35,* 1291–1301. http://dx.doi.org/10.1016/j.neubiorev.2011.02.003; McEwen, B. S., & McEwen, C. A. (2016). Response to Jerome Kagan's essay on stress. *Perspectives on Psychological Science, 11,* 451–455. http://dx.doi.org/10.1177/1745691616646635
26. See, e.g., Lin, N., Woelfel, M. W., & Light, S. C. (1985). The buffering effect of social support subsequent to an important life event. *Journal of Health and Social Behavior, 26,* 247–263. http://dx.doi.org/10.2307/2136756
27. McEwen, B., & McEwen, C. (2015). Social, psychological, and physiological reactions to stress. In R. Scott & S. Kosslyn (Eds.), *Emerging trends in the social and behavioral sciences* (pp. 1–15). New York, NY: Wiley. http://dx.doi.org/10.1002/9781118900772.etrds0311
28. Much has been written about the concept of coping, including the different coping mechanisms that persons employ in different contexts and at different stages of their lives. See, e.g., DeLongis, A., Folkman, S., & Lazarus, R. S. (1988). The impact of daily stress on health and mood: Psychological and social resources as mediators. *Journal of Personality and Social Psychology, 54,* 486–495. http://dx.doi.org/10.1037/0022-3514.54.3.486; Folkman, S., & Lazarus, R. S. (1988). Coping as a mediator of emotion. *Journal of Personality and Social Psychology, 54,* 466–475, http://dx.doi.org/10.1037/0022-3514.54.3.466; Folkman, S., Lazarus, R. S., Gruen, R. J., & DeLongis, A. (1986). Appraisal, coping, health status, and psychological symptoms. *Journal of Personality and Social Psychology, 50,* 571–579, http://dx.doi.org/10.1037/0022-3514.50.3.571; Folkman, S., Lazarus, R. S., Pimley, S., & Novacek, J. (1987). Age differences in stress and coping, *Psychology and Aging, 2,* 171–184; Folkman, S. (1991). The concept of coping. In A. Monat & R. Lazarus (Eds.), *Stress and coping: An anthology* (3rd ed., pp. 189–206). New York, NY: Columbia University Press; Gan, Y., & Liu, J. (2012). The mechanism by which interpersonal coping flexibility influences self-esteem. *Psychological Record, 62,* 735–746, http://dx.doi.org/10.1007/bf03395832; and Weisman, A. D. (1984). *The coping capacity: On the nature of being mortal.* New York, NY: Human Sciences Press.
29. Lazarus & Folkman (1984), *Stress, appraisal and coping,* p. 141.
30. See, e.g., Caspi, A., McClay, J., Moffitt, T. E., Mill, J., Martin, J., Craig, I. W., . . . Poulton, R. (2002). Role of genotype in the cycle of violence in maltreated children. *Science, 297,* 851–854. http://dx.doi.org/10.1126/science.1072290
31. According to Masten and Garmezy's risk factors model, "protective factors" consist of "1) personality dispositions of the child, 2) a warm, emotionally supportive family milieu, and 3) the presence of extended support systems." Masten & Garmezy (1985), Risk, vulnerability, and protective factors in the development of psychopathology, p. 14. Garmezy in particular saw protective factors as interacting with risk factors to mitigate their damage, writing that they were "those attributes of persons, environments, situations, and events that appear to temper predictions of psychopathology based upon an individual's at-risk status." Garmezy, N. (1983). Stressors of childhood. In N. Garmezy, & M. Rutter (Eds.), *Stress, coping, and development in children* (pp. 43–84). New York, NY: McGraw-Hill, p. 73. However, there is no reason why protective factors need to be restricted to a narrow set of positive life experiences instead of being extended to include a host of things known to enhance outcomes, or why these positive aspects or experiences would not have beneficial effects whether or not they act to mitigate the impact of risk factors.

32. See, e.g., Bai, G. J., Leon, S. C., Garbarino, J., & Fuller, A. K. (2016). The protective effect of kinship involvement on the adjustment of youth in foster care. *Child Maltreatment, 21,* 288–297. http://dx.doi.org/10.1177/1077559516669043; McCabe, K. M., & Clark, R. (1999). Family protective factors among urban African American youth. *Journal of Clinical Child Psychology, 28,* 137–150. http://dx.doi.org/10.1207/s15374424jccp2802_2; Taylor, R. D., Seaton, E., & Dominguez, A. (2008). Kinship support, family relations, and psychological adjustment among low-income African American mothers and adolescents. *Journal of Research on Adolescence, 18,* 1–22. http://dx.doi.org/10.1111/j.1532-7795.2008.00548.x
33. I should note that some researchers–particularly David Farrington, Rolf Loeber, Arnold Sameroff and their colleagues–have distinguished between protective factors and what they call "promotive" factors. They have used the latter term to underscore the fact that certain positive aspects of someone's life can enhance or improve their future outcomes in ways that are independent of any protection or buffering they may provide against risk factors. Although I agree with their point, to avoid making the model needlessly complex, I use "protective" factor to refer to life-enhancing, positive or beneficial aspects or elements in a person's life that increase the likelihood of desirable outcomes, either because they are a buffer against the risk factors to which someone has been subjected or because they independently improve a person's subsequent life chances. In actual fact, these are most often the very same kind of positive and beneficial aspects of someone's life as those that have been termed "promotive" factors.
34. Masten & Garmezy (1985), Risk, vulnerability, and protective factors in the development of psychopathology, p. 37.
35. van der Kolk, B. A., Roth, S., Pelcovitz, D., Sunday, S., & Spinazzola, J. (2005). Disorders of extreme stress: The empirical foundation of a complex adaptation to trauma. *Journal of Traumatic Stress, 18,* 389–400, p. 399. http://dx.doi.org/10.1037/e608902012-070
36. Masten & Garmezy (1985), Risk, vulnerability, and protective factors in the development of psychopathology, p. 38.
37. Masten & Garmezy (1985), Risk, vulnerability, and protective factors in the development of psychopathology, p. 38.
38. See, e.g., Norman, R. E., Byambaa, M., De, R., Butchart, A., Scott, J., & Vos, T. (2012). The long-term health consequences of child physical abuse, emotional abuse, and neglect: A systematic review and meta-analysis. *PLoS Medicine, 9,* e1001349. http://dx.doi.org/10.1371/journal.pmed.1001349; and Vachon, D. D., Krueger, R. F., Rogosch, F. A., & Cicchetti, D. (2015). Assessment of the harmful psychiatric and behavioral of different forms of child maltreatment. *JAMA Psychiatry, 72,* 1135–1142. http://dx.doi.org/10.1001/jamapsychiatry.2015.1792
39. Cloitre, M., Stolbach, B. C., Herman, J. L., van der Kolk, B., Pynoos, R., Wang, J., & Petkova, E. (2009). A developmental approach to complex PTSD: Childhood and adult cumulative trauma as predictors of symptom complexity. *Journal of Traumatic Stress, 22,* 399–408, p. 406. http://dx.doi.org/10.1002/jts.20444
40. See, e.g., McCord & Ensminger (1997), Multiple risks and comorbidity in an African American population.
41. Anda, R. F., Butchart, A., Felitti, V. J., & Brown, D. W. (2010). Building a framework for global surveillance of the public health implications of adverse childhood experiences. *American Journal of Preventive Medicine, 39,* 93–98. http://dx.doi.org/10.1016/j.amepre.2010.03.015. See also Kendall-Tackett, K. (2002). The health effects of childhood abuse: Four pathways by which abuse can influence health. *Child Abuse & Neglect, 26,* 715–730. http://dx.doi.org/10.1016/S0145-2134(02)00343-5
42. See, e.g., Downey, G., Khouri, H., & Feldman, S. (1997). Early interpersonal trauma and later adjustment: The meditational role of rejection sensitivity.

In D. Cicchetti & S. Toth (Eds.), *Developmental perspectives on trauma: Theory, research, and intervention* (pp. 85–114). Rochester, NY: University of Rochester Press; and Pietrzak, J., Downey, G., & Ayduk, O. (2005). Rejection sensitivity as an interpersonal vulnerability. In M. Baldwin (Ed.), *Interpersonal cognition* (pp. 62–84). New York, NY: Guilford Press.

43. See, e.g., Feldman, S., & Downey, G. (1994). Rejection sensitivity as a mediator of the impact of childhood exposure to family violence on adult attachment behavior. *Development and Psychopathology, 6,* 231–247; Frederick, J., & Goddard, C. (2008). Living on an island: Consequences of childhood abuse, attachment disruption and adversity in later life. *Child & Family Social Work, 13,* 300–310. http://dx.doi.org/10.1111/j.1365-2206.2008.00554.x
44. See, e.g., Cloitre, M., Khan, C., Mackintosh, M. A., Garvert, D. W., Henn-Haase, C. M., Falvey, E. C., & Saito, J. (2019). Emotion regulation mediates the relationship between ACES and physical and mental health. *Psychological Trauma: Theory, Research, Practice, and Policy, 11,* 82–89. http://dx.doi.org/10.1037/tra0000374
45. See, e.g., Dodge, K., Pettit, G., & Bates, J. (1994). Effects of physical maltreatment on the development of peer relations. *Development and Psychopathology, 6,* 43–55; Jaffe, P., Wolfe, D., Wilson, S., & Zak, L. (1986). Similarities in behavioral and social maladjustment among child victims and witnesses to family violence. *American Journal of Orthopsychiatry, 56,* 142–146; Mueller, N., & Silverman, N. (1989). Peer relations in maltreated children. In D. Cicchetti & V. Carlson (Eds.), *Child maltreatment: Theory and research on the causes and consequences of child abuse and neglect* (pp. 529–578). New York, NY: Cambridge University Press; Berenson, K., & Andersen, S. (2006). Childhood physical and emotional abuse by a parent: Transference effects in adult interpersonal relations. *Personality and Social Psychology Bulletin, 32,* 1509–1522. http://dx.doi.org/10.1177/0146167206291671; Massing-Schaffer, M., Liu, R., Kraines, M., Choi, J., & Alloy, L. (2015). Elucidating the relation between childhood emotional abuse and depressive symptoms in adulthood: The mediating role of maladaptive interpersonal processes. *Personality and Individual Differences, 74,* 106–111. http://dx.doi.org/10.1016/j.paid.2014.09.045; Perry, A., DiLillo, D., & Peugh, J. (2007). Childhood psychological maltreatment and quality of marriage: The mediating role of psychological distress. *Journal of Emotional Abuse, 7,* 117–142. http://dx.doi.org/10.1300/J135v07n02_07
46. See, e.g., Blanco, C., Rubio, J., Wall, M., Wang, S., Jui, C., & Kendler, K. (2014). Risk factors for anxiety disorders: Common and specific effects in a national sample. *Depression and Anxiety, 31,* 756–764; Kisely, S., Abajobir, A., Mills, R., Strathearn, L., Clavarino, A., & Najman, J. (2018). Child maltreatment and mental health problems in adulthood: Birth cohort study. *British Journal of Psychiatry, 213,* 1–6. Retrieved from https://www.cambridge.org/core/services/aop-cambridge-core/content/view/FEDE6971908492AC392A1DDDDB2E72CE/S0007125018002076a.pdf/child_maltreatment_and_mental_health_problems_in_adulthood_birth_cohort_study.pdf; and Moreno-Peral, P., Conejo-Ceron, S., Motrico, E. (2014). Risk factors for the onset of panic and generalised anxiety disorders in the general adult population: A systematic review of cohort studies. *Journal of Affective Disorders, 168,* 337–348. http://dx.doi.org/10.1016/j.jad.2014.06.021
47. Keltikangas-Jarvinen, L., & Heinonen, K. (2003). Childhood roots of hostility: Family factors as predictors of cognitive and affective hostility. *Child Development, 74,* 1751–1768. http://dx.doi.org/10.1046/j.1467-8624.2003.00636.x; Pierce, J., Abbey, A., & Wegner, R. (2018). Mediators of the association between childhood emotional maltreatment and young adult men's life satisfaction. *Journal of Interpersonal Violence, 33,* 595–616. http://dx.doi.org/10.1177/0886260515609584
48. Developmental psychologists Dante Cicchetti and Fred Rogosch have distinguished two interrelated concepts that are useful to keep in mind in understanding the

nature of cause-and-effect relationships between different kinds of traumas and risk factors, on the one hand, and the different life outcomes with which they are associated, on the other. Cicchetti, D., & Rogosch, F. (1996). Equifinality and multifinality in developmental psychopathology. *Development and Psychopathology, 8*, 597–600, p. 597. Thus, "multifinality" refers to the fact that the actual effect or outcome produced by any particular trauma or risk factor (or set of them) can vary depending on other components in a person's life course. I note throughout this book that criminal behavior is only one of a number of possible negative outcomes to which early traumas and risks are causally related. Similarly, "equifinality" refers to the fact that, especially in an "open system" such as a person's life course, "the same end state may be reached from a variety of different initial conditions and through different processes."

49. Office of Juvenile Justice and Delinquency Prevention (1995, May). *Guide for implementing the comprehensive strategy for serious, violent, and chronic juvenile offenders*. Washington, DC: United States Department of Justice, p. 4 (emphases added).
50. Masten & Garmezy (1985), Risk, vulnerability, and protective factors in the development of psychopathology, p. 25 (internal citation omitted).
51. Dubrow, N., & Garbarino, J. (1989). Living in the war zone: Mothers and young children in a public housing development. *Child Welfare, 68*, 3–20. See also Joan McCord's introductory chapter on urban violence and the chapters that follow: McCord, J. (1994). Inner city life: Contributions to violence. In National Research Council (Ed.), *Violence in urban America: Mobilizing a response* (pp. 100–104). Washington, DC: National Academies Press.
52. Nightingale, C. (1994). *On the edge: A history of poor black children and their American dreams*. New York, NY: Basic Books, p. 10. See also Anderson, E. (1990). *Streetwise: Race, class, and social change in an urban community*. Chicago, IL: University of Chicago Press; Canada, G. (1995). *Fist stick knife gun: A personal history of violence in America*. Boston, MA: Beacon Press; Coyle, D. (1993). *Hardball: A season in the projects*. New York, NY: G.P. Putnam; Kotlowitz, A. (1991). *There are no children here*. New York, NY: Doubleday; Rodriguez, L. (1993). *Always running,* la vida loca: *Gang days in L.A.* Willimantic, CT: Curbstone Press.
53. Masten & Garmezy (1985), Risk and protective factors in the development of psychopathology, p. 25.
54. Stouthamer-Loeber, M., Loeber, R., Wei, E., Farrington, D., & Wikstrom, P. (2002). Risk and promotive effects in the explanation of persistent serious delinquency in boys. *Journal of Consulting and Clinical Psychology, 70*, 111–123, p. 111. http://dx.doi.org/10.1037/0022-006X.70.1.111 There are numerous studies that have reached essentially this same conclusion. See also, e.g., Basto-Pereira, M., Miranda, A., Ribeiro, S., & Maia, A. (2016). Growing up with adversity: From juvenile justice involvement to criminal persistence and psychosocial problems in young adulthood. *Child Abuse & Neglect, 62*, 63–75. http://dx.doi.org/10.1016/j.chiabu.2016.10.011; Evans, G., Li, D., & Whipple, S. (2013). Cumulative risk and child development. *Psychological Bulletin, 139*, 1342–1396. http://dx.doi.org/10.1037/a0031808; and Layne, C., Greeson, J., Ostrowski, S. (2014). Cumulative trauma exposure and high risk behavior in adolescence: Findings from the National Child Traumatic Stress Network core data set. *Psychological Trauma: Theory, Research, Practice, and Policy, 6*(Suppl. 1), S40–S49. http://dx.doi.org/10.1037/a0037799
55. Anda, R. F., Butchart, A., Felitti, V. J., & Brown, D. W. (2010). Building a framework for global surveillance of the public health implications of adverse childhood experiences. *American Journal of Preventive Medicine, 39*, 93–98. http://dx.doi.org/10.1016/j.amepre.2010.03.015

56. McEwen & McEwen (2016), *Response to Jerome Kagan's essay on stress,* p. 452.
57. D'Andrea, W., Ford, J., Stolbach, B., Spinazzola, J., & van der Kolk, B. A. (2012). Understanding interpersonal trauma in children: Why we need a developmentally appropriate trauma diagnosis. *American Journal of Orthopsychiatry, 82,* 187–200. http://dx.doi.org/10.1111/j.1939-0025.2012.01154.x This proposed formulation extends and refines work that van der Kolk has done on what he termed "disorders of extreme stress" and the kind of complex adaptations traumatized persons often undertake in response to their mistreatment. See, e.g., Ford, J. (2017). Complex trauma and developmental trauma disorder. *Adolescent Psychiatry, 7,* 220–235. http://dx.doi.org/10.2174/2210676608666180112160419; Rahim, M. (2014). Developmental trauma disorder: An attachment-based perspective. *Clinical Child Psychology and Psychiatry, 19,* 548–560. http://dx.doi.org/10.1177/1359104514534947; Streeck-Fischer, A. (2000). Down will come baby, cradle and all: Diagnostic and therapeutic implications of chronic trauma on child development. *Australian and New Zealand Journal of Psychiatry, 34,* 903–918. http://dx.doi.org/10.1080/000486700265; van der Kolk, B., & Fisler, R. (1994). Childhood abuse and neglect and loss of self-regulation. *Bulletin of the Menninger Clinic, 58,* 145–168; van der Kolk, B. (2005). Developmental trauma disorder: Toward a rational diagnosis for children with complex trauma histories. *Psychiatric Annals,* 35, 401–408. http://dx.doi.org/10.3928/00485713-20050501-06; and van der Kolk, B., Roth, S., Pelcovitz, D., Sunday, S., & Sinazzola, J. (2005). Disorders of extreme stress: The empirical foundation of a complex adaptation to trauma. *Journal of Traumatic Stress, 18,* 389–399. http://dx.doi.org/10.1002/jts.20047
58. D'Andrea, Ford, Stolbach, Spinazzola, & van der Kolk (2012), Understanding interpersonal trauma in children: Why we need a developmentally appropriate trauma diagnosis, p. 188. They cite the fact that persons who have been exposed to childhood and adolescent risk factors and trauma respond well to "trauma-informed" interventions as further support for at least considering "a diagnosis based upon the interrelated sequelae of childhood victimization" (p. 194).
59. D'Andrea., Ford, Stolbach, Spinazzola, & van der Kolk (2012), Understanding interpersonal trauma in children: Why we need a developmentally appropriate trauma diagnosis, p. 189.
60. McEwen, B., & McEwen, C. (2015). Social, psychological, and physiological reactions to stress. In R. Scott & S. Kosslyn (Eds.), *Emerging trends in the social and behavioral sciences* (pp. 1–15). New York, NY: Wiley. http://dx.doi.org/10.1002/9781118900772.etrds0311
61. Skeem, J. L., Winter, E., Kennealy, P. J., Louden, J. E., & Tatar, J. R., II. (2014). Offenders with mental illness have criminogenic needs, too: Toward recidivism reduction. *Law and Human Behavior, 38,* 212–224. http://dx.doi.org/10.1037/lhb0000054
62. Skeem, Winter, Louden, & Tatar (2014), Offenders with mental illness have criminogenic needs, too: Toward recidivism reduction, p. 221.
63. Skeem, Winter, Louden, & Tatar (2014), Offenders with mental illness have criminogenic needs, too: Toward recidivism reduction, p. 221.
64. Skeem, Winter, Louden, & Tatar (2014), Offenders with mental illness have criminogenic needs, too: Toward recidivism reduction, p. 221.
65. Skeem, Winter, Louden, & Tatar (2014), Offenders with mental illness have criminogenic needs, too: Toward recidivism reduction, p. 222.
66. Penner, E. K., Viljoen, J. L., Douglas, K. S., & Roesch, R. (2014). Procedural justice versus risk factors for offending: Predicting recidivism in youth. *Law and Human Behavior, 38,* 225–237, p. 229. http://dx.doi.org/10.1037/lhb0000055
67. Andrews, D. A., & Bonta, J. (2010). Rehabilitating criminal justice policy and practice. *Psychology, Public Policy, and Law, 16,* 39–55, http://dx.doi.org/10.1037/

a0018362; Bonta, J., & Andrews, D. A. (2017). *The psychology of criminal conduct* (6th ed.). New York, NY: Routledge.

68. American Psychiatric Association. (2013). *Diagnostic and statistical manual of mental disorders* (5th ed.). Arlington, VA: American Psychiatric Association, p. 473.
69. American Psychiatric Association (2013), *Diagnostic and statistical manual of mental disorders*, p. 474.
70. American Psychiatric Association (2013), *Diagnostic and statistical manual of mental disorders*, p. 661.
71. American Psychiatric Association (2013), *Diagnostic and statistical manual of mental disorders*, p. 662.
72. American Psychiatric Association (2013), *Diagnostic and statistical manual of mental disorders*, p. 661.
73. Skeem, J. L., Mulvey, E. P., & Lidz, C. W. (2000). Building mental health professionals' decisional models into tests of predictive validity: The accuracy of contextualized predictions of violence. *Law and Human Behavior, 24,* 607–628, p. 609.
74. Skeem, Milvey, & Lidz. (2000), Building mental health professionals' decisional models, p. 609.
75. Silver, E., Mulvey, E. P., & Monahan, J. (1999). Assessing violence risk among discharged psychiatric patients: Toward an ecological approach. *Law and Human Behavior, 23,* 237–255, p. 237.
76. Some of the research that I cited earlier on the relationship between maltreatment and "rejection sensitivity" and subsequent difficulties with attachment and social adjustment reflects just such a pattern. See, e.g., Downey, Khouri, & Feldman (1997), Early interpersonal trauma and later adjustment; Feldman & Downey (1994), Rejection sensitivity as a mediator; and Pietrzak, Downey, & Ayduk (2005), Rejection sensitivity as an interpersonal vulnerability.
77. Gerald Patterson has done an excellent job teasing apart the sequence of developmental events by which children may move from abusive backgrounds, to problematic styles of interpersonal behavior, to potential delinquent behavior. See, e.g., Patterson, G. R., DeBaryshe, B. D., & Ramsey, E. (1989). A developmental perspective on antisocial behavior. *American Psychologist, 44,* 329–335. http://dx.doi.org/10.1037/0003-066X.44.2.329. See also Patterson, G. R., & Dishion, T. J. (1985). Contributions of families and peers to delinquency. *Criminology, 23,* 63–79. http://dx.doi.org/10.1111/j.1745-9125.1985.tb00326.x
78. Uggen, C., & Wakefield, S. (2005). Young adults reentering the community from the criminal justice system and becoming an adult. In W. Osgood, E. M. Foster, C. Flanagan, & G. Ruth (Eds.), *On your own without a net: The transition to adulthood for vulnerable populations* (pp. 114–144). Chicago, IL: University of Chicago Press, p. 134 (references omitted).
79. Krugman, P. (1991). History and industry location: The case of the manufacturing belt. *American Economic Review, 81,* 80–83, p. 80.
80. Gawande, A. (2009, January 26). Getting there from here: How should Obama reform health care? *The New Yorker* 26–35, p. 30.
81. Pierson, P. (2000). Increasing returns, path dependence, and the study of politics. *American Political Science Review, 94,* 251–267, p. 251. http://dx.doi.org/10.2307/256011
82. Pierson (2000), Increasing returns, path dependence, and the study of politics, p. 251.
83. Pierson (2000), Increasing returns, path dependence, and the study of politics, p. 252. As Margaret Levi expressed it, once a person has "started down a track, the costs of reversal are very high. There will be other choice points, but the entrenchments of certain institutional arrangements obstruct an easy reversal of the initial

choice." Levi, M. (1997). A model, a method, and a map: Rational choice in comparative and historical analysis. In M. I. Lichbach, & A. S. Zuckerman (Eds.), *Comparative politics: Rationality, culture, and structure* (pp. 19–41). Cambridge, England: Cambridge University Press, p. 28.

84. Pierson (2000), Increasing returns, path dependence, and the study of politics, p. 253. See also the work Pierson summarized at this point in his article: Arthur, W. B. (1994). *Increasing returns and path dependence in the economy.* Ann Arbor: University of Michigan Press.

3

Criminogenic Trauma

Social History and the Life Course

It could have had any number of possible endings. But events unfold along a single track. As we make decisions and decisions are made for us, we shed the lives that might have been.

—DANIELLE ALLEN[1]

Several decades of psychological theory and research now document the basic proposition that events that occur in childhood and adolescence can profoundly influence and affect adult behavior. Psychologists have long known that children need to be provided with "dependable attachment, protection, guidance, stimulation, nurturance, and ways of coping with adversity" during their early years of growth and development.[2] But we also now know that a very high percentage of persons who violate the law have lacked many of these things in their early lives and have been exposed instead to forms of psychological trauma, including what I explained in the last chapter have been termed "risk factors." Of course, the two facts are not unrelated. We now know that certain risk factors and traumatic experiences can be highly criminogenic, especially when they occur in combination. As I discuss at length in this chapter, there is much evidence that a great many persons who commit crime were exposed to multiple, serious, and chronic criminogenic risks and traumas as children and adolescents, casting grave doubt on the causal emphasis that the crime master narrative places on the

http://dx.doi.org/10.1037/0000172-004
Criminality in Context: The Psychological Foundations of Criminal Justice Reform, by C. Haney

nature of the supposedly free and unencumbered choices they make, their allegedly defective traits, and their purported inherent badness.

The focus on the nature and significance of the background and social history of persons who subsequently engage in criminal behavior connects directly with a renewed emphasis in the discipline of psychology on the use of social historical research techniques,[3] or what is sometimes called "the study of lives,"[4] to understand the impact of early development over the entire life course.[5] As one researcher has noted, the social or life history approach "implies a holistic stance to social reality" and is the "method of choice when complex human events are at stake, when inquiries into the subjective realm of human beliefs, motives and actions in complex social matrices are involved."[6] This method is in many ways uniquely suited to provide insights into how the early backgrounds of persons who have violated the law have helped to shape their character, influenced the course of their later development, and affected their actions as adults.

This chapter examines a wide range of psychologically problematic and traumatic childhood experiences that we now know constitute significant criminogenic risk factors—events and experiences that have been shown to increase the likelihood that someone will engage in subsequent adolescent and adult criminal behavior.[7] Knowledge about the operation of these potent risk factors and their long-term effects on criminal behavior speaks directly to several issues that are at the core of fundamental criminal justice reform, including the question of how we should go about gauging individual culpability in criminal law, the way that we determine the nature and amount of punishment that is morally deserved in a criminal proceeding, and how we might create and implement more effective programs of preventive crime control. Because crime and violence can no longer be adequately explained through a master narrative that relies on individualistic, "free choice" assumptions, effective strategies of crime control must rely more on multilevel analyses that grant equal if not primary significance to social historical, situational, institutional, community, and structural variables.[8] In an attempt to begin at "the beginning," the remainder of this chapter reviews the role of a special set of early social historical forces in some detail. The focus broadens considerably in the chapters that follow.

As I noted in the preceding chapter, Ann Masten and Norman Garmezy's risk factors model provides a very useful conceptual framework for understanding the way that early life experiences impact subsequent development. In this chapter, I discuss the range of early social historical risk factors—experiences, events, and influences that occur over a person's life course—that have been shown to have later criminogenic consequences. Risk factors can occur at any point in someone's life course and have a negative impact on the behavior that follows. However, psychological development unfolds sequentially. Thus, the risk factors and traumas that occur early in life are especially significant, in part because of the vulnerability of the children who experience them and also because they may influence the number and impact of the risk factors and stressors that may follow.[9]

As summarized below, much crime is committed by persons whose social histories have been pervaded by multiple risk factors. In addition, their adult lives are often characterized by a surplus of tension-producing environmental stressors. The combination of these forces thwarts and inhibits the development and maintenance of prosocial and law-abiding patterns of behavior. When added up over the course of a single life, the aggregate effects of these multiple risk factors and stressors can have profound consequences for a wide range of problematic behaviors including, as I have said, adult criminal behavior.

RISK FACTORS AND DAMAGING CHILDHOOD EXPERIENCES: CHILD MALTREATMENT

There are numerous criminogenic risk factors that occur in childhood and that can be subsumed within one increasingly widely understood rubric: "child maltreatment." Child abuse or maltreatment has been defined variously as "the degree to which a parent uses negative, inappropriate control strategies with his or her child,"[10] or "acts of omission or commission by a parent or guardian that are judged by a mixture of community values and professional expertise to be inappropriate and damaging."[11] Whichever definition is employed, child maltreatment has been widely recognized as a significant social problem since at least the 1960s.[12] The importance of protecting children who have been or may be the targets of such abuse has been long acknowledged and generally accepted in law as well.[13] Researchers in the early 1970s estimated that the incidence of child maltreatment was actually much greater than had been previously known,[14] and, in 1974, Congress passed the Child Abuse Prevention and Treatment Act, designed to encourage government agencies to do more thorough reports and keep more accurate records in child abuse cases.[15] As I noted at the very outset of this book, what was not well understood in the 1960s and early 1970s, but clearly is now, is that child maltreatment and exposure to other risk factors can be psychologically harmful and—depending on their nature and severity—can have profound *long-term* negative effects on the victims.

By at least the mid-1970s, the cabinet-level agency that was then called the Department of Health, Education, and Welfare (it is now Health and Human Services) sponsored professional forums in which mental health practitioners were advised about the importance of extending counseling and therapy to the child victims and adult perpetrators of such abuse. Thus, for more than 40 years, there was widespread concern "that the personality or developmental damage . . . done to [abused] children is profound and lasting."[16] By 2005, clinical researchers were characterizing childhood trauma, including abuse and neglect, as "probably the single most important public health challenge in the United States" and were urging authorities to implement therapeutically "appropriate prevention and intervention"[17] in order to minimize or eliminate the potentially disabling long-term effects on persons subjected to it.[18]

Much of the early research on child abuse focused on the alleged psychopathology of abusers themselves and suggested various interventions that were designed to provide them with individual-level treatment.[19] Researchers soon broadened the scope of their analysis, as they recognized that the maltreatment of children was related to a host of structural and contextual variables that extended well beyond the possible mental health problems of the ostensibly abusive parents.[20] Recognizing that the maltreatment of children was not simply an individual-level phenomenon also meant acknowledging that effective treatment programs were needed to address the broad context of abuse by providing "services which will ameliorate the family's present circumstances."[21] Indeed, child abuse and neglect are "symptomatic of a whole *range* of family difficulties and dysfunctions, frequently including economic and environmental problems."[22]

Subsequent research continued to emphasize that child abuse was not only a widespread problem—"far more prevalent than incidence figures usually suggest"[23]—but one that needed to be understood in the larger family context in which it occurred.[24] For example, researchers concluded in the late 1980s that "abuse should not be viewed only as an isolated incident, but as *an environment*."[25] They recognized that children in these abusive environments were often subjected to multiple forms of maltreatment and lived in places where chaos, disruption, disorganization, and drug and alcohol abuse were also frequently present. For example, one representative study of a sample of serious child maltreatment cases brought before a metropolitan juvenile court found that substance abuse was "rampant" in the home, that poverty and neglect were "pervasive," and that "[m]ost families were headed by a single parent, and more than half were dependent on public welfare."[26] Other early research suggested that, although child maltreatment occurred across the entire socioeconomic spectrum, it tended to be concentrated among parents who had children when they were themselves relatively young, had unstable marriages, came from large families, were more likely to have engaged in crime, and who tended to move frequently.[27] More broadly and understandably, research indicated that parents who were themselves living under heightened levels of stress were more likely to engage in punitive approaches to disciplining their children.[28]

For purposes of analytical clarity, two forms of child maltreatment can be distinguished: direct and indirect. In the case of *direct* maltreatment, the young person is the direct recipient of the abusive behavior at the hands of a parent or caregiver, whether he or she was the intended target or not. In the case of *indirect* maltreatment, the child victim is the incidental recipient of the abusive behavior by virtue of being exposed as a bystander or observer to the abuse of others or to a set of abusive family dynamics. As with most attempts to precisely classify life experiences and label specific risk factors that typically blend together over time and are often experienced simultaneously, this is an imperfect distinction that is useful to my narrative but which should not obscure the fact that it is the *cumulative* effect of these various interacting adverse events that is most problematic. That is, the most prevalent and damaging forms often occur in conjunction with one another as their effects add up over time.[29] Moreover, as one group of researchers noted, rather than focusing on the consequences of specific forms of maltreatment, "[i]t is well documented that each type of maltreatment rarely occurs in isolation."[30]

Whether direct or indirect, forms of child maltreatment can be highly criminogenic, as the research discussed in the remainder of this chapter establishes. It can lead to a range of early emotional and behavioral problems that—absent caring and effective intervention—children and adolescents are not able to easily overcome. Although I discuss the results of research on different forms of child maltreatment separately, as I noted, many of them co-occur. These co-occurring and accumulating risk factors are not only hurtful and immediately harmful to the children exposed to them but also can have long-term, potentially criminogenic effects. This fact has significant implications for how we understand the nature of criminality and view, evaluate, and reform the nation's social policies, legal doctrines and penal practices, as well as its broader crime control strategies.

Direct Forms of Child Maltreatment

Pre- and Perinatal Risks

A developing child's exposure to potentially damaging risk factors can begin even before birth. For example, we have known for some time that children whose mothers consume significant amounts of alcohol during pregnancy may be born with fetal alcohol syndrome (FAS), a neurological disorder that can undermine subsequent physical development and may be associated with a range of behavioral problems in childhood and beyond.[31] Moreover, a number of studies have found that FAS and a related disorder with a broader range of nonetheless potentially serious effects—fetal alcohol spectrum disorder (FASD)[32]—may place children at greater risk of engaging in illegal behavior later in life. "Primary" FASD-related disabilities are defined as "the inherent functional problems" that are thought to stem from alcohol-related neurological damage. However, "secondary" FASD-related disabilities, which are defined as the "acquired difficulties which individuals with FASD may develop as they mature," include problems in school, difficulty with drug and alcohol use and abuse, and "trouble with authorities or being charged or convicted of a crime, confinement in a juvenile justice system, substance abuse, or mental health treatment programme."[33] Most importantly, these particular effects of FASD are rarely manifested in a vacuum. That is, it has been shown that children who suffer FASD often grow up in what has been termed "a state of double jeopardy"—that is, because prenatal alcohol exposure is closely related to exposure to what have been called "adverse caregiving environments" (i.e., settings where their other parenting needs are not being met), the most adversely affected FASD children are ones placed doubly at risk—first from the FASD itself and second from the kind of troubled households in which they are often raised.[34]

In addition, there is other evidence to suggest that certain behaviors that are generally unhealthy for mothers during their pregnancies—such as poor diet—may create physical problems in the developing fetus that can negatively impact their children's behavior later on and are associated with higher rates of later illegal behavior. For example, although the causal mechanisms are still unclear,[35] several studies have shown that children born to mothers who smoked during their pregnancies experience increased risk of later persistent criminal behavior.[36]

We also now know that children who are born to mothers who have been the victims of domestic violence during their pregnancy are more likely to suffer from a variety of physical and emotional problems in infancy, and that these complications "are associated with poor outcomes later in life."[37] In fact, in addition to premature births, birth complications, lower birth weight, and newborn illnesses, all of which can result from in utero exposure to domestic violence, this particular prenatal trauma appears to be related to dissociative symptoms in young children,[38] and can affect their temperament and sensitivity as they mature.[39] In addition, research has suggested that "the physical trauma [of prenatal domestic violence] as well as the biological correlates of maternal stress may affect brain development and thus permanently influence a child's reaction to stress."[40]

As with many risk factors that impinge on both children and their parents, domestic violence can have both direct adverse effects on children and can affect them secondarily because of the negative impact it has on the behavior of their abused parent. For example, as Alytia Levendosky and Anne Bogat observed, "Parenting begins during pregnancy. It has been documented that exposure to domestic violence during pregnancy has been associated with delayed prenatal care, which then may have deleterious effects on the fetus and the woman."[41] Put simply, the abuse of a pregnant mother is harmful to her *and* to her child, potentially affecting the fetus's neurobiological development and having a negative psychological effect on the mother. Among other things, it may create maternal trauma symptoms that interfere with the mother's ability to obtain the prenatal care that both she and her developing child likely need and impair her subsequent interactions with her children.[42]

There is also evidence that a variety of *perinatal* problems—events that occur at or during the time of delivery—can have adverse long-term effects on children, including an increased likelihood of behavioral problems that can include criminal behavior.[43] Problematic perinatal events include a range of complications at the time of birth (e.g., an especially long or difficult labor, an unusually stressful delivery, the use of forceps that may injure the fetus during delivery).[44] Elizabeth Kandel and Sarnoff Mednick found that delivery complications were associated with an increased likelihood of later illegal behavior but—to foreshadow an issue to which I return at the end of this chapter—this was true *only* for those children who were already regarded as "high risk" for other reasons (e.g., their parents' ongoing psychiatric problems).[45]

Attachment, Abandonment, and Traumatic Separation

The psychological importance of parental "attachment" was first explored in-depth in classic work done by John Bowlby in the 1950s.[46] Bowlby's research established the significance of continuing contact with a nurturing parental figure.[47] His insights have been relied on by scholars as providing the early empirical basis for the claim that "maternal deprivation" can impede healthy child development.[48] Bowlby's pathbreaking findings were soon broadened to include recognition that a child's needs could be addressed by other stable parent figures as long as the nurturing contact began early and remained consistent over a reasonably long developmental period.[49] Researchers used Bowlby's work as the basis for theorizing about "attachment theory" and the origins of "attachment disorders," arguing that a child's early, consistent bonding experiences are essential for the development of self-regulation, the capacity for empathy, and the ability to cope adequately with stress later in life. Their research suggests that disruptions in the development of these crucial attachment relationships can put people at greater risk for serious socioemotional problems in adulthood.[50]

Psychiatrist Allan Schore characterized attachment theory as "*the* dominant model of human social-emotional development" in contemporary behavioral science.[51] More broadly, social psychologists Mario Mikulincer and Phillip Shaver suggested that a history of stable early attachments is important to the development of a what they termed "attachment security," which is positively associated with a range of essential psychological skills and capacities, including emotional self-regulation,[52] compassion and empathy,[53] the ability to make and sustain long-term close personal relationships,[54] and the resiliency to survive and recover from trauma later in life.[55] Children who are prevented from developing positive attachments may be correspondingly challenged in these domains and may be more likely to experience difficulties in social interactions and in relating emotionally to others.

Attachment disorders can stem from a variety of early childhood experiences, including ones in which children are raised in environments where they are not adequately nurtured. In addition, they may come about as a result of parental loss or abandonment. Bowlby's contemporary Donald Winnicott wrote about this deprivation as "a loss of something good that has been positive in the child's experience up to a certain date, and that has been withdrawn"; When the withdrawal extends "over a period of time longer than that over which the child can keep the memory of the experience alive," it is experienced as a traumatic loss.[56] Winnicott also wrote about the cumulative effects of these kinds of early traumas, which he suggested were often present in the lives of children who suffered subsequent behavioral problems.[57]

Traumatic abandonment can take many forms including, in the most extreme sense, a parent or parental figure literally abandoning a child. More often it involves a sudden absence or loss of a parent (e.g., death, incarceration) which, even though it lacks the implication of rejection commonly associated with intentional abandonment, is experienced as profound deprivation and loss nonetheless. Many mental health professionals have noted that the feelings of abandonment and depression that follow the loss of a parent in childhood or adolescence appear to persist long after the event itself. They have concluded that the "loss of a parent in infancy, early childhood, latency or adolescence, is a traumatic event with the potential for long-lasting intrusive effects of the child" comparable to posttraumatic stress disorder (PTSD).[58] Others have acknowledged that losing a parent when the child is still immature "inflicts a massive trauma from which it is very difficult to recover."[59]

Similarly, therapists have found that parental abandonment places children at risk for adolescent and adult depression. Children who suffer such abandonment may experience feelings of "inadequacy, worthlessness, helplessness, hopelessness, rejection by others, and loneliness."[60] Judith Mishne suggested that such broad and long-lasting effects occur in part because parental abandonment is a more complex phenomenon than the mere loss of attachment. She noted that although less has been written about children who have been abandoned by their parents, the psychological consequences of this trauma are intensified by the *interpretations* that children have of the event and their inability to impose finality on their loss. Mishne contended that

> [w]e can hardly measure and compare the pain and grief and rage of children in the face of the devastation of a parent loss . . . [It represents a] profound blow to a child's self-esteem and [creates a] sense of degradation . . . due to having been given up, put aside, left, or lost.[61]

When families are in disarray, struggling to manage economic and emotional crises and chaos, and lack access to social safety nets that might help stabilize them, parents and parental figures may come and go more frequently and unpredictably. These family transitions can occur for myriad reasons, perhaps because a family member's stress-related emotional instability undermines lasting relationships, because one or another partner is forced to seek gainful employment elsewhere, or because criminal justice system interventions (such as parental imprisonment) destabilize the family unit.[62] But children—especially young children—often experience this coming and going as a series of sequential abandonments; they may develop an emotional shell or strategy of social disengagement to minimize the repeated psychological pain that might otherwise result.

Attachment-related problems are prevalent in the lives of many criminal defendants, whose most important emotional and psychological needs may not have been met from early stages in their lives. Bowlby and Winnicott both speculated that much antisocial behavior resulted from these early and sometimes prolonged forms of parental deprivation. For example, Bowlby wrote that children whose attachment needs have not been consistently met may come to view the world as "comfortless and unpredictable; and they respond either by shrinking from it or doing battle with it."[63] Michael Burstein noted that many children who suffered parental rejection, abandonment, or loss understandably reacted by becoming distressed, angry, and sometimes even aggressive. He cited research showing that abandonment placed children at risk of "rebelliousness, disobedience, temper tantrums, stealing and truancy."[64] Similarly, Marinus van IJzendoorn reported that "[i]nsecure attachment relationships are a risk factor in serious antisocial behavior" and that "[d]isorganized attachments . . . are associated with elevated aggression in childhood and with serious crimes in (young) adulthood."[65] A more recent meta-analysis of a number of published studies on the issue concluded that, although the relationship attenuated over time, problematic parental attachment "is linked to delinquency in boys and girls."[66]

Finally, it is important to note that the last several decades of mass incarceration in the United States have resulted in an unprecedented number of children experiencing the incarceration of one or both of their parents.[67] Parental imprisonment is a criminogenic risk factor in its own right[68] and also increases the likelihood that children will be exposed to other risks, traumas, and adversities over their life course.[69] Joseph Murray and David Farrington reported that, although the exact nature of the causal relationship was difficult to specify, the kind of family turmoil and separation that comes about as a result of parental imprisonment "certainly is a risk factor and its effects appear to be relatively strong, with multiple adverse outcomes" for children.[70] Indeed, "parental imprisonment roughly trebles the risk for child antisocial behavior."[71]

Child Neglect

Mental health workers have known for decades that parental neglect can take a significant toll on the physical, intellectual, social, and emotional development of children and compromise their long-term psychological adjustment.[72] Although child neglect often occurs in conjunction with other forms of maltreatment, it has its own independent and potentially very serious harmful consequences.[73] Researchers and clinicians define child neglect as occurring "when a basic need of a child is not met, regardless of the cause(s)."[74] They have argued for a broad view of neglect that "expands from a focus on individual factors (i.e., parental omissions in care)" to include "the contribution of community and societal factors" that are seen as "increasingly important."[75] The developmental consequences of neglect may be manifested very early in a child's life, so that even by preschool years some neglected children experience a range of difficulties that can include low self-esteem, poor behavioral control, and negative affect.[76] Chronic and severe neglect has longer term harmful effects on the children who experience it.[77]

In addition to the neglect that comes from a parent's physical absence or withdrawal from the family, or the inability to provide for the material needs of children, researchers have also identified a problematic pattern they describe as "psychologically unavailable caregiving" or "emotional neglect," one in which parents are physically present but "unresponsive to their children and, in many cases, passively rejecting of them."[78] In fact, one national study found that, although all forms of child maltreatment tended to co-occur with each other, as well as in conjunction with a broader set of family problems, emotional neglect was the single most common form of neglect (occurring alone in the case of some 6.2% of all of the children in the sample).[79] Perhaps because psychologically unavailable parents are themselves overwhelmed with economic and other demands in their lives, they appear to be "detached and uninvolved with their children, interacting with them only when it [is] necessary."[80] Moreover, some studies have shown that this kind of neglect "is chronic and, despite efforts by various social agencies, the caretaking environment does not improve." In any event, "[t]he effects of maltreatment, particularly in the case of children whose mothers are psychologically unavailable, are cumulative."[81] Moreover, the magnitude of the effects has been described as "striking." Specifically, "[c]hildren who were emotionally neglected at an early age were more impaired in many areas of functioning than children who were physically abused or neglected," including being more socially withdrawn, acting more aggressively and performing more poorly in school, and reporting significantly more suicide attempts later in adolescence.[82]

The relationship between parental neglect and the increased likelihood that a child will engage in subsequent delinquent behavior has been studied extensively, and the link is now well-established.[83] For example, Martha Erickson and Byron Egeland found that very young children who were emotionally neglected "exhibited higher levels of social problems, delinquency, and aggression" as teens.[84] Here, too, neglect is more criminogenic when it occurs in conjunction with other problematic risk factors. Thus, Daniel Maughan and Simon Moore found that frequent parental separations, disorganized and chaotic family dynamics, marital disharmony, and poor parental supervision were key components in neglectful family systems that increased the chance a neglected child would later become involved in illegal activities.[85]

Direct Physical and Emotional Abuse

In addition to abandonment and different forms of neglect, other kinds of child maltreatment can be much more overt, proactive, and intrusive. In the early 1960s, clinicians wrote about a distinctive pattern of behavior that they termed "battered child syndrome,"[86] in which physically abused children manifested a characteristic set of symptoms in response to the trauma that parental figures had inflicted on them.[87] In these initial studies, researchers and clinicians searched for the causes of the parents' abusive behavior,[88] identified many of what they believed were the immediate and perhaps long-term psychological consequences of this form of extreme mistreatment,[89] and offered a range of proposals aimed at providing therapy and prevention.[90]

A second generation of studies done in the 1970s and 1980s corroborated and refined many of the earlier observations about the harmful effects of physical abuse on the "battered child." It became increasingly clear that this kind of trauma could have severe psychological consequences. Although the children who experienced it had different susceptibilities to harm, they "most often suffer multiple damage."[91] Later studies focused on the *long-term* effects of childhood physical and sexual abuse. Among other things, those effects include adult depression,[92] anxiety disorders,[93] and susceptibility to PTSD.[94]

More recent research on the effects of direct and indirect exposure to violence reached similar conclusions about long-term consequences. Indeed, a task force assembled by an organization of the nation's attorneys general—the top state law enforcement officials from across the country—stated unequivocally that

> [e]ven after the violence has ended, these child survivors suffer from severe problems with anxiety, depression, anger, grief, and posttraumatic stress that can mar their relationships and family life and limit their success in school or work, not only in childhood but throughout their adult lives. Without services or treatment, even children who appear resilient and seem to recover from exposure to violence still bear emotional scars that may lead them to experience these same health and psychological problems years or decades later.[95]

In 2018, a group of psychological researchers comprehensively reviewed the existing data on whether "physical punishment," which they defined as "the use of physical force to cause a child to experience some degree of physical pain or discomfort," was causally related to adverse outcomes for children.[96] Published on the pages of the *American Psychologist*, their conclusion was unequivocal: "[p]hysical punishment increases the risk that children will experience detrimental outcomes and this risk is experienced equally across cultural groups, families, and neighborhoods."[97] The evidence was highly consistent and indicated, among other things, that "exposure to more physical punishment leads to more behavior problems," including more acting out and delinquent behavior.[98]

Beyond direct links to delinquency, it is now widely accepted by researchers and practitioners that abused and traumatized children are more likely to engage in violence as adults, giving rise to what has been called a "cycle of violence"[99] or the "intergenerational transmission of violence."[100] Developmental psychologists and others understand that, although extreme physical punishment may produce conformity in the immediate situation or setting in which it is administered, it tends to increase the probability of deviance later in life, including delinquency in adolescence and criminal behavior in adulthood.[101] Stated in the starkest terms, in general, "abused and neglected children demonstrate increased risk of becoming adult criminals and of becoming adult violent criminals."[102] Thus the physical mistreatment of children tends to reappear in the violent behavior of its adult victims.

We also know that there is sometimes a tragic symmetry to the social dynamics of crime and violence such that researchers may find "isomorphisms" in the relationship between childhood abuse and adult behavior. That is, the form of violence that is manifested when the child turns from victim to victimizer may be the same kind that was inflicted by the original abuser, so that persons who were physically abused as children are more likely to be physically violent as adults, those who were sexually abused are most likely to be sexually violent, and so on.[103] Indeed, sometimes the abuse is reenacted at more or less the same stage in life as it was experienced.[104]

However, these kinds of symmetrical relationships or patterns are by no means the only ones that emerge. In fact, physical and sexual abuse often produce *generalized* patterns of dysfunction and *diffuse* problems in adjustment.[105] Although it seems likely that a number of different mechanisms may be at work in different families and for different children, there is now little doubt that the violence and abuse that characterizes the lives of so many criminal defendants is intergenerationally transmitted. Indeed, some research has extended this logic to show that "[e]xposure to aggressive behavior is predictive of aggression across *three* generations for males."[106] In addition, a number of studies indicate that childhood sexual abuse may have powerful, diffuse, and potentially disabling effects on its victims even after they have reached adulthood, including—in addition to criminality—PTSD, depression, suicidal behavior, and sexual promiscuity.[107]

Notwithstanding what we know about the harmful effects of physical abuse on normal psychological development, researchers have emphasized that we "should not ignore the considerable harms imposed by *emotional* abuse, which rival those of physical abuse and neglect."[108] Byron Egeland distinguished emotional neglect (the kind of emotionally unavailable behavior that I discussed in the last section) from emotional abuse, which includes proactive forms of "[v]erbal hostility, taunting, belittling, and rejection."[109] There is now extensive research suggesting that "neglect and emotional abuse needs to be given at least as much attention as physical and sexual abuse as potential sources of long-term psychological dysfunction."[110]

Here, too, research conducted over the last several decades has clearly documented the criminogenic effects of direct maltreatment on the children subjected to it.[111] As I noted earlier, specific forms of child maltreatment rarely occur in isolation, the harmful consequences are more likely when there are multiple family problems or issues. For example, Gerald Patterson and his colleagues have concluded that a disproportionate number of children who subsequently engage in criminal behavior come from homes where there is a high degree of turmoil and in which parental discipline is both inconsistent and coercive.[112] Physical and emotional abuse and neglect are associated with so-called "externalizing" or acting out behavior in adolescence, which can lead teenagers into later illegal behavior.[113] Some studies have also found that a history of having been subjected to child abuse helps to predict not only whether someone will become involved in illegal behavior but also may influence the age at which this begins (i.e., abused children tend to engage in such behavior at an earlier age than nonabused children).[114] Other research has suggested that a child's history of maltreatment may influence whether he or she commits more serious forms of law-breaking.[115] In addition, one study found that even among a relatively homogeneous group of youthful parolees, most of whom had "substantial criminal records," exposure to various forms of child maltreatment significantly increased their risk of rearrest for violent crimes.[116]

Direct forms of maltreatment thus can significantly disrupt and damage a child's or adolescent's long-term life trajectory in all of the aforementioned ways.

In addition to direct maltreatment, there are many other *indirect* risks and traumas to which children can be exposed that are both harmful and potentially criminogenic.

Indirect Forms of Child Maltreatment

Parental Mental Health and Substance Abuse Problems

Children whose parents suffer from mental health or substance abuse problems are placed at risk of suffering similar problems when they reach adulthood.[117] For example, a National Academy of Sciences report concluded that parental depression puts vast numbers of children at risk of adverse life outcomes.[118] More specifically, "[d]epression in parents interferes with parenting quality and is associated with poor health and development (e.g., physical, psychological, behavior, social development and mental health) in their children at all ages."[119] Among other things, a parent's serious mental illness or substance abuse can be highly disruptive to the daily lives and living arrangements of the children under his or her care.[120]

Some of these destabilizing consequences stem from the fact that parents who are struggling with mental illness or substance abuse may be understandably preoccupied with their own psychological problems and less able to properly care for their children. Depending on the nature of the parent's mental illness or extent of substance abuse, he or she may also be less able to control their emotions and more likely to overreact to the stress of parenting in ways that are potentially harmful to their children. Thus, some researchers have found that "[p]arental mental health is the only significant predictor of recurrent abuse: parents with mental health problems are significantly more likely than other parents to reabuse their children."[121] Of course, this does not mean that all mentally ill parents abuse their children, rather that, in certain cases, mental illness is predictive of recurrent abuse.

In addition, there are broader, secondary effects of parental mental illness that can disrupt families and undermine parenting. The time and resources devoted to the mentally ill parent's care may limit the amount that the nonmentally ill parent can provide to his or her children. Moreover, parents who suffer from serious mental illness are significantly more likely to be unemployed and are approximately twice as likely to live in poverty compared to peers without mental illness.[122] These financial hardships may adversely affect their parenting and place special economic burdens on their children.

Finally, parental substance abuse represents a related form of child maltreatment. For example, an addicted parent may inadvertently model substance abuse as an apparently acceptable coping mechanism for his or her children or, conversely, seek to minimize or disguise the abuse by becoming deceptive or withholding in interpersonal family interactions. Much research on the adult children of alcoholics also suggests that the family dynamics associated with parental alcoholism can have a lifelong adverse impact on children.[123]

Beyond the generally negative effects that parental mental health and substance abuse problems can have on a child's life course, there is a large literature that establishes their roles as potential risk factors for later aggression and law-breaking.[124]

Exposure to Family Violence, Conflict, and Turmoil

Although reported rates of "family violence"—violence in which both the victim and perpetrator are biologically or legally related—declined somewhat in the United States during the 1990s, it still represents about 10% of all violence in the country.[125] Family violence—especially what is termed "intimate partner violence"—tends to be disproportionately perpetrated by men and directed at women.[126] *Witnessing* domestic violence—when "children see, hear, are directly involved in (i.e., attempt to intervene), or experience the aftermath of physical or sexual assaults that occur between their caregivers"[127]—is a traumatic experience that can serve as a risk factor for later psychological and behavioral problems. So, too, can exposure to emotional abuse and intense family conflict and turmoil, even if it does not involve physical violence. This means that children may be victimized by living in abusive homes, even if they are not the intended or immediate targets of that abuse. In fact, studies show that witnessing abuse can sometimes be as psychologically hurtful as direct victimization itself.[128]

I noted earlier that even prenatal exposure to domestic violence—children born to mothers subjected to intense conflict and physical abuse during pregnancy—increased the chances that they would suffer from a range of problems later on. Exposure in childhood also can have adverse developmental effects. Thus, "preschoolers who witnessed domestic violence had many more behavioral problems, more negative affect, responded less appropriately to situations, were more aggressive with peers, and had more ambivalent relationships with teachers than those from nonviolent families."[129] Researchers have reported that adults who were exposed to intimate partner violence as infants and young children later manifested trauma-related symptoms, including PTSD,[130] which was exacerbated in cases where their mothers also exhibited trauma-related symptoms.[131] Adults who were exposed to violence when they were young also suffered from later emotional problems, such as anxiety and depressive disorders,[132] and troubled peer relationships.[133]

Witnessing domestic abuse can also have criminogenic consequences. For example, one early study found that boys appeared to be more vulnerable to the effects of marital discord (perhaps because they felt some responsibility to attempt to stop it or because they were more directly affected by the aggressiveness of their same-sex parent). Although the researchers could draw no simple causal connections between witnessing abuse and subsequent adjustment problems, they concluded that "[b]esides inappropriate modeling of conflict resolution, these children are affected by their mothers' diminished effectiveness as a parent, negative changes in family status, and related factors that result from family violence."[134] Even though exposure to family violence and conflict often co-occur with more direct forms of maltreatment,[135] and the separate effects are difficult to disentangle,[136] we do know that many persons who engage in law-breaking as adults come from chronically abusive homes in which their caretakers (especially their mothers) and other siblings have been physically attacked in their presence,[137] sometimes despite their own attempts to intervene.

Multiple Family Transitions

The impact of major life transitions typically depends on the context in which they occur.[138] Certain transitions—for example, a parent's decision to divorce in order to reduce domestic conflict or to move to a different community in the hope of improving the family's economic situation—might have long-term positive consequences for the children involved. However, *multiple* such transitions can reflect economic or other forms of instability and signal ongoing psychological disruption. Indeed, multiple family transitions—frequent changes in the makeup of the family unit, in its living arrangements, and the locations where family members reside—can be emotionally destabilizing, especially when they entail the sudden, unpredictable, and uncontrollable loss of persons who were once important and who provided a source of love, support, and authority. Significant family transitions can also compromise effective parenting by creating added burdens for the parents and caretakers who remain, undermining their ability to care for their children. That is, maintaining sensitivity to a child's emotional needs, setting consistent limits, and a host of other essential parenting tasks require significant investments of time and personal resources that parents who are themselves in turmoil or the throes of significant life transitions may not be able to expend.[139]

Although mainstream American society has become reasonably sensitive to the painfulness and potentially life-altering consequences of divorce and parental separation as they impact middle-class children,[140] the negative impacts of such family transitions on poor and minority children are less often carefully and sensitively addressed, in part because counseling and other forms of support are often less readily available to them. Yet the combination of the greater rates at which such family transitions occur among the poor, the already more fragile economic status of poor families, and decreased availability of needed services in poor communities may make these kinds of frequent transitions even more problematic.

As one group of researchers put it, "[p]arents in non-intact homes . . . experience many challenges and struggles that hinder their ability to maintain a strong affective bond with their children"[141] and that, in turn, may account for some of the criminogenic effect of multiple family transitions. In addition, we know that "[m]arital transitions, including divorce and remarriage, are stressful for adults and children and often alter family processes in ways that contribute to declines in child well-being."[142] The negative consequences can include poorer school performance, lower levels of occupational success, higher incidence of depression, and even elevated rates of delinquency.

As one Department of Justice-sponsored report noted, there is "a consistent relationship between a greater number of family transitions and a higher level of delinquency and drug use."[143]

Extreme Residential Mobility

Whether or not it is related to the makeup and breakup of families per se, extreme residential mobility constitutes a risk factor in its own right. Here, too, mobility itself is not necessarily problematic; its long-term consequences for children will depend not only on the number of moves but also on the reasons they occur and whether life circumstances are improved or disadvantaged as a result.[144] For perhaps obvious reasons, there is some evidence to suggest that targeted moves (e.g., as part of an intervention designed to move families living in very poor areas to more economically stable ones) can have beneficial effects.[145] However, there is also some evidence that under certain circumstances even a *single* move that is explicitly designed to improve the well-being of the family in question can have a negative effect on the self-reported behavioral problems and depressive symptoms of adolescent boys.[146] Researchers noted that even a well-intentioned move to an ostensibly better neighborhood might have unexpected, gendered consequences because "the adjustment to new social networks in the new neighborhoods may have been more difficult for boys than for girls, for example owing to the disruption of friendships or adult role models."[147]

In any event, families that are in *repeated* transition for whatever reason—for example, those that are struggling under the weight of poverty and the residential instability that it creates, or parental instability that compels them to move from place to place—can subject children to frequent life changes that have a destabilizing effect on their psychological development.[148] The general psychological mechanisms at work are not difficult to understand. Frequent moves can instill a sense of helplessness in some children, especially when their sense of personal security is jeopardized by the decisions of others. The loss of close friends or a reliable social network can deprive children of a potentially supportive milieu that might have served as an important protective factor to buffer them from the impact of other risk factors. The challenge of facing new and unfamiliar people and places may create anxiety, social withdrawal, and lowered self-esteem. In addition, extreme residential mobility means that parents also must negotiate new challenges that may distract them from their children's emotional needs, as they absorb the stresses associated with repeated relocation.[149]

The potential effects of this risk factor are surprisingly large. Thus, researchers have found that frequent changes in residences are associated with a higher risk for suicidal behavior and psychotic disorders among children and adolescents, even when a host of individual and family psychiatric variables are controlled for.[150] They are also associated with lower levels of overall well-being (including heightened mortality) in adulthood,[151] and emotional and behavioral reactions that may be precursors to forms of illegal behavior. For example, researchers have identified a relationship between frequent moves and early initiation into drug use and subsequent drug-related problems. In addition,

> [s]tudies have found that young people who move frequently or are classified as recent movers are more likely than others to develop conduct disorder, commit deviant acts (e.g., theft, vandalism), engage in sexually promiscuous behavior, fail a grade, and misbehave toward teachers and classmates.[152]

Frequent School Transitions, School Bonding, Dropping Out

Extreme residential mobility not only necessitates changes in residences but also often in the schools that children attend. It may significantly compromise the family's social capital, sever attachment relationships, and undermine a child's academic performance. Thus, moving to a new neighborhood typically entails the added social disequilibrium of a school transition in which prior social and academic networks and norms are disrupted. Boys have an especially difficult time negotiating the transition into new school environments and are likely to encounter peer rejection and increasing alienation from their classmates.[153] As several researchers observed, the "increased turmoil in the lives of adolescents who have experienced family changes and instability of residential settings may produce greater difficult in bonding with teachers and schools and in investing in the academic process." This pattern, in turn, may "create higher risk for deviant behavior."[154] In addition, children and adolescents whose trauma histories render them especially sensitive to rejection.[155] They may be especially likely to perceive and react to signs of rejection in a new setting, putting in motion a pattern of withdrawal followed by longer term relational difficulties, including loneliness and aggression.[156]

Extreme residential mobility and frequent school transitions are related to several other interconnected, school-related risk factors.[157] Specifically, they are associated with poor school performance and low levels of school bonding that, in turn, can have long-term problematic consequences for children and adolescents. If students perform poorly and are unable to bond with others at school, they have less access to the positive socialization experiences that school can provide, and their engagement with other students and potentially beneficial activities and organizations will be curtailed. Students who are less engaged with school and less bonded with their classmates are more likely to become involved in problematic behaviors that can include delinquency and substance use and that may lead to dropping out of school.[158]

Although not every study has demonstrated a criminogenic effect of dropping out of high school, the reasons for dropping out and a young person's surrounding environment in the immediate aftermath appear to matter a great deal. As one study that found little or no criminogenic effect put it: "Leaving school and attaching yourself to another conventional institution (work) may have an entirely different set of consequences than dropping out with no direction."[159] Absent these conventional attachments and opportunities, however, young persons who drop out of high school are at significant risk of becoming involved in illegal behavior.[160]

Exposure to Community Violence

Children and adolescents may be exposed to violence in their communities—either as direct victims of aggression, as witnesses to the violent victimization of others, or by hearing about violence that is happening in their neighborhood.[161] All three kinds of exposure have been studied and appear to have significant negative consequences (although they are not equivalent in magnitude). For example, Patrick Fowler and his colleagues conducted a meta-analytic review of some 114 studies on the effects of exposure to community violence and concluded that both direct and secondary or vicarious exposure produced a range of potentially serious symptoms.[162] The adverse consequences of exposure included those they characterized as "internalizing" (i.e., creating emotional problems such as depression or anxiety-related issues) and "externalizing" (i.e., forms of "acting out" such as aggressive behavior and delinquency), as well as symptoms that met the diagnostic criteria for PTSD.

Not surprisingly, Fowler et al. found that direct victimization predicted stronger effects than witnessing or hearing about community violence. Exposure in general was most likely to lead to PTSD, followed by externalizing and then internalizing effects. Thus, "exposure to community violence appears to represent a unique form of trauma that is particularly associated with the development of PTSD, especially among children and adolescents."[163] It also often led to "externalizing behavior," especially among adolescents, who were more likely to suffer from behavioral problems following exposure to community violence than were younger children.

Follow-up research has stressed that the harmful effects of exposure to community violence are multidimensional in nature. There also appears to be some specificity to the negative outcomes that are likely to occur that depends in part on the form of exposure—whether children and adolescents are the direct victims, see violence being perpetrated, or hear about its occurrence—as well as the age at which it is experienced. In particular, witnessing violence has "a unique association with aggression, both concurrently and later in development."[164] In addition, Traci Kennedy and Rosario Ceballo suggested that effects of exposure to community violence are not necessarily stable or consistently additive but may change over time.[165] That is, children and adolescents who live in high-crime neighborhoods where they are exposed to continuous, chronic violence may initially react with feelings of depression and anxiety but later become emotionally numb or "desensitized" and adopt a more aggressive or angry posture in response.

CRIMINOGENIC EFFECTS OF CHILD MALTREATMENT

As the preceding pages have made clear, child maltreatment can take a number of different forms that often produce serious, long-term, negative consequences. Many of these consequences are criminogenic—increasing the chances that a person will engage in delinquency in adolescence and criminal behavior in adulthood.[166] Although it is difficult to predict precisely which adverse outcomes will befall any one person who has suffered child maltreatment, the relationship of these kinds of early traumas to subsequent delinquent and adult criminal behavior has nonetheless been well-established. As early as the mid-1970s, a national news magazine alerted readers to what it described as "an epidemic of child abuse." The article quoted one expert who warned of "the dangers of permanent harm to children" coming about as a result of the abuse. Specifically: "Of those who have been emotionally deprived . . . many become delinquents."[167] At roughly the same time, the entry in the 1975 edition of the *Textbook of Pediatrics* that dealt with child abuse contained this stark prediction: "The untreated [abusive] families tend to produce children who grow up to be juvenile delinquents and murderers, as well as the batterers of the next generation."[168]

In the preceding pages, I summarized many of the findings from the numerous studies that have been conducted since then. Although researchers have greatly refined, nuanced, and modified those early, dire predictions, they have confirmed a basic message about the potential for child maltreatment to have criminogenic consequences that last well into adulthood. One recent review correctly characterized the existing empirical literature linking child maltreatment with subsequent criminal behavior as "vast."[169]

However, exactly *how* and *why* children who have been subjected to early trauma and abuse are more likely to become involved in criminal behavior later in their lives are more complex issues. Childhood risk factors and traumas are harmful, but why do they lead to an increased likelihood of delinquency and crime? Even by the mid-1980s, when numerous studies corroborated earlier hypotheses about the connection between early maltreatment and later criminal behavior (including the Masten and Garmezy risk factors model summarized in the last chapter and relied heavily on here), the specific psychological mechanisms that explained the connection remained unclear.

That is no longer the case. Research done in the last several decades has deepened our understanding of the various ways that child and adolescent traumas and risks produce their criminogenic effects. Many of the early efforts to uncover the mechanisms by which these aggressive patterns were psychologically encoded and subsequently enacted focused on what was termed "identification with aggressor."[170] That is, abused children were thought to exhibit poor impulse control and to more readily act in aggressive ways in large part because they had learned to emulate the behavior of the powerful parent who had mistreated them but with whom they nonetheless "identified." We now know that the causal links are more complicated and varied.[171]

With the caveat that no single mechanism can possibly explain a phenomenon as complex as criminal behavior, this section reviews some of the psychological processes that help to account for the relationship between child maltreatment and later delinquency and crime.[172] Whether and how any one mechanism plays an important role depend on the specific risks and traumas to which someone has been subjected, as well as many other aspects of the risk factor model I outlined earlier, including the number, severity, and duration of the risks, the presence or absence of vulnerabilities and protective factors, the nature, number, and magnitude of the stressors, and the effectiveness of the coping adopted. In addition, several different mechanisms are likely to operate across or throughout a single person's social history or life trajectory.

One mechanism involves children's *diffuse reactions to the trauma of abuse*. We now know that maltreatment is a significant form of psychological trauma that can trigger a powerful stress response. Stress responses can have numerous developmental effects that include undermining the regulation of emotion, distorting the way information is cognitively processed, and affecting the control of behavior.[173] Those effects, in turn, can lead to a host of interpersonal problems.[174] In fact, the consequences of exposure to multiple, recurring traumas early in life typically last well into adulthood, leading to adverse outcomes that "are not simply more severe than the sequelae of single incident trauma, but are qualitatively different in their tendency to affect *multiple* affective and interpersonal domains."[175]

In a related way, exposure to childhood risks and traumas can lead generally to other kinds of psychological problems, such as lowered self-esteem as well as depression and anxiety disorders, that are themselves indirectly linked to later delinquency and adult criminal behavior. For example, in Hans Toch's sophisticated analysis of the "anatomy of violence," he observed that there are some people "who tend to interpret situations as threatening or goading or challenging or overpowering," turning otherwise "harmless encounters into duels, purges, struggles for survival, or harmless escapes."[176] But he also acknowledged that the tendency "likely originates most frequently in interpersonal relationships early in life," in an "upbringing [that] has been deficient in stability and emotional support, thus making it difficult for positive self-perceptions to develop."[177] In a different but related way, children who are exposed to risk factors and traumas may experience psychiatric problems, including some that are, in turn, related to subsequent criminal behavior. For example, one study found that more than half of young men with criminal records also had childhood psychiatric histories. The relationship between psychiatric history and serious crime in young adulthood was especially strong in cases where anxiety disorders or depressive disorders were combined with a substance abuse disorder.[178]

A different causal mechanism involves *psychological self-defense* against an abusive parent or hostile environment that a child experiences as psychologically life-threatening. The developmental role of aggression in protecting a child's sense of self against external threats has been explained this way: "Faced with profoundly insensitive or cruel parenting, the young child's representation of all mental life will be fragile. Ordinary frustration of aims will signal potential destruction of the reflective self, accompanied by intolerable anxiety."[179] We also now know that young children whose attachment needs have not been consistently or adequately met often come to view the world, in Bowlby's terms, as "comfortless and unpredictable; and they respond either by shrinking from it or doing battle with it."[180]

Some of the specific behaviors that are commonly adopted as a psychologically self-defensive response to this kind of trauma—aggressiveness, rebelliousness, and disobedience—can serve as precursors to more serious behavioral problems, including later criminality. As one reviewer put it: "Numerous authors have related aggressive behavior in children to the psychological rejection and the abandonment which followed. These reports note rebelliousness, disobedience, temper tantrums, stealing and truancy."[181] Child maltreatment can also leave children with a sense of hopelessness and the feeling that they lack the agency to achieve positive life outcomes that, in turn, form the basis for pessimistic, fatalistic expectations about their future,[182] ones that have been shown to be related to subsequent delinquent and criminal behavior.[183]

In addition, a less psychodynamic and more social contextual view of "identification with the aggressor" emphasizes its *social learning or modeling* aspects. We know that the family environment is clearly "a key factor in understanding the etiology and maintenance of aggressive behavior," and that these patterns of behaving are transmitted from one generation to another implicitly through modeling.[184] Watching authority figures engage in physical confrontations or seeing siblings or other relatives or neighbors behave violently may teach several problematic lessons, including reinforcing a child's own sense of vulnerability and suggesting that even close familial connections may be sacrificed to anger.[185] Exposure to family or community violence also can legitimize using force and physical confrontation to address conflict and disagreement. If parents handle conflict and stress through violent acting out, their children may be more likely to model this behavior and engage in it later. This lesson, especially, has potentially destructive long-term consequences.[186] Not surprisingly, then, researchers have found that abused children are more aggressive, showing more hostile, externalizing and negative social behavior with other people than nonabused children[187] and, as Joan McCord concluded, exposure to parental conflict and aggression is one of the "instigating conditions" for subsequent criminal behavior.[188]

Child maltreatment can also *block positive connections to other socializing institutions* outside the home. Criminologists Rolf Loeber and Magda Stouthamer-Loeber published a meta-analysis of all available research on the relationship between family characteristics and delinquency and concluded that "socialization variables, such as lack of parental supervision, parental rejection, and parent-child involvement are among the most powerful predictors of juvenile conduct problems and delinquency."[189] Among other things, children who live in tumultuous families and who experience frequent moves and school transitions have more difficulties bonding with classmates and more often suffer academic problems. Difficulties fitting in and performing well in school represent criminogenic risk factors not only because they limit or eliminate opportunities for positive socialization but also make children and adolescents more vulnerable to harsher and potentially criminogenic forms of school intervention (of the sort that I discuss in the next chapter). They also limit a young person's access to legitimate employment opportunities that require educational credentials.

Exposure to risk factors and traumas also *facilitates dysfunctional forms of coping* that can be criminogenic. Young children subjected to maltreatment begin as largely helpless victims struggling to survive a psychologically dangerous environment. Their ad hoc attempts to cope with the immediate threats around them may lead to later problematic outcomes that they could not possibly have anticipated. Yet, as one group of researchers put it, the "developmental processes set in motion by abusive families . . . [begin] a negative chain of events that leads to further victimization on the streets and subsequent adverse developmental consequences for the child."[190] Childhood trauma also can negatively alter the way that children perceive and respond to the persons and situations that they subsequently encounter. That is, "children with early internal models of available care and self-worth are more responsive to positive features of the environment and more resilient to stress," whereas children who have been abused—and, therefore, who may have failed to develop such positive internal models—are not.[191] Together these adaptations to early traumatic experiences can predispose children and adolescents to dysfunctional forms of coping, such as self-medication,[192] that increase the likelihood of subsequent delinquent and adult criminal behavior.

Thus, although early social history is certainly not "destiny" and does not irreparably predetermine later outcomes in life, childhood traumas and risk factors can profoundly alter likelihoods, probabilities, life chances and, ultimately, outcomes. The basic connections between trauma and maltreatment, on the one hand, and subsequent adolescent delinquent and adult criminal behavior, on the other, have been too well established to dispute. Study after study has confirmed the existence of unfortunate cycles and patterns in which many criminal defendants have become deeply enmeshed—ones that begin with maltreatment at home and whose effects radiate out into the larger community.

The risk factors model provides invaluable insights into the ways in which the persons who engage in criminal behavior—especially serious, persistent law-breaking—differ from most law-abiding citizens. Those differences lie largely in the lives they have lived and the nature and number of the risk factors and traumas they have experienced. The magnitude and duration of risks matter as well, as do the nature and number of vulnerabilities protective factors that impede or enhance the ability to cope with stressors.[193] Moreover, the effects of even early risks and multiple traumas are probabilistic rather than absolute, and not necessarily sufficient to produce criminal trajectories.

For example, in Emmy Werner's classic 40-year longitudinal study of children in Kauai, Hawaii, who were placed at risk by perinatal stress, she found that they were more likely to become involved in delinquent behavior later in life *only* when they also were exposed to poor environmental conditions, such as chronic poverty and "a disruptive family environment" (e.g., separation from the mother or father, marital discord, parental mental health problems).[194] In fact, a more extensive review of the literature on the long-term effects of prenatal, perinatal, and postnatal risk factors showed that these things were clearly related to later criminal behavior, the children's subsequent living environment played an important role in determining later outcomes.[195] That is, what Patricia Brennan and Sarnoff Mednick called the "dual hazard" of being exposed to both birth-related *and* social risks was the most problematic pattern and, conversely, "a healthy social environment was found to protect individuals at physical or medical risk for antisocial outcome[s]."[196]

The interconnectedness of risks and the chaining of negative consequences can occur at multiple levels. For example, although we know that direct forms of maltreatment increase the likelihood that an adolescent will engage in troubled behavior, the additional experience of an indirect form of maltreatment–say, a high number of family transitions (both in caretakers and residences)—increases that probability even more. Indeed, as Ellen Herrenkohl and her colleagues put it, some especially at-risk children,

> having experienced more transitions early in life, run the risk of becoming more difficult to care for and thus are more likely to experience unstable placements, whether with friends, relatives, or foster homes. In turn, the instability in their lives leads to ever greater behavior problems.[197]

Moreover, the risk factor of extreme residential mobility typically co-occurs with frequent school transitions that, in turn, predict poor academic performance, lower levels of bonding at school, and a higher likelihood of dropping out[198]—all of which are criminogenic risk factors in their own right.

The chaining of risk factors and consequential events in someone's social history is subject to the forces of path dependency that I described in the last chapter—the way in which later life options are sometimes irrevocably altered in unanticipated ways. One of the most insightful descriptions of this process at work appeared recently in Danielle Allen's compelling story of her cousin Michael's life, which ended tragically and violently when he was still in his 20s. She described his "familiar" narrative—a "kid from a troubled home, trapped in poverty, without a stable world of adults coordinating care for him, [who] starts pilfering, mostly out of impatience to have things." But the narrative took dramatic turn when Michael was arrested at age 15 for a more serious crime and was eventually sentenced to adult prison. At that point, Allen noted, "his life accelerated, like a cylinder in one of those pneumatic tubes, whisking off your deposit at a drive through bank."[199] The particular life-changing "pneumatic tube" that whisked Michael away—the criminal justice system—accelerated with rapid speed and brutal effect. When he emerged from prison some 10 years later, he had "shed the life that might have been"—in some ways that were obvious and in others that were not.

But the person who had been whisked away, and all the potential and possibility that he once possessed, was not something that he could fully regain or create anew.

CONCLUSION

The adverse childhood events and experiences reviewed in this chapter constitute the social historical context of crime. Contrary to the tenets of the crime master narrative, unencumbered free choice and inherent badness play little or no role. Most people engage in troubled, problematic behavior because bad things have happened *to* them and too little has been in their lives to turn the resulting troubled trajectories in a different direction. When childhood and adolescent risk factors and traumas occur in significant numbers in a young person's life, are suffered in severe or substantial amounts over long periods of time, and when their impact is felt in the absence of caring assistance and other protective factors to buffer their most damaging effects, then they very significantly worsen the odds that they can be effectively overcome later. This is especially true when, as I discuss in subsequent chapters, they lead to dysfunctional forms of coping that promise short-term relief but which have long-term exacerbating effects, when they are compounded by problematic and counterproductive institutional interventions, and are exacerbated by encounters with criminogenic situations and settings later in life.

As Jerome Kagan has reminded us, children and adolescents who have been subjected to maltreatment are not a homogeneous group, and their outcomes in life are certainly not all foreordained by the early traumas they experienced. Many of the adversities they confront, "acting alone" may not have truly "formative power."[200] Even acting in combination with other risks factors, whether and how much formative power they ultimately have often depends on a set of larger contexts, ones that include, as Kagan noted, "the child's social class, ethnicity, cultural background, historical era and the extent to which these categories marginalized the child in his or her community."[201] Indeed, as several following chapters will show, the *next* stages in a person's social history—their institutional experiences, the immediate social settings and situations they enter, and the operation and effect of larger structural variables—play critically important roles.

NOTES

1. Allen, D. (2017, July 24). The life of a South Central statistic. *The New Yorker*. Retrieved from https://www.newyorker.com/magazine/2017/07/24/the-life-of-a-south-central-statistic
2. Hamburg, D. A. (1993). The American family transformed. *Society, 30*, 60–69. http://dx.doi.org/10.1007/BF02695809
3. Elder, G. H. (1981). Social history and life experience. In D. H. Eichorn, J. A. Clausen, N. Haan, M. P. Honzik, & P. H. Mussen (Eds.), *Present and past in middle*

life (pp. 3–31). New York, NY: Academic Press. http://dx.doi.org/10.1016/B978-0-12-233680-5.50007-1; Gubrium, J. F., & Holstein, J. A. (1995). Biographical work and new ethnography. In R. H. Josselson & A. Lieblich (Eds.), *Interpreting experience: The narrative study of lives* (Vol. 3, pp. 45–58). Thousand Oaks, CA: Sage. A number of sociologists have also embraced this approach. See Shanahan, M. J., & Macmillan, R. (2008). *Biography and the sociological imagination: Contexts and contingencies*. New York, NY: W. W. Norton.

4. See, e.g., Polkinghorne, D. E. (1996). Narrative knowing and the study of lives. In J. E. Birren, G. M. Kenyon, J.-E. Ruth, J. J. F. Schroots, & T. Svensson (Eds.), *Aging and biography: Explorations in adult development* (pp. 77–99). New York, NY: Springer; White, R. (1992). Exploring personality the long way: The study of lives. In R. A. Zucker, A. I. Rabin, J. Aronoff & S. Frank (Eds.), *Personality structure in the life course: Essays on personology in the Murray tradition* (pp. 3–21). New York, NY: Springer.
5. See, e.g., Caspi, A., Bem, D. J., & Elder, G. H., Jr. (1989). Continuities and consequences of interactional styles across the life course. *Journal of Personality, 57,* 375–406. http://dx.doi.org/10.1111/j.1467-6494.1989.tb00487.x; See also Richards, M., & Light, P. (Eds.). (1986). *Children of social worlds: Development in a social context*. Cambridge, MA: Harvard University Press; Sroufe, L. A., Egeland, B., & Kreutzer, T. (1990). The fate of early experience following developmental change: Longitudinal approaches to individual adaptation in childhood. *Child Development, 61,* 1363–1373. http://dx.doi.org/10.2307/1130748
6. Ortiz, K. R. (1985). Mental health consequences of life history method: Implications from a refugee case. *Ethos, 13,* 99–120, p. 100. http://dx.doi.org/10.1525/eth.1985.13.2.02a00020
7. See, e.g., Denno, D. W. (1986). Victim, offender, and situational characteristics of violent crime. *Journal of Criminal Law & Criminology, 77,* 1142–1158. http://dx.doi.org/10.2307/1143671; Farrington, D. P. (1990). Implications of criminal career research for the prevention of offending. *Journal of Adolescence, 13,* 93–113. http://dx.doi.org/10.1016/0140-1971(90)90001-N; Gordon, R. A. (1967). Issues in the ecological study of delinquency. *American Sociological Review, 32,* 927–944. http://dx.doi.org/10.2307/2092846
8. See, e.g., Hepburn, J. R. (1973). Violent behavior in interpersonal relationships. *Sociological Quarterly, 14,* 419–429. http://dx.doi.org/10.1111/j.1533-8525.1973.tb00870.x; McEwan, A. W., & Knowles, C. (1984). Delinquent personality types and the situational contexts of their crimes. *Personality and Individual Differences, 5,* 339–344. http://dx.doi.org/10.1016/0191-8869(84)90072-2; Sampson, R., & Lauritsen, J. (1994). Violent victimization and offending: Individual-, situational-, and community-level risk factors. In National Research Council, A. J. Reiss, Jr., & J. A. Roth (Eds.), *Understanding and preventing violence: Social influences* (Vol. 3, pp. 1–114). Washington, DC: National Academies Press. http://dx.doi.org/10.17226/4421; Toch, H. (1985). The catalytic situation in the violence equation. *Journal of Applied Social Psychology, 15,* 105–123. http://dx.doi.org/10.1111/j.1559-1816.1985.tb02338.x; Wenk, E. A., & Emrich, R. L. (1972). Assaultive youth: An exploratory study of the assaultive experience and assaultive potential of California Youth Authority wards. *Journal of Research in Crime & Delinquency, 9,* 171–196. http://dx.doi.org/10.1177/002242787200900208; Wright, K. N. (1991). The violent and victimized in the male prison. *Journal of Offender Rehabilitation, 16,* 1–26. http://dx.doi.org/10.1300/j076v16n03_01
9. See, e.g., Kaplow, J. B., & Widom, C. S. (2007). Age of onset of child maltreatment predicts long-term mental health outcomes. *Journal of Abnormal Psychology, 116,* 176–187. http://dx.doi.org/10.1037/0021-843x.116.1.176
10. Wolfe, D. A. (1987). *Child abuse: Implications for child development and psychopathology*. Newbury Park, CA: Sage, p. 25.

11. Garbarino, J. (1989). The incidence of and prevalence of child maltreatment. In L. Ohlin & M. Tonry (Eds.), *Family violence* (pp. 219–261). Chicago, IL: University of Chicago Press.
12. For a sample of articles and book chapters published on the topic of child abuse as early as the 1960s, see note 10 in Chapter 2.
13. For a sample of legal discussions of the issue of child abuse published as early as the mid-1970s, see note 11 in Chapter 2.
14. For example, Richard Light estimated in 1973 that there were between 665,000 and 1,675,000 children each year who were subjected to abuse, sexual molestation, or serious neglect. See Light, R. (1973). Abused and neglected children in America: A study of alternative policies. *Harvard Educational Review, 43,* 556–598, p. 556. http://dx.doi.org/10.17763/haer.43.4.u25580361w3r843n
15. The Child Abuse Prevention and Treatment Act was enacted as Public Law 93-274 on January 31, 1974. It provided federal assistance to states to develop child abuse and neglect identification programs, created the National Center on Child Abuse and Neglect to administer a range of abuse-related research grant programs, and established a National Clearinghouse on Child Abuse and Neglect Information. Laws to establish a system of intervention on behalf of abused children and to provide services to their families had already been passed in several states. For example, California passed a child protective services law in 1969. See Eads, W. E. (1969). Observations on the establishment of a child protective services system in California. *Stanford Law Review, 21,* 1129–1155. http://dx.doi.org/10.2307/1227467
16. Klaus, S. (1977). *Innovative treatment approaches for child abuse and neglect: Current issues and directions for future research.* Washington, DC: Department of Health, Education, and Welfare, p. 9.
17. van der Kolk, B. A. (2005). Developmental trauma disorder: Toward a rational diagnosis for children with complex trauma histories. *Psychiatric Annals, 35,* 401–408, p. 401. http://dx.doi.org/10.3928/00485713-20050501-06
18. Numerous articles and books have connected early childhood maltreatment to adjustment problems in adulthood. See, e.g., Thornberry, T. P., Henry, K. L., Ireland, T. O., & Smith, C. A. (2010). The causal impact of childhood-limited maltreatment and adolescent maltreatment on early adult adjustment. *Journal of Adolescent Health, 46,* 359–365. http://dx.doi.org/10.1016/j.jadohealth.2009.09.011; Shengold, L. (1989). *Soul murder: The effects of childhood abuse and deprivation.* New Haven, CT: Yale University Press.
19. See, e.g., Spinetta, J. J., & Rigler, D. (1972). The child abusing parent: A psychological review. *Psychological Bulletin, 77,* 296–304. http://dx.doi.org/10.1016/0145-2134(84)90022-x; and Terr, L. C. (1970). A family study of child abuse. *The American Journal of Psychiatry, 127,* 665–671. http://dx.doi.org/10.1176/ajp.127.5.665
20. One of the seminal articles that both critiqued the individualistic model of abuse as psychopathology and proposed a more social contextual and structural analysis of the problem was Gelles, R. J. (1973). Child abuse as psychopathology: A sociological critique and reformulation. *American Journal of Orthopsychiatry, 43,* 611–621. http://dx.doi.org/10.1111/j.1939-0025.1973.tb00830.x. See also Giovannoni, J. M. (1971). Parental mistreatment: Perpetrators and victims. *Journal of Marriage and the Family, 33,* 649–657. http://dx.doi.org/10.2307/349437
21. Klaus (1977), *Innovative treatment approaches,* p. 7. See also Terr (1970), A family study of child abuse. Terr's study of the individual psychological characteristics of persons who had engaged in child abuse led her to conclude that a *family* therapy model was required to effectively address the problem.
22. Klaus (1977), *Innovative treatment approaches,* p. 4 (emphasis added).

23. Egeland, B., & Erickson, M. (1987). Psychologically unavailable caregiving. In M. R. Brassard, R. Germain, & S. N. Hart (Eds.), *Psychological maltreatment of children and youth* (pp. 110–120). New York, NY: Pergamon, p. 115. One study found that more than two out of three incidents of physical or sexual abuse previously suffered by the residents of a chemical dependency treatment center had never been reported to legal, social services, or mental health personnel. See Caviola, A. A., & Schiff, M. (1988). Behavioral sequelae of physical and/or sexual abuse in adolescents. *Child Abuse and Neglect, 12,* 181–188. http://dx.doi.org/10.1016/0145-2134(88)90026-9
24. For early observations about the larger context of abuse, see the Gelles, Giovannoni, and Newburger & Bourne articles cited earlier, as well as, Gil, D. G. (1975). Unraveling child abuse. *American Journal of Orthopsychiatry, 45,* 346–356. http://dx.doi.org/10.1111/j.1939-0025.1975.tb02545.x
25. Egeland, B., & Erickson (1987), Psychologically unavailable caregiving, p. 115 (emphasis added). See also Wiggins, J. A. (1983). Family violence as a case of interpersonal aggression: A situational analysis. *Social Forces, 62,* 102–123. http://dx.doi.org/10.2307/2578350; and Moore, T., Pepler, D., Weinberg, B., Hammond, L., Waddell, J., & Weiser, L. (1990). Research on children from violent families. *Canada's Mental Health, 38,* 19–23.
26. Murphy, J. M., Jellinek, M., Quinn, D., Smith, G., Poitrast, F. G., & Goshko, M. (1991). Substance abuse and serious child mistreatment: Prevalence, risk, and outcome in a court sample. *Child Abuse & Neglect, 15,* 197–211, p. 208. http://dx.doi.org/10.1016/0145-2134(91)90065-1. For similar results obtained with a larger British sample, see Creighton, S. J. (1985). An epidemiological study of abused children and their families in the United Kingdom between 1977 and 1982. *Child Abuse & Neglect, 9,* 441–448. http://dx.doi.org/10.1016/0145-2134(85)90052-3. This work shows that the lives of parents and/or caretakers of abused children were themselves characterized by early parenthood, marital instability, large families, high rates of unemployment, mobility, and their own criminal histories.
27. For example, Creighton (1985), An epidemiological study of abused children and their families in the United Kingdom between 1977 and 1982.
28. See, e.g., Passman, R. H., & Mulhern, R. K., Jr. (1977). Maternal punitiveness as affected by situational stress: An experimental analogue of child abuse. *Journal of Abnormal Psychology, 86,* 565–569. http://dx.doi.org/10.1037/0021-843X.86.5.565
29. For example, one group of researchers found that early exposure to multiple risks and traumas—what they termed "polyvictimization"—was especially critical in the process by which negative experiences produced long-term damaging effects. This was in part because early exposure to multiple traumas and risks made later exposure more likely, and the children and adolescents who had exposure over a greater number of developmental periods were the ones most likely to suffer later and more serious problems. Dierkhising, C. B., Ford, J. D., Branson, C., Grasso, D. J., & Lee, R. (2018). Developmental timing of polyvictimization: Continuity, change, and association with adverse outcomes in adolescence. *Child Abuse & Neglect, 87,* 40–50. http://dx.doi.org/10.1016/j.chiabu.2018.07.022. On the issue of accumulated risks and the way that specific risks are especially important at different developmental stages, see also Grasso, D. J., Dierkhising, C. B., Branson, C. E., Ford, J. D., & Lee, R. (2016). Developmental patterns of adverse childhood experiences and current symptoms and impairment in youth referred for trauma-specific services. *Journal of Abnormal Child Psychology, 44,* 871–886. http://dx.doi.org/10.1007/s10802-015-0086-8
30. Mills, R., Scott, J., Alati, R., O'Callaghan, M., Najman, J. M., & Strathearn, L. (2013). Child maltreatment and adolescent mental health problems in a large birth cohort. *Child Abuse & Maltreatment, 37,* 292–302, p. 300. http://dx.doi.org/10.1016/

j.chiabu.2012.11.008 Some researchers have termed this common co-occurrence "multi-type maltreatment," whereas others have used "polyvictimization." See Arata, C. M., Langhinrichsen-Rohling, J., Bowers, D., & O'Brien, N. (2007). Differential correlates of multi-type maltreatment among urban youth. *Child Abuse & Neglect, 31,* 393–415. http://dx.doi.org/10.1016/j.chiabu.2006.09.006; and Finkelhor, D., Ormrod, R. K., & Turner, H. A. (2007). Polyvictimization: A neglected component in child victimization. *Child Abuse & Neglect, 31,* 7–26. http://dx.doi.org/10.1016/j.chiabu.2006.06.008

31. See, e.g., Kelly, S. J., Day, N., & Streissguth, A. P. (2000). Effects of prenatal alcohol exposure on social behavior in humans and other species. *Neurotoxicology and Teratology, 22,* 143–149. http://dx.doi.org/10.1016/s0892-0362(99)00073-2; Roebuck, T. M., Mattson, S. N., & Riley, E. P. (1999). Behavioral and psychosocial profiles of alcohol-exposed children. *Alcoholism: Clinical and Experimental Research, 23,* 1070–1076. http://dx.doi.org/10.1111/j.1530-0277.1999.tb04227.x; Streissguth, A., & Kanter, J. (Eds.). (1997). *The challenge of fetal alcohol syndrome: Overcoming secondary disabilities.* Seattle: University of Washington Press; and Wass, T. S., Mattson, S. N., & Riley, E. P. (2004). Neuroanatomical and neurobehavioral effects of heavy prenatal alcohol exposure. In J. Brick (Ed.), *Handbook of the medical consequences of alcohol and drug abuse* (pp. 139–169). Binghamton, NY: Haworth Press.
32. The broader term "FASD" is used to describe a continuum of harmful effects of fetal exposure to alcohol. See, e.g., Nulman, I., Ickowicz, A., Koren, G., & Knittel-Keren, D. (2007). Fetal alcohol spectrum disorder. In I. Brown, & M. Percy (Eds.), *A comprehensive guide to intellectual and developmental disabilities* (pp. 213–227). Baltimore, MD: Paul H. Brookes; Premji, S., Benzies, K., Serrett, K., & Hayden, K. A. (2007). Research-based interventions for children and youth with a fetal alcohol spectrum disorder: Revealing the gap. *Child: Care, Health and Development, 33,* 389–397. http://dx.doi.org/10.1111/j.1365-2214.2006.00692.x; and Sokol, R. J., Delaney-Black, V., & Nordstrom, B. (2003). Fetal alcohol spectrum disorder. *JAMA, 290,* 2996–2999. http://dx.doi.org/10.1001/jama.290.22.2996
33. Premji, Benzies, Serrett, & Hayden (2007), Research-based interventions for children and youth with a fetal alcohol spectrum disorder, p. 390. In addition, see, e.g., Fast, D., Conry, J., & Loock, C. (1999). Identifying fetal alcohol syndrome among youth in the criminal justice system. *Journal of Developmental & Behavior Pediatrics, 20,* 370–372. http://dx.doi.org/10.1097/00004703-199910000-00012; Rasmussen, C., & Wyper, K. (2007). Decision making, executive functioning and risky behaviors in adolescents with prenatal alcohol exposure. *International Journal on Disability and Human Development, 5,* 405–416. http://dx.doi.org/10.1515/IJDHD.2007.6.4.405. There is also some evidence to suggest that "other risk factors are more important than prenatal exposure to alcohol in development of delinquent behavior." Lynch, M. E., Coles, C. D., Corley, T., & Falek, A. (2003). Examining delinquency in adolescents differentially prenatally exposed to alcohol: The role of proximal and distal risk factors. *Journal of Studies on Alcohol, 64,* 678–686, p. 684. http://dx.doi.org/10.15288/jsa.2003.64.678 Indeed, "Adolescent perception of life stress and adolescent substance use were strong predictors of delinquent behavior. Aspects of the family environment were potent predictors as well" (p. 685).
34. Coggins, T. E., Timler, G. R., & Olswang, L. B. (2007). A state of double jeopardy: Impact of prenatal alcohol exposure and adverse environments on the social communicative abilities of school-age children with fetal alcohol spectrum disorder. *Language, Speech, and Hearing Services in Schools, 38,* 117–127. http://dx.doi.org/10.1044/0161-1461(2007/012)
35. Fergusson, D. M. (1999). Prenatal smoking and antisocial behavior. *Archives of General Psychiatry, 56,* 223–224. http://dx.doi.org/10.1001/archpsyc.56.3.223

36. See, e.g., Räsänen, P., Hakko, H., Isohanni, M., Hodgins, S., Järvelin, M.-R., & Tiihonen, J. (1999). Maternal smoking during pregnancy and risk of criminal behavior among male offspring in the Northern Finland 1966 birth cohort. *The American Journal of Psychiatry, 156,* 857–862. http://dx.doi.org/10.1176/ajp.156.6.857
37. Levendosky, A., & Bogat, A. (2006). Domestic violence and infancy. In K. Freeark & W. Davidson (Eds.), *The crisis in youth mental health: Critical issues and effective programs.* (Vol. 3, pp. 1–26). Westport, CT: Praeger.
38. Yalch, M. M., Black, J. A., Martin, L., & Levendosky, A. A. (2016). Effects of prenatal and postbirth intimate partner violence on preschool-age children's dissociative symptoms. *Journal of Aggression, Maltreatment & Trauma, 25,* 741–752. http://dx.doi.org/10.1080/10926771.2016.1194937
39. See, e.g., Lin, Y., Xu, J., Huang, J., Jia, Y., Zhang, J., Yan, C., & Zhang, J. (2017). Effects of prenatal and postnatal maternal emotional stress on toddlers' cognitive and temperamental development. *Journal of Affective Disorders, 207,* 9–17. http://dx.doi.org/10.1016/j.jad.2016.09.010; and Quinlivan, J. A., & Evans, S. F. (2005). Impact of domestic violence and drug use in pregnancy on maternal attachment and infant temperament in teenage mothers in the setting of best clinical practice. *Archives of Women's Mental Health, 8,* 191–199. http://dx.doi.org/10.1007/s00737-005-0079-7
40. Levendosky & Bogat (2006), Domestic violence and infancy, p. 5, citing research reported in Schore, A. N. (2003). *Affect dysregulation and disorders of the self.* New York, NY: W. W. Norton. See also Robinson, M. (2013). How the first nine months shape the rest of our lives. *Australian Psychologist, 48,* 239–245. http://dx.doi.org/10.1111/ap.12022; Robinson, M., Mattes, E., Oddy, W. H., Pennell, C. E., van Eekelen, A., McLean, N. J., . . . Newham, J. P. (2011). Prenatal stress and risk of behavioral morbidity from age 2 to 14 years: The influence of the number, type, and timing of stressful life events. *Development and Psychopathology, 23,* 507–520. http://dx.doi.org/10.1017/S0954579411000241; and Tearne, J. E., Allen, K. L., Herbison, C. E., Lawrence, D., Whitehouse, A. J. O., Sawyer, M. G., & Robinson, M. (2015). The association between prenatal environment and children's mental health trajectories from 2 to 14 years. *European Child & Adolescent Psychiatry, 24,* 1015–1024. http://dx.doi.org/10.1007/s00787-014-0651-7
41. Klaus (1977), *Innovative treatment approaches,* p. 7 (internal references omitted).
42. Lannert, B. K., Garcia, A. M., Smagur, K. E., Yalch, M. M., Levendosky, A. A., Bogat, G. A., & Lonstein, J. S. (2014). Relational trauma in the context of intimate partner violence. *Child Abuse & Neglect, 38,* 1966–1975. http://dx.doi.org/10.1016/j.chiabu.2014.10.002
43. See, e.g., Kandel, E., & Mednick, S. A. (1991). Perinatal complications predict violent offending. *Criminology, 29,* 519–530. http://dx.doi.org/10.1111/j.1745-9125.1991.tb01077.x
44. Brennan, P., & Mednick, S. (1997). Medical histories of antisocial individuals. In D. M. Stoff, J. Breiling, & J. D. Maser (Eds.), *Handbook of antisocial behavior* (pp. 269–279). New York, NY: John Wiley.
45. Kandel, E., & Mednick, S. A. (1991). Perinatal complications predict violent offending. *Criminology, 29,* 519–529. http://dx.doi.org/10.1111/j.1745-9125.1991.tb01077.x
46. Bowlby was originally tasked by the United Nations and World Health Organization to study mental health issues among homeless and displaced children who had been orphaned or were separated from their families. He stated his main finding succinctly: "[W]hat is believed to be essential for mental health is that the infant and young child should experience a warm, intimate, and continuous relationship with his mother (or permanent mother-substitute) in which both

find satisfaction and enjoyment." Bowlby, J. (1951). Maternal care and mental health. *Bulletin of the World Health Organization, 3,* 355–533, p. 361.

47. Bowlby, J. (1973). *Attachment and loss.* New York, NY: Basic Books. (Original work published 1969)
48. See, e.g., Patton, R. G., & Gardner, L. I. (1962). Influence of family environment on growth: The syndrome of "maternal deprivation." *Pediatrics, 30,* 957–962. See also Caldwell, B. (1970). The effects of psychological deprivation on human development in infancy. *Merrill-Palmer Quarterly, 16,* 260–270.
49. Note that although primary attachments are formed in infancy, attachment-related experiences can occur in later years as well. See, e.g., Ainsworth, M. D. (1989). Attachments beyond infancy. *American Psychologist, 44,* 709–716. http://dx.doi.org/10.1037/0003-066X.44.4.709; Anderson, S. A., & Sabatelli, R. M. (1999). *Family interaction: A multigenerational developmental perspective.* Boston, MA: Allyn and Bacon.
50. Schore, A. N. (2003). *Affect dysregulation and disorders of the self.* New York, NY: W. W. Norton. See also Schore, A. (2002). The neurobiology of attachment and early personality organization. *Journal of Prenatal & Perinatal Psychology & Health, 16,* 249–263; and Ainsworth, M. S. (1991). The development of infant-mother attachment. *Review of child development literature, 3,* 1–94. For a more current and comprehensive synthesis of attachment theory and research, see Mikulincer, M., & Shaver, P. R. (2007). *Attachment in adulthood: Structure, dynamics, and change.* New York, NY: Guilford Press; and Schore, A. (2017). Modern attachment theory. In S. N. Gold (Ed.), *APA handbook of trauma psychology* (Vol. 1, pp. 389–401). Washington, DC: American Psychological Association. http://dx.doi.org/10.1037/0000019-000
51. Schore, A. N. (2004). Graduation address: Santa Barbara Graduate Institute. *Journal of Prenatal & Perinatal Psychology & Health, 19,* 107–114, p. 108 (emphasis added). Schore went on to describe a fundamental paradigm shift that encompasses many of the empirical developments and theoretical syntheses that I discuss at length:

    > The current intense interest in a number of disciplines in developmental research, at various levels of analysis, has both dramatically expanded the amount of factual knowledge and significantly altered the theoretical constructs that model the etiologies and treatment of the psychological and physical disorders of infancy, childhood, and adulthood. (p. 108)

52. Much of the work done by Mikulincer and Shaver demonstrates the beneficial effects of "attachment security" and explores the conditions under which it can be created or enhanced. See, e.g., Mikulincer, M., Shaver, P. R., & Pereg, D. (2003). Attachment theory and affect regulation: The dynamics, development, and cognitive consequences of attachment-related strategies. *Motivation and Emotion, 27,* 77–102. http://dx.doi.org/10.1023/A:1024515519160
53. See, e.g., Mikulincer, M., Gillath, O., Halevy, V., Avihou, N., Avidan, S., & Eshkoli, N. (2001). Attachment theory and reactions to others' needs: Evidence that activation of the sense of attachment security promotes empathic responses. *Journal of Personality and Social Psychology, 81,* 1205–1224; Mikulincer, M., & Shaver, P. R. (2005). Attachment security, compassion, and altruism. *Current Directions in Psychological Science, 14,* 34–38. http://dx.doi.org/10.1111/j.0963-7214.2005.00330.x
54. See Mikulincer, M., & Shaver, P. R. (2005). Attachment theory and emotions in close relationships: Exploring the attachment-related dynamics of emotional reactions to relational events. *Personal Relationships, 12,* 149–168. http://dx.doi.org/10.1111/j.1350-4126.2005.00108.x; Shaver, P. R., Schachner, D. A., & Mikulincer, M. (2005). Attachment style, excessive reassurance seeking, relationship processes,

and depression. *Personality and Social Psychology Bulletin, 31,* 343–359. http://dx.doi.org/10.1177/0146167204271709

55. See, e.g., Atwool, N. (2006). Attachment and resilience: Implications for children in care. *Child Care in Practice, 12,* 315–330. http://dx.doi.org/10.1080/13575270600863226; Faber, A. J., & Wittenborn, A. K. (2010). The role of attachment in children's adjustment to divorce and remarriage. *Journal of Family Psychotherapy, 21,* 89–104. http://dx.doi.org/10.1080/08975353.2010.483625; and Ortigo, K. M., Westen, D., DeFife, J. A., & Bradley, B. (2013). Attachment, social cognition, and posttraumatic stress symptoms in a traumatized, urban population: Evidence for the mediating role of object relations. *Journal of Traumatic Stress, 26,* 361–368. http://dx.doi.org/10.1002/jts.21815
56. Winnicott, D. W. (1984). [Writings.] In C. Winnicott, R. Shepard, & M. Davis (Eds.), *Deprivation and delinquency* (p. 124). London, England: Tavistock.
57. Winnicott (1984), *Deprivation and delinquency.* For a more recent, comprehensive summary of the lifelong consequences of early problematic caregiving on a child's subsequent attachment-related behavior, see Doyle, C., & Cicchetti, D. (2017). From the cradle to the grave: The effect of adverse caregiving environments on attachment and relationships throughout the lifespan. *Clinical Psychology, 24,* 203–217. http://dx.doi.org/10.1111/cpsp.12192
58. Freudenberger, H. J., & Gallagher, K. M. (1995). Emotional consequences of loss for our adolescents. *Psychotherapy, 32,* 150–153, p. 153. http://dx.doi.org/10.1037/0033-3204.32.1.150
59. Wolfenstein, M. (1969). Loss, rage, and repetition. *Psychoanalytic Study of the Child, 24,* 432–460, p. 444. http://dx.doi.org/10.1080/00797308.1969.11822702 See also Call, J. D., & Wolfenstein, M. (1976). Effects of adults on object loss in the first five years. *Journal of the American Psychoanalytic Association, 24,* 659–668. See also Caldwell, B. M. (1970). The effects of psychosocial deprivation on human development in infancy. *Merrill-Palmer Quarterly, 16,* 260–277.
60. Schonfeld, W. (1995). Depression in adolescence. In R. Marohn & S. Feinstein (Eds.), *Adolescent psychiatry: Developmental and clinical studies* (Vol. 20, pp. 31–38). Hillsdale, NJ: Analytic Press, p. 32. For examples of the long-term psychological consequences of parental separation or loss, see Agid, O., Shapira, B., Zislin, J., Ritsner, M., Hanin, B., Murad, H., . . . Lerer, B. (1999). Environment and vulnerability to major psychiatric illness: A case control study of early parental loss in major depression, bipolar disorder and schizophrenia. *Molecular Psychiatry, 4,* 163–172. http://dx.doi.org/10.1038/sj.mp.4000473; Faravelli, C., Sacchetti, E., Ambonetti, A., Conte, G., Pallanti, S., & Vita, A. (1986). Early life events and affective disorder revisited. *British Journal of Psychiatry, 148,* 288–295. http://dx.doi.org/10.1192/bjp.148.3.288; Freudenberger, & Gallagher (1995), Emotional consequences of loss for our adolescents; Hällström, T. (1987). The relationships of childhood socio-demographic factors and early parental loss to major depression in adult life. *Acta Psychiatrica Scandinavica, 75,* 212–216. http://dx.doi.org/10.1111/j.1600-0447.1987.tb02777.x; Roy, A. (1985). Early parental separation and adult depression. *Archives of General Psychiatry, 42,* 987–991. http://dx.doi.org/10.1001/archpsyc.1985.01790330067008
61. Mishne, J. (1979). Parental abandonment: A unique form of loss and narcissistic injury. *Clinical Social Work Journal, 7,* 15–33, p. 33. http://dx.doi.org/10.1007/bf00761356 See also Mishne, J. M. (1984). Trauma of parent loss through divorce, death, and illness. *Child and Adolescent Social Work Journal, 1,* 74–88; and Mishne, J. (1992). The grieving child: Manifest and hidden losses in childhood and adolescence. *Child and Adolescent Social Work Journal, 9,* 471–490. http://dx.doi.org/10.1007/bf00845409. See also Asper, K., & Rooks, S. (1993).

The abandoned child within: On losing and regaining self-worth. New York, NY: Fromm. http://dx.doi.org/10.5860/choice.31-3474

62. Some of the potential complexity and interconnections between these and other social historical variables are captured in Sykes, B., & Pettit, B. (2014). Mass incarceration, family complexity, and the reproduction of childhood disadvantage. *The Annals, 654*, 128–149. http://dx.doi.org/10.1177/0002716214526345
63. Fonagy, P., Target, M., Steele, M., Steele, H., Leigh, T., Levinson, A., & Kennedy, R. (1997). Crime and attachment: Morality, disruptive behavior, borderline personality disorder, crime, and their relationship to security of attachment. In L. Atkinson & K. J. Zucker (Eds.), *Attachment and psychopathology* (pp. 223–274). New York, NY: Guilford Press.
64. Burnstein, M. H. (1981). Child abandonment: Historical, sociological and psychological perspectives. *Child Psychiatry & Human Development, 11*, 213–221, p. 218. See also Liebman, F. H. (1992). Childhood abandonment/adult rage: The root of violent criminal acts. *American Journal of Forensic Psychology, 10*, 57–64; and Pemberton, D. A., & Benady, D. R. (1973). Consciously rejected children. *British Journal of Psychiatry, 123*, 575–578. http://dx.doi.org/10.1192/bjp.123.5.575. Abandonment is also one of the traumatic childhood events that is related to suicide risk among jail inmates. See Blaauw, E., Arensman, E., Kraaij, V., Winkel, F. W., & Bout, R. (2002). Traumatic life events and suicide risk among jail inmates: The influence of types of events, time period and significant others. *Journal of Traumatic Stress, 15*, 9–16. http://dx.doi.org/10.1023/a:1014323009493
65. van IJzendoorn, M. H. (1997). Attachment, emergent morality, and aggression: Toward a developmental socioemotional model of antisocial behavior. *International Journal of Behavioral Development, 21*, 703–727, p. 720. http://dx.doi.org/10.1080/016502597384631
66. Hoeve, M., Stams, G. J. J. M., van der Put, C. E., Dubas, J. S., van der Laan, P. H., & Gerris, J. R. M. (2012). A meta-analysis of attachment to parents and delinquency. *Journal of Abnormal Child Psychology, 40*, 771–785, p. 781. http://dx.doi.org/10.1007/s10802-011-9608-1
67. Wakefield, S., & Wildeman, C. (2014). *Children of the prison boom: Mass incarceration and the future of American inequality*. Oxford, England: Oxford University Press.
68. See, e.g., Muftić, L. R., Bouffard, L. A., & Armstrong, G. S. (2016). Impact of maternal incarceration on the criminal justice involvement of adult offspring: A research note. *Journal of Research in Crime and Delinquency, 53*, 93–111. http://dx.doi.org/10.1177/0022427815593988; and Roettger, M. E., Swisher, R. R. (2011). Associations of fathers' history of incarceration with sons' delinquency and arrest among Black, White, and Hispanic males in the United States. *Criminology, 49*, 1109–1148. http://dx.doi.org/10.1111/j.1745-9125.2011.00253.x
69. See, e.g., Foster, H., & Hagan, J. (2015). Punishment regimes and the multilevel effects of parental incarceration: Intergenerational, intersectional, and interinstitutional models of social inequality and systemic exclusion. *Annual Review of Sociology, 41*, 135–158. http://dx.doi.org/10.1146/annurev-soc-073014-112437; Giordano, P. C., & Copp, J. E. (2015). "Packages" of risk: Implications for determining the effect of maternal incarceration on child wellbeing. *Criminology & Public Policy, 14*, 157–168. http://dx.doi.org/10.1111/1745-9133.12118; and Roettger, M. E., & Dennison, S. (2018). Interrupting intergenerational offending in the context of America's social disaster of mass imprisonment. *American Behavioral Scientist, 62*, 1545–1561. http://dx.doi.org/10.1177/0002764218796995
70. Murray, J., & Farrington, D. P. (2008). The effects of parental imprisonment on children. *Crime & Justice, 37*, 133–206, p. 186. http://dx.doi.org/10.1086/520070. Although "[c]hildren of incarcerated parents are at risk for negative social and academic outcomes, including internalizing and externalizing behavior problems, substance abuse, adult offending and incarceration, truancy, and school failure,"

whether and how much children are adversely affected by parental incarceration depend on a host of variables; Poehlmann, J., Dallaire, D., Loper, A. B., & Shear, L. D. (2010). Children's contact with their incarcerated parents: Research findings and recommendations. *American Psychologist, 65*, 575–598, p. 575. http://dx.doi.org/10.1037/a0020279. See also Murray, J., Farrington, D. P., Sekol, I., & Olsen, R. F. (2009). Effects of parental imprisonment on child antisocial behaviour and mental health: A systematic review. *Campbell Systematic Reviews, 4*, 1–105. http://dx.doi.org/10.1002/CL2.47

71. Murray & Farrington (2008), *The effects of parental imprisonment on children*, pp. 186–187.
72. Bullard, D. M., Jr., Glaser, H. H., Heagarty, M. C., & Pivchik, E. C. (1969). Failure to thrive in the "neglected" child. *American Journal of Orthopsychiatry, 37*, 680–690. http://dx.doi.org/10.1111/j.1939-0025.1967.tb00509.x; Lewis, H. (1969). Parental and community neglect—Twin responsibilities of protective services. *Children, 16*, 114–118; Meier, E. (1964). Child neglect. In N. Cohen (Ed.), *Social work and social problems* (pp. 153–199). New York, NY: National Association of Social Workers.
73. See, e.g., Crouch, J. L., & Milner, J. S. (1993). Effects of child neglect on children. *Criminal Justice and Behavior, 20*, 49–65. http://dx.doi.org/10.1177/0093854893020001005; and Wilson, H. (1980). Parental supervision: A neglected aspect of delinquency. *British Journal of Criminology, 20*, 203–235. http://dx.doi.org/10.1093/oxfordjournals.bjc.a047169
74. Dubowitz, H., Black, M., Starr, R. H., Jr., & Zuravin, S. (1993). A conceptual definition of child neglect. *Criminal Justice and Behavior, 20*, 8–26, p. 23. http://dx.doi.org/10.117/0093854890200001003
75. Dubowitz, Black, Starr, & Zuravin (1993), A conceptual definition of child neglect, p. 10. See also Feerick, M. M., Knutson, J. F., Trickett, P. K., & Flanzer, S. M. (Eds.). (2006). *Child abuse and neglect: Definitions, classifications, and a framework for research*. Baltimore, MD: Paul H. Brookes.
76. Egeland, B., Sroufe, L. A., & Erickson, M. (1984). The developmental consequence of different patterns of maltreatment. *Child Abuse & Neglect, 7*, 459–469. http://dx.doi.org/10.1016/0145-2134(83)90053-4
77. See, e.g., Taillieu, T. L., Brownridge, D. A., Sareen, J., & Afifi, T. O. (2016). Childhood emotional maltreatment and mental disorders: Results from a nationally representative adult sample from the United States. *Child Abuse & Neglect, 59*, 1–12. http://dx.doi.org/10.1016/j.chiabu.2016.07.005
78. Egeland, B., & Erickson, M. (1987), Psychologically unavailable caregiving, p. 113. Crittendon described this simply as a parent's "failure to connect emotionally" with his or her child. Crittendon, P. (1999). Child neglect: Causes and contributors. In H. Dubowitz (Ed.), *Neglected children* (pp. 47–68). London, England: Sage, p. 78. See also Wark, M. J., Kruczek, T., & Boley, A. (2003). Emotional neglect and family structure: Impact on student functioning. *Child Abuse & Neglect, 27*, 1033–1043. http://dx.doi.org/10.1016/S0145-2134(03)00162-5
79. Taillieu, Brownridge, Sareen, & Afifi (2016), Childhood emotional maltreatment and mental disorder.
80. Egeland & Erickson (1987). *Psychologically unavailable caregiving*, p. 113.
81. Egeland & Erickson (1987). *Psychologically unavailable caregiving*, p. 116.
82. Egeland, B. (2009). Taking stock: Childhood emotional maltreatment and developmental psychopathology. *Child Abuse & Neglect, 33*, 22–26, p. 23. http://dx.doi.org/10.1016/j.chiabu.2008.12.004. See also Erickson, M., & Egeland, B. (1996). The quiet assault: A portrait of child neglect. In J. Briere, L. Berliner, J. A. Bulkley, C. Jenny, & T. Reid (Eds.), *The APSAC handbook of child maltreatment* (pp. 4–20). Thousand Oaks, CA: Sage; and Kisely, S., Abajobir, A. A., Mills, R., Strathearn, L., Clavarino, A., & Najman, J. M. (2018). Childhood maltreatment

and mental health problems in adulthood: Birth cohort study. *The British Journal of Psychiatry, 213,* 698–703. http://dx.doi.org/10.1192/bjp.2018.207

83. Harriet Wilson wrote about the relationship in the early 1960s. See Wilson, H. (1962). *Delinquency and child neglect.* London, England: Allen & Unwin. Not long after, Donald West and David Farrington began to publish the results of what they termed the "Cambridge Study of Delinquent Development," in which the role of child neglect was examined. See, e.g., West, D., & Farrington, D. (1973). *Who becomes delinquent? Second report of the Cambridge study in delinquent development.* Oxford, England: Crane Russak. For more recent findings on the effects of neglect on subsequent criminal behavior, see Grogan-Kaylor, A., & Otis, M. D. (2003). The effect of childhood maltreatment on adult criminality: A Tobit regression analysis. *Child Maltreatment, 8,* 129–137. http://dx.doi.org/10.1177/1077559502250810; and Ryan, J. P., Williams, A. B., & Courtney, M. E. (3013). Adolescent neglect, juvenile delinquency and the risk of recidivism. *Journal of Youth and Adolescence, 42,* 454–465. http://dx.doi.org/10.1007/s10964-013-9906-8
84. Egeland (2009). Taking stock: Childhood emotional maltreatment and developmental psychopathology, p. 23.
85. Maughan, D., & Moore, S. C. (2010). Dimensions of child neglect: An exploration of parental neglect and its relationship with delinquency. *Child Welfare, 89,* 47–65. See also Chen, W.-Y., Propp, J., deLara, E., & Corvo, K. (2011). Child neglect and its association with subsequent juvenile drug and alcohol offense. *Child and Adolescent Social Work Journal, 28,* 273–290. http://dx.doi.org/10.1007/s10560-011-0232-2
86. See, e.g., Kempe, C. H., Silverman, F. N., Steele, B. F., Droegemueller, W., & Silver, H. K. (1962). The battered-child syndrome. *JAMA, 181,* 17–24. http://dx.doi.org/10.1001/jama.1962.03050270019004
87. See, e.g., Galdston, R. (1965). Observations on children who have been physically abused and their parents. *The American Journal of Psychiatry, 122,* 440–443. http://dx.doi.org/10.1176/ajp.122.4.440; Zalba, S. R. (1966). The abused child: I. A survey of the problem. *Social Work, 11,* 3–16. http://dx.doi.org/10.1093/sw/11.4.3; Zalba, S. R. (1967). The abused child: II. A typology for classification and treatment. *Social Work, 12,* 70–79. http://dx.doi.org/10.1093/sw/12.1.70
88. See, e.g., Brown, J. A., & Daniels, R. (1968). Some observations on abusive parents. *Child Welfare, 47,* 89–94; Elmer, E., & Gregg, G. S. (1967). Developmental characteristics of abused children. *Pediatrics, 40,* 596–602; Melnick, B., & Hurley, J. R. (1969). Distinctive personality attributes of child-abusing mothers. *Journal of Consulting and Clinical Psychology, 33,* 746–749. http://dx.doi.org/10.1016/0145-2134(80)90006-x; Steele, B., & Pollock, C. (1968). A psychiatric study of parents who abuse infants and small children. In R. Helfer (Ed.), *The battered child* (pp. 421–432). Chicago, IL: University of Chicago Press; Weston, J. (1968). The pathology of child abuse. In R. Helfer (Ed.), *The battered child* (pp. 61–86). Chicago, IL: University of Chicago Press; Wasserman, S. (1967). The abused parent of the abused child. *Children, 14,* 175–179.
89. See, e.g., Curtis, G. C. (1963). Violence breeds violence—Perhaps? *The American Journal of Psychiatry, 120,* 386–387. http://dx.doi.org/10.1176/ajp.120.4.386; See also Silver, L. B., Dublin, C. C., & Lourie, R. S. (1969). Does violence breed violence? Contributions from a study of the child abuse syndrome. *The American Journal of Psychiatry, 126,* 404–407, in which the authors wrote, "Violence does appear to breed violence. . . . The child who experiences violence . . . has the potential of becoming a violent member of society in the future" (p. 407).
90. See, e.g., Holter, J. C., & Friedman, S. B. (1968). Principles of management in child abuse cases. *American Journal of Orthopsychiatry, 38,* 127–138; Paulson, M., & Blake, P. (1969). The physically abused child: A focus on prevention. *Child Welfare, 48,* 86–95.

91. Garbarino (1989), The incidence of and prevalence of child maltreatment, p. 221.
92. For example, Portegijs, P. J. M., Jeuken, F. M. H., van der Horst, F. G., Kraan, H. F., & Knottnerus, J. A. (1996). A troubled youth: Relations with somatization, depression and anxiety in adulthood. *Family Practice, 13,* 1–11. http://dx.doi.org/10.1093/fampra/13.1.1
93. See, e.g., Cutajar, M. C., Mullen, P. E., Ogloff, J. R. P. Thomas, S. D., Wells, D. L., & Spataro, J. (2010). Psychopathology in a large cohort of sexually abused children followed up to 43 years. *Child Abuse & Neglect, 34,* 813–822. http://dx.doi.org/10.1016/j.chiabu.2010.04.004; Gilbert, R., Widom, C. S., Browne, K., Fergusson, D. Webb, E., & Janson, S. (2009). Burden and consequences of child maltreatment in high-income countries. *The Lancet, 373,* 68–81. http://dx.doi.org/10.1016/S0140-6376(08)61706-7; Moreno-Peral, P., Conejo-Cerón, S., Motrico, E., Rodríguez-Morejón, A., Fernández, A., García-Campayo, J., . . . Bellón, J. Á. (2014). Risk factors for the onset of panic and generalised anxiety disorders in the general adult population: A systematic review of cohort studies. *Journal of Affective Disorders, 168,* 337–348. http://dx.doi.org/10.1016/j.jad.2014.06.021; and Stein, M. B., Walker, J. R., Anderson, G., Hazen, A. L., Ross, C. A., Eldridge, G., & Forde, D. R. (1996). Childhood physical and sexual abuse in patients with anxiety disorders in a community sample. *The American Journal of Psychiatry, 153,* 275–277. http://dx.doi.org/10.1176/ajp.153.2.275
94. See, e.g., Bremner, J. D., Southwick, S. M., Johnson, D. R., Yehuda, R., & Charney, D. S. (1993). Childhood physical abuse and combat-related posttraumatic stress disorder in Vietnam veterans. *The American Journal of Psychiatry, 150,* 235–239. http://dx.doi.org/10.1176/ajp.150.2.235
95. Listenbee, R. L., Jr., Torre, J., Boyle, G., Cooper, S. W., Deer, S., Durfee, D. T., . . . Taguba, A. (2012, December 12). *Report of the Attorney General's National Task Force on Children Exposed to Violence.* Washington, DC: U.S. Department of Justice, p. 12. Retrieved from https://www.justice.gov/defendingchildhood/cev-rpt-full.pdf
96. Gershoff, E. T., Goodman, G. S., Miller-Perrin, C. L., Holden, G. W., Jackson, Y., & Kazdin, A. E. (2018). The strength of the causal evidence against physical punishment of children and its implications for parents, psychologists, and policymakers. *American Psychologist, 73,* 626–638, p. 626. http://dx.doi.org/10.1037/amp0000327
97. Gershoff, Goodman, Miller-Perrin, Holden, Jackson, Y., & Kazdin, (2018). The strength of the causal evidence against physical punishment of children, p. 634.
98. Gershoff, Goodman, Miller-Perrin, Holden, Jackson, & Kazdin, (2018). The strength of the causal evidence against physical punishment of children, p. 630. The latter conclusion was based in part on work by Andrew Grogan-Kaylor. See, e.g., Grogan-Kaylor, A. (2004). The effect of corporal punishment on antisocial behavior in children. *Social Work Research, 28,* 153–162. http://dx.doi.org/10.1093/swr/28.3.153; and Grogan-Kaylor, A. (2005). Corporal punishment and the growth trajectory of children's antisocial behavior. *Child Maltreatment, 10,* 283–292. http://dx.doi.org/10.1177/1077559505277803
99. Dodge, K. A., Bates, J. E., & Petit, G. S. (1990). Mechanisms in the cycle of violence. *Science, 250,* 1678–1683. http://dx.doi.org/10.1126/science.2270481; Widom, C. S. (1989). Child abuse, neglect, and adult behavior: Research design and findings on criminality, violence, and child abuse. *American Journal of Orthopsychiatry,* 59, 355–367; Widom, C. S. (1989). The cycle of violence. *Science, 244,* 160–166. http://dx.doi.org/10.1126/science.2704995
100. See, e.g., Truscott, D. (1992). Intergenerational transmission of violent behavior in adolescent males. *Aggressive Behavior, 18,* 327–335. http://dx.doi.org/10.1002/1098-2337(1992)18:5<327::AID-AB2480180502>3.0CO;2-O. Truscott's early study reported that "violent adolescent behavior was found to be associated with being physically and verbally aggressed against by the father" (p. 332).

101. For example, Straus, M. A. (1991). Discipline and deviance: Physical punishment of children and violence and other crime in adulthood. *Social Problems, 38,* 133–154. http://dx.doi.org/10.2307/800524
102. Rivera, B., & Widom, C. S. (1990). Childhood victimization and violent offending. *Violence and Victims, 5,* 19–35, p. 20.
103. For example, Dutton and Hart found that some 41% of the federal prison inmates they studied had been victims of some form of serious child abuse. Those who had been abused were not only 3 times more likely to have engaged in violent crime than those who were not, but the researchers also found that specific forms of child abuse were associated with specific, similar forms of adult violence. See Dutton, D. G., Hart, S. D. (1992). Evidence for long-term, specific effects of childhood abuse and neglect on criminal behavior in men. *International Journal of Offender Therapy and Comparative Criminology, 36,* 129–137. http://dx.doi.org/10.1177/0306624X9203600205
104. See, e.g., McCormack, A., Rokous, F. E., Hazelwood, R. R., & Burgess, A. W. (1992). An exploration of incest in the childhood development of serial rapists. *Journal of Family Violence, 7,* 219–228. http://dx.doi.org/10.1007/BF00979029. These authors reported that "early sexual abuse is responded to by reenactment behavior as an attempt to manage the confusion and stress generated by the sexual activities" (p. 226).
105. For example, one study of a random sample of male prisoners incarcerated in a rural state in the Northeastern United States found that fully 40% of them had been the victims of childhood sexual abuse, a much higher percentage than had committed sex-related offenses. Researchers found that the prisoners who had been sexually abused as children also were significantly more likely to manifest diagnosable psychiatric disorders than those who had not been victimized in this way. Fondaraco, K. M., Holt, J. C., & Powell, T. A. (1999). Psychological impact of childhood sexual abuse on male inmates: The importance of perception. *Child Abuse & Neglect, 23,* 361–369. http://dx.doi.org/10.1016/S0145-2134(99)00004-6
106. Doumas, D., Margolin, G., & John, R. S. (1994). The intergenerational transmission of aggression across three generations. *Journal of Family Violence, 9,* 157–175, p. 169 (emphasis added). http://dx.doi.org/10.1007/BF01531961. In any event, scholars and researchers have known for decades that abusive parenting and poor psychosocial functioning by parents that also often includes criminal behavior tends to replicate itself in the adults who were once its childhood victims. See, e.g., Rutter, M., Quinton, D., & Liddle, C. (1990). Parenting in two generations: Looking backwards and looking forwards. In N. Madge (Ed.), *Families at risk* (pp. 60–98). London, England: Heinemann; Tolman, R. M., & Bennett, L. W. (1990). A review of quantitative research on men who batter. *Journal of Interpersonal Violence, 5,* 87–118. http://dx.doi.org/10.1177/088626090005001007
107. See, e.g., Browne, A., & Finkelhor, D. (1986). The impact of child sexual abuse: A review of the research. *Psychological Bulletin, 99,* 66–77. http://dx.doi.org/10.1037/0033-2909.99.1.66; Liem, J. H., & Boudenwyn, A. C. (1999). Contextualizing the effects of childhood sexual abuse on adult self- and social functioning: An attachment theory perspective. *Child Abuse & Neglect, 23,* 1141–1157. http://dx.doi.org/10.1016/S0145-2134(99)00081-2; Maniglio, R. (2009). The impact of sexual abuse on health: A systematic review of reviews. *Clinical Psychology Review, 29,* 647–657. http://dx.doi.org/j.cpr.2009.08.003; Molnar, B. E., Berkman, L. F., & Buka, S. L. (2001). Psychopathology, childhood sexual abuse and other childhood adversities: Relative links to subsequent suicidal behavior in the US. *Psychological Medicine, 31,* 965–977. http://dx.doi.org/10.1017/S0033291701004329; Molnar, B., Buka, S., & Kessler, R. (2001). Child sexual abuse and subsequent psychopathology: Results from the National Comorbidity Study. *American Journal of Public Health, 91,* 753–760. http://dx.doi.org/10.2105/AJPH.91.5.753; Paolucci,

E. O., Genuis, M. L., & Violato, C. (2001). A meta-analysis of the published research on the effects of child sexual abuse. *Journal of Psychology, 135,* 17–36. http://dx.doi.org/10.1080/00223980109603677; Silverman, A. B., Reinherz, H. Z., & Giaconia, R. M. (1996). The long-term sequelae of child and adolescent abuse: A longitudinal community study. *Child Abuse & Neglect, 20,* 709–723. http://dx.doi.org/10.1016/0145-2134(96)00059-2; Statham, D. J., Heath, A. C., Madden, P. A., Bucholz, K. K., Bierut, L., Dinwiddie, S. H., . . . Martin, N. G. (1998). Suicidal behavior: An epidemiological and genetic study. *Psychological Medicine, 28,* 839–855.

108. Vachon, D. D., Krueger, R. F., Rogosch, F. A., & Cicchetti, D. (2015). Assessment of the harmful psychiatric and behavioral effects of different forms of child maltreatment. *JAMA Psychiatry, 72,* 1135–1142, p. 1141 (emphasis added). http://dx.doi.org/10.1001/jamapsychiatry.2015.1792
109. Egeland (2009). Taking stock: Childhood emotional maltreatment and developmental psychopathology, p. 22.
110. Mills, Scott, Alati, O'Callaghan, Najman, & Strathearn (2013). Child maltreatment and adolescent mental health problems, p. 300.
111. See, e.g., Allen, B. (2010). Childhood psychological abuse and adult aggression: The mediating role of self-capacities. *Journal of Interpersonal Violence, 20,* 1–18; Horan, J., & Widom, C. (2015). Cumulative childhood risk and adult functioning in abused and neglected children grown up. *Development and Psychopathology, 27,* 927–941; Widom, C. (2017). Long-term impact of childhood abuse and neglect on crime and violence. *Clinical Psychology: Science and Practice, 24,* 186–202.
112. See Reid, J., Patterson, G., & Snyder, J. (2002). *Antisocial behavior in children and adolescents: A developmental analysis and model for intervention.* Washington, DC: American Psychological Association.
113. See, e.g., Mills, Scott, Alati, O'Callaghan, Najman, & Strathearn, (2013). Child maltreatment and adolescent mental health problems.
114. Lake, E. S. (1995). Offenders' experiences of violence: A comparison of male and female inmates as victims. *Deviant Behavior, 16,* 269–290. http://dx.doi.org/10.1080/01639625.1995.9968002
115. Lewis, D. O., Shanok, S. S., Grant, M., & Ritvo, E. (1983). Homicidally aggressive young children: Neuropsychiatric and experiential correlates. *The American Journal of Psychiatry, 140,* 148–153. http://dx.doi.org/10.1176/ajp.140.2.148. This article describes a number of ways in which the early lives of "homicidally aggressive" young patients differed those of other troubled children and concluding, among other things, that "the households in which these children were raised were filled with violence."
116. Lattimore, P. K., Visher, C. A., & Linster, R. L. (1995). Predicting rearrest for violence among serious youthful offenders. *Journal of Research on Crime and Delinquency, 32,* 54–83, p. 76. http://dx.doi.org/10.1177/0022427895032001003
117. See, e.g., Leijdesdorff, S., van Doesum, K., Popma, A., Klaassen, R., & van Amelsvoort, T. (2017). Prevalence of psychopathology in children of parents with mental illness and/or addiction: An up to date narrative review. *Current Opinion in Psychiatry, 30,* 312–317. http://dx.doi.org/10.1097.YCO.0000000000000341. An international survey of nine countries estimated that between 5.3% and 6.7% of the more than 50,000 respondents were exposed to this specific risk factor and that it was one component of disrupted family functioning that was strongly associated with adult mental health problems. See Kessler, R. C. McLaughlin K. A., Green, J. G., Gruber, M. J., Sampson, N. A., Zaslavsky, A. M., . . . Williams, D. R. (2010). Childhood adversities and adult psychopathology in the WHO World Mental Health Surveys. *British Journal of Psychiatry, 197,* 378–385. http://dx.doi.org/10.1192.bjp.bp.110.080499

118. England, M. J., & Sim, L. J. (Eds.). (2009). *Depression in parents, parenting, and children: Opportunities to improve identification, treatment, and prevention*. Washington, DC: National Academies Press.

119. England & Sim (2009), *Depression in parents, parenting, and children*, p. 5.

120. See, e.g., Anda, R. F., Whitfield, C. L., Felitti, V. J., Chapman, D., Edwards, V. J., Dube, S. R., & Williamson, D. F. (2002). Adverse childhood experiences, alcoholic parents, and later risks of alcoholism and depression. *Psychiatric Services, 53,* 1001–1009. http://dx.doi.org/10.1176/appi.ps.53.8.1001; Burstein, M., Stanger, C., Kamon, J., & Dumenci, L. (2006). Parent psychopathology, parenting, and child internalizing problems in substance-abusing families. *Psychology of Addictive Behaviors, 20,* 97–106. http://dx.doi.org/10.1037/0893-164X.20.2.97; Dam, K., & Hall, E. O. (2016). Navigating in an unpredictable daily life: A metasynthesis on children's experiences living with a parent with severe mental illness. *Scandinavian Journal of Caring Sciences, 30,* 442–457. http://dx.doi.org/10.1111/scs.12285; Jaffee, S. R., Belsky, J., Harrington, H., Caspi, A., Moffitt, T. E. (2006). When parents have a history of conduct disorder: How is the caretaking environment affected? *Journal of Abnormal Psychology, 115,* 309–319. http://dx.doi.org/10.1037/0021-843X.115.2.309; Murphy, G., Peters, K., Wilkes, L. M., & Jackson, D. (2016). Adult children of parents with mental illness: Losing oneself. Who am I? *Issues in Mental Health Nursing, 37,* 668–673. http://dx.doi.org/10.1080/01612840.2016.1178359; Ranning, A., Munk Loursen, T., Thorup, A., Hjorthøj, C., & Nordentoft, M. (2016). Children of parents with serious mental illness: With whom do they grow up? A prospective, population-based study. *Journal of the American Academy of Child & Adolescent Psychiatry, 55,* 953–961. http://dx.doi.org/10.1016/j.aac.2016.07.776; and Reupert, A., & Maybery, D. (2016). What do we know about families where parents have a mental illness? A systematic review. *Child & Youth Services, 37,* 98–111. http://dx.doi.org/10.1080/0145935X.2016.1104037

121. Kruttschnitt, C., McLeod, J. D., & Dornfeld, M. (1994). The economic environment of child abuse. *Social Problems, 41,* 299–315, p. 307. http://dx.doi.org/10.2307/3096935

122. Luciano, A., Nicholson, J., & Meara, E. (2014). The economic status of parents with serious mental illness in the United States. *Psychiatric Rehabilitation Journal, 37,* 242–250. http://dx.doi.org/10.1037/prj0000087

123. See, e.g., Giglio, J. J., & Kaufman, E. (1990). The relationship between child and adult psychopathology in children of alcoholics. *International Journal of the Addictions, 25,* 263–290; Hall, C. W., & Webster, R. E. (2002). Traumatic symptomatology characteristics of adult children of alcoholics. *Journal of Drug Education, 32,* 195–211. http://dx.doi.org/10.2190/U29W-LF3W-748L-A48M; Harter, S. L. (2000). Psychosocial adjustment of adult children of alcoholics: A review of recent empirical literature. *Clinical Psychology Review, 20,* 311–337; Klostermann, K., Chen, R., Kelley, M. L., Schroeder, V. M., Braitman, A. L., Mignone, T. (2011). Coping behavior and depressive symptoms in adult children of alcoholics. *Substance Use & Misuse, 46,* 1162–1168. http://dx.doi.org/10.3109/10826080903452546; and Mathew, R. J., Wilson, W. H., Blazer, D. G., & George, L. K. (1993). Psychiatric disorders in adult children of alcoholics: Data from the Epidemiologic Catchment Area project. *The American Journal of Psychiatry, 150,* 793–800. http://dx.doi.org/10.1176/ajp.150.5.793

124. See, e.g., Caudill, B. D., Hoffman, J. A., Hubbard, R. L., Flynn, P. M., & Luckey, J. W. (1994). Parental history of substance abuse as a risk factor in predicting crack smokers' substance abuse, illegal activities, and psychiatric status. *American Journal of Drug and Alcohol Abuse, 20,* 341–354; Farrington, D. P., Jolliffe, D., Loeber, R., Stouthamer-Loeber, M., & Kalb, L. M. (2001). The concentration of offenders in families, and family criminality in the prediction of boy's delinquency.

Journal of Adolescence, 24, 579–596. http://dx.doi.org/10.1006/jado.2001.0424; Preski, S., & Shelton, D. (2001). The role of contextual, child and parent factors in predicting criminal outcomes in adolescence. *Issues in Mental Health Nursing, 22,* 197–205; Prochnow, J. E., & DeFronzo, J. V. (1997). The impact of economic and parental characteristics on juvenile misconduct. *Journal of Emotional and Behavioral Disorders, 5,* 119–124. http://dx.doi.org/10.1177/106342669700500026; Tzoumakis, S., Dean, K., Green, M. J., Zheng, C., Kariuki, M., Harris, F., . . . Laurens, K. R. (2017). The impact of parental offending on offspring aggression in early childhood: A population-based record linkage study. *Social Psychiatry and Psychiatric Epidemiology, 52,* 445–455. http://dx.doi.org/10.1007/s00127-017-1347-3

125. Durose, M. R., Harlow, C. W., Langan, P. A., Motivans, M. A., Rantala, R. R., & Smith, E. L. (2005). *Family violence statistics: Including statistics on strangers and acquaintances* (NCJ 207846). Washington DC: Bureau of Justice Statistics. http://dx.doi.org/10.1037/e412162005-001
126. According to the Bureau of Justice Statistics, about three quarters of the perpetrators of family violence are men and about three quarters of the victims are women. See Durose, Harlow, Langan, Motivans, Rantala, & Smith (2005), *Family violence statistics: Including statistics on strangers and acquaintances.*
127. Evans, S. E., Davies, C., & DiLillo, D. (2008). Exposure to domestic violence: A meta-analysis of child and adolescent outcomes. *Aggression and Violent Behavior, 13,* 131–140, p. 132. http://dx.doi.org/10.1016/j.avb.2008.02.005
128. This literature is extensive. See, e.g., Bogat, G. A., DeJonghe, E., Levendosky, A. A., Davidson, W. S., & von Eye, A. (2006). Trauma symptoms among infants exposed to intimate partner violence. *Child Abuse & Neglect, 30,* 109–125. http://dx.doi.org/j.chiabu.2005.09.002; Fantuzzo, J., Boruch, R., Beriama, A., Atkins, M., & Marcus, S. (1997). Domestic violence and children: Prevalence and risk in five major U.S. cities. *Journal of the American Academy of Child & Adolescent Psychiatry, 36,* 116–122. http://dx.doi.org/10.1097/00004583-199701000-00025; Graham-Bermann, S. A., & Levendosky, A. A. (1998). Traumatic stress symptoms in children of battered women. *Journal of Interpersonal Violence, 13,* 111–128. http://dx.doi.org/10.1177/088626098013001007; Holden, G. W., & Ritchie, K. L. (1991). Linking extreme marital discord, child rearing, and child behavior problems: Evidence from battered women. *Child Development, 62,* 311–327; Kitzmann, K. M., Gaylord, N. K., Holt, A. R., & Kenny, E. D. (2003). Child witnesses to domestic violence: A meta-analytic review. *Journal of Consulting & Clinical Psychology, 71,* 339–352. http://dx.doi.org/10.1037/0022-006x.71.2.339; Rosenberg, M. S. (1987). Children of battered women: The effects of witnessing violence on their social problem-solving abilities. *Behavior Therapist, 10,* 85–89; Rosenberg, M., & Giberson, R. (1991). The child witness of family violence. In R. Ammerman & M. Hersen (Eds.), *Case studies in family violence* (pp. 231–253). New York, NY: Plenum Press; Stagg, V., Wills, G. D., & Howell, M. (1989). Psychopathology in early childhood witnesses of family violence. *Topics in Early Childhood Special Education, 9,* 73–87. http://dx.doi.org/10.1177/027112148900900206; and Zeanah, C., & Scheeringa, M. (1997). The experience and effects of violence in infancy. In J. Osofsky (Ed.), *Children in a violent society* (pp. 97–123). New York, NY: Guilford Press.
129. Levendosky & Bogat (2006), Domestic violence and infancy, p. 5.
130. Levendosky, A. A., Bogat, G. A., & Martinez-Torteya, C. (2013). PTSD symptoms in young children exposed to intimate partner violence. *Violence Against Women, 19,* 187–201. http://dx.doi.org/10.1177/1077801213476458
131. Bogat, G. A., DeJonghe, E., Levendosky, A. A., Davidson, W. S., & von Eye, A. (2006). Trauma symptoms among infants exposed to intimate partner violence. *Child Abuse & Neglect, 30,* 109–125. http://dx.doi.org/10.1016/j.chiabu.2005.09.002

132. Wolfe, D. A., Crooks, C. V., Lee, V., McIntyre-Smith, A., & Jaffe, P. G. (2003). The effects of children's exposure to domestic violence: A meta-analysis and critique. *Clinical Child and Family Psychology Review, 6,* 171–187. http://dx.doi.org/10.1023/A:1024910416164
133. Camacho, K., Ehrensaft, M. K., & Cohen, P. (2012). Exposure to intimate partner violence, peer relations, and risk for internalizing behaviors: A prospective longitudinal study. *Journal of Interpersonal Violence, 27,* 125–141. http://dx.doi.org/10.1177/0886260511416474
134. Wolfe, D., Jaffe, P., & Wilson, S. (1988). A multivariate investigation of children's adjustment to family violence. In G. Hotaling & D. Sugarman (Eds.), *Family abuses and its consequences* (pp. 228–239). Newbury Park, CA: Sage.
135. Herrenkohl, T. I., Sousa, C., Tajima, E. A., Herrenkohl, R. C., & Moylan, C. A. (2008). Intersection of child abuse and children's exposure to domestic violence. *Trauma, Violence & Abuse, 9,* 84–99. http://dx.doi.org/10.1177/1524838008314797
136. Park, A., Smith, C., & Ireland, T. (2012). Equivalent harm? The relative roles of maltreatment and exposure to intimate partner violence in antisocial outcomes for young adults. *Children and Youth Services Review, 34,* 962–972. http://dx.doi.org/10.1016/j.childyouth.2012.01.029
137. See, e.g., Buka, S. L., Stichick, T. L., Birdthistle, I., & Earls, F. J. (2001). Youth exposure to violence: Prevalence, risks and consequences. *American Journal of Orthopsychiatry, 71,* 298–310; Herrera, V. M., & McCloskey, L. A. (2001). Gender differences in the risk of delinquency among youth exposed to family violence. *Child Abuse & Neglect, 25,* 1037–1051; Tajima, E. A., Herrendohl, T. I., Huang, B., & Whitney, S. D. (2004). Measuring child maltreatment: A comparison of prospective parent reports and retrospective adolescent reports. *American Journal of Orthopsychiatry, 74,* 424–435. http://dx.doi.org/10.1037/0002-9432.74.4.424; Moylan, C. A., Herrenkohl, T. I., Sousa, C., Tajima, E. A., Herrenkohl, R. C., & Russo, M. J. (2010). The effects of child abuse and exposure to domestic violence on adolescent internalizing and externalizing behavior problems. *Journal of Family Violence, 25,* 53–63. http://10.1007/s10896-009-9269-9; and Oakley, C., Harris, S., Fahy, T., Murphy, D., & Picchioni, M. (2016). Childhood adversity and conduct disorder: A developmental pathway to violence in schizophrenia. *Schizophrenia Research, 172,* 54–59. http://dx.doi.org/10.1016/j.schres.2016.01.047
138. See, e.g., Wheaton, B. (1990). Life transitions, role histories, and mental health. *American Sociological Review, 55,* 209–223. http://dx.doi.org/10.2307/2095627
139. See, e.g., Hetherington, E., & Clingempeel, W. G. (1992). *Coping with marital transitions: A family systems perspective.* Chicago, IL: University of Chicago Press; Laub, J. H., & Sampson, R. J. (1988). Unraveling families and delinquency: A reanalysis of the Gluecks' data. *Criminology, 26,* 355–380. http://dx.doi.org/10.111/j.1745-9125.1988.tb00846.x; Brown, S. L. (2006). Family structure transitions and adolescent well-being. *Demography, 43,* 447–461. http://dx.doi.org/10.1353/dem.2006.00
140. See, e.g., Amato, P. R. (2000). The consequences of divorce for adults and children. *Journal of Marriage and the Family, 62,* 1269–1287. http://dx.doi.org/10.1111/j.1741-3737.2000.01269.x
141. Schroeder, R. D., Osgood, A. K., & Oghia, M. J. (2010). Family transitions and juvenile delinquency. *Sociological Inquiry, 80,* 579–604, p. 582. http://dx.doi.org/10.1111/j.1475-682X.2010.00351.x
142. Brown (2006), Family structure transitions and adolescent well-being, p. 448.
143. Thornberry, T. P., Smith, C. A., Rivera, C., Huizinga, D., & Stouthamer-Loeber, M. (1999). *Family disruption and delinquency.* Washington, DC: U.S. Department of Justice, p. 4. See also Capaldi, D. M., & Patterson, G. R. (1991). Relation of parental transition to boys' adjustment problems: I. A linear hypothesis: II. Mothers at risk for transitions and unskilled parenting. *Developmental Psychology, 27,* 489–504.

http://dx.doi.org/10.1037/0012-1649.27.3.489; Fergusson, D. M., Horwood, L. J., & Linskey, M. T. (1992). Family change, parental discord and early offending. *Journal of Child Psychology and Psychiatry, 33,* 1059–1075. http://dx.doi.org/10.111/j.1469-7610.1992.tb00925.x; Suh, G. W., Fabricius, W. V., Stevenson, M. M., Parke, R. D., Cookston, J. T., Braver, S. L., & Saenz, D. S. (2016). Effects of the interparental relationship on adolescents' emotional security and adjustment: The important role of fathers. *Developmental Psychology, 52,* 1666–1678. http://dx.doi.org/10.1037/dev0000204; and Stevenson, M. M., Fabricius, W. V., Braver, S. L., & Cookston, J. T. (2018). Associations between parental relocation following separation in childhood and maladjustment in adolescence and young adulthood. *Psychology, Public Policy, and Law, 24,* 365–378. http://dx.doi.org/10.1037/e406762005-001

144. See, e.g., Hango, D. W. (2006). The long-term effect of childhood residential mobility on educational attainment. *Sociological Quarterly, 47,* 631–664; Humke, C., & Shaefer, C. (1995). Relocation: A review of the effects of residential mobility on children and adolescents. *Psychology: A Journal of Human Behavior, 32,* 16–24; and Roy, A. L., McCoy, D. C., & Raver, C. C. (2014). Instability versus quality: Residential mobility, neighborhood poverty, and children's self-regulation. *Developmental Psychology, 50,* 1891–1896. http://dx.doi.org/10.1037/a0036984; and Rosenbaum, J. E. (1995). Changing the geography of opportunity by expanding residential choice: Lessons from the Gautreaux program. *Housing Policy Debate, 6,* 231–269. http://dx.doi.org/10.1080/10511482.1995.9521186
145. Keels, M., Duncan, G. J., Deluca, S., Mendenhall, R., & Rosenbaum, J. (2005). Fifteen years later: Can residential mobility programs provide a long-term escape from neighborhood segregation, crime, and poverty? *Demography, 42,* 51–73. http://dx.doi.org/10.1353/dem.2005.0005
146. Osypuk, T. L., Tchetgen, E. J., Acevedo-Garcia, D., Earls, F. J., Lincoln, A., Schmidt, N. M., & Glymour, M. M. (2012). Differential mental health effects of neighborhood relocation among youth in vulnerable families: Results from a randomized trial. *Archives of General Psychiatry, 69,* 1284–1294. http://dx.doi.org/10.1001/archgenpsychiatry.2012.449
147. Osypuk, Tchetgen, Acevedo-Garcia, Earls, Lincoln, Schmidt, & Glymour (2012). *Differential mental health effects of neighborhood relocation,* p. 1290.
148. This appears to be especially true in the case of children who are already experiencing maltreatment. See Herrenkohl, E. C., Herrenkohl, R. C., & Egolf, B. P. (2003). The psychosocial consequences of living environment instability on maltreated children. *American Journal of Orthopsychiatry, 73,* 367–380. http://dx.doi.org/10.1037/0002-9432.73.4.367
149. See, e.g., Wills, T. A., & Cleary, S. D. (1996). How are social support effects mediated? A test with parental support and adolescent substance use. *Journal of Personality and Social Psychology, 71,* 937–952. It is tempting to view the dry-sounding term "extreme residential mobility" superficially, and discount the way it feels to the children subjected to it. However, consider the description by African American writer Brent Staples of the pattern of instability that characterizes many poor families:

> We moved all the time. We went on and on like bedouins with couches, tables, and mattresses jumbled in the backs of pickup trucks. We moved as the family grew. We moved when my parents were separated and again when they reconciled. We moved when we fell behind in the rent. We moved when the sheriffs put our furniture on the sidewalk. We moved after the family had pounded a house to pieces. We'd had seven different addresses by the time I reached the eighth grade. That's why I was never where I was. The move was out there lurking, just off the mental shore. Best to be ready when it came.

Staples, B. (1994). *Parallel time: Growing up in Black and White.* New York, NY: Pantheon, p. 11.

150. See, e.g., Haynie, D. L., South, S. J., & Bose, S. (2006). Residential mobility and attempted suicide among adolescents: An individual-level analysis. *Sociological Quarterly, 47,* 693–721. http://dx.doi.org/10.1111/j.1533-8525.2006.00063.x; Paksarian, D., Eaton, W. W., Mortensen, P. B., & Pedersen, C. B. (2015). Childhood residential mobility, schizophrenia, and bipolar disorder: A population-based study in Denmark. *Schizophrenia Bulletin, 41,* 346–354. http://dx.doi.org/10.1093/schbul/sbu074; Qin, P., Mortensen, P. B., & Pedersen, C. B. (2009). Frequent change of residence and risk of attempted and completed suicide among children and adolescents. *Archives of General Psychiatry, 66,* 628–632. http://dx.doi.org/10.1001/archgenpsychiatry.2009.20
151. Oishi, S., & Schimmack, U. (2010). Residential mobility, well-being, and mortality. *Journal of Personality and Social Psychology, 98,* 980–994. http://dx.doi.org/10.1037/a0019389
152. DeWit, D. J. (1999). Frequent childhood geographic relocation: Its impact on drug use initiation and the development of alcohol and drug-related problems among adolescents and young adults. *Addictive Behaviors, 23,* 623–634, p. 623 (internal citations omitted). See also Parente, M. E., & Mahoney, J. L. (2009). Residential mobility and exposure to neighborhood crime: Risks for young children's aggression. *Journal of Community Psychology, 37,* 559–578. http://dx.doi.org/10.1002/jcop.20314
153. See, e.g., Vernberg, E. M. (1990). Experiences with peers following relocation during early adolescence. *Journal of Orthopsychiatry, 60,* 466–472. http://dx.doi.org/10.1037/h0079160
154. Herrenkohl, Herrenkohl, & Egolf (2003), The psychosocial consequences of living environment instability on maltreated children, p. 377. In addition, see Eckenrode, J., Rowe, E., Laird, M., & Brathwaite, J. (1995). Mobility as a mediator of the effects of child maltreatment on academic performance. *Child Development, 66,* 1130–1142; Hagan, J., MacMillan, R., & Wheaton, B. (1996). New kid in town: Social capital and the life course effects of family migration on children. *American Sociological Review, 61,* 368–385. http://dx.doi.org/10.2307/2096354; Tucker, C. J., Marx, J., & Long, L. (1998). "Moving on": Residential mobility and children's school lives. *Sociology of Education, 71,* 111–129. http://dx.doi.org/10.2307/26732544
155. Downey, G., Khouri, H., & Feldman, S. (1997). Early interpersonal trauma and later adjustment: The meditational role of rejection sensitivity. In D. Cicchetti & S. Toth (Eds.), *Developmental perspectives on trauma: Theory, research, and intervention* (pp. 85–114). Rochester, NY: University of Rochester Press; and Pietrzak, J., Downey, G., & Ayduk, O. (2005). Rejection sensitivity as an interpersonal vulnerability. In M. Baldwin (Ed.), *Interpersonal cognition* (pp. 62–84). New York, NY: Guilford Press.
156. London, B., Downey, G., Bonica, C., & Paltin, I. (2007). Social causes and consequences of rejection sensitivity. *Journal of Research on Adolescence, 17,* 481–506. http://dx.doi.org/10.1111/j.1532-7795.2007.00531.x
157. See, e.g., Dupere, V., Archambault, I., Dion, E., Leventhal, T., & Anderson, S. (2014). School mobility and school-age children's social adjustment. *Developmental Psychology, 51,* 197–210. http://dx.doi.org/10.1111/j.1532-7795.2007.00531.x; and South, S. J., Haynie, D. L., & Bose, S. (2007). Student mobility and school dropout. *Social Science Research, 36,* 68–94. http://dx.doi.org/10.1016/j.ssresearch.2005.10.001. Exceptions to this rule can occur when families move in order to improve their residential or home environment. See, e.g., Hango, D. W. (2006), The long-term effect of childhood residential mobility on educational attainment.
158. See, e.g., Fite, P. J., Hendrickson, M., Rubens, S. L., Gabrielli, J., & Evans, S. (2013). The role of peer rejection in the link between reactive aggression and academic performance. *Child & Youth Care Forum, 42,* 193–205. http://dx.doi.org/10.1007/s10566-013-9199-9; Henry, K. L., Knight, K. E., & Thornberry, T. P.

(2012). School disengagement as a predictor of dropout, delinquency, and problem substance use during adolescence and early adulthood. *Journal of Youth and Adolescence, 41,* 156–166; Jose, P. E., Ryan, N., & Pryor, J. (2012). Does social connectedness promote a greater sense of well-being in adolescence over time? *Journal of Research on Adolescence, 22,* 235–251. http://dx.doi.org/10.1111/j.1532-7795.2012.00783.x; Najaka, S. S., Gottfredson, D. C., & Wilson, D. B. (2001). A meta-analytic inquiry into the relationship between selected risk factors and problem behavior. *Prevention Science, 2,* 257–271. http://dx.doi.org/10.1023/A:1013610115351; and Wang, M. T., & Fredricks, J. A. (2014). The reciprocal links between school engagement, youth problem behaviors, and school dropout during adolescence. *Child Development, 85,* 722–737. http://dx.doi.org/10.1111/cdev.12138

159. Sweeten, G., Bushway, S. D., & Paternoster, R. (2009). Does dropping out of school mean dropping into delinquency? *Criminology, 47,* 47–91, p. 79. http://dx.doi.org/10.1111/j.1745-9125.2009.00139.x
160. See, e.g., Thornberry, T. P., Moore, M., & Christenson, R. L. (1985). The effect of dropping out of high school on subsequent criminal behavior. *Criminology, 23,* 3–18. http://dx.doi.org/10.1111/j.1745-9125.1985.tb00323.x; and Hatt, B. (2011). Still I rise: Caught between the worlds of schools and prisons. *Urban Review, 43,* 476–490. http://dx.doi.org/10.1007/s11256-011-0185-y. Dropping out is often the culmination of a series of earlier problematic events, and its effects on subsequent delinquent and criminal behavior depend in part on the reasons a young person decides to leave school. See, e.g., Drapela, L. A. (2004), Does dropping out of high school cause deviant behavior? An analysis of the national education longitudinal study. *Deviant Behavior, 26,* 47–62. http://dx.doi.org/10.1080/016396290503006; and Sweeten, Bushway, & Paternoster (2009). Does dropping out of school mean dropping into delinquency?
161. Witnessing violence in the community appears to be more prevalent than witnessing parental violence and has independently harmful effects (including PTSD and major depressive disorder) that vary with nature of the perceived threat. See Zinzow, H. M., Ruggiero, K. J., Resnick, H., Hanson, R., Smith, D., Saunders, B., & Kilpatrick, D. (2009). Prevalence and mental health correlates of witnessed parental and community violence in a national sample of adolescents. *Journal of Child Psychology and Psychiatry, 50,* 441–450. http://dx.doi.org/10.1111/j.1469-7610.2008.02004.x
162. Fowler, P. J., Tompsett, C. J., Braciszewski, J. M., Jacques-Tiura, A. J., & Baltes, B. B. (2009). Community violence: A meta-analysis on the effect of exposure and mental health outcomes of children and adolescents. *Development and Psychopathology, 21,* 227–259. http://dx.doi.org/10.1017/S0954579409000145
163. Fowler, Tompsett, Braciszewski, Jacques-Tiura, & Baltes (2009), Community violence, p. 248.
164. Elsaesser, C. (2018). The longitudinal relations between dimensions of community violence exposure and developmental outcomes among adolescent ethnic minority males. *Psychology of Violence, 8,* 409–417, p. 414. http://dx.doi.org/10.1037/vio0000140. Elsaesser found that although each form of exposure appeared to have distinct immediate effects on psychological development, all forms of exposure had problematic consequences later in life. In addition, a child's or adolescent's relationship to the *source* of the community violence—whether it was someone he or she knew or was a stranger—also had an impact. Exposure to violence that was perpetrated by persons that a child or adolescent knew personally had a significantly greater impact.
165. Kennedy, T. M., & Ceballo, R. (2016). Emotionally numb: Desensitization to community violence exposure among urban youth. *Developmental Psychology, 52,* 778–789. http://dx.doi.org/10.1037/dev0000112

166. For examples of very early published reports that described the relationship between child maltreatment and later aggression, see Curtis (1963), Violence breeds violence—Perhaps; Eron, L. D., Walder, L. O., Toigo, R., & Lefkowitz, M. M. (1963). Social class, parental punishment for aggression, and child aggression. *Child Development, 34,* 849–867; Kopernik, L. (1964). The family as a breeding ground of violence. *Corrective Psychiatry and the Journal of Social Therapy, 10,* 315–322; Lefkowitz, M. M., Walder, L. O., & Eron, L. D. (1963). Punishment, identification, and aggression. *Merrill-Palmer Quarterly, 9,* 159–174; Silver, Dublin, & Lourie (1969), Does violence breed violence?; Yarrow, M., Campbell, J., & Burton, R. (1968). Theories and correlates of child aggression. In M. Radke-Yarrow, J. Campbell, & R. Burton (Eds.), *Child rearing: An inquiry into research and methods* (pp. 55–93). San Francisco, CA: Jossey-Bass.
167. Authorities face up to the child-abuse problem. (1976, May 3). *U.S. News & World Report,* pp. 83–84, p. 84. See also Sargent, D. (1971). The lethal situation: Transmission of urge to kill from parent to child. In J. Fawcett (Ed.), *Dynamics of violence* (pp. 105–113). Chicago, IL: American Medical Association; and Silver, L. B., Dublin, C. C., & Lourie, R. S. (1969). Does violence breed violence? As early as the 1970s, the pattern by which a "battered child tends to become a battering parent" was well enough established to be referred to as the "*classical* battered-child syndrome." Lystad, M. H. (1975). Violence at home: A review of the literature. *American Journal of Orthopsychiatry, 45,* 328–345, p. 334 (emphasis added). http://dx.doi.org/10.1111/j.1939-0025.1975.tb02544.x
168. Schmitt, B., & Kempe, C. (1975). Neglect and abuse of children. In V. Vaughan & R. McKay (Eds.), *Nelson textbook of pediatrics* (p. 111). Philadelphia, PA: W. B. Saunders.
169. Kerig, P., & Becker, S. (2015). Early abuse and neglect as risk factors for the development of criminal and antisocial behavior. In J. Morizot, & L. Kazemian (Eds.), *The development of criminal and antisocial behavior: Theory, research, and practical applications* (pp. 181–199). Cham, Switzerland: Springer International, p. 185. In addition to the articles cited elsewhere in this chapter, see also Hawkins, J., Herrenkhol, T., Farrington, D., Brewer, D. (2000). *Predictors of youth violence.* Juvenile Justice Bulletin. Washington, DC: U.S. Department of Justice; Ireland, T., & Widom, C. S. (1994). Childhood victimization and risk for alcohol and drug arrests. *International Journal of the Addictions, 29,* 235–274; Juon, H.-S., Doherty, E. E., & Ensminger, M. E. (2006). Childhood behavior and adult criminality: Cluster analysis in a prospective study of African Americans. *Journal of Quantitative Criminology, 22,* 193–214. http://dx.doi.org/10.1007/978-3-319-08720-7_12; Logan-Greene, P., & Jones, A. S. (2015). Chronic neglect and aggression/delinquency: A longitudinal examination. *Child Abuse & Neglect, 45,* 9–20. http://dx.doi.org/10.1016/j.chiabu.2015.04.003
170. For example, Silver, Dublin, & Lourie (1969), Does violence breed violence?
171. See, e.g., Kerig, P., & Becker, S. (2015), Early abuse and neglect as risk factors for the development of criminal and antisocial behavior.
172. Note also that a "criminogenic" risk factor is identified by the specific outcome to which it leads—juvenile or adult criminal behavior. But each one is part of a large category of risks and adverse experiences that can produce other problematic outcomes in life, among which criminal behavior is only one. For example, see Holmes, J. A. (2013). New paradigm: Developmental psychopathology. *British Journal of Psychiatry, 202,* 311. http://dx.doi.org/10.1192/bjp.202.4.31a. Holmes characterizes developmental psychopathology as "the current cutting edge," focusing on the way that "the interaction of adverse development processes"—risk factors and traumas—"within the social milieu sows the seeds for psychiatric disorder" (p. 311).

173. See Wilson, K. R., Hansen, D. J., & Li, M. (2011). The traumatic stress response in child maltreatment and resultant neuropsychological effects. *Aggression and Violent Behavior, 16*, 87–97. http://dx.doi.org/10.1016/j.avb.2010.12.007
174. Especially when children experience maltreatment in multiple ways and on a recurrent basis, they can suffer what has been termed "complex PTSD" or, in the childhood-specific term I referenced in the last chapter, "developmental trauma disorder." See, e.g., Cloitre, M., Stolbach, B. C., Herman, J. L., van der Kolk, B., Pynoos, R., Wang, J., & Petkova, E. (2009). A developmental approach to complex PTSD: Childhood and adult cumulative trauma as predictors of symptom complexity. *Journal of Traumatic Stress, 22*, 399–408. http://dx.doi.org/10.1002/jts.20444; and Van der Kolk, B. (2005). Developmental trauma disorder: Toward a rational diagnosis for children with complex trauma histories. *Psychiatric Annals, 35*, 401–408. http://dx.doi.org/10.3928/00485713-20050501-06
175. Cloitre, Stolbach, Herman, van der Kolk, Pynoos, Wang, J., & Petkova (2009). A developmental approach to complex PTSD, p. 405 (emphasis added). In addition, Bessel van der Kolk and his colleagues have found that

> [h]istories of childhood physical and sexual assaults also are associated with a host of other psychiatric problems in adolescence and adulthood: substance abuse, borderline and antisocial personality, as well as eating, dissociative, affective, somatoform, cardiovascular, metabolic, immunological, and sexual disorders.

van der Kolk, B. A., Roth, S., Pelcovitz, D., Sunday, S., & Spinazzola, J. (2005). Disorders of extreme stress: The empirical foundation of a complex adaptation to trauma. *Journal of Traumatic Stress, 18*, 389–300, p. 390 (internal references omitted). http://dx.doi.org/10.1002/jts.20047

176. Toch, H. (2017). *Violent men: An inquiry into the psychology of violence* (25th anniversary ed.). Washington, DC: American Psychological Association, p. 183.
177. Toch (2017), *Violent men*, p. 181, 182. On the relationship between self-esteem and delinquency and crime, see Mier, C., & Ladny, R. T. (2018). Does self-esteem negatively impact crime and delinquency? A meta-analytic review of 25 years of evidence. *Deviant Behavior, 39*, 1006–1022. http://dx.doi.org/10.1080/01639625.2017.1395667; and Trzesniewski, K. H., Donnellan, M. B., Moffitt, T. E., Robins, R. W., Poulton, R., & Caspi, A. (2006). Low self-esteem during adolescence predicts poor health, criminal behavior, and limited economic prospects during adulthood. *Developmental Psychology, 42*, 381–390. http://dx.doi.org/10.1037/0012-1649.42.2.381
178. Copeland, W. E., Miller-Johnson, S., Keeler, G., Angold, A., & Costello, E. J. (2007). Childhood psychiatric disorders and young adult crime: A prospective, population-based study. *The American Journal of Psychiatry, 164*, 1668–1675. http://dx.doi.org/10.1176/appi.ajp.2007.06122026
179. Fonagy, P., Moran, G. S., & Target, M. (1993). Aggression and the psychological self. *International Journal of Psychoanalysis, 74*, 471–485, p. 475.
180. Bowlby (1973), *Attachment and loss*, p. 208.
181. Burnstein, M. H. (1981). Child abandonment: Historical, sociological and psychological perspectives. *Child Psychiatry & Human Development, 11*, 213–221, p. 218. Others have suggested a pattern by which feelings of abandonment, in particular, instigate "acting out" behavior in adolescents that often leads to delinquent behavior:

> [Against] a background of emotional deprivation, the adolescent patient experiences a loss of a person who has been one of the few pillars of support to his immature personality. He then becomes depressed and starts to act out to protect himself from this feeling. By the time he is referred, he may have embarked on his acting-out behavior.

Schonfeld (1995), Depression in adolescence, p. 32.

182. See, e.g., Ackerman, B., & Brown, E. (2010). Physical and psychosocial turmoil in the home and cognitive development. In G. Evans & T. Wachs (Eds.), *Chaos and its influence on children's development: An ecological perspective* (pp. 35–47). Washington, DC: American Psychological Association; Feiring, C., Cleland, C. M., & Simon, V. A. (2009). Abuse-specific self-schemas and self-functioning: A prospective study of sexually abused youth. *Journal of Clinical Child & Adolescent Psychology, 39,* 35–50. http://dx.doi.org/10.1080/15374410903401112; and Sirin, S. R., Diemer, M. A., Jackson, L. R., Gonsalves, L., & Howell, A. (2004). Future aspirations of urban adolescents: A person-in-context model. *International Journal of Qualitative Studies in Education, 17,* 437–456. http://dx.doi.org/10.1080/0951839042000204607
183. Brumley, L. D., Jaffee, S. R., & Brumley, B. P. (2017). Pathways from childhood adversity to problem behaviors in young adulthood: The mediating role of adolescents' future expectations. *Journal of Youth and Adolescence, 46,* 1–14. http://dx.doi.org/10.1007/s10964-016-0597-9
184. Doumas, Margolin& John (1994). The intergenerational transmission of aggression across three generations, p. 157–158. That is: "children learn to aggress by observing aggression, particularly that of their parents who are familiar and powerful models." See also McCord, J. (1994). Aggression in two generations. In L. Huesmann (Ed.), *Aggressive behavior: Current perspectives* (pp. 241–251). New York, NY: Plenum.
185. As one group of researchers observed, "[p]arental maltreatment of children is essentially an interpersonal phenomenon and, as such, it would be expected to have major effects on children's social behavior and their understanding of social relationships." Salzinger, S., Feldman, R. S., Hammer, M., & Rosario, M. (1991). Risk for physical child abuse and the personal consequences for its victims. *Criminal Justice and Behavior, 18,* 64–81, p. 74 (citations omitted). http://dx.doi.org/10.1177/0093854891018001006. Another early reviewer suggested that harsh punishment "both frustrates the child and provides him a model" with which to discharge that frustration. Lystad (1975), Violence at home, p. 330. Modeling also may help to explain the recent finding that exposure to domestic violence and community violence is associated with higher levels of "gun violence involvement and with the presence of gun-specific risk factors (i.e., gun ownership, gun carrying, and gun arrests)." Wamser-Nanney, R., Nanney, J. T., Conrad, E., & Constans, J. I. (2019). Childhood trauma exposure and gun violence risk factors among victims of gun violence. *Psychological Trauma: Theory, Research, Practice, and Policy, 11,* 99–106, p. 104. http://dx.doi.org/10.1037/tra0000410. That is, exposure to violence in the home and community may teach the importance maintaining a capacity to achieve forceful control over others.
186. For examples of research that indicates that witnessing the physical abuse of others can be psychologically damaging, see Kleinman, M. (1987). Children—Witnesses to, and victims of, domestic violence. *New Jersey Psychologist,* 13–16; Rosenberg, M. S. (1987). Children of battered women: The effects of witnessing violence on their social problem-solving abilities. *Behavior Therapist, 10,* 85–89; Wolfe, D., Jaffe, P., & Wilson, S. (1988). A multivariate investigation of children's adjustment to family violence; Fantuzzo, J. W., & Mohr, W. K. (1999). Prevalence and effects of child exposure to domestic violence. *Future of Children, 9,* 21–32. http://dx.doi.org/10.2307/1602779; Kuther, T. L. (1999). A developmental-contextual perspective on youth covictimization by community violence. *Adolescence, 34,* 699–714, and references cited therein; and Pelcovitz, D., Kaplan, S. J., DeRosa, R. R., Mandel, F. S., & Salzinger, S. (2000). Psychiatric disorders in adolescents exposed to violence and physical abuse. *American Journal of Orthopsychiatry, 70,* 360–369, and to the earlier published references cited therein.
187. Salzinger, Feldman, Hammer, & Rosario (1991). Risk for physical child abuse, p. 74 (emphasis added).

188. McCord, J. (1991). The cycle of crime and socialization practices. *The Journal of Criminal Law & Criminology, 82,* 211–228. http://dx.doi.org/10.2307/1143796
189. Loeber, R., & Stouthamer-Loeber, M. (1986). Family factors as correlates and predictors of juvenile conduct problems and delinquency. In M. Tonry & N. Morris (Eds.), *Crime and justice* (Vol. 7). Chicago, IL: University of Chicago Press, p. 29. And, in the 1990s, see Sampson, R., & Laub, J. (1993). *Crime in the making: Pathways and turning points through life.* Cambridge, MA: Harvard University Press, http://dx.doi.org/10.1086/449112. Sampson and Laub concluded that "[e]rratic, threatening, and harsh discipline, low levels of supervision, and parental rejection all independently contribute to delinquency" (p. 119).
190. Whitbeck, L. B., Hoyt, D. R., & Ackley, K. A. (1997). Abusive family backgrounds and later victimization among runaway and homeless adolescents. *Journal of Research on Adolescence, 7,* 375–392, pp. 376–377. http://dx.doi.org/10.1207/s15327795jra0704_2
191. Sroufe, Egeland, & Kreutzer (1990). The fate of early experience following developmental change, p. 1371.
192. For example, one study found that a high rate of physical and sexual abuse appeared in the reported histories of adolescent residents of a drug dependency treatment center. Those residents who had been abused also had higher incidences of acting out behavior, were more likely to have been runaways, had prior involvement with the law, and engaged in sexual promiscuity more often than those in the nonabused group. See Caviola & Schiff (1988), Behavioral sequelae of physical and/or sexual abuse in adolescents.
193. Consistent with the risk factors model I have presented, data from a national trauma network found that children who became involved in the juvenile justice system tended to have high rates of trauma exposure that typically began early in life, was experienced in multiple contexts, and persisted over time. See Dierkhising, C. B., Ko, S. J., Woods-Jaeger, B., Briggs, E. C., Lee, R., & Pynoos, R. S. (2013). Trauma histories among justice-involved youth: Findings from the National Child Traumatic Stress Network. *European Journal of Psychotraumatology, 4(1),* 20274. Advance online publication. http://dx.doi.org/10.3402/ejpt.v4i0.20274
194. Werner, E. E. (1989). High-risk children in young adulthood: A longitudinal study from birth to 32 years. *American Journal of Orthopsychiatry, 59,* 72–81; Werner, E. E. (1993). Risk, resilience, and recovery: Perspectives from the Kauai longitudinal study. *Development and Psychopathology, 5,* 503–515. http://dx.doi.org/10.1017/S095457940000612X; Werner, E. E., & Smith, R. (1977). *Kauai's children come of age.* Honolulu: University of Hawaii Press; Werner, E. E., & Smith, R. (1982). *Vulnerable but invincible: A longitudinal study of resilient children and youth.* New York, NY: McGraw Hill. A study conducted in Montreal, Canada, found much the same thing—that serious delivery complications interacted with "family adversity" to predict a greater likelihood of engaging in illegal behavior in childhood and adolescence. See Arseneault, L., Tremblay, R. E., Boulerice, B., & Saucier, J. F. (2002). Obstetrical complications and violent delinquency: Testing two developmental pathways. *Child Development, 73,* 496–508. A different study showed that the combination of birth complications and the presence of an additional, different risk factor—in this case, parental rejection—significantly increased the likelihood of violence behavior in early adulthood. See Raine, A., Brennan, P., & Mednick, S. A. (1994). Birth complications combined with early maternal rejection at age 1 year predispose to violent crime at age 18 years. *Archives of General Psychiatry, 51,* 984–988. http://dx.doi.org/10.1001/archpsyc.1994.03950120056009
195. Brennan & Mednick (1997), Medical histories of antisocial individuals, p. 276.
196. Brennan & Mednick (1997), Medical histories of antisocial individuals, p. 276. Similarly, Gerald Patterson and his colleagues found that early exposure to risk factors, including a "disrupted" family dynamics, frequent family transitions, and

social disadvantage, placed them on a life trajectory in which delinquent and criminal behavior were more likely. See Patterson, G. R., Forgatch, M. S., Yoerger, K. L., & Stoolmiller, M. (1998). Variables that initiate and maintain an early-onset trajectory for juvenile offending. *Development and Psychopathology, 10,* 531–547. http://dx.doi.org/10.1017/S0954579498001734

197. Herrenkohl, Herrenkohl, & Egolf (2003). The psychosocial consequences of living environment instability on maltreated children, p. 378.
198. Moreover, these relationships are affected by family structure and parental involvement. For example, see Astone, N. M., & McLanahan, S. S. (1996). Family structure, parental practices, and high school completion. *American Sociological Review, 56,* 309–320. http://dx.doi.org/10.2307/2096106; Coleman, J. S. (1988). Social capital in the creation of human capital. *American Journal of Sociology, 94,* S95–S120; Hagan, J., MacMillan, R., & Wheaton, B. (1996), New kid in town: Social capital and the life course effects of family migration on children.
199. Allen, D. (2017, July 24). The life of a South Central statistic. *The New Yorker.* https://www.newyorker.com/magazine/2017/07/24/the-life-of-a-south-central-statistic
200. Kagan, J. (2013). Contextualizing experience. *Developmental Review, 33,* 273–278, p. 276. http://dx.doi.org/10.1016/j.dr.2013.07.003
201. Kagan (2013). Contextualizing experience, p. 274.

4

Institutional Failure

State Intervention as Criminogenic Risk

We survive by turning the work into routine, by engaging in only small bits of the totality at a time, and by distancing ourselves from the client, particularly from the client's experience of her or his own situation.

—NILS CHRISTIE[1]

In our society [total institutions] are forcing houses for the changing of persons; each is a natural experiment on what can be done to the self.

—ERVING GOFFMAN[2]

In writing about two notorious figures in American criminal justice history—Gary Gilmore and Willie Bosket—sociologist Mercer Sullivan noted that the extreme levels of violence in which they had engaged were "overdetermined" by numerous forces, many of whose effects began to register long before either man was institutionalized.[3] Sullivan argued, as I argue in this book, that many of those same forces "also affect a vastly larger and less pathologically involved population who pass through the criminal justice system."[4] In addition to the powerful, overdetermined set of forces that affected Gilmore, Bosket, and many others long before they were institutionalized, however, the eventual overlay of the "horrendous effects of reformatory and prison brutality" are also apparent in their lives. As Sullivan cautioned, the possibility that the criminal justice system "itself is deeply implicated in its own current rapid expansion is a

http://dx.doi.org/10.1037/0000172-005
Criminality in Context: The Psychological Foundations of Criminal Justice Reform,
by C. Haney

matter of the gravest concern."[5] The present chapter explores that grave concern at some length.

As I noted in the preceding chapter, the victimization of children has received a considerable amount of sympathetic attention from the public, the media, and concerned professionals over the last several decades.[6] However, a decidedly different attitude prevails once "abused children" themselves violate the law and cross into the category of "juvenile offenders." As one commentator observed, the policies by which children are processed in the juvenile justice system reflects the unfortunate fact that "*children in trouble* have increasingly been regarded, and thus treated, as 'offenders' first, and 'children' (or more specifically 'children in need') second, if at all."[7]

The irony, of course, is that the formerly sympathetic victims of abuse very often become the perpetrators of juvenile crime; they are the same children, although they are hardly treated in the same way. Far too many of them are subjected to "the corrosive and brutalizing inhumanity of custodial institutions," where they are abused again, this time within "a culture of bullying, intimidation and almost routine self-harm" that prevails inside a number of the juvenile institutions where they continue to be routinely sent.[8] C. Wright Mills has taught that "[t]o understand the biography of an individual, we must understand the significance of the roles he has played and does play," and that to understand these roles "we must understand the institutions of which they are a part."[9] In the case of "children in trouble"—either as "troubled children," children engaged in "troublesome" behavior, or some combination of the two—powerful institutions often impact their biographies at early and formative stages. For this reason, especially careful attention must be paid to the nature of the places of which they are often *forced* to become a part and the roles that they are required to play once inside them.

As I discuss in detail in this chapter, although the state intervenes ostensibly "in the best interests of the child," functioning *in loco parentis*, many of these interventions are so psychologically harmful that they represent risk factors in their own right, ones that increase the likelihood that children exposed to them will suffer subsequent emotional problems and engage in delinquent and even criminal behavior later in life. Yet, until recently, political and legal policymakers have given relatively little official recognition to the likely long-term consequences of exposure to these harsh and potential damaging practices and places. There has correspondingly been very little public recognition of their potential to adversely affect a child's entire life course. Indeed, the plight of wards inside the nation's juvenile justice institutions received so little attention in the past that, for years many jurisdictions failed to accurately *count* the number of such children, let alone adequately provide for their needs.[10] Notwithstanding improvements made in many jurisdictions in recent years,[11] the studies reviewed and information presented in this chapter document the continued lack of adequate and appropriate services for children who have experienced disastrous life circumstances, many of whom suffer from serious emotional problems as a result.[12] These data and observations underscore the fact that many such children have been inadequately or badly treated in certain (but certainly not all) public educational settings, social service or "child welfare" agencies, as well as by juvenile justice institutions that have too few resources, too little time, and insufficient expertise with which to reverse the effects of years of pre-existing trauma and set a life gone astray back on course.[13]

Several caveats are in order, as I begin a fairly detailed summary of the nature of these interventions and their potentially criminogenic consequences for children. For one, my focus extends beyond traditional "juvenile justice institutions" to include aspects of the foster care system and also practices and procedures that now prevail inside many public school systems. The traumatic experiences and criminogenic risks that precede and precipitate more direct juvenile justice system contacts often include these seemingly less intrusive and ostensibly more benign but nonetheless potentially harmful interventions. Early childhood, family, and other risks and traumas of the sort described in preceding chapters often lead to early state intervention of some kind, long before placement in a juvenile justice institution. This includes foster care placement (in the case of children whose home lives are regarded as problematic and potentially damaging) and harsh forms of school discipline in the case of at least some children whose classroom behavior is judged to be unacceptable.

The second caveat is that I make a concerted effort in this chapter to include some examples from past as well as present institutional failures and to provide geographically diverse illustrations of problematic forms of juvenile justice system interventions. Horrendous juvenile justice institutions have been with us for a very long time and have had criminogenic effects on generations of children and adolescents. Many persons who are still confined in adult correctional institutions were exposed decades ago to the kinds of places that I describe in the pages that follow. The criminogenic effects of that exposure help to explain their later criminal behavior. In addition, the fact that state political officials, legal decision-makers, and juvenile justice policy-makers have been made aware of these inadequacies and abuses for decades but have been unable or unwilling to correct them speaks to their deeply structural, seemingly endemic, nature. Although the kinds of problematic institutions that I discuss in the following pages are by no means universal, they are nonetheless frequent and are frequently intractable fixtures in a larger juvenile justice system that still too often emphasizes punitive forms of social control over more benign child welfare-oriented approaches.

FROM CHILD WELFARE TO THE CONTROL OF "JUVENILE OFFENDERS"

The term "iatrogenic" is used in medical and psychiatric contexts to describe the way in which a physician, "through his [or her] diagnosis, manner, or treatment," may induce or foster other symptoms or disorders, including the very ones he or she is attempting to cure.[14] Unfortunately, it is a term that also accurately describes the paradoxical effects of institutional intervention on the lives of many young persons who have broken the law.[15] That is, in the interests of addressing behavioral and other problems suffered by children who have come to the attention of the legal authorities, a great many of them are institutionalized in juvenile (and even adult) correctional facilities where their problems are made worse or new ones are created.

Of course, institutional practices, procedures, and conditions can and do vary widely, and juvenile justice interventions are not necessarily inherently harmful. Indeed, dedicated and well-trained social service agency workers and juvenile justice personnel have saved many children from worse fates and helped facilitate life-altering positive changes. Juvenile justice system interventions that are caring and properly designed often have resulted in truly beneficial outcomes.[16] Yet, there are still too many of them that do much more harm than good and have a powerfully criminogenic effect.

For example, Steven Lerner's study of California juvenile institutions conducted in the mid-1980s reached the "specific and urgent" recommendation that "our present system for dealing with youthful offenders needs drastic overhauling," in large part because of the extent to which it "return[ed] to freedom young men and women who have been brutalized by their institutional experience."[17] This fact led Lerner to conclude that such institutions actually "promote crime rather than deter it, and increase the criminal population at great expense to the rest of us."[18]

Robert Sampson and John Laub's influential analysis of data collected by Sheldon and Eleanor Glueck well over a half century ago on the causes of delinquency and adult criminality confirmed that some of most important negative effects of juvenile justice system intervention stemmed from the tendency to stigmatize young people, take them out of the mainstream of normal socialization and, in part as a result, to constrict their occupational opportunities in the future. As they put it, "the connection between official childhood misbehavior and [negative] adult outcomes may be accounted for in part by the structural disadvantages and diminished life chances accorded institutionalized and stigmatized youth."[19] Thus, Sampson and Laub viewed juvenile incarceration as having an *indirect* criminogenic effect, such that longer periods of confinement increased the likelihood of subsequent criminality by virtue of the way that they undermined the job stability of juveniles attempting to make a successful transition to adulthood. Indeed, they suggested that because "incarceration appears to cut off opportunities and prospects for stable employment later in life," even if its direct effect appears to be zero or even negative (that is, that it serves as a deterrent), "its indirect effect may well be criminogenic."[20]

However, the data they analyzed were collected from a specific Northeastern locale (central Boston) and in a different historical era—most of the juveniles the Gluecks studied would have first been institutionalized in Massachusetts the late-1930s.[21] More recent cohorts of children growing up in different parts of the country may have been subjected to forms of institutional mistreatment that were more *directly* harmful and traumatic. In such cases, juvenile institutionalization may do more than simply stigmatize and separate children and adolescents—as life-altering as that may be—but also may inflict additional direct trauma beyond the accumulated risk factors that I discussed in the last chapter.

Thus, mistreatment at the hands of juvenile justice institutions can operate as its own independent risk factor in the lives of children, increasing the likelihood not only of subsequent troubled and problematic adolescent behavior but also, ultimately, adult criminality. These troubling institutional histories may begin when children are relatively young—often long before any actual "delinquent" behavior has occurred. Unlike adults, children can be institutionalized, or at least subjected to drastic state intervention, because officials conclude that their parents cannot properly care for them. But each intervention has the capacity to increase the likelihood that the next one will occur. Children typically exercise no "choice" over any of these interventions, especially in the initial stages of the process, when they are too young to make remotely autonomous decisions and, in any event, are rarely given an opportunity to even express a preference let alone directly influence their immediate fate. Yet once caught in this iatrogenic spiral of intervention and institutionalization, they face difficult if not impossible odds attempting to extricate themselves from its consequences.

As the following pages suggest, institutional risks and traumas can be introduced very early into someone's social history, long before the "juvenile justice system" has formally intervened.

FOSTER CARE AS FLAWED INTERVENTION

In an average year, hundreds of thousands of children are formally retained in the foster care system in the United States.[22] Of course, children are typically placed in foster care in response to evidence that they are being maltreated, and their placements are intended to protect them from further exposure to the traumas and risk factors to which they already have been exposed.[23] However, studies indicate that supposedly temporary foster care placements outside of the home often lead to extended periods of time during which children are kept separated from their families, including many instances in which they are subjected to neglectful and even overtly harmful mistreatment. Decades ago, researchers began to report on the tendency for foster care placements to "drift" into troublesome patterns that disrupted the lives of children and left them in even more unstable environments than the ones they had been in. The patterns included frequent moves, "bandying (the children) from placement to placement and keeping their lives in limbo during their precious developmental years."[24] Children in foster care are thus vulnerable to forms of "retraumatization"—exposure to the same traumatic risk factors in their foster homes that led to their removal from their homes of origin, and repeatedly so—in each subsequent placement, done under the banner of providing "protective" care.[25]

These problems with the nation's foster care system are not remnants of some distant past when the effects of traumatic childhood experiences on developmental trajectories were not well understood. Notwithstanding the many unsettling accounts of the way the foster care system once operated, in supposedly less enlightened times,[26] many of the same or similar practices persist. Rather than infrequent aberrations, these problems are still widespread, and they are not restricted to the nation's poorest states. Many thousands of children across the country still spend time living in uncaring and abusive foster care placements that adversely affect them, sometimes with long-term criminogenic consequences.

For example, a highly critical report was completed at the turn of the 21st century on the quality of foster care in California—a state that at the time was neither poor nor thought to be particularly regressive in its approach to the provision of social services. At the time, California was home to over 100,000 foster children (approximately 20% of the nation's total). Yet the state permitted foster homes to be "licensed" without first determining "the suitability or ability of [the foster parents] to effectively parent children or to provide an emotionally healthy environment for children."[27] In addition, once children were taken from their homes, they remained in foster care *on average* for more than 2 years. A study of statewide practices also found evidence that "[c]hildren taken from their parents are often bounced from foster home to foster home. Some are returned to parents who abuse them again. Others are even abused by their foster families."[28] More than a decade later, another investigative report concluded that "the state's private foster family system—the largest in the nation—has become more expensive and more dangerous than the government-run homes it has largely replaced."[29]

Many studies of children who have been placed in the child welfare system have found that they suffer from a host of untreated problems that may be exacerbated during their stay in foster care. For example, one study showed that children in foster care were twice as likely to have been held back a grade, four times as likely to be expelled from school and, even by age 17, were reading at approximately a seventh-grade level. The children also were more likely to have contact with the legal and mental health systems—more than a third had spent at least a night in a correctional facility and a quarter reported having been prescribed psychotropic medications. Many other children had multiple foster care placements—nearly 40% of the children had been in four or more foster homes and most moves necessitated school changes as well.[30] Of course, these are vulnerable children to begin with, ones whose prior exposure to risks and traumas helps to account for these problematic outcomes. But there is little or no evidence that the foster care system in many jurisdictions is capable of providing the enhanced and enriched services they need.

Children in foster care are also at greater risk of being overmedicated with psychotropic medications.[31] In fact, in 2011, the federal government called on states to develop plans to monitor the use of these drugs with foster youth.[32] Although a number of states failed to respond to the request, data from California included a number of unsettling facts. For example, the rate at which foster care children in California were being prescribed psychotropic medications over the 10-year period from 2004 to 2014 was 3.5 times the national rate for those children who were not in foster care.[33]

Here, too, one explanation for such high medication rates may be that foster children have significantly worse trauma histories than most others their age and, as a result, have greater mental health needs overall. However, the California data indicated that the *majority* of the psychotropics prescribed to foster children were antipsychotic medications, ones not commonly used to treat trauma. They are also medications that have some of the most serious side effects associated with them. As a critical report on the practice noted,

> Of the tens of thousands of foster children placed on psychotropic drugs over the past 10 years, nearly 60 percent were prescribed an antipsychotic: the class of psychotropic medications with the highest risks. That figure stunned experts in the field and alarmed officials who oversee the state's foster care system. The Food and Drug Administration authorizes antipsychotics for children only in cases of severe mental illness, but evidence suggests doctors often prescribe them to California foster children for behavior problems—a legal but controversial practice that critics say should be limited.[34]

Each year, an estimated 20,000 adolescents leave the foster care system and attempt to live independently. They are at high risk of criminal justice system involvement and, as some studies show, this is especially true for those who have suffered frequent placement transitions and those not enrolled in school or employed at the time of their release from foster care.[35] Because children placed in foster care are, by definition, more likely to have suffered childhood maltreatment—including many of the very criminogenic risk factors and traumas that were discussed in the last chapter[36]—they are already at higher risk of entering the juvenile and adult criminal justice systems.

Some studies indicate that the intervention of the child welfare system (including foster care placement) produces mixed results, at least in some jurisdictions. That is, it lowers the overall likelihood of criminal behavior for some categories of children but increases it for others.[37] However, other studies reached more negative conclusions, finding that foster care placement itself resulted in an overall increase in the likelihood of criminal justice system involvement.[38] For example, one study of children "on the margin" of foster care placement in Cook County, Illinois (some of whom went into foster care and others of whom remained at home), reported that the foster care children were significantly more likely to engage in criminal behavior later in life—2 to 3 times as likely to be arrested, convicted, and imprisoned.[39] Other research has indicated that the mere fact of having had juvenile justice system involvement increased the stigma and social exclusion faced by children who were aging out of foster care, significantly limiting their access to conventional opportunities (e.g., school, work) and increasing their likelihood of becoming involved in crime as adults.[40]

Young persons who are placed in foster care are a highly traumatized population overall and meet the criteria for posttraumatic stress disorder (PTSD) at higher rates than youth not in foster care.[41] It is also the case that those with histories of prefoster care maltreatment (especially neglect and physical abuse) are more likely to experience abuse in the course of their foster care placements.[42] Whether or not they have suffered prefoster care mistreatment, they face a host of challenges in the transition to adulthood following foster care placement and generally do not fare well, with low levels of subsequent education and employment and higher levels of mental health and criminal justice system contact than others their age, leading researchers to conclude that the United States lacks "a developmentally appropriate and social inclusive system of support for vulnerable youth in transition to adulthood."[43]

These despairing accounts are not limited to private foster care home placements but apply to group homes as well.[44] Even in state-run facilities intended to care for the *most* troubled children—programs that correspondingly receive the most generous state allocations to provide services—often fall far short of agreed-upon professional standards. For example, in Alameda County, California, where the city of Oakland is located, there is just one emergency group home for emotionally disturbed teenagers. State agencies have repeatedly cited it for violations that included "providing insufficient food and clothing, mishandling of residents' money and medications, and abusive treatment by an inadequately trained staff."[45] The record of violations spanned a 10-year period, and the obstacles to finding timely remedies were substantial, including the fact that the licensing division responsible for monitoring these kinds of facilities was able to inspect only about a third of them each year. As one commentator concluded, the shortcomings of this particular facility, "which serves young people who often come from backgrounds of abuse and neglect, illustrate the difficulties that state and local governments have in regulating facilities that care for even the most vulnerable populations."[46]

Group homes that house intellectually disabled children—some of whom are at greater risk of ending up in the criminal justice system as adults[47]—are often even more problematic. For example, a statewide investigative journalism report on some 2,000 of these state-run homes in New York found that "employees who sexually abused, beat, or taunted residents were rarely fired, even after repeated offenses, and in many cases were simply transferred to other group homes run by the state."[48] Oversight of these facilities appeared to have gotten worse rather than better in recent years. Thus, the New York state agency charged with investigating accusations that residents were being mistreated had at one time actively pursued such complaints but apparently stopped doing so:

> These days, the commission is more likely to play down allegations of abuse than to root them out. And its resources are limited. In 2009, it investigated

less than two percent of allegations of abuse or neglect of the disabled by employees.[49]

A reform-minded new state administration proposed a series of changes that commentators noted were "a sign of the agency's problems," in part because they purported to initiate practices (e.g., reporting episodes of physical and sexual abuse) that were already required by law.[50] Moreover, the progress in the increased reporting of abuse that the new head of the oversight agency announced nonetheless "suggested that there are hundreds of serious allegations [of sexual abuse] that are still not being reported."[51]

Of course, as I noted, the tragic irony and greatest cause for concern is that virtually, by definition, the children in these foster care and related child welfare settings have already been exposed to high numbers of risk factors and traumas that are then compounded by additional neglect and maltreatment in the very systems that are supposed to protect them.

CRIMINALIZING CLASSROOM MISBEHAVIOR: THE SCHOOL-TO-PRISON PIPELINE

There is another set of problematic institutional policies and practices now in place that can adversely affect the lives of at-risk children and have potentially criminogenic consequences. The use of so-called zero tolerance discipline policies in public schools has not only increased the total number of school suspensions and expulsions that children incur but also placed a large number of them at greater risk of juvenile and adult criminal justice confinement. As one critic noted, "[a]fter years of campaigns aimed at keeping children at risk in school, the zero tolerance effort seeks instead to identify troublesome students and get them out of school."[52] Children who are "out of school" have to go somewhere, of course, and too often that has meant placing them on a path that includes eventual incarceration.

Indeed, because most zero tolerance policies include a provision that requires school officials to report infractions to law enforcement, these children become "known" to the legal system; as a result, their behavior is more likely to be closely monitored and sanctioned in ways that can have long-lasting negative consequences. Zero tolerance also discourages (and, in some instances, actually prevents) school officials from inquiring into the reasons for the rules infraction or exploring the potentially mitigating context in which it occurred. This is the "zero" part of the equation—*no* explanatory extenuation or mitigation of sanctions is typically permitted. Among other things, this means that students whose troublesome behavior is the result of family turmoil or their pre-existing emotional or psychological problems are still at risk of being expelled. Removed from whatever programs and services that might be available within the school system to address their personal issues in more caring and benign ways, many are shunted into the juvenile justice system instead.

Moreover, students whose problematic classroom behavior is the result of unidentified or untreated learning disorders may find their education-related problems reinterpreted, mislabeled, and mistreated as willful delinquency. As one commentator observed, "[a]s student misconduct is increasingly criminalized, more and more children with learning disabilities are entering the juvenile justice system."[53] Not surprisingly, children who are already "at risk,"[54] including a disproportionate number of African American and Latino children, are the ones most adversely affected by these policies.[55]

Zero tolerance and other harsh disciplinary policies are often administered by what are commonly called "school resource officers" (SROs) who operate in most school districts as formal extensions of local law enforcement. Beginning in the mid-1990s, "police in schools became the norm for many school districts, with nearly one billion dollars spent by federal agencies during this time period . . . employing over 17,000 officers nationally."[56] Most SROs are police officers who are employed directly by local law enforcement agencies; they, thus, do not work directly for nor answer to the school systems in which they function.

The various "get tough" policies that have been introduced into public schools, especially in urban school districts, have been characterized by critics as creating a "school-to-prison pipeline." Thus, troublesome classroom behavior that would have been handled in less drastic or intrusive ways in past times is now essentially criminalized, precipitating a traditional criminal justice response that can ensnare students in juvenile justice processes and institutions. As one commentator has noted, although the school-to-prison pipeline operates with more ferocity in some places and on some groups than others, the "overall trend in school criminalization has accelerated since the early 1990s across the socio-economic and geographic spectrum."[57]

The criminogenics of the school-to-prison pipeline are in part direct and follow from the adverse impact of early and unwarranted contact with the juvenile justice system. But some are indirect, ranging from the creation of a distinctly "penal" atmosphere within the school itself (e.g., metal detectors, surveillance cameras, police presence),[58] as well as in the way that suspensions and expulsions jeopardize students' chances of finishing high school which, in turn, places them at greater risk of engaging in subsequent delinquent and criminal behavior.[59] Whether direct or indirect, the effects of these practices are iatrogenic for many students, turning schools into places fraught with criminogenic risk rather than educational opportunity.

INSTITUTIONAL ABUSE: RECENT HISTORICAL CONTEXT

As far back as the 1930s, Clifford Shaw and other sociologists wrote about the ways in which juvenile justice institutions could socialize children into adult criminal careers, by exposing them to negative role models, stigmatizing them through the negative effects of labeling, and subjecting them to adverse conditions of confinement.[60] By the 1960s, government commissions recommended that juvenile crime be addressed primarily through family and community interventions; institutionalization was to be used only as an absolute last resort.[61] The recommendation was premised in part on documented instances of abuse and mistreatment in many individual state-run juvenile institutions and a "Great Society" shift toward social welfare solutions to social problems, such as poverty and crime.[62]

However, even in the 1960s, there was little sustained commitment to systemic juvenile justice reform. The progressive rhetoric of the time was never matched by the realities that juveniles confronted in many institutions across country. Eventually, the hopeful rhetoric was replaced with the same kind of "get tough" sentiments and policies that came to dominate crime and punishment practices at a national level. In the last several decades of the 20th century, a "penal harm" movement swept across the country that explicitly embraced the goal of making lawbreakers suffer,[63] and it helped to make an already harsh juvenile justice system even harsher.[64] Indeed, the widespread mistreatment and punitive ethos that already prevailed in many parts of the nation's juvenile justice system was not harsh enough for some politicians and policymakers. Their calls to treat children in even more draconian ways were eventually heeded in many jurisdictions, and the juvenile justice system, in general, shifted from rehabilitation to retribution and punishment instead.

With the nature of this shift in mind, note that the small sample of the documented cases of excessive punishment, deprivation, and physical abuse that I summarize in the pages that follow actually *predated* calls to increase punishment at the expense of rehabilitation. Moreover, they are merely a small sample from a much larger database of systemic failures and punitive excesses. They provide a baseline against which to judge late 20th-century claims that the juvenile system had become far "too lenient"—claims that led lawmakers in many parts of the country to "toughen" their laws to become even more punitive.

To take just one example from the 1960s, juvenile detention centers in Ohio were described as so "overcrowded, stifling" that children had to be detained in the city's adult jail.[65] A few years later, more graphic descriptions of conditions inside the state's main juvenile facility surfaced,[66] which included the observation that it was a "time bomb of human dynamite," where the concept of rehabilitation for the young men confined there was "almost farcical."[67] Another Ohio youth facility was described as "a place to make grown men cry" and "an overcrowded warehouse for wayward boys" with dormitories that were compared to "jungles."[68]

Similar accounts of mistreatment in juvenile institutions in numerous other states are contained in court cases filed in the decades since the 1960s. For example, in the 1970s, psychologist Stanley Brodsky reported on the nature of conditions at a so-called industrial school in Puerto Rico, where many at-risk children were sent.[69] Brodsky found that conditions at the facility were "inhumane, that the care was harsh and inadequate, and that no meaningful treatment services were available." Other 1970s cases surfaced inhumane treatment and conditions elsewhere in the country. For example, a federal judge in Texas found that correctional officers in the state's youth facilities "administered various forms of physical abuse, including slapping, punching, and kicking," and an extreme practice known as "racking" in which children were forced to stand against the wall with their hands in their pockets while being "struck a number of times by blows from the fists of correctional officers."[70]

A federal court in Indiana reached similar conclusions in the 1970s about the Indiana Boys School, condemning its use of corporal punishment—"supervised beatings by use of a thick board for violating institutional rules"—as well as the excessive and unjustified use of solitary confinement, and the forced administration of psychotropic drugs in lieu of less drastic interventions.[71] During the same time period, a federal judge in New York condemned what he characterized as "very serious constitutional abuses" that occurred at a state juvenile facility, including the punitive use of isolation, the use of hand and feet restraints to control juvenile wards, and the overuse of psychotropic medications such as Thorazine.[72]

A federal court in Oregon found that the state's major juvenile facility had been subjecting its wards to substandard living conditions as well as "inhumane, degrading, and 'punitive'" disciplinary practices. These included excessively segregating the young inmates—in any given month placing over half of them in "dark and depressing" isolation cells that were infested with insects, had blood and feces covering the walls, and smelled of urine.[73] In another case, a federal district judge in Mississippi found that the state's major "training school" for incarcerated juveniles subjected them to harmful conditions of confinement, failed to provide meaningful rehabilitative services, and employed cruel and unusual isolation units to discipline and control them.[74] In the late 1970s, a class action lawsuit was filed in Oklahoma challenging overall conditions of confinement in the state's juvenile justice system,[75] including reports that young wards in these facilities had been "shackled, hog-tied, sexually and physically abused, placed in solitary confinement as punishment and that workers have withheld food and other necessary items as punishment."[76] In the early 1980s, a series of scathing reports written about the Oklahoma system corroborated the juveniles' earlier accounts, including "brutal attacks, sexual assaults, or punitive, ramrod discipline by state employees that medical experts call[ed] 'appalling' and barbaric.'"[77]

Although they were not yet the subject of systemwide litigation, a number of juvenile institutions in California that were evaluated in the late 1970s and early 1980s suffered from a host of similar, widespread problems. Steven Lerner's investigative report was based on tours and interviews conducted at most of the major juvenile facilities in the state and concluded that the "institutional environment" at the California Youth Authority training schools was "in many ways detrimental to the health and behavior" of thousands of wards who were confined in them. The author cautioned that "not enough attention has been paid to the negative impact which remarkably stressful living conditions at the Youth Authority have on its institutionalized population."[78]

Data like these rarely garner much attention outside the local jurisdictions where individual lawsuits are filed or investigative reports are published. Yet the shocking observations and sobering conclusions reached in this small sample of early court cases and reports were not "outliers" that pertained only to facilities or state systems that operated far outside prevailing norms. In fact, several comprehensive studies of the nation's overall juvenile justice system that were conducted over the same several decades reached scathing conclusions, cataloging its destructive and criminogenic effects on the children housed there. The sheer scope of these criticisms underscored the overarching, structural nature of the problems.

For example, in the mid-1970s, the Ford Foundation sponsored a nationwide examination of juvenile justice facilities. Its author, Charles Silberman, was shocked by "the sheer quantity of punishment meted out by a system that boasts of having replaced punishment with rehabilitation."[79] He lamented the sad fact that the "overwhelming majority of detained juveniles receive no help worthy of the name"[80] and concluded that "[y]oungsters sent to juvenile detention centers and training schools are likely to be brutalized rather than rehabilitated."[81]

It was not an isolated critique. Another Ford Foundation-sponsored report compiled by the Vera Institute at roughly the same time reached almost identical conclusions. It is worth quoting at length:

> [The] cycle of neglect, rejections, transfer, and failure reinforces [the juvenile's] sense that he belongs nowhere and fans the alienation that contributes to violent behavior. The seemingly endless chain of policemen, probation officers, judges, social workers, doctors, and correction officers who pass through his life, rarely to reappear, conditions the child to expect little from relationships with adults except professional curiosity, indifference, or interference.[82]

The next decade saw similar, sweeping indictments of the nation's juvenile justice system. For example, a major study sponsored by the Department of Justice was published in the early 1980s, when support for punishment-oriented responses to juvenile crime was on the rise.[83] It, too, reached overarching conclusions about the negative effects of juvenile institutionalization that, because of the broad scope and careful design of the research, were difficult to ignore. The most problematic finding was that juvenile justice system intervention was not only ineffective overall but appeared to be counterproductive; that is, children who were brought into the juvenile system did significantly worse than those with comparable offenses who were not.[84]

In 1991, a federally-funded assessment of the nature and quality of conditions and care in juvenile justice facilities across the country helped explain why they were criminogenic.[85] Among other things, the study found that three-quarters of incarcerated children were housed in facilities that afforded substandard living conditions, many of which were plagued by overcrowding.

Thus, between 1987 and 1991, the percentage of juveniles who were confined in facilities in which the daily population exceeded the design capacity of the institution increased from 36% to 47%. These crowded living conditions were associated with increased rates of violence, suicidal behavior, and the use of isolation as a form of institutional control.

Near the end of the 1990s, the American Bar Association and the Justice Department (DOJ) issued a joint report on the state of juvenile justice institutions in the United States. Echoing the concerns expressed in the DOJ's earlier nationwide study, the authors acknowledged that such institutions were "increasingly overcrowded," "significantly deficient," and held a disproportionate number of young minority men incarcerated for property and drug-related crimes.[86] They expressed concern not only over the "[w]ell documented deficiencies" in conditions of confinement but also the poor quality and limited availability of treatment and educational services, inadequate security, and ineffective suicide prevention practices and policies. Moreover, as they noted, "[s]ubjecting youth to abusive and unlawful conditions of confinement serves only to increase rates of violence and recidivism and to propel children into the adult criminal justice system."[87]

Although the individual cases and comprehensive reports reviewed to this point pertain to conditions that existed decades ago, several things are important to note. The first is that, in the aggregate, over the years in which these facilities and others like them were in operation, tens of thousands of juveniles passed through them. The effects of the abusive treatment and egregious conditions are likely to have lasted a lifetime. For some, as many of the authors of the studies concluded, the experiences were undoubtedly criminogenic, leaving the young victims more rather than less likely to engage in criminal behavior as adults. In addition, in many cases, the destructive consequences likely reverberated across future generations. For example, some children traumatized by extreme institutional abuse were likely to have suffered long-term emotional consequences, including ones that may have compromised their future parenting.[88] In addition, in the case of those whose institutional abuse as juveniles contributed to their subsequent incarceration as adults, their own children may have been adversely affected by their prison-related absences.[89]

Further, despite the many persistent and troubling accounts of mistreatment and the adverse consequences of juvenile institutionalization—repeatedly documented in the kind of court cases and commissioned national studies I have cited—the juvenile justice system became even harsher in the 1990s and first decade of this century. In many ways it adopted the punitive values, perspectives, and practices of the adult correctional system that inflicted increasingly severe punishment at the expense of rehabilitation.[90] Indeed, notwithstanding obligatory rhetoric about continuing to act "in the best interests of the child," the nation's juvenile justice system operated in ways that were strikingly similar to its adult counterpart. The public, in turn, was encouraged in the mid-1990s to fear juvenile offenders as "superpredators"[91] who represented a ticking "teenage time bomb"[92] about to unleash a "coming bloodbath" perpetrated by hordes of the "young and the ruthless."[93] Thus, the crime master narrative that, in the past, had been applied almost exclusively to adult lawbreakers, was employed with a vengeance to explain and punish the behavior of children and adolescents, their developmental immaturity notwithstanding.

Although none of the dire predictions of this era came to pass, lawmakers pointed to at least some fearful members of the public (whose fear they and the media played a role in creating) to justify treating juvenile crime in much the same harshly punitive way that the nation now handled serious adult criminality. Yet, despite the extremist and sensationalized rhetoric that surrounded the alleged rise in juvenile crime, there was also evidence to suggest that many members of the public were either ambivalent about or opposed to many of the most punitive changes in juvenile justice laws and policies.[94] Nonetheless, by the late 1990s, some 28 states had changed juvenile laws to explicitly emphasize punishment as one of the primary (if not only) purpose of juvenile justice intervention. As Richard Redding put it, "There has been a gradual shift away from rehabilitation models of juvenile justice in favor of retributive and punitive models."[95]

An important manifestation of this changed perspective was reflected in the increasingly widespread practice of remanding youthful lawbreakers directly into the adult criminal court system and processing them as if they were adults. Despite extensive psychological research that distinguishes the behavioral and decision-making capacities of children and adolescents,[96] most states revised their laws to make it easier to "transfer, waive, refer, remand, or certify" juveniles both for trial and sentencing in adult court.[97] Worse still, virtually all of these newly enacted laws included provisions that allowed for the incarceration of children in adult prisons—prisons from which, for virtually the entire 20th century, they had been barred from being housed as a matter of law.

Whatever the precise political considerations that motivated the decisions to enact these laws, their potential psychological consequences were profound.[98] Incarcerating juveniles in adult facilities not only increased the chances that they would suffer additional trauma but also the likelihood that they would recidivate once released. In one study, for example, comparisons of a carefully matched sample of youth who were handled either in juvenile or adult court system showed that 30% of the adult court transfers were rearrested during the year after their release as opposed to 19% of those processed in the juvenile courts.[99]

Moreover, the brutal mistreatment and deprived conditions that had been documented years earlier inside many juvenile institutions persisted, despite the notoriety that was brought to them and litigation that was directed at changing them. For example, several decades *after* Steven Lerner's exposé on the California Youth Authority was published in the 1980s, a panel of outside experts issued a series of reports describing a host of deplorable conditions and harmful practices still in operation there. Among other things, they identified a "climate of violence [that] has engendered high levels of fear among wards and staff that affect virtually all aspects of daily operations." The widespread fear, in turn, resulted in an "extensive use of force, especially chemical agents" directed at the wards.[100] The practices were abusive and excessive, and even included using chemical agents to punish wards while they were "physically restrained or otherwise under control."[101] In addition, there were "a significant number of mentally ill wards held in the lockup units due to the lack of more appropriate treatment and housing alternatives."[102]

Similarly, fully 23 years after many of the harshest practices in the Mississippi's juvenile system were condemned in the litigation that I cited earlier, the Department of Justice found that many of the *same* deplorable conditions—a lack of medical and mental health care, staff vacancies of nearly 40 percent of necessary levels, enforced military "training" for wards, and the like—persisted.[103] Moreover, investigative reports indicated that although the State continued to require parents to place their children in this system, ostensibly in order to receive mental health care, the children were confined instead in facilities where they received little or no actual treatment, were not afforded even the basic educational programs that were mandated by law, and where many of them were placed in restraints and straitjackets, pepper sprayed, and put in isolation.[104]

In fact, patterns of juvenile justice system mistreatment and malfeasance continued well into the first decade of the 21st century. For example, the results of a joint investigation into juvenile facilities in New York State, conducted by Human Rights Watch and the American Civil Liberties Union, were detailed in report issued in September, 2006. It described the state's juvenile residential centers as among the worst in the world.[105] In the aftermath of that report, State officials vowed to overhaul the entire system in order to eliminate the widespread abuses that were identified. However, a few years later, the U.S. Department of Justice issued its own scathing report describing the severe mistreatment that was *still* taking place in a number of these facilities.[106] Federal investigators found that "[e]xcessive physical force was routinely used to discipline children," which "result[ed] in broken bones, shattered teeth, concussions and dozens of other serious injuries."[107] Moreover, despite high prevalence of mental health and substance abuse problems from which the children in the facilities suffered—three-quarters struggled with drug or alcohol problems and over half had been diagnosed with mental disorders—the Justice Department found that they were not being provided with remotely adequate treatment.[108]

By 2011, Richard Mendel's comprehensive report on behalf of the Annie Casey Foundation noted that over the previous four decades there had been some 57 lawsuits that "resulted in a court-sanctioned remedy in response to alleged abuse or otherwise unconstitutional conditions in juvenile facilities" throughout the country.[109] Nearly all—52 in total—"included allegations of systemic problems with violence, physical or sexual abuse by facility staff, and/or excessive use of isolation or restraint."[110] Additionally, as I have also suggested, Mendel made clear that these were not isolated incidents but "a sustained pattern of maltreatment" that, by implication, had been sustained for decades.[111]

The horrific conditions of confinement and overall patterns of mistreatment that have characterized the nation's juvenile justice system for decades inflict long-lasting trauma. As a result, many children already victimized by child maltreatment before entering the juvenile justice system absorb even more psychological harm as a result of their institutionalization. This kind of "retraumatization"—one whose dynamics I discuss in more depth later in this chapter—represents a significant risk factor for future criminal behavior.

THE CRIMINOGENICS OF JUVENILE INSTITUTIONALIZATION

Analyses of the devastating impact of juvenile justice system abuse are numerous and long-standing. In the 1970s, when many of the lawsuits over unconstitutional conditions were first filed, juvenile justice researchers Clemens Bartollas, Stuart Miller, and Simon Dinitz appropriately labeled the victimization of juveniles inside the very institutions where they had been sent to be helped as a "paradox." Among other things, they noted the loss of personal identity that wards often experienced, the atmosphere of fear, exploitation, and distrust that typically prevailed, and what they characterized as "the degrading manner in which juveniles are treated by staff." More specifically, they described "[t]he barking of orders, the harsh tone of voice, and the deriding comment [that] have long been found in juvenile institutions and contribute to the reason why staff tend to be looked upon as hostile, indifferent, condescending, and self-seeking."[112]

Bartollas and his colleagues described the extraordinary adaptations that wards made as they tried to cope with an institutional environment that was both a "punishment-centered bureaucracy" and a "terrifying . . . social world."[113] They characterized many of the living units in the facilities that they examined as "worse than the streets,"[114] and described them as places where young inmates learned to "feign bravery and toughness so convincingly that he is not challenged."[115] They concluded that even in the best juvenile institutions "very little correction, training, or adjustment occurs—or can, in fact, occur under present circumstances and social policies."[116]

Later commentators and analysts reached similar, equally sobering, conclusions about these criminogenic consequences. In the early 1980s, one of them cautioned about the way in which juvenile institutions instilled a view of the social world as essentially "impersonal, unstable and uncaring," and forced children to internalize a value system that was ultimately dysfunctional in the world outside the institution.[117] Such places not only failed to address the long-term needs of the children who were confined in them but actually taught one group of wards how to better exploit the others, while the more defenseless children learned "the contours of victimization, often emerging traumatized."[118] Rather than providing wards with the opportunities to develop more functional and prosocial models of behavior, to seek help for emotional problems many had developed in response to earlier traumas (that were likely at the root of their illegal behavior), or to obtain badly needed social and educational skills, the institutions placed them in settings where their time was "consumed in [a] survival struggle."[119]

The institutionalization of juveniles also appears to strengthen (and, in some cases, initiate) gang ties that may increase their later involvement in gang-related criminality. In the mid-1990s, sociologist Joan Moore found that so-called "state-raised" young persons who experienced frequent juvenile incarceration were the most committed to street gangs. She warned that the practice of incarcerating increasing numbers of young people at increasingly earlier ages would have the effect of creating cohorts of adolescents (and perhaps even preadolescents) with intensely hostile attitudes and deeper commitments to crime-oriented gangs.[120] Her warning went largely unheeded and her predictions came to pass, especially in urban areas where poor and minority youth were disproportionately placed in juvenile institutions.[121]

At the turn of the 21st century, psychologist Richard Redding wrote that, in many jurisdictions, the juvenile justice system had also become "a 'dumping ground' for mentally ill, learning disabled, or behaviorally disordered juveniles," many of whom had prior involvement with the mental health system but ended up in correctional institutions "because the mental health system has failed to serve their needs."[122] Indeed, more recent data indicate that staggering numbers of young persons are still being brought into the juvenile detention system suffering from some form of psychological disorder. For example, Linda Teplin and her colleagues found that nearly two thirds of males and nearly three quarters of females in the Cook County Juvenile Detention Center met the criteria for at least one psychiatric diagnosis.[123]

Although reforms implemented in recent years have reduced the overall numbers of children confined in the juvenile justice system nationwide, it is estimated that there are still well over 50,000 adolescents confined in juvenile facilities across the country, with perhaps as many as 10,000 confined in adult institutions.[124] As Christopher Mallett noted, "[t]he most common placement—for up to 40% of these adolescents—is a locked, long-term state or privately contracted prison-like facility that holds hundreds of young offenders at any one time and provides minimal rehabilitative services."[125] Additionally, as investigative journalist Nell Bernstein observed, despite the recent improvements and seemingly sincere commitments to bring about long-term and lasting reform,

> no ceremony, it seems—no report, reform, or road map—can put an end to the chronic violence and violation that are part and parcel of institutional justice. After countless cleansing rituals—investigations, commissions, regulations, and reforms—the abuse continues.[126]

This is, as she noted, the "*real* recidivism problem": institutional recidivism.[127]

ON THE NATURE OF RETRAUMATIZATION

The criminogenics of exposure to neglectful and abusive juvenile institutions need to be understood in the larger context of a child's life trajectory—indeed, as an extension of the social history that preceded it.[128] For many young persons subjected to institutional trauma—harsh and uncaring treatment by authority figures ostensibly responsible for their well-being—the experience is all too familiar. The cruelty of the institutions that play significant roles in "raising" at-risk children may reinforce aspects of the "forceful parenting" that many of them have already received at home, compounding the emotional impact and deepening whatever dysfunctional adaptations at least some of them may have felt necessary to undertake.[129]

However, abusive juvenile justice institutions go far beyond merely resonating with a forceful parental philosophy. They also expose children to a range of criminogenic traumas and risk factors that are psychologically analogous to those many of them suffered in their homes and neighborhoods. These institutional experiences add to the psychologically destructive impact of earlier childhood mistreatment and, in this sense, represent a form of "retraumatization"—*repeated* trauma-related experiences and events of the sort that can adversely affect their entire life course.[130]

There are unfortunately many unsettling parallels between conventional forms of child maltreatment and the kind of mistreatment and trauma that children are subjected to in abusive juvenile institutions. For example, the juvenile justice system often subjects children to forms of instability that are reminiscent of the chaotic homelife from which they have been taken. Such instability may occur early in the process, when state custody involves foster care placements that, as I noted earlier, can "drift" into patterns of "bandying (the children) from placement to placement and keeping their lives in limbo during their precious developmental years."[131] The adverse effects of extreme residential mobility that I discussed in Chapter 3 are likely to be compounded when the succession of placements they experience involves not only changes in freeworld residences and neighborhoods but also transitions into new families and caretakers. Moreover, the same kinds of unexpected, unpredictable, and seemingly purposeless changes also often occur *within* institutional settings, when children are repeatedly moved or transferred from one unit or facility to another, especially when it is done for little more than administrative convenience rather than an ostensible therapeutic or program-related reason.

Dysfunctional juvenile institutions have additional characteristics and features that strikingly parallel those that exist inside the kind of abusive and neglectful environments from which many institutionalized children have come. They include the dangerousness of their immediate circumstances, the imminent threat of physical, sexual, and psychological abuse, the rigid and overly punitive control, and the neglect of basic needs by "caretakers" who occupy positions of authority. As I also noted earlier, many juvenile institutions also force children to adopt violent survival strategies and to employ combative or psychologically remote and suspicious styles of interacting, defenses that they later may find difficult to relinquish. Some learn to engage in aggressive behavior from which—in less dangerous and threatening settings—they would otherwise have refrained.

Many juvenile institutions are still characterized by the "constant threat and occasional use of violence" that engenders a familiar emotional response for the children who struggle to overcome the "terrifying nature" of the facility in which they have been placed.[132] Unless a new ward is physically strong and intimidating, he "must either outsmart and outtalk those who attempt to exploit him, or he must feign bravery and toughness so convincingly that he is not challenged."[133] If these performances fail, he may be physically victimized, even subjected to "the most devastating blow of all" in the form of sexual exploitation.[134] In the dysfunctional context of a harsh institutional setting, otherwise dysfunctional behavior patterns such as aggression become adaptive, even necessary. As I say, some young persons who enter these environments already have begun to embrace these self-defensive behavioral styles in reaction to the abusive homes or dangerous neighborhoods from which they came.

Institutionalization can undermine healthy psychological and social development, especially for children with pre-existing emotional problems. It also deprives children of opportunities for normal social and peer group interaction, removes them from the rhythms and rituals of the adolescent social world, minimizes their contact with positive family role models, and threatens them with long-lasting stigmatization through the application of negative labels and treatment by staff that emphasizes their deviant status. Indeed, "[s]ociety's definition of juvenile offenders as deviants and of their acts as reprehensible is brought home again and again in the institutional milieu."[135]

All other things being equal, the longer the exposure, the more ingrained the patterns are likely to become and the greater the risk that a stigmatized sense of self and an institutionally-oriented value system will be internalized and become more resistant to change. Because children who are institutionalized for lengthy periods of time may pass through key developmental stages while they are confined in these atypical settings, an institutional identity may be literally the only one that they are able to acquire. This was poignantly underscored in writer Danielle Allen's biographical account of the plight of her younger cousin, who was incarcerated in the middle of his teenage years and was transformed by the unique transitions he and others were forced to undergo while institutionalized:

> The years between ages fifteen and twenty-six are structured with recognizable milestones: high school, driver's license, college, first love, first job, first serious relationship, perhaps marriage, possibly a child. For those who pass adolescence in prison, none of these rites of passage go away; it's just that they take on a massively distorted shape. It's sort of like a fun-house mirror. These life events don't get ticked off on some sort of regular schedule of progression but get racked up, unpredictably so, over the course of a hard-fought existential struggle. And extra rites of passage, unknown, say, to the high school senior, get added in.

> First long-term separation from family. First racial melee. First administrative segregation, also known as first solitary confinement. First sodomization.[136]

No part of my analysis is intended to suggest that everyone who enters a juvenile facility emerges on an unwavering path to adult criminality. We know that is not the case. So-called "age-crime" curves indicate that most people who engage in crime when they are young end up desisting as they mature.[137] Yet, what we know about the nature of many juvenile justice institutions suggests that many of them desist in spite of rather than because of the poor conditions and abusive treatment to which they were subjected. Their institutional experiences present them with additional traumas and risk factors with which to contend. Not surprisingly, the type of institution—the nature of the context—matters as well. As one study found, although "mere intervention by the juvenile justice system seems to have a negative effect, its impact increases as the type of intervention imposed becomes more intense and constrictive."[138]

The criminogenics of these forms of retraumatization are relatively straightforward. Repeated trauma places children and adolescents at greater risk for a wide range of problematic adult behaviors, including criminality. In addition, children who have adopted the aggressive and hypervigilant norms of juvenile institutions may internalize patterns of behavior that are likely to lead to subsequent contact with the adult criminal justice system. Those whose psychological development has been shaped by painful transitions forced on them in institutional settings may grow into adulthood with a marginalized, atypical, and stigmatized sense of self that can preclude their integration into more prosocial contexts and networks.

Shocking legal case studies, pointed scholarly analyses, and sobering comprehensive national assessments conducted over the last several decades have reached strikingly similar conclusions about brutal forms of mistreatment and the harmful effects of harsh institutional life on children and adolescents. Numerous researchers and practitioners have expressed strongly worded warnings about the urgent need to massively overhaul the nation's juvenile justice system, accompanied by thoughtful recommendations about how to do so.[139] However, at least until very recently, rather than heeding calls to implement alternative approaches to delinquency, politicians and legal policymakers pushed the juvenile justice system even closer to the punishment-oriented model of adult corrections. As a result, juvenile institutions continued to be plagued with a range of serious problems that had predictably long-lasting, harmful, and often criminogenic effects on the young persons confined in them.

It is important to note that politically and legally mandated reforms introduced over the last two decades have fortunately mitigated some of the worst abuses.[140] Perhaps most significantly, the rate at which young people were being committed to juvenile justice institutions in the United States began to drop dramatically in 2001 and has continued to do so since then.[141] Whether the long-overdue reforms can be maintained or are eliminated as the juvenile justice system falls prey to a well-documented "cycle" in which badly needed and long-overdue reforms are short-lived and the system returns to the troubled and traumatizing practices and conditions that once prevailed, frankly, remains to be seen.[142]

Yet many abusive practices and institutions have persisted.[143] Despite the significant progress made in recent years and the promising trend toward reform, the juvenile justice system *in general* still lacks adequate funding and operates without the resources needed to deliver proper programming and treatment. Many states still place children in intimidating and alienating institutional settings that are in dire need of better-trained and more carefully overseen staff. Although there are certainly better and worse juvenile justice institutions, and a number of less intrusive interventions with admirable rehabilitative programs that clearly "work,"[144] the practice of confining children in problematic institutions continues. It functions as an iatrogenic, criminogenic risk factor in its own right. Thus, it is still the case that many children—including ones that have already been exposed to poverty, abuse, and instability, and the like—find their lives further compromised rather than enhanced by these state-initiated interventions.

CONCLUSION

Jennifer Freyd and her colleague Carly Smith have used the term "institutional betrayal" to describe a special form of trauma that occurs "when an institution causes harm to an individual who trusts or depends upon that institution."[145] They argued that it can produce "exacerabative effects" in the form of higher rates of dissociation, anxiety, sexual dysfunction, and other trauma-related outcomes. The concept applies with special force and effect in the case of many of the institutions discussed in this chapter.

Children exposed to early traumas and risk factors are too often placed in settings that compound rather than ameliorate or address their problems. As the present chapter has made clear, many state-initiated interventions—ostensibly undertaken in the best interests of the child—frequently have paradoxically negative effects on the lives of the children who are subjected to them. The interventions are often woefully inadequate, clearly hurtful and harmful, and may be criminogenic. Whether in substandard foster care, punishment-oriented schools, or harsh juvenile justice institutions, the day-to-day experiences in these settings often parallel or replicate prior mistreatment, representing a form of retraumatization that worsens the effects of criminogenic influences in already troubled lives. In this way, then, the state ironically acts as an abusive parent, attempting to correct problems that may have originated in the home or community but doing so in ways that are all too familiar to the young people subjected to its control. Absent a different kind of more nurturing intervention to reduce the effects of trauma and risk factors, state intervention too often represents a problematic and life-changing "turning point"[146] that leads children and adolescents to resolve their internal struggle over who to be—indeed, over who they can become—in negative and potentially criminogenic ways.

Institutionalization in juvenile justice facilities, in particular, often worsens pre-existing problems by forcing children to learn habits of thinking and acting that will be deeply dysfunctional elsewhere in society and later in their lives. Institutional trauma and abuse may have long-term emotional consequences, including a stigmatized, diminished sense of self that often persists into adulthood. The harshest and most punitive such environments can compel institutionalized children and adolescents to embrace an exploitative value system, to distance themselves from others, adopt aggressive interactional styles, and to place individual survival above all else. These are problematic ways of being that may be difficult to relinquish once they have been adopted. Despite widespread knowledge that early exposure to harsh institutional settings is not only traumatic but can also be criminogenic, it is still too frequently—often enthusiastically—mandated in the name of crime reduction.[147]

However poorly the unencumbered "free choice" crime master narrative accounts for *adult* criminal behavior, it is even less valid when applied to *children* and *adolescents* who lack the capacity to foresee or reflect on many of the long-term consequences of their actions. The institutional placements are thus ones they truly did not choose but whose effects they nonetheless incur. Rather than ameliorating the problems for which they are ostensibly designed, many of these institutional arrangements, practices, and procedures serve as the mechanisms by which the kind of structural disadvantages I discuss in later chapters are deepened and further inscribed on the psyches of the young people already most affected by them. We still too often take our society's most traumatized and disadvantaged children—those at greatest risk of later lawbreaking—and subject them to forms of institutional mistreatment that a substantial amount of research now indicates drastically limits their options, autonomy, and potential for future success.

NOTES

1. Christie, N. (1982). *Limits to pain: The role of punishment in penal policy*, p. 12. Oxford, England: Robertson.
2. Goffman, E. (1961). *Asylums. Essays on the social situation of mental patients and other inmates*. Garden City, NY: Anchor Books, p. 12.
3. As the biographies of both men made clear—Gilmore's written by his brother, Mikal, and Bosket's by long-time *New York Times* legal reporter Fox Butterfield—each man lived a terribly traumatic and troubled life, was subjected to harsh institutional treatment where they resided, and grew up to commit notorious crimes. Gilmore's life ended when, in 1976, he became the first person executed in the "modern" era of the death penalty; Bosket, who is now nearing 60 years old, has spent virtually his entire adult life in prison, much of it in solitary confinement.
4. Sullivan, M. L. (1996). Biography of heinous criminals: Culture, family violence, and prisonization. *Journal of Research in Crime and Delinquency, 33*, 354–377, p. 376. http://dx.doi.org/10.1177/0022427896033003007. This is a review of the books

Shot in the Heart by M. Gilmore and *All God's Children: The Bosket Family and the American Tradition of Violence* by F. Butterfield.

5. Sullivan (1996), Biography of heinous criminals, p. 376.
6. For example, Finkelhor, D., & Dzuiba-Leatherman, J. (1994). Victimization of children. *American Psychologist, 49,* 173–183. http://dx.doi.org/10.1037/0003-066X.49.3.173
7. Goldson, B. (2000). "Children in need" or "young offenders"? Hardening ideology, organizational change and new challenges for social work with children in trouble. *Child & Family Social Work, 5,* 255–265, p. 256 (emphasis added). http://dx.doi.org/10.1046/j.1365-2206.2000.00161.x. Goldson described the "ideological imperative which dichotomizes the 'undeserving' from the 'deserving,' the 'threats' from the 'threatened,' the 'dangerous' from the 'endangered' and the 'damaging' from the 'damaged' and 'vulnerable.'" Although these ideologically driven dichotomies are "specious," as Goldson noted, they have operational as well as symbolic significance (p. 256).
8. Goldson (2000), Children in need, p. 258.
9. Mills, C. W. (1957). *The sociological imagination* (p. 161). Oxford, England: Oxford University Press.
10. Lerman, P. (1991). Counting youth in trouble in institutions: Bringing the United States up to date. *Crime & Delinquency, 37,* 465–480. http://dx.doi.org/10.1177/0011128791037004004
11. Bernard, T. J., & Kurlychek, M. C. (2010). *The cycle of juvenile justice* (2nd ed.). New York, NY: Oxford University Press.
12. Cohen, R., Preiser, L., Gottlieb, S., Harris, R., Baker, J., & Sonenklar, N. (1993). Relinquishing custody as a requisite for receiving services for children with serious emotional disorders: A review. *Law and Human Behavior, 17,* 121–134. http://dx.doi.org/10.1007/BF01044541
13. For example, Greene, M. B. (1993). Chronic exposure to violence and poverty: Interventions that work for youth. *Crime & Delinquency, 39,* 106–124. http://dx.doi.org/10.1177/0011128793039001007; Zigler, E., Taussig, C., & Black, K. (1992). Early childhood intervention: A promising preventative for juvenile delinquency. *American Psychologist, 47,* 997–1006. http://dx.doi.org/10.1037/0003-066x.47.8.997
14. Iatrogenic. (n.d.). In Oxford English Dictionary online, http://dictionary.oed.com. British author Aldous Huxley once described an epidemic as "iatrogenic" in that it was "produced and fostered by the very physicians who were supposed to be restoring the patients to health." Huxley, A. (1952). *Devils of Loudun*. London, England: Chatto & Windus, p. 219.
15. I am not the first to make this connection. See Gatti, U., Tremblay, R. E., & Vitaro, F. (2009). Iatrogenic effect of juvenile justice. *Journal of Child Psychology and Psychiatry, 50,* 991–998. http://dx.doi.org/10.1111/j.1469-7610.2008.02057.x. See also Dierkhising, C. B., Lane, A., & Natsuaki, M. N. (2013). Victims behind bars: A preliminary study of abuse during juvenile incarceration and post-release social and emotional functioning. *Psychology, Public Policy, and Law, 20,* 181–190. http://dx.doi.org/10.1037/law0000002
16. The research suggesting that there are positive outcomes that can come from proper, caring juvenile justice interventions is long-standing. See, e.g., Simpson, J., Eynon, T., & Reckless, W. (1963). Institutionalization as perceived by the juvenile offender. *Sociology and Social Research, 48,* 13–23.
17. Lerner, S. (1986). *Bodily harm: The pattern of fear and violence at the California Youth Authority.* Bolinas, CA: Commonweal Research Institute, p. 46. See also Abbott, D. E., & Carter, J. (2006). *I cried, you didn't listen: A survivor's exposé of the California Youth Authority.* Oakland, CA: AK Press; and Krisberg, B. A., & Austin, J. F. (1993). *Reinventing juvenile justice.* Thousand Oaks, CA: Sage.

18. Lerner (1986), *Bodily harm*, p. 47.
19. Sampson, R. J., & Laub, J. H. (1993). *Crime in the making: Pathways and turning points through life*. Cambridge, MA: Harvard University Press, p. 135. http://dx.doi.org/10.1177/0011128793039003010. They also wrote about what they describe as the "knifing off" of opportunities that comes about as a result of juvenile incarceration; that is, the way in which serious delinquency cuts out the opportunity for a conventional life later on (p. 142).
20. Sampson & Laub (1993), *Crime in the making*, p. 168. See Chapter 7 in their book for a detailed discussion of this issue.
21. The participants in the original Glueck study were, on average, between 14 and 15 years old in 1939, the year the study began. The researchers collected longitudinal data on them through with two separate follow-ups, one when the participants were about 25 years old and the final follow-up when they were 32 (with data collection ending in 1963). See Sampson & Laub (1993), *Crime in the making*, Chapter 2, for a detailed description of the Glueck data and methodology by which they were collected.
22. According to the latest Adoption and Foster Care Analysis and Reporting System (AFCARS) Report maintained by the Department of Health and Human Services, there were nearly a half million (437,465) children in foster care as of September 30, 2016. See https://www.acf.hhs.gov/sites/default/files/cb/afcarsreport24.pdf
23. See, e.g., Turney, K., & Wildeman, C. (2017). Adverse childhood experiences among children placed in and adopted from foster care: Evidence from a nationally representative survey. *Child Abuse & Neglect, 64*, 117–129. http://dx.doi.org/10.1016/j.chiabu.2016.12.009
24. Cooper, C. S., Peterson, N. L., & Meier, J. H. (1987). Variables associated with disrupted placement in a select sample of abused and neglected children. *Child Abuse & Neglect, 11*, 75–86. http://dx.doi.org/10.1016/0145-2134(87)90035-4
25. See, e.g., Nunno, M. A., & Motz, J. K. (1988). The development of an effective response to the abuse of children in out-of-home care. *Child Abuse & Neglect, 12*, 521–528. http://dx.doi.org/10.1016/0145-2134(88)90069-5; Weinberg, L. (2007). *The systematic mistreatment of children in the foster care system: Through the cracks*. New York, NY: Haworth Press. For a broader discussion and application of the concept of retraumatization, see Duckworth, M. P., & Follette, V. M. (Eds.). (2012). *Retraumatization: Assessment, treatment, and prevention*. New York, NY: Routledge.
26. See, e.g., Pelton, L. H. (1987). Not for poverty alone: Foster care population trends in the twentieth century [Special issue]. *Journal of Sociology & Social Welfare, 14*, 37–62.
27. See *California child and family services review: Statewide assessment* (August, 2002). Sacramento, CA: California Department of Social Services. See, especially, p. 108. The report cannot have come as a surprise to California officials. A decade earlier, the watchdog Little Hoover Commission had informed the governor and legislature that the state's foster care system had "failed miserably" to safeguard the lives and future of the tens of thousands of children who were "cast adrift" in it. Little Hoover Commission (1992, April). *Mending our broken children: Restructuring foster care in California*. Sacramento, CA: Little Hoover Commission.
28. McCormick, E. (2002, December 1). Alarming breakdowns in state foster care. *San Francisco Chronicle*, A1, A20, p. A20. The report was conducted by the California Department of Social Services as part of a nationwide review initiated by the U.S. Department of Health and Social Services (DHHS). California was the first among many states slated for these DHSS-ordered statewide reviews of their foster care systems. State officials said they expected to "fail" the review and expected that other states would as well. One public official was quoted as saying, "There's a growing national consensus that the system we have now . . . has not served children as well as we would have liked" (p. A20).

29. Therolf, G. (2013, December 18). Private foster care system, intended to save children, endangers some. *Los Angeles Times*. Retrieved from http://www.latimes.com/local/la-me-foster-care-dto-htmlstory.html. The *Times* analysis also found that those living in private agencies' homes were a third more likely to endure emotional or sexual abuse. Although the largest foster care system, California was not alone in providing dangerously substandard care for foster children. For example, a lawsuit filed against the foster care system in Arizona alleged that the state "pulls children from tumultuous family lives only to place them in more turbulent circumstances in the care of the state's child welfare system." Rojas, R. (2015, March 25). In Arizona, struggles to overhaul foster care. *The New York Times*, pp. A16, A20, at p. A16. The system began a long overdue restructuring when a whistleblower revealed that more than 6,500 complaints about abuse and neglect had been lodged but completely ignored. Yet the necessary overhaul was itself delayed. The governor "acknowledged that the state had come up 'woefully short' and ousted the director of the Department of Child Safety" (p. A16), but documents filed in the lawsuit "paint[ed] a picture on ongoing dysfunction," including a failure to address "the adverse conditions faced by children already in the state's foster care system" (p. A20).
30. Davey, M. (2004, February 24). Youths leaving foster care are found facing obstacles. *The New York Times*, p. A10, reporting on a Chapin Hall Center study, which can be found at Courtney, M. E., Terao, S., & Bost, N. (2004). *Midwest evaluation of the adult functioning of foster youth: Conditions of youth preparing to leave state care*. Chicago, IL: Chapin Hall Center for Children at the University of Chicago. Retrieved from https://www.chapinhall.org/wp-content/uploads/Midwest-Study-Youth-Preparing-to-Leave-Care.pdf
31. See, e.g., Alavi, Z., & Calleja, N. G. (2012). Understanding the use of psychotropic medications in the child welfare system: Causes, consequences, and proposed solutions. *Child Welfare, 91*, 77–94; and Longhofer, J., Floersch, J., & Okpych, N. (2011). Foster youth and psychotropic treatment: Where next? *Children and Youth Services Review, 33*, 395–404. http://dx.doi.org/10.1016/j.childyouth.2010.10.006
32. Kutz, G. D. (2011). *Foster children: HHS guidance could help states improve oversight of psychotropic prescriptions*. Washington, DC: U.S. Government Accountability Office. See also Burton, T. M. (2011, December 2). Foster kids are overly medicated, report says, *The Wall Street Journal*, p. A4. Retrieved from https://www.wsj.com/articles/SB10001424052970204397704577072743861074270
33. de Sa, K. (2014, August 24). Drugging our kids: Children in California's foster care system are prescribed unproven, risky medications at alarming rates. *Santa Cruz Sentinel*, pp. A1, A7–A8.
34. de Sa (2014). *Drugging our kids*, p. A7.
35. Barn, R., & Tan, J.-P. (2012). Foster youth and crime: Employing general strain theory to promote understanding. *Journal of Criminal Justice, 40*, 212–220. http://dx.doi.org/10.1016/j.jcrimjus.2012.01.004; Courtney, M. E., Dworsky, A., Brown, A., Cary, C., Love, K., & Vorhies, V. (2011). *Midwest evaluations of adult functioning of former foster youth: Outcomes at age 26*. Chicago, IL: Chapin Hall Center for Children at the University of Chicago. Retrieved from https://www.chapinhall.org/wp-content/uploads/Midwest-Eval-Outcomes-at-Age-26.pdf; Ryan, J. P., Hernandez, P. H., & Herz, D. (2007). Developmental trajectories of offending for male adolescents leaving foster care. *Social Work Research, 31*, 83–93. http://dx.doi.org/10.1093/swr/31.2.83
36. See, e.g., Rebbe, R., Nurius, P. S., Ahrens, K. R., & Courtney, M. E. (2017). Adverse childhood experiences among youth aging out of foster care: A latent class analysis. *Children and Youth Services Review, 74*, 108–116. http://dx.doi.org/10.1016/j.childyouth.2017.02.004; Salazar, A. M., Keller, T. E., Gowen, K., & Courtney, M. E. (2013). Trauma exposure and PTSD among older adolescents in

foster care. *Social Psychiatry and Psychiatric Epidemiology, 48,* 545–551. http://dx.doi.org/10.1007/s00127-012-0563-0; Turney, & Wildeman (2017), Adverse childhood experiences among children placed in and adopted from foster care: Evidence from a nationally representative survey.

37. See, e.g., Jonson-Reid, M., & Barth, R. P. (2000). From maltreatment report to juvenile incarceration: The role of child welfare services. *Child Abuse and Neglect, 24,* 505–520. http://dx.doi.org/10.1016/S0145-2134(00)00107-1; Jonson-Reid, M., & Barth, R. P. (2000). From placement to prison: The path to adolescent incarceration from child welfare supervised foster or group care. *Children and Youth Services Review, 22,* 493–516. http://dx.doi.org/10.1016/S0190-7409(00)00100-6
38. For a thoughtful discussion of the legal implications of this fact, see Pollack, D., Eisenberg, K., & Sundarsingh, A. (2012). Foster care as a mitigating circumstance in criminal proceedings. *Temple Political & Civil Rights Law Review, 22,* 45–67.
39. Doyle, J. J., Jr. (2008). Child protection and adult crime: Using investigator assignment to estimate causal effects of foster care. *Journal of Political Economy, 116,* 746–770. http://dx.doi.org/10.1086/590216. The author distinguishes cases "at the margin" from those where the children were "in such danger that all investigators would agree that the child should be placed in care" (p. 767). See also Doyle, J. J., Jr. (2013). Causal effects of foster care: An instrumental-variables approach. *Children and Youth Services Review, 35,* 1143–1151. http://dx.doi.org/10.1016/j.childyouth.2011.03.014
40. See, e.g., Crawford, B., Pharris, A. B., & Dorsett-Burrell, R. (2018). Risk of serious criminal involvement among former foster youth aging out of care. *Children and Youth Services Review, 93,* 451–457. http://dx.doi.org/10.1016/j.childyouth.2018.08.027; Lee, J. S., Courtney, M. E., Harachi, T. W., & Tajima, E. A. (2015). Labeling and the effect of adolescent legal system involvement on adult outcomes for foster youth aging out of care. *American Journal of Orthopsychiatry, 85,* 441–451. http://dx.doi.org/10.1037/ort0000090; Lee, J. S., Courtney, M. E., & Tajima, E. (2014). Extended foster care support during the transition to adulthood: Effect on the risk of arrest. *Children and Youth Services Review, 42,* 34–42. http://dx.doi.org/10.1016/j.childyouth.2014.03.018; and Yang, J., McCuish, E. C., & Corrado, R. R. (2017). Foster care beyond placement: Offending outcomes in emerging adulthood. *Journal of Criminal Justice, 53,* 46–54. http://dx.doi.org/10.1016/j.jcrimjus.2017.08.009
41. Salazar, Keller, Gowen, & Courtney (2013), Trauma exposure and PTSD among older adolescents in foster care.
42. Katz, C. C., Courtney, M. E., & Novotny, E. (2017). Pre-foster care maltreatment class as a predictor of maltreatment in foster care. *Child and Adolescent Social Work Journal, 34,* 35–49. http://dx.doi.org/10.1007/s10560-016-0476-y
43. Osgood, D. W., Foster, E. M., & Courtney, M. E. (2010). Vulnerable populations and the transition to adulthood. *Future of Children, 20,* 209–229, p. 291. http://dx.doi.org/10.1353/foc.0.0047
44. See, e.g., Behar, L., Friedman, R., Pinto, A., Katz-Levy, J., & Jones, W. G. (2007). Protecting youth placed in unlicensed, unregulated residential "treatment" facilities. *Family Court Review, 45,* 399–413. http://dx.doi.org/10.1111/j.1744-1617.2007.00155.x; and Pavkov, T. W., Negash, S., Lourie, I. S., & Hug, R. W. (2010). Critical failures in a regional network of residential treatment facilities. *American Journal of Orthopsychiatry, 80,* 151–159. http://dx.doi.org/10.1111/j.1939-0025.2010.01018.x
45. Bundy, T. (2011, March 20). Unclear oversight yields repeated violations at home for troubled youth. *The New York Times,* p. 29A.
46. Bundy (2011), Unclear oversight yields repeated violations at home for troubled youth, p. 29A.

47. For a discussion of some of the factors that account for the overrepresentation of intellectually disabled persons in the criminal justice system, see Haney, C. (2006). *Reforming punishment: Psychological limits to the pains of imprisonment.* Washington, DC: American Psychological Association, pp. 244–247. Reliable data on the prevalence of developmental or intellectual disability in the criminal justice system are difficult to acquire, in part because of the inconsistent ways in which it is assessed (if at all). In my summary of published literature reviews on the topic, I estimated the consensus of the studies placed the prevalence rate at "somewhere between 3–10%." Haney (2006), *Reforming punishment,* p. 252, and, particularly on p. 253, Table 8.2. Joan Petersilia offered a similar estimate a decade earlier. See Petersilia, J. (1997), Justice for all? Offenders with mental retardation and the California corrections system. *Prison Journal, 77,* 358–380.
48. Hakim, D. (2011, March 13). At state-run homes, abuse and impunity. *The New York Times,* pp. 1, 22–23, p. 1.
49. Hakim (2011), At state-run homes, abuse and impunity, p. 23, referring to the Commission on Quality of Care and Advocacy for Persons with Disabilities.
50. Hakin, D. (2011, June 14). State official cites progress in reporting abuse at group homes. *The New York Times,* p. A18.
51. Hakin (2011), State official cites progress in reporting abuse at group homes, p. A18.
52. Blumenson, E. D., & Nilsen, E. S. (2002). How to construct an underclass, or how the war on drugs became a war on education. *Journal of Gender, Race and Justice, 6,* 61–109, p. 64 (emphasis added). See also the conclusion of two researchers to the effect that "school personnel may simply be dumping problem students out on the streets, only to find them later causing increased violence and disruption in the community." Skiba, R., & Peterson, R. (1999). The dark side of zero tolerance: Can punishment lead to safe schools? *Phi Delta Kappan, 80,* 372–376, 381–382, p. 376.
53. Block, A., Special education law and delinquent children: An overview. *Juvenile Justice Fact Sheet,* Institute of Law, Psychiatry & Public Policy, University of Virginia (undated), p. 9. This is because "[f]or many special education students, particularly those who carry the label 'emotionally disturbed,' delinquent behavior such as threatening comments, property destruction, and aggression towards others is often a manifestation of their disability." Block, p. 7. Yet school administrators, who are legally prevented from expelling children for their behavior if it is a direct manifestation of a disability, appear increasingly willing to file criminal charges against them.
54. Reyes, P. (1989). Factors that affect the commitment of children at risk to stay in school. In J. Jakebrink (Ed.), *Children at risk* (pp. 18–31). Springfield, IL: Charles C. Thomas.
55. For example, see the conclusion of a 12-city study to the effect that "in disproportionate numbers, it is African American and Latino students whose futures are wrecked by zero-tolerance." Gordon, R., Della Piana, L., & Keleher, T. (2000, March). *Facing the consequences: An examination of racial discrimination in U.S. public schools.* Oakland, CA: Applied Research Center, p. 10. Retrieved from https://files.eric.ed.gov/fulltext/ED454323.pdf
56. Mallett, C. A. (2016). The school-to-prison pipeline: A critical review of the punitive paradigm shift. *Child & Adolescent Social Work Journal, 33,* 15–24, p. 20. http://dx.doi.org/10.1007/s10560-015-0397-1
57. Hirschfield, P. J. (2008). Preparing for prison? The criminalization of school discipline in the USA. *Theoretical Criminology, 12,* 79–101, p. 81. http://dx.doi.org/10.1177/1362480607085795
58. See, e.g., Kupchik, A., & Monahan, T. (2006). The new American school: Preparation for post-industrial discipline. *British Journal of Sociology of Education, 27,*

617–631. http://dx.doi.org/10.1080/01425690600958816; Rabinowitz, J. (2006). Leaving homeroom in handcuffs: Why an over-reliance on law enforcement to ensure school safety is detrimental to children. *Cardozo Public Law, Policy & Ethics Journal, 4,* 153–194. An April, 2014, *New York Times* editorial noted that "[c]omplaints about dangerous disciplinary practices involving shock weapons"—primarily Tasers—"are cropping up all over the country. The problem has its roots in the 1990s, when school districts began ceding even routine disciplinary duties to police and security officers, who were utterly unprepared to deal with children." Torturing children at school [Editorial]. (2014, April 12). *The New York Times,* p. A18. See also Lyons, W., & Drew, J. (2006). *Punishing schools: Fear and citizenship in American public schools.* Ann Arbor: University of Michigan Press; and Monahan, T., & Torres, R. (2010). *Schools under surveillance: Cultures of control in public education.* New Brunswick, NJ: Rutgers University Press.

59. See, e.g., Christie, C. A., Jolivette, K., & Nelson, C. M. (2005). Breaking the school to prison pipeline: Identifying school risk and protective factors for youth delinquency. *Exceptionality, 13,* 69–88. http://dx.doi.org/10.1207/s15327035ex1302_2; and Lochner, L., & Moretti, E. (2004). The effect of education on crime: Evidence from prison inmates, arrests, and self-reports. *American Economic Review, 94,* 155–189. http://dx.doi.org/10.1257/000282804322970751. Scott and Saucedo described how such school-to-prison pipeline scenarios can unfold:

> Once expelled, students who face poverty, the absence of a high school diploma, and a culture of street crime will find it almost impossible to find gainful employment. For many, the drug trade will seem to be one of the only potential sources of revenue.

Scott, R., & Saucedo, M. (2012). Mass incarceration, the school-to-prison pipeline, and the struggle of "secure communities" in Illinois. *Journal of Educational Controversy, 7,* Article 7. http://cedar.wwu.edu/jec/vol7/iss1/7. See also Wolf, K. C., & Kupchik, A. (2016). School suspensions and adverse experiences in adulthood. *Justice Quarterly, 34,* 407–430. http://dx.doi.org/10.1080/07418825.2016.1168475

60. See, e.g., Shaw, C. R. (1930). *The jack-roller: A delinquent boy's own story.* Chicago, IL: University of Chicago Press; Shaw, C. R., & McKay, H. D. (1931). *Social factors in juvenile delinquency: A study of the community, the family, and the gang in relation to delinquent behavior for the National Commission on Law Observance and Enforcement* (Vol. 2, No. 13). Washington, DC: Government Printing Office.

61. For example, the preamble to the Juvenile Delinquency and Youth Offenses Control Act signed by President Kennedy in 1961 noted that "[d]elinquency and youth offense occur disproportionately among school dropouts, unemployed youth faced with limited opportunities and with employment barriers, and youth in deprived family situations." Quoted in LaFree, G., Drass, K. A., & O'Day, P. (1992). Race and crime in postwar America: Determinants of African-American and White rates, 1957–1988. *Criminology, 30,* 157–188. http://dx.doi.org/10.1111/j.1745-9125.1992.tb01101.x

62. Despite its promise, the "Great Society" era of progressive social policy was short-lived, with most programs lasting only a few years after President Lyndon Johnson began them in the mid-1960s. Richard Nixon moved to end many of them after his election in 1968. See, e.g., Etzioni, A. (1970). Consensus and reforms in the "Great Society." *Sociological Inquiry, 40,* 113–122. http://dx.doi.org/10.1111/j.1475-682X.1970.tb00987.x; Haveman, R. H. (1987). *Poverty policy and poverty research: The Great Society and the social sciences.* Madison: University of Wisconsin Press. In his 1965 State of the Union Address, President Johnson pledged to "discover the causes of crime and [recommend] better ways to prevent it," in part by "search[ing] out answers to the problem of crime and delinquency." Johnson, L. B. (1965). State of the Union Message. *Current History, 48,* 176–182, p. 178.

63. See, e.g., Cullen, F. T. (1995). Assessing the penal harm movement. *Journal of Research in Crime and Delinquency, 32,* 338–358. http://dx.doi.org/10.1177/0022427895032003005
64. See, e.g., the discussions in Drinan, C. H. (2018). *The war on kids: How American juvenile justice lost its way.* New York, NY: Oxford University Press; Nellis, A. (2016). *A return to justice: Rethinking our approach to juveniles in the system.* Lanham, MD: Rowman and Littlefield (especially Chapter 4).
65. Timmons, D. (1960, March 13). Troubled youths to get airy haven. *Dayton Daily News.*
66. Stout, N. (1964, August 14). BIS needs larger staff, more psychiatric facilities. *The Dispatch.*
67. "The bomb is the antique and largely mis-named Boys Industrial School," a place whose "lack of personnel, facilities and time make the concept of rehabilitation for the youthful inmates almost farcical." Stout, N. (1964, August 10). Some can hear tick-ticking of human bombs at BIS. *The Dispatch.*
68. LaRochelle, T. (1967, February 19). Fairfield School for Boys was a place to make grown men cry. *Akron Beacon Journal.*
69. Brodsky, S. L. (1982). Correctional change and the social scientist: A case study. *Journal of Community Psychology, 10,* 128–132. http://dx.doi.org/10.1002/1520-6629(198204)10:2<128::AID-JCOP2290100205>3.0.CO;2-K. This study reported on conditions at the Industrial School at Mayaguez, Puerto Rico.
70. In addition, correctional officers at this Texas facility "administer[ed] blows to the face with both open and closed hands." *Morales v. Turman,* 364 F. Supp. 166, 170 (E.D. Tex., 1973). Jerome Miller, one of the experts who participated in the *Morales* litigation, described some of what he saw:

    > I'd spent a week or so touring Texas reform schools, where I saw kids beaten, tied, locked in isolation, forced to run till they dropped, hauling dirt from one pile to another and back again, gassed and maced while locked in closet like cells, and chased by bloodhounds and shotgun-toting guards.

    Miller, J. G. (1991). *Last one over the wall. The Massachusetts experiment in closing reform schools.* Columbus: Ohio State University Press, p. 215. The *Morales* court also found that children were being tear gassed as a form of punishment, and that the staff left them in unnecessarily severe solitary confinement cells for excessive periods of time. Even though nearly one quarter of the inmates in the six Texas facilities that were the focus of the litigation were Mexican American, and some could speak little or no English, the judge in *Morales* found that "[t]he speaking of Spanish by inmates is, or has been in the past, discouraged and has been in the past the subject of disciplinary action by [Texas] personnel." See 364 F. Supp. at 172–173.
71. *Nelson v. Heyne,* 355 F. Supp. 451, 454 (N.D. Ind. 1972).
72. The judge noted that the staff used handcuffs and plastic straps to bind the boys to their beds and other places in the facility "for hours at a time." Moreover, the children were "bound in this manner with a device connecting hands and feet behind their backs and have been left lying on their stomachs on the floor." *Pena v. New York State Division for Youth,* 419 F. Supp. 203, 211 (S.D.N.Y. 1976).
73. *Gary H. v. Hegstrom,* 831 F.2d 1430, 1434, 1435 (9th Cir. 1987), quoting *Gary H. v. Hegstrom,* No. CV 77-1039-BU 85-3730, slip op. at 18–19 (D. Or. Dec. 17, 1984). Although the opinions in the *Gary H.* case were written in the mid- to late-1980s, they addressed conditions of confinement that existed in the Oregon juvenile facility during the previous decade. Indeed, as the Ninth Circuit Court of Appeals noted, the unconstitutional conditions persisted even after "the original plaintiffs [had] become adults." *Gary H. v. Hegstrom,* 831 F. 2d at 1432.
74. *Morgan v. Sproat,* 432 F. Supp. 1130 (S.D. Miss. 1977).

75. *Terry D., et al. v. L.E. Rader, et al.* Case No: 5:78-cv-00004 (W.D. Okla. 1978).
76. Darkness to light, *Tulsa World*, February 24, 2002, p. 11. The lawsuit stalled as attorneys for both sides tried to negotiate a settlement. Outside investigative reports put pressure on the state to resolve the issues, but the case dragged on for more than a decade.
77. A legacy of shocking conditions and scandalous practices was uncovered that dated back many years. The investigative reports were based on detailed reviews of files obtained from numerous juvenile justice agencies and institutions, extensive interviews with Oklahoma juveniles who were confined in these facilities, and many staff members who worked in them that described "large, monolithic, strictly-secured institutions on remote campuses" in which a history of practices was uncovered that was "so macabre that it would make Charles Dickens wince." This and the other quotes in this section were taken from the Gannett News Service special report "Oklahoma Shame," published in 1982, which compiled the series of articles that had been previously published about the Oklahoma juvenile justice system. The articles described practices that apparently were widespread throughout the system. For example, a veteran social worker at one Oklahoma "training school" told investigators that "[s]tudents assigned at Boley would leave the institution with little knowledge other than training in unnatural sex and other undesirable activities." An independent Oklahoma City consulting firm concluded that three of the largest and "most notorious institutions" should be closed because they had "outlived their usefulness." Other reports spoke of "rampant child abuse" and various inhumane practices that "fester within [the state's] system of residential homes and training schools." There were admitted instances of children being hog-tied, and officials acknowledged that children confined at one facility were sometimes placed "in solitary cells for as long as 20 or 30 days at a time." The director of the state's juvenile system at the time conceded that such practices "would drive you and I stark raving crazy."
78. Lerner, S. (1982). *The CYA report: Conditions of life at the California Youth Authority.* Bolinas, CA: Common Knowledge Press, p. 8. For an evaluation of the harmful conditions of confinement in various California Youth Authority facilities, see also Lerner (1986), *Bodily harm.* In addition to the Youth Authority facilities in California, other juvenile facilities in the state were reportedly to be in crisis. For example, here is how conditions inside the state's largest youth holding facility were described in the mid-1990s:

    > Central Juvenile Hall, along with LA's two other detention halls, have a rated capacity to hold thirteen hundred kids. Most days they hold more than two thousand children in custody. The halls have responded to the crunch of kids and the escalating tensions and violence that result by issuing caustic pepper spray to their staff members, a measure long resisted but now embraced.

    Humes, E. (1996). *No matter how loud I shout: A year in the life of juvenile court.* New York, NY: Simon & Schuster, p. 360.
79. Silberman, C. E. (1978). *Criminal violence, criminal justice.* New York, NY: Random House, p. 320. Also in the mid-1970s, the National Advisory Commission on Criminal Justice Standards and Goals observed that although the nation's juvenile justice institutions were successful at meting out punishment to young lawbreakers, they typically accomplished very little else. The Commission concluded that juvenile justice facilities appeared to "relieve the community of responsibility by removing the young offender," but they also simultaneously "make successful integration unlikely. They change the committed offender, but the change is more likely to be negative than positive." National Commission on Criminal Justice Standards and Goals (1973). *Task force report on corrections.*

Washington, DC: Government Printing Office, p. 597. The report noted that although juvenile institutions gave the impression of protecting the community, "the protection does not last," in part because far too few juveniles were rehabilitated enough to refrain from future crime.

80. Silberman (1978), *Criminal violence, criminal justice*, p. 330.
81. Silberman (1978), *Criminal violence, criminal justice*, p. 312.
82. Strasburg, P. A. (1978). *Violent delinquents: A report to the Ford Foundation from the Vera Institute of Justice*. New York, NY: Monarch, p. 125. At around the same time period that these reports were published, a number of harsh commentaries written by former juvenile justice staff members appeared decrying the harmful long-term effects of confinement in the facilities where they had worked. In one case, ex–juvenile detention officers described a "negative dehumanized environment" in which "authoritarian-punitive" programs and "humiliating living conditions" threatened the self-esteem of the young people confined in them. Fetrow, R., & Fetrow, A. (1974). How a pre-trial facility can destroy the self-esteem of the juvenile. *International Journal of Offender Therapy and Comparative Criminology, 18*, 227–232, pp. 228, 230. http://dx.doi.org/10.1177/0306624X7401800303. They concluded that "[i]n this limited arena of interaction, the youngster is often traumatized for life . . . [and] in a state of chronic anxiety with nothing to maintain his self-esteem." (p. 231).
83. Shannon, L. (1982). *Assessing the relationship of adult criminal careers to juvenile careers: A summary.* Washington, DC: Department of Justice, Office of Juvenile Justice and Delinquency Prevention. The study examined three birth cohorts (born in 1942, 1949, and 1955) in a sample that totaled over 6,000 persons who had continuous residence in the same community—Racine, Wisconsin. The longitudinal design focused on their juvenile and adult police and court records at designated periods over time.
84. That is,

    > [I]t is apparent that the consequences of processing have been continuing misbehavior and continuing involvement while similar persons who have not become so heavily involved in the system are less likely to continue to engage in behavior which results in their names appearing in the public records.

    Shannon (1982), *Assessing the relationship*, p. 15. An article published that same year helped to explain why. It described the typical juvenile institution as one that "engenders a constant struggle for survival" in an environment where wards "spend much of their time either exploiting weaker youths or defending themselves against victimization." Davi, D. T. (1982). Chance, change and challenge in juvenile corrections. *Juvenile & Family Court Journal, 33*, 45–50, p. 47. http://dx.doi.org/10.1111/j.1755-6988.1982.tb01517.x
85. Parent, D. G., Lieter, V., Kennedy, S., Livens, L., Wentworth, D., & Wilcox, S. (1994). *Conditions of confinement: Juvenile detention and corrections facilities*. Washington, DC: Office of Juvenile Justice and Delinquency Prevention. See also Otto, R., Greenstein, J., Johnson, M., & Friedman, R. (1992). Prevalence of mental disorders among youth in the juvenile justice system. In J. Cocozza (Ed.), *Responding to the mental health needs of youth in the juvenile justice system* (pp. 7–48). Seattle, WA: The National Coalition for the Mentally Ill in the Criminal Justice System.
86. Puritz, P., & Scali, M. A. (1998). *Beyond the walls: Improving conditions of confinement for youth in custody* (p. xi). Washington, DC: Department of Justice.
87. Puritz & Scali (1998), *Beyond the walls*, p. xi. The tendency for institutional placements to become punitive and excessively controlling—even those that initially are conceived as less restrictive alternatives—seems widespread. Teresa O'Neill's study of "secure accommodation" facilities—the quaint British term for facilities in which children too young to be imprisoned were housed—found that they

were dominated by a concern for control that quickly led to the use of more serious sanctions (like locking the children in their rooms, taking away all of their possessions, and sometimes even turning off the electricity in the unit). O'Neill's interviews suggested that even those staff members who actively participated in the widespread "macho" institutional culture understood that secure accommodation was ultimately an ineffective way to deal with the troubled children who were under their control. O'Neill, T. (2001). *Children in secure accommodation: A gendered exploration of locked institutional care for children in trouble.* London, England: Jessica Kingsley.

88. Ann Nurse's study of "youth prisons" in the California Youth Authority documented the harsh nature of the day-to-day institutional life to which young male wards were subjected. In addition to the direct psychological impact of their authoritarian treatment, Nurse was concerned about how the treatment would compromise the wards' later attempts at parenting. She noted that "the young men are exposed to a model of control maintained through fear and monitoring," one that becomes a "potent" model of parenting that often teaches these young men "to use punishment as a way to manage their children." Nurse, A. M. (2002). *Fatherhood arrested: Parenting from within the juvenile justice system.* Nashville, TN: Vanderbilt University Press, p. 53 (internal citation omitted). As I point out later in this chapter, there is another potential dimension to this dynamic. Some young men in these environments have already been exposed to such a dysfunctional model of parenting and are "reexperiencing" authoritarian, harshly punitive treatment, administered this time by institutional staff members rather than parental figures in their homes.
89. I discuss the effects of parental incarceration in greater detail in Chapter 8.
90. Feld, B. C. (1999). *Bad kids: Race and the transformation of the juvenile court.* New York, NY: Oxford University Press.
91. I discussed the origins and use of the term "superpredators" in notes 113–118 in Chapter 1.
92. Zoglin, R. (1996, January 15). Now for the bad news: A teenage time bomb. *Time Magazine,* 52–53.
93. James Alan Fox, then the president of the American Society of Criminology, quoted in Krajicek, D. (1999, April). "Superpredators": The making of a myth. *Youth Today,* 1.
94. See Schiraldi, V., & Soler, M. (1998). The will of the people? The public's opinion of the Violent and Repeat Juvenile Offender Act of 1997. *Crime & Delinquency, 44,* 590–601. http://dx.doi.org/10.1177/0011128798044004007
95. Redding, R. E. (1997). Juveniles transferred to criminal court: Legal reform proposals based on social science research. *Utah Law Review, 3,* 709–763, p. 713, n. 23 (including the references cited therein).
96. This research is too extensive to review in detail. However, for overviews and representative examples, see Arnett, J. J. (1992). Reckless behavior in adolescence: A developmental perspective. *Developmental Review, 12,* 339–373. http://dx.doi.org/10.1016/0273-2297(92)90013-R; Grisso, T. (1996). Society's retributive response to juvenile violence: A developmental perspective. *Law and Human Behavior, 20,* 229–247. http://dx.doi.org/10.1007/BF01499022; Grisso, T. (1997). Juvenile competency to stand trial: Questions in an era of punitive reform. *Criminal Justice, 12,* 5–11; Steinberg, L., & Cauffman, E. (1996). Maturity of judgment in adolescence: Psychosocial factors in adolescent decision making. *Law and Human Behavior, 20,* 249–272. http://dx.doi.org/10.1007/BF01499023; Woolard, J. L., Reppucci, N. D., & Redding, R. E. (1996). Theoretical and methodological issues in studying children's capacities in legal contexts. *Law and Human Behavior, 20,* 219–228. http://dx.doi.org/10.1007/BF01499021

97. Redding (1997), Juveniles transferred to criminal court, p. 714. As I noted earlier, there were some 47 states and the District of Columbia that had substantially changed their juvenile justice laws by the end of the 1990s "to include more transfers of youth to adult court, more mandatory minimum sentences, and more incarceration." Puritz & Scali (1998), *Beyond the walls*, p. xi.
98. The increasing numbers of juveniles who were adjudicated and punished as though they were adults included many first-time lawbreakers "who are not likely to offend again, many who themselves have been victims or otherwise are vulnerable, and many whose choices were the consequence of immature judgments rather than antisocial behavior," and even though there was a long-standing consensus among experts that such experiences were likely to be especially traumatic and damaging. Grisso (1996), Society's retributive response to juvenile violence, p. 240. For an early discussion of some of the trauma and damage, see Johnson, R. (1978). Youth in crisis: Dimensions of self-destructive conduct among adolescent prisoners. *Adolescence, 13,* 461–482. For a broad-based discussion of the overall trends toward policies of adult transfer, see Fagan, J. & Zimring, F. E. (2000). *The changing borders of juvenile justice: Transfer of adolescents to the criminal court.* Chicago, IL: University of Chicago Press. Even the Justice Department acknowledged that, by 1998, the increased incarceration of juveniles in adult correctional institutions had "exacerbated the unlawful conditions found in many facilities where youth are held." Puritz & Scali (1998), *Beyond the walls*, p. xi. In one state, for example, a long list of abusive and harmful conditions to which juveniles were exposed in adult jails were documented, including "grim cells lacking natural direct natural lighting and crawling with cockroaches, rodents, and other vermin," deficient to nonexistent education and mental health services, regular and severe incidents of violence, and arbitrary and excessive terms of punishment and long stays in segregation. Human Rights Watch. (1999) *No minor matter: Children in Maryland's jails.* New York, NY: Author, at p. 2.
99. See Bishop, D. M., Lanza-Kaduce, L., & Frazier, C. E. (1998). Juvenile justice under attack: An analysis of the causes and impact of recent reforms. *University of Florida Journal of Law and Public Policy, 10,* 129–155; Bishop, D. M., Frazier, C. E., Lanza-Kaduce, L., & Winner, L. (1996). The transfer of juveniles to criminal court: Does it make a difference? *Crime & Delinquency, 42,* 171–191; Winner, L., Lanza-Kaduce, L., Bishop, D. M., & Frazier, C. E. (1996). The transfer of juveniles to criminal court: Reexamining recidivism over the long term. *Crime & Delinquency, 43,* 548–563. In addition, there was evidence to suggest that, at least in some jurisdictions, juveniles whose cases were processed adult criminal court were actually sentenced more severely than their young adult counterparts. Kurlychek, M. C., & Johnson, B. D. (2004). The juvenile penalty: A comparison of juvenile and young adult sentencing outcomes in criminal court. *Criminology, 42,* 485–515. http://dx.doi.org/10.1111/j.1745-9125.2004.tb00527.x
100. Krisberg, B. (2003). General corrections review of the California Youth Authority, December 23, p. 42. Retrieved from https://www.nccdglobal.org/sites/default/files/publication_pdf/ca-youth-authority.pdf. Staff members "complained that they lacked enough time to even talk to the wards on each shift, and were consequently not aware of the emotional state of the wards under their supervision" (p. 43). At the same time, they reported being "given very little guidance in working with very emotionally troubled, and often mentally ill, wards" (p. 46).
101. Krisberg (2003), *General corrections review*, p. 50.
102. Krisberg (2003), *General corrections review*, p. 51. The report also noted that

> [O]n any given day, between 10–12 percent of wards were housed in units in which they were confined to their rooms for 23 hours a day, with one hour permitted outside their rooms under close supervision. During this one hour that they are out

of their rooms, the wards may be in wrist and leg shackles, or they are moved to small cage-like confinement areas. (p. 51)

The latter was based on observations from a report filed a few years earlier by the Office of the Inspector General (2000, June 28), *Statewide Review of California Youth Authority Lockup Units*, which described "a system of disciplinary detention fraught with identified and potential constitutional rights violations; and a mental health delivery system in complete disarray" (quoted in Krisberg, p. 50).

103. Cited in Cohen, F. (2004). The limits of the judicial reform of prisons: What works, what does not. *Criminal Law Bulletin, 40*, 421–465, at p. 439.
104. See Halbfinger, D. M. (2003, September 1). Care of juvenile offenders in Mississippi is faulted. *The New York Times*, p. A11. See also Pear, R. (2003, September 1). Mental health care poor for some children in state custody. *The New York Times*, p. 1.
105. Human Rights Watch/American Civil Liberties Union (2006, September). *Custody and control: Conditions of confinement in New York's juvenile prisons for girls.*
106. Confessore, N. (2009, August 24). 4 youth prisons in New York used excessive force. *The New York Times*, quoting from Letter from Acting Assistant Attorney General Loretta King to New York Governor David Patterson, August 14, 2009. Retrieved from http://www.nytimes.com/2009/08/25/nyregion/25juvenile.html?_r=2&hpw. See also Task Force on Transforming Juvenile Justice (2009, December). *Charting a new course: A blueprint for transforming juvenile justice in New York State.* New York, NY: Vera Institute. Retrieved from https://storage.googleapis.com/vera-web-assets/downloads/Publications/charting-a-new-course-a-blueprint-for-transforming-juvenile-justice-in-new-york-state/legacy_downloads/Charting-a-new-course-A-blueprint-for-transforming-juvenile-justice-in-New-York-State.pdf
107. Confessore (2009), 4 youth prisons in New York used excessive force.
108. Confessore (2009), 4 youth prisons in New York used excessive force. Many of the same things could be said about Florida's notorious Arthur G. Dozier School for Boys, which was not closed until 2011. The Dozier School was described in the press as "synonymous with beatings, abuse, forced labor, neglect and, in some instances, death" over the course of its 100-year history. Alvarez, L. (2013, February 9). At boys' home, seeking graves and the reason. *The New York Times*, A1. Retrieved from https://www.nytimes.com/2013/02/10/us/10dozier.html?searchResultPosition=4. A number of first-person accounts of the brutality have appeared in print. See, e.g., Fisher, R. G. (2010). *The boys of the dark: A story of betrayal and redemption in the deep South.* New York, NY: St. Martin's Press; and Kiser, R. D. (2009). *The white house boys: An American tragedy.* Deerfield Beach, FL: Health Communications. See also Kimmerle, E. H. (2014). Forensic anthropology in long-term investigations: 100 cold years. *Annals of Anthropological Practice, 38*, 7–21. http://dx.doi.org/10.1111/napa.12039
109. Mendel, R. (2011). *No place for kids: The case for reducing juvenile incarceration* (p. 5). Baltimore, MD: Annie E. Casey Foundation.
110. Mendel (2011), *No place for kids*, p. 5.
111. Mendel (2011), *No place for kids*, p. 5.
112. Bartollas, C. F., Miller, S. J., & Dinitz, S. (1976). *Juvenile victimization: The institutional paradox.* New York, NY: Halsted, at p. 11.
113. Bartollas, Miller, & Dinitz (1976), *Juvenile victimization*, p. 197.
114. Bartollas, Miller, & Dinitz (1976), *Juvenile victimization*, p. 271.
115. Bartollas, Miller, & Dinitz (1976), *Juvenile victimization*, p. 12.
116. Bartollas, Miller, & Dinitz (1976), *Juvenile victimization*, p. 271. See also Bartollas, C. (1982). Survival problems of adolescent prisoners. In R. Johnson & H. Toch (Eds.), *The pains of imprisonment* (pp. 165–180). Beverly Hills, CA: Sage.
117. Davi (1982), Chance, change and challenge in juvenile corrections, p. 47.
118. Davi (1982), Chance, change and challenge in juvenile corrections, p. 47.

119. Davi (1982), Chance, change and challenge in juvenile corrections, p. 47.
120. Moore, J. (1996). Bearing the burden: How incarceration weakens inner-city communities. Paper read at The Unintended Consequences of Incarceration, Conference at the Vera Institute of Justice, New York, NY. See also Moore, J., & Pinderhughes, R. (1993). *In the barrios: Latinos and the underclass debate*. New York, NY: Russell Sage Foundation.
121. For a description this process in operation in highly racially/ethnically segregated California juvenile justice institutions, see Lopez-Aguado, P. (2016). "I would be a bulldog": Tracing the spillover of carceral identity. *Social Problems, 63*, 203–221. http://dx.doi.org/10.1093/socpro/spw001
122. Redding, R. E. (2001). Barriers to meeting the mental health needs of juvenile offenders in the Virginia juvenile justice system. *Juvenile Justice Fact Sheet* (p. 9). Charlottesville: Institute of Law, Psychiatry & Public Policy, University of Virginia.
123. Teplin, L. A., Abram, K. M., McClelland, G. M., Mericle, A. A., Dulcan, M. K., & Washburn, J. J. (2006, April). Psychiatric disorders of youth in detention. *Juvenile Justice Bulletin*. Washington, DC: Office of Juvenile Justice and Delinquency Prevention. See also Fazel, S., Doll, H., & Langström, N. (2008). Mental disorders among adolescents in juvenile detention and correctional facilities: A systematic review and metaregression analysis of 25 surveys. *Journal of the American Academy of Child & Adolescent Psychiatry, 47*, 1010–1019. http://dx.doi.org/10.1097/CHI.ObO13e31817eecf3; and Wasserman, G. A., McReynolds, L. S., Schwalbe, C. S., Keating, J. M., Jones, S. A. (2010). Psychiatric disorder, comorbity, and suicidal behavior in juvenile justice youth. *Criminal Justice and Behavior, 37*, 1361–1376. http://dx.doi.org/10.1177/0093854810382751
124. National Juvenile Justice and Delinquency Prevention Coalition. (2013). *Promoting safe communities: Recommendations for the 113th Congress*. Washington, DC: Government Printing Office.
125. Mallett, C. A. (2015). The incarceration of seriously traumatised adolescents in the USA: Limited progress and significant harm. *Criminal Behaviour and Mental Health, 25*, 1–9. http://dx.doi.org/10.1002/cbm.1946
126. Bernstein, N. (2014). *Burning down the house: The end of juvenile prison* (p. 298). New York, NY: The New Press.
127. Bernstein (2014), *Burning down the house: The end of juvenile prison*, p. 290 (emphasis added).
128. Following the logic of the preceding chapters, the young persons likely to be housed juvenile detention facilities are also likely to have been exposed to a disproportionate number of childhood and adolescent risks and traumas. See, e.g., Blackburn, A. G., Mullings, J. L., Marquart, J. W., & Trulson, C. R. (2007). The next generation of prisoners: Toward an understanding of violent institutionalized delinquents. *Youth Violence and Juvenile Justice, 5*, 35–56. http://dx.doi.org/10.1177/1541204006295156; Logan-Greene, P., & Jones, A. S. (2015). Chronic neglect and aggression/delinquency: A longitudinal examination. *Child Abuse & Neglect, 45*, 9–20. http://dx.doi.org/10.1016/j.chiabu.2015.04.003; and Wood, J., Foy, D. W., Layne, C., Pynoos, R., & James, C. B. (2002). An examination of the relationships between violence exposure, posttraumatic stress symptomatology, and delinquent activity: An "ecopathological" model of delinquent behavior among incarcerated adolescents. *Journal of Aggression, Maltreatment & Trauma, 6*, 127–147. http://dx.doi.org/10.1300/J146v06n01_07
129. As Carl Nightingale noted, institutions of social control began to play increasingly larger roles in the lives of inner-city children in the 1990s. In at least some cases, their harshness reinforced the lessons of the "forceful parenting" the children already received at home. Nightingale, C. H. (1994). *On the edge: A history of poor Black children and their American dreams*. New York, NY: Basic Books, p. 95. In fact,

some of the potentially destructive effects of normatively ineffective, stigmatizing, harsh juvenile justice system institutions were recognized long before this. Cf. Schur, E. M. (1973). *Radical non-intervention: Rethinking the delinquency problem.* Englewood Cliffs, NJ: Prentice-Hall.

130. See, e.g., Duckworth & Follette (2012), *Retraumatization: Assessment, treatment, and prevention.* See also Yehuda, R., & Spertus, I., & Golier, J. (2001). Relationship between childhood traumatic experiences and PTSD in adults. In S. Eth (Ed.), *PTSD in children and adolescents. Review of Psychiatry* (Vol. 20, pp. 117–158). Washington, DC: American Psychiatric Association; Glodich, A. (1998). Traumatic exposure to violence: A comprehensive review of the child and adolescent literature. *Smith College Studies in Social Work, 68,* 321–345; Straker, G., & Moosa, F. (1994). Interacting with trauma survivors in contexts of continuing trauma. *Journal of Traumatic Stress, 7,* 457–465; Everstine, D. S., & Everstine, L. (1993). *The trauma response: Treatment for emotional injury.* New York, NY: W. W. Norton.
131. Cooper, C. S., Peterson, N. L., & Meier, J. H. (1987). Variables associated with disrupted placement in a select sample of abused and neglected children. *Child Abuse & Neglect, 11,* 75–86. http://dx.doi.org/10.1016/0145-2134(87)90035-4
132. Bartollas, Miller, & Dinitz (1976), *Juvenile victimization,* p. 12.
133. Bartollas, Miller, & Dinitz (1976), *Juvenile victimization,* p. 12. One ward's compelling account of life inside a California Youth Authority facility included this observation:

> If a boy gave any sign of being in fear, he was tested immediately. Survival depended solely on how well he hid his normal feelings, his need to reach out, to feel loved and cared for. At [this facility], the worst mistake a kid could make was to show a sign of being normal. It remains the same to this day.

Abbott & Carter (2006), *I cried, you didn't listen,* p. 63

134. Bartollas, Miller, & Dinitz (1976), *Juvenile victimization,* p. 12. In her investigative report on juvenile institutions throughout the country, Nell Bernstein devoted an entire chapter to the issue of sexual abuse, which she termed "an open secret." See Bernstein (2014), *Burning down the house,* Chapter 6. She noted: "The widespread understanding that incarceration is likely to include the threat of sexual violation is among the darkest aspects of our juvenile prison system" (p. 105). See also Beck. A. J., Cantor, D., Hartge, J., & Smith, T. (2013, June). *Sexual victimization in juvenile facilities reported by youth, 2012: National survey of youth in custody, 2012.* Washington, DC: Department of Justice, indicating that 9.5% of incarcerated juveniles reported having been sexually assaulted at least once in the course of the previous year since admission.
135. Bartollas, Miller, & Dinitz (1976), *Juvenile victimization,* p. 11. The authors elaborated on some of the ways in which staff–inmate relationships can become distorted in juvenile institutions:

> Working in a "punishment-centered bureaucracy" induces staff to take advantage of the system whenever possible. Staff power over inmates is the greatest in the institution, and they frequently use it to their own advantage. Indeed, even management techniques which seem beneficial are sometimes harmful to boys. (p. 197)

136. Allen, D. (2017). *Cuz: The life and times of Michael A* (p. 81). New York, NY: Norton.
137. See, e.g., Farrington, D. P., Piquero, A. R., & Jennings, W. G. (2013). *Offending from childhood to late middle age: Recent results from the Cambridge Study in Delinquent Development.* New York, NY: Springer; and Sweeten, G., Piquero, A., & Steinberg, L. (2013). Age and the explanation of crime, revisited. *Journal of Youth and Adolescence, 42,* 921–938. http://dx.doi.org/10.1007/s10964-013-9926-4
138. Gatti, Tremblay, & Vitaro (2009), Iatrogenic effects of juvenile justice, p. 996.

139. See, e.g., Bartollas, Miller, & Dinitz (1976), *Juvenile victimization;* and Feld (1999), *Bad kids: Race and the transformation of the juvenile court.*
140. See, e.g., National Research Council. (2013). Reforming juvenile justice: A developmental approach. Washington, DC: National Academies Press; Scott, E. S., & Steinberg, L. (2008). *Rethinking juvenile justice.* Cambridge, MA: Harvard University Press.
141. See Pew Charitable Trust. (2015, November). Juvenile commitment rate drops 53%. Retrieved from https://www.pewtrusts.org/~/media/assets/2015/11/jjcommitment_infog-(8).pdf?la=en. The Office of Juvenile Justice and Delinquency Prevention reported that in 2016 that slightly over 45,000 juveniles were housed in residential facilities on any given day in the United States. OJJDP (2016), *Statistical briefing book.*
142. Dan Macallair ended his comprehensive history of the California Youth Authority by reflecting on the state's recent reforms. He offered a cautionary observation about the potential impermanency of the improvements in California that may apply to other states as well:

    > As confidence in the system grows, commitments accelerate and institutional populations swell. The increased commitments then result in political pressure to expand institutional capacity in order to accommodate the rising population. As county commitments increase, the cycle of decay accelerates, leading to deteriorating conditions, and staff abuse. Within a short time, the institutional system returns to its historical pattern.

    Macallair, D. E. (2015). *After the doors were locked: A history of youth corrections in California and the origins of twenty-first century reform.* Lanham, MD: Rowman & Littlefield, p. 250.
143. See, e.g., Dierkhising, Lane, & Natsuaki (2014), Victims behind bars. They found that nearly all (96.8%) of the children housed in secure juvenile facilities that they studied in California reported experiencing some kind of abuse there (including physical, sexual, and/or psychological abuse, denial of food, and excessive time in solitary confinement) and that the frequency of the abuse was related to subsequent PTSD, depressive symptoms, and continued postrelease criminal behavior. See also Willow, C. (2015). *Children behind bars: Why the abuse of child imprisonment must end.* Bristol, England: Policy Press. http://dx.doi.org/10.2307/j.ctt1t88zj2
144. For a plea issued in the "get tough" era to implement some of the most promising such programs, see Butts, J. A., & Mears, D. P. (2001). Reviving juvenile justice in a get-tough era. *Youth & Society, 33,* 169–198. http://dx.doi.org/10.1177/0044118X01033002003
145. Smith, C. P., & Freyd, J. J. (2014). Institutional betrayal. *American Psychologist, 69,* 575–587, p. 578.
146. Sampson & Laub (1993), *Crime in the making,* p. 8.
147. See, e.g., Gatti, Tremblay, & Vitaro (2009), Iatrogenic effect of juvenile justice; and Dierkhising, Lane, & Natsuaki (2013), Victims behind bars.

5

Criminogenic Contexts

Immediate Situations, Settings, and Circumstances

What social psychology has given to an understanding of human nature is the discovery that forces larger than ourselves determine our mental life and our actions—that chief among these forces [is] the power of the social situation.

—MAHZARIN R. BANAJI[1]

Under certain circumstances, it is not so much the kind of person a man is as it is the kind of situation in which he is placed that determines his actions.

—STANLEY MILGRAM[2]

This chapter addresses another important aspect of the relationship between social context and criminal behavior. Unlike the last several chapters that focused on accumulated *past* contexts—the developmental risk factors that are embedded in social and institutional histories—I concentrate here on the more immediate influence of the situation or setting in which criminal behavior occurs. Sociologist Kai Erickson once wrote that "[b]ehavior which qualifies one man for prison may qualify another for sainthood, since the quality of the act itself depends so much on the circumstances under which it was performed and the temper of the audience which witnessed it."[3] Although it is not my intention to argue that the circumstances under which most crime is performed can or should qualify its perpetrators for sainthood, our understanding of the moral quality of the act itself, the nature and amount of punishment that

http://dx.doi.org/10.1037/0000172-006
Criminality in Context: The Psychological Foundations of Criminal Justice Reform, by C. Haney

is warranted, and its implications for effective crime control policy are very much altered by an appreciation of the extent to which context matters.

The crime master narrative sees the "motivation to offend" as residing in some kind of criminal trait or evil disposition that is inherent within a lawbreaker. In this way, as Julie Horney noted, crime is seen as "the behavior that results when opportunities (or situations) exist that allow that disposition to manifest itself."[4] Instead, as she also observed, the social contextual model that I describe in this chapter focuses on "the inextricable linkage between situation and behavior," so that "crime and criminality become inseparable."[5] By locating the origins of criminal behavior in the fixed traits of those who engage in it, the crime master narrative implies a level of cross-situational consistency and intransigence that social behavior in general does not have.

As in earlier chapters, my analysis builds on the insights of contemporary psychological theory and data. It stands in direct opposition to the crime master narrative, in which criminal behavior is seen as the product of free choices made by perpetrators who act unencumbered not only by their past but also largely unaffected by present circumstances. We now know that there are many social contexts and situations that exert an extremely powerful influence over the shape and direction of the behavior that occurs within them. Crime is no exception to this general rule. That is, criminal behavior often results as much or more from the circumstances in which it transpires as the characteristics of the people who engage in it.

Criminologists Michael Gottfredson and Travis Hirschi observed that "[c]rimes are short-term, circumscribed events that presuppose a peculiar set of necessary conditions (e.g., activity, opportunity, adversaries, victims, goods)."[6] But this seems to imply that, typically, the criminal intent or propensity to violate the law already exists, needing only the right situation—the necessary conditions—to be expressed. A broader and more inclusive contextual model of crime also takes into account those instances in which elements or aspects of the immediate situation or context contribute to the very formation of the motive, impulse, or perceived need to commit the crime itself. Thus, from the broader perspective I develop in this chapter, the effort expended to establish the overall superiority of one or another specific contextual theory is somewhat misplaced. Instead, the explanatory value of each perspective varies from context to context so that, in any given life, the operation of several sets of contextual forces and dynamics are likely to be operative at different points or places in time.

For example, in some instances, the operative criminogenic or crime-producing context consists of "micro-events"—immediate provocations, affronts, or inducements—that help to precipitate criminal acts. In other instances, the criminogenic environment is broader and more "macro" or structural in nature. That is, characteristics of certain communities and neighborhoods—prevailing norms and expectations that seem to legitimize criminal behavior, limited opportunities for employment, a greater likelihood of encountering interpersonal conflict, and so on—combine to greatly increase the chances that residents will engage in criminal behavior. Thus, criminogenic contexts need to be considered at both micro and macro levels. In addition, at the end of this chapter, I discuss social histories, institutional interventions, and present circumstances that are typically highly interrelated and intertwined over a life course. Among other things, this means that persons who have the highest number or severity of criminogenic risk factors in their backgrounds or social histories are more likely to live in precisely those neighborhoods and communities where harsh institutional interventions more frequently occur and where problematic, precipitating situations and adverse circumstances predominate. People who have lived troubled, disadvantaged early lives frequently find themselves in troubled, disadvantaged circumstances as adults, and the unfortunate combination of the two elements—the personal historical and situational—increases the likelihood that they will engage in criminal behavior.

THE SITUATIONAL REVOLUTION

As I noted in passing in Chapter 2, the crime master narrative was challenged over the last several decades by emerging scientific knowledge that established the importance of the contextual or situational determinants of social behavior. Much of the research was conducted as part of a broader paradigm shift in social and personality psychology. This shift included empirical and analytical critiques of the traditional view that all social behavior (including criminal behavior) was caused primarily, if not exclusively, by a set of enduring traits or stable characteristics that resided entirely inside the persons who performed it. This widely held traditional view was what social psychologist Hazel Markus termed "the independent model of the person," in which all actions were thought to derive from personal agency that, in turn, was governed by the "internal states, capacities, motivations, and dispositions" within.[7] Beginning in the late 1960s, however, a number of psychologists began questioning these once seemingly unassailable assumptions. They eventually amassed impressive data of their own showing that social behavior was highly "situationally specific"—that is, that people's actions often varied dramatically as a function of the social contexts in which they took place.[8]

Researchers have remained as clear about these insights and their implications as they were when they began writing about them more than a generation ago. As Walter Mischel put it: "[O]ne of the core conclusions that needs to be drawn from 50 years of research is that the situation of the moment plays an enormously powerful role in the often automatic activation and regulation of complex human social behavior."[9] There is now widespread awareness among psychologists and other social scientists that it is impossible to fully understand how and why people act as they do without a careful examination of what one researcher has termed "the reality imperatives—situational demands, opportunities, and barriers" that shape lives.[10] The more powerful and extreme those imperatives, the less the behavior can be correctly attributed to personal characteristics or—as I discuss at length in a later chapter—to "free choice."

Some of the impact of situational forces and factors is immediate (e.g., reactions that people have to threats and provocations or the way that social pressures and stressors can elicit behavior that likely would not have otherwise occurred). But some of the impact is gradual and cumulative. Thus, even in adulthood, repeated exposure to certain environments and situations can have lingering, long-lasting effects. In fact, this kind of exposure to certain problematic situations may be at the root of seemingly chronic psychological conditions and disorders as well as what appear to be stable states and traits in people. For example, researchers have found that clinical syndromes like depression, people's tendency to engage in altruistic behavior, and the ability to cope effectively with the obstacles and challenges they face in life often stem from environmental factors rather than internal predispositions or individual traits.[11]

Just as with new knowledge about the critical importance of social history—background trauma and risk factors—this new perspective on social behavior has obvious relevance for the way we understand criminality, assess culpability, and mete out punishment, as well as for the development of more effective crime control policies. Many of the studies that I review in this chapter demonstrate that certain contexts and situations play an extremely important role in the occurrence of a broad range of problematic behaviors that include cheating, criminality, aggression, violence, and even homicide. Indeed, some studies have found that even persons who are supposedly operating at very high levels of "moral development" (as measured by a personality trait inventory) are willing to engage in dishonest behavior under situational conditions in which they are offered some minimal incentives and where they believe there is a low probability of detection.[12] Clearly, some personality characteristics (including prosocial, altruistic traits) can be overridden by certain very powerful situations.

CRIMINOGENIC SITUATIONS AND CRIMINAL BEHAVIOR

As recently as the mid-1980s, Anthony Mawson could accurately observe that, compared with all of the attention that historically had been given to personality or dispositional factors in explaining criminal behavior, "little is known about the role of situational factors and other types of short-term influences" on crime. More broadly, he noted that a variety of "recent life events or crises such as becoming unemployed, running out of money, losing a girlfriend, or being beaten up," may have a more important causal role in determining whether someone would engage in crime than previously acknowledged.[13] He proposed that various forms of what he termed "transient criminality" should be recognized as stemming largely from environmental influences rather than any enduring characteristics of the persons who engaged in it.[14] In part because of the broader "situational revolution" that commenced a half-century ago, much more is now known in psychology about a broad range of criminogenic situations.[15]

In addition to immediate, precipitating events, we also now know that situational stress can accumulate over time and that exposure to certain kinds of past stressful situations is related to problematic behavior in the present.[16] Moreover, there is a relationship between aggregate levels of situational "life stress" and specific forms of criminal behavior.[17] Even persistence of repetitive patterns of criminal behavior can often be attributed to a person's continued presence in criminogenic situations (rather than what would otherwise be seen as trait-based behaviors emanating from a person's "character"). Thus, the fact that someone continues to engage in lawbreaking may be caused by the fact that they remain mired in criminogenic circumstances rather than any personality-based, enduring criminal tendencies or traits or a stubborn insistence to make "bad choices" to engage in crime.

As I noted in Chapter 2, more sophisticated approaches to violence prediction and violence risk assessment now incorporate an explicitly contextual or "ecological" perspective into what were previously highly individualistic and exclusively person-centered inquiries.[18] Of course, the value of this approach is not limited to the prediction of *future* violent or criminal behavior. Because it can be incorporated effectively into the way that we understand *past* criminality as well, this new approach has significant implications not only for the way that we think about the nature of crime but also for prevailing views of legal culpability, the wisdom of our current punishment-laden crime control policies, and the creation of situationally oriented strategies of crime prevention.

CRIMINOGENIC CONTEXTS IN GENERAL

As I have argued in previous chapters, the nexus between various background risk factors such as childhood abuse and neglect and adverse institutional interventions places persons at risk for subsequent criminal behavior. Simply put, persons who have suffered these traumatic social and institutional histories are more likely to engage in crime. But the remainder of this chapter tells much of the rest of the story of why and how crime occurs when and where it does. I first discuss some of the research that illustrates the way that social contexts in general can influence criminal behavior, and then, later in the chapter, integrate this broad perspective on social situational variables with some of the social historical factors that I discussed earlier to present a more complex contextual explanation of criminal behavior.

I argue that the chances that someone will engage in criminal behavior are affected not only by child maltreatment, institutional malfeasance, and other traumatic events to which they have been exposed earlier in their lives but also by specific situations—the places in which they subsequently live, interact, and behave as adolescents and adults. We know, for example, that unemployment and employment in poor quality jobs are systematically related to high arrest rates among young adults.[19] The social and economic pressure to succumb to crime as well as the frequency and salience of criminal opportunities also vary by neighborhood and by more immediate social situations or circumstances. But, as I discuss later, there is more to the story than that.

Precipitating Contexts, Provocative Events, and Situational Stressors

Much of the research on the immediate contextual determinants of crime has been conducted by social psychologists who tend to focus by training on situational rather than dispositional influences on behavior. For example, contrary to traditional claims that violence occurs "mainly out of people's persistent internal drives," social psychologist Leonard Berkowitz has long-maintained that human aggression is "largely reactive, a response to situational conditions."[20] Berkowitz acknowledged that some persons may be more likely to respond aggressively than others, but has been quick to add that "appropriate situational stimuli" are virtually always required to provoke the violent reaction.

These "provocative" situational stimuli can occur in a number of settings, including ones in which people have been socialized to believe that they will win peer approval if they are aggressive (and disapproval if they are not) or have learned "that aggression is a desirable way of solving their conflicts."[21] Aggressive behavior also occurs in response to social conditions and barriers that repeatedly thwart or frustrate people in their attempts to achieve desired goals (even if the barriers are not caused by someone else's deliberate mistreatment, but especially when they are). Sociologists have suggested that, in addition to material deprivation per se, economic inequality or relative deprivation "engenders alienation, despair, and pent-up aggression, which find expression in frequent conflicts, including a high incidence of criminal violence."[22]

Not surprisingly, perhaps, persons who are already frustrated, irritated, or angry respond to the presence of what have been termed "aggression cues" (e.g., verbal or physical provocations, presence of aggression-related stimuli such as weapons) in social situations and are more likely to engage in aggression when the situational cues are present than when they are not.[23] The likelihood of violence and criminal behavior is significantly affected by situational factors in a wide range of different settings and kinds of interactions, including intimate partner relationships,[24] police–citizen interactions,[25] and in institutions such as jails and prisons.[26]

Similarly, when people are subjected to treatment that causes physical or psychological pain, or when they are subjected to noxious environmental conditions or placed in settings that they associate with past aversive or unpleasant events, they are more likely to react aggressively. Berkowitz concluded that whatever the specific external determinant of aggression in any particular instance, "violence in our society is best lessened by reducing [the] external determinants" that produce it.[27]

Berkowitz's important insights have been well known for years yet little acted upon in the criminal justice system or society at large, despite the fact that other prominent experts long embraced them. For example, at the start of the 1980s, when policies of mass incarceration were beginning to be enthusiastically pursued in the United States, well-known forensic psychiatrist Frank Ochberg argued to police officials that, although violence could be categorized in a number of ways, "[n]o violent act occurs in complete isolation," and that "[s]ettings, environmental factors, and triggering events are part of any violent act."[28] For this reason, he argued, effective policies of violence prevention must include attempts to modify the settings in which it commonly occurs.[29] Yet, as I noted, the nation remained deeply committed to an extreme version of the crime master narrative that demonized and dehumanized lawbreakers. Crime control policies moved aggressively in the opposite direction.

Among the "settings and environments" in which crime and violence are more likely to occur are ones characterized by "deindividuation" and "depersonalization." That is, we know that when people live and interact under conditions of relative anonymity (i.e., are deindividuated), or when they are in situations where their sense of self-awareness and concern for social evaluation are reduced (i.e., are depersonalized), they are, in turn, more likely to engage in illegal and aggressive behavior.[30] For example, one study concluded that aggressive behavior "is facilitated by situations that alter the individual's sense of self,"[31] and another found that impulsive and cyclical forms of aggressive behavior were related to the lowered sense of personal responsibility and diffused responsibility that deindividuation creates.[32] A number of other researchers used this insight to explain certain forms of gang-related behavior.[33]

A variety of studies have used Thomas Holmes and Richard Rahe's measure of "stressful life events"[34] to establish the relationship between stress and a wide range of negative outcomes, including physical and mental illness as well as crime.[35] Note that, as I acknowledged in Chapter 2, Holmes and Rahe developed their scale with a group of largely middle-class respondents. As a result, the list of events they judged to be "stressful" omitted ones more commonly encountered in criminogenic settings, such as experiencing homelessness, suffering drug or alcohol addiction, or witnessing violent confrontations. Despite these limitations, one early study showed that parents who engaged in child maltreatment were under significantly greater stress—nearly twice as much according to the Holmes and Rahe scale—as parents who did not.[36] In another study, a sample of male prisoners reported that they experienced an escalation of stressful life events in the year immediately preceding incarceration as compared with the 4 years before that, leading the researchers to conclude that criminal behavior could be conceptualized as similar to the "signs and symptoms of an illness"—as the manifestation of compromised or deteriorated coping in response to external stressors.[37]

This research is consistent with Mawson's basic model of "transient criminality" that I mentioned earlier in this chapter. He suggested that persons were at greater risk of engaging in illegal behavior when they encountered incongruous or stressful events, "particularly in a context of diminished social supports."[38] For example, high levels of stress have been shown to precipitate impulsive violent crimes, including cases in which the aggression is an expression of stress-related generalized anger and less instrumentally and logically related to the stressors that precipitated it.[39] In addition, persons who experience a high number of stressful life events that occur in the stress- and conflict-ridden communities where they live are generally more likely to engage in criminal behavior.[40]

More recent research has gone beyond the claim that stress in general is necessarily criminogenic and has linked particular kinds of stress to particular forms of criminal behavior. That is, in some instances, the kind of immediate situational or life stress appears to be directly related to the criminal behavior that it precipitates. For example, Edwin Lemert's classic work on the etiology of check forgery showed that a large percentage of persons who committed this crime had been laid off from their jobs, had suffered gambling losses, been on alcoholic binges, or were in trouble in their military service at some time in the period preceding their crimes.[41] Similarly, Richard Felson and his colleagues have shown that the experience of financial stress is related to property crimes (e.g., theft, sale of illicit drugs) and the experience of family stress (interpersonal conflicts) is related to assault.[42]

In addition, there is reason to believe that early stress and adversity—which may come about as a result of the kind of child maltreatment that I discussed in Chapter 3—can have cumulative effects, both on how much stress persons are likely to encounter later in life and on their capacity to manage it effectively if and when they do. That is, such adversity can negatively affect the nature and effectiveness of the coping mechanisms at their disposal. Of course, there is also a link between the risk factors that someone is exposed to early in life and the type of settings and situations that they are likely to encounter later on. This is one of the ways in which someone's early social history continues to matter well into adulthood; past experience connects to present circumstance in ways that have important implications for behavior over the entire life course.

The research that I have cited in previous chapters underscores how and why living through a trauma- and risk-filled childhood and adolescence increases someone's chances of confronting difficult—stressful—circumstances and situations later in adulthood. For example, we know that harsh parenting or the loss of a parental figure early in life can place someone at risk of a variety of psychological difficulties later on, in part because these experiences can impede the development of sustaining attachments to others.[43]

Developmental and social psychologists also now understand the importance of secure attachments later in life, and acknowledge the benefits of finding social settings and close relationships in which people can feel safe, trusting, and accepted, and have the sense that they "belong." Persons who suffered early disordered attachments or who were not able to establish any at all in childhood are less likely to find these nurturing relationships later in life.

Worse still, perhaps, they may be less able to benefit from whatever positive situations they do enter. That is, "children with early internal models of available care and self-worth are more responsive to positive features of the environment and more resilient to stress" as they mature.[44] Conversely, a background of traumatic abuse not only operates to place children in problematic and compromising situations later on—ones that they often are less able to handle—but also can undermine their ability to take advantage of supportive experiences or well-intentioned people whom they may encounter.

This kind of destructive nexus between early trauma, the subsequent lack of opportunities to find positive and supportive environments, and the inability to respond appropriately to positive experiences or available resources helps give risk factors and traumas their lasting potency and some of their most pernicious effects.

Social Identity and Criminal Contexts: Affronts, Embeddedness, and Coercion

Classic research done decades ago by sociologists Richard Felson and Henry Steadman was instrumental in advancing an explicit "situational approach to violence" that underscored the importance of carefully analyzing the precise characteristics of the immediate circumstances under which violent behavior occurs. Felson and Steadman examined the situational determinants of certain extreme forms of violent crime—specifically, homicides and assaults that were not committed as incidental to some other crime and that were serious enough to result in incarceration.[45] When they "microanalyzed" these incidents by examining both the motives of the perpetrators and the sequence of events that immediately preceded the violent encounter, several characteristic patterns emerged. For one, Felson and Steadman found that the violence was often precipitated by an "identity attack"—an insult or challenge to the perpetrator's sense of self. This identity attack was followed by an escalating pattern in which the victim attempted to verbally influence the antagonist. When these initial influence attempts failed, they led to threats that were followed by expressions of intentions to retaliate.

In the final stages of the violent encounter, the verbal conflict ended and a physical conflict began. Felson and Steadman found that both the perpetrators and victims of this kind of violence were likely to share a self-concept that seemed to require them to counterattack and retaliate when aggressed against. Obviously, the more people with this particular self-concept or social identity who live within a single neighborhood or community, the greater the likelihood that these escalating sequences of violent actions will unfold. Also, as perhaps would be expected, they found that violent encounters were more likely to occur in situations where one of the participants had a weapon. Surprisingly, however, the person who initially possessed the weapon more often than not ended up being the victim by the end of the violent interaction.

Felson and Steadman's findings fit a framework suggested even earlier by John Hepburn, who argued that violations of "relational rules"—expectations about how people should be interacting with one another in a given situation—often served as potent provocations to violent interpersonal interactions.[46] Because such violations were frequently perceived as threats to the situated identities of the participants, they created pressures to react forcefully in order to protect or defend their challenged sense of self. Hepburn suggested that, even though parties often tried to negotiate their respective identities with one another, and used "threat reduction tactics" to defuse the impending conflict, the presence of several contextual variables significantly increased the likelihood that violence would occur. Specifically, violence was more likely if participants were already exposed to environments that legitimized the use of violence or had prior experience with violent interactions or behavior. It was also more likely if one or both participants were intoxicated. In addition, if there was an audience present to witness the conflict, or if the participants perceived that there was a high personal cost associated with their failure to preserve their situated identity, then the probability of violent behavior was increased.[47]

In a related way, much evidence suggests that these characteristic ways of responding to insults, affronts, and "identity attacks" are not primarily the product of individual difference variables that reflect damaged psyches, misguided personal choices, or other trait-based predispositions. Many times they originate in the social norms of certain neighborhoods in which, to use Elijah Anderson's term, a "code of the streets" prevails that governs the use of violence and sets out those circumstances that are understood to precipitate it.[48] Under "the code," which operates as a broad set of situational pressures, interpersonal "respect" is of paramount importance. Although it is often defined in unique ways, respect itself is always highly valued—even glorified—and is governed by its own set of rules. Those rules, in turn, dictate whether and when disrespect must be responded to forcefully, in order to prevent a corresponding loss of face or, perhaps, an escalation of violence. Thus, "'Don't punk out.' 'If somebody messes with you, you got to pay them back.' 'If someone disses you, you got to straighten them out.'"[49] The code, as Anderson described it, is not the product of cultural dysfunction or personal pathology. Instead, it is a highly rational adaptation to a set of contingencies in which someone's safety in an otherwise tense, materially deprived, and potentially dangerous environment depends on his or her ability to follow agreed-upon interpersonal rules of engagement.

More recently, U.S. Department of Justice–sponsored research explored the "developmental relationships" between Anderson's thesis on "street code values," other neighborhood and family characteristics, and subsequent violent behavior.[50] As Anderson had previously noted, "in the troublesome public environment of the inner city, as people increasingly feel buffeted by forces beyond their control, what one deserves in the way of respect becomes more and more problematic and uncertain."[51] Especially in certain inner-city settings—where there is a "profound sense of alienation from mainstream society and its institutions," including from the police and judicial system—publicly establishing and maintaining "street credibility" represents a form of self-defense, demonstrating to others that you are not susceptible to being exploited, and are capable of "taking care of yourself," which, as Anderson put it, "translates into a sense of physical and psychological control."[52] In fact, the researchers testing his assertions concluded that "the stress of living in a poor and violent environment can cause young people to adopt the code of the street as a lifestyle guide," and that this, in turn, "is a powerful predictor of violent conduct, amplified by the effects of negative neighborhood characteristics."[53]

Other contextual models of criminality have focused on the role of peer influences—the notion that delinquency is predominately a social act or form of group behavior, such that young persons whose peers are involved in criminal activity are more likely to engage in such behavior themselves. Mark Warr summarized his years of research on this relationship by concluding that "peer influence is the principal proximate cause of most criminal conduct."[54] Relatedly, researchers Bill McCarthy and John Hagan used the term "criminal embeddedness" to describe the degree to which people living in criminogenic contexts become immersed in a network of interpersonal relationships that increase their exposure to crime-prone role models. In some instances, this network includes what are in essence "tutelage" relationships in which persons less experienced in crime are influenced in a direct way by more sophisticated criminal actors who are present in the particular neighborhoods where they live.[55] In this case, the process of "getting into street crime" requires the ability to acquire and exercise some of the very same social skills—in particular, a heightened sensitivity to people and the ability to learn effectively from others—that, in other contexts, would lead to more prosocial and conventionally acceptable forms of success.

Finally, Mark Colvin proposed a situational theory of criminal behavior that focuses on the role of what he termed "coercive" settings and life circumstances, ones that generate enough emotional and physical pain in people that they feel compelled to react against it. This kind of coercion can take the form of actual forceful actions or threats to use force by others that deprive persons of emotional and material necessities or significantly constrain them from achieving desired options. Coercive treatment can occur at home, in school, in a variety of external settings (such as neighborhoods and institutions), and includes levels of economic deprivation that generate feelings of severe stress and desperation. Colvin argued that coercive contexts become criminogenic when their victims begin "to view the world as an all-encompassing experience of coercion that can only be overcome through coercion," and behave accordingly.[56] Consistent with the perspective I have developed throughout, just as with childhood trauma and risks and forms of institutional failure and abuse, no single instance or isolated such experience is likely to engender criminal behavior; rather, it is "the overall mosaic of coercion one experiences that affects criminality."[57]

"NEIGHBORHOOD DISADVANTAGE"

Many contextual influences on criminal behavior are broader based and operate at a more structural than microanalytic or interpersonal level. For example, a group of sociological researchers have used the term "neighborhood disadvantage" to describe the nexus or cluster of interrelated factors that often accompany poverty and amplify its negative effects on early development as well as adult behavior.[58] The ecological features that make up this cluster can contribute to the disruption of the social organization of the neighborhood, undermine shared community norms, and weaken any generalized or collective support for positive family socialization. As two commentators summarized it, "neighborhood disadvantage provides a strong measure of environmental risk."[59]

Not surprisingly, neighborhood disadvantage can have criminogenic effects. For example, high rates of unemployment place economic stress on families and may undermine their overall stability. In addition, as Vonnie McLoyd noted, poverty often confronts people with "an unremitting succession of negative life events . . . in the context of chronically stressful ongoing life conditions such as inadequate housing and dangerous neighborhoods that together increase the exigencies of day-to-day existence."[60] Thus, under the risk factors model developed in Chapter 2, poverty and neighborhood disadvantage represent immediate stressors—the "exigencies of day-to-day existence"—with the potential to exacerbate the negative effects of the difficult, risk factor-filled social histories that many of their residents have endured. As psychologist Kenneth Clark observed many years ago, persons who are forced to live in disadvantaged neighborhoods and "whose daily experience tells them that almost nowhere in society are they respected and granted the ordinary dignity and courtesy afforded to others, will, as a matter of course, begin to doubt their own self-worth."[61] This, in turn, can make lawbreaking more likely.[62]

There are several other ways that neighborhood disadvantage can help to create a context that facilitates, provokes, or precipitates criminality. Disadvantaged neighborhoods are often characterized by high levels of transience and mobility that contribute to an overall sense of impermanence and disorganization that, in turn, can undermine the development of stable, consistent, and consensual community norms. Robert Sampson and John Laub have emphasized important role that positive connections to stable community institutions—school, work, family—have on desistance from crime, even for persons who are otherwise "at risk." Of course, in order to connect to these things, they have to be present and accessible. In places with high levels of neighborhood disadvantage, they often are not.

Thus, when neighborhood disadvantage isolates residents from mainstream institutions, it makes criminal behavior more likely. That is, people "are far less able to access conventional means to achieve general societal goals, to support family socialization of conventional values and norms, and to exert effective control over the behavior of residents."[63] The poverty that characterizes the lives of residents who live in such neighborhoods creates strong pressures to engage in illegal activities, and the neighborhoods themselves often have fewer mechanisms by which they may formally or informally limit what residents do.

Historian Randolph Roth argued that there is a "feelings and beliefs" component to the crime of homicide that is related to the nature of the connections and engagements people make with their surrounding environment, especially governmental structures. Thus, he found that historically in the United States and Western Europe, in addition to objective social conditions, homicide rates have tended to rise when persons did not feel that the governmental agencies and agents were legitimate and trustworthy, were stable and unbiased enough to fairly redress their wrongs and safeguard their well-being, felt politically and emotionally disconnected from their fellow citizens, and did not believe that they were part of a legitimate hierarchy in which they could participate, succeed, and be respected without resorting to violence.[64] His theory of the way feelings and beliefs affect homicide rates at a national level seems applicable to violence in more localized settings, where residents of disadvantaged neighborhoods are treated in ways that disenfranchise and alienate them from government representatives and agencies.

Beyond undermining the contact that residents have with mainstream sources of social support and control, neighborhood disadvantage maximizes their proximity to illegal activities. That is, neighborhoods characterized by high levels of poverty, unemployment, broken families, and transience or mobility "increase the likelihood of the emergence (and lack of effective control) of illegitimate opportunity structures and dysfunctional lifestyles, including an illicit economy (gambling, prostitution, extortion, theft, drug distribution networks), substance abuse, violence, and delinquent gangs."[65]

In addition, the prevalence of single-parent families in disadvantaged neighborhoods and the economic burdens that are shouldered by the parents who are present can limit the amount of time that children are able to spend with or around positive role models. Adolescents and young adults who live in chronically disadvantaged areas are more likely to be exposed to a "criminogenic street context" that increases the likelihood that they will participate in the activities that are going on around them.[66] As noted earlier, the neighborhoods themselves also are characterized by an overall sense of impermanence and disorganization that, in turn, undermines the development of stable, consistent, and consensual community norms. Thus, disadvantaged neighborhoods can produce criminogenic effects in part because they maximize the pressures to engage in crime, in part because they increase people's proximity to illegal activities, and in part because there are fewer resources and stable institutions to serve as countervailing pressures to refrain. All of these factors are related to higher crime rates.

As I noted briefly in Chapter 2, in recognition of the important role of these situational factors, some contemporary approaches to the prediction of violent behavior by patients who are being released from mental hospital stays now explicitly incorporate "enduring features of the patient's life situation," the "foreseeable events or stressors" that a person is likely to encounter in the community,[67] and even more macro or "ecological" variables such as neighborhood disadvantage. Taking social and contextual factors directly into account—examining socioeconomic status and the characteristics of the neighborhoods to which persons are returned—greatly improves predictive accuracy. For example, one such study found that examining whether neighborhoods were plagued by "concentrated poverty"—specifically, "the extent of disadvantage in the neighborhood contexts into which each patient was discharged"—greatly enhanced the accuracy of their risk assessments.[68] The researchers concluded that the "clinical implications of these findings lie in emphasizing the importance of assessing contextual conditions as well as individual characteristics when predicting and managing the risk for violence posed by discharged patients."[69]

This insight applies equally well to a broad range of other persons and settings—including criminal defendants and parolees—who should not be presumptively viewed by legal decision-makers "as either being 'dangerous' or 'not dangerous,' but instead . . . as possibly doing some type of [violent] act . . . if certain situations either persist or present themselves."[70] However, the implications of the insight that "certain situations" can have a significant influence on whether criminal behavior is likely to occur extend beyond improving predictive accuracy or nuancing judgments about a person's legal status. This perspective underscores not only the importance of taking a person's social circumstances carefully and consistently into account but also the value of *addressing* those circumstances proactively, in the name of preventive crime control.

My analysis of situational factors in crime causation has concentrated thus far on their impact on whether and how often crime occurs under certain kinds of circumstances or settings. However, there is one characteristic of a social context that has a direct effect not only on whether crime occurs but, if so, its nature and severity: the presence of firearms. Although this is a controversial political issue, and the empirical evidence is complex,[71] a number of studies have shown a relationship between increased gun ownership and crime, whether the guns are owned legally or illegally.[72] We also know that states with higher levels of firearm ownership have higher rates of firearm assaults, firearm robberies, and firearm homicides.[73] Easy access to guns raises the risk of serious violence, in part because of the greater injury that a perpetrator is enabled to inflict.[74] The National Rifle Association's often-repeated refrain to the effect that "guns don't kill people, people do"[75] is very much an extension of the increasingly defunct crime master narrative, one that insists on separating the behavior from the characteristics of the context in which it occurs and focusing only on the actor, who is viewed as having independently brought the crime about. Yet the presence of firearms in any situation or confrontation changes it, and the greater the lethal capacity of the firearm, the greater the change effected. In this case, the change in the nature of the context too often means that the consequences of actions that stem from passing anger that might have quickly subsided, a misunderstanding that could otherwise have been resolved, or a mental illness that might have been effectively treated are rendered more tragic and irreversible.

"SECONDARY" RISK FACTORS: MEDIATING THE LEGACIES OF SOCIAL HISTORY IN ADULTHOOD

Although traumatic social histories, problematic institutional interventions, and adverse surrounding circumstances are conceptually distinct and can be analytically separated—as I have done up to this point by discussing them in different chapters—in reality, they are highly interconnected. They typically co-occur over a life course in ways that can amplify their overall effect. There are several obvious ways in which this is so. For one, many victims of early childhood mistreatment live in neighborhoods that are also plagued by broadly criminogenic social conditions. Because the consequences of early childhood deprivation and maltreatment often reverberate through an entire life course, early trauma predisposes children to socioemotional difficulties that increase the chances of entering a variety of "bad situations," including repeated contact with harsh institutions. Without positive, sustained, and nurturing intervention and assistance—precisely the sort that they may not be able to obtain, either from their immediate families or from the chronically underfunded institutions where they are often placed—their early problems tend to persist into adulthood.

The risk factors model reminds us that a person's early exposure to traumas and risks can have adverse effects on their subsequent coping. This means that people who have been victimized as children and adolescents tend to encounter stressors later in life that they may be ill-equipped to handle. For example, their ability and opportunity to find and maintain nurturing or sustaining relationships to buffer them from the harsh circumstances and structural hardships that surround them may be compromised. Earlier maltreatment may undermine the development of healthy and competent adult identities. Through no fault or moral failing of their own, these patterns can lead to even more stressors in subsequent stages of their lives.

As persons who have been victimized and mistreated as children and adolescents grow older, fragile and problematic coping not only may become increasingly tenuous and problematic, but also more difficult for others to tolerate or excuse. Juvenile misbehavior that is seen as a sign of immaturity or youthful indiscretion is reacted to more sympathetically than the same or worse behavior from an older, presumably more mature teen who presents as "adult-like." The crime master narrative would have us believe that at some point in one's development—the age of 18 appears to be the legal consensus on the cut-off point—all persons are somehow able to cast off the influence of what came before, act completely autonomously and free of the burdens of the past, and function largely impervious to the pressures of the present.[76] However, there is no psychological principle of which I am aware that cleanly or definitively disconnects past from present within a single social history. Instead, as children mature, both the residue of their early developmental and institutional histories *and* the impact of current circumstances continue to play important roles in guiding subsequent patterns of behavior.

Moreover, the natural difficulty that all of us have in accurately placing other people's behavior in context—what is termed "the fundamental attribution error"—is intensified as behaviors become more extreme, threatening, and even criminal.[77] Not surprisingly, irritating, troublesome, and illegal behavior tends to be judged unsympathetically by observers, and certainly by its targets or victims. However, it is no less a product of the events that preceded it or the circumstances in which it occurred. The connection to earlier trauma or present provocation remains, whether or not it is immediately "visible" to someone who witnesses the later behavior. Yet, when the crime master narrative is activated, the natural tendency to pass negative judgment on an actor's inherent character, worth, and "badness," and to impute individual blame is intensified.

Because harmful past experiences can shape present decision-making, the victims of early trauma and risk factors often develop patterns and styles of coping with difficult situations that are themselves problematic and self-fulfilling in nature. People who have had bad things happen to them are often more likely to make bad choices—ill-advised or ill-considered choices to pursue options that lead to even more challenging situations that are especially difficult to successfully manage. This increases the chances that even more bad things will follow, including added conflicts, pressures, and temptations that occur more frequently in the stressful, chaotic places where they are more likely to live. Their own problematic and dysfunctional but ultimately understandable reactions and adaptations to the increasingly dire circumstances they must attempt to navigate and overcome add to the dynamic. For example, children and adolescents who adapt to the mistreatment and rejection they have experienced in the past by becoming more aggressive or emotionally distant from their peers may provoke even more rejection; the possibility of ever-escalating misbehavior and disconnection from others becomes more likely.[78]

In fact, two common but especially unfortunate adaptations to past risks and traumas—substance abuse and gang affiliation—can greatly amplify the effects of an adverse social history by generating criminogenic contexts of their own.

Self-Medicating Through Drug and Alcohol Abuse

Many young victims of childhood trauma turn to drugs and alcohol as a form of "self-medication" that reduces their immediate emotional pain.[79] Many children in abusive environments are also exposed to drug and alcohol use by the adult role models around them, offering available, seemingly acceptable strategies to handle the depression from which they often suffer.[80] Yet, alcohol and drug abuse can lead to criminogenic outcomes, ones that are not necessarily apparent to or easily anticipated by the young persons who adopt them. Although *researchers* know that "[e]arly illicit drug use does indeed imply higher likelihood of future offences . . . [I]t is connected with a higher risk for future criminality at all levels of behavioural risks in adolescence,"[81] the children and adolescents who employ these self-medicating strategies typically do not.

Of course, access to illegal drugs and the prevalence of drug dealing varies somewhat by setting or locale. In many poor communities, young people may be socialized into an illegal drug culture by the pull of powerful economic forces. For some, drugs not only represent a way to self-medicate but also an apparent pathway into self-sufficiency, or at least a way to supplement limited or nonexistent opportunities to make money in more legitimate ways. In many such communities the drug culture and illicit drug economy combine to produce a significant set of criminogenic pressures:

> The roles of drug pusher, pimp, and (illegal) hustler have become more and more attractive. Street-smart young people who operate in this underground economy are apparently able to obtain big money more easily and glamorously than their elders. . . . Because they appear successful, they become role models for still younger people. Members of the older generation, many of whom are not doing so well financially, find it hard to compete, and in frustration some accommodate the younger people.[82]

Indeed, one of the most negative aspects of the widespread use of crack cocaine that transformed many urban communities in the 1980s and early 1990s was the increased participation of many people living in these inner-city neighborhoods in what they perceived to be the only "business opportunity" available to them. As James Inciardi described them, the available career paths included

> the "peewees" and "wannabees," those street gang acolytes in grade school and junior high who patrol the streets with walkie-talkies in the vicinity of crack houses, serving in networks of lookouts, spotters, and steerers, and who aspire to be 'rollers' (short for high rollers) in the drug distribution business."[83]

Substance abuse can be criminogenic in a number of other ways. For example, drug addicts may become involved in selling drugs in order to support their habits. Other effects of drug addiction can be indirectly criminogenic. For example, heavy levels of cocaine and methamphetamine use may lead to long periods of sleeplessness and increased paranoia, which in turn may increase overreactions or aggressive responses in interpersonal interactions. At another level, regular contact with the illicit drug subculture—necessary to get illegal drugs and maintain an addiction—exposes users to a range of criminal behavior, role models, and lifestyles. The more frequent their contact and connections, the more likely they are to become integrated into the criminal activity that surrounds them.[84]

Thus, the use of certain kinds of illegal drugs, especially, places users in more frequent contact with criminal lifestyles, may create dependencies that require access to significant financial resources to maintain, and may impair judgment and lower inhibitions. In certain instances, the latter may lead to the misperception and misinterpretation of social cues, hypersensitivity to threats or personal affronts, and more aggressive responses to perceived provocations and interpersonal conflicts.[85]

The potential criminogenic effects of drug use depend in part on which drugs are used, and how much and for how long. For example, studies suggest that "polydrug" use (some combination of heroin or other opioids, cocaine, hallucinogens, methamphetamines, and barbiturates) is especially problematic.[86] That is perhaps because polydrug users are more likely to continue their use, and chronic use may lead to more continuous and more serious illegal behavior.[87] Drug selling, even in adolescence, can also have criminogenic effects,[88] placing teens in contact with an illicit drug subculture at a still early developmental stage.

At least in some cases, addiction also may become such a powerful motivator that it overcomes otherwise strong inhibitions against engaging in crime and, for some addicts, may increase the level of violence that they feel compelled to engage in. Thus, researchers who studied the dramatic increase in crack use that occurred several decades ago concluded that it gave rise to a new level of addiction-driven behavior. Desperate crack addicts, termed "zombies" by community residents, were known for their single-minded pursuit of the drug:

> [Crack is] a cheap but highly addictive drug that brings about a brief euphoria, then a sudden "crash" that leaves the user with an intense craving, or "jonesing," for more. While smoking the drug, "all they can think of is where they gon' get the next blast." One pursues it until one's resources are depleted. Addiction is widely believed to be instantaneous and permanent in effect, rendering the addict "a fool for crack."[89]

To be clear, there are many people who use drugs who do not engage in any other forms of illegal behavior. Many of the criminogenic aspects of drug use stem from the illegal, expensive, and stigmatized nature of the activity, not the inherent effects of the drugs. However, although illegal drug use does not necessarily lead to other forms of criminal behavior, its criminogenic effects are reflected in the fact that there is a high level of drug use among people who commit crimes and, among people who use certain drugs, there is a higher level of criminal behavior.[90] As two researchers have summarized, "Although drug use does not appear to initiate a criminal career, a large volume of research clearly indicates that frequency of drug use has a strong impact on the extent, direction, and duration of that (criminal) career."[91] In short, as I suggested earlier, street drug use places users in an environment where criminal behavior may be expected, accepted, and respected. Draconian drug policies that not only criminalize drug possession but can result in the imposition of harsh prison sentences necessarily place drug users at the margins of conventional society and at risk of criminal justice system processing (that can itself be highly criminogenic). This helps explain the interconnection between using illegal drugs and engaging in other forms of criminal behavior that occurs in the lives of many street drug users.[92]

Moreover, the long-term effects of drug abuse can reverberate back into the lives of the children whose parents are in the throes of addiction and whose behavior has suffered as a result. Although the myth of "crack babies" who were supposedly "born addicted" has been definitively debunked,[93] children whose parents become addicted to drugs are at greater risk of child abuse, neglect and, in extreme cases, abandonment which, in turn, can have significant criminogenic consequences.[94]

Alcohol use and abuse also can have separate criminogenic effects.[95] A surprisingly high percentage of persons report having used alcohol just before they engaged in criminal behavior. For example, one survey of probationers and prisoners indicated that nearly 40% of them reported that they were drinking alcohol at the time of the crime or just before.[96] The consumption of alcohol can increase the likelihood that adolescents will engage in delinquent behavior.[97] Moreover, alcohol use in adolescence is significantly related to such use in adulthood. Here, too, a self-medicating strategy often adopted in the aftermath of trauma and abuse has a longer-term counterproductive and criminogenic effect.

Creating Identity Through Gang Membership

Gang membership is another adaptation often taken in response to adverse developmental histories, impoverished and disadvantaged life circumstances, and to the bleak futures that many adolescents believe they will face when they eventually reach adulthood. The lure of neighborhood gangs comes primarily from the promise of social support, personal companionship and camaraderie, and economic opportunities, especially in environments where these things are difficult for young people to obtain any other way. Although gangs may facilitate alcohol and drug use and involve their members in illicit trafficking,[98] these are by no means their only or even primary attractions.[99]

Instead, gang membership is typically motivated and at times seemingly compelled by a host of other factors, including the perception of external threat and the attempt to impose order on chaotic surrounding circumstances.[100] As

James Vigil's early studies of urban Latino gangs showed, membership stemmed largely from the "absence of a secure cultural (and personal) identity," brought about by the structural marginality of the groups from which their members originated.[101] Indeed, the "multiple marginality" that researchers described applies to many criminal defendants who must cope with "the effects of barrio life, low socioeconomic status, culture conflict, and impaired development of self-esteem which arise in a complex of ecological, socioeconomic, cultural, and psychological factors."[102] Similarly, Luis Rodriguez has written eloquently for several decades about the pull of gang life in the Los Angeles neighborhoods where he grew up. He acknowledged that, for many young people, "a gang embraces who they are, gives them the initiatory community they seek and the incipient authority they need to eventually control their lives."[103] Thus, adolescents often turn to gangs in large part to obtain the "things other institutions, including schools and families, often fail to provide."[104]

The fact that marginalized young people turn to gangs to fulfill the needs and garner the opportunities that the larger society has otherwise denied them is reflected in statistics showing urban gang membership is concentrated in disenfranchised communities, especially among disempowered racial and ethnic groups. Facing poverty and structural disadvantage, alienating life circumstances, and few positive social networks to direct them toward organized prosocial activities or other outlets to which they can turn, gang memberships seems like a promising way to address a range of these otherwise unmet needs.

One particularly poignant example of these factors at work was illustrated in a study of Vietnamese street gangs that arose in the United States, which began among groups of orphaned street youth from Vietnam. Once in the United States, they "reestablished ties with the only social network available to them," namely, other isolated and dislocated youths whom they had known on the streets of Saigon and in the refugee camps where they had been taken.[105] Even those Vietnamese gang members who were not orphaned or housed in the refugee camps "lacked adult supervision in the United States because of the economic pressures on second wave refugee families."[106] These economic pressures meant that, in traditional extended family households where all adults were expected to work, parents were "often moonlighting at more than one job in order to survive"[107] and, therefore, unavailable to provide guidance and supervision.

Martin Sanchez-Jankowski's comparative study of ethnic gangs challenged the notion that their members typically joined because of personal pathology or wholly out of nefarious intentions. He argued instead that "the vast majority of gang members are quite energetic and are eager to acquire many of the same things that most members of American society want: money, material possessions, power, and prestige."[108] He suggested further that the violence in which they often engaged was an extension of their prior socialization and should be considered "appropriate behavior in an environment whose socioeconomic conditions are pathological."[109] Virtually all of the gang members he studied came from impoverished neighborhoods and relied on gangs in their quest for the good life in large part because other avenues to attain it had been foreclosed.

In this way, then, gang membership not only provides an alternative to isolation and idleness but also, for some, appears to promise opportunities to acquire income of some sort. This is why "both unemployment and dropping out of the labor force because of an absence of legitimate opportunities" are pathways into criminal behavior. Especially for "high risk" young people, "illegitimate activities at this stage [of their lives] offer far more visible sources of income than do legitimate ones."[110] Thus, far from a free and autonomous choice to forego otherwise plentiful, attractive options that are supposedly equally available to them and to instead engage in illicit and sometimes violent behavior, gang membership is often a forced adaptation, one that feels compelled by a very powerful set of social contextual factors. Societal- and institutional-level discrimination, the lack of employment opportunities, and strained or nonexistent community support networks mean that many young people "are more likely to seek alternative, albeit delinquent, means of securing prestige and economic success. Gangs provide a mechanism for these adolescents to achieve financial gain and status in their communities."[111]

Negative social historical influences, including the traumatic effects of prior exposure to powerful interpersonal and familial criminogenic factors, can also play a role. For example, Jerald Belitz and Diana Valdez have emphasized the importance of familial dysfunction, parental abuse, and institutional mistreatment in the backgrounds of the gang members with whom they have worked.[112] In their view, the roots of at least some gang-related aggression may lie in their clients' reactions to traumatic past life experiences. For these young men and women "[h]ostility and aggression mask an underlying depression and/or posttraumatic stress disorder, which are experienced in response to emotional or physical abuse, losses or deprivation."[113] More recently, Jane Wood, Constantinos Kallis, and Jeremy Coid similarly documented the comparatively high levels of past trauma and stress in the lives of the gang members they studied.[114]

Many adolescents who have suffered psychological, physical, and sexual abuse in the home or exposure to violence in their neighborhood, and who may face later retraumatization in juvenile correctional facilities, have received little or no counseling or therapy for whatever emotional and psychological effects they may have suffered as a result. Social stigma and cultural taboos can combine with a lack of appropriate community or neighborhood counseling resources and the limited availability of role models to follow, closing off opportunities for them to effectively address these underlying issues.[115] When young people with early trauma histories who suffer from these unacknowledged problems and unmet psychological needs also have few if any opportunities to develop more prosocial identities, gang membership represents a seemingly attractive way to fill the void.[116]

And yet, in ways that are rarely apparent when the initial benefits of joining a gang appear to be most salient, gang membership can worsen many of the very problems that recruits had hoped to resolve or avoid. It is an adaptation that may seem entirely rational and functional at the outset—responding to the need for self-protection in a dangerous neighborhood, a desire to overcome familial and social alienation, the chance to connect to a close social group, achieve a desirable neighborhood status, or alleviate economic woes. Yet many young people are initially drawn into gang life with no clear vision of the increasingly serious forms of criminal behavior that likely await them. Of course, street gangs can apply strong pressure to members to comply and may punish those who do not.[117] Ironically, at a personal level, the gang affiliation that many members expected would offer them social support and even, in some cases, protection from neighborhood violence actually results in exposure to greater levels of violence and even more "bleak future expectations."[118]

Here, too, a seemingly sensible adaptation to a set of impinging contextual and structural pressures over which people have little control carries long-term negative consequences that are difficult to foresee at the time the "choice" is made to embrace it. Once having joined, gang membership has a powerful effect on its members' behavior "because it leads to a change in [their] attitudes and beliefs."[119] In addition to these psychological changes, gang membership puts them on problematic life paths, including ones that involve delinquent and criminal behavior, along with mounting pressures to travel down one or another of them. Moreover, there are a number of serious criminal justice implications that now have even worse life-altering consequences than in the past (but are no less difficult to anticipate or foresee).

For example, many states have passed statutes that add "gang enhancements" to the punishment that is meted out for criminal convictions if juries find the acts were engaged in for "the benefit" of the gang or "in furtherance" of its interests.[120] There are a number of vagaries in the ways these laws are applied in criminal prosecutions and trials, making their actual legal consequences impossible to anticipate in advance. For example, most afford law enforcement a tremendous amount of discretion in defining and determining who actually is a gang member and in deciding which activities that a defendant engaged in were for the "benefit of the gang."[121] So-called gang databases are notoriously unreliable and overinclusive.[122] The pretrial and sentencing implications of being labeled a "gang member" and engaging in "gang-related" activity are nonetheless severe.[123]

In addition, there are less official, more subtle consequences of gang membership that also can have destructive effects on someone's life course. Media accounts of the "evils" of gang membership characterize gang-related activities as especially dangerous and threatening in ways that invest members with particularly fearsome qualities—as in newspaper headlines that refer to gangs as "the monster of crime" and their members as monstrous representatives of the gangs' criminal designs.[124] As one gang researcher noted decades ago, the media helped create and reinforce a "folkloric myth" concerning gangs in our society, one in which gangs themselves were given "demonic qualities."[125] As he put it, gangs have not only been depicted as physically threatening to law-abiding citizens, "but also as undermining the morals and values of the society as a whole." Indeed, they were even characterized as the "carriers of moral disease within the social body" of our society.[126] Over the past several decades, that mythology has only grown.[127]

As a result, the allegation of gang membership now carries substantial surplus meaning in criminal cases where it is made. Because gang members are presumed to be broadly involved in and deeply committed to criminal activity and, especially, violent crime, the mere suggestion that a criminal act is "gang-related" or that a criminal defendant is "gang-affiliated" carries a strong implication of guilt and enhanced culpability; the characterization simultaneously undermines the presumption of innocence and exaggerates the impulse to punish. Because gang-related crime is assumed to be more calculated and heinous, and gang members are perceived as more intractably devoted to criminality, gang allegations or accusations also function to implicitly increase the apparent seriousness of the crimes that suspected gang members are thought to have engaged in. This is not to suggest that many street and prison gangs do not involve their members in serious violent crime; they often do. However, law enforcement officials tend to automatically assume high levels of involvement in and commitment to illegal activity by persons identified as gang members and to subject suspected gang members to greatly increased surveillance and policing.[128] They are also likely to decontextualize gang-related behavior and overattribute responsibility for serious violence that occurs in urban areas to gang activity or to the gangs' involvement in drug trafficking.[129]

As the previously cited research underscored, none of these characterizations is entirely accurate and many are flatly incorrect.[130] Moreover, even though gang membership may represent a response to the effects of past mistreatment and structural disadvantage, and may be highly situational and transitory, the "gangster" label has long-term implications that are difficult to dispel once it has been applied. The popular stereotype of gang membership includes "essentialist" implications that feed the demonic myth—either that gang members are somehow intrinsically different than other young people or that once someone has joined or even associated with a gang they are permanently transformed (as though something essential has been altered within them that cannot be changed). This essentialism plays directly into broader mythologies about violent crime that are used to justify greatly enhanced punishment—as if "gang violence" is somehow worse than other kinds in part because of what is implied about its perpetrators.

Like most essentialist notions that are derived from the crime master narrative, these too are mistaken. To the contrary, what we know about youth gangs, at least, suggests both that their members "drift" in and out of criminal activity and that young people sometimes "drift" in and out of gangs as well.[131] Moreover, as I have suggested, although gang membership may facilitate criminal behavior, in part because "the normative support it provides for delinquent behavior generate[s] a context in which such behavior flourishes,"[132] that context can be changed or supplanted by the introduction of meaningful alternatives. Thus, there is no evidence that gang members are essentially different from their peers or that they are permanently transformed by their membership. The permanency of their affiliation depends primarily on a broader set of life circumstances—for example, whether other attractive alternatives or ways of being become available to them or, conversely, if they are incarcerated in juvenile justice or adult institutions where the pressure to affiliate may be much stronger—including becoming literally a matter of day-to-day safety and survival.

We know that gang identities are psychologically similar to many of the various other kinds of identities that adolescents explore in the natural transition to adulthood. These transitional adaptations can be redirected and reshaped in more positive directions *if* surrounding circumstances and situations facilitate such change. The fact that at least some adolescent gang members are troubled, traumatized, and marginalized at the outset may help to explain the nature of the activities in which they become involved—especially the drug use and aggressive behavior—but it does not render them more sinister or irredeemable as a result. Here, too, the adaptation to a set of very powerful social historical and social contextual forces can be modified by addressing the effects of past trauma and altering the circumstances and opportunity structures under which young people attempt to overcome them.

THE CRIMINOGENICS OF ADULT IMPRISONMENT

Ironically, and problematically, adult jail and prison environments constitute another potentially powerful criminogenic context in the lives of many young adults who have already experienced the kind of troubled and traumatizing social and institutional histories I have described thus far.[133] Like juvenile incarceration that often precedes it, prison life can be iatrogenic, affecting a person's future life course in ways that are the opposite of those ostensibly intended.[134]

In fact, a number of direct empirical studies, literature reviews, and meta-analyses have reported on the criminogenic effects of imprisonment. Thus, not only does prison life fail to put most prisoners on a path toward more law-abiding lifestyles, but the experience of having been incarcerated appears to increase the probability of engaging in crime.[135] A careful examination of the context of imprisonment helps to explain why. Frances Cullen, Cheryl Jonson, and Daniel Nagin provided a useful summary of the "social experience" of imprisonment: "For a lengthy period of time, [prisoners] associate with other offenders, endure the pains of imprisonment, risk physical victimization, are cut off from family and prosocial contact on the outside, and face stigmatization as 'cons,'" a label that not only serves as a social obstacle or impediment to connecting with others but also can "foster anger and a sense of defiance" among prisoners themselves.[136]

Some of the criminogenic effects of imprisonment are direct, immediate, and personal. That is, to adapt to and survive the dangers and the rigors of prison life, prisoners are forced to drastically modify their everyday habits and ways of being. Elsewhere I have written about the process of "prisonization"—a powerful form of socialization that, among other things, instills an overdependency on external structures and routines to which prison administrations require strict adherence. Prisonization can also foster the development of a tough veneer in which prisoners learn to suppress expressions of weakness or vulnerability. Guarding against exploitation that is prevalent in prison, many prisoners adopt a generalized mistrust of others. Some learn to strike out in response to minimal provocations and signs of interpersonal "disrespect." All of these adaptations are highly functional inside prison and problematic virtually everywhere else.[137]

During the era of mass incarceration, conditions and practices inside many American prisons became increasingly harsh, adversely affecting the day-to-day lives of persons housed there.[138] For example, the overwhelming influx of prisoners that occurred during the last four decades led to unprecedented levels of overcrowding inside many of the nation's correctional systems.[139] In addition, in part as a largely expedient response intended to maintain control inside potentially unstable overcrowded facilities, correctional administrators began to resort to an especially painful and potentially destructive form of prison discipline—the use of long-term solitary confinement. Each one of these two extremes of imprisonment—overcrowding and solitary confinement—is potentially criminogenic, both during incarceration itself and in the aftermath, as formerly incarcerated persons attempt to re-enter free society.

Overcrowding touches virtually every aspect of a prisoner's day-to-day existence and greatly amplifies the stress of prison life. Not surprisingly, a large literature on overcrowding has documented a range of adverse effects that occur when prisons have been filled to near capacity and beyond.[140] Crowding significantly worsens the quality of institutional life, interferes with the delivery of necessary services (e.g., programming and medical and mental health care), and increases the destructive potential of imprisonment. It has been shown to increase negative affect among prisoners, elevate their blood pressure, lead to greater numbers of prisoner illness complaints, result in high levels of stress that "can lead to physical and psychological impairment," and decrease overall levels of well-being.[141]

At the opposite end of the social spectrum, solitary confinement deprives prisoners of meaningful social contact and positive environmental stimulation. It, too, has been shown to have very serious, potentially debilitating, and sometimes even fatal consequences. Solitary confinement is stressful and painful and capable of producing a number of direct, adverse psychological reactions.[142] In addition, the long-term deprivation of meaningful contact with others can destabilize one's sense of self and instill "social pathologies" that come about as a result of being forced to adapt to the lack of meaningful social contact. Because humans are social beings whose personal identities are rooted in and maintained through social interaction, long-term isolated prisoners are literally at risk of losing their grasp on who they are—of how and whether they are connected to a larger social world.[143]

The use of this draconian form of prison confinement increased during the era of mass incarceration,[144] and estimates of the number of prisoners who were housed in solitary confinement on any given day during this period reached as high as 100,000 or more.[145] There is evidence that the effects of solitary confinement linger beyond the experience itself[146] and may include increased rates of recidivism compared with those of formerly incarcerated persons who were never forced to live in conditions of isolated confinement.[147]

In any event, whether or not prisoners have ever been housed in overcrowded mainline prisons or placed in debilitating forms of solitary confinement, they are often changed by the experience of imprisonment in ways that increase the likelihood that they will engage in illegal behavior once released. Some of the most serious psychological aftereffects of incarceration can compromise longer term economic and social reintegration in ways that prove criminogenic.[148] In addition, another often overlooked criminogenic aspect of prison confinement stems from the way that imprisonment facilitates and, in some instances, even compels *in*-prison crimes that are different from and sometimes more serious than those for which prisoners were originally sentenced. Indeed, because many correctional institutions function as though the people confined there are not fully human—performing what have been characterized as "waste management" functions[149]—it is all too easy for inmates to slip into applying this worldview to each other—seeing their fellows as lacking in value and somehow deserving of the degraded and diminished treatment they receive—while at the same time fighting against the tendency to apply it to oneself. Extreme forms of sexual and racial violence too often result, frequently engaged in by persons who have never done such things in the past.[150] Correctional officers are also subjected to the criminogenic situational pressures of the prison environment that can precipitate abusive behavior that would be considered criminal in another context and that is uncharacteristic of their free-world behavior.[151]

In addition, the criminogenic long-term effects of imprisonment are compounded by a set of "collateral consequences" that formerly incarcerated persons confront once they are released back into the free world. For example, in addition to the direct negative effects of imprisonment on prisoners themselves, there is much evidence that prison adversely and directly affects their subsequent employment opportunities. Formerly incarcerated persons have higher rates of unemployment and earn lower wages when they do find jobs.[152] The long periods of time from which prisoners are removed from the job market (during which time they are unlikely to obtain marketable job skills), and the stigma that employers attach to their prison records contribute to these employment effects. In fact, Becky Pettit and Bruce Western characterized imprisonment as "an illegitimate timeout that confers enduring stigma."[153] As they pointed out, this stigma deters employers from hiring for even low wage jobs, and the existence of a prison record also can create formal legal barriers for certain skilled and licensed occupations.

Unfortunately, the collateral consequences of imprisonment jeopardize more than post-prison employment opportunities. Amounting to what Gabriel Chin termed "the new civil death,"[154] they operate to marginalize formerly incarcerated persons and distance them from a wide range of public benefits and opportunities, including in housing, education, and political participation. Forced disengagement with the surrounding community and the added economic and social burdens of confronting these obstacles can significantly contribute to the long-term criminogenic effects of incarceration.[155]

CONCLUSION

In this chapter, I have argued that criminal behavior can only be fully understood in context—by examining aspects of the immediate circumstances and situations, and larger neighborhoods and communities, and even the institutions in which it occurs. I have suggested that contemporary psychological thinking requires placing a much greater emphasis on criminogenic contexts than current political and legal analyses of criminal behavior do. The psychological insights I have summarized about the powerful social contextual influences on criminal behavior call into question the crime master narrative's narrow, exclusive focus on supposedly free choices made by allegedly inherently bad people. As I discuss in greater detail in the closing chapter of this book, no effective strategy of crime control can continue to overlook the situational and social structural roots of criminality. Preventive interventions must address and alter the situations and contexts that have the most destructive criminogenic impact, reducing both the need and the opportunity for persons to engage in criminal behavior.[156] A deeper appreciation of the contextual determinants of crime also poses a challenge to the fairness and wisdom of holding individuals alone fully accountable and punishing them severely for their wrongdoing when, in many instances, they have adapted and reacted to a set of powerful structural and situational pressures over which they had little or no capacity to control, change, or resist.

Cornel West, writing at the peak of the mass incarceration movement in the United States when other commentators were warning about a menacing wave of "superpredators" that was supposedly poised to sweep across the nation,[157] instead lamented what he called "the collapse of meaning" in many communities, ones filled with the kind of criminogenic immediate situations and circumstances that I have discussed in this chapter. He wisely observed that "the eclipse of hope and absence of love of self and others" operated in tandem with economic deprivation in ways that tended to break people's "link to the supportive networks—family, friends, school—that sustain some sense of purpose in life."[158] West noted more generally that

> [W]e must acknowledge that structures and behavior are inseparable, that institutions and values go hand in hand. How people act and live are shaped—though in no way dictated or determined—by the larger circumstances in which they find themselves. These circumstances can be changed, their limits attenuated, by positive actions to elevate living conditions.[159]

The next two chapters build on the insight that "structures and behavior are inseparable" by analyzing the ways in which the kinds of past social histories and immediate criminogenic situations, settings, and circumstances I have discussed in this and the previous chapters are themselves part of a larger set of structural arrangements. Those structures are the legacy of a set of policy choices that reflect an often unspoken set of social, institutional, and political values. They operate to directly and adversely impact the day-to-day lives and living conditions of large groups of people in our society in ways that can have broad and powerful criminogenic consequences.

NOTES

1. Banaji, M. R. (2001). Ordinary prejudice. *Psychological Science Agenda, 14*(Jan.–Feb.), 8–11, p. 8.
2. Milgram, S. (1965). Some conditions of obedience and disobedience to authority. *Human Relations,* 18, 57–76 (1965), p. 75. http://dx.doi.org/10.1177/001872676501800105
3. Erikson, K. T. (1966). *Wayward Puritans: A study in the sociology of deviance* (pp. 4–5). New York, NY: Wiley.
4. Horney, J. (2006). An alternative psychology of criminal behavior. *Criminology, 44,* 1–16, p. 13.
5. Horney (2006), An alternative psychology of criminal behavior, p. 13.
6. Gottfredson, M. R., & Hirschi, T. (1990). *A general theory of crime* (p. 137). Stanford, CA: Stanford University Press.
7. Markus, H. R. (2008). Pride, prejudice, and ambivalence: Toward a unified theory of race and ethnicity. *American Psychologist, 63,* 651–670, p. 655. http://dx.doi.org/10.1037/0003-066X.63.8.651
8. Mischel, W. (1968). *Personality and assessment.* New York, NY: Wiley; and Mischel, W. (1990). Personality dispositions revisited and revised: A view after three decades. In L. A. Pervin (Ed.), *Handbook of personality: Theory and research* (pp. 111–134). New York, NY: Guilford Press.
9. Mischel, W. (1997). Was the cognitive revolution just a detour on the road to behaviorism? On the need to reconcile situational control and personal control. In R. S. Wyer, Jr. (Ed.), *The automaticity of everyday life: Advances in social cognition* (Vol. 10, pp. 181–186). Mahwah, NJ: Lawrence Erlbaum, p. 183. Mischel noted further: "[T]he significance of the situation in the regulation of human social behavior remains formidable, even after three decades of cognitive revolution" (p. 183).
10. Moen, P. (1995). Introduction. In P. Moen, G. H. Elder, Jr., & K. Lüscher (Eds.), *Examining lives in context: Perspectives on the ecology of human development* (pp. 1–11). Washington, DC: American Psychological Association. http://dx.doi.org/10.1037/10176-019
11. See, e.g., Brown, T. L., Phillips, C. M., Abdulla, T., Vinson, E., & Robertson, J. (2011). Dispositional versus situational coping: Are the coping strategies African

Americans use different for general versus racism-related stressors? *Journal of Black Psychology, 37*, 311–335. http://dx.doi.org/10.1177/0095798410390688; Clary, E. G., & Miller, J. (1986). Socialization and situational influences on sustained altruism. *Child Development, 57*, 1358–1369. http://dx.doi.org/10.2307/1130415; Guest, A. M., & McRee, N. (2009). A school-level analysis of adolescent extracurricular activity, delinquency, and depression: The importance of situational context. *Journal of Youth and Adolescence, 38*, 51–62. http://dx.doi.org/10.1007/s10964-008-9279-6; Hammen, C. (1990). Vulnerability to depression: Personal, situational, and family aspects. In R. E. Ingram (Ed.), *Contemporary psychological approaches to depression: Theory, research, and treatment* (pp. 59–69). New York, NY: Plenum Press. http://dx.doi.org/10.1007/978-1-4613-0649-8_5; Jex, S. M., Adams, G. A., Bachrach, D. G., & Sorenson, S. (2003). The impact of situational constraints, role stressors, and commitment on employee altruism. *Journal of Occupational Health Psychology, 8*, 171–180. http://dx.doi.org/10.1037/1076-8998.8.3.171; and Ouwehand, C., DeRidder, D. T. D., & Bensing, J. M. (2006). Situational aspects are more important in shaping proactive coping behaviour than individual characteristics: A vignette study among adults preparing for ageing. *Psychology & Health, 21*, 809–825. http://dx.doi.org/10.1080/14768320500537639. More broadly, Mirowsky and Ross demonstrated the ways in which the subjective experience of psychological distress varies as a function of general social conditions and social position. See Mirowsky, J., & Ross, C. E. (2003). *Social causes of psychological distress* (2nd ed.). Hawthorne, NY: Aldine de Gruyter.

12. See, e.g., Leming, J. S. (1978). Cheating behavior, situational influence, and moral development. *The Journal of Educational Research, 71*, 214–217. http://dx.doi.org/10.1080/00220671.1978.10885074
13. Mawson, A. (1987). *Situational criminality: A model of stress-induced crime*, p. 18. New York, NY: Praeger.
14. Mawson (1987), *Situational criminality: A model of stress-induced crime*, p. 20. I should note that Mawson's model was not entirely situational in nature and contained a number of intrapsychic mechanisms of questionable validity and utility. However, it did acknowledge something that, at the time, represented a challenge of sorts to the crime master narrative.
15. The perspective presented here is highly compatible with aspects of what is termed "criminal opportunity theory" in sociology. Thus: "[C]riminal opportunity theory has emphasized the 'normality' of criminal acts, arguing that offending and victimization emerge from socialization and social interaction rather than personal pathology. . . . [I]t maintains that criminal acts emerge from the circumstances in which individuals find themselves." Wilcox, P., Land, K., & Hunt, S. (2003). *Criminal circumstance: A dynamic multicontextual criminal opportunity theory*. New York, NY: Aldine de Gruyter, p. 16.
16. See, e.g., Gessner, T., O'Connor, J., Mumford, M. D., Clifton, T. C., & Smith, J. (1994). Situational influences on destructive acts. *Current Psychology, 13*, 303–325. http://dx.doi.org/10.1007/BF02686890
17. Harries, K. (1995). The ecology of homicide and assault: Baltimore City and County, 1989–91. *Studies on Crime & Crime Prevention, 4*, 44–60; Vaux, A., & Ruggiero, M. (1983). Stressful life change and delinquent behavior. *American Journal of Community Psychology, 11*, 169–183.
18. See, e.g., Silver, E., Mulvey, E. P., & Monahan, J. (1999). Assessing violence risk among discharged psychiatric patients: Toward an ecological approach. *Law and Human Behavior, 23*, 237–255. http://dx.doi.org/10.1023/A:1022377003150
19. Allen, E., & Steffensmeier, D. (1989). Youth, underemployment, and property crime: Differential effects of job availability and job quality on juvenile and young adult arrest rates. *American Sociological Review, 54*, 107–123. http://dx.doi.org/10.2307/2095665

20. Berkowitz, L. (1989). Situational influences on aggression. In J. Groebel & R. Hinde (Eds.), *Aggression and war: Their biological and social bases* (pp. 91–100). Cambridge, England: Cambridge University Press.
21. Berkowitz (1989), Situational influences on aggression, p. 94. Even the Karmapa Lama, the young man who has been mentored by the Dali Lama and discussed as his possible successor, who eschews violence as a matter of religious principle, acknowledged: "For any living being, when you feel the force of being cornered time and again, more and more, the time comes when you have nothing else left except to explode." Quoted in Symmes, P. (2009, March 2). Tibet's rising son, *Newsweek*, 31–33, p. 33.
22. Blau, J., & Blau, P. (1982). The cost of inequality: Metropolitan structure and violent crime. *American Sociological Review, 47,* 114–129, p. 126. http://dx.doi.org/10.2307/2095046. See also Williams, K. (1984). Economic sources of homicide: Reestimating the effects of poverty and inequality. *American Sociological Review, 49,* 283–289. http://dx.doi.org/10.2307/2095577
23. See, e.g., Carlson, M., Marcus-Newhall, A., & Miller, N. (1990). Effects of situational aggression cues: A quantitative review. *Journal of Personality and Social Psychology, 58,* 622–633. http://dx.doi.org/10.1037/0022-3514.58.4.622
24. See, e.g., Cleary Bradley, R. P., & Gottman, J. M. (2012). Reducing situational violence in low-income couples by fostering healthy relationships. *Journal of Marital and Family Therapy, 38,* 187–198. http://dx.doi.org/10.1111/j.1752-0606.2012.00288.x; Wilkinson, D., & Hamerschlag, S. (2005). Situational determinants in intimate partner violence. *Aggression and Violent Behavior, 10,* 333–361. http://dx.doi.org/10.1016/j.avb.2004.05.001
25. See, e.g., Bramsen, I. (2018). How violence happens (or not): Situational conditions of violence and nonviolence in Bahrain, Tunisia, and Syria. *Psychology of Violence, 8,* 305–315. http://dx.doi.org/10.1037/vio0000178; Toch, H. (1985). The catalytic situation in the violence equation. *Journal of Applied Social Psychology, 15,* 105–123. http://dx.doi.org/10.1111/j.1559-1816.1985.tb02338.x
26. See, e.g., Cooke, D., Wozniak, E., & Johnstone, L. (2008). Casting a light on prison violence in Scotland: Evaluating the impact of situational risk factors. *Criminal Justice and Behavior, 35,* 1065–1078. http://dx.doi.org/10.1177/0093854808318867; Gadon, L., Johnstone, L., & Cooke, D. (2006). Situational variables and institutional violence: A systematic review of the literature. *Clinical Psychology Review, 26,* 515–534. http://dx.doi.org/10.1016/j.cpr.2006.02.002; Steinke, P. (1991). Using situational factors to predict types of violence. *Journal of Offender Rehabilitation, 17,* 119–132. http://dx.doi.org/10.1300/J076v17n01_09; and Welsh, E., Bader, S., & Evans, S. (2013). Situational variables related to aggression in institutional settings. *Aggression and Violent Behavior, 18,* 792–796.
27. Berkowitz (1989), Situational influences on aggression, p. 100 (emphasis added).
28. Ochberg, F. (1980). On preventing aggression and violence. *The Police Chief, 67,* 52–56.
29. Ochberg (1980), On preventing aggression and violence, p. 52.
30. See, e.g., Prentice-Dunn, S., & Rogers, R. (1980). Effects of deindividuating situational cues and aggressive models on subjective deindividuation and aggression. *Journal of Personality and Social Psychology, 39,* 104–113. http://dx.doi.org/10.1037/0022-3514.39.1.104; Prentice-Dunn, S., & Rogers, R. (1989). Deindividuation and the self-regulation of behavior. In P. Paulus (Ed.), *Psychology of group influence* (pp. 87–109). Hillsdale, NJ: Lawrence Erlbaum; Taylor, L., O'Neal, E., Langley, T., & Butcher, A. (1991). Anger arousal, deindividuation, and aggression. *Aggressive Behavior, 17,* 193–206. http://dx.doi.org/10.1002/1098-2337(1991)17:4%3C193::AID-AB2480170402%3E3.0.CO;2-B; Zimbardo, P. (1995). The psychology of evil: A situationist perspective on recruiting good people to engage in anti-social acts. *Japanese Journal of Social Psychology, 11,* 125–133.

31. Bovasso, G. (1997). The interaction of depersonalization and deindividuation. *Journal of Social Distress and the Homeless, 6,* 213–228. http://dx.doi.org/10.1007/BF02939566
32. Paloutzian, R. F. (1975). Effects of deindividuation, removal of responsibility, and coaction on impulsive and cyclical aggression. *The Journal of Psychology, 90,* 163–169. http://dx.doi.org/10.1080/00223980.1975.9915771
33. See, e.g., Sun, K. (1993). The implications of social psychological theories of group dynamics for gang research. *Journal of Gang Research, 1,* 39–44.
34. Holmes, T. H., & Rahe, R. H. (1967). The social adjustment rating scale. *Journal of Psychiatric Research, 11,* 213–218. http://dx.doi.org/10.1016/0022-3999(67)90010-4
35. See, e.g., Paykel, E. S. (2001). The evolution of life events research in psychiatry. *Journal of Affective Disorders, 62,* 141–149. http://dx.doi.org/10.1016/S0165-0327(00)00174-9
36. Justice, B., & Justice, R. (1976). *The abusing family.* New York, NY: Human Sciences Press. More recent research also found a relationship between parental stress and maltreatment. See, e.g., Taylor, C., Guterman, N., Lee, S., & Rathouz, P. (2009). Intimate partner violence, maternal stress, nativity, and the risk for maltreatment of young children. *American Journal of Public Health, 99,* 175–183. http://dx.doi.org/10.2105/AJPH.2007.126722; Warren, E., & Font, S. (2015). Housing insecurity, maternal stress, and child maltreatment: An application of the family stress model. *Social Service Review, 89,* 9–39. http://dx.doi.org/10.1086/680043; and Pei, F., Wang, X., Yoon, S., & Tebben, E. (2019). The influences of neighborhood disorder on early childhood externalizing problems: The roles of parental stress and child physical maltreatment. *Journal of Community Psychology, 47,* 1105–1117. http://dx.doi.org/10.1002/jcop.22174
37. Masuda, M., Cutler, D., Hein, L., & Holmes, T. (1978). Life events and prisoners. *Archives of General Psychiatry, 35,* 197–203. http://dx.doi.org/10.1001/archpsyc.1978.01770260075009. Prison itself is stressful, as I discuss later in this chapter, and its stressfulness has been shown to increase the likelihood that prisoners will contract certain kinds of physical illnesses. See Massoglia, M. (2008). Incarceration as exposure: The prison, infectious disease, and other stress-related illnesses. *Journal of Health and Social Behavior, 49,* 56–71. http://dx.doi.org/10.1177/002214650804900105. Exposure to powerful stressors—sometimes termed "traumatic life events"—also increases the level of suicide risk among jail inmates. See Blaauw, E., Arensman, E., Kraaij, V., Winkel, F., & Bout, R. (2002). Traumatic life events and suicide risk among jail inmates: The influence of types of events, time period and significant others. *Journal of Traumatic Stress, 15,* 9–19. http://dx.doi.org/10.1023/A:1014323009493
38. Mawson (1987), *Situational criminality,* p. 247. The relationship between forms of generalized stress and criminality is also postulated in sociological "strain theory." See, e.g., Agnew, R. (2006). *Pressured into crime: An overview of general strain theory.* New York, NY: Oxford University Press. From a related perspective, Bruce Dohrenwend summarized his decades of research on life stress by noting that the studies "provide strong evidence" that stress and environmental adversity play an important role in the occurrence of a range of later problematic outcomes, including posttraumatic stress disorder (PTSD), major depression, alcoholism, substance use disorders, and lawbreaking. He concluded further that the likelihood of developing these types of adversity-related disorders was a function of the number and centrality of negative changes that took place in a person's life following exposure to the environmental stressors that, in turn, was a function of the nature of the adversities and personal characteristics of the individuals who experienced them. Dohrenwend, B. (2000). The role of adversity and stress

in psychopathology: Some evidence and its implications for theory and research. *Journal of Health and Social Behavior, 41,* 1–19. http://dx.doi.org/10.2307/2676357

39. Hartman, A., & Nicolay, R. (1966). Sexually deviant behavior in expectant fathers. *Journal of Abnormal Psychology, 71,* 232–234. http://dx.doi.org/10.1037/h0023360; Rada, R. (1978). Psychological factors in rapist behavior. In R. Rada (Ed.), *Clinical aspects of the rapist* (pp. 21–85). New York, NY: Grune and Stratton.
40. See the discussion of "neighborhood disadvantage" and related references later in this chapter.
41. Lemert, E. (1953). An isolation and closure theory of naïve check forgery. *The Journal of Criminal Law, Criminology, and Police Science, 44,* 296–307. http://dx.doi.org/10.2307/1139226
42. Felson, R., Osgood, D., Horney, J., & Wiernik, C. (2012). Having a bad month: General versus specific effects of stress on crime. *Journal of Quantitative Criminology, 28,* 347–363. http://dx.doi.org/10.1007/s10940-011-9138-6. See also Slocum, L., Simpson, S., & Smith, D. (2005). Strained lives and crime: Examining individual variation in strain and offending in a sample of incarcerated women. *Criminology, 43,* 1067–1110. http://dx.doi.org/10.1111/j.1745-9125.2005.00033.x. Slocum et al. found that "strain" was a dynamic concept with different dimensions that nonetheless were related to increased violence, drug use, and property crime. See also De Coster, S., & Kort-Butler, L. (2006). How general is general strain theory? Assessing the determinacy and indeterminacy across life domains. *Journal of Research in Crime and Delinquency, 43,* 297–325. http://dx.doi.org/10.1177/0022427806291272 (They found that the effects of stress tended to "spillover" in the domains were the stress was experienced [i.e., that stress experienced at school was related to delinquency at school and that stress experienced in the family setting was related to delinquency at home]).
43. See the previous chapter's discussion of and references to Bowlby, Ainsworth, and Shaver.
44. Sroufe, L., Egeland, B., & Kreutzer, T. (1990). The fate of early experience following developmental change: Longitudinal approaches to individual adaptation in childhood. *Child Development, 61,* 1363–1373, p. 1371. http://dx.doi.org/10.2307/1130748
45. Felson, R., & Steadman, H. (1983). Situational factors in disputes leading to criminal violence. *Criminology: An Interdisciplinary Journal, 21,* 59–74. http://dx.doi.org/10.1111/j.1745-9125.1983.tb00251.x. See also Steadman, H. (1982). A situational approach to violence. *International Journal of Law and Psychiatry, 5,* 171–186. http://dx.doi.org/10.1016/0160-2527(82)90004-8
46. Hepburn, J. (1973). Violent behavior in interpersonal relationships. *Sociological Quarterly, 14,* 419–429. http://dx.doi.org/10.1111/j.1533-8525.1973.tb00870.x. Although the motivations were expressed in somewhat different ways, researchers have found that assaults committed by women were impulsive acts that nonetheless followed a situational logic. That is, women were more likely to react violently when a victim's initial behavior appeared to have implications for defending the aggressor's physical well-being or upholding their public self-concept. Sommers, I., & Baskin, D. (1993). The situational context of violent female offending. *Journal of Research in Crime and Delinquency, 30,* 136–162. http://dx.doi.org/10.1177/0022427893030002002
47. In a related way, Randall Collins has offered a "general theory of violence as a situational process." He has "micro-analyzed" the circumstances under which violence occurs, concluding that potentially violent situations "are shaped by an emotional field of tension and fear" in which actual violence "is a structural property of situational fields, not a property of individuals." Collins, R. (2008). *Violence: A micro-sociological theory*. Princeton, NJ: Princeton University Press, p. 19.

48. Anderson, E. (1994, May). The code of the streets: How the inner-city environment fosters a need for respect and a self-image based on violence. *The Atlantic Monthly*, 81–94, p. 82.
49. Anderson (1994), The code of the streets, p. 86. See also Anderson, E. (1999). *Code of the street: Decency, violence, and the moral life of the inner city*. New York, NY: W. W. Norton.
50. Stewart, E., & Simons, R. (2009, February). *The code of the street and African American adolescent violence* (National Institute of Justice, Research in Brief). Washington, DC: National Institute of Justice. For a more detailed discussion of this research, see Stewart, E., & Simons, R. (2006). Structure and culture in African American adolescent violence: A partial test of the "code of the street" thesis. *Justice Quarterly, 23*, 1–33. http://dx.doi.org/10.1080/07418820600552378; and Stewart, E., & Simons, R. (2010). Race, code of the street, and violent delinquency: A multilevel investigation of neighborhood street culture and individual norms of violence. *Criminology, 48*, 569–605. http://dx.doi.org/10.1111/j.1745-9125.2010.00196.x
51. Stewart & Simons (2009), *The code of the street*, p. 2 (quoting Elijah Anderson).
52. Stewart & Simons (2009), *The code of the street*, p. 3 (quoting Elijah Anderson).
53. Stewart & Simons (2009), *The code of the street*, p. ii. Ironically, although subscribing to the code of the streets may seem to be functional and even necessary to residents in the neighborhood contexts in which it is embraced, there is evidence that African Americans who subscribe to it are at even greater risk of arrest and conviction. See Mears, D., Stewart, E., Warren, P., & Simons, R. (2016). Culture and formal social control. The role of the code of the street on police and court decision-making. *Justice Quarterly, 34*, 217–247. http://dx.doi.org/10.1080/07418825.2016.1149599
54. Warr, M. (2002). *Companions in crime: The social aspects of criminal conduct*. New York, NY: Cambridge University Press, p. 136 (emphasis in original). See also Walters, G. (2018). Resistance to peer influence and crime desistance in emerging adulthood: A moderated mediation analysis. *Law and Human Behavior, 42*, 520–530. http://dx.doi.org/10.1037/lhb0000293
55. See, e.g., McCarthy, B., & Hagan, J. (1995). Getting into street crime: The structure and process of criminal embeddedness. *Social Science Research, 24*, 63–95. http://dx.doi.org/10.1006/ssre.1995.1003
56. Colvin, M. (2000). *Crime and coercion: An integrated theory of chronic criminality*. New York, NY: St. Martin's Press, p. 50. What Colvin termed "social psychological deficits"—the behaviors adopted in response to coercion—are perhaps better described as social psychological adaptations—forced adjustments to a set of otherwise toxic environments and forms of mistreatment.
57. Colvin (2000), *Crime and coercion*, p. 86. See also Baron, S. (2009). Differential coercion, street youth, and violent crime. *Criminology, 47*, 239–268. http://dx.doi.org/10.1111/j.1745-9125.2009.00144.x; Colvin, M., Cullen, F., & Vander Ven, T. (2002). Coercion, social support, and crime: An emerging theoretical consensus. *Criminology, 40*, 19–42; and Unnever, J., Colvin, M., & Cullen, F. (2004). Crime and coercion: A test of core theoretical propositions. *Journal of Research in Crime and Delinquency, 41*, 244–268. http://dx.doi.org/10.1111/j.1745-9125.2002.tb00948.x
58. Elliott, D., Wilson, W., Huizinga, D., Sampson, R., & Rankin, B. (1996). The effects of neighborhood disadvantage on adolescent development. *Journal of Research in Crime and Delinquency, 33*, 389–426. http://dx.doi.org/10.1177/0022427896033004002
59. Vanderbilt-Adriance, E., & Shaw, D. (2008). Protective factors and the development of resilience in the context of neighborhood disadvantage. *Journal of Childhood Abnormal Psychology, 36*, 886–901, p. 888.

60. McLoyd, V. C. (1990). The impact of economic hardship on black families and children: Psychological distress, parenting, and socioeconomic development. *Child Development, 61*, 311–346, p. 318. http://dx.doi.org/10.2307/1131096
61. Clark, K. (1965). *Dark ghetto: Dilemmas of social power*. New York, NY: Harper and Row, pp. 63–64.
62. See, e.g., Mier, C., & Ladny, R. T. (2018). Does self-esteem negatively impact crime and delinquency? A meta-analytic review of 25 years of evidence. *Deviant Behavior, 39*, 1006–1022. http://dx.doi.org/10.1080/01639625.2017.1395667; and Trzesniewski, K. H., Donnellan, M. B., Moffitt, T. E., Robins, R. W., Poulton, R., & Caspi, A. (2006). Low self-esteem during adolescence predicts poor health, criminal behavior, and limited economic prospects during adulthood. *Developmental Psychology, 42*, 381–390. http://dx.doi.org/10.1037/0012-1649.42.2.381
63. Elliott, Wilson, Huizinga, Sampson, & Rankin (1996), p. 384.
64. Roth, R. (2009). *American homicide* (p. 18). Cambridge, MA: Harvard University Press.
65. Elliott, Wilson, Huizinga, Sampson, & Rankin (1996), p. 384.
66. See, e.g., De Coster, S., Heimer, K., & Wittrock, S. (2006). Neighborhood disadvantage, social capital, street context, and youth violence. *The Sociological Quarterly, 47*, 723–753. http://dx.doi.org/10.1111/j.1533-8525.2006.00064.x
67. Skeem, J., Mulvey, E., & Lidz, C. (2000). Building mental health professionals' decisional models into tests of predictive validity: The accuracy of contextualized predictions of violence. *Law and Human Behavior, 24*, 607–628, p. 609. http://dx.doi.org/10.1023/A:1005513818748
68. Silver, E., Mulvey, E., & Monahan, J. (1999). Assessing violence risk among discharged psychiatric patients: Toward an ecological approach. *Law and Human Behavior, 23*, 237–255, p. 242. http://dx.doi.org/10.1023/A:1022377003150
69. Silver, Mulvey, & Monahan (1999), Assessing violence risk among discharged psychiatric patients, p. 250.
70. Mulvey, E. P., & Lidz, C. W. (1995). Conditional prediction: A model for research on dangerousness to others in a new era. *International Journal of Law and Psychiatry, 18*, 129–143, p. 135 (emphasis added). http://dx.doi.org/10.1016/0160-2527(95)00002-Y
71. See, e.g., Fagan, J., & Wilkinson, D. (1998). Guns, youth violence, and social identity in inner cities. *Crime and Justice, 24*, 105–188. http://dx.doi.org/10.1086/449279; Kleck, G. (2015). The impact of gun ownership rates on crime rates: A methodological review of the evidence. *Journal of Criminal Justice, 43*, 40–48. http://dx.doi.org/10.1016/j.jcrimjus.2014.12.002
72. Khalil, U. (2017). Do more guns lead to more crime? Understanding the role of illegal firearms. *Journal of Economic Behavior & Organization, 133*, 342–361. http://dx.doi.org/10.1016/j.jebo.2016.11.010
73. Monuteaux, M., Lee, L., Hemenway, D., Mannix, R., & Fleegler, E. (2015). Firearm ownership and violent crime in the U.S.: An ecologic study. *American Journal of Preventive Medicine, 49*, 207–214. http://dx.doi.org/10.1016/j.amepre.2015.02.008; Roberts, D. (2009). Intimate partner homicide: Relationships to alcohol and firearms. *Journal of Contemporary Criminal Justice, 25*, 67–88. http://dx.doi.org/10.1177/1043986208329771
74. Hoskin, A. (2011). Household gun prevalence and rates of violent crime: A test of competing gun theories. *Criminal Justice Studies, 24*, 125–136. Richard Delgado, Jeffrey Fagan, and Deanna Wilkinson have recognized that, as Fagan summarized it "the presence of weapons also can escalate simple disputes into lethal violence," as well as that "the widespread presence of firearms in everyday social interactions" may represent the "most direct and unique form of social toxin" present in immediate environments where lethal violence occurs. Fagin, J. (1999). Context and culpability in adolescent crime. *Virginia Journal of Social Policy and Law, 6*,

507–581, p., 555, 559. See, also Fagan & Wilkinson (1998), Guns, youth violence, and social identity in inner cities, and Delgado, R. (1985). Rotten social background: Should the criminal law recognize a defense of severe environmental deprivation? *Law & Inequality, 3,* 9–90. In addition, there is evidence that in environments where there is easy access to firearms, adolescents feel peer pressure to carry and are more likely to use them. See, e.g., Wilkinson, D. L., McBryde, M. S., Williams, B., Bloom, S., & Bell, K. (2009). Peers and gun use among urban adolescent males: An examination of social embeddedness. *Journal of Contemporary Criminal Justice, 25,* 20–44. http://dx.doi.org/10.1177/1043986208328449. Thus, being embedded in a network of weapons-carrying friends not only increases the availability of weapons but may lead "low-status adolescents [to] impress" their higher status peers by "daring to carry weapons too." Dijkstra, J. K., Lindenberg, S., Veenstra, R., Steglich, C., Isaacs, J., Card, N. A., & Hodges, E. V. E. (2010). Influence and selection processes in weapon carrying during adolescence: The roles of status, aggression, and vulnerability. *Criminology, 48,* 187–220, p. 207. http://dx.doi.org/10.1111/j.1745-9125.2010.00183.x

75. Hennigan, D. (2016). *"Guns don't kill people, people kill people," and other myths about guns and gun control.* Boston, MA: Beacon Press.
76. To take just one example with which I have a special connection, consider California Governor Pete Wilson, whose political reputation was based in part on his ardent support for programs to combat child maltreatment. However, when Wilson was asked in 1992 to consider clemency for Robert Alton Harris, then scheduled to be the first man executed in California in some 25 years, Wilson rejected the plea. He did so despite the fact that Harris had endured years of horrendous abuse throughout his childhood and adolescence, suffered from fetal alcohol syndrome, and was literally abandoned by his family when they drove off to another state, leaving him alone in an agricultural field to fend for himself. Wilson summarized his logic this way: "As great as is my compassion for Robert Harris the child, I cannot excuse or forgive the choice made by Robert Harris the man." Chaing, H. (1992, April 17). Wilson denies Harris clemency. *San Francisco Chronicle,* pp. A1, A17, at p. A1. See also Haney, C. (1997). Psychological secrecy and the death penalty: Observations on "the mere extinguishment of life." *Studies in Law, Politics, and Society, 16,* 3–69.
77. See, e.g., Jones, E., & Nisbett, R. (1971). The actor and the observer: Divergent perceptions of the causes of the behavior. In E. Jones, D. Kanouse, H. Kelley, R. Nisbett, S. Valins, & B Weiner (Eds.), *Attribution: Perceiving the causes of behavior* (pp. 79–94). Morristown, NJ: General Learning Press; and Ross, L., & Nisbett, R. (1991). *The person and the situation.* New York, NY: McGraw Hill.
78. Gerald Patterson and his colleagues have done an excellent job teasing apart the sequence of developmental events by which children move from abusive backgrounds, to problematic styles of interpersonal behavior, to delinquency. See, e.g., Patterson, G., DeBaryshe, B., & Ramsey, E. (1989). A developmental perspective on antisocial behavior. *American Psychologist, 44,* 329–335, p. 331. http://dx.doi.org/10.1037/0003-066X.44.2.329. See also Patterson, G., & Dishion, T. (1985). Contributions of families and peers to delinquency. *Criminology, 23,* 63–79. http://dx.doi.org/10.1111/j.1745-9125.1985.tb00326.x
79. See, e.g., Rosenkranz, S., Muller, R., & Henderson, J. (2012). Psychological maltreatment in relation to substance abuse problem severity among youth. *Child Abuse and Neglect, 36,* 438–448. http://dx.doi.org/10.1016/j.chiabu.2012.01.005; Roy, A. (1999). Childhood trauma and depression in alcoholics: Relationship to hostility. *Journal of Affective Disorders, 56.* 215–218. http://dx.doi.org/10.1016/S0165-0327(99)00044-0; Thornberry, T. P., Henry, K. K., Ireland, T. O., & Smith, C. A. (2010). The causal impact of childhood-limited maltreatment and adolescent

maltreatment on early adult adjustment. *The Journal of Adolescent Health, 46,* 359–365. http://dx.doi.org/10.1016/j.jadohealth.2009.09.011

80. See, e.g., Khantzian, E. (1990). Self-regulation and self-medication factors in alcoholism and the addictions: Similarities and differences. In M. Galanter (Ed.), *Recent developments in alcoholism: Combined alcohol and other drug dependence* (Vol. 8, pp. 255–271). New York, NY: Plenum Press; Kosten, T., & Krystal, J. (1988). Biological mechanisms in posttraumatic stress disorder: Relevance for substance abuse. In M. Galanter (Ed.), *Recent developments in alcoholism* (Vol. 6, pp. 49–68). New York, NY: Plenum Press; Lacoursiere, R., Godfrey, K., & Ruby, L. (1980). Traumatic neurosis in the etiology of alcoholism: Viet Nam combat and other trauma. *The American Journal of Psychiatry, 137,* 966–968. http://dx.doi.org/10.1176/ajp.137.8.966
81. Stenbacka, M., & Stattin, H. (2007). Adolescent use of illicit drugs and adult offending: A Swedish longitudinal study. *Drug and Alcohol Review, 26,* 397–403, p. 401. http://dx.doi.org/10.1080/09595230701373875. See also Langevin, R., Ben-Aron, M., Wortzman, G., Dickey, R., Handy, L. (1987). Brain damage, diagnosis, and substance abuse among violent offenders. *Behavioral Sciences and the Law, 5,* 77–94. http://dx.doi.org/10.1002/bsl.2370050108; Langevin, R., Paitich, D., Orchard, B., Handy, L., & Russon, A. (1982). The role of alcohol, drugs, suicide attempts and situational strains in homicide committed by offenders seen for psychiatric assessment. *Acta Psychiatrica Scandinavica, 66,* 216–228. http://dx.doi.org/10.1111/j.1600-0447.1982.tb00931.x; Parker, R. N. (1995). Bringing "booze" back in: The relationship between alcohol and homicide. *Journal of Research in Crime and Delinquency, 32,* 3–38. http://dx.doi.org/10.1177/0022427895032001001
82. Anderson (1994), *Code of the street: Decency, violence, and the moral life of the inner city,* p. 77.
83. Inciardi, J. (1993). Drug-involved offenders: Crime-prison-treatment. *Prison Journal, 73,* 253–256, p. 253. http://dx.doi.org/10.1177/0032855593073003001
84. Goldstein, P. (1989). Drugs and violent crime. In N. Wiener & M. Wolfgang (Eds.), *Pathways to criminal violence* (pp. 16–48). Newbury Park, CA: Sage.
85. See, e.g., Holcomb, W. R., & Anderson, W. P. (1983). Alcohol and multiple drug abuse in accused murderers. *Psychological Reports, 52,* 159–164. http://dx.doi.org/10.2466/pr0.1983.52.1.159. They found that among a sample of persons charged with first degree or capital murder, alcohol at the scene of the crime and evidence of multiple drug use by the perpetrator intensified the severity of the violence.
86. See, e.g., Chaiken, J. M., & Chaiken, M. R. (1990). Drugs and predatory crime. *Crime and Justice, 13,* 203–239. http://dx.doi.org/10.1086/449176
87. French, M. T., McGeary, K. A., Chitwood, D. D., McCoy, C. B., Inciardi, J. A., & McBride, D. (2000). Chronic drug use and crime. *Substance Abuse, 21,* 95–109. http://dx.doi.org/10.1080/08897070009511422
88. See, e.g., Menard, S., & Mihalic, S. (2001). The tripartite conceptual framework in adolescence and adulthood: Evidence from a national sample. *Journal of Drug Issues, 31,* 905–939. http://dx.doi.org/10.1177/002204260103100406
89. Anderson (1994), *Code of the street: Decency, violence, and the moral life of the inner city,* p. 87.
90. See, e.g., Harrison, L., & Gfroerer, J. (1992). The intersection of drug use and criminal behavior: Results from the national household survey on drug abuse. *Crime and Delinquency, 38,* 422–443. See also McBride, D., & McCoy, C. (1994). The drugs-crime relationship: An analytical framework. *Prison Journal, 73,* 257–278, to the effect that: "Regardless of the exact nature of the relationship, the existing data suggest that, increasingly, drug use, particularly cocaine use, has become integrated with a high level of international, national, and local street violence" (p. 271).

91. McBride & McCoy (1994), *The drugs-crime relationship: An analytical framework*, p. 268.
92. See, e.g., Stephens, R. (1991). *The street addict role*. New York: State University of New York Press; see also Williams, T. (1989). *The cocaine kids: The inside story of a teenage drug ring*. Reading, MA: Addison-Wesley.
93. See, e.g., Day, N., & Richaerdson, G. (1993). Cocaine use and crack babies: Science, the media, and miscommunication. *Neurotoxicology and Teratology, 15*, 293–294. http://dx.doi.org/10.1016/0892-0362(93)90025-J; Lyons, P., & Rittner, B. (1998). The construction of the crack babies phenomenon as a social problem. *American Journal of Orthopsychiatry, 68*, 313–320. http://dx.doi.org/10.1037/h0080340
94. See, e.g., Freisthler, B., Wolf, J. P., Wiegmann, W., & Kepple, N. J. (2017). Drug use, the drug environment, and child physical abuse and neglect. *Child Maltreatment, 22*, 245–255. http://dx.doi.org/10.1177/1077559517711042
95. See, e.g., Bushman, B., & Cooper, H. (1990). Effects of alcohol on human aggression: An integrative research review. *Psychological Bulletin, 107*, 341–354. http://dx.doi.org/10.1037/0033-2909.107.3.341; and Martin, S. E., Maxwell, C. D., White, H. R., & Zhang, Y. (2004). Trends in alcohol use, cocaine use, and crime: 1989–1998. *Journal of Drug Issues, 34*, 333–359. http://dx.doi.org/10.1177/002204260403400205
96. Greenfeld, L. A., & Henneberg, M. A. (2001). Victim and offender self-reports of alcohol involvement in crime. *Alcohol Research & Health, 25*, 20–31.
97. See, e.g., Popovici, I., Homer, J. F., Fang, H., & French, M. T. (2012). Alcohol use and crime: Findings from a longitudinal sample of U.S. adolescents and young adults. *Alcoholism: Clinical and Experimental Research, 36*, 532–543. http://dx.doi.org/10.1111/j.1530-0277.2011.01641.x. See also Graham, K. (2009). They fight because we let them! Applying a situational crime prevention model to barroom violence. *Drug and Alcohol Review, 28*, 103–109. http://dx.doi.org/10.1111/j.1465-3362.2008.00038.x
98. Fagan, J. (1989). The social organization of drug use and drug dealing among urban gangs. *Criminology, 27*, 633–669. http://dx.doi.org/10.1111/j.1745-9125.1989.tb01049.x; Sullivan, M. (1989). *"Getting paid": Youth crime and work in the inner city*. Ithaca, NY: Cornell University Press.
99. In fact, the media stereotype that youth gangs are primarily responsible for drug distribution and sales in the inner city do not appear to be entirely accurate. See, e.g., Fagan, J., & Chin, K. L. (1989). Initiation into crack and cocaine: A tale of two epidemics. *Contemporary Drug Problems, 16*, 579–618; Klein, M. W., Maxson, C. L., & Cunningham, L. C. (1993). "Crack," street gangs, and violence. *Criminology, 29*, 623–650. http://dx.doi.org/10.1111/j.1745-9125.1991.tb01082.x
100. See, e.g., van der Kolk, B. (1987). The role of the group in the origin and resolution of the trauma response. In B. van der Kolk (Ed.), *Psychological trauma* (pp. 153–172). Washington, DC: American Psychiatric Publishing:

    > When faced with an external threat, people tend to band together in groups to protect themselves . . . the degree to which individuals seek this kind of protection depends on both their internal sense of security and the intensity of the external threat (p. 155).

    See also Macdonald, K. (2003). Marginal youth, personal identity, and the contemporary gang: Reconstructing the social world? In L. Dontos, D. Brotherton, & L. Barrios (Eds.), *Gangs and society: Alternative perspectives* (pp. 62–74). New York, NY: Columbia University Press: "The gang is a response to social disorganization: It produces order in a world of disorder . . . where the self is constantly vulnerable to the lack of respect," gang membership becomes a preferred "strategy to defend subjectivity . . . where social domination is increasingly experienced in terms of personal failure" (p. 66, 70).

101. Vigil, J. D. (1983). Chicano gangs: One response to Mexican urban adaptation in the Los Angeles area. *Urban Anthropology, 12,* 45–75, p. 47.
102. Vigil, J. D. (1988). *Barrio gangs: Street life and identity in Southern California*. Austin: University of Texas Press.
103. Rodríguez, L. (1994, November 21). Throwaway kids: Turning youth gangs around. *The Nation, 259,* 605–609, p. 605. See also Cromwell, P., Taylor, D., & Palacios, W. (1992). Youth gangs: A 1990s perspective. *Juvenile and Family Court Journal, 43,* 25–31. http://dx.doi.org/10.1111/j.1755-6988.1992.tb00731.x; Hagedorn, J. (1988). *People and folks: Gangs, crime and the underclass in rust belt city*. Chicago, IL: Lakeview; Moore, J. W. (1985). Isolation and stigmatization in the development of an underclass: The case of Chicano gangs in East Los Angeles. *Social Problems, 33,* 1–10. http://dx.doi.org/10.2307/800627
104. Rodríguez (1994), *Throwaway kids,* p. 605.
105. Smith, M., & Tarallo, B. (1995). Who are the "good guys"? The social construction of the Vietnamese "other." In M. Smith & J. Feagin (Eds.), *The bubbling cauldron: Race, ethnicity, and the urban crisis* (pp. 50–75). Minneapolis: University of Minnesota Press.
106. Smith & Tarallo (1995), Who are the good guys?, p. 20. "Second wave" is a term that has been given to Vietnamese refugees who came to the United States in the late 1970s, at a time when many had been threatened with or forced into "reeducation" camps in Vietnam and included "boat people" who faced harrowing experiences at sea before arriving in this country. They also tended to come from more rural environments, were less educated, and brought fewer economic resources with them. All of these factors meant that they generally faced a more difficult transition to U.S. society than "first wave" refugees.
107. Smith & Tarallo (1995), Who are the good guys?, p. 20.
108. Sanchez-Jankowski, M. (1991). *Islands in the street: Gangs and American urban society* (p. 312). Berkeley: University of California Press.
109. Sanchez-Jankowski (1991), *Islands in the street,* p. 312.
110. Sviridoff, M., & Thompson, J. W. (1983). Links between employment and crime: A qualitative study of Rikers Island releasees. *Crime & Delinquency, 29,* 195–212, p. 211. http://dx.doi.org/10.1177/001112878302900201. Another early study of gangs, this one done in Midwestern cities, reached similar conclusions about the economic circumstances that make gang membership more attractive:

> An economically and socially marginal youth who has dropped out of or been expelled from school, and/or is without job skills, is in deep trouble . . . To make matters worse, the military, a traditionally available alternative career path for the poor, is increasingly inaccessible due to the higher quality of applicants generated by an economy with relatively few attractive entry-level positions for unskilled workers.

Huff, C. (1989). Youth gangs and public policy. *Crime and Delinquency, 35,* 524–537, p. 527. http://dx.doi.org/10.1177/0011128789035004001
111. Belitz, J., & Valdez, D. (1997). A sociocultural context for understanding gang involvement among Mexican-American male youth. In J. Garcia & M. Zea (Eds.), *Psychological interventions and research with Latino populations* (pp. 56–72). Boston, MA: Allyn and Bacon, p. 59.
112. Belitz, J., & Valdez, D. (1994). Clinical issues in the treatment of Chicano male gang youth. *Hispanic Journal of Behavioral Sciences, 16,* 57–74. http://dx.doi.org/10.1177/07399863940161005
113. Belitz & Valdez (1994), Clinical issues in the treatment of Chicano male gang youth, p. 61. James Vigil has reached similar conclusions in rich ethnographic studies of East Los Angeles neighborhoods in which he has contrasted families whose children became involved in gangs with those who did not. Many of the families whose children were more likely to join gangs faced greater economic strains and had less social capital. In addition, he noted that

> Abuse is also present in many of the households, be it abuse of people or abuse of substances, and it further complicates parenting efforts of heads of households. . . . Where parents err, the children seek other guides, and when parents aren't there, the children are up for grabs, especially when the streets become the behavioral environment.

Vigil, J. (2007). *The projects: Gang and non-gang families in East Los Angeles*. Austin: University of Texas Press, p. 158.

114. Wood, J. L., Kallis, C., & Coid, J. W. (2017). Differentiating gang members, gang affiliates, and violent men on their psychiatric morbidity and traumatic experiences. *Psychiatry, 80*, 221–235.
115. See Belitz & Valdez (1994), Clinical issues in the treatment of Chicano male gang youth, for suggested alternative approaches for treatment. For more recent studies that document the role of a broad range of risk factors that help to account for gang membership, gang associations, and "gang-like" behavior, see Bishop, A., Hill, K., Gilman, A., Howell, J., Catalano, R., & Hawkins, J. (2017). Developmental pathways of youth gang membership: A structural test of the social development model. *Journal of Crime and Justice, 40*, 275–296. http://dx.doi.org/10.1080/0735648X.2017.1329781; Howell, J., & Egley, A. (2005). Moving risk factors into developmental theories of gang membership. *Youth Violence and Juvenile Justice, 3*, 334–354. http://dx.doi.org/10.1177/1541204005278679; Eitle, D., Gunkel, S., & Van Gundy, K. (2004). Cumulative exposure to stressful life events and male gang membership. *Journal of Criminal Justice, 32*, 95–111. http://dx.doi.org/10.1016/j.jcrimjus.2003.12.001; Quinn, K., Pacella, M., Dickson-Gomez, J., & Nydegger, L. (2017). Childhood adversity and continued exposure to trauma and violence among adolescent gang members. *American Journal of Community Psychology, 59*, 36–49. http://dx.doi.org/10.1002/ajcp.12123; and Thompson, K., & Braaten-Antrim, R. (1998). Youth maltreatment and gang membership. *Journal of Interpersonal Violence, 13*, 328–345. http://dx.doi.org/10.1177/088626098013003002
116. As one legal commentator summarized, "Gangs are a product of urban decay. Many young people who grow up without economic opportunity and in struggling families and communities turn to gangs for a sense of belonging, a source of respect and support." Ford, R. (1994). Juvenile curfews and gang violence: Exiled on main street. *Harvard Law Review, 107*, 1693–1710, p. 1693–1694. http://dx.doi.org/10.2307/1341824
117. For example, Esbensen, F., & Huizinga, D. (1993). Gangs, drugs, and delinquency in a survey of urban youth. *Criminology, 31*, 565–589. http://dx.doi.org/10.1111/j.1745-9125.1993.tb01142.x; Maxson, C. L., Gordon, M. A., & Klein, M. W. (1985). Differences between gang and nongang homicides. *Criminology, 23*, 209–222. http://dx.doi.org/10.1111/j.1745-9125.1985.tb00334.x
118. Quinn, Pacella, Dickson-Gomez, & Nydegger (2017), *Childhood adversity and continued exposure to trauma and violence among adolescent gang members*, p. 49.
119. Matsuda, K., Meide, C., Taylor, T., Freng, A., & Esbensen, F. (2012). Gang membership and adherence to the "code of the street." *Justice Quarterly*, 1–29, p. 18. http://dx.doi.org/10.1080/07418825.2012.684432
120. See, e.g., Yoshino, E. (2008). California's criminal gang enhancements: Lessons from interviews with practitioners. *Southern California Review of Law and Social Justice, 18*, 117–152.
121. See, e.g., McGinnis, C., & Eisenhart, S. (2010). Interrogation is not ethnography: The irrational admission of gang cops as experts in the field of sociology. *Hastings Race and Poverty Law Journal, 7*, 111–159. Even former prosecutors recognize the excesses of gang-related laws and prosecutorial practices that include overbroad definitions of what constitutes gang membership, overfiling gang allegations, using the threat of draconian gang enhancements to coerce plea bargains, and the prejudicial impact of gang testimony at trial. See, e.g., Caldwell, H. (2015).

Reeling in gang prosecution: Seeking a balance in gang prosecution. *University of Pennsylvania Journal of Law and Social Change, 18,* 341–375.

122. For example, even the California State Auditor concluded that the state's gang database, "CalGang," suffered from poor oversight and contained questionable, unreliable information that likely impinged on constitutional and privacy rights. See California State Auditor (2016). *The CalGang criminal intelligence system.* Sacramento: California State Auditor. See also Wright, J. (2005). The constitutional failure of gang databases. *Stanford Journal of Civil Rights & Civil Liberties, 2,* 115–142.
123. See, e.g., Howell, K. (2011). Fear itself: The impact of allegation on pre-trial detention. *St. Thomas Law Review, 23,* 620–659.
124. Massarella, L. (2004, January 13). Gangs becoming "monster of crime," police officials say, rising violence calls for federal, state aid. *San Jose Mercury News,* p. 11A. Retrieved from https://www.nl.newsbank.com. In fact, in this one short article reporting on statements made at a "meeting of high-ranking federal and local police officers," law enforcement officials were quoted as characterizing gangs not only an "emerging monster of crime," but also "like a cancer" and "a disease."
125. Sanchez-Jankowski (1991), *Islands in the street,* p. 308.
126. Sanchez-Jankowski (1991), *Islands in the street,* p. 308.
127. Sociologist Victor Rios has written persuasively about the fear-mongering and demonization that was directed particularly at youth of Color over the last several decades, leading to harsher juvenile justice practices and policies. See Rios, V. (2008). The racial politics of youth crime. *Latino Studies, 6,* 97–115. http://dx.doi.org/10.1057/lst.2008.10; and Rios, V. (2011). *Punished: Policing the lives of Black and Latino boys.* New York, NY: New York University Press. For a discussion of related demonizing imagery applied to groups of young men of Color, see Welch, M., Price, E., & Yankey, N. (2002). Moral panic over youth violence: Wilding and the manufacture of menace in the media. *Youth & Society, 43,* 3–30. http://dx.doi.org/10.1177/0044118X02034001001
128. See, e.g., Chesney-Lind, M., Rockhill, A., Marker, N., & Reyes, H. (1994). Gangs and delinquency: Exploring police estimates of gang membership. *Crime, Law, and Social Change, 21,* 201–228. http://dx.doi.org/10.1007/BF01307964; and Tapia, M. (2011). Gang membership and race as risk factors for juvenile arrest. *Journal of Research in Crime and Delinquency, 48,* 364–395. http://dx.doi.org/10.1177/0022427810393013
129. See, e.g., Meehan, P. J., & O'Carroll, P. W. (1992). Gangs, drugs, and homicide in Los Angeles. *American Journal of Diseases of Children, 146,* 683–687.
130. Indeed, Mercer Sullivan found that the cliques and gangs he studied were "quasi-familial groupings that served to protect their members from outsiders." Sullivan (1989), *Getting paid,* p. 110. He concluded that this kind of group

    > was by no means a specialized criminal organization; it was rather a multi-functional, quasi-familial grouping in the context of which these youths discussed school, jobs, their families, and girlfriends or played handball, raced pigeons, and engaged in many other activities besides economic crimes.

    Sullivan (1989), *Getting paid,* p. 125.
131. For example, Thornberry, T. P., Krohn, M. D., Lizotte, A. J., & Chard-Wierschem, D. (1993). The role of juvenile gangs in facilitating delinquent behavior. *Journal of Research in Crime and Delinquency, 30,* 55–87. http://dx.doi.org/10.1177/0022427893030001005
132. Thornberry, Krohn, Lizotte, & Chard-Wierschem (1993), The role of juvenile gangs in facilitating delinquent behavior, p. 79.
133. My discussion of these issues focuses primarily on the potentially criminogenic effects of prison rather than jail environments, in part because they have been

studied much more extensively. Yet there are several reasons to at least acknowledge the possibility that jails have similar adverse effects and to take them into account. For one, although stays in jail are briefer, far more people are incarcerated in jails than prison, with more than ten million persons per year admitted to these facilities in 2016. Zeng, Z. (2018, February). *Jail inmates in 2016*. Washington, DC: Bureau of Justice Statistics. Although one study found that nearly two out of every three jail inmates suffered from a mental health problem, three quarters drug or alcohol abuse and dependency or both and a quarter acknowledged having suffered physical or sexual abuse, a much smaller percentage received mental health treatment during confinement than persons confined in prisons. James, D. J., & Glaze, L. E. (2006). *Mental health problems of prison and jail inmates*. Washington, DC: Bureau of Justice Statistics. Jail inmates are also subjected to the many of the same kind of harsh disciplinary practices as prisoners, including solitary confinement. See, e.g., Haney, C., Weill, J., Bakhshay, S., & Lockett, T. (2016). Examining jail isolation: What we don't know can be profoundly harmful. *Prison Journal, 96,* 126–152. http://dx.doi.org/10.1177/0032885515605491

134. The criminogenic effects of adult imprisonment can be conceptualized as social historical factors as well as well as immediate criminogenic contexts. I have chosen to discuss them in this chapter in part because exposure typically occurs in adulthood, making its effects less obviously developmental in nature, and also because of the powerful and direct criminogenic pressures that exist inside the immediate environment of prison.
135. See, e.g., Bales, W., & Piquero, A. (2012). Assessing the impact of imprisonment on recidivism. *Journal of Experimental Criminology, 8,* 71–101. http://dx.doi.org/10.1007/s11292-011-9139-3; Bernburg, J., Krohn, M., & Rivera, C. (2006) Official labeling, criminal embeddedness, and subsequent delinquency: A longitudinal test of labeling theory. *Journal of Research in Crime and Delinquency, 43,* 67–88. http://dx.doi.org/10.1177/0022427805280068; Chen, K., & Shapiro, J. (2007). Do harsher prison conditions reduce recidivism? A discontinuity-based approach. *American Law & Economics Review,* 9, 1–29. http://dx.doi.org/10.1093/aler/ahm006; Cullen, F., Jonson, C., & Nagin, D. (2011). Prisons do not reduce recidivism: The high cost of ignoring science. *Prison Journal, 91*(Suppl.), 48S–65S. http://dx.doi.org/10.1177/0032885511415224; Gaes, G., & Camp, S. (2009). Unintended consequences: Experimental evidence for the criminogenic effect of prison security level placement on post-release recidivism. *Journal of Experimental Criminology, 5,* 139–162. http://dx.doi.org/10.1007/s11292-009-9070-z; Jaman, D., Dickover, R., & Bennett, L. (1972). Parole outcome as a function of time served. *British Journal of Criminology, 12,* 5–34. http://dx.doi.org/10.1093/oxfordjournals.bjc.a046355; Nagin, D. S., Cullen, F. T., & Jonson, C. L. (2009). Imprisonment and reoffending. In M. Tonry (Ed.), *Crime and justice: A review of research* (Vol. 38, pp. 115–200). Chicago, IL: University of Chicago Press; Nieuwbeerta, P., Nagin, D. S., & Blokland, A. A. (2009). The relationship between first imprisonment and criminal career development: A matched samples comparison. *Journal of Quantitative Criminology, 25,* 227–257; Petrosino, A., Turpin-Petrosino, C., & Guckenburg, S. (2010). *Formal system processing of juveniles: Effects on delinquency*. Oslo, Norway: The Campbell Collaboration; Smith, P., Goggin, C., & Gendreau, P. (2002). *The effects of prison sentences and intermediate sanctions on recidivism: General effects and individual differences*. Ottawa, Ontario: Solicitor General of Canada; Spohn, C., & Holleran, D. (2002). The effect of imprisonment on recidivism rates of felony offenders: A focus on drug offenders. *Criminology, 40,* 329–347. http://dx.doi.org/10.1111/j.1745-9125.2002.tb00959.x; and Vieraitis, L., Kovandzic, T., & Marvell, T. (2007). The criminogenic effect of imprisonment: Evidence from state panel data, 1974–2002. *Criminology and Public Policy, 6,* 589–622. http://dx.doi.org/10.1111/j.1745-9133.2007.00456.x

136. Cullen, Jonson, & Nagin (2011), Prisons do not reduce recidivism, p. 53S. Here is how Mikal Gilmore, the brother of Gary Gilmore—the first person to be executed in the United States in the "modern era" of the death penalty—described the way that the experience of imprisonment had affected him:

> [Gary] had seen things in prison. He told me about those things. He had seen people maimed—he saw a man get his hands cut off—and he had seen men murdered. He'd seen so fucking many assaults, and when he was younger, he himself had been assaulted. Beaten. Raped. Terrorized. But he learned to go with it. As he got older and bigger and meaner, he became the assaulter. After that, they had nothing they could scare him with . . .

Gilmore, M. (1994). *Shot in the heart*. New York, NY: Doubleday, p. 341.

137. See, e.g., Haney, C. (2003). The psychological impact of incarceration: Implications for post-prison adjustment. In J. Travis, & M. Waul (Eds.), *Prisoners once removed: The impact of incarceration and reentry on children, families, and communities* (pp. 33–66). Washington, DC: Urban Institute Press; Haney, C. (2005). *Reforming punishment: Psychological limits to the pains of imprisonment*. Washington, DC: American Psychological Association; and Haney, C. (2012). Prison effects in the age of mass imprisonment. *Prison Journal, 92*, 1–24.
138. Haney, C. (2008). Counting casualties in the war on prisoners. *University of San Francisco Law Review, 43*, 87–138. See also Irwin, J. (2004). *The warehouse prison: Disposal of the new dangerous class*. Los Angeles, CA: Roxbury.
139. The Bureau of Justice Statistics reported in 2012 that there were still nine state prison systems and the massive Federal Bureau of Prisons that were operating at 130% or more of their design capacity. Carson, A., & Sabol, W. (2012, December). *Prisoners in 2011*. (Bureau of Justice Statistics Special Report, BJS 239808). Washington, DC: Department of Justice.
140. Haney, C. (2006). The wages of prison overcrowding: Harmful psychological consequences and dysfunctional correctional reactions. *Washington University Journal of Law & Policy, 22*, 265–293; and Haney, C. (2015). Prison overcrowding. In B. Cutler & P. Zapf (Eds.), *APA handbook of forensic psychology* (pp. 415–436). Washington, DC: American Psychological Association.
141. Paulus, P., McCain, G., & Cox, V. (1978). Death rates, psychiatric commitments, blood pressure, and perceived crowding as a function of institutional crowding. *Journal of Environmental Psychology & Nonverbal Behavior, 3*, 107–116, p. 115. http://dx.doi.org/10.1007/BF01135608. See also Lawrence, C., & Andrews, K. (2004). The influence of perceived prison crowding on male inmates' perception of aggressive events. *Aggressive Behavior, 30*, 273–283. http://dx.doi.org/10.1002/ab.20024; Ostfeld, A. (1987). *Stress, crowding, and blood pressure in prison*. Hillsdale, NJ: Lawrence Erlbaum; and Paulus, P., Cox, V., & McCain, G. (1988). *Prison crowding: A psychological perspective*. New York, NY: Springer-Verlag.
142. See, e.g., Andersen, H. S., Sestoft, D., Lillebaek, T., Gabrielsen, G., Hemmingsen, R., & Kramp, P. (2000). A longitudinal study of prisoners on remand: Psychiatric prevalence, incidence and psychopathology in solitary vs. non-solitary confinement. *Acta Psychiatrica Scandinavica, 102*, 19–25. http://dx.doi.org/10.1034/j.1600-0447.2000.102001019.x; Cloyes, K., Lovell, D., Allen, D., & Rhodes, L. (2006). Assessment of psychosocial impairment in a supermaximum security unit sample. *Criminal Justice and Behavior, 33*, 760–781. http://dx.doi.org/10.1177/0093854806288143; Grassian, S. (2006). Psychiatric effects of solitary confinement. *Washington University Journal of Law and Policy, 22*, 325–383; and Haney, C. (2003). Mental health issues in long-term solitary and "supermax" confinement. *Crime and Delinquency, 49*, 124–156. http://dx.doi.org/10.1177/0011128702239239
143. Haney, C. (2008). A culture of harm: Taming the dynamics of cruelty in supermax prisons. *Criminal Justice and Behavior, 35*, 956–984. http://dx.doi.org/10.1177/

0093854808318585; Haney, C. (2009). The social psychology of isolation: Why solitary confinement is psychologically harmful. *Prison Service Journal UK, 181*, 12–20; Haney, C. (2018). Restricting the use of solitary confinement. *Annual Review of Criminology, 1*, 285–310. http://dx.doi.org/10.1146/annurev-criminol-032317-092326

144. Gibbons, J., & Katzenbach, N. (2006). *Confronting confinement: A report of the Commission on Safety and Abuse in America's Prisons*. New York, NY: Vera Institute of Justice.
145. See, e.g., Gibbons & Katzenbach (2006), *Confronting confinement*. In 2017, President Obama estimated "that as many as 100,000 inmates are currently held in solitary confinement—a figure that includes juveniles and people with mental illness." Obama, B. H. (2017). The President's role in advancing criminal justice reform. *Harvard Law Review, 130*, 811–866, p. 830. In addition, see Association of State Correctional Administrators (2015). *Time in cell: The ASCA Liman 2014 national survey of administrative segregation in prison*. New Haven, CT: The Liman Program, Yale Law School, and Association of State Correctional Administrators, whose estimates were somewhat lower but still substantial.
146. See, e.g., Human Rights in Trauma Mental Health Lab (2017). Mental health consequences following release from long-term solitary confinement in California. Palo Alto, CA: Stanford University; and Kupers, T. (2016). The SHU post-release syndrome: A preliminary report. *Correctional Mental Health Report, 17*, 81–85; and Brinkley-Rubinstein, L., Sivaraman, J., Rosen, D. L., Cloud, D. H., Junker, G., Proescholdbell, S., Shanahan, M. E., & Ranapurwala, S. I. (2019). Association of restrictive housing during incarceration with mortality after release. *JAMA Network Open, 2*, e1912516. http://dx.doi.org/10.1001/jamanetworkopen.2019.12516
147. The data are somewhat mixed but suggestive on this specific issue. Compare Butler, D., Steiner, B., Makarios, M., & Travis, L. (2017). Assessing the effects of exposure to supermax confinement on offender postrelease behaviors. *Prison Journal, 97*, 275–295. http://dx.doi.org/10.1177/0032885517703925; Lovell, D., Johnson, L., & Cain, K. (2007). Recidivism of supermax prisoners in Washington State. *Crime & Delinquency, 53*, 633–656. http://dx.doi.org/10.1177/0011128706296466; Mears, D., & Bales, W. (2009). Supermax incarceration and recidivism. *Criminology, 47*, 1131–1166. http://dx.doi.org/10.1111/j.1745-9125.2009.00171.x; Motiuk, L., & Blanchette, K. (2001). Characteristics of administratively segregated offenders in federal corrections. *Canadian Journal of Criminology, 41*, 131–143.
148. See, e.g., Turney, K., Wildeman, C., & Schnittker, J. (2012). As fathers and felons: Explaining the effects of current and recent incarceration on major depression. *Journal of Health and Social Behavior, 53*, 465–481. http://dx.doi.org/10.1177/0022146512462400
149. See, e.g., Simon, J. (1993). From confinement to waste management: The post-modernization of social control. *Focus on Law Studies, 8*, 4–8.
150. See, e.g., Haney, C. (2011). The perversions of prison: On the origins of hypermasculinity and sexual violence in confinement. *American Criminal Law Review, 48*, 121–141. For a different perspective on this issue, see Gifford, B. (2019). Prison crime and the economics of incarceration. *Stanford Law Review, 71*, 71–135.
151. For an early, experimental demonstration of how even a simulated prison environment can dramatically modify the behavior of college student participants randomly assigned to either prisoner or guard roles, see Haney, C., Banks, W., & Zimbardo, P. (1973). Interpersonal dynamics in a simulated prison. *International Journal of Criminology and Penology*, 1, 69–97. For a discussion of the situational characteristics that may facilitate abusive staff behavior in real prisons, see Haney, C. (2016). *On structural evil: Disengaging from our moral selves* [*Review of the book Moral disengagement: How people do harm and live with themselves, by A. Bandura*].

PsycCRITIQUES, 61. http://dx.doi.org/10.1037/a0040160; and Weill, J., & Haney, C. (2017). Mechanisms of moral disengagement and prisoner abuse. *Analyses of Social Issues and Public Policy, 17*, 286–318. http://dx.doi.org/10.1111/asap.12142

152. For a review, see Western, B., Kling, J., & Weiman, D. (2001). The labor market consequences of incarceration. *Crime and Delinquency, 47*, 410–427. http://dx.doi.org/10.1177/0011128701047003007
153. Pettit, B., & Western, B. (2004). Mass imprisonment and the life course: Race and class inequality in U.S. incarceration. *American Sociological Review*, 69, 151–169, p. 155.
154. Chin, G. (2012). The new civil death: Rethinking punishment in the era of mass incarceration. *University of Pennsylvania Law Review, 160*, 1789–1833, p. 1789.
155. Chin, G. (2018). Collateral consequences and criminal justice: Future policy and constitutional directions. *Marquette Law Review, 102*, 233–260; Meek, A. (2014). Street vendors, taxicabs, and exclusion zones: The impact of collateral consequences of criminal convictions at the local level. *Ohio State Law Journal, 75*, 1–56; and Mauer, M., & Chesney, M. (2002). *Invisible punishment: The collateral consequences of mass imprisonment*. New York, NY: The New Press.
156. See, e.g., Clarke, R. V. (1985). Delinquency, environment and intervention. *Journal of Child Psychology & Psychiatry and Allied Disciplines, 26*, 505–523. http://dx.doi.org/10.1111/j.1469-7610.1985.tb01639.x; Sampson, R., & Lauritsen, J. (1994). Violent victimization and offending: Individual-, situational-, and community-level risk factors. In A. Reiss, & J. Roth (Eds.), *Understanding and preventing violence* (Vol. 3, pp. 1–114). Washington, DC: National Academies Press.
157. See, e.g., the discussion of the superpredator mythology at notes 113–118 in Chapter 1.
158. West, C. (1993). *Race matters* (p. 5). New York, NY: Vintage Press.
159. West (1993), *Race matters*, p. 12.

6

Poverty

Structural Risk and Criminal Behavior

The "have-nots" in every society always have been subject to greater pressure to commit crimes and to fewer constraints than their more affluent fellow citizens. This is, indeed, a tragic byproduct of social and economic deprivation.

—JUSTICE LEWIS POWELL[1]

Highlighting the behavioral pathologies and, especially, the criminality of the poor was an important means of transforming their image from needy to undeserving. By emphasizing street crime and by framing that problem as the consequence of bad people making bad choices, conservatives made it much less likely that members of the public would empathize with the plight of the poor and support measures to assist them.

—KATHERINE BECKETT AND THEODORE SASSON[2]

Sociologist Loïc Wacquant argued that the incarceration boom of the last quarter of the 20th century was in essence a policy that both by design and consequence resulted primarily in "punishing the poor."[3] Thus, "fewer than half of inmates [in U.S. prisons] held a full-time job at the time of their arraignment, and two-thirds issue from households with annual income amounting to less than *half* of the so-called poverty line."[4] Of course, Wacquant understood that the poor in virtually every society are the most likely to suffer its criminal sanctions. That is in part because, as Anatole France's aphorism reminded us, "the law in all its majesty draws no distinctions among

http://dx.doi.org/10.1037/0000172-007
Criminality in Context: The Psychological Foundations of Criminal Justice Reform,
by C. Haney

people but forbids the rich and poor alike from begging on the streets and sleeping in the public parks."[5] Although the criminal law may be applied evenhandedly in theory, many of its provisions in fact prohibit behavior in which only the poor are compelled to engage. Thus, whenever a nation intensifies its system of punishment, as the United States did over the last several decades, the poor are disproportionately impacted.

However, the criminogenic impact of poverty on a person's life course can extend far beyond the functionally unequal application of the laws. Poverty operates in many ways as kind of a core or "gateway" risk factor into criminality, shaping the lives of many young people who experience its effects along multiple dimensions that can persist across an entire lifetime. The psychological effects of poverty have been increasingly studied and understood over the last several decades, as research on the broad range of risk factors that I summarized in Chapter 3 burgeoned more generally. Until this period of increased interest, frankly, research on the immediate and long-term impact of social class on a person's well-being and life course was, as social psychologist Bernice Lott observed, a "glaring omission" in the field of psychology (although poverty and income inequality were studied broadly in the fields of sociology and economics).[6]

A National Academy of Sciences Committee recently reported that although the "official poverty level"—taking only direct income into account—had not changed appreciably in the United States over the last 50 years, "supplemental poverty"—taking near-cash government assistance (e.g., Supplemental Nutrition Assistance Program or SNAP) into account—had declined significantly (from 28.4% in 1967 to 15.6% in 2016).[7] Yet the U.S. still leads other Western nations with whom we often compare ourselves on most measures of poverty—in large part because "[t]he United States spends less to support low income families with children than peer English-speaking countries do"[8]—and has nearly twice the number of children in "deep poverty" as the next-ranked of these nations.[9] Latino children in the United States experience the highest rates of poverty (21.7%), followed by Black children (17.8%), both of which are more than double the percentage of White children (7.9%).[10] The Committee reached important conclusions not just about the extent of childhood poverty but also its long-term impact: "We find overwhelming evidence from this literature that, on average, a child growing up in a family whose income is below the poverty line experiences worse outcomes than a child from a wealthier family in virtually every dimension," including those that are the focus of this book—delinquency and crime.[11]

The myriad ways that poverty contributes to crime have now been extensively studied in psychology as well and the criminogenic effects of economic disadvantage on individual social histories are increasingly well-understood. A number of studies have established a relationship between various measures of poverty and different forms of criminal behavior, including serious violent crime.[12] The powerful criminogenics of economic disadvantage can operate at multiple levels. We now know that poverty can have direct physical and psychological effects that are damaging in their own right, ones that operate to narrow a person's life options and opportunities. Direct poverty-related risk factors include the deprivation of the material things that children need in order to thrive, potentially higher levels of exposure to environmental toxins and hazards, and increased transience and instability that is driven by economic scarcity.

Poverty also indirectly exposes children and adolescents to other potentially damaging risk factors and traumas. For example, poverty may adversely impact parents, saddling them with unmanageable financial burdens that compromise or interfere with their relationships with their children and may even increase the likelihood of maltreatment. Poverty also affects the nature of the institutions with which persons come into contact and on which they depend for their continued well-being. Poor children and adolescents are more likely to endure intervention from harsher or more inept institutions, and to be consigned as young adults to live in communities with scant employment opportunities, surrounded by higher levels of crime and violence. Finally, as I noted, poverty operates as a kind of gateway risk factor, helping to ensure that—because of the host of hazards and other problematic circumstances that economic deprivation brings about—poor children are more likely to be exposed to multiple *other* risk factors that can have life-altering, criminogenic consequences.

There is a key caveat that is important to state at the outset of this chapter, one that applies to the next as well. In both instances, I am making a structural-not individual-level critique. In the grand tradition of "blaming the victim" that too often serves to obfuscate meaningful analyses of structurally based social problems in the United States,[13] the poor are often blamed for their own economic victimization, through the suggestion that flaws in their personal characteristics, a presumed lack of talent or ambition, some set of supposedly problematic family values or habits, or a mythical "culture of poverty" account for their material disadvantages. They do not. Thus, nothing I will say about the effects of economic deprivation and income inequality is intended to imply that the significant challenges that poor persons must overcome to achieve positive, successful life outcomes in American society are a function of their alleged personal, familial, or cultural deficits.

My colleague, social psychologist Heather Bullock, has written extensively about the fact that, to the extent they are portrayed in the media at all, images of the poor tend to characterize them in terms of their personal defects and shortcomings, as "dishonest, dependent, lazy, uninterested in education, and promiscuous."[14] As she and others have also shown, however, these stereotypes are inaccurate, invidious misconceptions that divert attention from the underlying structural causes of poverty and interfere with the broad-based economic reforms that are required to address it.

Of course, apart from their problematic role with respect to poverty-related policies, such portrayals play directly into the crime master narrative. In the final analysis, by this view, poverty, like crime, is seen as a personal choice. To the extent that poverty is strongly related to criminal behavior, proponents of the crime master narrative individualize the link and shift ultimate responsibility onto the poor themselves. The public has been taught to see the poor as "morally deficient and responsible for their plight,"[15] and because they supposedly lack the talent, initiative, and work ethic to succeed in conventional ways, by implication, many of them turn to crime instead.

To the contrary, as the research reviewed in this chapter shows, the origins of poverty's criminogenic effects are structural in nature. Indeed, one of the tragedies of economic deprivation and income inequality is that it squanders and thwarts human potential, cutting many people off from the even more significant things they likely would have been able to accomplish in their lives.[16] The material deprivation, the lack of opportunity, and the increased exposure to other criminogenic risk factors can also lead people to engage in criminal activities from which they otherwise would have refrained.

DIRECT EFFECTS OF POVERTY

In recent years, increased attention has been given to the mechanisms by which poverty has significant psychological consequences for the children who experience it. Although poverty is not always a chronic condition—that is, more people tend to go through "spells" of poverty than are mired in long, insurmountable periods of economic disadvantage—the durations tragically tend to last longer when they begin early in a child's life. That is, "[c]hildren who are born into poverty seem to be faced with an extremely long period of disadvantage."[17]

Many of the negative effects of poverty on children are the direct result of various forms of physical and psychological deprivation that can impair their health and well-being in the course of early development and beyond. One ethnographer studying children growing up in a poor urban neighborhood acknowledged their impressive resourcefulness in coping with poverty, but was nonetheless forced to conclude that there were many cases in which these admirable adaptive skills were still "no match for the physical toll of poverty and its constant frustrations and humiliations."[18]

Immediate Developmental Effects of Poverty

Not surprisingly, poverty is related to prenatal malnourishment and often to premature birth, low birth weight, and a range of interrelated medical conditions.[19] As I noted in Chapter 3, a variety of potential risk factors and traumas occur at or around the time of birth that can have a range of long-term adverse effects on children that are psychological as well as medical in nature. Because successfully avoiding these things or mitigating their harmful consequences often depends on access to proper medical care during and after pregnancy, poor children are at greater risk of suffering these maladies and less likely to have them properly treated in the aftermath.

There is also evidence that poverty can negatively impact children's cognitive development, especially when it is experienced over a long duration and for children who are being raised in low-income neighborhoods (suggesting that part or all of the differential in cognitive development may be explained by differences in the quality of schooling and access to supplemental educational and other resources).[20] As would be expected, this also translates into negative effects on poor children's "life chances." That is, poverty, especially when it impacts children early in life, not only can negatively affect preschool performance but also "is associated with low test scores later in childhood as well as school failure, school disengagement, and dropping out of school."[21] All of these outcomes limit children's options and opportunities to succeed in conventional ways and are associated with later delinquent and criminal behavior.

In addition, research conducted on "environmental justice" has established that "historically disadvantaged groups . . . are burdened disproportionately by environmental hazards."[22] Because poor areas are more often plagued by toxic wastes and dangerous chemicals, poor persons are at greater risk of being exposed to potentially damaging environmental toxins.[23]

David Pellow summarized the literature on environmental justice this way:

> [H]undreds of studies have documented that people of color, people of lower socioeconomic status, indigenous and immigrant populations, and other marginalized communities are disproportionately affected by ecologically harmful infrastructures such as landfills, mines, incinerators, polluting factories, and destructive transportation systems, as well as by the negative consequences of ecologically harmful practices, such as climate change/disruption and pesticide exposure.[24]

Among the most harmful and criminogenic form of exposure is lead poisoning, which has been associated with a range of serious behavioral problems later in life, including delinquent and criminal behavior.[25] As Robert Sampson and Alix Winter recently noted, "lead poisoning takes its toll very early in life—almost out of the starting gate."[26]

Poor nutrition, inconsistent eating habits, and hunger caused by food scarcity also leave many economically disadvantaged children susceptible not only to malnutrition and related physical problems but also to a host of adverse psychological outcomes. They include, as Carl Nightingale put it, the way in which "[f]rustration at their parents' inability to provide and memories of those adults' defensive responses to requests for food and clothes inevitably help engender . . . mistrust and manipulative behavior."[27] Being hungry in a world where most others are not helps to explain why poverty "often engenders a deep sense of personal failure and humiliation."[28]

Childhood poverty has a number of additional long-term psychological consequences. Researchers have documented the persistent despair and emotional distress that severe economic deprivation can bring about. One early survey found that welfare status or perceived financial stress was significantly related to children's emotional and behavioral problems—specifically, to higher levels of depression, antisocial behavior, and impulsivity.[29] Children who lack the resources and socialization to seek professional help for these emotional problems may be tempted to cope by "self-medicating." Early illicit drug use places them at risk of later addiction and, as I discussed in the last chapter, other forms of illegal behavior may follow.

In fact, some researchers have suggested that economic insecurity—a state of uncertainty about one's financial stability—is associated with increased levels of physical pain. As they conclude, "it physically hurts to be economically insecure," primarily because of the feelings of lack of control it creates.[30] In addition to the sheer painfulness of poverty and the stress of insecurity and sense of lost control it brings about, there is evidence that the very high levels of stress that children living in impoverished circumstances frequently experience—especially when poverty is suffered on a long-term basis—can impair the development of appropriate biological stress responses and even undermine later executive functioning.[31] Some studies have suggested that the stress of "[s]ustained poverty in early childhood increases the likelihood of weak self-regulatory skills with important implications for school performance" and may even affect cognitive development.[32]

Whatever the exact cause, the educational disadvantages that poor children face are especially problematic and potentially criminogenic. They can interfere with a child's ability to connect to the potentially positive socializing influence of school environments, undermine the potential protective factor of school achievement, and limit employment options later in life.[33] These kinds of negative consequences may be moderated by effective parenting or, as I discuss later in this chapter, exacerbated when parenting behavior is itself adversely affected.[34]

Poverty also can have the direct effect of pushing children too rapidly toward adult status and roles. When interpersonal resources within the family must be devoted more to economic survival than to childrearing, younger children tend to grow up "undersocialized."[35] As two developmental researchers put it, conditions of economic deprivation have been found to create "an accelerated pace toward adult status, a pace responsive to the 'downward extension of adultlike obligations' in hard times, and also produced families that resembled an understaffed environment—that is, one with an excess of tasks relative to able members,"[36] which tends to result in inadequate socialization experiences for, at least, younger children.

We know also that, all other things being equal, children who suffer economic deprivation are less likely to be hopeful, self-directed, and confident about their future than those who grow up under better economic conditions.[37] To the extent to which children perceive fewer prosocial options for eventual success, or correspondingly feel that they have less to lose than their more confident and optimistic counterparts, they may perceive the potential costs and benefits of criminal behavior very differently.

Chaos, Residential Instability, Transience, and Homelessness

Poverty—especially chronic, long-lasting poverty—can have direct effects on nearly every aspect of a child's life. Some may impair healthy development in ways that are known to be criminogenic. As I discussed in Chapter 3, developmental psychologists know well that children require a degree of stability in order to prosper and that "instability" has a number of problematic developmental effects. In this context, instability can occur along a number of dimensions, including the frequency, co-occurrence, nature, and magnitude of the changes involved. Several researchers have conceptualized the totality of these dimensions as "ecological instability"—which they defined as "frequent changes occurring in multiple developmental contexts across early childhood"—and found that most or all measures were associated with decreased school readiness.[38] However, because of the lack of resources to help control their surroundings and the significant economic strains family members regularly confront, poor families are especially susceptible to what has been termed "environmental chaos."[39] Defined to include such things "unpredictability in everyday activities" and "a general lack of routinization and structure in daily life,"[40] environmental chaos can have long-term problematic effects on child and adolescent development,[41] including difficulty in later behavioral adjustment.[42] Although environmental chaos is certainly not unique to poor families, their increased chances of experiencing it are potentially problematic, in part because it often occurs in a larger community context that is also characterized by instability.

Other studies have shown that there are additional events and experiences that poor families are more likely to experience that can lead to later adjustment problems among children, even the increased risk of criminal behavior. They include divorce, single parenthood at the time of birth or throughout childhood, and the death of a parent.[43] The additional economic burdens and social stressors that even a dedicated single parent must shoulder in order to provide consistent, nurturing care for his or her children can interfere with effective parenting. Indeed, Gerald Patterson and his colleagues have shown that, whatever the underlying cause, frequent family transitions are especially problematic when they lead to disruptions in parenting and are combined with already existing social disadvantage.[44]

As with many of the specific risk factors that *can* have long-term criminogenic effects, the determination of whether and how they do, as David Farrington and his colleagues put it with respect to the so-called broken homes effect, is "nuanced," and particular poverty-related influences "can lead to distinct outcomes in a myriad of ways."[45] Thus, the degree to which these particular risks and traumas ultimately affect and undermine a child's immediate environment will depend on a host of other factors that are part of the larger context in which he or she is raised, all of which, in turn, can limit or exacerbate any potentially criminogenic consequences.[46] However, here, too, Farrington et al. have shown that frequent family transitions are especially problematic when they result in disruptive parenting and are combined with social disadvantage.[47]

In addition, poverty can force families to move frequently, subjecting children to residential and other forms of instability. For example, under- or unemployed parents may have to move frequently because their tenuous position in tight labor markets requires them to live wherever they can find work. Families on the edge of economic collapse may be forced to adopt more transient lifestyles in which parents are buffeted from job to job at the slightest economic shift or because they literally cannot afford to stay in one place for very long.[48]

Children for whom poverty has taken such a toll often grow up in families that not only move repeatedly but many times without plan or purpose; their parents may suffer multiple separations and divorces, and there is often a constant stream of new adults in their lives. Forced transience and family chaos that are born of poverty can take a toll on parents as well, sometimes creating social and personal instability or engendering interpersonal conflicts. Of course, children are at the mercy of their family's economic vulnerability and the instability and lack of structure that accompanies persistent poverty. Their social and developmental histories are frequently pervaded by this kind of geographical chaos and instability; they lack a sense of rootedness or memories of a "place" where they feel that they truly belong.

Children who are captives of such chronic transience and family turmoil may feel that there is little or nothing in their lives that is constant or that lasts long enough to allow them to make genuine emotional investments. They may lack the permanence they need to structure their own internal lives or use as the basis upon which to build stable identities. Older children may be catapulted into caretaker or protective roles in relation to their younger siblings, long before they have acquired the maturity to properly play them. In any event, children in environments that are not only economically deprived but also in environments in which family life has become chaotic and unpredictable as a result typically suffer the greatest adverse effects.

Housing instability and housing insecurity can affect children in a number of potentially harmful ways.[49] In extreme cases, of course, poor families can become homeless. Homeless children may be forced to grow up under circumstances in which traditional school and community ties are difficult to establish and maintain. Indeed, we now know that homelessness is a tragic social problem in part because of the lasting emotional consequences it can have on those children who persistently endure it.[50] Chronically homeless children may grow up alienated, feeling understandably insecure in the unpredictable and hostile world around them.

The problem of homelessness continues to plague American society, and it has not been adequately addressed in recent years. National estimates place the number of young adults between the ages of 12 and 24 who are homeless during the course of any given year at between 1.6 million and 2.1 million, with as many as nearly a half million homeless on any given day.[51] Some homeless children have fled their families of origin to escape abuse, but many have not: "The percentage of homeless youth who report having previously been in foster care or another institutional setting (such as juvenile detention or a mental health facility) . . . varies across studies, ranging between 21 and 53 percent."[52] Many states lack adequate social services targeted to the needs of this large population of young people who are, in turn, left to fend for themselves.[53]

One study of a large sample of adolescents identified another dimension to the potential criminogenic effects of homelessness, beyond the chaos and unpredictability it introduced into their lives. McCarthy and Hagan found that homelessness made children vulnerable to becoming "embedded" in the criminal networks they encountered in the streets, where they were also more likely to be exposed to so-called tutelage relationships in which more sophisticated, typically older youths and adults "schooled" them in ways of surviving that included engaging in criminal behavior.[54]

Poverty-Related Stress and Parenting

Whether or not they have been homeless, we know that many persons who have committed crime have experienced high levels of poverty and economic deprivation throughout their lifetime. Research has identified many of the intermediate steps along the pathway from this early experience to adult criminality. As I noted in passing earlier, in addition to its direct effects, many of the adverse consequences of poverty are indirect. Thus, we know that poverty forces adult family members to adapt to scarcity in ways that negatively affect them and their interpersonal relationships and, in turn, their children's development. Decades ago, James Garbarino suggested that many of the effects of poverty on child development might be mediated by the impact that socio-economic stress had on parents,[55] and subsequent research has born this out. As he observed, children require stable and secure environments, positive parental involvement, a strong prosocial belief system, connection to a caring, just community, and access to basic resources in order ensure their healthy development.[56] Yet poverty can and often does interfere with parents' ability to provide many if not most of these things.

As one review of the literature on the familial effects of economic hardship on parenting summarized, "research evidence continues to accumulate suggesting that economic hardship . . . has an adverse influence on the psychological well-being of family members and on the quality of family relationships."[57] It can adversely affect parenting in at least three different ways: by increasing parental stress and its potential consequences, by contributing to marital disharmony and conflict, and by changing the nature and amount of interaction parents are able to have with children.[58] Thus, there is a "spillover" of poverty into children's lives from the way it can affect "all aspects of their most salient proximal environment—their family."[59]

In Chapter 2, I discussed some of the research that has established a significant relationship between life stress and negative outcomes, including studies that used a stress scale developed by Thomas Holmes and Richard Rahe.[60] I noted then that the Holmes and Rahe scale had been designed on the basis of data collected from (and appeared to be intended to be used with) samples of largely middle-income participants. In the context of the present discussion, however, it is useful to consider what a poverty-based version of that scale might look like—to underscore the comparative magnitude of the stressors that many chronically poor parents experience. Thus, for example, suppose what Holmes and Rahe described in their scale as a "change in health of family members" included the fact that the respondent's family lacked the means with which to obtain health care and, therefore, could only seek medical attention for dire health emergencies; or that the work-related stressors Holmes and Rahe listed (e.g., "business readjustment," "change in financial state," "change to a different line of work") meant not only that the respondent had lost his or her job but was chronically unemployed or largely unemployable because of a lack of education, job skills, or a prison record that employers regarded as disqualifying; or that what Holmes and Rahe described as a "change in eating habits" really meant dealing with chronic food insecurity, scarcity, and hunger; or that what was termed a "change in living conditions" in their life stress scale (along with the rest of their residence-related items) actually meant that the respondent and his or her family were forced to live homeless on the streets or in a car; or that the "death of a spouse" or "death of a close family member" (that the Holmes and Rahe scale asked about) was actually one brought about by neighborhood violence that the respondent directly witnessed. It is not difficult to imagine how these kinds of more poverty-sensitive stressful life events might have negative consequences that could negative affect many aspects of a family's functioning.

Not surprisingly, perhaps, some studies have reported a relationship between the stress-related effects of poverty and harsh or abusive parenting. Thus an early literature review noted in the 1980s that there was a "growing consensus" among researchers that "the maltreatment of children results, in part, from stress."[61] Under the stress of severe economic hardship, parents may struggle to maintain their own stability and equanimity and, because they lack the resources with which to seek help, their problems may go unaddressed and worsen. Thus, the damaging effects of poverty on children may be greatest when parents are overwhelmed by it and their ability to serve in consistent caretaker roles is compromised. Early research on the indirect negative effects of poverty on child development indicated not only that maltreatment was more prevalent among the "persistently poor" but also found that whether or not a parent had mental health problems was "the only significant predictor of recurrent abuse."[62] Other research suggested that the stress of having limited financial support and little social support from the surrounding community contributed to parental depression and greater amounts of child maltreatment.[63]

It is certainly *not* the case that poor people are somehow "predisposed" to emotional problems that lead to child maltreatment. Instead, poverty imposes greater levels of economic stress and frustration on parents that may undermine their well-being and force them to live structurally disadvantaged neighborhoods where little or no help is forthcoming. Children who live in poor neighborhoods that are characterized by few if any effectively functioning social service agencies or institutions, where there is low social cohesion and high residential turnover, and a concentration of other problematic social conditions are at highest risk of maltreatment.[64] Poor parents who are themselves at risk and under heightened levels of stress—for example, by virtue of having younger children to care for, being especially young parents, or functioning as single parents who lack a partner with whom to share responsibilities—are more likely to resort to forceful and potentially abusive practices with their children.[65] Thus, as one study showed, "areas with the highest maltreatment rates were those with the intertwined conditions of poverty, unemployment, female-headed households, racial segregation, abandoned housing, and population loss."[66] The combination of high levels of neighborhood poverty and little social cohesion appears to exacerbate some forms of child maltreatment.

Although positive parenting can moderate and reduce the negative effects on poverty in children,[67] researchers have documented the ways in which economic hardship produces psychological distress for both children and parents, making parenting in the midst of scarcity especially challenging. As public policy scholar Robert Putnam put it,

> Everyday stress levels vary across families, of course, but a vast body of research links parental stress with less sensitive, less responsive parenting, and thus with bad outcomes for kids. Stressed parents are both harsher and less attentive parents. Economic stress, in particular, disrupts family relations, fosters withdrawn and inconsistent parenting, and directly increases chronic stress among children.[68]

Glen Elder's visual representation of this process is depicted in Figure 6.1. It illustrates one pathway through which poverty can lead to adverse outcomes for children, depending on whether and how it impacts parents.

The sheer stress of poverty makes parents more vulnerable to negative life events of all sorts, and may limit their opportunities to engage in supportive and involved parenting.[69] In one study, for example, economic hardship decreased parental nurturance and increased inconsistent parental discipline, which in turn increased levels of depression and loneliness among children. Similarly, the same researchers found that the increasingly inconsistent parental discipline that occurred in response to economic hardship was related to their children's increased delinquency and drug use.[70] Thus, when poverty-related stressors undermine parents' ability to provide nurturing care and leads to more inconsistent discipline, the children's risk of adverse outcomes such as depression, drug use, and delinquency can increase.

A British study of some 30,000 children documented the long-term effects of economic disadvantage over their life course. Although the relationships were complex, the researchers found that the negative influences of

FIGURE 6.1. Linkages Between Family Hardship and Child Outcomes

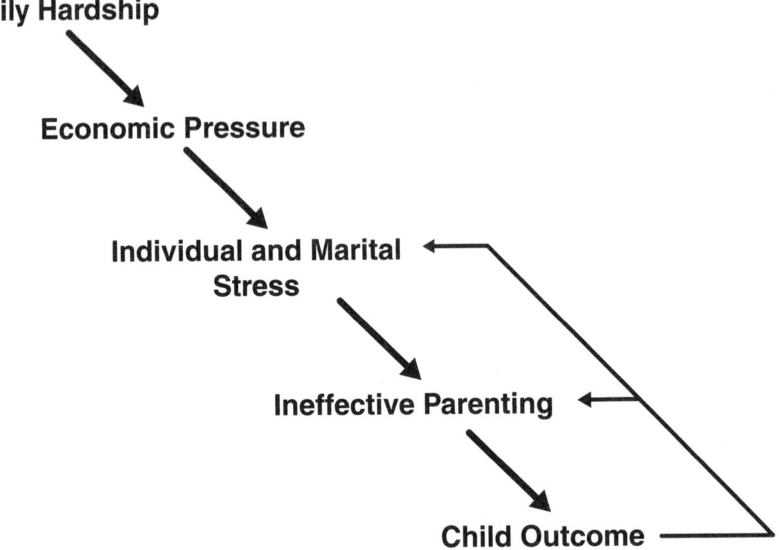

From "Time, Human Agency, and Social Change Perspectives on the Life Course," by G. Elder, 1994, *Social Psychology Quarterly, 57,* p. 12. Copyright 1994 by Sage. Reprinted with permission.

poverty were additive over time—"being born into a relatively disadvantaged family increases the probability of accumulating risks associated with that disadvantage"—and that poverty had an adverse impact on adult competencies and outcomes.[71]

In addition, the extra burdens shouldered by impoverished parents may indirectly affect their children's cognitive development. Early, classic research by Betty Hart and Todd Risley documented the nature and consequences of differences in language experiences between children from disadvantaged, working class, and professional families.[72] They found the sheer number of words to which poor children were exposed by age three was significantly lower than for children raised in working class or professional families, as were the number of "encouragements" (as opposed to "discouragements") they received. Not only were these differentials extremely large, they also appeared to have significant consequences for the children's future learning potential. Thus, "the number of different words of all types the parent said per hour was more strongly related to all of the child's accomplishments at age 3" and, it turned out, into third grade as well.[73]

Here, too, the differences in parenting practices are contextually driven. Rather than reflecting "bad" parenting practices that are freely chosen by poor parents who suffer from alleged emotional or intellectual deficits of their own, or operate within a supposed "culture of poverty" in which caring for children is deemphasized or misguided, economically disadvantaged parents are instead reacting directly (and understandably) to the stress of the sometimes seemingly insurmountable economic challenges they face.

POVERTY AND ADVERSE COMMUNITY CONTEXT

The African proverb that "it takes an entire village to raise a child" attained prominence in the 1990s in discussions about child rearing and child development, in part because it was the title of a well-known book by then First Lady and long-time children's advocate Hillary Rodham Clinton.[74] The proverb underscores the degree to which children are dependent on the broader context in which they grow up or, as some commentators have put it, "children must be seen in relation to their family, and families must be seen in relation to their community."[75] However, some economically disadvantaged children spend too little time in a single community to establish any relational ties to the institutions or people in the places where they live. Many others grow up in communities where social disorganization and the press of poverty are so widespread that they preclude other "villagers" from taking any helpful role in their upbringing. Indeed, as one study of the "human ecology of child maltreatment" concluded,

> A family's own problems seem to be compounded rather than ameliorated by the neighborhood context, dominated as it is by other needy families. Under such circumstances, strong support systems are most needed but least likely to operate. The high-risk area needs outside intervention to increase its capacity to fend for itself and to strengthen families as a way of reducing the demands they place on already tenuous informal helping networks.[76]

In addition to the combination of many poor and needy families living in a single geographical area that lacks sufficient "informal helping networks," many such impoverished communities lack an adequate formal social welfare infrastructure to help address their basic problems and needs.

Thus, beyond the way that poverty can adversely affect a young person's developmental trajectory and shape a social history in its early stages, it can significantly influence the nature of the immediate situations and circumstances that a child enters later in life. If people's opportunities and options have been compromised and limited by their exposure to numerous primary risk factors during childhood and adolescence, then they are more likely to live in environments that expose them to other kinds of secondary risk factors. Indeed, because many people continue to be mired in poverty as a result of the structural barriers they still confront and, in some cases, because they are still affected by the legacies of the childhood traumas and maltreatment to which they were exposed earlier, they are more likely to be forced by circumstance to live in areas characterized by what I described in Chapter 5 as "neighborhood disadvantage."

As I noted then, neighborhood disadvantage refers to a set of interrelated community characteristics that often accompany poverty and amplify its negative effects in ways that can be criminogenic.[77] For example, high rates of unemployment place economic stress on residents that may, in turn, undermine family stability. The transience and instability that pervade disadvantaged neighborhoods help to create an overall sense of impermanence and disorganization that also can impede the development of stable, consistent, and consensual community norms. All of these factors are related to higher crime rates.

Additionally, crime is more prevalent in disadvantaged neighborhoods because "[i]ndividuals who are poor are confronted with an unremitting succession of negative life events . . . in the context of chronically stressful, ongoing life conditions such as inadequate housing and dangerous neighborhoods that together increase the exigencies of day-to-day existence."[78] Thus, under the risk factors model, poverty and neighborhood disadvantage represent *immediate* stressors—the "exigencies of day-to-day existence"—with the potential to exacerbate the negative effects of the difficult, risk-filled social histories that many residents already have endured.[79] Living in severely disadvantaged neighborhoods also can change the way people think about themselves, undermine their sense of self, and make them more likely to give in to the desperation they feel.

Finally, as Mercer Sullivan documented in his study of several different groups of urban adolescents, children who grow up in poorer neighborhoods often lack social capital that provides access to a social safety net that can buffer them from the worst consequences of their adolescent mistakes. In some instances, the poor neighborhoods he analyzed were simultaneously less tolerant of the adolescents' transgressions but also less capable of providing them with the assistance they needed to avoid repeatedly engaging in the same troublesome behavior.[80] They were thus more at risk of more frequent and more prolonged criminal justice system involvement.

POVERTY AND INSTITUTIONAL DISADVANTAGE

Impoverished neighborhoods often lack sufficient infrastructure and resources with which to address the basic needs of their residents. A group of sociologists summarized it this way: in many poor neighborhoods, families are "isolated from mainstream institutions. They are far less able to access conventional means to achieve general societal goals, to support family socialization of conventional values and norms, and to exert effective control over the behavior of residents."[81]

Because of the role that schools play as a primary socializing agents in childhood and adolescence, the substandard quality of the educational institutions to which poor families have access and the punitive disciplinary practices that characterize many of the schools that poor children attend can significantly affect their life outcomes.[82] There is a tragic arc to this cycle, one that begins with something that parents are unable to avoid—poverty—and can end with something many that children are unable to overcome—school failure and all that it implies for their subsequent life course. Thus, substandard and understaffed schools that are unable to engage students or interest them in the process of learning contribute to academic disengagement and alienation. The "school-to-prison pipeline" and related harsh disciplinary practices discussed in Chapter 4 are more likely to be implemented in schools that serve disadvantaged students, leading to more juvenile justice system involvement and less educational engagement. But low levels of school bonding, poor academic performance, truancy, expulsion, and dropping out all occur with greater frequency among economically disadvantaged students and in schools located in low-income neighborhoods. [83] They are also all risk factors in their own right, increasing the likelihood of subsequent delinquent and criminal behavior.[84]

In addition, although the educational achievement gap between economically disadvantaged students and others is not a simple function of differentials in school funding,[85] it is at least in part related to differences in levels of educational expenditures.[86] Despite concerted efforts made over the last several decades to reduce the inequities in funding, significant differences still exist between and within state school systems.[87] Moreover, in addition to research that has found "compelling evidence that money does matter" in school performance, we also know that "resources can meaningfully improve long-term outcomes for students."[88] Thus, the long-term outcomes that are affected by school spending include not only educational attainment (the years of education completed) but also later economic outcomes (wages and incidence of poverty). Although levels of school spending affect all groups, increases in expenditures are especially advantageous in the case of students attending schools in low-income districts.[89]

There are other dimensions to the relationship between poverty and educational disadvantage. Research shows that neighborhood public schools have higher concentrations of students from low income families than their percentages in the surrounding community, in part because many higher income parents have options to send their children to private, charter, or magnet schools. The high correlation between the income levels within a school and the academic performance of its individual students means that "elevated concentrations of poverty in public schools are likely to have a particularly deleterious impact on young children whose families are already economically disadvantaged."[90]

The "income-achievement gap" in the United States is sizable and has been growing since 1980 (a period during which the Black–White gap was actually decreasing).[91] Not surprisingly, school risk factors (e.g., teachers' lack of experience, high turnover, poor building quality) are interrelated to community risk factors such as neighborhood disadvantage, so that poorer schools tend to be located in the communities with higher concentrations of economically disadvantaged families. The accumulation of these risks affects levels of school-wide achievement.[92] Gloria Ladson-Billings was correct to warn that the "culture of poverty" explanation for poor children's school performance is disturbing not only because it is factually incorrect but also because it "absolves social structures—governmental and institutional—of responsibility for the vulnerabilities that poor children regularly face."[93]

Michelle Fine and her colleagues have written eloquently about the many ways in which the kinds of schools to which poor children, especially poor children of Color, are consigned in many parts of American society may not only fail to properly educate them but also generate negative feelings and teach long-term "civics lessons" that may eventually lead to juvenile crime.[94] Among other things, impoverished children in these dilapidated, underfunded, and undermanned schools experience forms of "psychological and social devastation,"[95] including a sense of alienation, betrayal, and anger. Their poor educational experiences can disadvantage them in the competition to enter college and marginalize them in the workforce. These imposed economic vulnerabilities can generate resentment born of the betrayal of the once-believable promise of a quality education and promising future.

In fact, in part because of the way in which individual- and family-level poverty is replicated and amplified by institutional disadvantages, early economic disadvantage is actually a risk factor for later poverty. That is, a child who spends half or more of his or her early years in poverty has more than a 40% chance of living in poverty at age 35.[96] This speaks not only to the power of poverty to negatively affect an entire life course but also to the lack of meaningful and supportive institutional infrastructure in American society to provide meaningful, viable pathways out of economic disadvantage.

STRUCTURAL DISADVANTAGE: POVERTY AS A GATEWAY RISK FACTOR

Implicit in much of what I have said so far, poverty increases the likelihood of exposure to numerous other risk factors that are known to have long-term adverse—and sometimes criminogenic—consequences. In this way, as I have suggested, it functions as a gateway to other potentially damaging risk factors in childhood and adolescence. Thus, researchers have acknowledged that "living in a poor, dangerous neighborhood virtually guarantees exposure to risk factors outside the home that affect child development," and that "neighborhood disadvantage provides a strong measure of environmental risk."[97]

The combination of poverty-related stress and the lack of an effective and responsive social welfare infrastructure inside many poor communities can prove insurmountable. One commentator observed nearly 50 years ago that most poor families were "systematically shunted into community systems which are predominately punitive and regulatory, and conversely diverted away from those systems which are supportive and enhancing of parental role performance."[98] This is still the case.[99] The combination of added economic stressors and diminished community assistance helps explain why persistent poverty may be related to child maltreatment. In fact, one group of researchers concluded that long-term or chronic poverty was systematically related to patterns of *repeated* maltreatment. Thus, children who were abused on multiple occasions were more likely to live "in families with intergenerational histories of poverty."[100] When economic stress overwhelms parents, their parenting practices and other aspects of their lives are likely to be adversely affected, with potential consequences for their children.

Gary Evans and his colleagues have meticulously documented the ways in which poverty exposes children to multiple, cumulative environmental and psychosocial risk factors.[101] As depicted in the Figure 6.2, sizable numbers of children from poor families are exposed to multiple risks that accumulate in their lives, as compared to children from middle-class families who typically experience only a few.

Although the group-level linkages from childhood poverty to adult crime and violence are sometimes complicated and contingent, they are rarely difficult to disentangle or to understand in individual cases. As I summarized in the preceding pages, poverty exposes children to a host of risk factors in the home, school, and community that affect them directly, and it has other

FIGURE 6.2. Cumulative Risk Exposure in Relation to Poverty

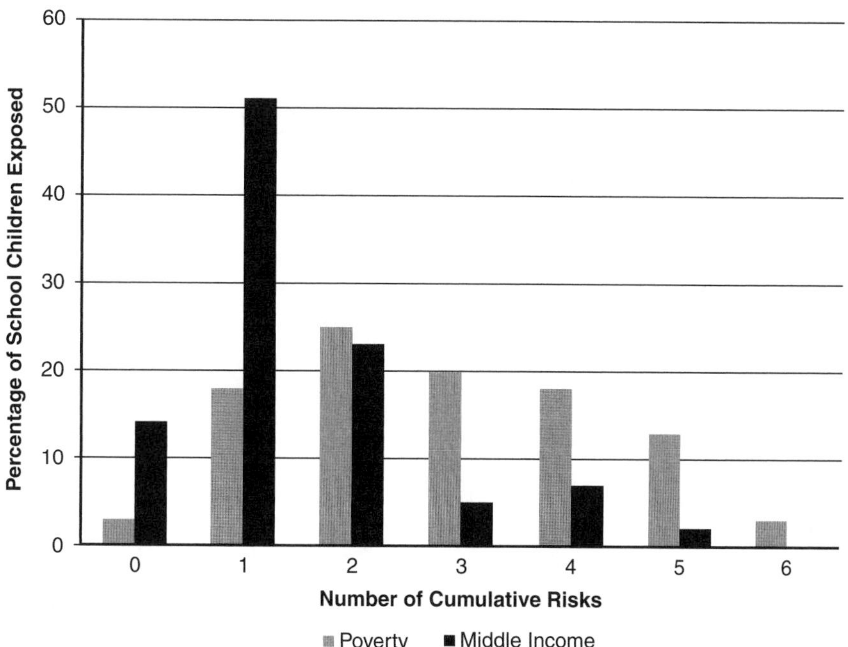

The percentage of poor and nonpoor children exposed to cumulative physical and psychosocial environmental risks. The mean number of multiple stressors is significantly higher ($p < .001$) for the poverty sample compared with the middle-income sample. From "The Environment of Childhood Poverty," by G. Evans, 2004, *American Psychologist, 59*, p. 87. Copyright 2004 by the American Psychological Association.

more indirect effects that operate largely through the impact poverty has on parents. Especially because of the lack of effective social service and child welfare agencies and organizations to assist children and their parents in poor neighborhoods, they are at greater risk of problematic life outcomes, including becoming involved in delinquent and criminal behavior.

For example, David Farrington, Rolf Loeber and their colleagues found that the combination of high numbers of risk factors and few protective or promotive factors has "the same relation to persistent serious delinquency in different neighborhoods," but that there were higher rates of delinquency in poor neighborhoods because children there were exposed to greater numbers of risks and had the benefit of fewer protective factors.[102] Candace Kruttschnitt, Jane McLeod, and Maude Dornfield have shown that long-term poverty can create a larger *context* for abuse, violence, and criminality in which the children are reared: "The problems of these families, then, are inextricably tied to both past and present experiences of economic deprivation and associated antisocial behaviors."[103] Indeed, Kruttschnitt, McLeod, and Dornfield concluded that "[v]iolence does occur at all income levels but it is more often repeated among the persistently poor."[104] Over the long run, these effects tend to recur, and become intergenerational. For example, in instances where poverty leads to violence—particularly if it results in parental imprisonment—it increases the chances of continuing poverty for the next generation of children.

At another level, poverty and material deprivation can increase levels of personal frustration. Indeed, chronic poverty can result in a state of *chronic* frustration. Depending upon the circumstances—in particular, the reasons a person perceives that his or her desired goals are persistently blocked—the kind of frustration may produce greater levels of "angry aggression."[105] Numerous studies provide empirical support for the commonsense proposition that the kind of frustration that makes people angry also can lead to aggressive behavior, even crime.[106] In this context, relative deprivation—the perception that one is economically deprived compared to similar others—is especially frustrating. As Gwynn Nettler noted, "the principal interpretation given for the association between economic inequality and violent crime has focused on the process of relative deprivation as a stimulant to hostility."[107] In extreme cases, it may even help to account for the relationship that researchers have found between poverty and homicide.[108]

These immediate effects of poverty not only can directly influence the course of child development but also lead to behavioral adaptations that can have longer-term negative consequences. For example, if and when the connections between poverty, frustration, negative affect or anger, and aggression do manifest themselves in childhood and adolescence, they increase the chances of exposure to other risk factors, such as early drug use and juvenile incarceration, both of which are likely to amplify the earlier negative effects. The fact that these relationships may be manifested in complicated and contingent ways does not lessen the force with which they can influence and impair a life course.

The last chapter discussed the way that substance abuse can serve as a dysfunctional adaptation to the emotional distress that earlier exposure to risk factors and traumas can produce. I characterized it as a "dysfunctional" adaptation precisely because of its long-term tendency to worsen rather than ameliorate distress, thus serving as a risk factor of its own that is sometimes criminogenic. Poverty, too, is a risk factor for substance abuse, which may set a similarly dysfunctional process in motion. More specifically, economic deprivation is associated with depression and a sense of hopelessness that many persons are tempted to alleviate through self-medication, especially if they lack access to conventional forms of treatment. The eventual endpoint of this adaptation is typically difficult for persons to anticipate at the outset but can further mire them in the same kind of impoverished conditions that caused their initial distress. The authors of one study described one of the ways this can occur, noting that "substance abuse compounds the factors that may influence the onset of poverty, such as being fired for being drunk on the job." But poverty, in turn, also "compounds the factors that influence substance use through the greater proximity of bars and outlets that sell alcohol in low income neighborhoods."[109]

At another level, if poor children are more likely grow up in families where their parents use drugs or alcohol to alleviate their own feelings of despair, the parents' adaptation can increase the chances of child maltreatment and also provide the children with a role model for self-medication in response to emotional pain. In either case, if this increases the risk of substance abuse for the children, it will be more difficult for them to extricate themselves from the disadvantaged circumstances that originally set this process in motion.[110] As I say, these pathways are many and varied, but they are influenced directly and indirectly by the structural condition of economic disadvantage and income inequality.

CONCLUSION

Poverty increases exposure to a host of potentially harmful risk factors, including ones known to be criminogenic. In fact, the relationship between poverty and crime has been so long and widely understood that it was essentially assumed in one of the early, classic criminological studies. Thus, the original Glueck data from the 1940s on which Robert Sampson and John Loeb relied for their influential analyses of the role of risk factors and turning points in delinquency and criminality held the broader contextual factor of poverty constant. That is, *all* of the young men from whom the Gluecks collected data, and whose life trajectories Sampson and Loeb analyzed, came from "underprivileged neighborhoods"—socially disorganized communities that Sampson and Loeb described as "regions of poverty, economic dependence, and physical deterioration," and lived in homes that generally were "crowded, and often lacking in basic necessities like sanitary facilities, tubs/showers, and central heating."[111] The Gluecks understood in the 1940s, and we understand even better now, that crime is concentrated in environments characterized by economic hardship and deprivation. This chapter has synthesized much of what is known about the social and psychological dynamics of that relationship.[112]

To concede that poor persons succumb to the economic pressures that surround them is not intended to diminish the nature of their struggle or the resiliency with which they wage it. It is, instead, a way of acknowledging the magnitude of the forces aligned against their success. Law professor Thomas Ross reminds that, despite what I have written about the potential damaging effects of poverty, historically, "the story of people in poverty in this country has been a story of strength and success."[113] As with any analysis that is focused on criminogenic effects—by definition those persons for whom the obstacles became insurmountable—it is easy to overlook that "[a]gainst all odds, facing social stigma and working through maddening systems of public assistance, the poor have survived." In fact, they have survived and often overcome these odds because, as Ross observed, "[m]any poor women and men have kept their families together and maintained safe and decent lives in the midst of conditions that would seem to make family disintegration inescapable."[114]

Yet it is also true that there are many mechanisms by which structural inequality is inscribed on the psyches, social relations, institutional experiences, and life chances of the poor. Few people freely choose to be poor and to endure the deprivation, marginalization, and stigma that it often entails in our society. However, as a result of preexisting structural arrangements over which they have no control, poor children are disproportionately subjected to treatment and exposed to living conditions that make delinquency and crime more likely. They live in stressed and sometimes fragile families that are under dire economic pressures and at risk of unraveling, and in communities plagued by neighborhood disadvantage that engenders crime. The limited arenas that they are permitted to enter and the scarce opportunities they are afforded later in life typically devalue many of the very habits and skills they have developed in response to the severe deprivations and inequalities to which they have been subjected.[115] They have significantly fewer lawful options through which to achieve economic stability, professional success, and overall well-being. Yet we continue to individualize blame for succumbing to context-driven lawbreaking and rely heavily on a crime master narrative that holds them fully accountable, as if the paths they followed were chosen on a level playing field. It is the primary way that the criminal justice system itself contributes to the obfuscation of "the entrenched and embedded character of social equality" and its myriad personal, familial, and community consequences.[116]

NOTES

1. *Furman v. Georgia*, 408 U.S. 238, 447 (1972).
2. Beckett, K., & Sasson, T. (2000). *The politics of injustice: Crime and punishment in America* (p. 53). Thousand Oaks, CA: Sage.

3. Wacquant, L. (2009). *Punishing the poor: The neoliberal government of social insecurity.* Durham, NC: Duke University Press. http://dx.doi.org/10.1215/9780822392255
4. Loury, G. C. (2008). *Race, incarceration and American values* (p. 60). Cambridge, MA: MIT Press. The quote is attributed to L. Wacquant.
5. France, A. (1894). *The red lily.*
6. Lott, B. (2002). Cognitive and behavioral distancing from the poor. *American Psychologist, 57,* 100–110, p. 101. http://dx.doi.org/10.1037/0003-066X.57.2.100. See also Kraus, M. W., & Stephens, N. M. (2012). A road map for an emerging psychology of social class. *Social and Personality Psychology Compass, 6,* 642–656. http://dx.doi.org/10.1111/j.1751-9004.2012.00453.x
7. National Academies of Sciences, Engineering, and Medicine. (2019). *A roadmap to reducing child poverty.* Washington, DC: National Academies Press, p. 55–57. http://dx.doi.org/10.17226/25246
8. National Academies of Sciences, Engineering, and Medicine (2019), *A roadmap to reducing child poverty,* p. 9.
9. National Academies of Sciences, Engineering, and Medicine (2019), *A roadmap to reducing child poverty,* p. 61. The NAS defined "poverty" threshold as $25,000 for a family of four. "Deep poverty was defined as family resource levels that are less than half the poverty line" (p. 19).
10. National Academies of Sciences, Engineering, and Medicine (2019), *A roadmap to reducing child poverty,* p. 42.
11. National Academies of Sciences, Engineering, and Medicine (2019), *A roadmap to reducing child poverty,* p. 67. The Committee noted, even more directly, that "[t]he weight of the causal evidence indicates that income poverty itself causes negative child outcomes, especially when it begins in early childhood and/or persists throughout a large share of a child's life" (p. 89).
12. See, e.g., Ellen, I. G., Lacoe, J., & Sharygin, C. A. (2013). Do foreclosures cause crime? *Journal of Urban Economics, 74,* 59–70. http://dx.doi.org/10.1016/j.jue.2012.09.003; Fajnzylber, P., Lederman, D., & Loayza, N. (2002). What causes violent crime? *European Economic Review, 46,* 1323–1357. http://dx.doi.org/10.1016/S0014-2921(01)00096-4; Karmen, A. (2000). Poverty, crime, and criminal justice. In W. C. Heffernan & J. Kleinig (Eds.), *From social justice to criminal justice: Poverty and the administration of criminal law* (pp. 25–46). New York, NY: Oxford University Press.
13. Ryan, W. (1971). *Blaming the victim.* New York, NY: Random House; Lugo-Ocando, J. (2015). *Blaming the victim: How global journalism fails those in poverty.* London, England: Pluto Press. http://dx.doi.org/10.2307/j.ctt183p3tc
14. Bullock, H. E. (1995). Class acts: Middle-class responses to the poor. In B. Lott & D. Maluso (Eds.), *The social psychology of interpersonal discrimination* (pp. 118–159). New York, NY: Guilford Press, p. 125. See also Bullock, H. E., Wyche, K. K., & Williams, W. R. (2001). Media images of the poor. *Journal of Social Issues, 57,* 229–246. http://dx.doi.org/10.1111/0022-4537.00210
15. Chafel, J. A. (1997). Societal images of poverty: Child and adult beliefs. *Youth & Society, 28,* 432–463, p. 438. http://dx.doi.org/10.1177/0044118X97028004003
16. Williams, T., & Kornblum, W. (1994). *The uptown kids: Struggle and hope in the projects.* New York, NY: Grosset/Putnam.
17. Bane, M. J., & Ellwood, D. T. (1986). Slipping in and out of poverty: The dynamics of spells. *Journal of Human Resources, 21,* 1–23, p. 17. http://dx.doi.org/10.2307/145955
18. Nightingale, C. H. (1994). *On the edge: A history of poor Black children and their American dreams* (p. 55). New York, NY: Basic Books.
19. See, e.g., Scrimshaw, N. S. (1969). Early malnutrition and central nervous system function. *Merrill-Palmer Quarterly of Behavior and Development, 15,* 375–388; and Gardner, L. I. (1972). Deprivational dwarfism. *Scientific American, 227,* 76–82.

20. Duncan, G. J., Brooks-Gunn, J., & Klebanov, P. K. (1994). Economic deprivation and early childhood development. *Child Development, 65,* 296–318. http://dx.doi.org/10.2307/1131385
21. Duncan, G. J., Yeung, W. J., Brooks-Gunn, J., & Smith, J. R. (1998). How much does childhood poverty affect the life chances of children? *American Sociological Review, 63,* 406–423, p. 420. http://dx.doi.org/10.2307/2657556
22. Zilney, L. A., McGurrin, D., & Zahran, S. (2006). Environmental justice and the role of criminology: An analytical review of 33 years of environmental justice research. *Criminal Justice Review, 31,* 47–62, p. 57. http://dx.doi.org/10.1177/0734016806288258. See also Bullard, R., & Wright, B. (2003). Environmental justice for all. In S. Plous (Ed.), *Understanding prejudice and discrimination* (pp. 448–462). New York, NY: McGraw Hill; and Taylor, D. E. (2000). The rise of the environmental justice paradigm: Injustice framing and the social construction of environmental discourses. *American Behavioral Scientist, 43,* 508–580. http://dx.doi.org/10.1177/0002764200043004003
23. See, e.g., Downey, L., Crowder, K., & Kemp, R. J. (2017). Family structure, residential mobility, and environmental quality. *Journal of Marriage and Family, 79,* 535–555. http://dx.doi.org/10.1111/jomf.12355; Holton, W. C. (2004). Rich map poor map. *Environmental Health Perspectives, 112,* 176–179. http://dx.doi.org/10.1289/ehp.112-a176; Maantay, J. (2001). Zoning, equity, and public health. *American Journal of Public Health, 91,* 1033–1041; and Morello-Frosch, R., Zuk, M., Jerrett, M., Shamasunder, B., & Kyle, A. D. (2011). Understanding the cumulative impacts of inequalities in environmental health: Implications for policy. *Health Affairs, 30,* 879–887. http://dx.doi.org/10.1377/hlthaff.2011.0153
24. Pellow, D. N. (2016). Toward a critical environmental justice studies: Black Lives Matter as an environmental challenge. *Du Bois Review: Social Science Research on Race, 13,* 221–236, p. 222. http://dx.doi.org/10.1017/S1742058X1600014X
25. See, e.g., Denno, D. W. (1993). Considering lead poisoning as a criminal defense. *Fordham Urban Law Journal, 20,* 377–385; Dietrich, K. N., Douglas, R. M., Succop, P. A., Berger, O. G., & Bornschein, R. L. (2001). Early exposure to lead and juvenile delinquency. *Neurotoxicology and Teratology, 23,* 511–518. http://dx.doi.org/10.1016/S0892-0362(01)00184-2; Nevin, R. (2000). How lead exposure relates to temporal changes in IQ, violent crime, and unwed pregnancy. *Environmental Research, 83,* 1–22. http://dx.doi.org/10.1006/enrs.1999.4045; Stretesky, P. B., & Lynch, M. J. (2001). The relationship between lead exposure and homicide. *Archives of Pediatric Adolescent Medicine, 155,* 579–582. http://dx.doi.org/10.1001/archpedi.155.5.579; Stretesky, P. B., & Lynch, M. J. (2004). The relationship between lead and crime. *Journal of Health and Social Behavior, 45,* 214–229. http://dx.doi.org/10.1177/002214650404500207; and Wright, J. P., Dietrich, K. N., Ris, M. D., Hornung, R. W., Wessel, S. D., Lanohear, B. P., . . . Rae, M. N. (2008). Association of prenatal and childhood blood lead concentrations with criminal arrests in early adulthood. *PLoS Medicine, 5,* e101, 0732–0739. http://dx.doi.org/10.1371/journal.pmed.0050101
26. Sampson, R. J., & Winter, A. S. (2018). Poisoned development: Assessing childhood lead exposure as a cause of crime in a birth cohort followed through adolescence. *Criminology, 56,* 269–301, p. 294. http://dx.doi.org/10.1111/1745-9125.12171. See also Persico, C., Figlio, D., & Roth, J. (2016, May). *Inequality before birth: The developmental consequences of environmental toxicants* (NBER Working Paper 22263). Cambridge, MA: National Bureau of Economic Research.
27. Nightingale (1994), *On the edge: A history of poor Black children and their American dreams,* p. 55.
28. Nightingale (1994), *On the edge: A history of poor Black children and their American dreams,* p. 55.

29. Takeuchi, D. T., Williams, D. R., & Adair, R. K. (1991). Economic stress in the family and children's emotional and behavioral problems. *Journal of Marriage and Family, 53,* 1031–1041. See also Lorant, V., Deliège, D., Eaton, W., Robert, A., Philippot, P., & Ansseau, M. (2003). Socioeconomic inequalities in depression: A meta-analysis. *American Journal of Epidemiology, 157,* 98–112; Uddin, M., Jansen, S., & Telzer, E. H. (2017). Adolescent depression linked to socioeconomic status? Molecular approaches for revealing premorbid risk factors. *Bioessays, 39,* 1–7. http://dx.doi.org/10.1002/bies.201600194
30. Chou, E. Y., Parmar, B. L., & Galinsky, A. D. (2017). Economic insecurity increases physical pain. *Psychological Science, 27,* 443–454, p. 443. http://dx.doi.org/10.1177/0956797615625640
31. See, e.g., Blair, C., & Raver, C. C. (2012). Child development in the context of adversity: Experiential canalization of brain and behavior. *American Psychologist, 67,* 309–318. http://dx.doi.org/10.1037/a0027493; Blair, C., & Raver, C. C. (2015). School readiness and self-regulation: A developmental psychobiological approach. *Annual Review of Psychology, 66,* 711–731. http://dx.doi.org/10.1146%2Fannurev-psych-010814-015221; Blair, C., Raver, C. C., Granger, D., Mills-Koonce, R., Hibel, L., & Family Life Project Key Investigators. (2011). Allostasis and allostatic load in the context of poverty in early childhood. *Development and Psychopathology, 23,* 845–857. http://dx.doi.org/10.1017/S0954579411000344; Evans, G. W. (2003). A multimethodological analysis of cumulative risk and allostatic load among rural children. *Developmental Psychology, 39,* 924–933. A multimethodological analysis of cumulative risk and allostatic load among rural children; and Raver, C. C., Blair, C., Garrett-Peters, P., & Family Life Project Key Investigators. (2015). Poverty, household chaos, and interparental aggression predict children's ability to recognize and modulate negative emotions. *Development and Psychopathology, 27,* 695–708. http://dx.doi.org/10.1017/S0954579414000935
32. McEwen, B., & McEwen, C. (2015). Social, psychological, and physiological reactions to stress. In R. A. Scott & S. M. Kosslyn (Eds.), *Emerging trends in the social and behavioral sciences: An interdisciplinary, searchable, linkable resource* (pp. 1–15). New York, NY: Wiley. http://dx.doi.org/10.1002/9781118900772.etrds0311
33. See, e.g., Reardon, S. F. (2013, May). The widening income achievement gap. *Educational Leadership, 70,* 10–16.
34. See, e.g., Blair, C., Granger, D. A., Willoughby, M., Mills-Koonce, R., Cox, M., Greenberg, M. T., . . . Family Life Project Key Investigators. (2011). Salivary cortisol mediates the effect of poverty and parenting on executive functioning in childhood. *Child Development, 82,* 1970–1984. http://dx.doi.org/10.1111/j.1467-8624.2011.01643.x.; Evans, G. W., Kim, P., Ting, A. H., Tesher, H. B., and Shannis, D. (2007). Cumulative risk, maternal responsiveness, and allostatic load among young adolescents. *Developmental Psychology, 43,* 341–351. http://dx.doi.org/10.1037/0012-1649.43.2.341; and Hackman, D. A., Gallop, R., Evans, G. W., & Farah, M. J. (2015). Socioeconomic status and executive function: Development trajectories and mediation. *Developmental Science, 18,* 686–702. http://dx.doi.org/10.1111/desc.12246
35. See, e.g., Elder, G. H., Jr., & Caspi, A. (1988). Economic stress in lives: Developmental perspectives. *Journal of Social Issues, 44,* 25–45. http://dx.doi.org/10.1111/j.1540-4560.1988.tb02090.x
36. Elder & Caspi (1988), Economic stress in lives, p. 33.
37. Duncan, Brooks-Gunn, & Klebanov (1994), Economic deprivation and early childhood development; Elder, G. H., Jr. (1979). Historical change in life patterns and personality. In P. B. Baltes & O. G. Brim, Jr. (Eds.), *Life span development and behavior* (Vol. 2, pp. 117–159). New York, NY: Academic Press.
38. Fomby, P., & Mollborn, S. (2017). Ecological instability and children's classroom behavior in kindergarten. *Demography, 54,* 1627–1651, p. 1644. http://dx.doi.org/10.1007/s13524-017-0602-2

39. See, e.g., Evans, G. W., Gonnella, C., Marcynyszyn, L. A., Gentile, L., & Salpekar, N. (2005). The role of chaos in poverty and children's socioemotional adjustment. *Psychological Science, 16,* 560–565. http://dx.doi.org/10.1111/j.0956-7976.2005.01575.x; Evans, G. W., & Wachs, T. D. (Eds.). (2010). *Chaos and its influence on children's development: An ecological perspective.* Washington, DC: American Psychological Association. http://dx.doi.org/10.1037/12057-000
40. Bronfenbrenner, U., & Evans, G. W. (2000). Developmental science in the 21st century: Emerging questions, theoretical models, research designs, and empirical findings. *Social Development, 9,* 115–125, p. 121. http://dx.doi.org/10.1111/1467-9507.00114
41. See, e.g., Kamp Dush, C. M., Schmeer, K. K., & Taylor, M. (2013). Chaos as a social determinant of child health: Reciprocal associations? *Social Science & Medicine, 95,* 69–76. http://dx.doi.org/10.1016/j.socscimed.2013.01.038; Klemfuss, J. Z., Wallin, A. R., & Quas, J. A. (2018). Attachment, household chaos, and children's health. *Families, Systems, & Health, 36,* 303–314. http://dx.doi.org/10.1037/fsh0000303; Tucker, C. J., Sharp, E. H., Van Gundy, K. T., & Rebellon, C. J. (2017). Household chaos, relationships with parents, and adolescents' future beliefs. *Journal of Family Studies, 23,* 229–242. http://dx.doi.org/10.1080/13229400.2015.1090327. Not surprising, the timing and intensity of the chaos as well as the level of maternal distress with which it is associated can influence the magnitude of the negative effects. See Coley, R. L., Lynch, A. D., & Kull, M. (2015). Early exposure to environmental chaos and children's physical and mental health. *Early Childhood Research Quarterly, 32,* 94–104. http://dx.doi.org/10.1016/j.ecresq.2015.03.001
42. See, e.g., Ross, L. T., & Hill, E. M. (2002). Childhood unpredictability, schemas for unpredictability, and risk taking. *Social Behavior and Personality, 30,* 453–473. http://dx.doi.org/10.2224/sbp.2002.30.5.453; Shapero, B. G., & Steinberg, L. (2013). Emotional reactivity and exposure to household stress in childhood predict psychological problems in adolescence. *Journal of Youth and Adolescence, 42,* 1573–1582. http://dx.doi.org/10.1007/s10964-013-9954-0; Valiente, C., Lemery-Chalfant, K., & Reiser, M. (2007). Pathways to problem behaviors: Chaotic homes, parent and child effortful control, and parenting. *Social Development, 16,* 249–267. http://dx.doi.org/10.1111/j.1467-9507.2007.00383.x; and Vernon-Feagans, L., Willoughby, M., Garrett-Peters, P., & Family Life Project Key Investigators. (2016). Predictors of behavioral regulation in kindergarten: Household chaos, parenting, and early executive functions. *Developmental Psychology, 52,* 430–441. http://dx.doi.org/10.1037/dev0000087
43. See, e.g., Osborne, C., & McLanahan, S. (2007). Partnership instability and child well-being. *Journal of Marriage and Family, 69,* 1065–1083. http://dx.doi.org/10.1111/j.1741-3737.2007.00431.x; Sauvola, A., Koskinen, O., Jokelainen, J., Hakko, H., Järvelin, M.-R., & Räsänen, P. (2002). Family type and criminal behaviour of male offspring: The Northern Finland 1966 birth cohort study. *International Journal of Social Psychiatry, 48,* 115–121. http://dx.doi.org/10.1177/002076402128783163; and Wells, L. E., & Rankin, J. H. (1991). Families and delinquency: A meta-analysis of the impact of broken homes. *Social Problems, 38,* 71–93.
44. Patterson, G. R., Forgatch, M. S., Yoerger, K. L., & Stoolmiller, M. (1998). Variables that initiate and maintain an early-onset trajectory for juvenile offending. *Development and Psychopathology, 10,* 531–547. http://dx.doi.org/10.1017/S0954579498001734
45. Theobald, D., Farrington, D. P., & Piquero, A. R. (2013). Childhood broken homes and adult violence: An analysis of moderators and mediators. *Journal of Criminal Justice, 41,* 44–52, p. 50. http://dx.doi.org/10.1016/j.jcrimjus.2012.12.003. See also Ackerman, B. P., Kogos, J., Youngstrom, E., Schoff, K., & Izard, C. (1999).

Family instability and the problem behaviors of children from economically disadvantaged families. *Developmental Psychology, 35,* 258–268. http://dx.doi.org/10.1037/0012-1649.35.1.258; and Jaffee, S. R., Hanscombe, K. B., Haworth, C. M. A., Davis, O. S. P., & Plomin, R. (2012). Chaotic homes and children's disruptive behavior: A longitudinal cross-lagged twin study. *Psychological Science, 23,* 643–650. http://dx.doi.org/10.1177/0956797611431693

46. A high number of family transitions also appears to exacerbate the negative effects of other forms of child maltreatment. See, e.g., Herrenkohl, E. C., Herrenkohl, R. C., & Egolf, B. P. (2003). The psychosocial consequences of living environment instability on maltreated children. *American Journal of Orthopsychiatry, 73,* 367–380. http://dx.doi.org/10.1037/0002-9432.73.4.367
47. Others have shown that all forms of child maltreatment may lead to subsequent delinquent behavior, especially when there are cumulative risks present combined with economic disadvantage. See, e.g., Mersky, J. P., & Reynolds, A. J. (2007). Child maltreatment and violent delinquency: Disentangling main effects and subgroup effects. *Child Maltreatment, 12,* 246–258. http://dx.doi.org/10.1177/1077559507301842
48. Extreme of residential mobility and the psychological adjustments it necessitates help to account for its long-term adverse mental health consequences. See, e.g., Oishi, S., & Schimmack, U. (2010). Residential mobility, well-being, and mortality. *Journal of Personality and Social Psychology, 98,* 980–994. http://dx.doi.org/10.1037/a0019389
49. See, e.g., Cutts, D. B., Meyers, A. F., Black, M. M., Casey, P. H., Chilton, M., Cook, J., & Frank, D. (2011). U.S. housing insecurity and the health of very young children. *American Journal of Public Health, 101,* 1508–1514. http://dx.doi.org/10.2105/AJPH.2011.300139; and Ziol-Guest, K. M., & McKenna, C. C. (2014). Early childhood housing instability and school readiness. *Child Development, 85,* 103–113. http://dx.doi.org/10.1111/cdev.12105
50. See, e.g., Begun, S., Bender, K. A., Brown, S. M., Barman-Adhikari, A., & Ferguson, K. (2018). Social connectedness, self-efficacy, and mental health outcomes among homeless youth: Prioritizing approaches to service provision in a time of limited agency resources. *Youth & Society, 50,* 989–1014. http://dx.doi.org/10.1177/0044118X16650459; Bender, K., Ferguson, K., Thompson, S., Komlo, C., & Pollio, D. (2010). Factors associated with trauma and posttraumatic stress disorder among homeless youth: The importance of transience. *Journal of Traumatic Stress, 23,* 161–168. http://dx.doi.org/10.1002/jts.20501; and Molnar, J. M., Rath, W. R., & Klein, T. P. (1990). Constantly compromised: The impact of homelessness on children. *Journal of Social Issues, 46,* 109–124. http://dx.doi.org/10.1111/j.1540-4560.1990.tb01801.x
51. Foster, L. (2020). *Estimating California's homeless youth population.* CA Homeless Youth Project: Sacramento (2010), p. 3, Retrieved from http://www.research.policyarchive.org/95913.pdf, quoting *Understanding homeless youth: Numbers, characteristics, multisystem involvement and intervention options: Hearings before the U.S. House Committee on Ways and Means, Subcommittee on Income Security and Family Support* (2007) (testimony of Martha R. Burt). Retrieved from http://www.urban.org/UploadedPDF/901087_Burt_Homeless.pdf
52. Foster, *Estimating California's homeless youth population,* p. 3, quoting Toro, P. A., Dworksy, A., & Fowler, P. J. (2007). *Homeless youth in the United States: Recent research findings and intervention approaches,* pp. 6–4. Retrieved from http://aspe.hhs.gov/hsp/homelessness/symposium07/toro/index.htm
53. For example, "Nearly two-thirds of California counties have no services targeted for the state's estimated 200,000 homeless youth." Lin, J. (2011, January 26). Most California counties lacking programs for homeless youths. *San Francisco Chronicle,* p. C3.

54. McCarthy, B., & Hagan, J. (1995). Getting into street crime: The structure and process of criminal embeddedness. *Social Science Research, 24,* 63–95. http://dx.doi.org/10.1006/ssre.1995.1003
55. Garbarino was among the first psychologists to write about and document this relationship. He has studied and written about it for decades. See, e.g., Garbarino, J. (1976). A preliminary study of some ecological correlates of child abuse: The impact of socioeconomic stress on mothers. *Child Development, 47,* 178–185; Garbarino, J. (1992). The meaning of poverty in the world of children. *American Behavioral Scientist, 35,* 220–237. http://dx.doi.org/10.1177/0002764292035003003
56. Garbarino (1992), The meaning of poverty in the world of children.
57. Conger, K. J., Rueter, M. A., & Conger, R. D. (2000). The role of economic pressure in the lives of parents and their adolescents: The family stress model. In L. J. Crockett & R. K. Silbereisen (Eds.), *Negotiating adolescence in times of social change* (pp. 201–223). Cambridge, England: Cambridge University Press.
58. In addition to the sheer amount of additional time poor parents must spend on managing the economic challenges they confront, there is some evidence that poverty-related concerns actually consume significant amounts of a person's mental resources; that is, "the very context of poverty imposes load and impedes cognitive capacity." Mani, A., Mullainathan, S., Shafir, E., & Zhao, J. (2013). Poverty impedes cognitive function. *Science, 341,* 976–980, p. 980. http://dx.doi.org/10.1126/science.1238041
59. Conger, Rueter, & Conger (2000), The role of economic pressure, p. 217.
60. See, e.g., Holmes, T. H., & Rahe, R. H. (1967). The social readjustment rating scale. *Journal of Psychosomatic Research, 11,* 213–218. http://dx.doi.org/10.1016/0022-3999(67)90010-4; and Holmes, T., & Masuda, M. (1974). Life changes and illness susceptibility. In B. S. Dohrenwend & B. P. Dohrenwend (Eds.), *Stressful life events: Their nature and effects* (pp. 45–72). New York, NY: Wiley.
61. Steinberg, L. D., Catalano, R., & Dooley, D. (1981). Economic antecedents of child abuse and neglect. *Child Development, 52,* 975–985, p. 975. http://dx.doi.org/10.2307/1129102. As Duva and Metzger summarized, "The stress of living in harsh, deprived conditions can have a disabling effect on parenting capacities, resulting in inconsistent discipline, failure to respond to a child's emotional needs, or failure to prevent or address a potential risk to safety." Duva, J., & Metzger, S. (2010). Addressing poverty as a major risk factor in child neglect: Promising policy and practice. *Protecting Children, 25,* 63–74, p. 65.
62. Kruttschnitt, C., McLeod, J. D., & Dornfeld, M. (1994). The economic environment of child abuse. *Social Problems, 41,* 299–315, p. 307. http://dx.doi.org/10.2307/3096935. See also Newland, R. P., Crnic, K. A., Cox, M. J., Mills-Koonce, W. R., & Family Life Project Key Investigators. (2013). The family model stress and maternal psychological symptoms: Mediated pathways from economic hardship to parenting. *Journal of Family Psychology, 27,* 96–105. http://dx.doi.org/10.1037/a0031112.
63. Barnhart, S., & Maguire-Jack, K. (2016). Single mothers in their communities: The mediating role of parenting stress and depression between social cohesion, social control and child maltreatment. *Children and Youth Services Review, 70,* 37–45. http://dx.doi.org/10.1016/j.childyouth.2016.09.003. See also Pereira, M., Negrão, M., Soares, I., & Mesman, J. (2015). Predicting harsh discipline in at-risk mothers: The moderating effect of socioeconomic deprivation severity. *Journal of Child and Family Studies, 24,* 725–733. http://dx.doi.org/10.1007/s10826-013-9883-2
64. Several possible causal mechanisms may account for this relationship. See Coulton, C. J., Crampton, D. S., Irwin, M., Spilsbury, J. C., & Korbin, J. E. (2007). How neighborhoods influence child maltreatment: A review of the literature and

alternative pathways. *Child Abuse & Neglect, 31*, 1117–1142. http://dx.doi.org/10.1016/j.chiabu.2007.03.023. See also Freisthler, B., Merritt, D. H., & LaScala, E. A. (2006). Understanding the ecology of child maltreatment: A review of the literature and directions for future research. *Child Maltreatment, 11*, 263–280. http://dx.doi.org/10.1177/1077559506289524; and McLeigh, J. D., McDonell, J. R., Lavenda, O. (2018). Neighborhood poverty and child abuse and neglect: The mediating role of social cohesion. *Children and Youth Services Review, 93*, 154–160. http://dx.doi.org/10.1016/j.childyouth.2018.07.018

65. Gelles, R. J. (1992). Poverty and violence toward children. *American Behavioral Scientist, 35*, 258–274. http://dx.doi.org/10.1177%2F0002764292035003005. See also Scaramella, L. V., Neppl, T. K., Ontai, L. L., & Conger, R. D. (2008). Consequences of socioeconomic disadvantage across three generations: Parenting behavior and child externalizing problems. *Journal of Family Psychology, 22*, 725–733. http://dx.doi.org/10.1037/a0013190
66. Coulton, C. J., Korbin, J. E., Su, M., & Chow, J. (1995). Community level factors and child maltreatment rates. *Child Development, 66*, 1262–1276, p. 1271. http://dx.doi.org/10.2307/1131646
67. Positive parenting is also a buffer against the long-term negative health effects of poverty as well. See, e.g., Miller, G. E., Lachman, M. E., Chen, E., Gruenewald, T. L., Karlamangla, A. S., & Seeman, T. E. (2011). Pathways to resilience: Maternal nurturance as a buffer against the effects of childhood poverty on metabolic syndrome at midlife. *Psychological Science, 22*, 1591–1599. http://dx.doi.org/10.1177/0956797611419170
68. Putnam, R. D. (2015). *Our kids: The American dream in crisis.* New York, NY: Simon & Shuster, p. 130 (footnote omitted).
69. See, e.g., McLoyd, V. C. (1990). The impact of economic hardship on Black families and children: Psychological distress, parenting, and socioeconomic development. *Child Development, 61*, 311–346 (1990). See also Rutter, M., & Giller, H. (1983). *Juvenile delinquency: Trends and perspectives.* New York, NY: Guilford Press. These authors concluded that "Serious socioeconomic disadvantage has an adverse effect on the parents, such that parental disorders and difficulties are more likely to develop and good parenting is impeded" (p. 185).
70. Lempers, J. D., Clark-Lempers, D., & Simons, R. L. (1989). Economic hardship, parenting, and distress in adolescence. *Child Development, 60*, 25–39. http://dx.doi.org/10.2307/1131068
71. Schoon, I., Sacker, A., & Bartley, M. (2003). Socio-economic adversity and psychosocial adjustment: A developmental-contextual perspective. *Social Science & Medicine, 57*, 1001–1015, p. 1012. http://dx.doi.org/10.1016/s0277-9536(02)00475-6. See also Duncan, C. M. (1996). Understanding persistent poverty: Social class context in rural communities. *Rural Sociology, 61*, 103–124. http://dx.doi.org/10.1111/j.1549-0831.1996.tb00612.x; and Wagmiller, R. L., Lennon, M. C., Kuang, L., Alberti, P. M., & Aber, J. L. (2008). The dynamics of economic disadvantage and children's life chances. *American Sociological Review, 71*, 847–866. http://dx.doi.org/10.1177%2F000312240607100507
72. Hart, B., & Risely, T. (1995). *Meaningful differences in the everyday experience of young American children.* Baltimore, MD: Brookes. The study was based on approximately 2.5 years of monthly observations of 42 economically and racially diverse families in Lawrence, Kansas.
73. Hart & Risely (1995), *Meaningful differences*, p. 146. See also Dearing, E. (2008). The psychological costs of growing up poor. *Annals of the New York Academy of Sciences, 1136*, 324–332. http://dx.doi.org/10.1196/annals.1425.006; and Walker, D., Greenwood, C., Hart, B., & Carta, J. (1994). Prediction of school outcomes based on early language production and socioeconomic factors. *Child Development, 65*, 606–621.

74. Clinton, H. R. (1996). *It takes a village, and other lessons children can teach us*. New York, NY: Simon & Schuster. See also Lerner, R., & McKinney, M. (1993). It takes an entire village to raise a child. [Review of the book *Children and families in the social environment*, by J. Garbarino]. *Contemporary Psychology, 38*, 783–784.
75. Lerner & McKinney (1993), It takes an entire village, p. 783.
76. Garbarino, J., & Sherman, D. (1980). High-risk neighborhoods and high-risk families: The human ecology of child maltreatment. *Child Development, 51*, 188–198, p. 198.
77. Elliott, D. S., Wilson, W. J., Huizinga, D., Sampson, R. J., Elliott, A., & Rankin, B. (1996). The effects of neighborhood disadvantage on adolescent development. *Journal of Research in Crime and Delinquency, 33*, 389–426. http://dx.doi.org/10.1177%2F0022427896033004002; and Sampson, R. J. (2012). Neighborhood inequality, violence, and the social infrastructure of the American city. In W. F. Tate, IV (Ed.), *Research on schools, neighborhoods, and communities: Toward civic responsibility* (pp. 11–28). Lanham, MD: Rowman and Littlefield.
78. McLoyd (1990), The impact of economic hardship on Black families and children, p. 318.
79. McLoyd (1990), The impact of economic hardship on Black families and children, p. 318.
80. Sullivan, M. L. (1989). *"Getting paid": Youth crime and work in the inner city*. Ithaca, NY: Cornell University Press.
81. Elliott, Wilson, Huizinga, Sampson, Elliott, & Rankin (1996), The effects of neighborhood disadvantage on adolescent development, p. 394. In addition, poor communities are especially vulnerable to social hazards and natural disasters and many lack the institutional resilience to respond and recover in a timely fashion if and when they do occur. This means that the long-term effects for residents are likely to linger. See Bergstrand, K., Mayer, B., Brumback, B., & Zhang, Y. (2015). Assessing the relationship between social vulnerability and community resilience to hazards. *Social Indicators Research, 122*, 391–409. http://dx.doi.org/10.1007/s11205-014-0698-3
82. Duncan, G. J., & Murnane, R. J. (2014). *Restoring opportunity: The crisis of inequality and the challenge for American education*. Cambridge, MA: Harvard Education Press; Konstantopoulos, S., & Borman, G. (2011) Family background and school effects on student achievement: A multilevel analysis of the Coleman data. *Teachers College Record, 113*, 97–132; and Reardon, S. F. (2011). The widening academic achievement gap between the rich and the poor: New evidence and possible explanations. In G. J. Duncan & R. J. Murnane (Eds.), *Whither opportunity? Rising inequality, schools, and children's life chances* (pp. 91–117). New York, NY: Russell Sage Foundation. http://dx.doi.org/10.4324/9780429499821-33
83. See, e.g., Galster, G., Marcotte, D. E., Mandell, M., Wolman, H., & Augustine, N. (2007). The influence of neighborhood poverty during childhood on fertility, education, and earnings outcomes. *Housing Studies, 22*, 723–751. http://dx.doi.org/10.1080/02673030701474669; and Newcomb, M. D., Abbott, R. D., Catalano, R. F., Hawkins, J. D., Battin-Pearson, S., & Hill, K. (2002). Mediational and deviance theories of late high school failure: Process roles of structural stains, academic competence, and general versus specific problem behavior. *Journal of Counseling Psychology, 49*, 172–186. http://dx.doi.org/10.1037/0022-0167.49.2.172
84. See, e.g., Mazerolle, L., Bennett, S., Antrobus, E., Cardwell, S. M., Eggins, E., & Piquero, A. R. (2018). Disrupting the pathway from truancy to delinquency: A randomized field trial test of the longitudinal impact of a school engagement program. *Journal of Quantitative Criminology*, 1–27. http://dx.doi.org/10.1007/s10940-018-9395-8; Henry, K. L., Knight, K. E., & Thornberry, T. P. (2012). School disengagement as a predictor of dropout, delinquency, and problem substance use during adolescence and early adulthood. *Journal of Youth and Adolescence,*

41, 156–166. http://dx.doi.org/10.1007/s10964-011-9665-3; Rocque, M., Jennings, W. G., Piquero, A. R., Ozkan, T., & Farrington, D. P. (2017). The importance of school attendance: Findings from the Cambridge study in delinquent development on the life-course effects of truancy. *Crime & Delinquency, 63*, 592–612. http://dx.doi.org/10.1177%2F0011128716660520

85. See, e.g., Ladd, H. F. (2012). Education and poverty: Confronting the evidence. *Journal of Policy Analysis and Management, 31*, 203–227. http://dx.doi.org/10.1002/pam.21615; Whipple, S. S., Evans, G. W., Barry, R. L., Maxwell, L. E. (2010). An ecological perspective on cumulative school and neighborhood risk factors related to achievement. *Journal of Applied Developmental Psychology, 31*, 422–427. http://dx.doi.org/10.1016/j.appdev.2010.07.002
86. See, e.g., Jackson, C. K., Johnson, R., & Persico, C. (2016). The effects of school spending on educational and economic outcomes: Evidence from school finance reforms. *The Quarterly Journal of Economics, 131*, 157–218. http://dx.doi.org/10.1093/qje/qjv036
87. See, e.g., Cascio, E. U., & Reber, S. (2013). The poverty gap in school spending following the introduction of Title I. *American Economic Review, 103*, 423–427. http://dx.doi.org/10.1257/aer.103.3.423
88. Jackson, C. K., Johnson, R. C., & Persico, C. (2015). Boosting educational attainment and adult earnings: Does school spending matter after all? *Education Next, 15*, 68–76, p. 70.
89. See Lafortune, J., Rothstein, J., & Schanzenbach, D. W. (2016, February). *School finance reform and the distribution of student achievement* (Working Paper 22011). Cambridge, MA: National Bureau of Economic Research. http://dx.doi.org/10.3386/w22011
90. Saporito, S., & Sohoni, D. (2007). Mapping educational inequality: Concentrations of poverty among poor and minority students in public schools. *Social Forces, 85*, 1227–1253, p. 1246. http://dx.doi.org/10.1353/sof.2007.0055
91. See, e.g., Reardon (2013), The widening income achievement gap, p. 12. Sirin, S. R. (2005). Socioeconomic status and academic achievement: A meta-analytic review of research. *Review of Educational Research, 75*, 417–453. http://dx.doi.org/10.3102%2F00346543075003417
92. See, e.g., Whipple, Evans, Barry, & Maxwell (2010), An ecological perspective on cumulative school and neighborhood risk factors.
93. Ladson-Billings, G. (2017). "Makes me wanna holler": Refuting the "culture of poverty" discourse in urban schooling. *Annals of the American Academy of Political and Social Science, 673*, 80–90, p. 82. http://dx.doi.org/10.1177%2F0002716217718793
94. Fine, M., Burns, A., Payne, Y. A., & Torre, M. E. (2004). Civic lessons: The color and class of betrayal. *Teachers College Record, 106*, 2193–2223. http://dx.doi.org/10.1111/j.1467-9620.2004.00433.x. Fine and her colleagues found that California public schools that were located in predominately poor communities tended to be ones with facilities that were "in desperate disrepair," that employed faculty who were "underqualified and turning over at alarming rates," and were using instructional materials that were "fully inadequate to the task of educating for rigor and democracy" (p. 2195).
95. Fine, Burns, Payne, & Torre (2004), *Civic lessons*, p. 2194.
96. Fass, S., Dinan, K. A., & Aratani, Y. (2009). *Child poverty and intergenerational mobility*. New York, NY: National Center for Children in Poverty.
97. Vanderbilt-Adriance, E., & Shaw, D. S. (2008). Protective factors and the development of resilience in the context of neighborhood disadvantage. *Journal of Abnormal Child Psychology, 36*, 887–901, p. 888. http://dx.doi.org/10.1007%2Fs10802-008-9220-1
98. Giovannoni, J. M. (1971). Parental mistreatment: Perpetrators and victims. *Journal of Marriage and the Family, 33*, 649–657, p. 656. http://dx.doi.org/10.2307/349437

99. Chapter 4 discussed the potential criminogenic impact of punitive public schools, a flawed foster care system, and harsh juvenile institutions. These are places and practices to which poor children are disproportionately, if not exclusively, subjected.
100. Kruttschnitt, C., McLeod, J. D., & Dornfeld, M. (1994). The economic environment of child abuse. *Social Problems, 41,* 299–315, p. 309–310. http://dx.doi.org/10.2307/3096935. They also lived in families "with a generalized history of violence, which in some cases explained their parents' criminal histories" (p. 310).
101. Evans, G. W. (2004). The environment of childhood poverty. *American Psychologist, 59,* 77–92. http://dx.doi.org/10.1037/0003-066X.59.2.77
102. See, e.g., Stouthamer-Loeber, M., Loeber, R., Wei, E., Farrington, D. P., & Wikström, P.-O. H. (2002). Risk and promotive effects in the explanation of persistent serious delinquency in boys. *Journal of Consulting and Clinical Psychology, 70,* 111–123, p. 111. http://dx.doi.org/10.1037//0022-006x.70.1.111. Thus, "The average number of risk effects decreased as the [socioeconomic status] of the neighborhood became higher. With regard to the promotive effects, the average number increased as the neighborhood [socioeconomic status] increased" (p. 121).
103. Kruttschnitt, McLeod, & Dornfeld 1994, The economic environment of child abuse, p. 309–310. See also Day, J., Ji, P., DuBois, D. L., Silverthorn, N., & Flay, B. (2016). Cumulative social-environmental adversity exposure as predictor of psychological distress and risk behavior in urban youth. *Child & Adolescent Social Work Journal, 33,* 219–235. http://dx.doi.org/10.1007/s10560-015-0421-5
104. Kruttschnitt, McLeod, & Dornfeld (1994), The economic environment of child abuse, p. 310.
105. See, e.g., Berkowitz, L. (1989). Frustration-aggression hypothesis: Examination and reformulation. *Psychological Bulletin, 106,* 59–73. http://dx.doi.org/10.1037/0033-2909.106.1.59
106. Studies have looked directly at the relationship between the kind of frustration that comes from perceived disadvantage or deprivation and aggression. See, e.g., Greitemeyer, T., & Sagioglou, C. (2016). Subjective socioeconomic status causes aggression: A test of the theory of social deprivation. *Journal of Personality and Social Psychology, 111,* 178–194. http://dx.doi.org/10.1037/pspi0000058; Greitemeyer, T., & Sagioglou, C. (2017). Increasing wealth inequality may increase interpersonal hostility: The relationship between personal relative deprivation and aggression. *Journal of Social Psychology, 157,* 766–776. http://dx.doi.org/10.1080/00224545.2017.1288078; and Kraus, M. W., Horberg, E. J., Goetz, J. L., & Keltner, D. (2011). Social class rank, threat vigilance, and hostile reactivity. *Personality and Social Psychology Bulletin, 37,* 1376–1388. http://dx.doi.org/10.1177/0146167211410987 See also Barlett, C. P., & Anderson, C. A. (2014). Bad news, bad times, and violence: The link between economic distress and aggression. *Psychology of Violence, 4,* 309–321. http://dx.doi.org/10.1037/a0034479
107. Nettler, G. (1984). *Explaining crime* (3rd ed.). New York, NY: McGraw Hill, p. 229. See also Coccia, M. (2017). A theory of general causes of violent crime: Homicides, income inequality and deficiencies of the heat hypothesis and of the model of CLASH. *Aggression and Violent Behavior, 37,* 190–200. http://dx.doi.org/10.1016/j.avb.2017.10.005
108. See, e.g., Huff-Corzine, L., Corzine, J., & Moore, D. C. (1991). Deadly connections: Culture, poverty, and the direction of lethal violence. *Social Forces, 69,* 715–732; Williams, K. R. (1984). Economic sources of homicide: Reestimating the effects of poverty and inequality. *American Sociological Review, 49,* 283–289. http://dx.doi.org/10.2307/2095577
109. Kost, K. A., & Smyth, N. J. (2002). Two strikes against them? Exploring the influence of a history of poverty and growing up in an alcoholic family on alcohol

problems and income. *Journal of Social Science Research, 28,* 23–52, p. 25. http://dx.doi.org/10.1300/J079v28n04_02

110. For a recent meta-analytic review of studies reporting this relationship, see Halpern, S. C., Schuch, F. B., Scherer, N. J., Sordi, A. O., Pachado, M, Dalbosco, C., . . . Von Diemen, L. (2018). Child maltreatment and illicit substance abuse: A systematic review and meta-analysis of longitudinal studies. *Child Abuse Review, 27,* 344–360. http://dx.doi.org/10.1002/car.2534
111. Sampson, R. J., & Laub, J. H. (1993). *Crime in the making: Pathways and turning points through life.* Cambridge, MA: Harvard University Press, p. 27. http://dx.doi.org/10.1177/0011128793039003010. The Gluecks' own interpretation of their data was problematic. As Sampson and Laub noted, "[o]n most accounts, the Gluecks simply viewed delinquents and their families as inferior" (p. 43). Among the problematic proposals that followed from this view, the Gluecks aspired to create a system whereby authorities could identify "potential delinquents at school age, perhaps even as early as age 2 or 3" to provide therapeutic intervention that would prevent subsequent criminal behavior (p. 44).
112. Some of that complexity is captured in opinion writer Nicholas Kristof's observation that

> [D]isadvantage is less about income than environment. The best metrics of child poverty aren't monetary, but rather how often a child is read to or hugged. Or, conversely, how often a child is beaten, how often the home descends into alcohol-fueled fistfights, whether there is lead poisoning, whether ear infections go untreated. That's a poverty that is far harder to escape. Some think success is all about "choices" and "personal responsibility." Yes, these are real, but it's so much more complicated than that.

Kristof, N. (2015, August 9). U.S.A., land of limitations? Biggest factor for success isn't hard work but how our lives started. *The New York Times,* Sunday Review, p. 9.

113. Ross, T. (1991). The rhetoric of poverty: Their immorality, our helplessness. *Georgetown Law Journal, 79,* 1449–1547, p. 1543. See also Anderson, E. (1999). *Code of the streets: Decency, violence, and the moral life of the inner city.* New York, NY: Norton; Dohan, D. (2003). *The price of poverty: Money, work, and culture in the Mexican-American barrio.* Berkeley: University of California Press; and Newman, K. S. (1999). *No shame in my game: The working poor in the inner city.* New York, NY: Knopf/Russell Sage.
114. Ross (1991), The rhetoric of poverty, p. 1543.
115. For extended discussions of some of the nuance and complexity in the processes by which this occurs, compare Lareau, A. (2003). *Unequal childhoods: Class, race, and family life.* Berkeley: University of California Press, and Willis, P. (1977). *Learning to labor: How working class kids get working class jobs.* New York, NY: Columbia University Press.
116. Pellow (2016), Toward critical environmental justice studies, p. 224.

7

The Criminogenics of Race in a Divided Society

Racialized Criminality and Biographical Racism

It may be impossible to overstate the significance of race in defining the basic structure of American society.

—MICHELLE ALEXANDER[1]

By virtually every measure of social and economic well-being, African Americans are significantly disadvantaged compared with their White counterparts. They suffer widespread and significant health disparities compared with Whites,[2] the gap in median income between Black and White men has returned to 1950 levels,[3] Blacks are much more likely to be victimized by crime (including homicide),[4] are nearly 4 times more likely than Whites to experience homelessness in their lifetimes,[5] and there are pervasive differences between Black and White children on a host of indices of overall "well-being."[6] These persistent and pervasive differences in life circumstances add up over a life course and, in any individual social history, amount to what I have previously termed "biographical racism."[7] It is the accumulation of race-based social and economic obstacles, indignities, and disadvantages, experienced across an entire lifetime, significantly influencing the social histories of persons of Color in American society.

The social, institutional, and economic differentials that biographical racism creates translate into heightened exposure to criminogenic risks and traumas. W. E. B. DuBois wrote more than a century ago about the injuries of racial mistreatment and their effects on criminal behavior. He observed that

http://dx.doi.org/10.1037/0000172-008
Criminality in Context: The Psychological Foundations of Criminal Justice Reform, by C. Haney

"[t]he connection of crime and prejudice is neither simple or direct. . . . The connections are more subtle and dangerous; it is the atmosphere of rebellion and discontent that unrewarded merit and reasonable but unsatisfied ambition make."[8] In fact, alleged or actual racial differences in crime rates reflect differences in exposure to societally-imposed criminogenic conditions as well as racially discriminatory treatment at the hands of the nation's institutions of justice.

To be sure, the nature of our still racially divided society virtually ensures these outcomes. In the clearest possible example, if poverty is a gateway criminogenic risk factor, and I have argued at length in Chapter 6 that it is, then the race-based structural poverty that has persisted almost unabated in the United States from the emancipation of African Americans to the present day plays a central role in their over-representation in the criminal justice system.

Social psychologist Colin Leach has highlighted an important psychological nexus at the core of racist regimes, even—perhaps especially—ones such as ours that claim to have achieved formal legal equality (e.g., "equal protection"). In such regimes, he wrote, it is imperative that the "ascription of inferior intelligence, effort, culture or morality suggests that the ethnic group should be treated less well than one's own."[9] The stereotype of the moral inferiority of certain racial groups has been fiercely preached in our society and relative inequality of treatment manifested with a vengeance in our nation's criminal justice system.

THE PSEUDOSCIENTIFIC MERGING OF RACE AND CRIME

Racism played a critically important role in the historical development of the American criminal justice system. The 19th-century pseudoscientific doctrines that I referred to in Chapter 1 as "embodied individualism"—the widely accepted theories that located the causes of criminal behavior entirely inside the physical make-up of its perpetrators—all had distinctly racist components to them. Just as the individualistic crime master narrative still dominates thinking about crime and punishment in the United States, the legacies of these long-discredited racist views about the nature of criminality also persist.

The first of these embodied individualistic theories, craniometry, was a framework that, as I noted, had dominated the discipline of anthropology during the 19th century.[10] It was also "an essentially racist or ethnocentric enterprise"[11] that helped to racialize American society's understanding of the nature of criminality. In addition to supposedly providing insights into individual-level traits and characteristics, craniometric measurements of skull size and shape were used to classify racial groups into a hierarchy of value, merit, and worth.[12]

Racist ideologues, such as Madison Grant, used the "doctrine of the skull" to argue both that certain individuals and even whole groups of people were innately inferior as well as innately immoral.[13] Published in 1916, Grant's unapologetically racist tract, *The Passing of the Great Race,* received a warm reception from members of the public and from scholarly reviewers and numerous legislators alike, who used it as one of the "scientific" bases for restrictive immigration laws. The enthusiasm with which it was greeted reflected the degree to which biologically based racism and doctrines of racial exclusiveness were widely and openly accepted in American society well into the 20th century.[14]

Similarly, like craniometry before it, phrenology also had a distinctly racist component. It is difficult to overestimate "how thoroughly phrenology was embedded in American culture and society" for much of the 19th century and how deeply implanted its biologically based racist assumptions became.[15] Phrenologists held "an essentialist view of humanity in which racial differences were immutable and racial hierarchies were clear."[16] The alleged inferiority of Blacks was thought to include their moral as well as intellectual "desolation."[17]

Eugenics eventually supplanted both craniometry and phrenology and was far more influential, becoming the basis for a full-fledged social and political movement. Of course, eugenics was foremost a theoretical framework, holding that everyone's essential human traits and capacities were rooted in their genetic makeup. But eugenicists also contended that genetically determined traits and capacities were unevenly distributed between different racial and ethnic groups. They arranged these separate groups into an overall hierarchy of merit or worth on the basis of their supposed collective genetic endowment, with Nordic Whites at the top. As a racist sociopolitical policy, eugenic assertions about the relative inferiority of certain groups and individuals were translated into a host of draconian laws and policies designed to enhance racial purity and address a wide range of supposedly genetically determined social problems (such as crime). Allegedly biologically and genetically "defective" persons and groups were not only scorned as inferior beings but actually targeted for extinction by, among other things, restricting or prohibiting their immigration and procreation.

The eugenics belief that individual characteristics, such as intellectual capacity and criminality, were genetically determined *and* that they were directly related to race was openly and widely embraced, including by many prominent and otherwise respectable politicians. Victoria Nourse noted that even the "great progressive" president Theodore Roosevelt was a eugenics enthusiast who warned that "the failure of the better classes to breed at the same rate as their inferiors" could lead to "race death."[18] Eugenicists advocated that societies could only improve themselves by enhancing their genetic "purity" and purging themselves of their most defective members, primarily through selective breeding and sterilization. These ideas had a profound influence on the operation of the late 19th and early 20th century criminal justice system. In addition to the sterilization of persons deemed genetically "unfit" and "degenerate," eugenics was used as the basis for broadening the reach of the criminal justice system itself.

For example, historian Miroslava Chavez-Garcia examined the role that eugenics played in the origins and rapid growth of California's vast network of juvenile justice institutions in the late 19th and early 20th century. As she showed, eugenics provided the supposed "scientific" inspiration and justification for "the process through which troublesome and otherwise unwanted youths were sorted, classified, and transferred among juvenile justice institutions across the state."[19] Well into the early decades of the 20th century, California employed an army of "eugenics fieldworkers" who combed the state, administering "abbreviated intelligence tests" and constructing "pedigree charts" that supposedly traced the "biological influence of inherited dysgenic traits"—such as "feeblemindedness," "sexual immorality," and "excitability"—through several generations in order "to prove the researchers' scientific contentions about the connection among heredity, intelligence, delinquency, and, ultimately, race."[20] Although large numbers of poor whites were also subjected to the same techniques and classified accordingly, in practice, as Chavez-Garcia documented, "wayward youth of color" were "more likely to be criminalized, racialized, and pathologized as deviant and defective boys in need of further institutionalization and, ultimately, sterilization."[21]

The fourth pseudoscientific theory of embodied individualism that I discussed in Chapter 1, instinct theory, was also used to convey a pernicious racist message in the 19th and early 20th centuries. The professional prominence of its main advocate, William McDougall, who was described in the 1920s as having "made in total as great a contribution to the science as any living psychologist"[22] and in historical accounts as one of "titans in psychology,"[23] underscored the widespread acceptance of his views. In fact, McDougall asserted that instincts were not only the "primary innate tendencies" that governed people's behavior, but also that they served as the basis of relative strengths in the "native constitutions" of individuals of different races. He used this supposed hierarchy of native constitutions to make incendiary claims about the "racial stocks" of different nations and voice the alarmist warning that "the reproduction of the inferior classes" threatened the very existence of democracy, which he viewed as a weak and ill-conceived form of government. McDougall warned that "the civilization of America is doomed" unless it effectively dealt with its "most immediately urgent evil, the high birth-rate of the admittedly and grossly unfit," which he though must be accomplished through a combination of "sterilization and institutional segregation."[24]

All four pseudoscientific theories shared a basic core consistency with respect to crime, namely, that the tendency to engage in criminal behavior was an embodied trait that was more prevalent among disfavored racial groups. For example, one especially prominent commentator was Oliver Wendell Holmes, Sr. His son, as I noted in Chapter 1, was influential U.S. Supreme Court Justice Oliver Wendell Holmes, Jr., author of the infamous *Buck v. Bell* opinion that authorized sterilization in order to limit future generations of "defectives." Holmes Sr. was himself an enthusiastic proponent of eugenics who subscribed wholeheartedly to its racialized view of criminal behavior. Thus, Holmes Sr.

thought that serious criminality was perpetrated by persons who were born with a "villainous low forehead and poisoned instincts, and bred among creatures of the Races Maudites [cursed races] whose natural history has to be studied like that of beasts of prey and vermin."[25]

The racist origins and implications of these prominent theories and their simultaneous application to understanding crime and criminals were woven together to effectively establish the unshakable belief that the causes of crime resided inside the defectiveness of the individuals who engaged in it. They were also woven into the equally ardently held view that those defects were disproportionately possessed by certain disfavored and genetically inferior groups, primarily African Americans. For example, in his meticulous historical analysis of the "inseparable linking of the two social categories of race and crime" during the 19th and early 20th centuries,[26] Khalil Gibran Muhammad focused on a fundamental difference in the way that high rates of crime and incarceration among white immigrants and African Americans were explained and responded to. Although many recently arrived European immigrant groups were initially demonized and criminally stereotyped during this era, their eventual assimilation into the larger White society led to a greater willingness to explain their criminality in terms that acknowledged their economic woes. In contrast, Black criminality continued to be attributed almost exclusively to the inherent "nature" of the perpetrators.[27] In fact, instead of using the known criminogenic effects of poverty to explain Black criminality, as was increasingly done with immigrant Whites, the prevalence of alleged criminal traits among Blacks was turned on its head and used to explain their poverty.[28]

In this way, the supposed inherent characteristics of African Americans were thought to doom them to inferiority and to predispose them to badness. Unfortunately, contemporary examples of these implicit beliefs in operation are too numerous to comprehensively catalogue. Indeed, Michelle Alexander has argued persuasively that "today mass incarceration defines the meaning of blackness in America: black people, especially black men, are criminals."[29] They range from the animalistic nature of the depictions of African American perpetrators of crime,[30] to the ease with which incendiary racists claims are made in response to high profile crimes alleging African American involvement,[31] to one of the nation's most prominent criminologists, James Q. Wilson, asserting that there are racial differences in the propensity to commit crime.[32]

There are repeated examples of this in the media but perhaps none so dramatic as the coverage of the so-called Central Park Five case in which, in 1989, an accused group of African American teenagers was depicted in animalistic terms in the press, which described them as a "wolf pack" and coined the term "wilding" to describe their alleged behavior. Among other extreme and dehumanizing statements made about them, political commentator and one-time presidential candidate Patrick Buchanan referred to the boys as "savages" and advocated that one of them be publicly hanged in Central Park, in the manner of a lynching.[33] That same year, at the height of the subsequently debunked "crack baby scare," syndicated *Washington Post* conservative opinion writer Charles Krauthammer wrote a widely distributed article that began with the assertion that Black women were giving birth to a "bio-underclass" whose "biological inferiority is stamped at birth." In a variation of a long-standing eugenics theme, Krauthammer warned that the babies' "permanent inferiority" would doom them to "a menial life of severe deprivation" and their allegedly increasing numbers would "become a threat to communal life as a whole."[34] But Krauthammer was not alone in perpetrating these biologically based invidious, frightening, and ultimately invalid claims, as a recent *New York Times* editorial mea culpa admitted.[35]

Jennifer Eberhardt and her colleagues have demonstrated the depth and breadth of the ways in which this pernicious mindset continues to operate. They conducted a series of experiments in which they showed, among other things, that there is a deep-seated implicit association of Blacks with criminality;[36] that Black children appear to be seen as more inherently culpable than Whites (and therefore more appropriately judged and punished as adults)[37]; that Blacks are more likely to be perceived as innately less human and more capable of committing violent crime compared with Whites[38]; and that the degree to which someone's facial characteristics appear "stereotypically Black" actually influences the likelihood that persons are willing to condemn them to death.[39]

The 19th-century pseudoscientific assertions about African Americans have thus become so deeply embedded in our society as to function, not just as a passing stereotype but, as a kind of durable cultural archetype, one that "naturally" associates racial characteristics with criminality. Unfortunately, no matter how flawed, fallacious, and pernicious, the belief and the archetype have managed to persist into modern times. Residues of these badly flawed, racist theories of crime remain implanted in contemporary mindsets in the form of strongly held albeit implicit beliefs about the supposed predispositions of African Americans to engage in criminal behavior. It is difficult to imagine a more hurtful and potentially harmful legacy with which to grapple.

STRUCTURAL RACISM: POVERTY, RACE, AND CRIME

Race and poverty remain inextricably bound in the United States.[40] African American children, particularly, are more likely to live under conditions of *chronic* poverty. For example, between 1970 and the mid-1980s, during the first decade and a half of the period in which policies of mass incarceration drastically increased the numbers of persons confined inside the nation's prisons, the poverty rate among Black children actually rose from 42.5% to 45.1%.[41] Although poverty rates have declined overall since then, racial and ethnic differentials remain. For example, in 2000 approximately 33% of African American children lived at or below the poverty line, as did 27.2% of Latino children (compared with 9.3% for Whites).[42]

More recently, 2014 reporting on poverty levels for families (rather than children-only), indicated that 25.5% of Black and 22.8% of Latino families lived in poverty (compared with 9.9% of White families).[43] Patrick Sharkey showed that minorities are not only "stuck in place" but tend to be stuck in poor places from which they cannot easily extricate themselves. Thus, he found that young African Americans (between the ages of 13 and 28) were 10 times more likely to live in poor neighborhoods than young Whites, but also, in a pattern he termed "the intergenerational transmission of context" (specifically, the context of poverty), that two thirds of African American families who lived in the poorest quarter of neighborhoods a generation ago continued to live there.[44] In light of the powerful criminogenic effects of economic and neighborhood disadvantage, these facts alone go a long way toward explaining the overrepresentation of persons of Color in the juvenile and adult criminal justice systems.

In fact, African American poverty and income inequality is so intractable in the United States that it even affects those who begin at the highest income levels. Researchers at the National Bureau of Economic Research have shown that even among the comparatively few African American men born to relatively wealthy families, few are can escape the racial pull of economic inequality.[45] Although income distributions tend to improve somewhat for Latinos across generations, they do not for African Americans and Native Americans. The large, persistent differences in wages and employment status that exist between Black and White men cannot be explained by differences in any of a host of family characteristics (such as parental marital status, education, and wealth). Even for Black and White boys who grew up in the same neighborhoods, "black boys have lower incomes in adulthood than white boys in 99% of Census tracks."[46]

On the other hand, the researchers did find that the nature of the communities in which the children were raised helped alleviate racial disparities. That is, although the race-based economic differentials were greater in low poverty neighborhoods, both Black and White boys who were raised in communities with lower levels of race bias and higher rates of father presence tended to fare better as adults. Young Blacks who moved to better areas (low poverty rates, less racism, greater father presence) had significantly better long-term income outcomes. The authors of this study concluded that "environmental conditions have causal effects on racial disparities," and that the Black–White income gap can be reduced by improving those conditions. Unfortunately, they also noted that fewer than 5% of black children actually "grow up in environments that foster upward mobility."[47]

Even a college degree, long touted as a "great equalizer" that levelled the economic playing field in a way that would enable lower income students to obtain higher wages and eventually increase their accumulated wealth, does not have the same effect for graduates of Color as it does for White graduates. For example, describing a "shockingly clear" pattern, William Emmons and Bryan Noeth found that "White and Asian college grads do much better than their counterparts without college, while college-grad Hispanics and blacks do much worse proportionately."[48] Of course, Blacks and Latinos who attend college are better off than those who do not, but the effect is not remotely as large for them as it is for Whites or Asians, meaning that the economic incentive for them to attend and graduate from college is not remotely the same, especially when the high levels of college-related debt that many face upon graduation is taken into account. In fact, as Emmons and Noeth put it, "borrowing too much to get a piece of the American dream often undermines any hope of sustaining it."[49] Because students of Color typically have fewer family resources at their disposal with which to help finance their education to begin with, this pattern is particularly problematic for them.

There is another important dimension to the structural poverty to which racial and ethnic minorities are subjected in American society. Although official de jure housing segregation supposedly ended in the United States by the 1960s, de facto segregation has continued and, in some ways, intensified since then. Richard Rothstein's historical analysis of housing laws explains why. He demonstrated that "until the last quarter of the twentieth century, racially explicit policies of federal, state, and local governments defined where whites and African Americans could live."[50] Far from reflecting "free choice" (e.g., that "Black families prefer to live with each other") or personal shortcomings (e.g., that Blacks "lack the wherewithal to move to better neighborhoods"), housing segregation was instead "public policy that explicitly segregated every metropolitan area in the United States." The policy was "so systematic and forceful that its effects endure to the present time."[51]

The resulting patterns of housing segregation have been manifested in numerous parts of the country, in what historian Matthew Lassiter termed "spatial apartheid." To take just one example of how it operated in one geographical area, in the metropolitan New Orleans area from the 1930s through the 1980s, twice as many federally backed homeowner loans went to suburbanites as went to residents of Orleans Parish (where the residents were primarily persons of Color). African Americans complained that retail services, such as restaurants and corner groceries, were drained out of their neighborhoods as the large number of White residents departed. They argued that racism was the primary motivation for White flight as well as the differential pattern of federal funding. Lassiter concluded that the resulting demographic shift in New Orleans and other U.S. cities led to the ascendance of a politically potent White suburban population, whose ostensibly color-blind, individualist rhetoric defending suburbanization actually masked a form of post-Jim Crow spatial apartheid that was based on class and race.[52]

These forces have operated in tandem to keep many African Americans mired in poverty, living in what Lauren Krivo and Dana Peterson have identified as the kind of "extremely disadvantaged neighborhoods" where violence is more likely.[53] It has ensured their continuing residential segregation, which "is associated with more crime as well as a variety of other social problems for disadvantaged nonwhite communities."[54]

RACIAL DISCRIMINATION AS MACRO- AND MICROAGGRESSION

There are a number of widespread, painful, and potentially criminogenic forms of racial oppression to which persons of Color are subjected at an interpersonal level in American society. As Carl Nightingale noted, notwithstanding the progress made since the 1960s in quelling overt expressions of racism in this society, significant numbers of African American and Latino children "still encounter expressions of racial hatred, live in racially segregated neighborhoods, and endure the suspicion widespread among many people in positions of authority."[55] This, too, represents a form of abuse that, as I will detail, exacerbates other kinds of maltreatment and may have long-term criminogenic effects.

The direct experience of racism and racial discrimination is itself a powerful primary risk factor that jeopardizes the long-term well-being of persons subjected to it. On a structural or macro level, it operates to socially, economically, and politically marginalize persons of Color, limiting the places where they can live, their access to high quality education and employment, and their level of civic engagement. It also has a psychological component. Not surprisingly, numerous studies have shown that racial stigma and being subjected to expressions of racial prejudice are pernicious and potentially damaging.

In fact, the negative impact of what have been termed racial "microaggressions" has been increasingly recognized in the psychological literature.[56] Microaggressions consist of the "everyday slights, insults, putdowns, invalidations, and offensive behaviors that people of color experience in daily interactions."[57] Although they are sometimes discounted as minor, and even dismissed as little more oversensitivity on the part of persons who complain about them,[58] microaggressions can be profoundly hurtful and harmful. Indeed, when microaggressions accumulate over time, they may amount to a form of racial trauma that has significant negative consequences, including adversely affecting cognitive functioning and a person's overall mental and physical health.[59]

Beyond the accumulation of day-to-day microaggressions, the experience of racial discrimination more broadly—"unfair, differential treatment on the basis of race"[60]—is psychologically painful and can have a number of potentially long-term negative consequences. In addition to undermining physical health,[61] the experience of racism leads to heightened levels of psychological distress,[62] depression and anxiety,[63] and negative mood and lowered self-esteem.[64] It is so hurtful and potentially harmful that it is identified as a risk factor for mental illness.[65] Indeed, mental health professionals regard racial discrimination as a form of "traumatic stress"[66]—even as a form of violence[67]—that can undermine behavioral adjustment in a wide range of settings.[68] It also can lead to an increased likelihood of delinquent and criminal behavior.[69]

RACE AND MALTREATMENT

We know that "Black children suffer disproportionately from virtually every form of stress affecting full and healthy development."[70] The early stages of the biographical racism to which they are exposed includes the fact "[t]oo many black children live in conditions of poverty that deprive them of necessary medical care, adequate housing, food, and clothing."[71] In some instances, these structurally imposed forms of deprivation can also translate into somewhat higher rates of child maltreatment.[72]

For example, the National Incidence Study of Child Abuse and Neglect (NIS) compiles and maintains a federally funded database on national rates of child maltreatment. There have been four such NIS surveys, conducted in 1980, 1986, 1993, and 2005–2006. The research has produced one consistent finding over the years: "Throughout its history, the NIS has consistently demonstrated that socioeconomic factors are strongly predictive of child maltreatment."[73] Although each of the NIS estimates have provided valuable national data on the extent of child maltreatment, the last survey yielded an unprecedented finding. For the first time, the maltreatment rates for Black children significantly differed from those of Whites. Specifically: "Black children experienced a significantly higher rate of physical abuse, overall abuse, and overall maltreatment."[74] The NIS researchers offered two explanations for the new finding—first, that significant improvements in the overall design of the study (especially a larger sample and better measures) had yielded more precise and comprehensive results and, second, that the deteriorating economic circumstances of Black families had subjected them to more of the pressures and influences that help produce maltreatment.

The latter explanation was buttressed by the most recent NIS data that revealed significant differences in income levels for the families of the children who were studied. Nearly half of Black children (45.9%) in the study lived in "low socioeconomic status" families, as compared to little more than one in seven White children (15%). The households of fully a third of Black children (32.6%) participated in some kind of poverty program, whereas fewer than one in ten (8.2%) of White children's did.[75] Moreover, although household income increased for all racial groups between 1993 and 2006 (the two most recent NIS assessments), "improvements in household incomes for White children far outpaced those of the Black children."[76] In fact, the authors of the study speculated that it was likely that the measure of socioeconomic status used may have systematically underestimated the income differentials of Black and White children at each level so that, for example, Black children were actually worse off economically than was reflected in the category to which they were assigned in the study. This led them to argue that the fact that Black children in households at higher socioeconomic levels were still at greater risk of maltreatment was "because they are poorer than the White children in these households."[77]

Here, too, the explanation for these differentials is rooted in the structural disadvantage that families of Color confront, which persist in part as a result of proactive policies and practices designed to maintain them and in part because of the lack of government-sponsored programs and support in many poor minority communities aimed at alleviating them. As Robert Crutchfield noted: "Blaming parents who were themselves the victims of our collective failures one generation earlier does nothing to break the cycle. With joblessness and labor market marginality, we set the stage for social and economic disadvantage."[78] Thus, the potential criminogenic consequences are best addressed by attacking the structural racism that produces them.

THE SOCIAL HISTORICAL IMPACT OF INSTITUTIONAL RACISM

The kind of neglectful and abusive institutional treatment and trauma that I discussed in Chapter 4 is imposed more often on minority children, whose lives are more often touched and redirected by forceful state intervention.[79] Thus, the data suggest that African American children, especially, are more often drawn into the so-called child welfare system in the United States and subjected to its often harsh and potentially criminogenic influences. At the turn of the 21st century, Dorothy Roberts reported that although African American children constituted 17% of the nation's children, they represented 42% of all children in foster care in the United States.[80] In some communities the disparities were even more dramatic. For example, African American children constituted 95% of all of the children in foster care in city of Chicago.[81] Moreover, once they were in the system, Roberts noted that African American children were less likely to receive in-home services, less likely to receive mental health services, and more likely to be institutionalized for their emotional problems.[82]

Roberts concluded that these disparities could be explained in large part by the way that the child welfare system operates to reinforce stereotypes about the "unfitness" of Black families and need for them to be supervised by Whites. As a consequence, family autonomy and self-determination among Black Americans is undermined, and their ability to collectively overcome broader forms of "institutionalized discrimination" is neutralized.[83] Roberts argued further that the child welfare system tended to confuse parenting problems that stemmed primarily from poverty with ones that were the product of parental malice or incompetence. Instead of addressing poverty and assisting parents in overcoming it, the system focused on—and often responded punitively to—the outward manifestations of having been exposed to poverty. What is defined by child welfare agencies as inadequate and neglectful parenting often reflects a class-biased lack of understanding about the ways in which poor parents are forced to manage a wide range of daunting day-to-day economic challenges and contingencies. Rather than addressing the underlying problem by providing direct services designed to cushion the effects of poverty, the child welfare system responds with "state intervention [that] is punitive in nature."[84]

There are other patterns and processes at work that help to funnel African American children into harsh institutional settings. Remarkably, differential treatment of African American children in the public school system begins in *preschool*. Thus, the Office of Civil Rights reported that although Black children represented 18% of children enrolled in preschool, they accounted for nearly half (48%) of the preschoolers who received "more than one out-of-school suspension." Overall, Black students are suspended at a rate 3 times that of Whites, and although they constitute 16% of student enrollment, they make up 27% of students referred to law enforcement and 31% of students subjected to a school-related arrest.[85]

Access to secondary public education is in theory intended to serve as a potential pathway out of poverty and into better opportunities in the labor market. For structurally disadvantaged minority youth, however, it often fails to achieve this goal. Some of the failures of public education for these groups take the form of "benign neglect"—simply ignoring their educational and other needs. Yet there is often a harder edge to the treatment they receive in later grades. For example, Jesmyn Ward described the way the young African American men with whom she grew up in her small Mississippi hometown were eventually treated:

> Years later that benign neglect would turn malignant and would involve illegal strip searches of middle schoolers accused of drug dealing, typing these same students as troublemakers, laying a thick paper trail of imagined or real discipline offenses, and once the paper trail grew thick enough, kicking out the students who endangered the blue-ribbon rating with lackluster grades and test scores.[86]

As I noted in Chapter 4, there is a process at work in some school systems that is even more sinister than the one Ward observed in her rural community—a "school-to-prison pipeline" that serves to effectively channel some students into the juvenile and eventually adult criminal justice system.[87] Young students of Color are at greater risk of being put in this pipeline. The increased risks occur in a number of ways, including being "sent to the office" more often than other students, even when their behavior, the nature of the schools they attend, and other variables are controlled for.[88] Minority students are also singled out disproportionately for school discipline in response to nebulous, low-level infractions (e.g., "excessive noise," "disrespect"). This often represents a first step in a process that can escalate into higher rates of school suspension that are, in turn, related to court referrals. The differentials are large—one study found that, even after controlling for socioeconomic differences, African American children in middle school were more than twice as likely to be sent to the principal's office or suspended, and 4 times as likely to be expelled than their White counterparts.[89] As Lizbet Simmons put it, "the punitive dynamics that influence the early educational experience of African American youths lead to youth exclusion, alienation, and invisibility and help generate correctional trajectories."[90]

As a *New York Times* editorial decrying harsh school discipline practices noted, concern over juvenile and school crime in the 1980s led to a number of changes in public schools that "tighten[ed] disciplinary policies and increase[ed] the number of police patrolling the schools," producing a "repressive environment in which young people are suspended, expelled, or even arrested over minor misbehaviors."[91] This "criminalizing" of routine school disciplinary problems entangled many children, "sometimes permanently, in the criminal justice system."[92] But a 2013 study of New York City public schools showed that the "entanglements" were not evenly distributed across races; the school-to-prison pipeline operated to capture far more children of Color than others. Thus, Black students in New York were 4 times more likely to be suspended than White students, and Hispanic students were twice as likely. When it came to the more drastic step of actually arresting students, the racial disproportion was much more dramatic: Blacks students were 14 times and Hispanic students 5 times more likely to be arrested for school-based incidents than their White peers.[93] The disproportions were not due to "higher rates of misbehavior." Instead: "[T]here appeared to be a differential pattern of treatment, originating at the classroom level, wherein African American students are referred to the office for infractions that are more subjective in interpretation."[94]

To help explain these racial differences more generally, Ann Ferguson has theorized about various ways that public schools help to construct "bad boys" out of young African American male students.[95] For example, differences in "manners, style, body language, and oral expressiveness" subtly but systematically appear to influence the way in which teachers apply school rules and label African American students, ultimately placing them "at the bottom rung of the social order."[96] Of course, the process of characterizing student behavior and disciplining those who misbehave is a natural part of the socialization process for students of all races. However, when students of Color are singled out for discipline, they are likely to be stigmatized and, in turn, often alienated from the people and places that treat them this way. Moreover, "[i]n the case of African American boys, misbehavior is likely to be interpreted as symptomatic of ominous criminal proclivities"[97] and the long-term consequences of such characterizations may "substantially increase one's chance of ending up in jail."[98]

In addition, there is evidence of racial inequality in the assignment of African American children to special education classes. Nationwide statistics indicate that they are 3 times more likely to be labeled with an intellectual disability and twice as likely to be labeled emotionally disturbed as their White counterparts.[99] Moreover, once they have been diagnosed as suffering from intellectual disability, they are more likely than White students to be separated from mainstream classrooms, and relegated to underfunded and poorly implemented programs that provide them with marginal educational experiences and minimal employment skills. The long-term effects of this practice contribute to higher rates of unemployment and, correspondingly, a greater risk of incarceration among young African American adults.[100]

Students of Color are also much more likely to be identified as members of gangs, and subject to heightened scrutiny by the police and differential treatment in the juvenile justice system. The social processes by which their overrepresentation in gang databases occurs is at least in part a function of the neighborhoods in which many students of Color live as well as racial and ethnic stereotyping among school and law enforcement officials. As one commentator noted, gangs are often located in socially and economically disadvantaged urban centers where there are concentrations of minority youth.[101] Whether or not they are actual "members" of the gang,

> young persons living in a neighborhood under the control of a particular gang will likely be associated with that gang, and many of their acquaintances and neighbors, and even friends, will be members of the local gang. People with childhood friends or acquaintances who later became gang members may cause them to be mistaken as gang members themselves. They may even dress like their gang member neighbors, even if they themselves are not gang members.[102]

Despite the questionable reliability of the gang labels that are applied in the creation of the gang databases, they have severe consequences for the young people to whom they are attached, including significantly harsher criminal justice system treatment (such gang enhancements at the time of sentencing). Law enforcement casts an especially wide net in its effort to identify actual or potential gang members and it can ensnare a large number of young people of Color. In California, for example, the state law enforcement database on gang membership—the so-called CalGang Database—in 2000 contained a list of some 250,000 alleged gang members, 90% of whom were Latino or African American.[103]

DISPROPORTIONATE MINORITY CONFINEMENT

As Judith Cox and James Bell noted, "[t]he juvenile justice system is full of implicit messages legitimizing the notion that youth of color are beyond rehabilitation, thereby making it permissible to warehouse them in conditions of confinement that are often overcrowded and dangerous."[104] Minority overrepresentation in the juvenile justice system was identified decades ago, and has been widely acknowledged—even taken for granted—in the intervening years. Indeed, it has been given its own acronym—"DMC" (for "disproportionate minority confinement"). Historically, the racially disproportionate chances of being incarcerated and disparities in the length of incarceration have been substantial.[105] In fact, minority youth represent the majority of children held in juvenile facilities—a long-standing pattern that has been well-documented nationwide since at least the 1990s.

In 1992, an amendment to the Juvenile Justice and Delinquency Prevention Act of 1974 required states that were receiving funding under the Juvenile Justice and Delinquency Prevention Act to analyze the extent of DMC in their respective juvenile justice systems. As a result of being more carefully studied and regularly reported on throughout 1990s, the full extent of the problem became increasingly apparent. For example, a nationwide study done in the mid-1990s showed that the proportion of incarcerated minority youth exceeded their percentage in the general population in every state but one—Vermont. The disparities in the other states were sizable, with the proportion incarcerated averaging about 280% more than their proportion in the population.[106]

A federally mandated assessment of the quality of conditions and nature of care in juvenile justice facilities across the country published in the mid-1990s found that the rapid expansion of the size of the juvenile justice system was due in part to disproportionate increases in the incarceration of minority youth: between 1987 and 1991, as their percentages in juvenile correctional facilities grew from 53% to 63%.[107] In addition to a high percentage of minority children in juvenile institutions, the researchers found that, in the sample of the nearly 100 facilities that they inspected, approximately 73% of the children had reported mental health problems during their intake screening, and 57% reported that they had received treatment for mental health problems *prior* to their incarceration.[108] However, there was no evidence that these increasingly overcrowded and perennially underfunded facilities were able to address such extremely high levels of mental health needs among the children in their custody.

The disproportionate incarceration of minority youth continued throughout the decade of the 1990s. Although they comprised 34% of the U.S. population in 1997, they represented 62% of children who were incarcerated that year. African American children with no prior admissions to the juvenile justice system were 6 times more likely to be incarcerated in a public facility than White children with the same background who were charged with the same offense. If the African American children had one or two prior admissions, then they were 7 times more likely to be incarcerated than Whites with the same background. Moreover, African American youth who were held in custody remained an average of 61 days longer than Whites. And the disparity in length of confinement was particularly pronounced for drug offenses, for which African American juveniles were confined an average of 90 days longer than their White counterparts.[109]

Because much past juvenile justice agency-level reporting failed to distinguish "Latino" juveniles from others, many previous statistical comparisons focused primarily on African Americans versus Whites.[110] But what is known about the differential treatment of Latino youth by the juvenile justice system is not encouraging. For example, data collected in the late 1990s indicated that Latino children were overrepresented in juvenile detention centers in some 39 states.[111] On the basis of 1997 data,

Latino children with no prior admissions to the juvenile justice system were 3 times more likely to be incarcerated in a public facility than White children with the same background. Those who had been committed one or two times before were twice as likely to be incarcerated as White children with the same background histories. Latino children also tended to be held in custody an average of 112 days longer than White children. In the case of drug offenses, Latino youth tended stay in custody more than twice as long as their White counterparts (306 days vs. 144 days).[112]

Although in-depth research on DMC was first conducted decades ago, and widespread concerns over the troubling racial disproportions were voiced shortly thereafter, more recent data have documented very similar, equally problematic overall patterns.[113] Thus, in 2015, children of Color represented a majority of those confined in secure residential facilities: Black youth comprised 42% of those confined nationally, and Hispanic and Native American youth another 24%. In some states, the disproportionate minority confinement was even more dramatic. For example, in California, Black and Hispanic children comprised fully 83% of those confined in juvenile facilities. In Maryland and New Jersey, for example, they were over 80%, and in the District of Columbia, the figure was a staggering 97%.[114] On the basis of 2015 data, African American children in the United States were more than 4 times as likely and Hispanic children were almost twice as likely as Whites to be confined in a residential facility.[115]

Perhaps because it has come to be regarded as an unfortunate fact of life in juvenile justice systems across the country, the long-term impact of DMC is sometimes discounted in published research on the topic. Studies instead tend to focus more on whether DMC results from discrimination or some other factor (such as higher rates of youthful lawbreaking). One sophisticated study of race and criminal justice decision-making illustrates this point. Researchers analyzed data from a large sample of juvenile defendants sentenced in two very different cities—Phoenix and Philadelphia—and concluded in both places that "we find no evidence, in our sample of serious offenders, that ethnic minority youth are more likely than White youth to be placed in secure confinement, either with or without controlling for other factors."[116] Indeed, they appeared to have found exactly that—that race did not predict whether the young person was sentenced either to probation or to a juvenile facility, at least in the two cities that were studied. However, what went unnoticed—or, at least, was not commented on—was the fact that youth of Color made up the great majority of juveniles who came before the juvenile courts for sentencing—some 62% in Phoenix and fully 87% in Philadelphia.[117]

Whatever the cause, discrimination or something else, the fact that so many youth of Color are "justice-involved" at such young ages has potentially criminogenic implications. Even in cities where racial discrimination by officials is not directly at fault, contact with juvenile justice institutions is likely to profoundly and adversely affect the trajectories of significant numbers of minority children and adolescents.[118]

In fact, African American and Latino children continue to be overrepresented at literally every stage of juvenile justice system processing—they are overrepresented in arrests, in referrals to juvenile court, and among those juveniles who are held in detention awaiting the disposition of their case. They are more likely to be formally charged in juvenile court, more likely to have their case waived from juvenile to adult court (which typically results in the incarceration in even harsher adult, rather than juvenile, penal institutions), and more likely to receive a case disposition that requires an out-of-home placement (e.g., a commitment to a locked institution).[119] There is thus clear evidence that the criminogenic effects of juvenile institutionalization that I discussed in Chapter 4 are inequitably distributed across racial and ethnic groups in our society.

In addition to DMC that pertains specifically to juvenile institutions, a number of states also passed laws over the last several decades that were intended to streamline the process by which juveniles could be transferred to adult courts and, therefore, be subjected to adult punishments (including imprisonment in adult penal facilities).[120] As I noted earlier, the Justice Department reported in 1998 that "[f]orty-seven of the fifty States and the District of Columbia have substantially changed their juvenile justice laws in recent years to include more transfers of youth to adult court, more mandatory minimum sentences, and more incarceration," and that many of those transfers were to facilities in which "unlawful conditions" prevailed.[121]

Here, too, the racial disproportions have been striking. For example, in one state where incarcerated children were exposed to substandard adult jail conditions, nearly 75% of the children transferred to adult criminal courts in one were African American, despite representing less than 30% of the state's overall population.[122] The General Accounting Office reported similar disproportions for numerous other states.[123] More recent data reveal similar patterns—race significantly influences juvenile court decision-making,[124] including the determination of whether a juvenile case will be handled in adult court and, if it is, the nature of the disposition that results.[125]

Despite a lack of evidence that it reduces juvenile crime and may instead expose children to especially toxic forms of punishment that increase the likelihood of later criminal behavior,[126] the practice of treating children as adults in certain cases and jurisdictions, including placing them in adult prisons, continues (albeit on a much reduced pace in recent years).[127]

DISPROPORTIONATE ADULT IMPRISONMENT

As I noted in Chapter 5, the experience of adult imprisonment can be highly criminogenic. Long-standing racial differentials in rates of incarceration in the United States mean that, throughout the nation's history, African Americans have been far more likely to have been exposed to this criminogenic risk factor than other persons.[128] The racial differentials in incarceration rates became even more striking during the era mass incarceration that began in the mid-1970s, and many minority communities were devastated as a result. In fact, as recently as the early 1990s, the high overall rates of incarceration in the United States were driven largely by the extraordinarily high rates among African Americans. In contrast, the rate of incarceration of White males in the United States still compared favorably with the low rates in most Western European nations, including those in countries regarded as the most progressive and least punitive in the world. Although the rate of incarceration for Whites in the United States began to rise in the late 1980s, and eventually surpassed those in Western European nations, it never came remotely close to approximating the incarceration rate for African Americans. Indeed, by the early 1990s, the United States was imprisoning African American men at a rate that was approximately *4 times* that of Black men in South Africa.[129]

There has been extensive research and commentary about the predictably devastating consequences that these differential rates of imprisonment have had on African Americans at individual, family, and community levels.[130] Michael Tonry succinctly summarized the overall impact:

> It is not hard to conclude that the machinery of the criminal justice system produces devastatingly reduced life chances for black Americans. If the aim were to reduce black men's chances of earning a decent living, or being successfully married and a good father, or being socialized into pro-social values, it is hard to see how the justice system could do those things more effectively.[131]

It is difficult to overstate the harm that has been incurred as a result of these draconian policies—most directly on the prisoners of Color subjected to the pains of imprisonment and its lasting effects, but also more broadly on the persons closest to them. There are intergenerational psychological, social, and economic consequences for the children who have grown up in households directly affected by incarceration.[132] For example, as I noted in passing in Chapter 3, parental imprisonment is a powerful risk factor that can have a host of negative consequences for children whose parents are imprisoned, including "roughly trebling the risk for child antisocial behavior."[133] The era of mass incarceration meant that parental imprisonment became an increasingly common event in the United States over the last several decades, especially in communities of Color. The Bureau of Justice Statistics reported in 2007 that there were some 1.7 million children in the United States who had a parent in prison, an 82% increase since 1991.[134] Several years later, the estimates had grown to approximately 2.7 million, including one in nine African American children who had at least one incarcerated parent.[135] The specific consequences of parental incarceration can vary, in part as a function of which parent is imprisoned, interpersonal relations within the family before, during, and after incarceration, the developmental stage and educational level of the child at the time the parent's time in prison occurs, and the psychological impact of (especially) the father's incarceration on the mother. However, most research shows that "paternal incarceration is detrimental for children" and that the effects consistently include increased "antisocial and nonnormative behavioral outcomes."[136] The continued extraordinary levels of overincarceration in African American communities underscore the long-term significance of this issue for Black parents and their children.

RACE, CRIME, AND COMMUNITY

I have argued so far that whatever differential crime rates may exist between different racial and ethnic groups, they derive in large part from what I called biographical racism—the accumulation of a wide range of race-based inequalities, inequities, and injustices that persons of Color experience over the course of their lifetime. In addition to the effects of having been raised in environments that are still marred by racism and discrimination, many young persons of Color have been exposed to forms of institutional mistreatment that have their own powerful criminogenic effects. In this way, the juvenile and adult justice systems are themselves implicated in and may paradoxically amplify the effects of exposure to past criminogenic risks and traumas and current community contexts.

In addition, many minority children and adolescents live in communities plagued by violence. Not surprisingly, then, they report being exposed to violently traumatic events at much higher rates than other groups,[137] and may suffer posttraumatic stress disorder (PTSD) as a result.[138] As I noted in an earlier chapter, researchers have concluded that children who grow up in certain urban housing projects are exposed to traumatic violence comparable to children living in "war zones" and may suffer the same kinds of psychological aftereffects and, therefore, need the same kinds of treatment as those children.[139] Yet, the communities in which many children of Color live often lack a supportive infrastructure to which they can turn for help. Moreover, when they do seek assistance, they may encounter local agency and organization representatives who actually contribute to their traumatization—the "suspicion widespread among many people in positions of authority" to which Nightingale referred.[140]

Although much of the attention that is devoted to racial injustice has concentrated on urban or inner-city areas, there are rural communities where its effects are also acutely felt. In Jesmyn Ward's personal memoir (from which I quoted in an earlier chapter), she described what the weight of racism felt like in the rural community where she was raised, and the way it surrounded and shaped the trajectories of the young people who were subjected to it:

> My entire community suffered from a lack of trust: we didn't trust society to provide the basics of a good education, safety, access to good jobs, fairness in the justice system. And even as we distrusted the society around us, the culture that cornered us and told us we were perpetually less, we distrusted each other. We did not trust our fathers to raise us, to provide for us. Because we trusted nothing, we endeavored to protect ourselves, boys becoming misogynistic and violent, girls turning duplicitous, all of us hopeless. Some of us turned sour from

> the pressure, let it erode our sense of self until we hated what we saw, without and within. And to blunt it all, some of us turned to drugs.[141]

Whether they live in urban or rural areas of the United States, persons of Color have a fundamentally different relationship with and experience of law enforcement than do Whites. As law professor Paul Butler starkly put it, "[t]here has never, not for one minute in American history, been peace between black people and the police."[142] The differential experiences start early in the socialization process and are produced in part by what Victor Rios termed the "hypercriminalization" of young persons of Color—the ways in which the police automatically code their "everyday behaviors and styles" as "deviant, risky, threatening, or criminal, across social contexts."[143] In fact, there is evidence that Black children begin to be coded differently by law enforcement and others as early as age ten, from which point forward they begin to be seen as older than their actual chronological age and also as inherently more "guilty."[144]

Ronald Weitzer and Steven Tuch conducted a national survey of adults from different metropolitan areas that documented the accumulation of these problematic encounters over a lifetime. They found that a third of African Americans reported being stopped on the streets of their city for "no good reason" (about 3 times the White percentage), fully three fourths believed Blacks were treated worse than Whites, and half thought the police used excessive force (more than 3 times the percentage among Whites).[145] As the authors concluded, these "racial disparities are not simply a matter of opinion" but rather reflect "real differences in police practices" in minority neighborhoods where police misconduct is concentrated.[146] Another study found that the "tens of thousands of law enforcement home raids [that] are conducted annually, disproportionately occurring in minority communities," actually produce symptoms that meet the diagnostic criteria for PTSD, including nightmares, suicidality, and reacting to law enforcement as "triggering" stimuli.[147]

In fact, there is now some direct evidence that so-called proactive policing of minority youth has criminogenic consequences. Phillip Goff and his colleagues recently found that the more often young African American and Latino boys were stopped by the police, the more likely they were to become involved in subsequent delinquent behavior.[148] Although the relationship was partially mediated by the degree to which the police contact was experienced as psychologically stressful—boys who reported suffering greater psychological distress as a result of the encounters later manifested more criminogenic effects—it was independent of their prior delinquent behavior. That is,

> Boys who reported little or no delinquent behavior at one wave were just as likely to be stopped 6 months later as were boys who reported any or a great deal of delinquency. Moreover, regardless of whether a boy had committed any prior delinquent acts, a police stop was associated with more frequent delinquent behavior in the future.[149]

In a related way, then, the fact that African Americans and Latinos are "over-stopped, over-frisked, over-searched, and over-arrested"[150] not only contributes to strained and potentially fatal interactions with the police but also may serve as the basis for a worldview in which communities of Color have less confidence in, are less willing to rely on, and have a "reservoir of bad will" toward conventional law enforcement agencies.[151]

Of course, problematic face-to-face encounters with the police are just the first stage in criminal justice system processing at which racial factors may affect legal decision-making. The implicit bias that I discussed earlier makes the task of completely disentangling the role that race plays within the criminal justice system difficult if not impossible; it potentially affects so many subjective judgments that occur *after* persons of Color have been taken into custody. They include: the kind of behavior and amount of evidence that prosecutors conclude justify criminally charging a suspect and with which offense(s); judgments about whether defendants can be released on their own their recognizance pretrial or need to post bail (and if so, how much); the perceived public safety interest and estimate of the likelihood that a defendant will be convicted that justify continuing to proceed with prosecution (or not); what constitutes a fair and just plea bargain and whether one will be offered; the jurors' prior beliefs about a defendant's probable legal guilt, level of moral blameworthiness, and the quantum of evidence they will require to convict at trial; a judge's estimate of a convicted person's future dangerousness, fitness for rehabilitation, and overall culpability at the time of sentencing; a prison classification officer's assessment of likely institutional adjustment; a disciplinary hearing officer's view of the guilt and punishment deserved for any in-prison rule violation; a parole board member's prediction about someone's likely success in postprison reentry; and a parole officer's judgment about whether and when a parolee's behavior constitutes an actionable violation. *All* of these judgments and more are subject to the subtle influence of race-based implicit biases.

The cumulative effects of these decisions, in turn, are potentially criminogenic, but in a different sense from the way I have been using that term. Rather than affecting the likelihood that persons will engage in illegal behavior, these criminogenic factors affect whether and to what degree their behavior will be officially characterized and treated as criminal and with what criminal justice system consequence. They directly affect a host of decisions and outcomes in which the crime master narrative is directly implicated, including the likelihood that a person will be arrested, kept in pretrial detention, prosecuted, convicted, sentenced to prison, receive a long prison sentence, be classified as a maximum security prisoner, be sent to disciplinary segregation, retained in prison, and returned to custody after release.[152] In fact, because no aspect of criminal justice decision-making appears to be exempt from the influence of racial factors, it is difficult to know what baseline statistic to select as a neutral point from which to calculate race effects.

CONCLUSION

Racial injustice remains deeply embedded in American society. Many persons of Color live in the most crime-prone, criminogenic, and overpoliced neighborhoods in the nation. They are thus more likely to be compelled to crime, victimized by it, suspected of having engaged in it, and punished more harshly if and when they are convicted of it. In part because they are more often the targets of criminal justice system scrutiny, young minority men are more likely to experience the criminalizing effects of juvenile and adult incarceration. As William Chambliss summarized, "[y]oung African-American and Latino men are defined [by the police] as a criminal group, arrested for minor offenses over and over again, and given criminal records which justify long prison sentences."[153] They return to communities that are often ill-equipped to assist them, where criminogenic factors and forces to which they earlier succumbed persist, and they are stigmatized in ways that jeopardize their long-term, successful reentry.

Indeed, the increased scholarly attention focused on the lives of young African Americans and Latinos in the nation's inner cities has exposed the grim realities of surviving the mean streets that many previous decades of economic and political neglect have produced. Many autobiographical and ethnographic accounts published in the 1990s—when the policies that produced the era of mass incarceration were still well underway—provided a detailed backdrop for understanding how basic structural disadvantages can generate a pervasive network of day-to-day challenges and obstacles that pervaded their lives.[154] These textured and compelling stories offer powerful testimony about the resiliency and personal strength that the authors mustered in the face of nearly overwhelming odds. But they also provided clear evidence of the persistent press of sociopolitical and economic forces that shape and narrow the choices that are available to and made by individual actors in these settings. The behavior that results is often less the product of rational or conscious decision-making than, at times, a reaction to "[f]eelings of sheer humiliation and embarrassment, disappointment and frustration, grief and loneliness, and fear and anxiety (especially concerning suspicion, rejection, and abandonment)," as well as anger and outright resistance created by the racial injustice to which they continue to be subjected.[155]

In accounting for the significantly higher rates of incarceration of persons of Color in U.S. society, the late Norval Morris acknowledged that to the degree to which they engaged in higher rates of "prisonable" crime, the differentials are a condemnation of the conditions to which they have been exposed rather than any innate criminal propensities or disproportionately faulty "free choices." As he put it,

> [I]f blacks and, to a lesser extent, Hispanics have been subjected to adverse social conditions stretching over generations—if opportunities for a contribution and rewarding life have been denied them by the lack of adequate health care and the lack of reasonable educational and employment opportunities, if their children and youths over generations have been subjected to the culture of the

inner-city streets, and if socially acceptably role models are denied them—then criminality becomes a much more normal and accepted social adaptation, passed on from generation to generation.[156]

The substantial social and economic barriers I have discussed in this chapter too often thwart and choke the expression of the extraordinary talent and energy that exists in communities of Color that could otherwise be channeled into personal achievement and professional success. Instead, many persons of Color must divert their skill, effort, and resources to the task of surviving economically deprived and hostile interpersonal environments including, in some instances, to engage in the sometimes illegal activities that such survival seems too commonly to require.[157] As Elijah Anderson and others have noted, many minority communities have large concentrations of "the unemployed, the underskilled, and the poorly educated" who, despite being highly intelligent and talented, have also been "demoralized by racism and the wall of social resistance facing them. In this context they lose perspective and lack an outlook and sensibility that would allow them to negotiate the wider system of employment and society in general."[158]

Race thus adds a critically important dimension to the contextual analysis of crime in American society. Personal, institutional, and structural racism establish a larger context that exposes many persons of Color to a host of other social historical risk factors, traumas, and immediate situational influences that can elicit or provoke criminal behavior. As Robert Sampson's research underscored, high crime rates in urban African American communities often stem from the structural linkages between unemployment, economic deprivation, and family disruption.[159] Others have found the same kind of connections between race-based inequality and violent crime,[160] even homicide.[161] The racial dimension to poverty in the United States in some ways deepens the stigma and renders it more chronic. In other ways it seems to heighten the sense of injustice, the righteous outrage that develops in what one commentator has termed a "subculture of exasperation."[162] But examining the role that race has played in the lives of many persons who have violated the law also underscores the fact that race does more than just make these other conditions worse. That is, racism—personal, institutional, and structural racism—can dominate the biographies of persons of Color, exposing them to adverse experiences that no one else in this society has. The legacies of these experiences can be and very frequently are transcended, but doing so requires shouldering a significant and often life-altering burden that others do not have.

NOTES

1. Alexander, M. (2010). *The new Jim Crow: Mass incarceration in the age of colorblindness* (p. 25). New York, NY: The New Press.
2. Adler, N. E., & Rehkopf, D. H. (2008). U.S. disparities in health: Descriptions, causes, and mechanisms. *Annual Review of Public Health, 29,* 235–252. http://dx.doi.org/10.1146/annurev.publhealth.29.020907.090852

3. Bayer, P., & Charles, K. K. (2018). Divergent paths: A new perspective on earnings differences between Black and White men since 1940. *The Quarterly Journal of Economics, 133,* 1459–1501. http://dx.doi.org/10.1093/qje/qjy003
4. See, e.g., Lo, C. C., Howell, R. J., & Cheng, T. C. (2013). Black–White differences in homicide victimization. *Aggression and Violent Behavior, 18,* 125–134. http://dx.doi.org/10.1016/j.avb.2012.11.006
5. Fusaro, V. A., Levy, H. G., & Shaefer, H. L. (2018). Racial and ethnic disparities in the lifetime prevalence of homelessness in the United States. *Demography, 55,* 2119–2128. http://dx.doi.org/10.1007/s13524-018-0717-0
6. O'Hare, W. P. (2016). Consistencies and differences across states in the well-being of non-Hispanic White, Hispanic, and Non-Hispanic Black Children in the United States. *Child Indicators Research, 9,* 1117–1137. http://dx.doi.org/10.1007/s12187-015-9355-x
7. Haney, C. (2004). Condemning the other in death penalty trials: Biographical racism, structural mitigation, and the empathic divide. *De Paul Law Review, 53,* 1557–1589.
8. Du Bois, W. E. B. (1899). *The Philadelphia Negro: A social study* (p. 351). New York, NY: Shocken.
9. Leach, C. W. (2005). Against the notion of a "new racism." *Journal of Community & Applied Psychology, 15,* 432–445, p. 442. http://dx.doi.org/10.1002/casp.841
10. Jackson, J. P., Jr. (2010). Whatever happened to the cephalic index? The reality of race and the burden of proof. *Rhetoric Society Quarterly, 40,* 438–458, p. 447. http://dx.doi.org/10.1080/02773945.2010.517233
11. Perrin, C., & Anderson, K. (2013). Reframing craniometry: Human exceptionalism and the production of racial knowledge. *Social Identities, 19,* 90–103, p. 94. It was also characterized as an "anxious attempt . . . to establish the existence of a uniquely human rationality or mind" (p. 95).
12. Ashley Montague described the flawed and "rather naïve belief" to which many 19th-century physical anthropologists subscribed:

    > It was believed that the form of the skull in particular remained constant in each race, and that different races typically showed different cranial indices. Hence, all one had to do was to measure skulls, calculate the indices, and draw the more or less "obvious" conclusions.

    Montague, A. (1960). Craniometry. In A. Montague, *A handbook of anthropometry: With a section on the measurement of body composition* (pp. 42–66). Springfield, IL: Charles C Thomas, p. 42. At the core of the craniometric pseudoscience was the so-called cephalic index, which craniometrists believed was the key to understanding racial groups as well as individuals. They argued that this measurement—"a ratio of the width of the head to the length of the head"—was impervious to external influences. It therefore served as the basis for the argument that any differences between the average cephalic indices of different racial groups were evidence of inherent rather than acquired capacities, ones that were not the result of experience, access to resources, or differential treatment. See Jackson (2010), Whatever happened to the cephalic index?, p. 448.
13. Grant was a wealthy New York socialite who dabbled in anthropology and genetics, as well as serving as a prominent purveyor and popularizer of racial nativism. He believed that "[m]oral, intellectual and spiritual attributes are as persistent as physical characters and are transmitted substantially unchanged from generation to generation." Grant, M. (1916). *The passing of the great race or the racial basis of European history*. New York, NY: Scribners, p. 226. Grant and others relied on the craniometrists' claim that the skull was impervious to environmental influences as their "scientific basis" for arguing against what Grant called a "fatuous belief" in the power of things like education and opportunity to alter people's outcomes

in life (p. 14). The obviously racist nature of the book's many assertions was made more palatable by virtue of the fact that they were extensions of the otherwise widely accepted craniometric pseudoscientific doctrine.

14. Alexander, C. C. (1962). Prophet of American racism: Madison Grant and the Nordic myth. *Phylon, 23,* 73–90, p. 84.
15. Branson, S. (2017). Phrenology and the science of race in Antebellum America. *Early American Studies: An Interdisciplinary Journal, 15,* 164–193, p. 165.
16. Branson (2017), Phrenology and the science of race in Antebellum America, p. 177. For example, post–Civil War researchers conducted autopsies on the brain size and weight of White and Black soldiers and compared them to determine their relative "intellectuality." See Haller, J. S., Jr. (1970). Concepts of race inferiority in nineteenth-century anthropology. *Journal of the History of Medicine and Allied Sciences, 25,* 40–51. http://dx.doi.org/10.1093/jhmas/XXV.1.40
17. Branson (2017), Phrenology and the science of race in Antebellum America, p. 178.
18. Nourse, V. F. (2008). *In reckless hands:* Skinner v. Oklahoma *and the near triumph of American eugenics.* New York, NY: W. W. Norton, p. 21.
19. Chavez-Garcia, M. (2012). *States of delinquency: Race and science in the making of California's juvenile justice system* (p. 8). Berkeley: University of California Press. http://dx.doi.org/10.1525/california/9780520271715.001.0001
20. Chavez-Garcia (2012), *States of delinquency,* p. 89.
21. Chavez-Garcia (2012), *States of delinquency,* p. 8. This occurred in part because, as Chavez-Garcia noted, "[g]enerally, fieldworkers had little understanding of the boys'—and families'—cultural, ethnic, or socioeconomic makeup, for they came from different worlds," in part because they "privileged Euro-American values and customs," and in part, because they believed science had demonstrated that Blacks and Mexicans were "biologically and racially inferior" (p. 91).
22. Quoted in Adams, D. (1939). William McDougall. *Psychological Review, 46,* 1–8, p. 1.
23. Roback, A. (1952). William McDougall and hormic psychology. In A. Roback (Ed.), *History of American psychology* (pp. 253–263). New York, NY: Library. http://dx.doi.org/10.1037/10800-021
24. McDougall, W. (1926). *Is America safe for democracy?* New York, NY: Charles Scribner, pp. 194, 195. See also Pastore, N. (1944). A social approach to William McDougall. *Social Forces, 23,* 148–152. McDougall's quest for racial purity and his apparent preference for authoritarian regimes over democratic ones, at a time when the specter of fascism was rising in Nazi Germany, undermined his influence and the outward legitimacy of the eugenics movement more generally. See Nourse (2008), *In reckless hands.*
25. Holmes, O. W., Sr. (1882). *The poet at the breakfast-table* (p. 226). Boston, MA: Houghton, Mifflin.
26. Muhammad, K. G. (2010). *The condemnation of blackness: Race, crime, and the making of modern urban America* (p. 80). Cambridge, MA: Harvard University Press. http://dx.doi.org/10.2307/j.ctvjsf4fx
27. See, especially, the discussion in Muhammad (2010), *The condemnation of blackness,* Chapter 4. Stuart Gilman noted that many writers in prominent medical journals in the late 19th and early 20th centuries "viewed ethics as genetically predisposed; treatable in some races (or individuals) and permanently diseased in others. Blacks and other degenerates would ultimately be written off as either untreatable or ethically terminal." Gilman, S. C. (1983). Degeneracy and race in the nineteenth century: The impact of clinical medicine. *Journal of Ethnic Studies, 10,* 27–50, p. 42.
28. Thus, in a book that Muhammad characterized as a "tour de force in the annals of post-emancipation writing on the Negro Problem," Frederick Hoffman claimed

that the "inherent traits" of Blacks (that included their alleged inborn criminality and immorality), as well as their "innate self-destructive tendencies," represented their "greatest hindrances to social and economic progress." Hoffman, F. (1896). *Race traits and tendencies of the American Negro*. New York, NY: American Economic Association. Quoted by Muhammad (2010), *The condemnation of blackness*, p. 35.

29. Alexander (2010), *The new Jim Crow*, p. 192. Moreover, in classic crime master narrative terms, "mass incarceration is predicated on the notion that an extraordinary number of African Americans but not all have freely chosen a life of crime and thus belong behind bars" (p. 235). For a discussion of the continued operation of genetic and biological determinism in contemporary White racial ideology—what the authors termed "ultimate attribution error"—see Byrd, W. C., & Ray, V. E. (2015). Ultimate attribution in the genetic era: White support for genetic explanations of racial difference and policies. *The Annals of the American Academy of Political and Social Sciences, 661*, 212–235. http://dx.doi.org/10.1177/0002716215587887
30. See, e.g., Goff, P. A., Eberhardt, J. L., Williams, M. J., & Jackson, M. C. (2008). Not yet human: Implicit knowledge, historical dehumanization, and contemporary consequences. *Journal of Personality and Social Psychology, 94*, 292–306. http://dx.doi.org/10.1037/0022-3514.94.2.292
31. See notes 33–35 and their accompanying text.
32. James Q. Wilson, arguably the most celebrated criminologist of his day, gave media interviews in the mid-1980s in which he opined that there was "overwhelming evidence" that "crime runs in families." See Leo, J., & Castronovo, V. (1985, October 21). Behavior: Are criminals born, not made? *Time Magazine*, p. 1. Retrieved from http://www.time.com/time/printout/0,8816,960148,00.html. He also gave credence to the notion that "genetic traits predispose some to criminality"; see Wilson, J. Q. (1985, September 30). "Genetic traits predispose" some to criminality: A conversation with James Q. Wilson. *U.S. News & World Report*, p. 54. Additionally, he speculated that "it's conceivable that there are genetic differences across all ethnic and racial groups such that . . . perhaps black children are more aggressive and harder to condition generally," see Katz, L., & Wilson, J. Q. (1985, November 13), Too Many of Us Are Prisoners of Crime, *USA Today*, p. A11.
33. Duru. N. J. (2004). The Central Park Five, the Scottsboro Boys, and the myth of the bestial Black man. *Cardozo Law Review, 25*, 1315–1365, p. 1351.
34. See Krauthammer, C. (1989, July 30) Children of cocaine. *The Washington Post*. Retrieved from https://www.washingtonpost.com/archive/opinions/1989/07/30/children-of-cocaine/41a8b4db-dee2-4906-a686-a8a5720bf52a/?noredirect=on&utm_term=.b56d44785f50
35. See Editorial Board. (2018, December 28). Slandering the unborn: How bad science and a moral panic, fueled in part by the news media, demonized mothers and defamed a generation. *The New York Times*. Retrieved from https://www.nytimes.com/interactive/2018/12/28/opinion/crack-babies-racism.html
36. Eberhardt, J. L., Goff, P. A., Purdie, V. J., & Davies, P. G. (2004). Seeing Black: Race, crime, and visual processing. *Journal of Personality and Social Psychology, 87*, 876–893. http://dx.doi.org/10.1037/0022-3514.87.6.876
37. Rattan, A., Levine, C. S., Dweck, C. S., & Eberhardt, J. L. (2012). Race and the fragility of the legal distinction between juveniles and adults. *PLoS ONE, 7*, e36680.
38. See, e.g., Goff, Eberhardt, Williams, & Jackson (2008), Not yet human: Implicit knowledge, historical dehumanization, and contemporary consequences; and Eberhardt, Goff, Atiba, Purdie, & Davies (2004). Seeing Black: Race, crime, and visual processing.
39. Eberhardt, J. L., Davies, P. G., Purdie-Vaughns, V. J., & Johnson, S. L. (2004). Looking deathworthy: Perceived stereotypicality of Black defendants predicts

capital-sentencing outcomes. *Psychological Science, 17,* 383–386. http://dx.doi.org/10.1111/j.1467-9280.2006.01716.x. Outside the laboratory, darker skin color and Afrocentric features of defendants appear to be associated with receiving harsher sanctions in the criminal justice system, irrespective of the defendants' actual race. See King, R. D., & Johnson, B. D. (2016). A punishing look: Skin tone and Afrocentric features in the halls of justice. *American Journal of Sociology, 122,* 90–124. http://dx.doi.org/10.1086/686941. For a review of a number of studies that have a relationship between skin color, stereotypic Afrocentric features and "looking dangerous," being presumed guilty, and receiving harsher punishment, see Bennett, M. W., & Plaut, V. (2018). Looking criminal and the presumption of dangerousness: Afrocentric facial features, skin tone, and criminal justice. *U.C. Davis Law Review, 51,* 745–803.

40. Duncan, G. J., & Rodgers, W. (1991). Has children's poverty become more persistent? *American Sociological Review, 56,* 538–550. http://dx.doi.org/10.2307/2096273
41. Bane, M. J., & Ellwood, D. T. (1986). Slipping in and out of poverty: The dynamics of spells. *Journal of Human Resources, 21,* 1–23. http://dx.doi.org/10.2307/145955. The percentage of White children living in poverty rose from 10.5% to 12.9% during this period.
42. Specifically, Daniel Lichter and his colleagues showed that the poverty rate for African American children decreased only modestly in these years, from 39.2% to about 33%, and for Latino children from 33.3% to 27.2% (as opposed to Whites, for whom it went from an already comparatively low 10.8% in 1990 to 9.3% in 2000). See Lichter, D. T., Qian, Z., & Crowley, M. L. (2005). Child poverty among racial minorities and immigrants: Explaining trends and differentials. *Social Science Quarterly, 86,* 1037–1059. They attributed the declines largely to increasing levels of maternal employment in minority communities. A different analysis of overall (as opposed to child-only) poverty data reported similar differentials, placing the poverty rate in the 1970s among African Americans as approximately 4 times the rate for Whites, and for Latinos at approximately 3 times the White rate. See Danziger, S., Reed, D., Brown, T. N. (2002). *Poverty and prosperity: Prospects for reducing racial/ethnic economic disparities in the United States.* Ann Arbor: University of Michigan. A University of Michigan report indicated that the relative poverty rates of Whites, African Americans, and Latinos had changed very little by the end of the 1990s, except that poverty rates among African Americans more closely approximated that of Latinos. See Danziger, Reed, & Brown (2002), *Poverty and prosperity.* The overall Latino poverty rate was estimated at 31% in the 2000 Census. U.S. Bureau of the Census, Population Division. (2000). *Current population survey.* Washington, DC: Government Printing Office. Poverty among Latino children is recognized as a long-standing problem. See Children's Defense Fund (1991). *Latino child poverty in the United States.* Washington, DC: Author.
43. Thiede, B. C., Kim, H., & Slack, T. (2017). Marriage, work and racial inequalities in poverty: Evidence from the United States. *Journal of Marriage and the Family, 79,* 1241–1257. http://dx.doi.org/10.1111/jomf.12427
44. See Sharkey, P. (2013). *Stuck in place: Urban neighborhoods and the end of progress toward racial equality.* Chicago, IL: University of Chicago Press, p. 39. See also Sharkey, P. (2008). The intergenerational transmission of context. *American Journal of Sociology, 113,* 931–969. http://dx.doi.org/10.1086/522804
45. Chetty, R., Hendren, N., Jones, M. R., & Porter, S. R. (2018, March). *Race and economic opportunity in the United States: An intergenerational perspective* (Working Paper 24441). Cambridge, MA: National Bureau of Economic Research. http://www.nber.org/papers/w24441 http://dx.doi.org/10.3386/w24441
46. Chetty, Hendren, Jones, & Porter (2018), *Race and economic opportunity,* p. 1.
47. Chetty, Hendren, Jones, & Porter (2018), *Race and economic opportunity,* p. 1.

48. Cohen, P. (2015, August 17). Racial wealth gap persists despite degree, study says. *The New York Times*, B1–B2, p. B1. Retrieved from http://www.nytimes.com/2015/08/17/business/racial-wealth-gap-persists-despite-degree-study-says.html, citing to Emmons, W. R., & Noeth, B. J. (2015). Why didn't higher education protect Hispanic and Black wealth? *Federal Reserve Bank of St. Louis Report*, Issue 12. Retrieved from https://www.stlouisfed.org/publications/in-the-balance/issue12-2015/why-didnt-higher-education-protect-hispanic-and-black-wealth
49. Cohen (2015), Racial wealth gap persists despite degree, study says, p. B2.
50. Rothstein, R. (2017). *The color of law: A forgotten history of how our government segregated America* (p. vii). New York, NY: W. W. Norton.
51. Rothstein (2017), *The color of law*, p. viii.
52. Landphair, J. (2007). "The forgotten people of New Orleans": Community, vulnerability, and the Lower Ninth Ward. *The Journal of American History, 94*, 837–645. http://dx.doi.org/10.2307/25095146
53. Krivo, L. J., & Peterson, R. D. (1996). Extremely disadvantaged neighborhoods and urban crime. *Social Forces, 75*, 619–648. See also Peterson, R. D., & Krivo, L. J. (2010). *Divergent social worlds: Neighborhood crime and the racial-spatial divide*. New York, NY: Russell Sage Foundation.
54. Krivo, L. J., Byron, R. A., Calder, C. A., Peterson, R. D., Browning, C. R., Kwan, M.-P., & Lee, J. Y. (2015). Patterns of residential segregation: Do they matter for neighborhood crime? *Social Science Research, 54*, 303–318, p. 314.
55. Nightingale, C. H. (1994). *On the edge: A history of poor Black children and their American dreams*. New York, NY: Basic Books, p. 10. In addition to Nightingale's, numerous other autobiographical and ethnographic accounts published in the early to mid-1990s documented the day-to-day struggle against the accumulation of these experiences as well as the toll that they could take over a lifetime. See, e.g., Anderson, E. (1990). *Streetwise: Race, class, and social change in an urban community*. Chicago, IL: University of Chicago Press (1990); Canada, G. (1995). *Fist stick knife gun: A personal history of violence*. Boston. MA: Beacon Press; Coyle, D. (1993). *Hardball: A season in the projects*. New York, NY: G. P. Putnam; Frey, D., *The last shot: City streets, basketball dreams*. Boston, MA: Houghton Mifflin (1994); Ladd, J. (1994). *Out of the madness: From the projects to a life of hope*. New York, NY: Warner; McCall, N. (1994). *Makes me wanna holler: A young Black man in America*. New York, NY: Random House; Kotlowitz, A. (1991). *There are no children here: The story of two boys growing up in the other America*. New York, NY: Doubleday; Rodriguez, L. (1993). *Always running, la vida loca: Gang days in L.A.* Los Angeles, CA: Curbstone; Staples, B. (1994). *Parallel time: Growing up in Black and White*. New York, NY: Pantheon; Zavella, P. (1995). Living on the edge: Everyday lives of poor Chicano/Mexican families. In A. Gordon, & C. Newfield (Eds.), *Mapping multiculturalism?* (pp. 362–386). Minneapolis: University of Minnesota Press. For a different but related perspective on many of these same issues that was published during approximately the same time period, see Sullivan, M. L. (1989). *"Getting paid": Youth crime and work in the inner city*. Ithaca, NY: Cornell University Press.
56. The term "microaggressions" was coined decades ago by psychiatry professor Chester Pierce. See Pierce, C. (1970). Offensive mechanisms: The vehicle for microaggressions. In F. Barbour (Ed.), *The Black 70s* (pp. 265–281). Boston, MA: Porter Sargent. In recent years, in part as a result of extensive research conducted by Derald Sue and his colleagues, the widespread nature and harmful consequences of racial microaggressions have been increasingly acknowledged. See, e.g., the recent special issue of *American Psychologist* devoted to racial trauma: Comas-Díaz, L., Hall, G. N., Neville, H. A., & Kazuk, A. E. (Eds.). (2019). Racial trauma: Theory, research, and healing. *American Psychologist, 74*, 1–161. http://dx.doi.org/10.1037/amp0000442. See also Sue, D. W. (2010). *Microaggressions in everyday life: Race, gender, and sexual orientation*. Hoboken, NJ: Wiley.

57. Sue, D. W., Alsaidi, S., Awad, M. N., Glaeser, E., Calle, C. Z., & Mendez, N. (2019). Disarming racial microaggressions: Microintervention strategies for targets, White allies, and bystanders. *American Psychologist, 74,* 128–142, p. 129.
58. See, e.g., Thomas, K. R. (2008). Macrononsense in multiculturalism. *American Psychologist, 63,* 274–275. http://dx.doi.org/10.1037/0003-066X.63.4.274
59. See, e.g., Clark, R., Anderson, N. B., Clark, V. R., & Williams, D. R. (1999). Racism as a stressor for African Americans: A biopsychosocial model. *American Psychologist, 54,* 805–816. http://dx.doi.org/10.1037/0003-066X.54.10.805; Nadal, K. L., Griffin, K. E., Wong, Y., Hamit, S., & Rasmus, M. (2014). The impact of racial microaggressions on mental health: Counseling implications for clients of color. *Journal of Counseling & Development, 92,* 57–66. http://dx.doi.org/10.1002/j.1556-6676.2014.00130.x; Nadal, K. L., Griffin, K. E., Wong, Y., Davidoff, K. C., & Davis, L. S. (2017). The injurious relationship between racial microaggressions and physical health: Implications for social work. *Journal of Ethnic & Cultural Diversity in Social Work, 26,* 6–17. http://dx.doi.org/10.1080/15313204.2016.1263813; Salvatore, J., & Shelton, J. N. (2007). Cognitive costs of racial prejudice. *Psychological Science, 18,* 810–815. http://dx.doi.org/10.1111/j.1467-9280.2007.01984.x; and Sue, D. W., Capodilupo, C. M., & Holder, A. M. B. (2008). Racial microaggressions in the life experience of Black Americans. *Professional Psychology: Research and Practice, 39,* 329–336. http://dx.doi.org/10.1037/0735-7028.39.3.329
60. Burrow, A. L., & Ong, A. D. (2010). Racial identity as a moderator of daily exposure and reactivity to racial discrimination. *Self and Identity, 9,* 383–402, p. 384. http://dx.doi.org/10.1080/15298860903192496
61. Guyll, M., Matthews, K. A., & Bromberger, J. T. (2001). Discrimination and unfair treatment: Relationship to cardiovascular reactivity among African American and European American women. *Health Psychology, 20,* 315–325. http://dx.doi.org/10.1037/0278-6133.20.5.315
62. See, e.g., Sellers, R. M., & Shelton, J. N. (2003). The role of racial identity in perceived racial discrimination. *Journal of Personality and Social Psychology, 84,* 1079–1092. http://dx.doi.org/10.1037/0022-3514.84.5.1079; Pieterse, A. L., Todd, N. R., Neville, H. A., & Carter, R. T. (2012). Perceived racism and mental health among Black American Adults: A meta-analytic review. *Journal of Counseling Psychology, 59,* 1–9. http://dx.doi.org/10.1037/a0026208. Discrimination is hurtful to a wide range of marginalized racial and ethnic groups. See, e.g., Garcini, L. M., Chen, M. A., Brown, R. L., Galvan, T., Saucedo, L., Cardoso, J. A. B., & Fagundes, C. P. (2018). Kicks hurt less: Discrimination predicts distress beyond trauma among undocumented Mexican immigrants. *Psychology of Violence, 8,* 692–701. http://dx.doi.org/10.1037/vio0000205
63. See, e.g., Banks, K. H., & Kohn-Wood, L. P. (2007). The influence of racial identity profiles on the relationship between racial discrimination and depressive symptoms. *Journal of Black Psychology, 33,* 331–354. http://dx.doi.org/10.1177/0095798407302540; Klonoff, E., Landrine, H., & Ullman, J. B. (1999). Racial discrimination and psychiatric symptoms among Blacks. *Cultural Diversity & Ethnic Minority Psychology, 5,* 329–339. http://dx.doi.org/10.1037/1099-9809.5.4.329
64. See, e.g., Broudy, R., Brondolo, E., Coakley, V., Brady, N., Cassells, A., Tobin, J. N., & Sweeney, M. (2007). Perceived ethnic discrimination in relation to daily moods and negative social interactions. *Journal of Behavioral Medicine, 30,* 31–43. http://dx.doi.org/10.1007/s10865-006-9081-4; Greene, M. L., Way, N., & Pahl, K. (2006). Trajectories of perceived adult and peer discrimination among Black, Latino, and Asian American adolescents: Patterns and psychological correlates. *Developmental Psychology, 42,* 218–236. http://dx.doi.org/10.1037/0012-1649.42.2.218
65. See, e.g., Williams, D. R., Neighbors, H. W., & Jackson, J. S. (2003). Racial/ethnic discrimination and health: Findings from community studies. *American Journal of*

Public Health, 93, 200–208. http://dx.doi.org/10.2105/AJPH.93.2.200; Williams, D. R., & Williams-Morris, R. (2000). Racism and mental health: The African American experience. *Ethnicity & Health, 5,* 243–268. http://dx.doi.org/10.1080/713667453. Leaune and his colleagues found a significant relationship between racial/ethnic minority status and symptoms of psychosis, which they attributed in part to greater levels of "chronic social stress" of the sort brought about by deprivation and discrimination. Leaune, E., Dealberto, M.-J., Luck, D., & Grot, S. (2019). Ethnic minority position and migrant status as risk factors for psychotic symptoms in the general population: A meta-analysis. *Psychological Medicine, 49,* 545–558, p. 555. http://dx.doi.org/10.1017/s0033291718002271. See also Anglin, D. M., Greenspoon, M., Lighty, Q., & Ellman, L. M. (2016). Race-based rejection sensitivity partially accounts for the relationship between racial discrimination and distressing attenuated positive psychotic symptoms. *Early Intervention in Psychiatry, 10,* 411–418. http://dx.doi.org/10.1111/eip.12184; Morgan, C., Charalambides, M., Hutchinson, G., & Murray, R. M. (2010). Migration, ethnicity, and psychosis: Toward a sociodevelopmental model. *Schizophrenia Bulletin, 36,* 655–664. http://dx.doi.org/10.1093/schbul/sbq051; and Oh, H., Cogburn, C. D., Anglin, D., Lukens, E., & DeVylder, J. (2016). Major discriminatory events and risk for psychotic experiences among Black Americans. *American Journal of Orthopsychiatry, 86,* 277–285. http://dx.doi.org/10.1037/ort0000158

66. See, e.g., Carter, R. T. (2007). Racism and psychological and emotional injury: Recognizing and assessing race-based traumatic stress. *The Counseling Psychologist, 35,* 13–105. http://dx.doi.org/10.1177/0011000006292033; Wei, M., Wang, K. T., Heppner, P. P., & Du, Y. (2012). Ethnic and mainstream social connectedness, perceived racial discrimination, and posttraumatic stress symptoms. *Journal of Counseling Psychology, 59,* 486–493. http://dx.doi.org/10.1037/a0028000
67. See, e.g., Helms, J. E., Guerda, N., & Green, C. E. (2012). Racism and ethnoviolence as trauma: Enhancing professional and research training. *Traumatology, 18,* 65–74. http://dx.doi.org/10.1177/1534765610396728; Sanders-Phillips, K. (2009). Racial discrimination: A continuum of violence exposure for children of color. *Clinical Child and Family Psychology Review, 12,* 174–195. http://dx.doi.org/10.1007/s10567-009-0053-4
68. See, e.g., Benner, A. D., Wang, Y., Shen, Y., Boyle, A. E., Polk, R., & Cheng, Y.-P. (2018). Racial/ethnic discrimination and well-being during adolescence: A meta-analytic review. *American Psychologist, 73,* 855–883. http://dx.doi.org/10.1037/amp0000204; Dotterer, A. M., McHale, S. M., & Crouter, A. C. (2009). Sociocultural factors and school engagement among African American youth: The roles of racial discrimination, racial socialization, and ethnic identity. *Applied Developmental Science, 13,* 61–73. http://dx.doi.org/10.1080/10888690902801442; Prelow, H. M., Mosher, C. E., & Bowman, M. A. (2006). Perceived racial discrimination, social support, and psychological adjustment among African American college students. *The Journal of Black Psychology, 32,* 442–454. http://dx.doi.org/10.1177/0095798406292677
69. See, e.g., Burt, C. H., Simons, R. L., & Gibbons, F. X. (2012). Discrimination, ethnic-racial socialization, and crime: A micro-sociological model of risk and resilience. *American Sociological Review, 77,* 648–677. http://dx.doi.org/10.1177/0003122412448648; Caldwell, C. H., Kohn-Wood, L. P., Schmeelk-Cone, K. H., Chavous, T. M., & Zimmerman, M. A. (2004). Racial discrimination and racial identity as risk or protective factors for violent behaviors in African American young adults. *American Journal of Community Psychology, 33,* 91–105. http://dx.doi.org/10.1023/B:AJCP.0000014321.02367.dd; Evans, S. Z., Simons, L. G., & Simons, R. L. (2016). Factors that influence trajectories of delinquency throughout adolescence. *Journal of Youth and Adolescence, 45,* 156–171. http://dx.doi.org/10.1007/s10964-014-0197-5; Gerrard, M., Stock, M. L., Roberts, M. E., Gibbons,

F. X., O'Hara, R. E., Weng, C. Y., & Wills, T. A. (2012). Coping with racial discrimination: The role of substance abuse. *Psychology of Addictive Behaviors, 26,* 550–560. http://dx.doi.org/10.1037/a0027711; Gibbons, F. X., O'Hara, R. E., Stock, M. L., Gerrard, M., Weng, C.-Y., & Wills, T. A. (2012). The erosive effects of racism: Reduced self-control mediates the relation between perceived racial discrimination and substance use in African American adolescents. *Journal of Personality and Social Psychology, 102,* 1089–1104. http://dx.doi.org/10.1037/a0027404; and Robinson, W. L., Paxton, K., & Jonen, L. (2011). Pathways to aggression and violence among African American adolescent males: The influence of normative beliefs, neighborhood, and depressive symptomatology. *Journal of Prevention & Intervention in the Community, 39,* 132–148. http://dx.doi.org/10.1080/10852352.2011.556572

70. Lassiter, R. (1987). Child rearing in Black families: Child-abusing discipline? In R. L. Hampton (Ed.), *Violence in the Black family: Correlates and consequences* (pp. 39–54). Lexington, MA: Lexington Books.
71. Lassiter (1987), Child rearing in Black families: Child-abusing discipline?, p. 39.
72. In addition to Lassiter (1987), Child rearing in Black families: Child-abusing discipline?, See also Daniel, J. H., Hampton, R. L., & Newberger, E. H. (1983). Child abuse and accidents in Black Families: A controlled comparative study. *American Journal of Orthopsychiatry, 53,* 645–653. http://dx.doi.org/10.1111/j.1939-0025.1983.tb03408.x; McLoyd, V. C. (1990). The impact of economic hardship on Black families and children: Psychological distress, parenting, and socioeconomic development. *Child Development, 61,* 311–346. http://dx.doi.org/10.2307/1131096
73. Sedlak, A. J., Mettenburg, J., Winglee, M., Cirarico, J., & Basena, M. (2010). *Fourth national incidence study of child abuse and neglect (NIS-4): Analysis Report.* Washington, DC: Department of Health and Human Services, Administration for Children and Families, p. 9. The study "gathers data from both (1) child protective service agencies and (2) community professionals who encounter maltreated children during the course of their work in a variety of agencies, including schools, hospitals, law enforcement, day care, and shelters" (p. 3).
74. Sedlak, Mettenburg, Winglee, Cirarico, & Basena (2010), *Fourth national incidence study of child abuse,* p. 4. Black children suffered physical harm and overall harm at rates that were approximately twice those of white children. See Figures 1.1 and 1.2, pp. 6, 7.
75. Sedlak, Mettenburg, Winglee, Cirarico, & Basena (2010), *Fourth national incidence study of child abuse,* defined "Low Socioeconomic Status" as having a household income (in 2006) of $15,000 or less, parent(s) who were not high school graduates, or the household participated in a poverty program. See Table 1.1, p. 8.
76. Sedlak, Mettenburg, Winglee, Cirarico, & Basena (2010), *Fourth national incidence study of child abuse,* p. 47.
77. Sedlak, Mettenburg, Winglee, Cirarico, & Basena (2010), *Fourth national incidence study of child abuse,* p. 49.
78. Crutchfield, R. (2014). *Get a job: Labor markets, economic opportunity, and crime* (p. 205). New York, NY: New York University Press. http://dx.doi.org/10.18574/nyu/9780814717073.001.0001
79. For example, a report on foster care in California at the start of the 21st century found that about two thirds of all foster children in the state were from two minority groups: African Americans (36%) and Latinos (28%). See *California child and family services review: Statewide assessment* (2002, August). Sacramento, CA: California Department of Social Services, p. 105. Although the level of overrepresentation had dropped significantly by 2009, African American children were still more than 5 times as likely as White children to be placed in foster care and were more likely to have "long stays" in foster care and less likely to be

reunited with their birth families. See Danielson, C., & Lee, H. (2010). *Foster care in California: Achievements and challenges*. San Francisco, CA: Public Policy Institute of California. More recent national statistics indicate that 23% of the total number children in the foster care system in the United States in 2016 were African American. Children's Bureau (2018, April). *Foster care statistics 2016*. Washington, DC: Department of Health and Human Services, p. 8. Retrieved from https://www.childwelfare.gov/pubPDFs/foster.pdf

80. Roberts, D. (2002). *Shattered bonds: The color of child welfare* (p. 8). New York, NY: Basic Civitas Books.
81. Roberts (2002), *Shattered bonds: The color of child welfare*, p. 9.
82. Roberts (2002), *Shattered bonds: The color of child welfare*, pp. 21–23.
83. Roberts (2002), *Shattered bonds: The color of child welfare*, p. ix.
84. Roberts (2002), *Shattered bonds: The color of child welfare*, p. 91.
85. Office for Civil Rights (2014, March). Data snapshot: School discipline. *Civil Rights Data Collection*. Issue Brief No. 1. Washington, DC: Department of Education, p. 1.
86. Ward, J. (2013). *Men we reaped: A memoir* (p. 111). New York, NY: Bloomsbury.
87. See, e.g., Wald, J., & Losen, D. J. (Eds.). (2003). Deconstructing the school-to-prison pipeline, *New Directions for Youth Development*, 99, 1–120.
88. See, e.g., Bradshaw, C. P., Mitchell, M. M., O'Brennan, L. M., & Leaf, P. J. (2010). Multilevel exploration of factors contributing to overrepresentation of Black students in office disciplinary referrals. *Journal of Educational Psychology, 102*, 508–520. http://dx.doi.org/10.1037/a0018450; Rocque, M. (2010). Office discipline and student behavior: Does race matter? *American Journal of Education, 116*, 557–581. http://dx.doi.org/10.1086/653629; and Nicholson-Crotty, S., Birchmeier, Z., & Valentine, D. (2009). Exploring the impact of school discipline on racial disproportion in the juvenile justice system. *Social Science Quarterly, 90*, 1003–1018. http://dx.doi.org/10.1111/j.1540-6237.2009.00674.x
89. Skiba, R. (2000). *The color of discipline: Sources of racial and gender disproportionality in school punishment*, Indiana Education Policy Center, Policy Research Report #SRS1, pp. 13, 16. Earlier reports on the same issue found some of these same patterns of racially discriminatory treatment in a number of public schools. For example, in Oakland, California, at a time when African American students comprised 28% of the students in the school system, they represented 53% of the suspensions. Commission for Positive Change in the Oakland Public Schools. (1992). *Keeping children in schools: Sounding the alarm on suspensions*. Oakland, CA: Author, p. 1. The issue received national attention in the early 1990s. See Hull, J. (1994, April 4). Do teachers punish according to race? *Time Magazine*, 30–31. Almost a decade later, the problem had not abated. See Morse, J. (2002, May 27). Learning while Black. *Time Magazine*, 50–53. See also a comprehensive statistical analysis sponsored by the *Seattle Post-Intelligencer* examining nearly 40,000 Seattle secondary school disciplinary records that found that African American students were more than twice as likely as any other group to be suspended or expelled. The statistical disparities remained even after the variables of poverty and living in a single-parent family (both of which also were associated with higher rates of school discipline) were taken into account. The differentials were particularly pronounced for vague or subjective offenses like "disobedience" and "interference with authority." Denn, R. (2002, March 15). Blacks are disciplined at far higher rates than other students, *Seattle Post-Intelligencer*.
90. Simmons, L. (2017). *The prison school: Educational inequality and school discipline in the age of mass incarceration* (pp. 23–24). Berkeley: University of California Press. http://dx.doi.org/10.1525/california/9780520281455.001.0001
91. Editorial (2013, May 30). The school-to-prison pipeline: A task force urges New York City schools to adopt new approaches to student discipline. *The New York Times*, p. A18.

92. Editorial (2013, May 30), The school-to-prison pipeline, p. A18.
93. Kaye, J. (2013, May). *Keeping kids in school and out of court: Report and recommendations.* New York, NY: New York City School-Justice Partnership Task Force, pp. 6–8.
94. Kaye (2013, May), *Keeping kids in school,* p. 6, quoting Skiba, R. J., Michael, R. S., Nardo, A. C., & Peterson, R. L. (2002). The color of discipline: Sources of racial and gender disproportionality in school punishment. *Urban Review, 34,* 327–342, p. 327. https://doi.org/10.1023/A:1021320817372
95. Ferguson, A. A. (2000). *Bad boys: Public schools in the making of Black masculinity.* Ann Arbor: University of Michigan Press. See also Barona, A., & Garcia, E. E. (Eds.). (1990). *Children at risk: Poverty, minority status, and other issues in educational equity.* Washington, DC: National Association of School Psychologists; Jonathan Kozol, J. (1991). *Savage inequalities: Children in America's schools.* New York, NY: Harper Collins. http://dx.doi.org/10.3998/mpub.16801
96. Ferguson (2000), *Bad boys: Public schools in the making of Black masculinity,* p. 51. Indeed, Ferguson noted that schools are "replete with symbolical forms of violence," in part because children who are regarded by authorities as "troublemakers" are themselves

    > conscious of the fact that school adults have labeled them as problems, social and educational misfits" and many are also aware "that what they bring from home and neighborhood–family, structure and history, forms of verbal and nonverbal expression, neighborhood lore and experiences–has little or even deficit value (p. 169).

97. Ferguson (2000), *Bad boys: Public schools in the making of Black masculinity,* p. 89.
98. That is because, "in the daily experience of being named as a 'troublemaker' regulated, and surveilled, access to the full resources of the school are increasingly denied as the boys are isolated in nonacademic spaces in school or banished to lounging at home or loitering on the streets." Moreover, time spent in the school detention center "means time lost from classroom learning; suspension, at school or at home, has a direct and lasting negative effect on the continuing growth of a child" so that "human possibilities are stunted at a crucial formative period of life." Ferguson (2000), *Bad boys: Public schools in the making of Black masculinity,* p. 230. See also Henning, K. N. (2013). Criminalizing normal adolescent behavior in communities of Color: The role of prosecutors in juvenile justice reform. *Cornell Law Review, 98,* 383–462. http://dx.doi.org/10.2139/ssrn.2128857
99. Losen, D., & Orfield, G. (Eds.). (2002). *Racial inequality in special education.* Boston, MA: Harvard Education Press.
100. Losen & Orfield (Eds.). (2002), *Racial inequality in special education,* p. 34.
101. Yoshino, E. R. (2008). California's criminal gang enhancements: Lessons from interviews with practitioners. *Southern California Review of Law and Social Justice, 18,* 117–152.
102. Yoshino (2008), California's criminal gang enhancements, p. 127 (footnotes omitted).
103. Yoshino (2008), California's criminal gang enhancements, pp. 127–128 (footnotes omitted).
104. Cox, J. A., & Bell, J. (2001). Addressing disproportionate representation of youth of Color in the juvenile justice system. *Journal of the Center for Families, Children & the Courts, 3,* 31–43, pp. 31–32.
105. In the not-too-distant past, there were also very significant, explicit differences in the *nature* of the juvenile institutions to which White and Black children were separately sent. These included those in the openly segregated juvenile justice systems that existed until relatively recently in many Southern states. African American children were sent to separate facilities, such as the notorious "Alabama School for Negro Children" at Mt. Meigs, or the Scotlandville facility that housed young African

American boys in Louisiana. At Mt. Meigs, for example, African American children were required "to spend large amounts of time performing manual farm labor for the sole purpose of producing income for the institution." Complaint in Intervention, filed November 8, 1969, by the U.S. Department of Justice, in the Middle District of Alabama in *Stockton v. Alabama Industrial School for Negro Children*, Civil Action No. 2834. Indeed, witnesses and legal documents also confirmed that the boys were "beaten around the head and on the back and legs with broom and mop handles, fan belts and fists . . . routinely . . . [and] without defined standards." See The Verified Proposed Findings of Fact by the United States and adopted by the Court in *Stockton*. Wilbert Rideau's firsthand account described Scotlandville this way:

> Staff members whipped every kid in the vicinity of a fight, theft, misbehavior, or other wrongdoing, even if they were only seeking information. Shocking tales of cruelty, brutality, and even deaths occasionally appeared in newspapers after someone escaped from the facility, but staffers were seldom held accountable.

Rideau, W. (2010). *In the place of justice: A story of punishment and deliverance*. New York, NY: Knopf, p. 14. For litigation filed some 15 years after *Brown v. Board of Education*, attempting address Louisiana's still racially segregated juvenile justice system, see *Major v. Sowers*, 297 F. Supp. 664 (E.D. La., 1969).

106. See Hamparian, D., & Leiber, M. J. (1997). *Disproportionate confinement of minority juveniles in secure facilities: 1996 National report*. Champaign, IL: Community Research Associates.
107. Parent, D. G., Lieter, V., Kennedy, S., Livens, L., Wentworth, D., Wilcox, S., & Abt Associates, Inc. (1994). *Conditions of confinement: Juvenile detention and corrections facilities*. Washington, DC: Office of Juvenile Justice and Delinquency Prevention. See also Bishop, D. M., & Frazier, C. E. (1988). The influence of race in juvenile justice processing. *Journal of Research in Crime and Delinquency, 25*, 242–263. http://dx.doi.org/10.1177/0022427888025003003
108. Parent, Lieter, Kennedy, Livens, Wentworth, Wilcox, & Abt Associates, Inc. (1994), *Conditions of confinement: Juvenile detention and corrections facilities*. See also Otto, R., Greenstein, J., Johnson, M., & Friedman, R. (1992). Prevalence of mental disorders among youth in the juvenile justice system. In J. Cocozza (Ed.), *Responding to the mental health needs of youth in the juvenile justice system* (pp. 7–48). Seattle, WA: The National Coalition for the Mentally Ill in the Criminal Justice System. Finally, see Redding, R. (n.d.). Barriers to meeting the mental health needs of juvenile offenders in the Virginia juvenile justice system. *Juvenile Justice Fact Sheet*, Charlottesville: Institute of Law, Psychiatry & Public Policy, University of Virginia, to the effect that the juvenile justice system is perceived as "a 'dumping ground' for mentally ill, learning disabled, or behaviorally disordered juveniles," many of whom had prior involvement with the mental health system but ended up in the juvenile justice system "because the mental health system has failed to serve their needs" (p. 9).
109. Data derived from DeComo, R. E. (1993). *The juveniles taken into custody research program: Estimating the prevalence of juvenile custody rates by race and gender*. San Francisco, CA: National Council on Crime and Delinquency.
110. As Poe-Yamagata and Jones noted, "[s]ince many data systems fail to disaggregate ethnicity from race, Latino youth are often counted as 'White.'" Poe-Yamagata, E., & Jones, M. (2000). *And justice for some: Differential treatment of youth of Color in the justice system*. San Francisco, CA: National Council on Crime and Delinquency, p. 1. See also Villarruel, A., & Walker, N. (2002). *Donde esta la justicia? A call to action on behalf of Latino and Latina youth in the U.S. Justice System*. Washington, DC: Building Blocks for Youth:

> Current methods for recording and gathering data obstruct attempts to understand the magnitude of the problem of over-representation and disparate treatment of

> Latino/a youth in the justice system. Critical pieces of information often are missing, variables are not specified in detail, terminology is inconsistently used, and information is not consistently reported across jurisdictions (p. 10).

111. See Human Rights Watch. "Race and Incarceration in the United States." Retrieved from http://hrw.org/backgrounder/usa/race/. "Juvenile detention centers" in this analysis included homes for neglected children, residential treatment centers, and detention centers. In some 22 states, the overrepresentation in juvenile detention centers was substantial, reflecting numbers of detained Latino children that were 200% or more of their percentage in the state population. In some areas where there were substantial numbers of Latino youth, the disparities were especially problematic. For example, in Los Angeles County in 1996–1998, Latino youth were arrested 2.3 times as often as White youth, prosecuted as adults 2.4 times as often as Whites, and imprisoned 7.3 times as often as their White counterparts. A Latino youth who committed a violent offense in this jurisdiction during this period was 12 times more likely to be incarcerated in the California Youth Authority as a White juvenile. See Villarruel & Walker (2002), *Donde esta la justiciar?*, p. 8.
112. See DeComo (1993), *The juveniles taken into custody research program*.
113. For example, one analysis of these data indicated that DMC rates for African American youth had declined somewhat between 1997 and 2006, Black youth were still 3.4 times more likely to be confined in juvenile institutions than Whites. See Davis, J., & Sorensen, J. R. (2013). Disproportionate minority confinement of juveniles: Examination of Black–White disparity in placements, 1997–2006. *Crime & Delinquency, 59,* 115–139. http://dx.doi.org/10.1177/0011128709359653; Mallett, C., & Stoddard-Dare, P. (2010). Predicting secure detention placement for African-American juvenile offenders: Addressing the disproportionate minority confinement problem. *Journal of Ethnicity in Criminal Justice, 8,* 91–103. http://dx.doi.org/10.1080/15377931003761011
114. Office of Juvenile Justice and Delinquency Prevention. (2019). *Easy access to Census of Juveniles in Residential Placement: 1997–2011*. Retrieved from http://www.ojjdp.gov/ojstatbb/ezacjrp/. Data are from a census of nearly 4,000 public and private juvenile facilities in the United States and include persons under the age of 21 who were assigned to a bed at a juvenile residential facility as a result of being charged with or adjudicated responsible for a criminal offense.
115. Office of Juvenile Justice and Delinquency Prevention. (2016). *Statistical briefing book*. Retrieved from https://www.ojjdp.gov/ojstatbb/corrections/qa08203.asp?qaDate=2015. See also Sedlak, A. J., & Bruce, C. (2016). *Survey of youth in residential placement: Youth characteristics and background. SYRP Report*. Rockville, MD: Weststat.
116. Cauffman, E., Piquero, A. R., Kimonis, E., Steinberg, L., Chassin, L., & Fagan, J. (2007). Legal, individual, and environmental predictors of court disposition in a sample of serious adolescent offenders. *Law and Human Behavior, 31,* 519–535, p. 531. http://dx.doi.org/10.1007/s10979-006-9076-2
117. Cauffman, Piquero, Kimonis, Steinberg, Chassin, & Fagan (2007), Legal, individual, and environmental predictors, p. 527.
118. See also Piquero, A. R. (2008). Disproportionate minority contact. *The Future of Children, 18,* 59–79. http://dx.doi.org/10.1353/foc.0.0013
119. See, e.g., Leonard, K., Pope, C., & Feyerherm, W. (Eds.). (1995). *Minorities in juvenile justice*. Thousand Oaks, CA: Sage; Amnesty International. (1998, November 20). *Betraying the young: Human rights violations against children in the U.S. justice system*. AI Index: AMR 51/057/1998; Snyder, H., & Sickmund, M. (1999). *Juvenile offenders and victims: 1999 National Report*. Washington, DC: Office of Juvenile Justice and Delinquency Prevention; Males, M., & Macallair, D. (2000). *The color of justice: An analysis of juvenile adult court transfers in California*. Washington, DC: Building Blocks for Youth; and Poe-Yamagata & Jones (2000), *And justice for some*.

120. The transfer of juveniles into the adult criminal court system can occur in one of three ways: a judicial transfer proceeding (in which judges decide whether "waiver" into the adult system is warranted), so-called direct file (in which some state laws give prosecutors the power to process the case in adult rather than juvenile court), and statutory or legislative waiver (in which certain criteria such as offense seriousness or prior record result in the automatic transfer of a juvenile case to adult court). In addition, as I noted in Chapter 4, there is some evidence to indicate that in some jurisdictions young persons whose cases have been moved from juvenile to the adult criminal justice system are actually treated more harshly than adults convicted of similar crimes. See Kurlychek, M. C., & Johnson, B. D. (2004). The juvenile penalty: A comparison of juvenile and young adult sentencing outcomes in criminal court. *Criminology, 42*, 485–515. http://dx.doi.org/10.1111/j.1745-9125.2004.tb00527.x
121. Puritz, P., & Scali, M. (1998). *Beyond the walls: Improving conditions of confinement for youth in custody* (p. xi). Washington, DC: Department of Justice.
122. Human Rights Watch. (1999). *No minor matter: Children in Maryland's jails* (pp. 20–21). New York, NY: Author.
123. General Accounting Office. (1995). *Juvenile justice: Juveniles processed in criminal court and case dispositions* (pp. 50–58). Washington, DC: Author.
124. See, e.g., Fader, J. J., Kurlychek, M. C., & Morgan, K. A. (2014). The color of juvenile justice: Racial disparities in dispositional decisions. *Social Science Research, 44*, 126–140. http://dx.doi.org/10.1016/j.ssresearch.2013.11.006
125. See, e.g., Kurlychek, M. C. (2018). Mitigation for minors: Exploring the nuances of social constructs and legal status in structuring sentences for youthful offenders. *Punishment & Society, 20*, 498–522. http://dx.doi.org/10.1177/1462474517708559
126. The potential deterrent versus criminogenic effect of handling juvenile cases in adult court appears to depend some on the jurisdiction as well as the nature of the transfer process. See, e.g., Fowler, E., & Kurlychek, M. C. (2018). Drawing the line: Empirical recidivism results from a natural experiment raising the age of criminal responsibility. *Youth Violence and Juvenile Justice, 16*, 263–278. http://dx.doi.org/10.1177/1541204017708017; Zane, S. N., Welsh, B. C., & Mears, D. P. (2016). Juvenile transfer and the specific deterrence hypothesis. *Criminology & Public Policy, 15*, 901–925. http://dx.doi.org/10.1111/1745-9133.12222
127. Thus,

> together the expansion of juvenile transfer laws and the proliferation of sentencing guidelines have led to a record number of youth being punished under adult sentencing guidelines, where sentencing options are more formally structured and typically more severe than in juvenile courts.

Johnson, B. D., & Kurlychek, M. C. (2012). Transferred juveniles in the era of sentencing guidelines: Examining judicial departures for juvenile offenders in adult criminal court. *Criminology, 50*, 525–564, p. 526. http://dx.doi.org/10.1111/j.1745-9125.2011.00270.x. See also Washburn, J. J., Teplin, L. A., Voss, L. S., Simon, C. D., Abram, K. M., & McClelland, G. M. (2008). Psychiatric disorders among detained youths: A comparison of youths processed in juvenile court and adult criminal court. *Psychiatric Services, 59*, 965–973. http://dx.doi.org/10.1176/ps.2008.59.9.965

128. Dunbaugh, F. (1979). Racially disproportionate rates of incarceration in the United States. *Prison Law Monitor, 1*, 205–225, p. 219.
129. King, A. E. O. (1993). The impact of incarceration on African American families: Implications for practice. *Families in Society: The Journal of Contemporary Human Services, 74*, 145–153. http://dx.doi.org/10.1177/104438949307400302. Thus, the rate at which White men were imprisoned nearly doubled between 1985 and 1995, growing from a rate of 528 per 100,000 in 1985 to a rate of 919 per 100,000 in 1995. However, the impact of incarceration on African American men, Hispanics, and women of all racial and ethnic groups was much greater. The number of African American men who were incarcerated rose from 3,544 per 100,000 in 1985 to a

rate of 6,926 per 100,000 in 1995. Also, between 1985 and 1995, the number of Hispanic prisoners rose by an average of 12% annually. Mumola, C., & Beck, J. (1997, June). *Prisoners in 1996* (NCJ 164619). Rockville, MD: Bureau of Justice Statistics. Although the disparities in incarceration rates between Whites and African Americans have decreased slightly since the mid-1990s, they remain extremely high. See, e.g., Enders, W., Percorino, P., & Souto, A.-C. (2019). Racial disparity in U.S. imprisonment across states and over time. *Journal of Quantitative Criminology, 35,* 365–392. http://dx.doi.org/10.1007/s10940-018-9389-6

130. There is a large amount of literature that documents these effects. In addition to Alexander (2010), *The new Jim Crow,* see, e.g., Crutchfield, R. D., & Weeks, G. A. (2015). The effects of mass incarceration on communities of Color. *Issues in Science and Technology, 32,* 109–119; Lee, H., McCormick, T., Hicken, M. T., & Wildeman, C. (2015). Racial inequalities in connectedness to imprisoned individuals in the United States. *DuBois Review: Social Science Research on Race, 12,* 269–282. http://dx.doi.org/10.1017/S1742058X15000065; and Schnittker, J., Massoglia, M., & Uggen, C. (2011). Incarceration and the health of the African American community. *Du Bois Review, 8,* 133–141. http://dx.doi.org/10.1017/S1742058X11000026

131. Tonry, M. (2009). Explanations of American punishment policies: A national history. *Punishment & Society, 11,* 377–394, p. 387. http://dx.doi.org/10.1177/1462474509334609

132. For especially thoughtful discussions of how the criminal justice system "infiltrates" the lives of families of Color and adversely affects their children, and the many ways in which the devastating cumulative consequences of this infiltration help to perpetuate and worsen racial inequality, see Foster, H., & Hagan, J. (2009). The mass incarceration of parents in America: Issues of race/ethnicity, collateral damage to children, and prisoner reentry. *The Annals of the American Academy of Political and Social Science, 623,* 179–194. http://dx.doi.org/10.1177/0002716208331123; and Pettit, B., & Gutierrez, C. (2018). Mass incarceration and racial inequality. *American Journal of Economics and Sociology, 77,* 1153–1182. http://dx.doi.org/10.1111/ajes.12241

133. Murray, J., & Farrington, D. P. (2008). The effects of parental imprisonment on children. *Crime & Justice, 37,* 133–206, pp. 186–187. http://dx.doi.org/10.1086/520070. See also Bell, M. F., Bayliss, D. M., Glauert, R., & Ohan, J. L. (2018). Using linked data to investigate developmental vulnerabilities in children of convicted parents. *Developmental Psychology, 54,* 1219–1231. http://dx.doi.org/10.1037/dev0000521; and Wildeman, C. (2014). Parental incarceration, child homelessness, and the invisible consequences of mass imprisonment. *The Annals of the American Academy of Political and Social Science, 651,* 74–96. http://dx.doi.org/10.1177/0002716213502921

134. For these and other data on trends in parental incarceration in the United States, see Glaze, L. E., & Maruschak, L. M. (2008). *Parents in prison and their minor children* (NCJ 222984). Washington, DC: Department of Justice Statistics; and Mumola, C. J. (2000). *Incarcerated parents and their children* (NCJ 182335). Washington, DC: Department of Justice Statistics. See also Schirmer, S., Nellis, A., & Mauer, M. (2009). *Incarcerated parents and their children, trends 1991–2007.* Washington DC: The Sentencing Project. As the Sentencing Project Report noted, according to 2004 data, more than half of parents housed in a state correctional facility had never had a personal visit from their children:

> A key factor in explaining the limited contact is that incarcerated parents are generally housed far from home. In 2004, 62% of parents in a state correctional facility and 84% in a federal correctional facility were housed more than 100 miles from their place of residence at arrest. . . . This finding indicates that children of incarcerated parents typically live too far from their parents to see them very often.

Schirmer, Nellis, & Maurer (2009), *Incarcerated parents and their children, trends 1991–2007,* p. 8.

135. National Resource Center on Children & Families of the Incarcerated. (2014). *Children and Families of the Incarcerated Fact Sheet.* Retrieved from http://nrccfi.camden.rutgers.edu/files/nrccfi-fact-sheet-2014.pdf
136. Foster, H., & Hagan, J. (2015). Punishment regimes and the multilevel effects of parental incarceration: Intergenerational, intersectional, and interinstitutional models of social inequality and systemic exclusion. *Annual Review of Sociology, 41,* 135–158, p. 141. http://dx.doi.org/10.1146/annurev-soc-073014-112437. For additional research on the complex relationship between parental incarceration and its effects on their children, see Murray, J. (2007). The cycle of punishment: Social exclusion of prisoners and their children. *Criminology & Criminal Justice, 7,* 55–81. http://dx.doi.org/10.1177/1748895807072476; Murray & Farrington (2008), The effects of parental imprisonment on children; Wildeman, C. (2009). Parental imprisonment, the prison boom, and the concentration of childhood disadvantage. *Demography, 46,* 265–280. http://dx.doi.org/10.1353%2Fdem.0.0052; Wildeman (2014), Parental incarceration, childhood homelessness, and the invisible consequences of mass imprisonment; *Annals of the American Academy of Political and Social Science, 651,* 74–96. http://dx.doi.org/10.1177%2F0002716213502921; Wildeman, C., Schnittker, J., & Turney, K. (2012). Despair by association? The mental health of mothers with children by recently incarcerated fathers. *American Sociological Review, 77,* 216–243. http://dx.doi.org/10.1177/0003122411436234; and Wildeman, C., & Turney, K. (2014). Positive, negative, or null? The effects of maternal incarceration on children's behavioral problems. *Demography, 51,* 1041–1068. http://dx.doi.org/10.1007/s13524-014-0291-z
137. See, e.g., Hatch, S. L., & Dohrenwend, B. P. (2007). Distribution of traumatic and other stressful life events by race/ethnicity, gender, SES and age: A review of the research. *American Journal of Community Psychology, 40,* 313–332. http://dx.doi.org/10.1007/s10464-007-9134-z; and Rich, J. A., & Grey, C. M. (2005). Pathways to recurrent trauma among young Black men: Traumatic stress, substance use, and the "Code of the Street." *American Journal of Public Health, 95,* 816–824. http://dx.doi.org/10.2105%2FAJPH.2004.044560
138. See, e.g., Schwartz, A. C., Bradley, R. L., Sexton, M., Sherry, A., & Ressler, K. J. (2005). Posttraumatic stress disorder among African Americans in an inner city mental health clinic. *Psychiatric Services, 56,* 212–215. http://dx.doi.org/10.1176/appi.ps.56.2.212; Smith, J. R., & Patton, D. U. (2016). Posttraumatic stress symptoms in context: Examining trauma responses to violent exposures and homicide death among Black males in urban neighborhoods. *American Journal of Orthopsychiatry, 86,* 212–223. http://dx.doi.org/10.1037/ort0000101; and Cross, D., Vance, L. A., Kim, Y. J., Fox, N., Jovanovic, T., & Bradley, B. (2018). Trauma exposure, PTSD, and parenting in a community sample of low-income, predominately African American mothers and children. *Psychological Trauma: Theory, Research, Practice, and Policy, 10,* 327–335. http://dx.doi.org/10.1037/tra0000264
139. Dubrow, N. F., & Garbarino, J. (1989). Living in the war zone: Mothers and young children in a public housing development. *Child Welfare, 68,* 3–20. See also Joan McCord's introductory chapter on urban violence and the chapters that follow: McCord, J. (1994). Inner city life: Contributions to violence. In National Research Council (Ed.), *Violence in urban America: Mobilizing a response* (pp. 100–104). Washington, DC: National Academies Press. See also Lowe, S. R., Galea, S., Uddin, M., & Koenen, K. C. (2014). Trajectories of posttraumatic stress among urban residents. *American Journal of Community Psychology, 53,* 159–172. http://dx.doi.org/10.1007/s10464-014-9634-6
140. Nightingale (1994), *On the edge: A history of poor Black children and their American dreams,* p. 10.
141. Ward (2013), *Men we reaped: A memoir,* p. 169.

142. Butler, P. (2017). *Chokehold: Policing Black men* (p. 2). New York, NY: The New Press.
143. Rios, V. M. (2011). *Punished: Policing the lives of Black and Latino boys.* New York, NY: New York University Press, p. xiv. See also Henning, K. (2017). Boys to men: The role of policing in the socialization of Black boys. In A. J. Davis (Ed.), *Policing the Black man: Arrest, prosecution, and imprisonment* (pp. 57–94). New York, NY: Pantheon.
144. Goff, P. A., Jackson, M. C., Di Leone, B. A., Culotta, C. M., DiTomasso, N. A., & DiTomasso, N. (2014). The essence of innocence: Consequences of dehumanizing Black children. *Journal of Personality and Social Psychology, 106,* 526–545. http://dx.doi.org/10.1037/a0035663
145. Weitzer, R., & Tuch, S. (2006). *Race and policing in America: Conflict and reform.* New York, NY: Cambridge University Press. http://dx.doi.org/10.1017/CBO9780511617256 Half of the African American respondents also thought that racial prejudice was "very common" among the police in their city, and half felt that they were stopped by the police just because of their race or ethnic background (again, both percentages were well over the percentage of Whites who felt the same way, despite living in the same communities).
146. Weitzer & Tuch (2006), *Race and policing in America,* p. 56. For an excellent discussion of the recent history of increasingly aggressive, expansive, and intrusive police practices in poor communities of Color, see Soss, J., & Weaver, V. (2017). Police are our government: Politics, political science, and the policing of race–class subjugated communities. *Annual Review of Political Science, 20,* 565–591. http://dx.doi.org/10.1146/annurev-polisci-060415-093825
147. Lopez, W. D., Novak, N. L., Harner, M., Martinez, R., & Seng, J. S. (2018). The traumatogenic potential of law enforcement home raids: An exploratory report. *Traumatology, 24,* 193–199. http://dx.doi.org/10.1037/trm0000148
148. Del Toro, J., Lloyd, T., Buchanan, K. S., Robins, S. J., Bencharit, L. Z., Smiedt, M. G., . . . Goff, P. A. (2019). The criminogenic and psychological effects of police stops on adolescent black and Latino boys. *PNAS Latest Articles,* 1–8. http://dx.doi.org/10.1073/pnas.1808976116
149. Del Toro, Lloyd, Buchanan, Robins, Bencharit, Smiedt, . . . Goff (2019), The criminogenic and psychological effects of police stops, pp. 6–7.
150. Ayres, I., & Borowsky, J. (2008). A study of racially disparate outcomes in the Los Angeles police department, Retrieved from http://www.aclu-sc.org/view/47, quoted in Unnever, J. D., & Gabbidon, S. L. (2011). *A theory of African American offending: Race, racism, and crime.* New York, NY: Routledge, p. 171. http://dx.doi.org/10.4324/9780203828564
151. Unnever, & Gabbidon (2011), *A theory of African American offending: Race, racism, and crime,* p. 172. Thus, as they put it: "[I]t is difficult for African Americans to believe that they should obey the law when they see it as a racist means to disrespect, harass, humiliate, bully, and unfairly imprison them" (p. 173).
152. For some recent discussions of the myriad points at which implicit bias, racially disproportionate practices, and other racial factors influence criminal justice outcomes, see Berdejó, C. (2018). Criminalizing race: Racial disparities in plea-bargaining. *Boston College Law Review, 59,* 1187–1249; Chin, W. Y. (2016). Racial cumulative disadvantage: The cumulative effects of racial bias at multiple decision points in the criminal justice system. *Wake Forest Journal of Law & Policy, 6,* 441–458; and Tonry, M. (2019). Predictions of dangerousness in sentencing: Déjà vu all over again. *Crime and Justice: A Review of Research, 48,* 439–482. http://dx.doi.org/10.1086/701895
153. Chambliss, W. J. (1994). Policing the ghetto underclass: The politics of law and law enforcement. *Social Problems, 41,* 177–194, p. 183. http://dx.doi.org/10.2307/3096929

154. See the references cited in note 55.
155. Nightingale (1994), *On the edge: A history of poor Black children and their American dreams*, p. 40.
156. Morris, N. (1995). The contemporary prison, 1965–present. In N. Morris & D. Rothman (Eds.), *The Oxford history of the prison: The practice of punishment in Western society* (pp. 202–231). New York, NY: Oxford University Press.
157. Williams, T., & Kornblum, W. (1994). *The uptown kids: Struggle and hope in the projects*. New York, NY: Grosset/Putnam.
158. Anderson (1990), *Streetwise: Race, class, and social change in an urban community*, p. 66.
159. Sampson, R. J. (1987). Urban Black violence: The effect of male joblessness and family disruption. *American Journal of Sociology, 93*, 348–382. http://dx.doi.org/10.1086/228748
160. For example, Blau, J. R., & Blau, P. M. (1982). The cost of inequality: Metropolitan structure and violent crime. *American Sociological Review, 47*, 114–129. http://dx.doi.org/10.2307/2095046
161. For example, Balkwell, J. W. (1990). Ethnic inequality and the rate of homicide. *Social Forces, 69*, 53–70. http://dx.doi.org/10.1093/sf/69.1.53
162. Harvey, W. (1986). Homicide among Black adults: Life in the subculture of exasperation. In D. Hawkins (Ed.), *Homicide among Black Americans* (pp. 153–171). Lanham, MD: University Press of America.

8

Individualistic Myths and the Disregard of Context

Deconstructing "Equally Free Autonomous Choice"

Everybody is given the privilege to compete—on an arena built by and for the middle classes. It is an arrangement perfectly suited for transforming structural inequalities into experience[s] of individual failure and guilt.

—NILS CHRISTIE[1]

People do not act as autonomous moral agents, impervious to the social realities in which they are enmeshed.

—ALBERT BANDURA[2]

There are very few important public policy arenas in which the fiction that human behavior is the exclusive product of truly "free and autonomous choice" persists. Criminal law is one of them. Viewed through its narrow frame, lawbreakers are routinely regarded as acting unencumbered by past history and unfettered by present circumstances. Remarkably, what historian Leonard Levy said about 19th-century American criminal law—that "guilt, like sin, is personal because each man is the captain of his own conduct" and that "the law pictured personal action as the result of the exercise of free will"[3]—accurately describes contemporary legal doctrines and practices.

Any attempt to fully integrate what is now known about the long-term, powerful influence of external forces and factors on criminal behavior is still met with much resistance throughout the nation's criminal justice system.

http://dx.doi.org/10.1037/0000172-009
Criminality in Context: The Psychological Foundations of Criminal Justice Reform,
by C. Haney

The crime master narrative's core behavioral assumption, and the one on which the prevailing model of legal responsibility is still based, posits that criminal acts are the simple product of bad and blameworthy choices. Despite decades of research that have significantly complicated the picture, the model has proven remarkably resistant to change. In fact, at times it seems invulnerable to empirical challenge—so to speak, "data proof."

The fact that the venerable free choice model that has dominated traditional legal thinking for so long remains stubbornly entrenched in criminal law and criminal justice institutions, firmly at the center of the powerful crime master narrative that pervades popular thinking about crime and punishment, impedes attempts to achieve meaningful and comprehensive criminal justice reform.[4] This chapter attempts to both explain that persistence and to undertake the difficult task of deconstructing the flawed thinking that is the basis for this culturally embedded view.

THE "NOT EVERYBODY" FALLACY

My critique of the entrenched free choice model at the heart of the crime master narrative requires an extended discussion of what I term the "not everybody fallacy." The fallacy begins with the simple and entirely accurate observation that "not everybody" who has experienced a traumatic, potentially criminogenic social and institutional history actually grows up to engage in criminal behavior as an adult. The same can be said about persons who enter powerfully criminogenic environments in adulthood—not everybody succumbs to the pressures and provocations that I discussed in Chapter 5. However, this fairly unremarkable and otherwise straightforward observation is often then used as the basis for the assertion that because "not everybody" who has been exposed to criminogenic risk factors behaves in the same way (i.e., does not engage in criminal behavior), social history and circumstance cannot possibly represent the primary causes of crime.

There are too many instances of this kind of dismissive rhetoric to comprehensively illustrate. But here is one representative example of how the fallacy is framed:

> Most poor people are law-abiding and most kids from broken homes are not delinquents. Children may bear the scars of neglect and deprivation for life, but most do not become criminals. The environment does have an effect, but people perceive and react to similar conditions of life very differently.[5]

The crime master narrative's explanation of these different reactions to purportedly similar conditions is *choice*; that is, persons who did end up engaging in criminal behavior were ones who simply *chose* to do bad, and those similarly situated persons who refrained from crime did so because of the better choices they made.

In this way, the empirically correct observation that people vary in their reactions to similar past social historical and immediate contextual conditions is turned into a superficially plausible, but ultimately illogical and fallacious, "disproof" of the causal role of criminogenic social factors. This misleading "not everybody" fallacy leads many citizens, legal decision-makers, and social policy analysts to reject the importance of social history and context in explaining criminal behavior and prevents them from developing the most appropriate and scientifically valid ways of responding to and, ideally, preventing it. Because this "not everybody" fallacy so often impedes clear thinking about the causes of crime and thwarts attempts to achieve meaningful criminal justice reform, it warrants a detailed discussion.

Note that in virtually all other contexts in which we attempt to understand and explain human social behavior—save those in which legal blame is being affixed and punishment is being meted out—we intuitively recognize the important ways that background and social history can significantly influence what we do and even shape who we are and what we are capable of becoming. Few people doubt the wisdom of the poet Wordsworth's observation that "the child is father of the man,"[6] or Alexander Pope's homily that "just as the twig is bent, the tree's inclined."[7] Thus, under most circumstances there is generally little dispute over whether experiences we have early in life influences the choices we make later or help to determine the behavior in which we subsequently engage.

Indeed, the relatively widespread attention and concern that are now appropriately focused on identifying and reporting child maltreatment in our society—and the vigor with which abusers are vilified and sometimes legally prosecuted—are based in part on the implicit recognition that early exposure to this kind of traumatic mistreatment can tragically alter the life course of its young victims.[8] Even several of the most conservative members of the current U.S. Supreme Court—Justices Alito, Roberts, and Thomas—approvingly quoted scientific experts to the effect that certain forms of child abuse are not only "grossly intrusive in the lives of children" but also "harmful to their normal psychological, emotional and sexual development in ways which no just or humane society can tolerate."[9]

In fact, Justice Alito explicitly acknowledged the empirical relationships that have been established in the scientific literature between sexual abuse and "later problems" in the lives of victims, including substance abuse, psychiatric illness, and criminal arrests. In part because "child-rape victims become society's problems as well," he argued in favor of allowing the perpetrators of this crime to be sentenced to death.[10] Tellingly, however, Alito has endorsed these propositions *only* in the context of holding individual abusers accountable (as I say, accountable enough to punish them by death). He inexplicably refuses to acknowledge the important criminogenic role of abuse in explaining adult criminal behavior when doing so would logically lead to mitigating or lessening the punishment meted out—for example, in cases where the victims of this abuse are themselves capital defendants whose life paths are characterized by some of the worst but predictable behavioral consequences of their earlier traumatic victimization.[11]

Widespread concerns about the damaging effects of child maltreatment exist despite the fact that we know that "not every" child who experiences abusive treatment will be affected in the *same* way. Indeed, in *general* discussions of child abuse, recognition that its long-term harms are highly variable and may significantly differ on a case-by-case basis does not detract in the least from public and professional recognition that it is a serious social problem, worthy of widespread concern and decisive intervention. The considerable range of different effects that abuse has on its victims later in their lives does not lessen our sense of urgency about developing effective social and legal policies to reduce or eliminate it, nor does the fact that the specific consequences of abuse may vary from person to person reduce the importance of trying to minimize the overall number of children who are victimized in this way and to provide caring services for those who have been potentially harmed. Nor would most sensible analysts of the long-term consequences of such abuse suggest that the different effects that are manifested by different individual victims can be explained simply by the willful choices that they subsequently make—that some victims freely "chose" to suffer life-long bouts of depression, others simply "chose" chronic alcohol or drug addiction, and still others miraculously "decided" not to be bothered in life-altering ways at all.

Similarly, most thoughtful legal analysts and members of the public readily accept the *general* proposition that childhood matters, profoundly. That is, few doubt that persons who have suffered abuse or maltreatment as children, have experienced significant poverty and racism in their lives, grown up in a conflict-ridden domestic or urban "war zone," or been victimized by stays in uncaring or brutalizing juvenile or adult institutions are more likely to suffer from a whole range of potentially serious emotional and behavioral problems in adulthood. Most would accept—again, in general terms—that some of the long-term problems that abuse victims might experience could well include an increased chance or likelihood of engaging in troubled, conflictual, and even criminal behavior. Moreover, few people would argue prospectively that concerns over the future consequences of the relatively high levels of child abuse, childhood poverty, or early, painful encounters with race-based inequalities that still plague our society are misplaced because, after all, the victims of these unfortunate experiences can and should simply "choose" to ignore, set aside, or rise above the scarring effects that may beset them later on.

Yet, when we attempt to take trauma- and risk factor-filled social histories systematically into account in assessing blameworthiness for *specific* crimes or judging the culpability of *particular* lawbreakers, we are still often met with a moralistic resistance that borders on the irrational. Similarly, when policies for controlling crime are proposed that depend less exclusively on punishing individuals after the fact and seek instead to preventively address structural and situational causes, clear thinking succumbs to confused rhetoric about "making excuses" and letting undeserving, manipulative criminals "get away with it."[12] Indeed, in the politically charged atmosphere in which these sometimes emotionally overwrought discussions occur, persons who propose empirically supported approaches to crime control that take social history and circumstantial factors explicitly into account are often the target of unwarranted ad hominem accusations about their alleged lack of "moral toughness" or membership in some kind of "criminals' lobby."[13]

Why this double standard? Part of the explanation appears to be rooted in history and tradition. If it is true that "law is frozen history,"[14] then these legal doctrines of responsibility are encased in several past centuries of prescientific thinking. As I noted at the outset of this book, judgments of legal responsibility were originally founded on a traditional model of psychological individualism, one fashioned and maintained without the benefit of the kind of contemporary knowledge and insight that we can now bring to bear on the question of crime causation. Long-standing criminal law doctrines and an imposing landscape of criminal justice institutions that were built in support of them were founded on these now increasingly untenable views. Fully integrating and embracing these new context-based perspectives would require us to relinquish aspects of a deeply entrenched belief system that has served the legal status quo quite well.[15]

As a result, two seemingly incompatible points of view co-exist simultaneously in the minds of many people. On the one hand, we intuitively appreciate the potentially destructive and even long-term criminogenic effects of certain harmful past experiences as well as certain crime-inducing present conditions such as abject poverty and dangerous levels of neighborhood disadvantage. Indeed, no one of us would voluntarily allow one of our own children or other loved ones to be exposed to these things, in part because we grasp the long-term effects that might be incurred. On the other hand, many people continue to act as though those things have no relevance whatsoever for case-by-case judgments that are made about personal responsibility and legal blameworthiness and refuse to acknowledge their importance in the creation of more intelligent and effective approaches to crime control.

In addition to the inertia that comes from such a history and established set of traditions, the apparent plausibility of the "not everybody" argument is buttressed by a highly consistent set of media stereotypes and periodic doses of politically inspired law-and-order rhetoric that repeatedly reinforce the crime master narrative. Both sources of crime-related "messaging" operate in tandem to serve as powerful forms of public miseducation about these issues, leaving many people irrationally skeptical about any social scientific or other explanation for criminal behavior that challenges the crime master narrative on which they have learned to rely.[16] The argument that what we now know about powerful criminogenic forces and factors should be taken into account in adjudicating responsibility and calibrating punishment is often met not only with skepticism but outright hostility. As I say, this hostility also helps to thwart criminal justice reform and the development of truly effective, humane crime control policies. Too often the fear of crime and anger toward those who commit it cloud our ability to think clearly about how a more just and effective criminal justice system can be created. Thus, the fallacious notions that continue to undergird the crime master narrative warrant careful debunking.

"FREE CHOICE" THROUGH THE LENS OF SOCIAL CONTEXTUALISM

As I have implied throughout this book, our legal system continues to ignore at its peril the social histories and present circumstances of persons held responsible for engaging in criminal behavior. That peril includes continuing to pursue crime control policies that are far less effective than they might be and employing doctrines of responsibility and culpability that are essentially unfair to many persons whose fates are adjudicated in the criminal justice system. In the remainder of this chapter, I discuss some of the mistaken behavioral assumptions, illogical inferences, and selective information processing that collectively account for the tendency to discount the clear implications of what we now know about the powerful influence of social history and social context.

Specifically, I will suggest that the "not everybody" fallacy and the outmoded model of unencumbered "free choice" on which it is based suffer from a number of logical and empirical problems. They include (a) the tendency to assume that variations in people's behavior and life outcomes must be the exclusive product of the different individual choices they have made; (b) failing to consider the fact that crime is often committed under circumstances where very little meaningful "choice-making" occurs or is even possible; (c) ignoring the damaging effects that multiple, chronic risk factors have on choice-making itself; (d) overlooking the fact that what appear to be nearly identical past histories and present circumstances are often significantly different in fact; (e) disregarding the aggregate impact of risk factors, as well as differences in their magnitude, duration, and the age at which they are encountered; and, finally, (f) failing to recognize that traumas and risk factors can produce a wide range of different problematic outcomes that depend in part on the presence or absence of protective factors or buffers, vulnerabilities, stressors, and available coping mechanisms in a person's life.

I discuss these various limitations of and qualifications to the crime master narrative, free choice model, and "not everybody" fallacy in more detail in each of the several sections that follow.

Behavioral Variation, Choice, and Context

This section discusses some of the general reasons why apparent variations in the way that different people behave within the same social context do not necessarily reflect different choices that they have made free of that context. Instead, the different ways that people react and adapt to the same immediate conditions and situations may be a function of their different socialization histories and the unique mix of different buffers and vulnerabilities that people bring into a given situation. Their specific reactions and adaptations nonetheless occur *in direct response to* the circumstances themselves (rather than independent of them) and are, therefore, hardly a function of some kind of unencumbered "free choice."

This is perhaps easier to see in domains of life or common experience that are far removed from the morally charged settings in which criminal responsibility is affixed and punishment meted out. In psychopharmacology, for example, different patients often react very differently to the same psychoactive drug.[17] Psychiatrists regularly prescribe different psychotropic medications to patients with the "same" psychiatric disorder because of differences in the ways the patients react, and they also carefully calibrate different doses of the same drug for different patients who are identically afflicted. Sometimes, these variations in patient reactions are based on measurable differences between them (e.g., age, gender, body weight). Most other times, though, there are a host of idiosyncratic factors that are difficult to precisely identify but nonetheless result in different reactions occurring with different patients.

Yet, none of these differences in outcome—whatever their origin—detract from the simple fact that the patients are responding to essentially the same common *internal* stimulus—in particular, the psychoactive drug that they have taken in interaction with their psychological condition. It is easy to see that their reactions—whatever they are and in whatever different ways they are manifested—would not have occurred without their having taken the drug. No one would plausibly argue that the range of individual variations that occur in reaction to the same drug are produced primarily by different "free choices" that are being made by the patients themselves.

Similarly, the different reactions that people have to powerful *external* stimuli—like childhood risk factors or criminogenic social contexts—do not require us to resort to "free choice" to explain. That is, these different patterns of responding are sometimes based on measurable differences between people's capacities or capabilities (e.g., resiliency). Other times they stem from idiosyncratic factors that may not be easy to identify and, therefore, defy precise description (just as in the case of varied reactions to psychoactive drugs). But in each case, the significant influences on the behavior—and the variations between people—include their past histories and key elements of the situation in which they act. Thus, history and context must be taken into account in order to fully understand and explain the individual variations that we observe in behavior.

Different life trajectories often can be explained by the different options available to persons as they cope and adapt to whatever challenges and stressors they confront. The variations in the options they actually have or perceive are available to them often reflect differences in their personal characteristics (e.g., gender, age) and the way those characteristics interact with their structural position, rather than the exercise of unencumbered "choice." For example, urban ethnographer Carl Nightingale has suggested that higher high school graduation rates and successful employment among inner-city African American girls might reflect their slight advantage in having what he termed "greater avenues for psychic expression" compared with boys.[18] That is, although the girls in the neighborhoods that he studied certainly were constrained in other ways, they were afforded somewhat more latitude to pursue the socially acceptable options to express and channel the structurally based anger and pain that they, too, felt as a result of the harsh surrounding circumstances in which they were raised. Unlike the boys, however, those options did not often place them in direct contact with the criminal justice system or the potentially criminogenic experiences it often entailed. In this way, the pathways afforded the girls did not so strongly disfavor or preclude them from staying in school or caring openly about their classroom performance. Nor were they as likely as the boys to be derided for persisting with their studies or for conscientiously pursuing whatever employment opportunities were available to them. Even though they appeared to be "in the same situation" as the boys, they were not. Yet, the incremental advantage—being given somewhat greater latitude to pursue socially acceptable options—was no more under their direct control than their "choice" of gender.

Conversely, early juvenile justice system intervention in the lives of boys and young men of Color placed them on a more problematic pathway than their noninstitutionalized peers. The greater rates at which these boys dropped out of school, the high rates of delinquency with which dropping out was associated, the boys' subsequent more frequent and more serious contacts with the criminal justice system, and the higher rates at which they adopted later and longer-term criminal life styles was not a simple function of "choice." That is, it was not the case that the boys simply "chose to be bad" and the girls did not.

In a related way, it is sometimes the case that variations in behavior in the "same" situation are the result of different subjective interpretations that persons have of the situations that they enter. In this way, they are not really "experiencing" the same environment (at least not in the same way), even though they appear to be. For example, psychologist Walter Mischel, whose early work helped precipitate the "situational revolution" and a contemporary reformulation of the field of personality psychology that I discussed earlier in this book,[19] acknowledged the importance of what he termed "situations inside the head," by which he meant "the person's chronic affective states, styles of encoding information, self-representations and expectations (e.g., about one's own efficacy), goals, values, self-regulatory strategies, and action scripts, all of which are likely to interact with and change the impact of the external stimulus."[20] Mischel argued that these mental representations of situations are often where the real power over behavior resides.

He also argued that it ought to be possible for people to influence these things on their own—"through self-generated strategies to change the mental representations" of the situation—just as they are influenced by the external situations.[21] These "self-generated strategies" sound a lot like choices, and

I suspect Mischel intended them to be understood as such. However, for many people, these kinds of strategies are as elusive as the changed behavior that they are presumably capable of directing. This is why bad habits are so difficult to relinquish and why problematic behavior patterns so often persist. Not everyone has the same access to knowledge about techniques for changing "mental representations" or the capacity to implement the techniques even when they do. Indeed, few such "self-generated" strategies are truly *self*-generated at all. Instead, they typically must be learned or brought about through changed circumstances (e.g., positive reinforcement for their use), and this, in turn, often requires outside intervention and support (e.g., counseling).

For example, relapse following treatment for drug and alcohol addiction is between 50% and 70% during the first year following treatment.[22] Weight loss and the successful cessation of cigarette smoking are so notoriously difficult to achieve that elaborate therapeutic regimens and entire industries have grown up to facilitate accomplishing the task.[23] Even more discrete health-related behaviors such as medication compliance are difficult to maintain or modify without assistance.[24] More generally, a number of studies have shown that simply having an expressed desire or intention to change problematic habits or some aspect of one's characteristic patterns of behavior is not sufficient to actually accomplish the goal. Instead, it typically requires additional, systematic intervention.[25]

Given the intractability of most ingrained behavior patterns, *all* of these contingencies—learning, changed circumstances, and outside intervention and support—must *repeatedly* and *consistently* occur before anyone's "self" can undo well-established but ultimately dysfunctional adaptations and begin to generate more appropriate alternative strategies. Unfortunately, access to the necessary knowledge and the resources with which to obtain outside intervention and support as well as the ease with which to implement any changed mental representations may be compromised by the past traumas and risk factors to which someone has been exposed and the problematic life circumstances with which he or she must presently cope. Moreover, these social history-based limitations and barriers are often compounded by structural disadvantages over which people also have little or no control and certainly do not "choose." Here, too, variations in behavior—so-called *self*-initiated change—is significantly influenced by past and present contexts rather than the simple product of "free choice."

Unpacking the Nature of "Choice"

The crime master narrative has given rise to and supports the legal presumption that lawbreakers routinely make morally blameworthy, free and autonomous choices to engage in criminal behavior. The law assumes not only that people intend the natural and probable consequences of their actions but also that those intentions are the product of a more or less *deliberative* process. Thus, lawbreakers supposedly first think about engaging in crime, decide that they will, and then proceed to do so. However, the ostensibly simple relationship that the law posits between thought and action is actually quite problematic.

We now know that this seemingly commonsense sequence—the proposition that people act only after they have engaged in deliberative thought—is not quite how the process typically unfolds in real life. In fact, a number of studies have raised questions about the conscious nature of "choice" in general, and whether most behavior, under "normal" circumstances, is preceded by a thoughtful consideration of options and a purposeful selection between alternative courses of action. That is, the simple notion that behavior is always preceded by conscious, deliberative thought has become increasingly untenable.

Thus, contemporary psychological research has established the "automaticity" in much of the social behavior in which people routinely engage—that is, its fundamentally unreflective nature. By this account, the perception of conscious, deliberative choice is generally constructed (and often reconstructed) *after* the fact—either by others, who attempt to make sense of a particular course of action by attributing intent to the person who took it, or by the actor himself, who examines his actions and interpolates an intervening thought process that, in fact, did not necessarily occur. Years ago, social psychologist Daryl Bem articulated what he termed "self perception theory," arguing that people routinely infer their own beliefs and motivations after the fact, by reflecting on their actions and interpreting them the way an outside observer would.[26] Thus, rather than having access to some private, internal decision-making process, we often "perceive ourselves" from the outside, and draw conclusions about what must have been going on internally to account for our behavior, including the "choices" we appear to have made.

More recently, John Bargh added significantly to our understanding of "choice-making." He has suggested that "much of everyday life—thinking, feeling, and doing—is automatic in that it is driven by current features of the environment" and mediated by our automatic cognitive processing of those features, rather than "by conscious choice or reflection."[27] Bargh has acknowledged that the environment that influences thought, emotion, and action is a "psychological situation"—which can include the internal reactions of the individual—rather than simply a set of objective, external circumstances. Nonetheless, he maintained that "goals can be activated automatically (without an act of will) and then may operate on environmental information without one's awareness or need to monitor the goal's progress."[28]

Bargh was equally clear that automaticity stems from "direct environmental effects for which no conscious involvement is required," a perspective that led him to conclude that much social behavior is caused "by some force other than an act of will."[29] He also rejected the notion that people can simply "choose" to neutralize or counteract the effects of the environment, arguing that "[s]uch acts of control require an awareness of the possibility of being influenced in ways other than those of which one is aware, and such occasions are few and far between."[30] Bargh directly disputed the notion that people almost always "intend"—in the sense of having thought through and decided to bring about—the natural probable consequences of their behavior. These insights directly challenge assumptions about "free choice" that still dominate the criminal law.

Beyond the questions that Bargh and others have raised about choice in general, there is a great deal of evidence that the nature of the choice-making that occurs in the course of much criminal behavior is especially compromised and problematic. Much crime is committed under circumstances in which little actual reflective thought—a sober consideration of the various reasons for and against a course of action and a rational decision about how to proceed—is feasible or even possible. Many criminal acts are impulsive or reactive rather than carefully premeditated,[31] and a high percentage of persons who violate the law are under the influence of drugs or alcohol when they do.

Indeed, there are numerous estimates of the role that drug and alcohol impairment plays in facilitating crime. Perhaps the most extensive is the U.S. Justice Department's Survey of Inmates, which includes self-reports of approximately 20,000 carefully sampled state and federal prisoners. These national surveys were administered every 6 to 7 years, and they produced stable patterns of results over time. According to data in the first two of the three most recent surveys—conducted in 1991 and again in 1997—approximately three quarters of state prisoners and four fifths of federal prisoners reported being what could be characterized as *"alcohol- or drug-involved"* or both, including *one half* of the state prisoners and a *quarter to a third* of federal prisoners who were using drugs or alcohol at the time of the offense for which they were convicted and sent to prison.[32] Although the third survey, conducted in 2004, did not include data for alcohol involvement or use at the time of the crime, the data for drug use was virtually identical to the earlier surveys. Thus, prisoners in 2004 reported the same rate of "regular" drug use as prisoners had reported in 1997 (69.2% vs. 69.6%, respectively), and the same percentage were using *at the time of their offense* (32.1% in 2004 vs. 32.6% in 1997).[33]

Another study that was conducted at roughly the same time as the last of the three Surveys of Inmates analyzed data from a large sample of arrestees and also confirmed the high percentage of drug and alcohol use among lawbreakers.[34] To determine the extent of drug and alcohol use by persons booked into jails and detention facilities around the country, civilian research teams worked in 39 separate monitoring sites and conducted direct interviews and drug testing within 48 hours of someone's arrest. The study found that over *two thirds* of the men who were assessed tested positive for one of five different drugs, with more than a third reporting "heavy" drug use and a slightly higher number being identified as "at risk for drug dependence."[35] Although an average of only about one in 10 of the arrestees tested positive for alcohol consumption at the time of arrest, nearly half reported having engaged in "binge drinking" within the last month, and more than a quarter were identified as "at risk of alcohol dependence."[36]

To be sure, drug and alcohol use can and does impair judgment, increase impulsivity, and impede careful decision-making. This fact serves as the legal justification for regulating the use of these substances and prohibiting some of them altogether; it is why, for example, persons found driving "under the influence" are prosecuted—based on the presumption that they are "impaired." Although it certainly does not play a role in every case and rarely serves as a legal excuse for criminal behavior, widespread drug and alcohol use by persons who engage in crime compromises the nature and quality of whatever choices they make and undermines the validity of the prevailing "free choice" model of criminality. It should also give pause to the presumptions about normatively "conscious, rational decision-making" that are routinely attached to defendants in the legal processes by which their criminal responsibility is determined and appropriate punishments calculated and meted out.

Of course, I am not suggesting that criminal behavior is never consciously chosen or that it is always the product of substance-impaired thinking that precludes rationality. Rather, I mean simply that it is important to be cognizant of the ways that what we mean by "choice" can and often should be problematized and, therefore, carefully assessed and analyzed rather than automatically presumed in the case of every criminal act. Moreover, as I discuss in the remainder of this chapter, even when criminal behavior has been demonstrably "chosen," it is worth considering—and under some circumstances taken explicitly into account—whether and how the choices that people make to engage in crime are significantly influenced by factors in their past and present over which they have little control.

The Contextual Determinants of "Choice-Making"

Setting aside the issues of whether and how often people make conscious choices that guide their everyday life and the degree to which crime-related choices are impaired by drug and alcohol use, truly meaningful choices can only be made when persons are able to perceive available options and then to pursue them. But the capacity to perceive and take advantage of viable options can be significantly limited by a person's troubled and traumatic past history. One of the most destructive legacies of childhood trauma is the way that it distorts child's or adolescent's' understanding of what is possible and truncates their view of viable future pathways. In addition to being deprived of material advantages, many chronically poor children grow up in environments where opportunities are not only drastically limited in actual fact but may be impossible for them to perceive at all.

Indeed, our self-perceptions are not necessarily any more freely chosen than the experiences that helped to create them. When formative experiences consist largely of trauma, abuse, and deprivation, subsequent life choices are hardly unencumbered by what preceded them. Child maltreatment can and often does diminish self-esteem and undermine a sense of agency, changing a child's perception of what he or she deserves in life or is capable of achieving. Similarly, racial discrimination is pernicious in part because it can condition its victims to limit themselves, pre-emptively foreclose plans and dreams, and abandon aspirations in advance of ever having pursued them. Editorial opinion writer Charles Blow's thoughtful commentary is relevant here. He observed that individual choices and broader systemic or structural disadvantages are "interwoven" in people's lives "like the fingers of clasped hands"—that is, that "[p]eople make choices within the context of their circumstances." Blow was especially concerned with the effect of racial bias, noting that the context or circumstances in which people make choices may be severely affected by such bias: "These biases do material damage as well as help breed a sense of despair, which in turn can have a depressive effect on aspiration and motivation."[37]

In this way, then, people's "bad choices" often reflect a conditioned inability to perceive and fully appreciate—rather than a conscious decision to willfully disregard—even the limited set of options that are, in fact, available to them. In addition, risk factors and traumas, such as abuse and neglect, often diminish their victims' optimism and the self-confidence needed to take advantage of whatever positive options and life paths they do perceive. There is a great deal of research in social psychology that demonstrates the multiple ways in which people's confidence levels, their experience of social anxiety, and the evaluations they make of their own performance can be altered by relatively modest negative feedback—including feedback that is actually incorrect or false.[38] Thus, even small differences in the messages persons receive from their environment about their options and abilities can shape their self-perceptions. Of course, the feedback that is often consistently generated over the course of psychologically embattled childhood and adolescence are far more powerful, persistent, and self-defining than any of the comparatively pallid messages that can be ethically used in laboratory research studies.

In a different but related way, the problematic short-term survival strategies that I discussed in Chapter 4 that are adopted in the wake of trauma can have profoundly negative long-term consequences. Because these detrimental outcomes are not readily apparent at the time the adaptations are made, few children and adolescents can foresee where they are likely to lead. Fewer still can fairly be said to have "freely chosen" the worst consequences that they may eventually bring about. Coping strategies to manage multiple risk factors and life traumas are often adopted under circumstances in which children and adolescents feel that their very psychological survival is at stake. But feelings of desperation often preclude sober reflection and cloud judgment. The inability to foresee where their forced choices ultimately will take them, especially if the available options seem reasonable or necessary at the time, is compounded if these pathways have been normalized in the communities where they live.

As one group of researchers described the process generally,

> [T]he evidence suggests that there are continuities in development that stem from the opening up or closing down of further opportunities—a train of events

> in which there are lasting sequelae as a result of a cumulative chain of indirect effects.[39]

Earlier choices can help create some options but invariably close down others. Yet these patterns—chains of linked events and the consequences that follow—are typically identifiable only after the fact and even then not always by the persons who have initiated them. Unlike academic researchers, who are positioned to observe the adaptations to and long-term consequences of childhood trauma—systematically and at a distance—children and adolescents who are groping for ways to cope with and overcome these experiences and who may seize on one or another short-term survival strategy to alleviate their immediate emotional distress or diminished sense of self cannot anticipate the future opportunities they are "closing down." This is reminiscent of the discussion of path dependence in Chapter 2 and the way that the "critical moments or junctures that shape the basic contours of social life" can operate to put people on a particular path that will prove difficult for them to modify, reverse, or otherwise exit.[40] The challenge is to know when a juncture is truly critical and to be able anticipate how difficult it will be to exit the path on which it may put you.

For example, Gerald Patterson and his colleagues have identified the causal connection between poor parenting (e.g., harsh, inconsistent discipline, little positive involvement, inadequate monitoring and supervision) and coercive, socially unskilled behavior on the part of the children who have been subjected to it. Patterson learned that this coercive behavior on the child's part—a predictable adaptation made in response to a dysfunctional family life—frequently led to social rejection and school failure. Moreover, he and his colleagues found that children typically reacted to these two unexpected and undesirable outcomes by adopting what the researchers termed "deviant peer group membership," which not only facilitated subsequent delinquent acts and substance abuse but also made a series of problematic adult life outcomes more likely. The negative consequences included "[becoming a] school dropout, uneven employment histories, substance abuse, marital difficulties, multiple offenses, incarceration, and institutionalization,"[41] none of which were likely "chosen" or foreseen at the time the seemingly reasonable—even necessary or compelled—adaptations were made.

Similarly, other developmental researchers have documented the ways in which "interactional styles" can have important consequences that exacerbate a child's early difficulties and produce a set of related problems that persist across an entire life course. For example, Avshalom Caspi and Daryl Bem observed that "a boy whose ill temper leads him to drop out of school may thereby limit his future career opportunities and unwittingly channel himself into frustrating life circumstances that further evoke a pattern of striking out explosively against the world."[42] Setting aside the fact that an "ill temper" is unlikely to emerge in a social historical vacuum, it is unrealistic to assume that a boy who makes the choice (for whatever reason) to drop out of school can meaningfully anticipate all of the ways in which his future career opportunities will be limited as a result. He is unlikely to foresee the "frustrating life circumstances" that the research tells us he is now more likely to encounter, and he certainly cannot appreciate in advance how it will feel to be mired in the midst of these compromised options. Like any of us at such an early stage of life, he surely lacks the self-awareness to know how much more often his tendency to strike out "explosively" will be evoked in the face of the more frequent, future frustrations that will result from his seemingly innocent (and rarely entirely "voluntary") decision to drop out of school. And he cannot possibly foresee what we know may be the final unfortunate step in this linked sequence of events—how much more crime-prone the preceding steps are likely to make him. It makes little sense to insist that the criminal "choices" this young man now seems more destined to make are somehow free and unencumbered by his past noncriminal choices and the present problematic life circumstances to which they have led him.

Of course, even managing to perceive a broader range of available choices or envision a hopeful alternative future does not guarantee that victims of childhood trauma or neighborhood violence can implement the actions required to attain them (especially if they have never seen them modeled in ways that they feel they can emulate), or that they can overcome other powerful structural disadvantages that they face. As Carl Nightingale wrote about the young girls whose lives he studied and to whom I referred earlier, the slight advantage they may have had over their male classmates in terms of the broader avenues of emotional expression available to them did not necessarily ensure that they could overcome the other forces at work in their lives, because "a slightly wider array of options to express pain does not by any means always reduce the power of girl's painful memories sufficiently to avoid inauspicious outcomes."[43]

It is also clear, except in the limited metaphysical way in which there are always "options" to behave differently, that past traumas and present criminogenic circumstances can impede a person's ability choose more auspicious outcomes. The habits of envisioning possible alternative courses of action, thinking through potential consequences of each, and devising strategies for planful behavior—indeed, choice-making and decision-making themselves—are behaviors that must be taught and learned. However, a number of children who subsequently engage in illegal behavior also grow up in environments that are so neglectful, chaotic, or threatening that they not only do not learn how to do these things well but do not know anyone who does. They are too often forced merely to react, struggling to survive the seemingly perilous world around them. This characteristic way of behaving is sometimes described as impulsivity, but most people are impulsive until they are taught otherwise.

In any event, all of these factors—the way that exposure to risks and traumas distorts and narrows the perceptions of available options, the difficulty of fully and accurately anticipating the long-term negative consequences of short-term survival strategies and adaptations to hardship and distress, and the sometimes insurmountable challenge of devising and implementing more positive alternative pathways in the absence of role models and structural supports—combine to ensure that choices made in such contexts are rarely "free" and rarely if ever unencumbered by past history and present circumstances.

Critical Variations in the "Same" Social Histories

In the classic "not everybody" argument used to ostensibly rebut social contextual explanations of crime, the paradigmatic case to which critics often point is the indisputable fact that siblings raised "in the same family" did not "turn out the same," especially when only some family members succumbed to the criminogenic forces around them by subsequently engaging in crime and others did not. The fact that siblings ostensibly exposed to the *same* trauma- and risk factor-filled environments during childhood ended up pursuing very *different* and more law-abiding life courses in adulthood supposedly definitively "disproves" the causal role of the family dynamics and community circumstances in explaining criminal behavior. But the argument is specious, and a moment's reflection tells us why. Even for persons raised under seemingly "identical" circumstances within the "same" family, individual lives are composed of a complex amalgam of experiences that vary widely from person to person (and sibling to sibling). No child grows up in literally the "same" family, at least not in any meaningful psychological sense.

The work of developmental contextualists further underscores the degree to which most processes of psychological change or influence are highly dependent on the *particular* social context or set of conditions in which they occur.[44] Thus: "[T]he import of any set of contextual conditions for psychosocial behavior and development can only be understood by specifying the context's relations to the specific, developmental features of the [persons] within it."[45] The theoretical perspective of life-span developmental psychology acknowledges a similar point: "Depending on the life conditions and experiences of a given individual, his or her developmental course can take many forms."[46]

Moreover, even small differences in contexts and circumstances can cause large differences in development and outcomes. Social psychologist Mahzarin Banaji and her colleagues have explored this fact at some length. They used the term "microenvironments" to refer to "the class of environmental influences that are pervasive and influential even though they are not easily perceived or comprehended because of their 'smallness.'"[47] The most illustrative "gross characterizations of environments" is the same one that is often featured in the "not everybody" fallacy to reach erroneous conclusions about the contextual causes of crime: "The best example is perhaps the continuing assumption that environments are more similar for children sharing the same family than those that are not."[48] However, Banaji and her colleagues observed that even small differences in these "same" family environments meant that experiences and formative developmental events were really not "shared" in the same way by family members, certainly not in the way that the superficial assertions or gross characterizations that characterize "not everybody" arguments typically imply that they are.

As Banaji reminded us, persons may share "the same gross environment (e.g., family) but not the same microenvironments (e.g., variations in treatment within family)," and these variations in microenvironments can be "a powerful predictor of behavior" that accounts for differences in actions and life courses between them.[49] In addition, even if the intrafamilial experiences of siblings are very similar, their lives outside the immediate family are unlikely to be remotely the same. Thus, very few children raised in the same family attend the same schools, have the same teachers and peers, and are subjected to the same neighborhood influences. These insights provide a useful corrective to the persistent tendency to equate what appear at first glance to be common experiences and life circumstances, and then to prematurely conclude that the "same" past history or present circumstance has produced very different outcomes that, therefore, must have been "chosen."

Moreover, to develop this analysis a bit further, there are several additional reasons why events and experiences within the same family do not have the same psychological effects on all of the children within it. For one, the effects of seemingly identical experiences differ as a function of *when* in the lives of different children they occur. Whether events are good or bad, their timing influences how they are experienced, interpreted, and reacted to by the children themselves. As one developmental psychologist described the "myth of developmental uniformity" in response to the trauma of child abuse,

> [T]he "same" type of maltreatment experienced at different points in development is not likely to produce uniform outcomes. . . . Because children at various developmental levels have qualitatively different tools for interpreting events, the "same" event is likely to produce qualitatively distinct meanings for children at different ages.[50]

Different development stages present children with different psychological challenges to confront and master. This means, commonsensically, that the age at which siblings experience a family crisis or hardship affects how they will be affected by it. The trauma of abandonment, divorce, or the death of a parent typically has very different psychological meaning and consequences for very young children than for teenagers. Michael Burnstein, who noted that "[n]umerous authors have related aggressive behavior in children to the psychological rejection and the abandonment which it followed," including "rebelliousness, disobedience, temper tantrums, stealing and truancy," also noted that the "[t]iming of the rejection or abandonment is crucial" to any sensitive and meaningful analysis of its likely effects.[51]

In addition, families go through "life cycles" of their own in which, at different stages, different challenges or crises are more likely.[52] Depending on which stage in the cycle a child is born, he or she is likely to experience "family life" very differently. For example, all other things being equal, children born into young families are more likely to experience economic hardship;

those whose parents are relatively inexperienced at childrearing are somewhat more likely to receive inconsistent, overly protective, or especially strict care; children who grow up during periods of marital disharmony are more likely to experience their family as unstable and uncaring, because their parents are distracted or preoccupied with their own problems; and so on.

Even more broadly, the particular historical period in which a family event occurs can have an effect on children who are at different stages of maturation when it occurs. For example, Glen Elder found that the lives of the children he studied were not only shaped by the immediate social circumstances but also by their encounters with larger economic trends and historical forces and their own developmental stages at the time those events occurred. Indeed, there were "noteworthy variations in developmental stage at the point of economic strain . . . and in the social timetable of age-related options or roles."[53] In this case, the younger cohort of boys that Elder studied were most affected by growing up in an historical period marked by economic deprivation: "[T]hese boys as adolescents ranked well below the non-deprived on goal orientation, self-competence, social skills, and assertiveness, a difference . . . that is linked to paternal impairment, hostile relations with father, and inconsistent discipline."[54]

Similarly, a number of studies have shown that the effects of economic hardship are often indirect, in ways that are mediated by whether and how the financial struggles affect the behavior of the parents. Thus, as I pointed out in Chapter 6, poverty is experienced differently by children whose parents are overwhelmed by it—when they cannot be as nurturing as they would like to because they are so consumed by the press of seemingly insurmountable economic burdens that they have little time and few psychological resources left to focus on anything else. The effects of poverty also vary as a function of the age, gender, and other characteristics of the children within a family.[55] For example, Elder and Caspi found that conditions of economic deprivation produced

> an accelerated pace toward adult status, a pace responsive to the 'downward extension of adultlike obligations' in hard times, and also produced families that resembled an understaffed environment—that is, one with an excess of tasks relative to able members,

which tended to result in the undersocialization of, at least, younger children.[56]

Other differences in outcome can be explained by different patterns of parenting in families that faced similar structural disadvantages but handled them differently, in ways that had significantly different consequences for their children. Certain kinds of positive parenting can buffer otherwise "at risk" children from ever committing crime. For example, Joan McCord found that maternal affection, nonpunitive and consistent discipline, and parental supervision functioned as effective protective factors that helped children withstand the effects of the otherwise potentially damaging influences in their lives. Conversely, she also learned that violence was more likely to be transmitted intergenerationally when aggressive fathers created social environments that were conducive to aggressive behavior.[57] Thus, the different life outcomes for children who come from families that struggled to overcome similar structural disadvantages can only be truly understood by looking carefully at the different patterns of parenting that occurred within them.

In fact, individual lives or family experiences that may look similar from a distance are easily differentiated by those who experienced them directly. Thus, most of us can readily acknowledge that our *own* siblings were not treated in exactly the same ways by our parents or significant others and, in that sense, we did not experience exactly the "same" family life as they. The ease with which this basic commonsensical point—one derived from personal experience—is set aside in discussions of the causes of criminal behavior is telling and problematic and underscores the illogic that surrounds debates over crime-related legal doctrines and public policies.

Beyond personal reflection, candid and carefully done biographies typically identify the distinct influences that helped to shape one sibling's life course but not that of another.[58] The notably more successful survivors of severe childhood trauma and mistreatment often provide accounts of their ultimate success that emphasize the role that chance or good fortune played at crucial turning points. They can often point to fortuitous circumstances or interventions that occurred at critical moments in their lives that their more troubled siblings typically did not experience. The serendipitous presence of a caring teacher, relative, friend, or counselor who acknowledged and reinforced the vulnerable child's personal value and worth can serve as a critical buffer that determines whether he or she succumbs to their traumatic social history or manages to overcome it.

Unfortunately, the life histories of many criminal defendants lack these benign interventions and other fortuitous buffers. The nearly complete absence of protective factors in an otherwise tragically difficult childhood may be the final factor that distinguishes them from their law-abiding siblings or childhood friends or from their neighborhood peers whose lives took different, more successful paths. Either because of their age, gender, or some idiosyncratic characteristic or factor, many of the most troubled children in a family were the targets of a disproportionate amount of parental maltreatment and even rage. Some shouldered an undue share of the family's financial burdens (perhaps being given or assuming responsibility for the well-being of their siblings), in whatever way they could, lawful or not. Others voluntarily interposed themselves in family conflicts and interpersonal violence and bore the brunt of these things themselves.

All of this means that children who appear to be in the "same situation"—even in the "same family"—are typically living in very different psychological environments. Their different outcomes in life are as much or more the product of the actual variations in their social historical, situational, and structural differences as any set of individual choices that they have supposedly freely made.

The Cumulative Effects of Multiple Risk Factors

The impact of criminogenic risk factors and social contexts is often dismissed through a simplistic "single factor" analysis that understates their collective role. For example, the indisputable fact that "not everybody" who is poor (even desperately poor) commits crime or that "not everybody" who has been severely abused or maltreated in their family or community reacts to the experience by engaging in criminal behavior is used as evidence that social historical factors in general cannot cause crime. Yet parsing and isolating one factor at a time ignores the fact that criminogenic life histories typically entail multiple traumas and numerous adverse childhood experiences that combine and interact with one another in formative ways that shape later outcomes.

In less politically charged contexts, sophisticated behavioral and medical models routinely explain complex behavior by taking *multiple* causes explicitly into account. Thus, for example, the fact that "not everybody" who smokes subsequently contracts cancer does not make cigarettes any less a carcinogen. Clearly, exposure to multiple carcinogens raises the odds of contracting the disease. In a similar way, it should be obvious that the fact that not everyone who is desperately poor or abused as a child commits crime does not make these experiences any less criminogenic or belie the relationship between multiple risk factors and adverse outcomes. Yet this otherwise commonsense model of psychological development is often ignored when the "not everybody" fallacy is asserted to defend the crime master narrative and the free choice assumptions on which it is based. As I have noted throughout this chapter, these kinds of flawed arguments—in this case, a single factor theory—seems to carry more weight in debates over doctrines of legal culpability and the development of alternative crime-control policies than in any other area of social science and policy analysis. In any event, we know that beyond the simple presence or absence of one or another specific damaging experience, the *additive* impact of multiple risk factors and the way that they interact with each other is what amplifies their separate effects.

Novelist John Wideman provided another perspective on the nuance and complexity that characterize life histories. In addition to the purely quantitative or additive models of risks and traumas, Wideman observed that various combinations of social forces and life circumstances subtly but powerfully mix together to determine outcomes. Reflecting on the two different trajectories followed by him and his brother—himself a successful writer, his brother convicted of serious crimes—he wrote,

> You never know exactly when something begins. The more you delve and backtrack and think, the more clear it becomes that nothing has a discrete, independent history; people and events take shape not in orderly, chronological sequence but in relation to other forces and events, tangled skeins of necessity and interdependence and chance that after all could have produced only one result: what is.[59]

Of course, the psychological data that have served as the empirical basis for much of this book help us isolate and untangle Wideman's "skeins of necessity and interdependence and chance." We know that the events that shape people's lives are made up of many forces and factors that have been carefully studied. We know that in some cases they include traumatic experiences, forms of deprivation and mistreatment, institutional malfeasance, and structural disadvantage that add up over a life course. And we know that they can collectively form a destructive whole that transcends even its most hurtful, potentially damaging individual parts.

Moreover, it is important to acknowledge that, in some cases the accumulation of trauma and risk is truly staggering. In fact, the backgrounds and social histories of persons who have committed very serious forms of violent crime are often characterized by an unremitting succession of multiple risk factors—one compounded upon another. They often suffer these risks and traumas in powerful "doses" and may experience them over the course of an entire lifetime. For example, in my own experience, many persons who have committed the most serious crimes—capital murder—were born into severe poverty, endured extreme abuse as children, suffered the sting of racial or ethnic prejudice and mistreatment, received substandard education at schools that often functioned as part of the "prison pipeline," and they were traumatized rather than treated inside the juvenile justice institutions where they were confined.[60] Later—often as stigmatized, unstable, drug-addicted, unemployed adults—they wandered in and out of adult prisons that did little more than warehouse them (or worse), and their problems were compounded rather than being effectively addressed.[61] The case of Lamar Jackson, which I discussed earlier in this book, is much closer to being normative than exceptional. There are unfortunately many capital defendants whose lives are much like his.

We cannot do justice to the cumulative psychological effects of these multiple risks by oversimplifying or by pulling them apart, one by one, to assert that "not everybody" who experienced any *one* of them behaved in one way or another. In fact, for many criminal defendants, the risk factors are so many and varied, as well as powerful and sustained, that the real issue is not why "not everybody" responded the way that they did but rather, whether and how anybody could have survived unscathed and why more people with remotely similar histories and circumstances do not succumb.

Of course, this raises the obvious counterfactual question: What about those people who *have* managed to escape their traumatic social histories without turning to crime? To some commentators, these counterfactual stories are what seem to make the "not everybody" argument so plausible. In fact, however, it is difficult to know exactly how many such exceptions there really are. We lack systematic data on persons who have experienced the *multiple, enduring,* and *severe* risk factors that are common in the lives of persons who have engaged in serious criminal behavior but who have themselves emerged seemingly unscathed. It may be that among the small group of people who have been exposed to multiple and powerful risks and traumas over a long period of time and during especially vulnerable developmental stages, the baseline of subsequent crime and violence is actually quite high and that, although they certainly exist, there are very few such counterfactual cases after all.

Notwithstanding our lack of precise knowledge about how many such cases there really are, most of us intuitively grasp how truly difficult it is to overcome significant numbers of traumas and risks, a lifetime of extreme hardship and disadvantage, to survive in "war zone" neighborhoods, or rise above abusive, dehumanizing institutional trauma. The persons who do manage this remarkable feat are often appropriately singled-out as extraordinary, acknowledged and admired for their noteworthy accomplishments. In fact, the noteworthiness of their success serves as indirect confirmation of the magnitude of the challenges that they have overcome. Moreover, although it is always tempting to attribute the success of people who have overcome great odds to their superior, seemingly internally driven "choice-making," there is often a different logic at work. No matter how extraordinary, few people can simply "choose" to successfully overcome the legacy of past trauma through the sheer exercise of "will." Subtle, seemingly insignificant advantages at an earlier time can produce significant differences in later life outcomes. Their trauma histories may have been somewhat less severe, the abuse and neglect that they suffered not quite as chronic and unremitting, or their hardships may have been buffered by outside intervention—someone who elevated their sense of self, validated their personal struggle, or identified previously unrecognized talents.

In any event, in most discourse and discussion about crime and punishment, the praise that we rightly bestow on the extraordinary persons who have somehow managed to transcend their exceptionally difficult life circumstances does not lessen the degree of judgment and condemnation routinely directed at persons who were unable to match these rare accomplishments. Outside the morally-charged context where criminal responsibility is assigned, culpability assessed, and where punishment is eventually meted out, it likely would be.

Considering the Full Range of Social Contextual Causes and Consequences

One final component of the "not everybody" fallacy derives from the deep and profoundly individualistic, dispositional bias that still dominates "commonsense" thinking about social behavior in general and "deviant" or unusual behavior (e.g., criminality) in particular. Many differences in life outcomes are still implicitly assumed to be primarily—if not exclusively—produced by differences in internal, personal characteristics. According to this stereotypic view, successful persons—especially those who have prevailed against great odds—are assumed to have tried harder, had more talent, or just been "better" people. In the context of criminal justice decision-making, persons who avoided falling prey to the criminogenic influences that surrounded them are viewed this way—as people who simply had a stronger conscience, better character, or more "mettle" to guide their successful, law-abiding, moral choices than those who succumbed. Conversely, the perpetrators of crime are thought to have been lazy or weak or "bad seeds" from the start, persons who willingly embraced a flawed or defective moral compass that consistently led them in the wrong direction or selfishly eschewed the right path to instead commit criminal acts of wanton self-indulgence.

As I have tried to show, these misattributional fictions are maintained in part because of a refusal to closely examine and analyze the different life histories and circumstances that help to account for people's success and failure in life. A serious, careful examination of the internal dynamics of adaptation and survival over a lifetime virtually always reveals a much more complicated social and structural logic at work. Even within the same family, as noted above, different life outcomes can be explained by differences in siblings' exposure to varying combinations of risks and protective factors or fortuitous access to opportunities that were given to some family members and denied to others.

With these things in mind, it is also important to acknowledge that the long-term, potentially destructive effects of trauma-filled social histories can manifest themselves in a *variety* of ways later in life. There are not only a number of different pathways (or combinations of risk factors) that can lead to the same outcome (in this case, criminal behavior)—what developmental psychologists call "equifinality"—but also different outcomes that can be reached as a result of the same or a similar path—what they term "multifinality."[62] Thus, even though "not everybody" who has been the victim of early deprivation, experienced severe abuse, or suffered the sting of racial mistreatment actually resorts to crime or violence, few emerge completely unaffected. Some persons with trauma- and risk-filled social histories turn feelings inward, where their deeply held pain becomes the source of a disabling psychiatric disorder or emotional problem. Some use drugs to anesthetize themselves early and often against the pain they feel and chronically struggle with lifelong addictions. And some of the people exposed to brutalizing experiences and harsh conditions will lead lives of quiet desperation, isolated from others and withdrawn from the social world.

Of course, as I noted, there *are* remarkable success stories, many persons who prevail despite the obstacles. But even among these people, there are few who truly untouched by chronic exposure to severe forms of childhood trauma and adverse life experiences. The line between internalized and externalized aggression is often fluctuating and blurred and hardly anyone is fully in control of the side on which they will fall, especially if the early traumas that produced it are chronic and severe enough. Variations in the kinds of adaptations that people make to these potentially overwhelming experiences and multiple traumas may tell us where to find many of them later in their lives—in mental hospitals, homeless shelters, street corners, or criminal courtrooms, or even notably living entirely successful, law-abiding lives—but these different life outcomes are based on great deal more than "free choice."

The social histories of some notorious criminal defendants help to illustrate this point. For example, Gary Gilmore was convicted of a brutal murder in Utah and became the first person to be executed in the United States in the modern era of capital punishment in the mid-1970s. However, he made a number of very serious attempts to take his own life before he ever took the life of anyone else. In fact, Gilmore's execution may have represented an especially high profile, poignant, and historically significant instance of state-assisted suicide. He insisted on waiving his appeals at a time when legal battles over the constitutionality of various aspects of capital punishment were still raging; there was every reason to believe that a competent team of appellate lawyers would have managed to save his life, if he had allowed them to proceed. Gilmore's younger brother Mikal—a successful writer who seemed to have emerged unscathed from the history of violence that plagued his family—wrote eloquently about the way in which a destructive childhood can take a different but nonetheless exacting toll on even those siblings who appear to have escaped its legacy. He concluded:

> What had gone wrong [in my life], I realized, was because of my past, something that had been set in motion long before I was born. It was what Gary and I shared, more than any blood tie: we were both heirs to a legacy of negation that was beyond our control or our understanding. Gary had ended up turning the nullification outward—on innocents, on [Gary's girlfriend] Nichole, on his family, on the world and its ideas of justice, finally on himself. I had turned the ruin inward. Outward or inward—either way, it was a powerfully destructive legacy.[63]

CONCLUSION

As this chapter was intended to show, the "not everybody" argument in some ways reflects deep confusion about the language of causality in psychology, using an unsophisticated and oversimplified concept of "choice" to uncritically defend an increasingly untenable and counterproductivce crime master narrative. As I have suggested, despite its commonsense appeal, the "not everybody" argument represents a flawed and specious way of conceptualizing what people do and why. A moment's reflection confirms the fact that virtually no event, experience, or social influence produces literally the same psychological effect on everyone. No matter how powerful a background factor or present situational influence, it is safe to assert that "not everyone" exposed to it will respond in exactly the same way. Indeed, if this were to become the threshold for widespread acceptance—true uniformity in response or outcome—then no social contextual variable could ever meet it, no matter its role in placing children or adults seriously at risk. It is a form of fallacious reasoning that *dis*proves far too much.

The crime master narrative and free choice model of behavior persist as legal fictions, firmly embedded in our history and culture, facilitating a flawed process by which criminal responsibility is determined and blame affixed on individuals and individuals alone. Although there may be some circumstances in which this outdated model may come somewhat closer to capturing the causal mechanisms actually at work (e.g., for example, when persons whose power and resources genuinely do afford them a wide range of behavioral options but who nonetheless intentionally choose to engage in wrongdoing), it fails in the much more normative cases in which it is repeatedly and unsparingly employed. I am not the first commentator to observe in this context that our current criminal law doctrines persist in holding most accountable those persons whose social histories and life circumstances afford them the least amount of autonomy, the fewest attractive alternatives, and the narrowest range of genuine choices.

With all of this in mind, the next chapter seeks to advance the cause of fundamental criminal justice reform by proposing a set of new legal policies and practices that are based on a more empirically and theoretically sound social contextual model of criminal behavior. These new and necessary approaches are designed to take social historical, contextual, and structural factors more explicitly into account and to implement more humane limits to the severe levels of punishment that we continue to impose in response to criminal wrongdoing.

NOTES

1. Christie, N. (1982). *Limits to pain*. Oxford, England: Robertson, p. 59.
2. Bandura, A. (2016). *Moral disengagement: How people do harm and live with themselves*. New York, NY: Worth, p. 10.
3. Levy, L. W. (1957). *The law of the Commonwealth and Chief Justice Shaw* (p. 321). New York, NY: Harper & Row.
4. Haney, C. (2000). Making law modern: Toward a contextual model of justice. *Psychology, Public Policy, and Law, 7*, 3–63.
5. Samenow, S. E. (1984). *Inside the criminal mind* (p. 13). New York, NY: Times Books.
6. From Wordsworth's 1807 poem "My Heart Leaps Up."
7. From Alexander Pope's poem, *Epistles to Several Persons*, "To Lord Cobham" (1734).
8. See, e.g., Sonkin, D. J. (Ed.). (1987). *Domestic violence on trial*. New York, NY: Springer; Humm, S. R. (1991). Criminalizing poor parenting skills as a means to contain violence by and against children. *University of Pennsylvania Law Review, 139*, 1123–1161. http://dx.doi.org/10.2307/3312384
9. From Justice Alito's dissenting opinion in *Kennedy v. Louisiana*, 554 U.S. 407, 468 (2008), quoting Bagley, C., & King, K. (1990). *Child sexual abuse: The search for healing*. London, England: Routledge, p. 2.
10. *Kennedy v. Louisiana*, 554 U.S. at 468.
11. For example, when he served on the Third Circuit Court of Appeals, Justice Alito discounted the significance of a death penalty defendant's attorneys to uncover and present the full details of the extensive history of brutal child abuse to which the defendant had been subjected and the fetal alcohol-related organic brain damage from which he likely suffered. See *Rompilla v. Horn*, 355 F.3d 233 (3rd Cir. 2004). But a year later—the same year Justice Alito was appointed to the U.S. Supreme Court—a majority of Justices overturned his decision in *Rompilla v. Beard*, 545 U.S. 374 (2005). Nonetheless, Justices Thomas, Scalia, and Alito have continued to refuse to acknowledge the mitigating significance of childhood trauma and risk factors in capital cases.

12. Dershowitz, A. M. (1994). *The abuse excuse: And other cop-outs, sob stories, and evasions of responsibility*. Boston, MA: Little, Brown.
13. Among others, President Ronald Reagan's Attorney General, Edwin Meese, famously called the American Civil Liberties Union a "criminals' lobby" in a 1981 speech to the California Peace Officers Association. Coleman, K. (1986, May 4). The roots of Ed Meese: Reagan's polemical Attorney General has prompted a major constitutional debate, surprising those who knew him in his pragmatic early days, *The Los Angeles Times*. Retrieved from http://articles.latimes.com/1986-05-04/magazine/tm-3972_1_ed-meese. More recently, Arkansas Senator Tom Cotton wrote an editorial criticizing proposed bipartisan prison reform legislation that promised no more than very modest reductions in certain federal prison sentences as "just a misguided effort to let serious felons out of prison," and he told readers that it was a way for "unaccountable politicians" to "gamble with your life." Cotton, T. (2018, November 15). Lame duck Congress' rush for criminal justice reform plan will hurt, not help. *USA Today*. Retrieved from https://www.usatoday.com/story/opinion/2018/11/15/tom-cotton-congresss-criminal-justice-reform-bill-opioids-laws-column/2003829002/
14. von Friedrich, C. (1961). Law and history. *Vanderbilt Law Review, 14*, 1027–1048.
15. See, e.g., the discussion in Haney (2002), Making law modern: Toward a contextual model of justice.
16. See, e.g., a discussion of these stereotypes in Haney, C. (2009). Media criminology and the death penalty. *De Paul Law Review, 58*, 689–740.
17. See, e.g., Otis, H., & King, J. (2006). Unanticipated psychotropic medication reactions. *Journal of Mental Health Counseling, 28*, 218–240. http://dx.doi.org/10.17744/mehc.28.3.9nvtlruygt0r7qca
18. Nightingale, C. (1994). *On the edge: A history of poor Black children and their American dreams*. New York, NY: Basic Books, p. 46. For a poignant and personal example of this dynamic as well as the role of "buffers" or protective factors in the life of a young Puerto Rican woman who grew up academically successful in an otherwise very poor and crime-ridden inner city, see Torres, M. (2009). From the bricks to the hall. *Harvard Educational Review, 79*, 594–600. http://dx.doi.org/10.17763/haer.79.4.l5138t7647713620
19. Mischel, W. (1968). *Personality and assessment*. New York, NY: Wiley.
20. Mischel, W. (1997). Was the cognitive revolution just a detour on the road to behaviorism? On the need to reconcile situational control and personal control. In R. Wyer (Ed.), *Advances in social cognition: The automaticity of everyday life* (Vol. 10, pp. 181–186). Mahwah, NJ: Lawrence Erlbaum, p. 182–183.
21. Mischel (1997), Was the cognitive revolution just a detour on the road to behaviorism?, p. 184.
22. See, e.g., O'Brien, C. P., & McLellan, A. T. (1996). Myths about the treatment of addiction. *The Lancet, 347*, 237–240. http://dx.doi.org/10.1016/S0140-6736(96)90409-2
23. See, e.g., Borland, C., Cooper, J., McNeill, A., O'Connor, R., & Cummings, K. (2011). Trends in beliefs about the harmfulness and use of stop-smoking medications and smokeless tobacco products among cigarette smokers: Findings from the ITC four-country survey. *Harm Reduction Journal, 8*, 8–11. http://dx.doi.org/10.1186/1477-7517-8-21; vanDellen, M. R., Boyd, S. M., Ranby, K. W., & Beam, L. B. (2016). Successes and failures in resisting cigarettes affect partner support for smoking cessation. *Psychology & Health, 32*, 221–233. http://dx.doi.org/10.1080/08870446.2016.1255945; Throsby, K. (2009). The war on obesity as a moral project: Weight loss drugs, obesity surgery and negotiating failure. *Science as Culture, 18*, 201–216. http://dx.doi.org/10.1080/09505430902885581
24. See, e.g., Bosworth, H. B., Blalock, D. V., Hoyle, R. H., Czajkowski, S. M., & Voils, C. I. (2018). The role of psychological science in efforts to improve cardiovascular

medication adherence. *American Psychologist, 73,* 968–980. http://dx.doi.org/10.1037/amp0000316

25. See, e.g., Hudson, N., Briley, D., Chopik, W., & Derringer, J. (2018). You have to follow through: Attaining behavioral change goals predicts volitional personality change. *Journal of Personality and Social Psychology.* Advance online publication. http://dx.doi.org/10.1037/pspp0000221; Hudson, N. W., & Fraley, R. C. (2015). Volitional personality trait change: Can people choose to change their personality traits? *Journal of Personality and Social Psychology, 109,* 490–507. http://dx.doi.org/10.1037/pspp0000021
26. Bem, D. J. (1967). Self-perception: An alternative interpretation of cognitive dissonance phenomena. *Psychological Review, 74,* 183–200. http://dx.doi.org/10.1037/h0024835
27. Bargh, J. (1997). The automaticity of everyday life. In R. Wyer (Ed.), *Advances in social cognition: The automaticity of everyday life* (Vol. 10, pp. 1–61). Mahwah, NJ: Lawrence Erlbaum, p. 2.
28. Bargh, J. (1997). Reply to the commentaries in "The automaticity of everyday life." In R. Wyer (Ed.), *Advances in social cognition: The automaticity of everyday life* (Vol. 10, pp. 231–246). Mahwah, NJ: Lawrence Erlbaum, p. 232. See also the discussion by Mahzarin Banaji on the ways in which these insights favor a new and deeper form of environmental determinism in understanding social behavior. Banaji, M., Blair, I., & Glaser, J. (1997). Environments and unconscious processes. In R. Wyer (Ed.), *Advances in social cognition: The automaticity of everyday life* (Vol. 10, pp. 63–74). Mahwah, NJ: Lawrence Erlbaum.
29. Bargh (1997), Reply to the commentaries, p. 243.
30. Bargh (1997), Reply to the commentaries, p. 243. He argued further:

    > I believe if one is scrupulously honest about the number of times per day that one actually takes more than a half-second to make a decision (one signature of a control or nonautomatic process), the number could be counted on one's fingers. . . . When it does happen—when we do override the automatic process—these occasions are memorable and salient precisely because they are effortful and unusual. As a consequence, we are misled by the greater availability of these occasions in memory into hugely overestimating how often we really do engage in acts of deliberate control. (p. 244)

31. This is more obvious in the case of youthful or immature lawbreakers. Thus: "[O]ffenders against persons . . . often act out of impulse during interpersonal conflict and may not necessarily plan to commit a crime." Redding, R. E. (1997). Juveniles transferred to criminal court: Legal reform proposals based on social science research. *Utah Law Review, 1997,* 709–763, p. 735. Even early studies of so-called psychopathic personalities conceded that "violent crimes are more likely to be impulsive than premeditated." Heilbrun, A. B. (1979). Psychopathy and violent crime. *Journal of Consulting and Clinical Psychology, 47,* 509–516, p. 513. http://dx.doi.org/10.1037//0022-006x.47.3.509
32. Mumola, C. (1999, January). *Substance abuse and treatment, state and federal prisoners, 1997.* (NCJ 172871,). Washington, DC: Bureau of Justice Statistics Special Report. See also Cook, P. J., & Moore, M. J. (1993). Violence reduction through restrictions on alcohol availability. *Alcohol Health & Research World, 17,* 151–156; Leukefeld, C. G. (1985). The clinical connection: Drugs and crime. *International Journal of the Addictions, 20,* 1049–1064. http://dx.doi.org/10.3109/10826088509047764; Wald, H., Flaherty, M., & Pringle, J. (1999). Prevention in prisons. In R. Ammerman, P. Ott, & R. Tarter (Eds.), *Prevention and societal impact of drug and alcohol abuse* (pp. 369–381). Mahwah, NJ: Lawrence Erlbaum.
33. Mumola, C., & Karberg, J. (2006, October). *Drug use and dependence, state and federal prisoners, 2004* (NCJ 213530). Washington, DC: Bureau of Justice Statistics.

34. Zhang, Z. X. (2003). *Drug and alcohol use and related matters among arrestees, 2003.* Chicago, IL: Arrestee Drug Monitoring Program. Retrieved from http://www.ncjrs.gov/nij/adam/ADAM2003.pdf
35. Zhang (2004), *Drug and alcohol use and related matters among arrestees, 2003,* Table 9. No more than about one in 20 had received outpatient drug treatment in the previous year and nearly the same small percentage reported inpatient drug treatment during the same period. See Table 14.
36. Zhang (2004), *Drug and alcohol use and related matters among arrestees, 2003,* Table 10.
37. Blow, C. (2014, August 18). Frustration in Ferguson, *The New York Times*, p. A19.
38. See, e.g., Smith, S. M., Norrell, J. H., & Saint, J. L. (1996). Self-esteem and reactions to ego threat: A (battle)field investigation. *Journal of Basic and Applied Social Psychology, 18,* 395–404. http://dx.doi.org/10.1207/s15324834basp1804_3; vanDellen, M. R., Campbell, W. K., Hoyle, R. H., & Bradfield, E. K. (2011). Compensating, resisting, and breaking: A meta-analytic examination of reactions to self-esteem threat. *Personality and Social Psychology Review, 15,* 51–74. http://dx.doi.org/10.1177/1088868310372950; Wild, J., Clarke, D. M., Ehlers, A., & McManus, F. (2008). Perception of arousal in social anxiety: Effects of false feedback during a social interaction. *Journal of Behavior Therapy and Experimental Psychiatry, 39,* 102–116. http://dx.doi.org/10.1016/j.jbtep.2006.11.003
39. Rutter, M., Quinton, D., & Liddle, C. (1983). Parenting in two generations: Looking backwards and looking forwards. In N. Madge (Ed.), *Families at risk* (pp. 60–98). London, England: Heineman.
40. Pierson, P. (2000), Increasing returns, path dependence, and the study of politics. *American Political Science Review, 94,* 251–267, pp. 251, 252. http://dx.doi.org/10.2307/2586011
41. Patterson, G. R., DeBaryshe, B. D., & Ramsey, E. (1989). A developmental perspective on antisocial behavior. *American Psychologist, 44,* 329–335, p. 331. http://dx.doi.org/10.1037//0003-066x.44.2.329. See also Patterson, G., & Dishion, T. (1985). Contributions of families and peers to delinquency. *Criminology, 23,* 63–79. http://dx.doi.org/10.1111/j.1745-9125.1985.tb00326.x
42. Caspi, A., Bem, D. J., & Elder, G. H., Jr. (1989). Continuities and consequences of interactional styles across the life course. *Journal of Personality, 57,* 375–406, p. 377. http://dx.doi.org/10.1111/j.1467-6494.1989.tb00487.x
43. Nightingale (1994), *On the edge: A history of poor Black children and their American dreams,* p. 46.
44. Developmental contextualism is in some ways an outgrowth of a contextualist philosophy of science that emerged at around the same time as the "situational revolution" in psychology. All three share the same basic assumption that "human activity does not develop in a social vacuum, but rather it is rigorously situated within a sociohistorical and cultural context of meanings and relationships." Rosnow, R., & Georgoudi, M. (1986). *Contextualism and understanding in behavioral science: Implications for research and theory.* New York, NY: Praeger, p. 5. Developmental contexualism is also intellectually connected to "community psychology," which emerged as a critical alternative to traditional individual-center clinical psychology models of behavior. See, e.g., Trickett, E. J., Barone, C., & Buchanan, R. M. (1996). Elaborating developmental contextualism in adolescent research and intervention: Paradigm contributions from community psychology. *Journal of Adolescence, 6,* 245–269, to the effect that "[a]t the epistemological core of community psychology lies the belief that individuals are inextricably embedded in an ecological context" (p. 250).
45. Lerner's work, especially, has emphasized the individuality of adolescent development and its responsiveness to the demands of social context. See, e.g., Lerner, R. M., & Kauffman, M. B. (1985). The concept of development in contextualism. *Developmental Review, 5,* 309–333. http://dx.doi.org/10.1016/0273-2297(85)90016-4.

See also Lerner, R., & Lerner, J. (1989). Organismic and social contextual bases of development: The sample case of early adolescence. In W. Damon (Ed.), *Child development today and tomorrow* (pp. 69–85). San Francisco, CA. Jossey-Bass.

46. Baltes, P. B. (1987). Theoretical propositions of life-span developmental psychology: On the dynamics between growth and decline. *Developmental Psychology, 23,* 611–626, p. 613. http://dx.doi.org/10.1037/0012-1649.23.5.611
47. Banaji, M., Blair, I., & Glaser, J. (1997). Environments and unconscious processes. In R. Wyer (Ed.), *Advances in social cognition: The automaticity of everyday life* (Vol. 10, pp. 63–74). Mahwah, NJ: Lawrence Erlbaum, p. 68.
48. Banaji, Blair, & Glaser (1997), Environments and unconscious processes, p. 68.
49. Banaji, Blair, & Glaser (1997), Environments and unconscious processes, p. 68.
50. Shir, S. (1987). The interpersonal legacy of physical abuse of children. In M. Straus (Ed.), *Abuse and victimization across the life span* (pp. 57–81). Baltimore, MD: Johns Hopkins University Press.
51. Burnstein, M. H. (1981). Child abandonment: Historical, sociological, and psychological perspectives. *Child Psychiatry & Human Development, 11,* 213–221, pp. 216–218. http://dx.doi.org/10.1007/bf00706520. See also Wolfenstein, M. (Ed.). (1976). Effects of adults on object loss in the first five years. *Journal of the American Psychoanalytic Association, 24,* 659–668. http://dx.doi.org/10.1177/000306517602400310; Mishne, J. (1992). The grieving child: Manifest and hidden losses in childhood and adolescence. *Child & Adolescent Social Work Journal, 9,* 471–490 http://dx.doi.org/10.1007/bf00845409; and Freudenberger, H. J., Gallagher, K. M. (1995). Emotional consequences of loss for our adolescents. *Psychotherapy: Theory, Research, Practice, Training, 32,* 150–153. http://dx.doi.org/10.1037/0033-3204.32.1.150
52. For example, Aldous, J. (1978). *Family careers: Developmental change in families.* New York, NY: John Wiley; Duvall, E. (1977). *Marriage and family development* (5th ed.). Philadelphia, PA: J. B. Lippincott. For some early discussions of the way in which the life cycles of families interact with race, see, e.g., Banks, J. (1987). A developmental perspective on Black family violence. In R. Hampton (Ed.), *Violence in the Black family: Correlates and consequences* (pp. 249–259). Lexington, MA: Lexington; and Hampton, R. L. (1982). Family life cycle, economic well-being, and marital disruption in Black families. *California Sociologist, 5,* 16–32.
53. Elder, G. H., Jr. (1981). Social history and life experience. In D. Eichorn, J. Clausen, N. Haan, M. Honzik, & P. Mussen (Eds.), *Present and past in middle life* (pp. 3–31). New York, NY: Academic Press, p. 3. See also Elder, G. H., Jr. (1974). *Children of the Great Depression.* Chicago, IL: University of Chicago Press; and Elder, G. H., Jr. (1979). Historical change in life patterns and personality. In P. Bates & O. Brim (Eds.), *Life-span development and behavior* (Vol. 2, pp. 117–159). New York, NY: Academic Press. http://dx.doi.org/10.1016/B978-0-12-233680-5.50007-1
54. Elder (1981), Social history and life experience, p. 19.
55. For example, Elder, G. H., Jr., Nguyen, T. V., & Caspi, A. (1985). Linking family hardship to children's lives. *Child Development, 56,* 361–375. http://dx.doi.org/10.2307/1129726
56. Elder, G. H., Jr., & Caspi, A. (1988). Economic stress in lives: Developmental perspectives. *Journal of Social Issues, 44,* 25–45, p. 33.
57. McCord, J. (1994). Aggression in two generations. In L. Huesmann (Ed.), *Aggressive behavior: Current perspectives* (pp. 241–251). New York, NY: Plenum; McCord, J. (1991). The cycle of crime and socialization practices. *Journal of Criminal Law & Criminology, 82,* 211–228. http://dx.doi.org/10.1007/978-1-4757-9116-7_10
58. Gilmore, M. (1991). Family album. *Granta, 37,* 10–52; Gilmore, M. (1994). *Shot in the heart.* New York, NY: Doubleday; Staples, B. (1994). *Parallel time: Growing up in Black and White.* New York, NY: Pantheon.
59. Wideman, J. (1984). Brothers and keepers. New York, NY: Holt, Rinehart and Winston, p. 19. Wideman's book examines how "people and events take shape,"

especially the differences between his own life course—as a successful writer and professor—and that of his younger brother who, despite being raised in the "same" family, faced a host of different challenges.

60. See, e.g., Haney, C. (1995). The social context of capital murder: Social histories and the logic of capital mitigation. *Santa Clara Law Review, 35,* 547–609; Haney, C. (2006). Exonerations and wrongful condemnations: Expanding the zone of perceived injustice in capital cases. *Golden Gate Law Review, 37,* 131–173 (2006); Haney, C. (2008). Evolving standards of decency: Advancing the nature and logic of capital mitigation. *Hofstra Law Review, 36,* 835–882. In a preliminary study of the backgrounds and social histories of persons tried for capital murder, Joanna Weill and I found that they were exposed to an average of 21 risk factors (of a possible 36 that were coded) in their lifetimes. Haney, C., & Weill, J. (2013). *Social histories of capital defendants.* Unpublished manuscript, University of California, Santa Cruz.
61. See, e.g., Haney, C. (1997). Psychological secrecy and the death penalty: Observations on "the mere extinguishment of life." *Studies in Law, Politics, and Society, 16,* 3–69; and Haney, C. (2009). On mitigation as counter-narrative: A case study of the hidden context of prison violence. *University of Missouri-Kansas City Law Review, 77,* 911–946.
62. As Dante Cicchetti and Fred Rogosch define it, *multifinality* means that "a particular adverse event should not necessarily be seen as leading to the same psychopathological or nonpsychopathological outcome in every individual." Cicchetti, D., & Rogosch, F. A. (1996). Equifinality and multifinality in developmental psychopathology. *Development and Psychopathology, 8,* 597–600, p. 598. http://dx.doi.org/10.1017/s0954579400007318. They also noted that "[t]he appreciation of equifinality and multifinality in development encourages theorists and researchers to entertain more complex and varied approached to how they conceptualize and investigate development and psychopathology" (p. 599). The truncated "not everybody" argument unfortunately does the opposite.
63. Gilmore (1991), Family album, p. 49. See also Gilmore (1994), *Shot in the heart.* For another social historical and contextual analysis of a destructive, violent legacy that analyzes some of the ways that the juvenile and criminal justice systems can exacerbate these problems, see Butterfield, F. (1995). *All God's children: The Bosket family and the American tradition of violence.* New York, NY: Alfred Knopf.

Reorienting the Law

Context-Based Legal Reforms

Making the criminalized human again and ending the tragedy of the punitive state will take new ways of thinking, a revitalized imagination, and reckoning with a historical legacy that weighs heavily on the present.

—TONY PLATT[1]

We must look now and in the future beneath the surface of the events immediately surrounding the commission of the crime and analyze the social and psychological background of the criminal. . . . The fact that he is guilty and possessed mens rea is a superficial fact when it comes to the determination of the kind and nature of the sanction to be imposed upon him.

—JUDGE JOHN BIGGS[2]

More than a decade ago now, several legal scholars expressed concern over an unfortunate "movement inward" that had dominated criminal law scholarship for much of the 20th century. They lamented the fact that many of their colleagues had become "content to accept technical legal rules instead of asking whether those rules accord with modern knowledge about human behavior." It was, they said, a state of affairs "in desperate need of correction."[3] I suggest in this chapter that what these scholars said about criminal law scholarship could be said with equal or greater force about criminal law doctrines and crime control policies more generally, not just about

http://dx.doi.org/10.1037/0000172-010
Criminality in Context: The Psychological Foundations of Criminal Justice Reform,
by C. Haney

those who study them. I argue further that asking seriously whether and how technical legal rules and policies "accord with modern knowledge about human behavior" is essential to and creates a very powerful impetus for broad-based criminal justice reform.[4]

As I pointed out in the opening chapter of this book, contemporary doctrines of criminal responsibility continue to be based largely on an anachronistic form psychological individualism that locates the causes of behavior exclusively inside the individuals who engage in it. It has been enshrined for centuries in our criminal laws and led to the creation of a crime master narrative with deep historical, cultural, and political roots. The simplistic notion that crime results from little more than bad people freely choosing to do bad things has been buttressed by venerable legal traditions and a set of imposing criminal justice institutions in which it serves as a basic operating assumption.

The formidable amount of data and theory I have reviewed in the preceding chapters, amassed over the past several decades, has remained tangential if not entirely irrelevant to this entrenched system. This means that a large body of scientific knowledge about the powerful influence of social historical and immediate situational factors on criminal behavior continues to be excluded or ignored at virtually every stage of criminal justice system processing. It plays little or no formal role in trial-level calculations of criminal responsibility and culpability, in decision-making about the nature and amount of punishment that should be meted out, or in considerations that might be given to alternative sentencing arrangements that can and perhaps should be made for persons convicted of crime. It also means that in the media and public discourse about crime, persons who are accused or convicted of committing crimes have continued to be demonized, dehumanized, and often severely punished, with little regard for or understanding of the roots of their behavior, notwithstanding the existence of a powerful set of societally created risks and traumas to which they have often been exposed.

In fact, as the United States adopted increasingly harsh crime control policies during the era of mass incarceration, adding to already unprecedented rates of imprisonment, lawmakers "doubled down" on the crime master narrative and the anachronistic model of behavior on which it is based. They expanded the reach of the criminal law, increased efforts to identify and prosecute as many individual lawbreakers as possible, and punished them more severely than in past times. Conversely, legal decision-makers gave increasingly little or no consideration to the very social historical and circumstantial factors that researchers from a wide range of social scientific disciplines were establishing had such a significant impact on criminal behavior. To take just one example, in the mid-1990s, when the crime master narrative was being used with great effect to drive up public support for mass incarceration and tougher criminal law doctrines, sociologist Mercer Sullivan noted, almost matter-of-factly, that "[t]he contribution of childhood abuse and neglect to later psychopathology, antisocial behavior, and criminality is well established in the psychological and criminological literature."[5] Yet these "well established" facts had no measurable impact whatsoever on harsh crime and punishment policies that were being pursued and intensified in the United States.

Ironically, then, the doubling down on harsh criminal justice practices occurred at precisely the same time that a vast amount of research was accumulating that raised fundamental questions about the validity of two previously unquestioned "givens"—the "free will" paradigm of criminal responsibility and the crime master narrative on which it is largely premised. As I say, both of these intertwined frameworks continued to dominate thinking about the nature of criminality, as lawmakers, courts, and prison policymakers ignored much of the mounting research and its implications for crime prevention and the administration of justice. In this chapter, I argue that truly integrating and applying what we now know about the social historical and circumstantial causes of criminal behavior into criminal justice decision-making provides an intellectual framework that can and should precipitate and guide a host of fundamental changes in criminal law doctrines and procedures. In addition, beyond the set of interrelated reforms designed to enhance the fairness of legal doctrines and criminal justice practices, integrating this new knowledge should also lead to a parallel set of paradigmatic shifts in the focus of the nation's overall approach crime control. Those shifts are discussed at length in the next chapter.

Unlike 19th-century legal policymakers who enshrined the free will model of criminal behavior and its companion crime master narrative, contemporary analysts now have a veritable mountain of empirical data on which to premise much more sophisticated approaches. We have the luxury of being able to shape new legal doctrines that are based on valid science and to use available data to systematically develop fairer legal doctrines and more effective and preventative strategies of crime control. The psychological insights I have summarized in preceding chapters underscore the need to radically revise the narrowly individualistic model of behavior that locates the causes of criminality entirely inside its perpetrators. As this research makes clear, we now know that the roots of criminal behavior can be traced to the harmful social contexts in which children and adolescents are raised, the tragic developmental histories that many of them have in common, the institutional malfeasance and mistreatment to which they too often have been subjected, and the criminogenic environments to which they continue to be exposed throughout much of their lives, including the social and economic disadvantage and race-based inequalities to which many of them have been subjected.

In fact, as I suggest in the pages that follow, the changed perspective brought about by the deconstruction of the crime master narrative is fundamental; it should compel a basic reorientation in a range of key criminal justice policies and practices. Integrating a more psychologically sophisticated contextual model of behavior that fully acknowledges the criminogenic effects of past history and present circumstance has profound implications for how we determine legal responsibility and culpability, what we regard as fair sentencing practices, and the prison policies and practices we pursue in the name of correctional reform. This chapter analyzes a number of those implications.

I should note at the outset that, although I do not discuss them in detail, I believe that it is necessary to pursue many of the recently proposed, eminently worthy criminal justice reforms that are aimed at curbing the massive amount of control and leverage that the system wields over people's lives—ranging from reform of the bail system, to eliminating excessive and escalating monetary fines, to placing limits on coercive aspects of the plea bargaining process, to curbing the enormous discretionary power of prosecutors.[6] From the perspective from which this book has been written, all of these reforms share a common implicit recognition that context matters. The entrenched criminal justice practices and policies that other commentators have argued must be targeted for reform are ones in which insurmountable power imbalances within criminal justice settings and situations compromise the rights and adversely affect the lives of criminal defendants. Notwithstanding the importance of these largely procedural reforms, my focus is on a different and more fundamental set of issues.

Although the recommendations I develop in this and the following chapter are largely theoretical in nature, they are also explicitly programmatic and, therefore, controversial. Drawing out the implications of the extensive body of research that I reviewed in earlier chapters is admittedly fraught with pitfalls and invites criticism of one or another specific proposal as well as inevitable charges of naiveté for suggesting that our entrenched criminal justice system could ever be fundamentally changed. It nonetheless must be done. I think it is incumbent on social scientists and others of us who write about new knowledge that we believe has important implications for and applications to law and social policy to be explicit about what, exactly, we mean. There are always a multitude of good, practical reasons why such deeply embedded and long-standing policies and practices "cannot possibly" be reformed in any significant way. And yet, on this issue at least, the time has come to make the case for why these interrelated legal reforms can and should be devised, debated, and eventually implemented.

A CONTEXT-BASED MODEL OF LEGAL RESPONSIBILITY

Doctrines of criminal responsibility reflect an inherently imprecise calculation. They imperfectly simplify an enormously complicated human inquiry into whether and how much blame lawbreakers deserve for the transgressions that they have committed (and, by implication, the quantity of punishment they should receive). The simplification is typically accomplished through a nearly exclusive focus on the individual lawbreaker and his internal state—specifically, his "state of mind" at the time that his criminal acts were presumably undertaken. In Justice Jackson's pithy formulation, crime is defined in law as "constituted only from concurrence of an evil-meaning mind with an evil-doing hand," an approach he correctly noted was "congenial to an intense individualism" that "took deep and early root in American soil."[7]

Given the centrality of specific states of mind in this profoundly important process, the categories that the law uses in making these all-important judgments are surprisingly crude and imprecise. Jackson himself commented on the "variety, disparity and confusion" that has attended "definitions of the requisite but elusive mental element" and conceded that courts have "devised working formulae, if not scientific ones."[8] As one legal commentator put it years ago: "A tradition of chronic imprecision in the elucidation of principles of criminal responsibility has existed in the common-law world for more than seven centuries."[9] From the perspective of modern psychological theory, the constricted nature of the categories is more problematic than just their "chronic imprecision." The nature of the enterprise is based entirely on psychological individualism (i.e., focusing on what allegedly transpired in the mind of the individual actor) and is wholly consistent with the crime master narrative (i.e., using the actor's state of mind to estimate the quantity of his or her "badness" or, as the California Supreme Court once put it, "appraising the quantum of [a lawbreaker's] moral turpitude and depravity").[10] Correspondingly, the categories themselves greatly narrow the scope of psychological inquiry that is permitted in order to establish the degree of criminal responsibility and level of culpability that are affixed in a criminal case.

Forensic experts and scholars have repeatedly pushed against these restrictive categories in the past, but with little success. For example, more than a half century ago, law professor Bernard Diamond, a highly respected and influential forensic psychiatrist in his day, advocated significantly broadening the scope of psychological evidence deemed relevant in criminal cases and making the legal categories to which such evidence was applied far less rigid. Diamond, who had already helped to shape a number of important criminal law doctrines,[11] argued that legally recognized states of mind should be arranged along a *continuum* rather than being cast invariably in "all or none" terms. In the late 1950s and early 1960s—long before death penalty trials were routinely bifurcated into separate and distinct guilt and penalty phases—Diamond suggested that jurors who voted to spare the lives of death-eligible persons (e.g., by recommending "mercy"), despite having convicted them of first-degree murder, were already operating with this implicit understanding. That is, he thought jurors intuitively understood that, even among the category of first-degree murderers, there were significant variations and distinctions in their degree of responsibility and culpability that the law at the time did not—but should—formally recognize. Diamond suggested further that the continuum that capital jurors had grasped was one that was increasingly understood and utilized by his colleagues in forensic psychiatry. Indeed, he argued that this view comported with a related, broader shift that was already underway in forensic mental health, namely what he described as a move "away from static, diagnostic, and classification psychiatry toward dynamic descriptions of the particular mental mechanisms which led up to the crime."[12]

The approach Diamond advocated seemed to foreshadow precisely the kind of contextualized, in-depth investigation into a death penalty defendant's background and social history that has become absolutely central to capital penalty trials since the mid-1970s.[13] Capital jurors are permitted to hear testimony and consider evidence that address the full range of social historical and circumstantial issues that I have discussed at length throughout this book, and they are instructed to take those things into account in deciding whether to sentence the defendant to life or death. Yet this kind of broad-based, searching inquiry, introduced with the imprimatur of the U.S. Supreme Court in capital cases decades ago,[14] still does not routinely occur in *any other* kind of criminal case.[15] However, Diamond thought it should, and I wholeheartedly agree.

Diamond also described more meaningful forensic evaluations and investigations that would require experts to spend "many more hours . . . with the defendants" in order to uncover the full range of psychological mechanisms that explained their behavior, and to interpret those mechanisms in the "framework of the defendant's life history." Indeed, Diamond advocated a "total approach" to understand the person whose actions were under scrutiny, one in which "everything that has happened" to the defendant "starting with his ancestors and going through the entire life history right up to the present moment" were regarded as potentially significant. And he urged that the "same totalistic approach should be carried over into the courtroom."[16] Here, too, he anticipated exactly the way that properly conducted death penalty trials now proceed and argued that it be done more broadly, in all kinds of criminal cases.[17]

Diamond's scholarly writing urging a more expansive, nuanced, and in-depth inquiry into criminal responsibility and a broader scope of inquiry by which it was established at trial was published in the late 1960s and early 1970s. Midway through the decade of the 1970s, of course, a fundamental shift in crime and punishment policy began in the United States.[18] This was the start of the "mean season" of correctional policy and the outset of the era of mass incarceration.[19] Nothing remotely resembling this kind of "liberalizing" of criminal law doctrine could or would be considered over the next several decades, as criminal law "reform," such as it was, moved in a decidedly different—essentially opposite—direction. Indeed, far from being broadened, the scope of evidence about a person's background or psychological makeup deemed relevant in criminal proceedings was increasingly narrowed until it all but disappeared. In the years that followed, attempts "to better understand the human complexities of the individual," as Diamond had put it, were essentially abandoned in the criminal justice system generally.[20] Among other things, legal defenses that involved mental states—the primary vehicle through which those human complexities had been explored in expert testimony—became even more narrowly focused and constrictive. In some instances, they were eliminated altogether.

The insanity defense is perhaps the most well-known example. Following the controversial verdict in the high-profile case of John Hinckley, who had attempted to assassinate President Ronald Reagan, many sweeping reforms were passed that were designed to limit the successful use of the defense itself. Two commentators described the case succinctly: "On June 21, 1982, a Washington, D.C. jury found John W. Hinckley Jr. Not Guilty by Reason of Insanity (NGRI) on all charges arising from his attempted assassination of President Reagan. No verdict in recent history has evoked so much public indignation."[21] The indignation was shared and amplified by lawmakers who responded by drastically narrowing the circumstances under which the insanity defense could be used, making it difficult to successfully mount, and altering the consequences for defendants when it was.[22]

Federal lawmakers acted especially quickly on the issue. For example, "[a]fter twenty-six different pieces of legislation were introduced in Congress to either abolish or restrict the insanity defense at the federal level, Congress enacted the Insanity Defense Reform Act of 1984," which tightened the substantive legal test for insanity, procedurally shifted the burden of persuasion from the prosecution to the defense (requiring the defendant to provide "clear and convincing" proof of his insanity), and limited the scope of admissible expert testimony.[23] By the end of the next year, "thirty-three states had followed the lead of Congress and re-evaluated the insanity defense as it applied in their respective state jurisdictions."[24]

These and other changes were clearly designed to limit the successful use of mental states defenses.[25] They dampened whatever enthusiasm might have existed for analyzing and presenting the kind of "psychodynamic framework of the defendant's life history" that Diamond had advocated as a better and more scientifically justified way to determine degrees of criminal responsibility. Not surprisingly—in light of the legal trends underway and the broader social and political forces that helped to bring them about—Diamond's optimism about introducing a more "totalistic" perspective to better understand criminal defendants and ensure fairer and more valid trial outcomes waned considerably.[26]

Diamond lamented the continued reliance on unduly narrow criminal law doctrines and practices that limited and even prohibited meaningful forensic inquiries into the causes of criminal behavior and consideration of the full range of psychological forces that may have significantly influenced a criminal defendant's behavior. Yet he continued to advocate in favor of *someday* implementing a more global and comprehensive approach in the criminal justice system, one that more fully considered the entire range social factors that undermined a defendant's "ability to make a free, rational, responsible decision when faced with the temptation or impulse to commit a crime."[27] He thought such factors specifically should include

> poverty, continued unemployment, chaotic living conditions, such as that associated with ghettos, and other social and environmental detrimental factors which could impair an individual's powers of free will without necessarily resulting in a disease or mental abnormality. Thus, proper attention could directly be given by the law to cultural deprivation and other external factors which override the individual's capacity for free choice.[28]

Of course, as the numerous studies I reviewed in the preceding chapters attest, the social histories and present circumstances of persons who have engaged in criminal behavior are replete with exposure to these and other specific risk factors and traumas as well as social and environmental conditions that collectively bear on issues of causality and the compromised nature of the "free choices" they typically make. The underlying premise of Diamond's recommended legal reforms—that criminal behavior is shaped by a myriad of powerful forces and influences that the perpetrators of crime certainly did not "freely choose" and over which they often have had little or no control—lacked the overwhelming empirical support that it now has. Thus, although Diamond's ideas on these issues may have been too innovative and provocative at the time he proposed them, the time has now come to seriously reconsider and devise ways to implement them.

There are a number of different ways that social historical and contextual evidence and analysis can be taken more explicitly and meaningfully into account. It is important to acknowledge that these are recommendations for *modifying* doctrines of responsibility, not a proposal to eliminate them or provide blanket absolution for persons who have broken the law. Some sense of personal responsibility is an essential component in empowering people to change their life circumstances and alter whatever path their social history has placed them on. Moreover, accountability is the hallmark of any meaningful system of criminal justice. But it must be fairly determined, in a realistic decision-making context that takes new knowledge about the social historical and contextual causes of criminal behavior much more conscientiously and systematically into account.

The first and perhaps most radical application of this new knowledge would be to recognize its legal relevance to determinations of criminal responsibility and culpability. That is, courts would permit it to be introduced at the time that the defendant's guilt is decided, to bear directly on the degree to which he or she can and should be held to account.[29] George Fletcher explained that the classic rationale for the law of excuses is to lessen an offender's responsibility and punishment whenever "his act seems to be attributable to circumstances rather than to his character. The act does not tell us what kind of person the actor is. The premise seems to be that if a violation of the law does not accurately reveal the actor's character, it is unjust to punish him for what he has done."[30] The deconstruction of the crime master narrative and a correspondingly greater emphasis on the role of social history and context in the criminal law limits instances in which legal decision-makers can or should routinely infer that criminal behavior alone "tells us what kind of person the actor is."

In fact, in the decades that followed Diamond's initial proposals, other authors made similar recommendations, with increasingly larger databases on which to rely, as research on the long-term effects of risk factors, trauma, and adverse childhood experiences mounted. For example, in the mid-1980s, Richard Delgado advanced a proposal to allow what he termed a "rotten social background" defense in criminal cases, concluding from his review of the social science literature "that life in a violent, overcrowded, stress-filled neighborhood can induce a state in which a resident reacts to certain stimuli with automatic aggression." Therefore, Delgado argued, "[s]ome defendants should be able to prove that they lived under such conditions and that these conditions were causally connected to the crimes charged."[31] With even more data on which to rely, in the late 1990s, Jeffrey Fagan presented a sophisticated contextual framework for understanding adolescent criminal behavior, acknowledging the way that people's decisions to engage in crime "are shaped through interactions with features of their environments, [and] are contingent on responses emanating from that context."[32] Although Fagan limited his analysis to adolescent crime, much of the framework he offered was applicable to adults as well and included many of the social historical and contextual factors that I summarized in the preceding chapters.

Adding to these earlier calls to use social science as the basis for revisiting these doctrines, more recent commentary suggests that these innovative changes are long overdue.[33] Without attempting to resolve legal debates over whether and how they are best fitted into existing legal defenses, and which ones most apply—justification, excuse, necessity, diminished capacity, or even nonjusticiability—the critical point is that these insights are now clearly relevant to issues of criminal responsibility and culpability and should be incorporated in ways that they have not been before. Even Stephen Morse who staunchly opposed the use of "severe environmental deprivation" as a separate defense since the mid-1970s has argued more recently in favor of a "generic mitigating excuse" that would be employed to establish "partial responsibility" in appropriate cases.[34]

In fact, debates over the precise category of legal defense into which evidence about social history and context best fits, or whether what has been termed "rotten social background"[35] or "severe environmental deprivation"[36] should be recognized as separate defenses, may be a distraction from the indisputable import of this new knowledge. In this regard, I agree with Jeffrey Fagan, who argued that the "relevance of social context to culpability does not require new theories or doctrines of law" because the constructs themselves "can be accommodated in existing categories of criminal law."[37] It is thus time to more explicitly acknowledge the legal relevance of broad categories of social historical and contextual evidence to inquiries into states of mind, whether or not there are separate defenses created or new verdicts made possible.

NEW MODELS OF SENTENCING

Beyond the proposal to modify doctrines of criminal responsibility and culpability to take these social factors and psychological forces explicitly into account in the guilt determination stage of a criminal trial, there is a second level of reform that follows directly from the deconstruction of the crime master narrative. Supplanting it with a more sophisticated and empirically supported model of the causes of criminal behavior will have significant implications for improving the fairness of a host of sentencing policies.

These implications provide strong rationales for reversing numerous trends that emerged over the last several decades. In addition to the restrictions that were placed on the use of mental states defenses during the era of mass incarceration, criminal laws and criminal justice system policies and practices repeatedly increased how often and for how long prison sentences were meted out in jurisdictions across the country. The United States quickly became an outlier in terms of the amount of prison pain the nation inflicted on persons found guilty of violating criminal laws. Among other things, widespread changes in sentencing laws were implemented that drastically reduced the amount of discretion that trial judges were permitted to exercise in imposing specific prison sentences following a criminal conviction. Increasingly, courts were required to limit their sentencing considerations to the nature of the crime for which the defendant was being punished and little or nothing else. In the mid-1970s and the decades that followed, legislatures enacted a range of these interrelated changes, including establishing sentencing commissions and promulgating sentencing guidelines,[38] mandatory minimum sentences,[39] statutorily-required enhancements[40] and, eventually, so-called three strikes laws.[41] Their consequences were draconian. For example, "The average prison time served by federal defendants more than doubled after the [Sentencing] Guidelines became effective."[42]

Together these changes in sentencing laws and practices excluded from the sentencing calculus much of what Norwegian criminologist Nils Christie termed "the whole question of social justice."[43] Sentencing hearings soon became highly abbreviated and pro forma affairs. With little or no discretion to be exercised and few if any options from which to pick, judges soon came to view evidence about the backgrounds, social histories, unique circumstances, and special characteristics of the defendants whom they were sending to prison—all of the things that extensive empirical research now indicates have a profoundly formative effects and continuing influence—as largely irrelevant.[44]

These mass incarceration–era sentencing reforms represented a particularly damaging application of the crime master narrative that resulted in unprecedented numbers of people spending previously unheard of amounts of time in prison. The demise of this outmoded and now indefensible model of criminal behavior should lead to the creation of an entirely different approach to sentencing and a fundamental revision of the principles by which punishment is meted out and alternative responses to criminal behavior employed.

Reforming the Federal and Other Guidelines

As I noted above, the vast array of social historical and contextual determinants of criminal behavior that I discussed in some detail in Chapters 3 through 6 were essentially *barred* from meaningful consideration under the federal sentencing guidelines for many years. In 2005, the U.S. Supreme Court decision in *United States v. Booker*[45] rendered the Guidelines "advisory," rather than "mandatory," and opened up opportunities and incentives for federal criminal defense attorneys to collect and present mitigation evidence at the time of sentencing (because federal judges now presumably were given greater latitude to fashion fairer "downward departures" from the harsh sentencing guidelines). However, *Booker* was by no means a panacea. Indeed, there is some evidence that at least some federal judges have imposed harsher sentences than in the past and that, in any event, the Guidelines still hold sway over the sentences that are being meted out in many jurisdictions, perhaps the result of what former federal judge Nancy Gertner acknowledged as "habits ingrained during twenty years of mandatory Guideline sentencing."[46]

In the spirit of frankly assessing how great a distance real reform will require us to travel, it is worth examining the deleterious logic of the Guidelines themselves. Among other things, the Guidelines required that unless child maltreatment was judged to have been "extraordinary," it could not be taken into consideration.[47] This unduly restrictive provision forced courts to reject or ignore a broad range of potentially relevant social history evidence that may have been compelling—including even "shocking" levels of abuse—thus discounting the well-established psychological significance of truly severe trauma and abject deprivation and a host of other risk factors that we know can impact a criminal defendant's life course.

For example, in *United States v. Brady,*[48] the Second Circuit noted that in determining whether downward departures in sentencing were appropriate, "the abuse must be *judged against that suffered by the typical defendant,* many of whom have unfortunately suffered severe abuse in their early lives."[49] The Court was explicit about what it saw as the need to employ this comparative, limiting standard. It was necessary, the judges said, because of "the sad fact that so many defendants have unfortunate pasts and we cannot apply a disfavored departure to many or most defendants."[50] Ironically, from the perspective developed in the previous chapters, the *Brady* Court employed the right facts to reach the wrong conclusion. The sheer prevalence of abuse in the lives criminal defendants may render it "ordinary," but that hardly makes it an inappropriate consideration in reaching just sentencing outcomes. Requiring courts to ignore the *normatively* troubled and traumatic lives of many criminal defendants and the powerful role played by past history and present circumstances is reminiscent of Justice Brennan's dissent in the Supreme Court's notorious *McCleskey v. Kemp* death penalty decision to the effect that his colleagues in the majority were afraid of dispensing "too much justice."[51]

The second prong of the Guideline standard that governed downward departures in federal sentencing also limited the degree to which child abuse and maltreatment, as well as other risk factors and traumas, could be taken into account. As the *Brady* court noted, the "causation requirement" mandated that even when a defendant suffered "horrific abuse that did not end with childhood," she was required to prove that this history of abuse "'contributed' to her commission of the offense" in order to prevail.[52] Thus, "the requirement of a causal nexus restrict[ed] the circumstances in which a departure on the grounds of abuse" to cases in which abuse created a mental condition that "leads to or causes the criminal conduct."[53] Depending on exactly how stringent the proof of a "casual nexus" a court required, it too could functionally preclude a great many defendants from obtaining downward departures.

The Guidelines' limiting principles notwithstanding, what we now know about the social historical and contextual roots of criminality underscores the importance of taking this knowledge into account in assessing the degree of culpability and the "just measure of pain" that should be meted out in response to wrongdoing.[54] We know that truly fair assessments of culpability and blameworthiness must extend beyond the Guidelines-based narrow focus on nothing more than the nature of the crime that the defendant was convicted of committing. More broadly, the determinate sentencing policies ushered in over the last several decades are long overdue for a set of liberalizing and broadening reforms, including devising new methods of determining degrees of culpability for purposes of deciding on sentence length and creating a range of new sentencing options that are less draconian and more context-sensitive than at present. The transition back to less rigid sentencing models should afford legal decision-makers much greater latitude in using background and contextual information to override presumptive prison sentences and implement alternatives, and to do so based on a valid and empirically grounded model of criminal behavior.

I have argued elsewhere that there were racial implications to the "decontextualized" sentencing calculations that various sentencing guidelines and grids, mandatory minimums, determinate sentencing laws, and other "discretion-less" approaches ushered in during the era of mass incarceration. Because the criminogenic influence of the race-based inequities to which many minority defendants were subjected were systematically excluded from consideration at the time of sentencing, they were subjected to a particularly perverse form of the "fundamental attribution error"—"systematically discounting the important social, historical and situational determinants of behavior (in this case, criminal behavior) and correspondingly exaggerating the causal role of dispositional or individual characteristics."[55] As Michael Tonry noted, "a first step toward reducing racial disproportions [in rates of imprisonment] is to loosen up sentencing laws and guidelines to let judges more often mitigate sentences to take account of offenders' personal circumstances."[56] Unfortunately, this "first step" that Tonry advocated more than two decades ago has yet to be taken in many jurisdictions. Nonetheless, a number of the preceding chapters provide the theoretical and empirical basis for establishing how and why a wide range of these "personal circumstances" matter, and they should be used to guide broad-based sentencing reforms.

Eliminating Narrow "Desert-Based" Sentencing Rationales

There are a number of additional sentencing reforms that should follow from replacing the crime master narrative with a more social historical and contextual model of criminal behavior. Among other things, the new narrative underscores the need to seriously reexamine the narrowly framed "just deserts" rationales that were introduced in the 1970s and 1980s and used as the basis on which harsher, decontextualized criminal sentencing was premised. Desert-based sentencing focused only on the severity of the crime in determining the magnitude of punishment supposedly deserved. As I noted with respect to the federal Guidelines, individualized factors (e.g., background factors or mitigating circumstances of the crime) were not only deemphasized but actually prohibited under this framework. As one federal judge succinctly put it, "Pure retribution, or 'just deserts,' ignores the handicapping effect of social, economic, and natural deprivation."[57]

The deconstruction of the crime master narrative promises to turn that approach on its head. That is, in addition to taking the background and life circumstances of the person convicted of violating the law into account, courts would be permitted to consider the nature and impact of the sanction imposed on the defendant, including its implications for his immediate context (especially for persons who are financially dependent on him or for whom he serves in a parenting or caretaker role). In addition, the consequences of the sanction for the larger community in which the person who broke the law resides are relevant, including whether and how that community can address its criminogenic aspects and contribute to making crime survivors whole. I develop some of these sentencing options at greater length at the end of this chapter and in the next, but they include restorative justice approaches that consider the broader social ecology in which crime occurs, is reacted to, and recovered or healed from.

Using the seriousness of a criminal conviction in lieu of more nuanced and individualized sentencing determinations was especially attractive to lawmakers and criminal justice decision-makers during the age of mass incarceration in which unprecedented numbers of prisoners needed to be processed, classified, and placed under correctional control. If the circumstances and needs of individual criminal defendants were ignored under desert-based sentencing in which only the seriousness of the offense mattered, they were similarly irrelevant in prison, where a "new penology" was emerging. As described by Jonathan Simon and Malcolm Feeley, correctional decision-makers began performing little more than an "actuarial" function in which calculations were made about the aggregate risk presented by large groups or categories of prisoners, seen collectively as "waste" to be "managed" rather than individuals whose needs were to be carefully assessed and meaningfully addressed.[58] It meshed perfectly with the rigid sentencing formulas and mandatory guidelines and grids that were being implemented over the same time period, jointly decontextualizing and dehumanizing our views of defendants as well as prisoners.[59] But adopting a broader and more nuanced contextual model of criminality would require us to modify all of this.

In fact, although desert theory was adopted in part in the pursuit of *uniformity* in sentencing, this proved to be an utterly unattainable goal.[60] In addition to failing to achieve its alleged purpose, desert-based sentencing glossed over a host of truly fundamental problems. As I have suggested throughout this book, taking a person's unique social history and circumstances into account is essential to understanding how and why they became involved in criminal activity. A meaningful appreciation of those factors can and should bear on the nature of the sanction a criminal defendant deserves, which suggests in turn that truly "just" sentences should be equitable—treat similarly situated persons the same—rather than equal—merely meting out equal sentences for "equal" crimes. Creating the kind of individualized and context-sensitive analyses of culpability required by equitable sentencing models would mean taking the full range of forces and factors that influenced the defendant's behavior into account. These more empirically informed causal models and more sophisticated assessments of culpability also call for the creation of more discretionary sentencing options—including community-based, restorative justice models that do not involve imprisonment. They allow decision-makers to properly and fairly respond to important variations in individual cases, defendants, and contexts.

Creating a new set of jurisprudential principles by which sanctions are calibrated with more careful attention to the specific dimensions of a criminal defendant's background and circumstances might also entail establishing a metric of culpability that is in some ways analogous to the one that two desert theorists actually advocated for "gauging criminal harm."[61] Proposed during the height of the just deserts movement, Andrew von Hirsch and Nils Joreborg's framework suggested calculating the harmfulness of a criminal act as a function of the degree to which it adversely impacted a crime survivor's ability to lead the "good life."[62] Under a broad restorative justice model that is consistent with the social contextual model of criminal behavior I presented in the preceding chapters, the full extent of the harm suffered by a crime survivor is clearly an important, legitimate consideration. Yet, calculations concerning the long-term or future harm that a lawbreaker's actions brought about—some of which may have been unintended, unanticipated, and perhaps even unknowable to him at the time he engaged in them—do not begin to exhaust the entire range of factors that are relevant to a fair assessment of culpability and the fashioning of a just and humane sanction.

In fact, the degree to which a *criminal actor*'s social history and present circumstances at the time of the crime significantly deviated from some agreed-upon representation of the "good life" also seems relevant to determining whether and what kind of punishment is fairly warranted and should be meted out for his transgressions.[63] As I noted earlier, the criminogenics of poverty and race in American society have guaranteed that ignoring past social history and present circumstances have operated to disadvantage poor defendants of Color most of all. Thus, it seems increasingly clear that if a truly fair deserts-based sentencing model could ever be justified, *at least* as much care and attention would need to be brought to bear on the lawbreaker's side of the equation.

In addition, it would also require seriously and carefully considering the nature of the "desert" imposed—perhaps applying a form of the "standard of living" or "quality of life" measure in order to calibrate the amount of penal pain that would be brought about by particular conditions of confinement, as a way of estimating the true magnitude of the punishment that a court was contemplating meting out. From a psychological perspective, simply counting the number of years (i.e., sentence length) a lawbreaker would be required to serve is a terribly imprecise scale on which to measure comparable deserts. Obviously, some prisons inflict more "deserts" than others on the persons confined inside them. Moreover, individual differences in vulnerability to confinement might also be factored into the equation.

In any event, facing these hard questions would at least force us to recognize that, as one legal commentator has noted, punishment "is not merely the quantity of time in prison. . . . What actually happens to prisoners—their daily pain and suffering inside prison—is the only true measure of whether the traditional concepts (justifying imprisonment) have meaning."[64] My point is simply that if a desert-based sentencing rationale is to have any continuing currency, we now possess the tools with which to broaden it considerably, so that a whole host of previously ignored factors—including the background and present circumstances of the lawbreaker (i.e., his or her deservingness) as well as the numerous variations in the painfulness and long-term consequences of the punishment (i.e., the actual desert)—are taken more formally into account.

Toward "Holistic Lawyering": Broadening the Role of Mitigation

As I noted previously, death penalty trials still represent the one legal proceeding in which meaningful, in-depth inquiries into the defendant's entire social history and the broader social context in which he or she acted are routinely conducted and where this kind of evidence may be fully presented to a jury in the course of the formal sentencing process. Jurors are allowed to consider the "moral guilt" or blameworthiness of the defendant in a broader and more expansive way than in any other kind of criminal case[65] and they are allowed to consider the role that background risk factors, traumas, institutional abuse, poverty, and racism played in shaping the defendant's life course. Moreover, this kind of presentation is not restricted to cases in which this kind of evidence bears directly on the specific capital crime for which the defendant is being sentenced.[66] As federal Judge Richard Paez recently put it, the jury's "exercise of mercy could stem from a defendant's tragic past and his endurance of unconscionable abuse, his cognitive defects, or some other personal, humanizing characteristic that has nothing to do with undermining or rebutting the prosecution's case."[67] The results of the inquiry into the psychologically significant events in the defendant's life are admitted for that broader purpose—to show how they adversely affected the course of that life. In so doing, the scope of relevant testimony is significantly broadened in the proceedings to allow precisely the kind of holistic inquiry that Bernard Diamond proposed decades ago.

Although capital defendants have typically been exposed to a greater number of risk factors and traumas throughout their lives—compared to many other persons who have broken the law—the importance of using social historical mitigation to better calibrate blameworthiness applies with equal force to criminal cases in general.[68] The "death is different" jurisprudence that undergirds the constitutional standards governing capital cases should not obscure the logic of employing the same kind of broad-based social historical inquiries in noncapital cases where they are equally relevant to fair and just sentencing. There is no obvious reason that "telling the client's story" should be limited to capital cases.[69] Moreover, the mitigating evidence that is surfaced in telling these stories should bear not only on the length of sentence that is justly imposed but also on whether alternatives to incarceration are warranted in light of evidence that documents the mitigating significance of a defendant's social history and present circumstances. Even in what should become increasingly less common cases in which courts decide that a prison sentence is absolutely necessary, a comprehensive mitigation investigation should bear directly on court recommendations and correctional decisions about the richness and array of rehabilitative options that the defendant should be given access to while incarcerated.[70] Of course, all of this will require a greater emphasis on—and corresponding increase in training, resources, and staffing—within the broader, noncapital criminal defense community to approach lawyering from a more holistic perspective. This holistic model of lawyering would become one in which, on a routine basis, clients' social histories and present circumstances would be painstakingly investigated, carefully analyzed, and effectively presented to influence the outcome of each case that defense attorneys handle.

Making the sentencing process fairer and more reliable by taking the full measure of the defendant's life history into account and permitting the broader use of mitigation in criminal cases will also improve the functioning of the criminal justice system in other ways. For example, by encouraging defense attorneys and experts to more carefully and routinely explore their clients' backgrounds and better understand the full range of the risk factors, traumas, institutional mistreatment, poverty, and discrimination to which they have been exposed, their complex needs can be better identified and more effectively addressed. As Miriam Gohara put it, defense attorneys will "realign their practices and professional standards accordingly,"[71] operating with increased sensitivity and responsiveness to their clients.[72]

Moreover, the collection and analysis of mitigation evidence in criminal cases in general would add to the growing database on the prevalence and severity of risk factors and traumas in society at large, including their life-changing impact on criminal defendants and the important role they play in generating crime. These expanded sentencing proceedings would represent another source of knowledge about the criminogenic effects of risk factors and traumas, and heighten awareness among members of the judiciary, lawmakers, and members of the public about the depth and breadth of these problems as well as the personal, social, and economic costs of failing to address them. Until these real-life stories are surfaced on more regularly and broadly, pockets of ignorance about the real causes of crime are likely to persist. Thus, permitting social historical and social contextual mitigation evidence to be introduced into criminal cases in general will further enlighten key constituencies about not only who commits crime but why.

A CONTEXTUALIST "WHAT WORKS": REHABILITATING JAILS AND PRISONS

Elsewhere I have written that "acknowledging the powerful influence of past and present contexts and situations on behavior has important implications for correctional policy and practice."[73] Obviously, if past and present contexts matter in society at large, then they matter in jails and prison too. The most important implications that can be drawn from this insight are two-fold. The first is that the effects of past exposure to risk factors, traumas, and institutional mistreatment must be taken seriously in any attempt to provide meaningful programming in correctional settings. The second and very much related implication is that jails and prisons themselves must be fundamentally restructured to minimize or eliminate their *re*traumatizing effects. Finally abandoning the crime master narrative and its focus on individuals as the primary or exclusive causal locus of behavior will shift more attention onto the powerful role of criminogenic situations and circumstances, underscoring the need to rehabilitate *places* in addition to (or sometimes instead of) people.

As noted earlier, the offense-based desert and retribution justifications for punishment and an emerging "new penology" both dominated in the era of mass incarceration. Together they contributed to a penal regime in which the severity of a criminal conviction governed sentencing and, at the same time, jail and prison officials embraced expedited procedures designed to "manage risks" in correctional decision-making. In addition, the unprecedented rates of incarceration and high levels of overcrowding in the nation's prison system and the explicit rejection of rehabilitation as the primary purpose of imprisonment combined to adversely affect the treatment of prisoners *after* they began serving their sentences.[74]

Only an extreme and truly cynical form of the crime master narrative could ever have legitimized operating prisons as a form of what was described as "human waste management."[75] The imminent demise of this increasingly anachronistic narrative should hasten the end of the cruel, dehumanizing, and destructive prison practices that harsh, mass incarceration-era regimes entailed. Reversing the harmful trends of the past several decades will require us not only to restore rehabilitation as a central goal of wholly a revised corrections agenda but also to significantly revise concept of rehabilitation itself, in light of the social contextual knowledge advanced in the preceding chapters. Thus, a fundamentally new approach to prison programming can and should be implemented that is characterized by its emphasis on context—the context from which most prisoners have come before their incarceration, the prison context in which they will be housed, and (as I discuss in the next chapter) the context to which they will return once released.

As psychiatrist Terry Kupers correctly summarized, a "large majority of prison inmates come from low-income, high-crime neighborhoods, and are likely to have been subjected to repeated and prolonged trauma and violence since childhood."[76] This fact has broad and deep implications both for the kinds of programming and treatment that must be made available inside prisons, the nature of the prison environments in which prisoners can be safely housed and for how long, and the attention that must be given to changing the nature of the environments to which prisoners return upon release.

More broadly, there are important implications to the explicit recognition that prisons are filled with many persons who share problematic, often traumatic, social histories. One is that effective programs of meaningful rehabilitation must be "trauma informed." This includes recognizing that "[t]he experience of arrest, jail, court processes, and prison can all *create* trauma" in the lives of prisoners.[77] Thus, criminal justice programs and places must be restructured as much as possible to avoid harming an already vulnerable population, entirely shifting and refocusing the current tenor and content of correctional rehabilitation in jails and prisons.[78] From this perspective, effective rehabilitation means acknowledging the often underappreciated future potential of the prison population, one filled with persons who can and will flourish in the right contexts. Here, too, the deconstruction of the crime master narrative will lead to a deemphasis on therapeutic programs that implicitly but consistently view prisoners as inherently defective patients and instead implement approaches that acknowledge them as multidimensional persons who can prosper and flourish in the right, properly structured settings and circumstances.

In a related way, a more trauma-centered approach to rehabilitation would acknowledge the basic social contextual point that in-prison programming is most effective when it directly addresses the broad range of past influences that have impacted a prisoner's life, and implicitly rejects the traditional individualistic notion that the source of problematic behavior must be located exclusively inside the person who engages in it. In fact, one comprehensive review of prison rehabilitation programs already reached this fundamentally social contextualist conclusion:

> An important supplementary finding concerns the extensiveness of interventions and the degree of involvement of services across a range of contexts of an individual's life, most importantly, that of the family. Broadly speaking, the more areas of a person's life on which it is possible to have an influence, even if

only an indirect one, the greater the likelihood of securing and maintaining change.[79]

In addition, by broadening the scope of the "intervention" and reframing the nature of the "patient," these new context-based correctional regimes will focus more directly on jails and prisons themselves, where serious and sustained efforts must be made to eliminate the degrading, dehumanizing, and confrontational aspects that characterize most such facilities.[80] When good things happen in correctional settings—and sometimes they do—it is too often in spite of the way in which these environments are structured and operated, not because of it. Precisely because many prisons and jails have become such problematically countertherapeutic and psychologically harmful environments, existing mechanisms must be bolstered or new ones created to enable meaningful reform and oversight efforts to be initiated and sustained.

With this in mind, a much more vigorous, contextually sophisticated prison jurisprudence is long overdue.[81] Justice Anthony Kennedy's recent recognition that "[p]risoners retain the essence of human dignity inherent in all persons," and that this dignity "animates the Eighth Amendment prohibition against cruel and unusual punishment,"[82] is an important start. But Eighth Amendment jurisprudence remains severely handicapped by the Prison Litigation Reform Act (PLRA),[83] which was passed at the height of the era of mass incarceration when many lawmakers and members of the public were not only ignorant about and unconcerned with the harsh realities of prison life, but also largely unaware of the life-altering consequences of being exposed to them. As Margo Schlanger and Giovanna Shay observed, this legislation interposed significant "obstacles to meritorious lawsuits" that challenged prison conditions, thus "undermining the rule of law in our prisons and jails."[84] This, in turn, "emboldens prison and jail officials" and "further dehumaniz[es] prisoners and promot[es] a culture of callousness."[85]

The crime master narrative contributed to this in an indirect but important way. Because people were supposed to be sent to prison for the bad things they presumably freely chose to do, and the "badder" the act, the longer the prison term they supposedly deserved, harsh prison conditions were relatively easy to justify (or at least, to tolerate or ignore). On the other hand, greater cognizance of the contributing influences of family, neighborhood, school, and community, and larger structural forces such as poverty and racism on criminal behavior should act as a motivating force to transform our nation's evolving standards of decency, changing the normative understanding of what prisoners "deserve," and ending a decades-long willingness to allow prisoners to suffer. With these things in mind, it is time to significantly amend the PLRA or to abandon it altogether.

Indeed, there is an overarching principle that should apply here, and the demise of the crime master narrative can hasten its more widespread acceptance in the United States. The Norwegian prison system is generally regarded as one of the most humane and effective in the world.[86] It operates penal institutions that are barely recognizable as such, at least when compared to their American counterparts. At the core of the Norwegian correctional philosophy is something they term "the principle of normality." The principle is described in some ways as a programmatic approach to the way that prison life should be structured—the notion that day-to-day life in prisons must resemble "normal life" as much as possible.[87] But there is a deeper, more fundamental assumption that I believe is at the heart of this principle—the belief that prisoners too are fundamentally normal, and that they are normatively worthwhile human beings. The Norwegians assume this so implicitly that they often fail to make it an explicit part of their statement of correctional principles. Yet, it both exemplifies the approach they take to persons who have violated the law and animates the rest of their penal philosophy. It is also the antithesis of the crime master narrative that has operated for so long and with such invidious force and effect in the United States. Frankly recognizing the ways in which the social histories and circumstances of *normal* people can adversely affect their life courses and increase the likelihood that they may someday violate the law—without compromising their personhood or the "essence of human dignity" that all persons retain—will make implementing a principle of normality inside our nation's prisons more likely.

The long-term crime control advantages of radically transforming the nature of prison confinement should become increasingly obvious. We know that adverse prison conditions can have negative effects on prisoners that often carry over to their postprison adjustment, increasing the chances that they will violate the law again. In the long run, this dynamic operates to keep prison populations high. Conversely, creating fundamentally new prison forms—a kind of newly designed setting that eventually will supplant what are now defined as prisons—that are well-managed, safe, and provide persons with badly needed services and opportunities will enhance their subsequent adjustment and redound to the benefit of the larger community.[88] It should be clear that providing prisoners with necessary and fully appropriate amounts of medical and mental health care, effective rehabilitative services and programs, and safe, secure, humane living conditions is not only a moral and constitutional obligation but also an essential part of an overall strategy of humane and effective crime control.

Implicit in this overarching call for the radical reconfiguring of the prison form is the need to drastically reduce and eventually eliminate the range of draconian practices that still exist in many correctional environments. If jails and prisons represent the concrete and steel embodiments of the crime master narrative's assumption that individuals alone are responsible for free-world crime, then harsh disciplinary sanctions such as solitary confinement represent the embodiment of that ill-conceived view as applied inside correctional facilities. Consider the wrongheadedness of this practice from the social contextual perspective I have developed throughout much of this book: persons who have demonstrated difficulties adjusting to one harsh environment (jail or prison) are placed in a much worse place (solitary confinement), where adjustment is far more difficult. Many remain there until and unless their behavior miraculously improves. Guided by the still-dominant crime master narrative, prison officials too often ignore the role that this much harsher context plays in generating additional infractions and prolonging stays in isolation. Solitary confinement regimes offer prisoners little or no assistance or insight into how to better control their behavior or better adjust and survive within the institution. Instead, prisoners are left to languish alone, in typically small and degraded cells, where they not only suffer but also often deteriorate in response to their poor treatment and deprived conditions.

Solitary confinement is thus a hurtful and often harmful correctional context in which prisoners are denied meaningful human contact and access to activities and services from which they could benefit. The crime master narrative serves as an overarching justification for this kind of punitive practice—in or out of jail and prison, bad people do bad things and have themselves "earned" the punishment imposed on them in response. It also serves as a basis for ignoring harmful consequences that come from exposure to toxic environments—through the mistaken assumption that people are relatively unaffected by the contexts or settings in which they placed, no matter the grave risk of sometimes permanent harm. Despite lacking any documented penological purpose,[89] prolonged solitary confinement represents little more than punishment for punishment's sake. The deconstruction of the crime master narrative serves as an important intellectual justification for significantly limiting and eventually ending the use of this painful, dangerous practice, one that so completely ignores the dictum that context matters.

This same dictum bears on fundamental jail and prison reform in another important way, one that is often lost sight of, even in otherwise very thoughtful proposals for correctional change. Because correctional officers are both affected by and form an essential part of existing prison environments,[90] they too must be invited to play a central role in the redesign of the nature of the facilities in which they work. They can and should assist in the creation and implementation of new forms of jail and prison programming, and help to devise methods and policies to ensure that humane correctional practices are employed on a day-to-day basis. We know that many contemporary jails and prisons simultaneously facilitate prisoner abuse *and* undermine the health and well-being of prison staff.[91] Thus, the morally disengaging aspects of jail and prison environments that foster the mistreatment of prisoners must be systematically analyzed and eliminated, for the benefit of staff as well as the persons whom they supervise.

Alison Liebling and her colleagues have written insightfully about the way that positive changes in the nature of the correctional officer role in turn change the prison climate to the benefit of prisoners and staff alike.[92] In fact, without the investment of correctional officers in the process of correctional change, meaningful jail and prison reform is unlikely to occur and certainly cannot be sustained. That investment should derive from the correctional officers' own enlightened self-interest, shaped and guided by significantly revamped forms of correctional training that definitively deconstruct the crime master narrative with which officers traditionally have been imbued. These new forms of training would be combined with newly reconfigured and elevated occupational roles that place officers in supportive rather than oppositional and repressive relationships with prisoners.

It is also important to acknowledge here a theme that I will develop at greater length in the following chapter. Prison itself should of course be radically reformed to minimize its needlessly painful aspects and eliminate its predictable long-term harms, and restructured to provide prisoners with a panoply of meaningful services and rehabilitative options inside. We are obligated as a society to make major investments in preparing prisoners for their eventual release. This obligation forces us to confront a long-ignored but now unavoidable reality—namely, that this kind of preparation is simply not possible inside most of the penal institutions that currently exist in the United States. Entirely new settings must be created that, like the Norwegian model, barely resemble the still degrading and dehumanizing American prison form. The deconstruction of the individual blame-oriented crime master narrative should hasten the time when "the principle of normality" and all that it implies will supplant the goal of "mak[ing] offenders suffer" that characterized the last several decades of this nation's criminal justice history.[93]

PSYCHOLOGY AND THE POLITICAL ECONOMY OF PRISONS

As I discussed at some length in Chapter 4, we now know that many juvenile and adult penal institutions operate in ways that exacerbate the very problems they are intended to solve. Incarceration not only adds to the psychic pain that persons with already traumatic social histories experience—representing a form of "retraumatization"—but it can also have destructive—even criminogenic—long-term consequences. This applies with equal and perhaps greater force to persons who have been convicted of engaging in violent criminal behavior. There is certainly nothing about prison that is likely to deter or deescalate future violence among persons who have learned to resort to it in the past. Quite the contrary. As Hans Toch wisely noted, "[v]iolence feeds on low self-esteem and self-doubt, and prison unmans and dehumanizes; violence rests on exploitation and exploitiveness, and prison is a power-centered jungle."[94] This means that safe and effective diversion programs, therapeutic alternatives to incarceration that respond more effectively to the causal factors that are actually implicated in the criminal behavior in question, and approaches that we know will avoid many of the predictably counterproductive consequences of conventional prisons must be considered for this group of lawbreakers as well.

In any event, given what we now know about how much "context matters," legal decision-makers and correctional policymakers cannot continue to operate, as Justice Blackmun once put it, "blind[ed] . . . to the realities of prison life."[95] Instead, as I noted earlier, heightened awareness of the long-term consequences of the pains of imprisonment should routinely guide more searching and consequential legal inquiries into prison conditions to eliminate cruel and unusual punishment. In addition, however, we also need a fundamental political recalibration of whether how much penal pain our society is justified in imposing in response to crime. The best way to limit the pains of imprisonment is to ensure the fewest number of persons necessary enter prison or prison-like settings.

Proposals to significantly reduce and limit the number of incarcerated persons are no longer controversial in the United States, after decades of mass incarceration. As a report of a National Academy of Sciences committee of scholars who studied the causes and consequences of high rates incarceration in the United States acknowledged, "[p]rison conditions can be especially hard on some people, particularly those with mental illness, causing severe psychological stress."[96] In part with this fact in mind, the report recommended that "federal and state policy makers should revise criminal justice policies to significantly reduce the rate of incarceration in the United States."[97]

Yet, despite the many thoughtful, well-intentioned efforts underway around the country, the reductions that have accrued to date are not remotely commensurate with the magnitude and urgency of the task. Notwithstanding modest decreases in the number of incarcerated persons in the years since 2009,[98] extraordinary numbers of persons remain imprisoned in the United States. The Sentencing Project has estimated that at the pace of current trends, it would take approximately 75 years to lower the U.S. prison population by half,[99] which likely would still leave the nation at or near the top of the world leaders in imprisonment. Many of the proposals I outline in this and the next chapter are intended to greatly accelerate the rate at which reductions in the prison population occur. In the interim, however, hundreds of thousands of persons will continue to be subjected to the pains of imprisonment, many in truly horrendous prisons.[100]

In one sense, the challenge of the next decade is to amass the same kind of political will and commitment of resources that produced the era of mass incarceration decades ago, but this time to reverse it. Yet, given the vested interests that now have a stake in preserving or enlarging the massive "prison industrial complex,"[101] significantly more energy and advocacy will be required to achieve necessary, meaningful reductions in our current prison population. A daunting, crisis-level challenge like mass incarceration demands a coordinated response that entails more than merely slowing the pace at which we do the same harmful things. Instead, we need the correctional equivalent of a "Green New Deal,"[102] in which prison industrial complex companies and interests that now operate in the service of a 19th-century penal technology that has massive psychological, social, economic, and environmental externalities are reconfigured, transitioning to support and participate in an innovative and much more effective and humane approach to the social problem of crime. In fact, there is reason for guarded optimism that this kind of broad-based political consensus necessary to support these efforts may finally have begun to coalesce.[103]

To be sure, there is a great distance that remains to be traveled. Yet, nation's policy about the amount of imprisonment it dispenses is based in part on what Franklin Zimring and Gordon Hawkins once termed "the political economy of prisons."[104] As they noted, there are no bedrock legal or constitutional principles that dictate how many people a nation puts in prison or for how long. That is, "the jurisprudence of imprisonment is rarely precise about the number of offenders who must be sent to prison or about the duration of their imprisonment."[105] Moreover, the amount of imprisonment a society regards as necessary or desirable cannot be straightforwardly inferred from the nature of its criminal laws. Thus, specific prison practices as well as overall levels of imprisonment may—and clearly do—vary widely, even between countries that have very similar statutes and legal traditions.[106]

In fact, the psychological assumptions that people in general make about crime and punishment—assumptions that help to explain *why* people are sent to prison, and that certainly influence what should happen to them while they are there—influence *how many* people the public believes should be sent to prison and how long they should be required to stay. Of course, there are many reasons to believe that even in a democracy these things are jealously guarded prerogatives of the state. Some historians have suggested that one motivation for the law's increased use of imprisonment in place of executions at the start of the 19th century in England was the troublesome gap between the public's views of the appropriate use of a particular punishment—the death penalty—and those held by the lawmakers. Specifically, there was "a growing resistance [among officials] to the idea that the state should share the infliction of the punishment with the community," whose members gathered—with increasingly unpredictable reactions—to watch it.[107]

As Michael Ignatieff observed, "imprisonment offered the state unparalleled control over the offender, enabling it to regulate the amount of suffering involved in any sentence, free from the jeers of the populace."[108] To be sure, inflicting legal punishment inside the prison rather than in the open public square distanced citizens further from the actions that were being taken in their name and kept them relatively ignorant about what really went on behind the prison walls. Even though there are no longer "crowds of outsiders" present at the moment of punishment, public opinion still influences the punishment norms that govern our society. Unfortunately, however, far from acting as "a rough check on custodial power,"[109] public sentiment in the recent past has been employed to raise the limits on what is considered appropriate levels of punishment.

Indeed, draconian legislation like three strikes laws passed during the recent "mean season" of corrections[110] was based on an extreme version of the crime master narrative. In essence, such laws enthusiastically advanced the 19th-century model of human nature that I have implicitly critiqued throughout much of this book, and they are at odds with what we now know about the social historical and circumstantial origins of criminal behavior. At the time they were passed, the laws were clear examples of a misguided form of "penal populism" at work,[111] as ginned up public sentiment was harnessed to distort the punishment process and ratchet up the number and length of the prison sentences that were meted out.

The crime master narrative operated with a vengeance during the era of mass incarceration, buttressing an invalid view of the causes of crime—who commits it and why—and convincing the voting public that the perpetrators of crime were inherently and irredeemably bad. But the crime master narrative simultaneously, albeit indirectly, increased widespread public ignorance about the real pains of imprisonment by implicitly suggesting that they were so insignificant to unfeeling prisoners and their families and communities as to be justifiably ignored in calculations about how many people should be subjected to them and for how long. These interconnected and profoundly uninformed views of the causes of crime and the impact of prison pain eased the political and legal limits to the punitive nature of imprisonment itself.

For example, as one legal commentator succinctly noted, "California's over-inclusive Three Strikes rule comes at the expense of a prevention-oriented approach to crime, which would confront the twin problems of poverty and racism that make individuals more likely to commit crime."[112] Of course, the barriers to meaningful criminal justice reform—ill-considered, media-driven, and politically-inspired crime control policies that failed to address any of the underlying structural and social contextual causes of crime—were not unique to California.[113] They were implemented throughout the nation, and, despite some modest reforms, most of them remain in place.

At some point, however, more informed voting majorities cognizant of the real causes of crime will demand more effective solutions to law-breaking in which the role of imprisonment is greatly diminished. Clear-eyed assessments of the inhumane consequences of the draconian laws that were passed during the last several decades will eventually precipitate calls for real reform and widespread repeal of pointlessly hurtful, counterproductive punishments. The unduly harsh prison sentences that were imposed on both nonviolent *and* violent lawbreakers must be reexamined and readjusted in light of the new knowledge summarized in many of the previous chapters. Alternative sentencing models must be created that use imprisonment as an absolute last resort, imposed for as short a time as absolutely necessary.[114]

In this regard, two criminal sentences in particular are largely incompatible with the new knowledge that I have presented in the preceding pages. Life-without-parole prison sentences and the death penalty both reflect an inherently essentialist view of human nature, implicitly assuming that crime emanates exclusively from within the unchanging and unchangeable characteristics of its perpetrators. This view is no longer intellectually sustainable. It ignores the transformative influence of social context on behavior and the capacity for redemptive change that maturation and different life circumstances can bring about.[115] In fact, the kind of permanent exile contemplated by these sentences—from society, in the case of life-without-parole and, in the case of the death penalty, from life itself—is so extreme that most citizens are unable to bring themselves to authorize it. Indeed, they ordinarily must be "moral disengaged" from the humanity of the persons on whom the sentences are to be imposed.[116]

Albert Camus wrote eloquently about making these kind of definitive judgments—"the final condemnation" that capital punishment required and which he staunchly opposed. He observed that this kind of categorical finality was incompatible with his preferred form of compassionate justice, one that he saw as rooted to the recognition that human beings not only share a "solidarity in error and aberration" but also "a common suffering."[117] From his perspective, passing a "definitive, irreparable" judgment on another person's life required decision-makers and society at large to not only ignore this common suffering but also to deny the human capacity for redemption and change. A more psychologically valid, context-sensitive model of behavior is compatible with Camus's more optimistic view—that human nature is inherently modifiable and therefore capable of growth and transformation. Indeed, if social contextualism teaches us anything it is that, under the right circumstances, all of us have the capacity to behave differently and better.

PROMOTING RESTORATIVE JUSTICE

Supplanting the crime master narrative with a more contextual view of the causes of criminal behavior adds an intellectual dimension to increasingly widespread programs of "restorative justice" that respond to crime in ways that directly involve the larger community and crime survivors in its long-term resolution. I frankly do not believe that restorative justice models could have emerged and been considered on such a widespread basis from within the exclusively individual-centered, 19th-century view of the causes of human behavior on which the crime master narrative is premised. However, a 21st-century understanding of these issues has created both the opportunity and urgency to bring about this kind of fundamental criminal justice change. Restorative justice programs bring to bear holistic perspectives on crime control by examining key aspects of the broader social and community context in which a crime has occurred and uses these perspectives to develop ways to address it.[118] As John Braithwaite argued, "the rule of law will amount to a meaningless set of formal sanctioning proceedings which will be perceived as arbitrary unless there is community involvement in moralizing about and helping with the crime problem."[119]

In fact, the underlying theoretical basis for the restorative justice model is entirely consistent with the social historical and contextualist views that I have advanced throughout this book. For example, Braithwaite's assessment of the waning utility of individualistic models of behavior echoes the discussion with which my analysis began:

> Individualism is an ideology which was useful during early capitalist development, but today we depend less and less on rugged individualists. Most economic activity occurs in bureaucratic organizations; scientific breakthroughs are increasingly the work of research teams; even contemporary artistic work is often located in public and private conglomerates, foundations, institutes.[120]

The proponents of restorative justice sometimes take the issue of crime causation for granted, moving quickly past it to concentrate most of their analysis on the advantages and techniques of restoration and reintegration. The argument they typically advance in favor of restorative justice programs is based at least in part on practical considerations—that restorative justice models work. Thus, many of its proponents spend little or no time addressing what, for many politicians and policymakers, is still a pressing, threshold question—why focus on community reintegration rather than individual punishment in the first place? The context-sensitive model of criminal behavior that I presented in the preceding chapters provides an intellectual foundation from which to address this issue. Because criminal behavior has causal roots and broad consequences in the context in which it occurs—a set of interacting family, community, institutional, and structural criminogenic influences and impacts—restorative justice models that engage all of these dimensions are better able to address crime in whatever form it occurs.

Restorative justice programs deemphasize, and where possible completely circumvent, the often counterproductive and even criminogenic institutional apparatus of the criminal justice system that I discussed in Chapters 4 and 5. In fact, Braithwaite argued that reliance on the state "as the all-powerful agent of social control" derives from the individualistic society in which our crime-control strategies originated.[121] As he noted, the state typically responds to increased public concerns about crime "the only way it can—by locking more people up, giving the police and business regulatory agencies more powers, trampling on the very civil liberties which are the stuff of individualist ideologies."[122] This unfortunate irony notwithstanding, "locking more people up" does little or nothing to heal crime survivors or impact problematic aspects of the community where the crime took place.

In fact, the crime master narrative and associated punitive practices narrow the horizons and limit the expectations of crime survivors by teaching them the unfortunate and erroneous lesson that the suffering of another person is all they need to alleviate their own. Instead we need to develop new and better societal responses to crime that promote genuine healing for crime survivors without adding to the overall levels of trauma in their communities. Restorative justice practices simultaneously acknowledge the personhood of lawbreakers and more meaningfully address the needs and preferences of crime survivors.

A less individualistic, more contextual system of justice can reduce our dependency on exclusively state-based sanctions by conceding the importance of something I discuss in the next chapter: community-based responses to crime that recognize the wisdom of involving residents and other stakeholders in the process.[123] Social contextualists understand that crime control programs that transform social relations and community dynamics are far more effective and have more lasting consequences than traditional individual-centered approaches. Thus, fair, effective, and humane crime control policies are based on the recognition that criminality is produced largely by the criminogenic aspects of the family, community, institutional, and structural contexts in which it is engendered and occurs.

Consistent with this view, restorative justice programs emphasize that the reintegration of the person who violated the law and the healing of crime survivors can often be made part of the same process. In addition to working explicitly to reintegrate persons back into their community, then, effective restorative justice programs also involve persons who have committed crimes in the task of addressing the needs of their victims as well as those of the larger community in which they reside. At the same time, and in a way that is diametrically opposed to the crime master narrative, this approach explicitly acknowledges the personhood of the lawbreaker him- or herself, and openly invites and legitimizes that person's participation in the life of the surrounding community. It also encourages and facilitates their contributions to the processes by which the community and its members can be made whole. Ideally, what is thus "restored" and even enhanced is a set of contextual relationships—between persons who have violated the law, crime survivors, and their shared community.

CONCLUSION

Deconstructing the outmoded crime master narrative and supplanting it with a radically different understanding of the causes of crime promises to bring about transformational legal change. In this chapter, I have outlined some of that change, including the modification of doctrines of legal responsibility based on a contextual model of criminal behavior, the implementation of broad, context-based sentencing reforms (including the limitation or elimination of some our current criminal law's most draconian punishments), a significant restructuring of the nature of prison life, a recalibration of the political economy of prisons to reflect the extremely limited role these institutions should play in a revamped and restructured criminal justice system, and bringing about the more widespread use of restorative justice rather than exclusively punitive models and processes in the criminal justice system generally. These are decidedly *not* calls to eliminate accountability for wrongdoing. Ironically, as Danielle Sered reminded us, our current system of harsh prison punishment is uniquely structured to *minimize* opportunities for genuine, heartfelt accountability or to circumvent them entirely. In fact, as she says, the present criminal justice system actually "creates obstacles to the ways responsible people could make right for what they have done."[124]

With the aspirational but achievable goals I have laid out in this chapter in mind, the foreseeable future will be a period of transition. Many persons who are currently imprisoned will still reenter communities that lack the resources to provide them with meaningful services to facilitate their successful reintegration. Unless formerly incarcerated persons are able to reside in communities where genuine opportunities for gainful employment, decent housing and healthcare, and the chance for full-fledged social and civic participation exist, even fundamental legal and prison reforms will matter very little in the long run. This social contextual insight explains many alleged past failures of rehabilitation. That is, even when especially dedicated prisoners gained access to well-designed prison programs and acquired positive skills, their effects dissipated when, in the typical case, the communities to which they returned lacked the resources, opportunities, and infrastructure to support them. Desistance from lawbreaking is not simply a matter of achieving the requisite personal change in prison, learning to "make better choices," or committing more forcefully to exercise the individual will to "do good," as the crime master narrative would have us believe. As I say, acquiring tools in prison with which to enable successful reintegration is an important first step that will likely not matter in the absence of a supportive community that provides viable options and needed assistance.

Recognizing the now undeniable empirical connections between context and criminality also provides a persuasive rationale for limiting the use of imprisonment, which by definition acts only on persons and not social situations or circumstances.[125] Yet no responsible proposal to drastically deemphasize the extent to which a nation resorts to imprisonment can ignore the question of what needs to be done *instead*. The next chapter examines that issue in detail, by discussing a range of largely preventative strategies of crime control that are based explicitly on the contextual insights that have been developed throughout this book. Relinquishing our dependence on the outmoded crime master narrative is an essential precondition for a host of additional changes that go well beyond the reform of internal criminal justice doctrines, practices, and procedures. The next chapter's proposals address our overall approach to crime control and the need to fundamentally reconfigure and recalibrate the basic balance between prevention and punishment.

NOTES

1. Platt, T. (2018). *Beyond these walls: Rethinking crime and punishment in the United States*, p. 255. New York, NY: St. Martin's Press.
2. Biggs, J. (1955). *The guilty mind: Psychiatry and the law of homicide* (pp. 192–193). New York, NY: Harcourt, Brace. In his long and distinguished career on the Third Circuit Court of Appeals, Judge Biggs was regarded as a "pioneer in the application of psychiatry to the law." Seitz, C. (1976). John Biggs, Jr. *Villanova Law Review, 22*, 584–586, p. 584.
3. Meares, T. L., Kahan, D. M., & Katyal, N. (2004). Updating the study of punishment. *Stanford Law Review, 56*, 1171–1210, p. 1171.
4. Elsewhere I have written about the overarching nature of the reforms that a truly "contextual model of law" would bring to many of our legal system's institutional arrangements, procedures, and practices. See Haney, C. (2002). Making law modern: Toward a contextual model of justice. *Psychology, Public Policy, and Law, 7*,

3–63. http://dx.doi.org/10.1037/1076-8971.8.1.3. The current chapter is focused more specifically at the related, but narrower, implications of a deconstruction of the crime master narrative.

5. Sullivan, M. L. (1996). Biography of heinous criminals: Culture, family violence, and prisonization. *Journal of Research in Crime and Delinquency, 33,* 354–377, p. 356. http://dx.doi.org/10.1177%2F0022427896033003007. He emphasized: "There is a high degree of consensus in criminology that childhood neglect and abuse are powerful, if not inevitable, predictors of future criminality" (p. 372).
6. A number of thoughtful scholars have discussed these proposals for reform. See, e.g., Barkow, R. (2019). *Prisoners of politics: Breaking the cycle of mass incarceration.* Cambridge, MA: Harvard University Press. http://dx.doi.org/10.4159/9780674238992; Bazelon, E. (2019). *Charged: The new movement to transform American prosecution and end mass incarceration.* New York, NY: Random House; and Lynch, M. (2016). *Hard bargains: The coercive power of drug laws in federal court.* New York, NY: Russell Sage Foundation. http://dx.doi.org/10.4159/9780674238992
7. *Morissette v. United States,* 342 U.S. 246, 251–252 (1952).
8. *Morissette v. United States,* 342 U.S. at 252.
9. Dubin, G. V. (1966). Mens rea reconsidered: A plea for a due process concept of criminal responsibility. *Stanford Law Review, 18,* 322–395, p. 324. http://dx.doi.org/10.2307/1227271. Similarly, see Packer, H. (1963). Mens rea and the Supreme Court. *1962 Supreme Court Review,* 107–152. http://dx.doi.org/10.1086/scr.1962.3108794 "One searches the treatises in vain for any articulation of underlying principles or for the construction of any analytical framework that would serve either to explain or to criticize the development of [this area of] the law" (p. 137). In addition to the lack of legal coherence and any defensible underlying rationale for existing categories of mens rea, the psychological processes by which legal decision-makers routinely infer states of mind are also problematic. See, e.g., Beattey, R., & Fondaraco, M. (2018). The misjudgment of criminal responsibility. *Behavioral Science and the Law, 36,* 457–469. http://dx.doi.org/10.1002/bsl.2354; Finkel, N. (1998). *Commonsense justice: Jurors' notions of the law.* Cambridge, MA: Harvard University Press; and Levinson, J. D. (2005). Mentally misguided: How state of mind inquiries ignore psychological reality and overlook cultural differences. *Howard Law Journal, 49,* 1–29.
10. *People v. Goedecke,* 65 Cal. 2d 850, 856 (1967).
11. Bernard Diamond was a noted scholar–practitioner whose innovative ideas sparked legal change in a number of areas of criminal law, especially with respect to mental state defenses. Among other things, he was the defense psychiatrist who testified in *People v. Gorshen,* 51 Cal. 2d 716 (1959), a case that was instrumental in creating the doctrine of "diminished capacity" in California. He also testified in *People v. Newton,* 8 Cal. App. 3d 359 (Cal. Ct. App. 1970), where his testimony was key to establishing the basis for a defense of unconsciousness to negate a requisite state of mind. Michael Tigar described Diamond as simply "the most prolific and perceptive proponent of mental condition defenses to specific intent crimes." Tigar, M. (1986). Crime talk, rights talk, and double-talk: Thoughts on reading the *Encyclopedia of crime and justice. Texas Law Review, 65,* 101–151, p. 147. In addition to his contributions on mental state defenses, Diamond's scholarly articles prompted courts to approach a number of important criminal law issues differently. For example, he helped to convince legal decision-makers to more carefully scrutinize—and, under certain circumstances, to prohibit—the testimony of hypnotized witnesses. See Diamond, B. (1980). Inherent problems in the use of pretrial hypnosis on a prospective witness. *California Law Review, 68,* 313–349. http://dx.doi.org/10.2307/3479989. For brief discussions of some of the impact of Professor Diamond's distinguished career

on the criminal law, see both the in memoriam comments in the *California Law Review* by California Supreme Court Justice Stanley Mosk and those by Diamond's colleague, Professor Jerome Skolnick. Mosk, S. (1990). In memoriam: A giant in the field. *California Law Review, 78,* 1431–1432; and Skolnick, J. (1990). In memoriam: Dr. Bernard L. Diamond. *California Law Review, 78,* 1433–1436. For a collection of and commentary on some of Professor Diamond's most widely cited published work, see Quen, J. (Ed.). (1994). *The psychiatrist in the courtroom: Selected papers of Bernard L. Diamond, M.D.* Hillsdale, NJ: Analytic Press.

12. Diamond, B. (1961). Criminal responsibility of the mentally ill. *Stanford Law Review, 14,* 59–86, pp. 82–83. http://dx.doi.org/10.2307/1226566
13. I have written several articles about how these kinds of sentencing hearings operate and what they are designed to accomplish. See, e.g., Haney, C. (2006). Exonerations and wrongful condemnations: Expanding the zone of perceived injustice in capital cases. *Golden Gate Law Review, 37,* 131–173; Haney, C. (2008). Evolving standards of decency: Advancing the nature and logic of capital mitigation. *Hofstra Law Review, 36,* 835–882 (2008); and Haney, C. (2009). On mitigation as counter-narrative: A case study of the hidden context of prison violence. *University of Missouri-Kansas City Law Review, 77,* 911–946.
14. The evolution of the legal doctrine establishing the right of a capital defendant to introduce a very broad range of "background and circumstance" evidence began with *Lockett v. Ohio,* 438 U.S. 586 (1978) and *Eddings v. Oklahoma,* 455 U.S. 104 (1982). The *constitutional requirement* that capital defense attorneys properly investigate and, where appropriate, effectively present mitigating social history evidence was established in *Williams v. Taylor,* 529 U.S. 362 (2000) and further elaborated in both *Wiggins v. Smith,* 539 U.S. 510 (2003) and *Rompilla v. Beard,* 545 U.S. 374 (2005).
15. Two important legal developments have created opportunities for social historical and contextual evidence to be presented as mitigation in noncapital cases. In *United States v. Booker,* 543 U.S. 220 (2005), the U.S. Supreme Court ruled that the federal sentencing guidelines (which, as I discuss later in this chapter, all but eliminated the presentation of this kind of evidence) were advisory rather than mandatory, providing federal defenders with an opportunity and incentive to gather and present mitigation of the sort that was previously introduced only in capital cases. The second important development involved two cases in which the Court first barred life-without-parole sentences for juveniles in nonhomicide cases committed before the defendant turned 18 (see *Graham v. Florida,* 560 U.S. 48 [2010]) and then prohibited mandatory life-without-parole sentences for any juvenile defendants (*Miller v. Alabama,* 567 U.S. 460 [2012]). Together these two cases created the need to develop and an opportunity to present extensive mitigation evidence in the sentencing (and resentencing) hearings held for this category of juvenile defendants. For a thoughtful discussion of some of the complexities involved in these proceedings, see Grisso, T., & Kavanaugh, A. (2016). Prospects for developmental evidence in juvenile sentencing based on *Miller v. Alabama. Psychology, Public Policy, and Law, 22,* 235–249. http://dx.doi.org/10.1037/law0000090. These complexities notwithstanding, I suggest later in this chapter that these legal developments should represent the beginning of a movement toward introducing background social history testimony in all appropriate criminal cases.
16. Diamond (1961), Criminal responsibility of the mentally ill, pp. 82–83 (emphasis added).
17. Diamond noted that when he had used this "totalistic approach," in cases where he had served as an expert witness, he had been better able to educate judges and juries, so that they could "better understand the human complexities of the

individual whom they must judge." The result, he argued, "inevitably must be greater justice for all." Diamond (1961), Criminal responsibility of the mentally ill, p. 83.

18. I have discussed these trends elsewhere. See, e.g., Haney, C. (1997). Psychology and the limits to prison pain: Confronting the coming crisis in Eighth Amendment law. *Psychology, Public Policy, and Law, 3*, 499–588. http://dx.doi.org/10.1037/1076-8971.3.4.499; Haney, C. (1998). Riding the punishment wave: On the origins of our devolving standards of decency. *Hastings Women's Law Journal, 9*, 27–78; and Haney, C. (2008). Counting casualties in the war on prisoners. *University of San Francisco Law Review, 43*, 87–138.
19. Cullen, F. (1995). Assessing the penal harm movement. *Journal of Research in Crime and Delinquency, 32*, 338–358. http://dx.doi.org/10.1177/0022427895032003005. There are a number of excellent chronicles of the rise of mass incarceration in the United States. See, e.g., Gottschalk, M. (2006). *The prison and the gallows: The politics of mass incarceration in America*. New York, NY: Cambridge University Press. http://dx.doi.org/10.1017/CBO9780511791093; Hinton, E. (2016). *From the war on poverty to the war on crime: The making of mass incarceration in America*. Cambridge, MA: Harvard University Press. http://dx.doi.org/10.4159/9780674969223; and Useem, B., & Piehl, A. (2008). *Prison state: The challenge of mass incarceration*. New York, NY: Cambridge University Press. http://dx.doi.org/10.1017/CBO9780511813573
20. See, e.g., Feeley, M., & Simon, J. (1992). The new penology: Notes on the emerging strategy of corrections and its implications. *Criminology, 30*, 449–474. http://dx.doi.org/10.1111/j.1745-9125.1992.tb01112.x
21. Hans, V. P., & Slater, D. (1983). John Hinckley Jr. and the insanity defense: The public's verdict. *Public Opinion Quarterly, 47*, 202–212, p. 202. http://dx.doi.org/10.1086/268780
22. For a discussion of some of the case's legal aspects and implications for the "reform" of the insanity defense, see Low, P., Jeffries, J., & Bonnie, R. (2008). *The trial of John W. Hinckley, Jr.: A case study in the insanity defense*. New York, NY: Foundation Press; Perlin, M. (1985). The things we do for love: John Hinckley's trial and the future of the insanity defense in the federal courts. *New York Law School Law Review, 30*, 857–868; and Steadman, H., Morrissey, J., Callahan, L., & McGreevey, M. (1993). *Before and after Hinckley: Evaluating insanity defense reform*. New York, NY: Guilford Press.
23. Fradella, H. (2007). From insanity to beyond diminished capacity: Mental illness and criminal excuse in the post-Clark era. *University of Florida Journal of Law and Public Policy, 18*, 7–92, p. 24 (footnotes omitted).
24. Fradella (2007), From insanity to beyond diminished capacity, pp. 27–8. Other state reforms eliminated the traditional insanity defense entirely. See, e.g., Nusbaum, D. (2002). Note, The craziest reform of them all: A critical analysis of the constitutional implications of "abolishing" the insanity defense. *Cornell Law Review, 87*, 1509–1572. Some legislatures substituted verdicts such as "guilty but mentally ill." See, e.g., Slobogin, C. (1985). The guilty but mentally ill verdict: An idea whose time should not have come. *George Washington Law Review, 53*, 492–527; and Woodmansee, M. A. (1996). The guilty but mentally ill verdict: Political expediency at the expense of moral principle. *Notre Dame Journal of Law, Ethics, and Public Policy, 10*, 341–386. The Arizona legislature employed the term "guilty except insane" for the alternative to the traditional insanity defense that it passed in 1994. The law defined insanity very narrowly—among other things, by explicitly excluding a number of psychiatric conditions that it said did *not* constitute insanity and also by excluding the consideration of psychosocial stressors that might have affected the defendant's behavior. See Ariz. Rev. Stat. Ann. § 13-502 (West Supp. 1997). For a discussion of the events in 1989 that led to the passage of the Arizona

law, see MelanCon, R. (1998). Arizona's insane response to insanity. *Arizona Law Review, 40,* 287–317.

25. For example, a number of states eliminated the "diminished capacity" defense, in which criminal defendants were permitted to introduce evidence that they lacked the capacity to form the requisite mental state or specific intent at the time of the criminal offense. As with the *Hinckley* verdict's effect on insanity defenses, the movement to eliminate the diminished capacity defense was precipitated in part by a high-profile jury verdict that generated public outcry, followed by what appeared to an extreme and politically motivated legislative response. In 1979, a jury convicted Dan White, a member of the San Francisco Board of Supervisors, of killing the city's mayor and another board member. Despite what the press had reported was clear evidence of premeditation and a strong case for two counts of first-degree murder, the jury found White guilty of voluntary manslaughter. In the aftermath of the verdicts (for which White was sentenced to just a little more than 7 years in prison), California and other states passed laws eliminating the defense or significantly restricting its use. For discussions of these events and the changes that followed, including their unintended consequences, see Comparet-Cassani, J. (1999). How the abolition of diminished capacity affected parity of sentencing in murder cases under the California determinate sentencing law. *Southwestern University Law Review, 29,* 51–108; and Fradella (2007), From insanity to beyond diminished capacity.
26. Some courts considered innovations similar to the ones Diamond recommended but ultimately refused to embrace them. For example, in a landmark case, *United States v. Brawner,* 471 F.2d 969 (D.C. Cir., 1972), the U.S. Court of Appeals for the District of Columbia bluntly declined: "We have rejected a broad 'injustice' approach that would have opened the door to expositions of e.g., cultural deprivation, unrelated to any abnormal condition of the mind" (p. 995). However, a concurrence in *Brawner* written by Judge David Bazelon, a jurist whose views on psychiatry and law were especially highly regarded at the time, acknowledged that psychiatrists had "vociferously criticized [an] approach to the problem of criminal responsibility on the ground that it did not correspond to the state of psychiatric knowledge." As Bazelon noted, the criticism was based in part on the crude, all-or-none quality of the determination:

    > In their view few if any persons could be said to be totally lacking in the capacity to distinguish right from wrong or to control their actions. At the same time psychiatrists believed that they could provide extensive insights into other aspects of behavior that were highly relevant to the problem of responsibility . . . [T]he traditional tests were deemed too narrow to allow consideration of such insights. (p. 1015)

    In fact, although Diamond was among the first to make these proposals, a number of jurists and scholars made—and disagreed over—similar recommendations not long after. For example, following his widely discussed dissent in *United States v. Alexander* (471 F.2d 923 [D.C. Cir. 1972]) arguing that a defendant's impoverished background should be taken explicitly into account in criminal proceedings, Judge David Bazelon debated these issues in print with law professor Stephen Morse in the mid-1970s. See Bazelon, D. (1976). The morality of the criminal law. *Southern California Law Review, 49,* 385–405; Morse, S. (1976). The twilight of welfare criminology: A reply to Judge Bazelon. *Southern California Law Review, 49,* 1247–1268; Bazelon, D. (1976). The morality of the criminal law: A rejoinder to Professor Morse. *Southern California Law Review, 49,* 1269–1274; and Morse, S. (1976). The twilight of welfare criminology: A final word. *Southern California Law Review, 49,* 1275–1276.
27. Diamond, B. (1973). From *Durham* to *Brawner*: A futile journey. *Washington University Law Quarterly, 1973,* 109–125, pp. 119–120.

28. Diamond (1973), From *Durham* to *Brawner*: A futile journey, p. 120. In fact, Diamond suggested that an *expanded* doctrine of diminished capacity—one "based upon social and cultural factors"—could someday be employed in determining the degrees of guilt and levels of responsibility. Diamond, B. (1978). Social and cultural factors as a diminished capacity defense in criminal law. *Bulletin of the American Academy of Psychiatry and Law, 6,* 195–208, p. 203. Thus, he argued that the jury's decision in the guilt phase of a murder case should "reflect the careful weighing of the particular factors of the defendant's background, the impact of those factors upon his mental faculties, and their relevance to the criminal act and mens rea" (p. 203). By focusing on the influence of social background factors on mental states—not just those cases in which it resulted in a "mental illness"—Diamond proposed allowing psychological testimony to be introduced in a much broader ranges of cases on a greater number of issues.
29. Although the modifications in doctrines of criminal responsibility and sentencing reforms that I propose in this chapter would likely decrease the overall amount of punishment meted out, it is also possible to conceive of ways that recognition of the actual criminogenic consequences of certain settings, circumstances, practices, and policies could lead to holding some persons more rather than less legally accountable. Thus, the actions of persons who knowingly engage in the creation and maintenance of criminogenic situations (i.e., ones known to engender or facilitate illegal behavior in others) might be held accountable, in lieu of or in addition to focusing exclusively upon the individual actor or perpetrator of crimes who succumbed to these situations. That is, more psychologically sophisticated notions of contextual causation may lead to the more active pursuit of legal liability for those persons responsible for creating and maintaining the situations that influenced or "caused" crime in the first place—those who are in some sense contextual accomplices to the illegal acts themselves. For example, in cases attempting to establish gun industry (civil rather than criminal) liability, courts have routinely viewed the intentional act of the individual shooter as a superseding cause that eliminated the manufacturer's responsibility for any ensuing harm. See, e.g., Jennings, E. (1997). Saturday night. Ten P.M.: Do you know where your handgun is? *Seton Hall Legislative Journal, 21,* 31–67; Mackarevich, G. (1983). Note, Manufacturers' strict liability for injuries from a well-made handgun. *William & Mary Law Review, 24,* 467–501. A more sophisticated appreciation of the power of context and situation in crime causation would undermine this defense. It would also assist cities seeking to recover the public costs associated with gun violence through product liability cases in which they have sued gun manufacturers for knowingly marketing and distributing guns without installing safety devices to prevent shootings. See, e.g., Polston, M., & Weil, D. (1997). Unsafe by design: Using tort actions to reduce firearm-related injuries. *Stanford Law & Policy Review, 8,* 13–21. See also Lytton, T. (Ed.). (2005). *Suing the gun industry.* Ann Arbor: University of Michigan Press. http://dx.doi.org/10.3998/mpub.102828; and Vernick, J. S., Rutkow, L., & Salmon, D. A. (2007). Availability of litigation as a public health tool for firearm prevention: Comparison of guns, vaccines, and motor vehicles. *American Journal of Public Health, 97,* 1991–1997. http://dx.doi.org/10.2105%2FAJPH.2006.092544
30. Fletcher, G. (1974). The individualization of excusing conditions. *Southern California Law Review, 47,* 1269–1309, p. 1271.
31. Delgado, R. (1985). Rotten social background: Should the criminal law recognize a defense of severe environmental deprivation? *Law and Inequality, 3,* 9–90, pp. 85–86.
32. Fagan, J. (1999). Context and culpability in adolescent crime. *Virginia Journal of Social Policy and the Law, 6,* 507–581, p. 511.

33. See, e.g., Cotton, M. (2005). A foolish consistency: Keeping determinism out of the criminal law. *Boston University Public Interest Law Journal, 15,* 1–48, to the effect that "[t]he distortions in the law that occur to preserve the free will assumption are themselves costs" that include "undermin[ing] some citizens' confidence in the intelligence of the idea that people freely choose their behavior and therefore are justly blamed" (p. 42); Kirchmeier, J. (2004). A tear in the eye of the law: Mitigating factors and the progression toward a disease theory of criminal justice. *Oregon Law Review, 83,* 631–730, to the effect that continuing to ignore the implications of "empirical evidence of the causes of human actions . . . reveals a criminal justice system with no moral foundation" (p. 727); O'Hanlon, S. (2009). Towards a more reasonable approach to free will in criminal law. *Cardozo Public Law, Policy and Ethics Journal, 7,* 395–428, to the effect that preserving the increasingly indefensible categorical presumption of free will "undermines the legitimacy of the legal system because it is insulated from scientific reality and often, in the name of justice, self-righteously ascribes criminal responsibility to people who are morally undeserving of such responsibility and associated punishment" (pp. 426–427). In addition, a number of scholars have called for a broad "poverty defense" to be explicitly incorporated into the criminal law. See, e.g., Duff, R. (2001). *Punishment, communication, and community*. New York, NY: Oxford University Press. http://dx.doi.org/10.1093/mind/111.442.392, to the effect that persons who have been "excluded from a fair share in, or a fair opportunity to acquire, the economic and material benefits others enjoy" and denied the "respect and concern due" them as persons should not be "called to account" for criminal acts they have committed (pp. 183–184); Gilman, M. (2013). The poverty defense. *University of Richmond Law Review, 47,* 495–553, to the effect that the kind of poverty defense that is already in use in some jurisdictions in child neglect cases can and should be employed in a wider variety of criminal cases to "shine a light on poverty, its effects, and the constrained choices it imposes" (p. 552); Green, S. (2010). Hard times, hard time: Retributive justice for unjustly disadvantaged offenders. *University of Chicago Legal Forum, 2010,* 43–71, to the effect that unless the law develops ways of formally taking into account the plight of lawbreakers "who, by virtue of their social circumstances, should be regarded as blameless . . . we run the risk of compounding the sins of distributive injustice with those of retributive injustice" (pp. 70, 71); and Tadros, V. (2009). Poverty and criminal responsibility. *Journal of Value Inquiry, 43,* 391–413. http://dx.doi.org/10.1007/s10790-009-9180-x, to the effect that "a kind of injustice is perpetrated by the state against the poor when it holds them responsible for their crimes . . . insofar as it does not fully recognize its own responsibility for the wrongdoing of the poor" (p. 410). See also Robertson, J. (2002). Closing the circle: When prior imprisonment ought to mitigate capital murder. *Kansas Journal of Law and Public Policy, 11,* 415–426, who argued that the "enduring and systematic brutalization of inmates" (p. 416) that occurs inside many U.S. prisons means that having been incarcerated should be considered a mitigating factor in capital sentencing.
34. Morse, S. (2003). Diminished rationality, diminished responsibility. *Ohio State Journal of Criminal Law, 1,* 289–308. Thus, partial responsibility would reflect "an explicitly normative judgment" made "by the community's representatives at the guilt phase, not by judges at sentencing." It would constitute an affirmative defense and, when successful, would result in juries reaching a separate verdict—"guilty but partially responsible" (p. 299).
35. See Delgado (1985), Rotten social background: Should the criminal law recognize a defense of severe environmental deprivation?
36. In 2011, the *Alabama Civil Rights & Civil Liberties Law Review* published a special issue devoted to a discussion of the potential role of "severe environmental

deprivation" in the criminal law. See *Alabama Civil Rights & Civil Liberties Law Review, 2*, 1–173.

37. Fagan (1999), Context and culpability in adolescent crime, p. 572. Fagan and I disagree a bit on whether injecting this new social historical and contextual scientific knowledge into existing criminal law defenses would require only a "little innovation," as he believes, or something more substantial, as I do.
38. See Freed, D. (1992). Federal sentencing in the wake of the guidelines: Unacceptable limits on the discretion of sentencers. *Yale Law Journal, 101*, 1681–1754. For a critique of U.S. Sentencing Commission by a then-sitting federal judge, who argued that the Commission was politicized and sometimes even more punitive than members of the public in whose name political figures claimed to be acting, see Gertner, N. (2008). The United States Sentencing Commission. In A. Freiberg & K. Gelb (Eds.), *Penal populism, sentencing councils, and sentencing policy* (pp. 103–111). Devon, England: Willan.
39. See, e.g., critical discussions of the nature and adverse impact of this sentencing "reform" in Luna, E., & Cassells, P. (2010). Mandatory minimalism. *Cardozo Law Review, 1*, 1–83. http://dx.doi.org/10.2139/ssrn.2181092; and Martin, J. S., Jr. (2004). Why mandatory minimums make no sense. *Notre Dame Journal of Law, Ethics & Public Policy, 18*, 311–317.
40. See, e.g., Burman, K. C. (2004). Firearm enhancements under the Federal Sentencing Guidelines. *University of Chicago Law Review, 71*, 1055–1076; Hartfield, L. (2006, May 30). Challenging crime of violence sentence enhancements. *The Champion*, 28–34; Hester, R., Frase, R. S., Roberts, J. V., & Mitchell, K. L. (2018). Prior record enhancements at sentencing: Unsettled justifications and unsettling consequences. *Crime and Justice, 47*, 209–254. http://dx.doi.org/10.1086/695400
41. Shinbein, I. (1996). Three strikes and you're out. A good political slogan to reduce crime but a failure in its application. *New England Journal of Criminal and Civil Commitment, 22*, 175–204; Turner, M., Sundt, J., Applegate, B., & Cullen, F. (1995). "Three strikes and you're out" legislation: A national assessment. *Federal Probation, 59*, 16–35; and Zimring, F., & Hawkins, G. (2001). *Punishment and democracy: Three strikes and you're out in California*. New York, NY: Oxford University Press.
42. Hofer, P. (2016). After ten years of Advisory Guidelines and thirty years of mandatory minimums, federal sentencing still needs reform. *University of Toledo Law Review, 47*, 649–693, p. 650. Moreover, the Guidelines, as written, were just the beginning of the problem. For an analysis of how federal prosecutors "seized, with gusto, the opportunity to join the national crime-fighting bonanza" and learned to "massage to Guidelines" to get the harsh sentences they wanted imposed, see Lynch (2016), *Hard bargains: The coercive power of drug laws in federal court*, generally and quoted at pp. 131–132.
43. Christie, N. (1993). *Crime control as industry: Towards gulags, Western style?* London, England: Routledge, p. 134. http://dx.doi.org/10.4324/9780203826263. See also Bagaric, M., Fischer, N., & Wolf, G. (2017). Bringing sentencing into the 21st century: Closing the gap between practice and knowledge by introducing expertise into sentencing law. *Hofstra Law Review, 45*, 785–850, to the effect that

    > The most pressing and important issue relating to sentencing law and practice is its continued disregard of knowledge and empirical evidence. Sentencing is the area of law where there is the greatest gap between practice and what knowledge tells us can be achieved. (p. 785)

44. See, e.g., Freed (1992), Federal sentencing in the wake of guidelines: Unacceptable limits on the discretion of sentencers.
45. *United States v. Booker*, 543 U.S. 220 (2005).

46. Gertner, N. (2009). Supporting advisory guidelines. *Harvard Law & Policy Review, 3*, 261–281, p. 270. See also Bowman, F. O., III (2014). Dead law walking: The surprising tenacity of the Federal Sentencing Guidelines. *Houston Law Review, 51*, 1227–1270, to the effect that

    > from the points of view of federal defendants in the mass and of the system that processes them from arrest to prison gate, perhaps the most surprising fact about Booker is just how small an effect it has actually had. (pp. 1229–1230)

    See also Hofer (2016), After ten years of Advisory Guidelines, p. 649, to the effect that "[f]ederal sentencing is a tragic mess." And also Divine, J. (2018). *Booker* disparity and data-driven sentencing. *The Hastings Law Journal, 69*, 771–833.
47. The guidelines specified that not even "[m]ental and emotional conditions . . . ordinarily relevant in determining whether a sentence should be outside the applicable guideline range" would be considered. U.S. Sentencing Guidelines, § 5H1.3
48. *United States v. Brady*, 417 F.3d 326 (2nd Cir. 2005).
49. *United States v. Brady*, 417 F.3d at 333 (emphasis added).
50. *United States v. Brady*, 417 F.3d at 334.
51. *McCleskey v. Kemp*, 481 U.S. 279, 339 (1987).
52. *United States v. Brady*, 417 F.3d at 334.
53. *United States v. Brady*, 417 F.3d at 334.
54. Ignatieff, M. (1978). *A just measure of pain: The penitentiary in the Industrial Revolution, 1750–1850*. New York, NY: Pantheon.
55. Haney, C. (2006). *Reforming punishment: Psychological limits to the pains of imprisonment* (p. 96). Washington, DC: American Psychological Association. http://dx.doi.org/10.1037/11382-000
56. Tonry, M. (1995). *Race, crime, and punishment in America* (p. 170). New York, NY: Oxford University Press.
57. *United States v. Hawkins*, 380 F. Supp. 2d 143, 151 (E.D.N.Y. 2005).
58. Feeley & Simon (1992), The new penology: Notes on the emerging strategy of corrections and its implications. Feeley and Simon focused on the way in which the waste management mentality affected correctional decision-making. Yet elements of this same kind of mind-set appear in the criminal jurisprudence and sentencing practices that emerged over this same time period.
59. For an extended critical discussion of the origins, applications, and pitfalls of desert-based sentencing, see Haney, C. (2012). Politicizing crime and punishment: Redefining "justice" to fight the "War on Prisoners." *West Virginia Law Review, 114*, 373–414.
60. For numerous examples of the many irrationalities, incoherencies, and inconsistencies that continue to plague the nation's criminal codes and sentencing statutes, see Barkow, E. (2019). *Prisoners of politics: Breaking the cycle of mass incarceration*. She, too, recognized the fundamental flaw in mandatory minimum sentencing laws:

    > They cut off consideration of relevant facts about culpability. They do not allow a judge to take account of the defendant's motive, age, economic circumstances, family situation, background, or other relevant mitigating circumstances. Everyone is lumped together regardless of individual differences. (p. 36)

61. von Hirsch, A., & Jareborg, N. (1991). Gauging criminal harm: A living-standard analysis. *Oxford Journal of Legal Studies, 11*, 1–38. http://dx.doi.org/10.1093/ojls/11.1.1
62. Here, too, the desert formulation begged many fundamental questions. What, after all, is the "good life," and who should define it? In general, desert-based sentencing did not provide very precise guidance about how to achieve fairer or

more meaningful calculations of the *exact* quantities of punishment or pain that should be meted out in response to any particular criminal act.

63. Of course, there is no way for the perpetrator of a crime to fully know or meaningfully anticipate the long-term impact of his or her criminal behavior on a crime victim's ability to lead a good and fulfilling life. For this reason, it seems inappropriate as the basis on which to calculate "desert," although it obviously should very much influence the nature of the restorative response that is warranted and guide the provision of crime survivor services.
64. Blecker, R. (1990). Haven or hell? Inside Lorton Central Prison: Experiences of punishment justified. *Stanford Law Review, 42,* 1149–1202, p. 1152. For a different debate over the question of "equity in sentencing," see the contrasting views expressed in Sherwin, R. (1990). Employing life expectancy as a guideline in sentencing criminal offenders: Toward a humanistic proposal for change. *Prison Journal, 70,* 125–127. http://dx.doi.org/10.1177%2F003288559007000116; and Acker, J. (1990). On confusing justice with mercy: A reply to Professor Sherwin. *Prison Journal, 70,* 128–130. http://dx.doi.org/10.1177%2F003288559007000117. Sherwin argued that sentencing tribunals should take age explicitly into account because differences in "the amount of time the offender is predicted to have left to live" (p. 125) mean that, for each year of time served, older offenders lose proportionately greater amounts of their remaining life. Acker responded that the mere fact that one has fewer years to look forward to does not necessarily mean that those years should or would be valued more. Notwithstanding the merits of each specific argument, the larger point is that there is no simple, precise way to calculate "desert." The apparent simplicity of the formulation was part of its rhetorical charm–equal time for equal crime. Beneath the surface of that glib formulation, however, lurked a host of daunting and, to my mind at least, insurmountable problems.
65. See, e.g., Haney (2006), Exonerations and wrongful condemnations: Expanding the zone of perceived injustice in capital cases.
66. As the Ninth Circuit put it: "While demonstrating such a causative 'nexus' between painful life experiences and the commission of the offense is one way in which mitigating evidence can be expected to alter a sentencing outcome, it is certainly not the only one." *Doe v. Ayers,* 782 F.3d 425, 462 (9th Cir. 2015), citing *Tennard v. Dretke,* 542 U.S. 274 (2004).
67. *Apelt v. Ryan,* 906 F.3d 834, 837 (9th Cir. 2018) (Paez, J., dissenting).
68. See, e.g., Gohara, M. (2013). Grace notes: A case for making mitigation the heart of noncapital sentencing. *American Journal of Criminal Law, 41,* 41–88. http://dx.doi.org/10.2139/ssrn.2433719
69. Monahan, E., & Clark, J. (Eds.). (2017). *Tell the client's story: Mitigation in criminal and death penalty cases.* Chicago, IL: American Bar Association.
70. Developing mitigation by compiling an extensive social or life history can be crucial to other important aspects of a criminal case and to the dignity and well-being of clients as well. See, e.g., Dudley, R., & Leonard, P. (2008). Getting it right: Life history investigation as the foundation for a reliable mental health assessment. *Hofstra Law Review, 36,* 963–988.
71. Gohara (2013), Grace notes: A case for making mitigation the heart of noncapital sentencing, p. 85.
72. Hugh Mundy has discussed the increased importance of teaching mitigation practices to students enrolled in clinical law courses and the long-term benefits of doing so. See, e.g., Mundy, H. (2013). It's not just for death cases anymore: How capital mitigation investigation can enhance experiential learning and improve advocacy in criminal defense clinics. *California Western Law Review, 50,* 31–73.

73. Haney (2006), *Reforming punishment: Psychological limits to the pains of imprisonment,* p. 303. Many of the issues discussed in this section are addressed at length in that volume, especially Chapter 10.
74. For a series of discussions about the nature of these changes that likened them to a "war on prisoners," see Haney (2008), Counting casualties in the war on prisoners; Haney, C. (2010). Demonizing the "enemy": The role of science in declaring the "war on prisoners." *Connecticut Public Interest Law Journal, 9,* 139–196; and Haney, C. (2012). Politicizing crime and punishment: Redefining justice to fight the war on prisoners. *West Virginia Law Review, 114,* 373–414.
75. Feeley & Simon, The new penology: Notes on the emerging strategy of corrections and its implications., p. 470.
76. Kupers, T. (1996). Trauma and its sequelae in male prisoners: Effects of confinement, overcrowding, and diminished services. *American Journal of Orthopsychiatry, 66,* 189–196, p. 193. http://dx.doi.org/10.1037/h0080170
77. Levenson, J. S., & Willis, G. M. (2018). Implementing trauma-informed care in correctional treatment and supervision. *Journal of Aggression, Maltreatment & Trauma, 28,* 481–501, p. 488 (emphasis added). http://dx.doi.org/10.1080/10926771.2018.1531959
78. See also Bloom, S., & Farragher, B. (2013). *Restoring sanctuary: A new operating system for trauma-informed systems of care.* New York, NY: Routledge. http://dx.doi.org/10.1093/acprof:oso/9780199796366.001.0001; Donisch, K., Bray, C., & Gewirtz, A. (2016). Child welfare, juvenile justice, mental health, and education providers' conceptualizations of trauma-informed practice. *Child Maltreatment, 21,* 125–134. http://dx.doi.org/10.1177/1077559516633304; and Kubiak, S., Covington, S., & Hiller, C. (2017). Trauma-informed corrections. In D. W. Springer & A. R. Roberts (Eds.), *Social work in juvenile and criminal justice systems* (pp. 92–104). Springfield, IL: Charles C Thomas; and Miller, N. A., & Najavits, L. M. (2012). Creating trauma-informed correctional care: A balance of goals and environment. *European Journal of Psychotraumatology, 3,* 1–8. http://dx.doi.org/10.3402%2Fejpt.v3i0.17246. Trauma-informed treatment practices have been appropriately advocated in the foster care and juvenile justice systems. See, e.g., Beyerlein, B., & Block, E. (2014). The need for trauma-informed care within the foster care system: A policy issue. *Child Welfare, 93,* 7–21; and Branson, C., Baetz, C., Horowtiz, S., & Hoagwood, K. (2017). Trauma-informed juvenile justice systems: A systematic review of definitions and core components. *Trauma: Theory, Research, Practice, and Policy, 9,* 635–646. http://dx.doi.org/10.1037/tra0000255
79. McGuire, J. (2002). Integrating findings from research reviews. In J. McGuire (Ed.), *Offender rehabilitation and treatment: Effective programmes and policies to reduce reoffending* (pp. 3–38). Chichester, England: John Wiley. http://dx.doi.org/10.1002/9780470713464.ch1
80. Social justice–oriented efforts that proceed under the banner of "abolishing prisons" lodge entirely legitimate critiques of the institution itself and of incremental efforts to change it, as well as setting entirely worthy aspirational goals. See, e.g., Davis, A. (2003). *Are prisons obsolete*? New York, NY: Random House; and McLeod, A. M. (2015). Prison abolition and grounded justice. *UCLA Law Review, 62,* 1156–1239. I believe that my own and others' social historical and contextual interpretations of the nature of criminal behavior and critiques of the criminogenic "context" of prison lead in exactly that direction. Cf. Binder, G., & Notterman, B. (2017). Penal incapacitation: A situationist critique. *The American Criminal Law Review, 54,* 1–56. However, a more realistic approach to abolition is to propose such significant change in the nature of the institution that what eventually results will bear little or no relationship to what we have come to think of as "prison."
81. See, e.g., Fathi, D. C. (2010). The challenge of prison oversight. *The American Criminal Law Review, 47,* 1453–1462.

82. *Brown v. Plata*, 563 U.S. 493, 510 (2011).
83. The PLRA—Pub. L. No. 104-134, §§801–810, 110 Stat. 1321—was passed in 1996. It places elaborate limitations on the nature and scope of prison litigation, narrowing the kind of prisoner claims that can be heard by the courts, narrowing the grounds on which prisoners could prevail, and making it more difficult to address adverse prison conditions through litigation.
84. Schlanger, M., & Shay, G. (2008). Preserving the rule of law in America's jails and prisons: The case for amending the Prison Litigation Reform Act. *University of Pennsylvania Journal of Constitutional Law, 11*, 139–154, p. 140.
85. Schlanger & Shay (2008), Preserving the rule of law in America's jails and prisons (p. 145).
86. See, e.g., Labutta, E. (2017). The prisoner as one of us: Norwegian wisdom for American prison practice. *Emory International Law Review, 31*, 329–359; and Moynihan, S. (2016). They don't do it like my clique: How group loyalty shapes the criminal justice systems in the United States and Norway. *Arizona Journal of International and Comparative Law, 33*, 423–450.
87. See, e.g., Høidal, A. (2018). Normality behind the walls: Examples from Halden Prison. *Federal Sentencing Reporter, 31*, 58–66. The Norwegians have implemented this model more effectively than any other prison system of which I am aware. However, a version of it has actually been proposed and was once implemented on a very limited basis in the United States as well. See Dora Schirro's description of the "parallel prison universe" that she attempted to create in the Missouri prison system that she oversaw, one based on the principle that "[l]ife inside prison should resemble life outside," so that prisoners "can acquire values, habits, and skills that will help them become productive, law-abiding citizens." Schirro, D. (2000). Correcting corrections: Missouri's parallel universe. In U.S. Department of Justice, *Sentencing and corrections: Issues for the 21st century. Papers from the executive sessions on sentencing and corrections* (No. 8). Washington, DC: Author, p. 1. Retrieved from https://www.ncjrs.gov/pdffiles1/nij/181414.pdf
88. See, e.g., Haney (2006), *Reforming punishment: Psychological limits to the pains of imprisonment*; and Liebling, A., & Maruna, S. (Eds.). (2005). *The effects of imprisonment*. Cullompton, England: Willan.
89. There is no clear-cut evidence that solitary confinement achieves any of the goals that are typically cited to justify its use. It has unpredictable and sometimes counterproductive effects on the overall number of assaults on staff and/or inmates throughout prison systems. See, e.g., Briggs, C. S., Sundt, J. L., Castellano, T. C. (2003). The effect of supermaximum security prisons on aggregate levels of institutional violence. *Criminology, 41*, 1341–1376. http://dx.doi.org/10.1111/j.1745-9125.2003.tb01022.x; and Sundt, J., Castellano, T., Briggs, C. (2008). The sociopolitical context of prison violence and its control: A case study of supermax and its effect in Illinois. *Prison Journal, 88*, 94–122. http://dx.doi.org/10.1177%2F0032885507310994. In addition, there is no evidence that it has any appreciable effect in reducing the size, number, or operation of prison gangs. See, e.g., Colvin, M. (1992). *The penitentiary in crisis: From accommodation to riot in New Mexico*. Albany: State University of New York Press; and Shalev, S. (2009). *Supermax: Controlling risk through solitary confinement*. Cullompton, England: Willan. http://dx.doi.org/10.4324/9781843927136. Moreover, neither short-term nor long-term stays in solitary confinement appear to achieve specific deterrent effects by reducing subsequent disciplinary infractions by prisoners who have experienced them. See, e.g., Morris, R. (2016). Exploring the effect of exposure to short-term solitary confinement among violent prison inmates. *Journal of Quantitative Criminology, 32*, 1–22. http://dx.doi.org/10.1007/s10940-015-9250-0; and Reiter,

K. A. (2012). Parole, snitch, or die: California's supermax prisons and prisoners, 1997–2007. *Punishment & Society, 14,* 530–563. http://dx.doi.org/10.1177%2F1462474512464007. And, ironically, there is some research to suggest that time spent in solitary confinement may increase the likelihood of postprison criminal behavior. See, e.g., Lovell, D., Johnson, L., Cain, K. (2007). Recidivism of supermax prisoners in Washington state. *Crime & Delinquency, 53,* 633–656. http://dx.doi.org/10.1177/0011128706296466; and Mears, D., & Bales, W. (2009). Supermax incarceration and recidivism. *Criminology, 47,* 1131–1166. http://dx.doi.org/10.1111/j.1745-9125.2009.00171.x

90. Haney, C., Banks, W., & Zimbardo, P. (1973). Interpersonal dynamics in a simulated prison. *International Journal of Criminology and Penology, 1,* 69–97; and Haney, C., & Zimbardo, P. (1977). The socialization into criminality: On becoming a prisoner and a guard. In J. Tapp & F. Levine (Eds.), *Law, justice, and the individual in society: Psychological and legal issues* (pp. 198–223). New York, NY: Holt, Rinehart, and Winston.
91. On moral disengagement and abuse, see Weill, J., & Haney, C. (2016). Mechanisms of moral disengagement and prisoner abuse. *Analyses of Social Issues and Public Policy, 17,* 286–318. http://dx.doi.org/10.1111/asap.12142. On the stressfulness of the correctional officer role, see Cullen, F., Link, B., Wolfe, N., & Frank, J. (1985). The social dimensions of correctional officer stress. *Justice Quarterly, 2,* 505–528. http://dx.doi.org/10.1080/07418828500088711; Dowden, C., & Tellier, C. (2004). Predicting work-related stress in correctional officers: A meta-analysis. *Journal of Criminal Justice, 32,* 31–47. http://dx.doi.org/10.1016/j.jcrimjus.2003.10.003; and Finney, C., Stergiopoulos, E., Hensel, J., Bonato, S., & Dewa, C. S. (2013). Organizational stressors associated with job stress and burnout in correctional officers: A systematic review. *BMC Public Health, 13,* 1–13. http://dx.doi.org/10.1186/1471-2458-13-82
92. See, e.g., Liebling, A. (2011). Moral performance, inhuman and degrading treatment and prison pain. *Punishment & Society, 13,* 530–550. http://dx.doi.org/10.1177%2F1462474511422159; and Liebling, A., Price, D., & Shefer, G. (2011). *The prison officer* (2nd ed.). Cullompton, England: Willan. http://dx.doi.org/10.4324/9780203832998
93. Cullen (1995), Assessing the penal harm movement, p. 340.
94. Toch, H. (2017). *Violent men: An inquiry into the psychology of violence* (25th anniversary ed.). Washington, DC: American Psychological Association, p. 224. http://dx.doi.org/10.1037/0000044-000
95. This was Justice Harry Blackmun's lament over the Supreme Court's "unduly narrow definition of punishment," in a case in which the Court held that

    > any pain and suffering endured by a prisoner that is not formally part of his sentence—no matter how severe or unnecessary—will not be held violative of the Cruel and Unusual Punishments Clause unless the prisoner establishes that some prison official intended the harm.

    Concurring opinion in *Farmer v. Brennan,* 511 U.S. 825, 855 (1994).
96. National Research Council. (2014). *The growth of incarceration in the United States: Causes and consequences* (p. 6). Washington, DC: National Academies Press.
97. National Research Council. (2014), *The growth of incarceration in United States,* p. 9. Indeed, the Committee concluded, based on all of the available scientific evidence, that

    > To minimize the harm from incarceration, we urge reconsideration of the conditions of confinement and programs in prison. . . . Given how damaging the experience of incarceration can be for some of those incarcerated and in some cases for their families and communities, we propose that steps be taken to improve the conditions

and programs in prisons in ways that will reduce the harmful effects of incarceration and foster the successful reintegration of former prisoners when they are released.

National Research Council (2014), *The growth of incarceration in United States,* p. 10.

98. The U.S. prison population peaked in 2009, with a total of 1,615,500 incarcerated in state or federal prison. By 2017, the total had decreased 8% (a decline of 126,100 prisoners). Bronson, J., & Carson, E. (2019, April). *Prisoners in 2017* (NCJ 252156). Washington, DC: Bureau of Justice Statistics, pp. 1–43, p. 3, Table 1.
99. Ghandnoosh, N. (2018, March). Can we wait 75 years to cut the prison population in half? *Policy Brief.* Retrieved from https://www.sentencingproject.org/publications/can-wait-75-years-cut-prison-population-half/
100. The depth of the dehumanization and cruelty that prevails in many of these places is typically kept from public view and even from scholarly analysis and commentary. Typically, the documentation only appears in court decisions that detail unconstitutional prison conditions, practices, and forms of treatment. See, e.g., *Madrid v. Gomez,* 889 F. Supp. 1146 (N.D. Cal. 1995); *Brown v. Plata,* 563 U.S. 493 (2011); *Braggs v. Dunn,* 257 F. Supp. 3d 1171 (M.D. Ala. 2017).
101. The term "prison industrial complex" was coined at the height of the era of mass incarceration by Eric Lotke to describe the subsidiary economic interests that offer specialized prison-related goods and services, from prison construction to security hardware to products marketed to prisoners (including food, toiletries, electronics, and access to telephones that are typically sold at greatly inflated prices). Lotke, E. (1996). The prison industrial complex. *Multinational Monitor, 17,* 18–21. See also Brewer, R., & Heitzeg, N. (2008). The racialization of crime and punishment: Criminal justice, color-blind racism, and the political economy of the prison industrial complex. *American Behavioral Scientist, 51,* 625–644. http://dx.doi.org/10.1177%2F0002764207307745; Gordon, A. (1990). Globalism and the prison industrial complex: An interview with Angela Davis. *Race and Class, 40,* 145–157. http://dx.doi.org/10.1177%2F030639689904000210; and Platt, T. (Ed.). (2004). Challenging the prison-industrial complex: A symposium. *Social Justice, 31,* 7–38.
102. For a discussion of the Green New Deal and its relationship to efforts that address "systemic injustice" more broadly, see Bhuyan, R., Wahab, S., & Park, Y. (2019). A Green New Deal for social work. *Affilia: Journal of Women and Social Work. 34,* 289–294. http://dx.doi.org/10.1177%2F0886109919861700. As Ashley Dawson put it, "we must rebuild our sense of collective possibility, and, with it, a state oriented to positive rather than merely punitive ends." Dawson, A. (2010). Why we need a Global Green New Deal. *New Politics, XII,* 88–94, p. 88.
103. For promising signs that this may be more possible now than at any time in the recent past, see Astor, M. (2019, May 17). On this issue, both sides concede they were wrong. *The New York Times,* p. A20, reporting on a Brennan Center for Justice report compiling recommendations from politicians and activists from across the political spectrum supporting a message of "a new bipartisan consensus on criminal justice." The message includes acknowledging that "the old consensus" that urged ever-increasing prison populations "was wrong" and touting support for wide-ranging criminal justice reform efforts. See also Chettiar, I., & Raghavan, P. (Eds.). (2019). *Ending mass incarceration: Ideas from today's leaders.* New York, NY: Brennan Center for Justice.
104. Zimring, F., & Hawkins, G. (1989). On the scale of imprisonment: Downes's *Contrasts in Tolerance. Law and Social Inquiry,* 527–538, p. 528.
105. Zimring & Hawkins. (1989). On the scale of imprisonment, p. 528.
106. See, e.g., Walker, J., Collier, P., & Tarling, R. (1990). Why are prison rates in England and Wales higher than in Australia? *British Journal of Criminology, 30,* 24–35. http://dx.doi.org/10.1093/oxfordjournals.bjc.a047978

107. Ignatieff (1978), *A just measure of pain: The penitentiary in the Industrial Revolution, 1750–1850*, p. 90.
108. Ignatieff (1978), *A just measure of pain: The penitentiary in the Industrial Revolution, 1750–1850*, p. 90.
109. Ignatieff (1978), *A just measure of pain: The penitentiary in the Industrial Revolution, 1750–1850*, p. 208.
110. See, e.g., Cullen (1995), Assessing the penal harm movement.
111. Cote-Lussier, C., & Carmichael, J. (2018). Public support for harsh criminal justice policy and its moral and ideological ties. *Psychology, Public Policy, and Law, 24*, 235–247; and Roberts, J., Stalans, L., Indermaur, D., & Hough, M. (2003) *Penal populism and public opinion: Lessons from five countries*. New York, NY: Oxford University Press.
112. Recent legislation, criminal procedure—sentencing—California enacts enhancements for prior felony convictions. *Harvard Law Review, 107*, 2123–2128, p. 2126.
113. For a discussion of some of the forces at work, see Haney (1998), Riding the punishment wave; Haney, C. (2009). Media criminology and the death penalty. *DePaul Law Review, 58*, 689–740; and Haney (2012), Politicizing crime and punishment: Redefining justice to fight the war on prisoners.
114. Mowatt, R. (1996, July 8). Millions spent on "3-strikes" offenders. *San Jose Mercury News*, pp. A-1, A-10.
115. These are virtual truisms among social psychologists. For example, Mahzarin Banaji and Deborah Prentice concluded their review of the literature on "the self in social contexts" by citing to the many "demonstrations of self-concept change during periods of life transition," which, as they noted, "suggest a powerful influence of changing contexts." These transition contexts include "the societal and cultural norms that shape the self and social behavior." Banaji, M., & Prentice, D. (1994). The self in social contexts. *Annual Review of Psychology, 45*, 297–332, p. 325. http://dx.doi.org/10.1146/annurev.ps.45.020194.001501. The context-sensitive changes affect a range of social behaviors, including those linked to a person's "self-regulatory processes" (p. 325).
116. Haney, C. (1997). Violence and the capital jury: Mechanisms of moral disengagement and the impulse to condemn to death. *Stanford Law Review, 49*, 1447–1486; Haney, C. (2005). *Death by design: Capital punishment as a social psychological system*. New York, NY: Oxford University Press.
117. Camus, A. (1960). Reflections on the guillotine. In *Resistance, rebellion, and death* (pp. 131–189). New York, NY: Modern Library.
118. See, e.g., Bazemore, G. (1998). Restorative justice and earned redemption: Communities, victims, and offender reintegration. *American Behavioral Scientist, 41*, 768–813. http://dx.doi.org/10.1177/0002764298041006003
119. Braithwaite, J. (1989). *Crime, shame, and reintegration*, p. 8. New York, NY: Cambridge University Press. http://dx.doi.org/10.1017/CBO9780511804618
120. Braithwaite (1989), *Crime, shame, and reintegration*, p. 168.
121. Braithwaite (1989), *Crime, shame, and reintegration*, p. 171.
122. Braithwaite (1989), *Crime, shame, and reintegration*, p. 171.
123. For example, as Braithwaite noted,

    > [A] responsibility of the probation officer could be to convince representatives of a young person's school, employer, sporting clubs, and other groups that are important to the offender to attend the court and offer their opinions on what they would be able to contribute to monitoring the offender's behavior in [the] future and to her rehabilitation.

    (1989), *Crime, shame, and reintegration*, p. 173.
124. Sered, D. (2019). *Until we reckon: Violence, mass incarceration, and a road to repair.* New York, NY: The New Press, p. 139. As she noted, the dehumanizing conditions

and sometimes brutal treatment to which prisoners are subjected are harsh and potentially destructive punishments that are essentially independent of or orthogonal to accountability:

> No one in prison is required to face the human impacts of what they have done, to come face to face with the people whose lives are changed as a result of their decisions, to own their responsibility for those decisions and the pain they have caused, and to do the extraordinarily hard work of answering for that pain and becoming someone who will not commit that harm again. (p. 91)

125. These issues are discussed in greater length in Haney (2006), *Reforming punishment: Psychological limits to the pains of imprisonment.*

10

Pursuing Social Justice

An Agenda for Fair, Effective, and Humane Crime Policy

What has been attempted has all the time been within the limits of available resources. Massive economic and social action has never been undertaken. . . . That would demand social reorganizations far beyond the power of criminological research workers.

—NILS CHRISTIE[1]

As the preceding chapters have made clear, we now understand the many ways in which criminal behavior is deeply rooted in the developmental and institutional histories of those who engage in it, as well as the social contexts in which it commonly occurs. Much criminal behavior can be traced to what Judge David Bazelon once called "accidents of birth."[2] Of course, the accidents that Bazelon had in mind were social and economic—not genetic—in nature. Whatever the legacies that the parents of even those persons who have committed serious crimes have bequeathed to their children, they are to be found less in their DNA than in their socioeconomic status, and the lives of deprivation and discrimination, child abuse and neglect, neighborhood disadvantage, and early exposure to violence that poverty too often engenders.

As I have argued throughout this book, conventional models of crime control are premised on the crime master narrative and its free choice assumptions about behavior. As a result, they depend almost exclusively on individual-level legal responses (primarily imprisonment). Yet that narrative and those underlying assumptions are increasingly anachronistic and

http://dx.doi.org/10.1037/0000172-011
Criminality in Context: The Psychological Foundations of Criminal Justice Reform, by C. Haney

intellectually unsustainable. In addition, their role in helping to perpetuate rather than alleviate structural injustices is especially problematic in a society plagued by increasing economic inequality and persistent racial disparities. A fundamentally different, social justice–oriented approach to crime and punishment is needed.

Indeed, if the last several decades of mass incarceration have demonstrated anything, it is that fluctuating crime rates are largely impervious to even drastically increased levels of punishment. In 2014, a several-year-long study by a National Academy of Sciences committee concluded that the long period of decline in crime rates in the United States that began in the 1990s had very little if anything to do with the starkly punitive era of mass incarceration in which it occurred.[3] Crime-control-by-imprisonment—still our nation's preferred approach—is no more than a partial and ultimately ineffective response that ignores the underlying causes of crime. Instead, the time has come to translate the empirically well-documented and theoretically sound social historical and contextual framework I have discussed throughout this book into a set of social policies that directly address the forces and factors that are most responsible for generating crime.

In the last chapter, I discussed many of the ways that numerous social contextual insights can and should be better integrated into existing legal doctrines and criminal justice practices and procedures. They are essential to ensuring and promoting greater fairness in determining criminal responsibility and, in turn, sanctioning wrongdoing. But, frankly, none of these important reforms will much matter unless we address the persistent and severe economic and racial disparities that continue to plague the nation. By driving a criminogenic cycle that simultaneously overpunishes and undervalues minorities and the poor and operates to keep crime rates unnecessarily high, these disparities help to ensure that our criminal justice institutions are filled to capacity and beyond.

A broad-based social historical and contextual approach to crime control will require a fundamental reframing of the current organization of the criminal justice system as well as a prioritizing of prevention over punishment. In this regard, the Dutch criminologist Louk Hulsman has written about what he called the "cultural organization" of the contemporary criminal justice system, one that constructs reality in such a way as to focus on only a specific incident—the crime—and to freeze the action at the time and place where it has occurred. Functioning to keep the crime master narrative firmly in place, this cultural organization facilitates the blaming of only a single individual—the perpetrator—and isolates him out from his environment and social context. The traditional perpetrator-oriented criminal justice system is not only "based on blame-allocation, and on a 'last judgment' view of the world" but also fails to provide "a context in which problematic situations can be defined and dealt with in an emancipatory way."[4] Both this outdated perspective and the larger cultural organization that supports it must be dismantled if genuine criminal justice reform is to succeed.

With this perspective in mind, I want to build directly on lessons of the earlier chapters that were devoted to identifying and analyzing the past and present contexts of criminality that have shaped the lives of the overwhelming majority of persons who have violated the law, and use these insights as the basis for an additional set of far-reaching proposals for even more fundamental reform. The last chapter discussed some of the ways that the legal system itself can and should be modified and restructured with this new knowledge in mind. Using that knowledge and adding to those reforms, the present chapter explicitly proposes a radical shift in the focus of our nation's crime control policies to free ourselves from the narrowly individualistic and ultimately ineffective framework that undergirds constrained and constricted traditional approaches.

CONTEXT-BASED CRIME PREVENTION

Effective crime control policies must go beyond merely reacting to crime and instead prioritize proactive and preventive interventions that directly address past and present contexts that promote crime. Although the more context-sensitive legal doctrines and policies and corresponding limitations on the use of imprisonment that I outlined in Chapter 9 are important and essential to pursue, their long-term, sustained impact will prove modest and fleeting unless many of these more fundamental structural reforms are implemented as well. Criminal laws and penal practices by definition address individual-level manifestations of past trauma and persistent structural inequality after the fact and, therefore, fail to eradicate root causes. Thus, at the same time these badly needed legal and prison reforms are implemented, a set of parallel and equally ambitious efforts also must be undertaken to address the full range of social, cultural, and economic forces and factors that promote, instigate, and precipitate criminal behavior. Programs of significant social and economic transformation are needed to address the myriad criminogenic risk factors and traumas *before* their predictable consequences have come to pass. This paradigmatic shift in the conceptual framework on which our crime control policies are based will require the full-scale implementation of broader social policies that include fundamental forms of socioeconomic change, a renewed commitment to extending and improving educational and employment opportunities, and a basic shift in the nation's political (not just criminological) priorities. These are long-term, idealistic goals, to be sure, but ones that are necessary to achieve. In fact, a number of them are already underway or well within our grasp.[5]

Optimizing the success of context-sensitive models of crime prevention also means taking into account the range of variations that occur within and between communities in which such programs are implemented.[6] Community interventions designed to address the risk of delinquency and crime should employ an approach that clinicians term "multisystemic," but reframed to comprehensively address as many aspects of a person's social context and social network as possible. This kind of multisystemic approach would explicitly acknowledge the multidetermined nature of social behavior, including criminal behavior. As I have emphasized throughout this book, we now understand that criminal behavior occurs within a social context or an "ecology" that is made up of family, school, work, peers, and neighborhood, all of which are interconnected.[7] The long-term success of these interventions depends on the degree to which they take into account and target those interconnected aspects of someone's operative life space.

For example, there are a number of existing crime control programs that already effectively address some of the adverse effects of criminogenic social histories and present circumstances that can and should be implemented on a more widespread basis. Thus, early childhood intervention programs aimed at reducing or eliminating the impact of risk factors and that seek to maximize the number of protective factors that operate in the lives of children have long-term crime control implications. The best of these programs acknowledge the larger family context in which risk and protective factors are generated by providing services and assistance to parents and other members of the families in which the children live. Effective programs start early, provide sustained and long-term support, and are premised on the principle that the social contexts in which young children mature are the most appropriate targets at which to direct preventative efforts.[8] The success of these programs demonstrate that early childhood intervention can be a powerful form of crime prevention.[9]

Child Protective Services (CPS) functions as the main governmental agency that intervenes in cases of suspected maltreatment in the United States. The laws that were passed in the early 1970s that brought CPS into existence were well-intended attempts to address the increasingly acknowledged problem of child maltreatment. Since then, there has been a substantial investment in the CPS model, which has raised public awareness of the widespread scope and long-term impact of child maltreatment.[10] It has improved state and local recordkeeping and the accuracy of data on the prevalence of abuse and neglect and had beneficial effects on the lives of many children seriously at risk. Yet, recent research suggests that the mere fact of CPS intervention, including those cases in which allegations of maltreatment in a household are substantiated, does not necessarily alleviate the effect of other risk factors in children's lives. Nor does it necessarily improve family functioning in the long run or reduce anxious or aggressive behaviors that at-risk children may manifest as they mature.[11] Researchers have rightly characterized these oversights as "missed opportunities" because the contact that CPS workers have with members of a family in which maltreatment may have occurred could be far more robust and address a much greater range of problems than at present.

For example, Matthew Stagner and Jiffy Lansing proposed a new framework for preventing child abuse and neglect based on a concept that has been recently applied in health care and social welfare.[12] The "investment-prevention" framework differs from the traditional CPS response to maltreatment by focusing on preventing maltreatment from occurring in the first place. Whereas the traditional model identified risk factors for maltreatment and focused on the alleged deficiencies of primary caretakers, the new model relies on principles from developmental and ecological psychology to strengthen existing protective factors by building on and improving family and social networks. The goal is to directly enhance and reinforce the ability of parents to care for their children by identifying the specific strengths of the parents and the protective factors to which the children have access at particular developmental stages. Rather than focusing exclusively on ways to minimize harm to the child, this approach aims to maximize the child's potential by enhancing aspects his or her social and family context, in part by strengthening the capacity of parents and communities to care for their children in ways that promote well-being.

An overarching national strategy of crime prevention also would critically reexamine the nature and effect of the nation's foster care programs. Foster care policies reflect a societal-level choice about when and how to intervene in the lives of at-risk children. Historically, these policies have ignored the myriad problems of the poor families from which most foster children come and avoided grappling with the entrenched nature of the poverty in which many of their parents have become mired.[13] Other alternatives—direct assistance to families in need, provision of child care to unemployed or working poor families, increased access to intensive outpatient drug and alcohol programs, and opportunities to attend parenting classes and receive related services—all represent promising solutions to the problems of at-risk children and their caretakers. Indeed, these broader based programs are premised on a sound contextual insight: at risk children can be helped by providing the assistance that their families need to overcome the life challenges that can create instability and may lead to neglectful and abusive parenting.

In fact, a range of transitional services already exist that can increase an adolescent's successful movement from foster care to independent living in adulthood, reducing the chances of subsequent involvement in the criminal justice system. Thus, foster youth "who report employment at the onset of the transition" from foster care or those "who have future educational aspirations" experience "reduced risk for arrest in adulthood."[14] Some child welfare systems also provide foster youth with "extended foster care support" that continues beyond the first stage of the transition. This support in turn reduces subsequent involvement with the adult criminal justice system. Such extended support includes "financial and other support for educational and vocational programs, financial literacy training and employment services, housing assistance programs, employment support, life skills classes, medical insurance, support for teen parenting, and legal advice."[15] This kind of extended foster care support should become a central component of national programs of both social welfare *and* crime control.

On a different front, the relationship between economic disadvantage and child maltreatment can be fully addressed only by attacking poverty and its broader effects (rather than by punishing adult parents who are themselves the victims of that poverty).[16] In fact, these kinds of poverty-related early intervention programs have been in operation in certain parts of the country for decades. As one evaluation of a successful program concluded,

> [The results] underscore the need for high-quality learning environments for impoverished infants, toddler, and preschoolers. This study demonstrates that if such children are given high-quality educational experiences during the preschool years, their academic performance and school progress may be significantly enhanced through middle adolescence.[17]

Perhaps because of the importance of positive school experiences in enhancing early socialization, the benefits of education-centered programs that are directed at improving academic performance often extend more broadly into other aspects of the children's lives. I have argued that poverty is a gateway risk factor that increases a child's chances of being exposed to a range of other potentially damaging and criminogenic risks. Conversely, it appears that high quality early education programs are gateway protective factors that, in close conjunction with programs designed to reduce poverty itself, can provide children with a pathway out of economic disadvantage, neutralizing the criminogenic effects of poverty, and making positive life outcomes more likely. Even programs such as Head Start, originally intended to address the problem of school failure among low-income children, have been shown to result in significant reductions in juvenile crime.[18]

Other programs that provide low-income children with preschool, as well as continuing social and academic services in the first several grades of elementary school, have resulted in significantly higher rates of school completion, lower numbers of children repeating grades or being placed in special education classes, *and* lower rates of juvenile arrests.[19] For example, as one evaluation of one of the better-known programs concluded: "Evidence gathered over twenty-two years indicates that the High/Scope Perry Preschool Program, reduced high school dropout and demand for welfare assistance, increased participants' adult earnings and property wealth, and *cut crime in half.*"[20] Moreover, it was cost effective. Researchers estimated that the program provided taxpayers with a return of $7.16 for every dollar that was invested in it.

Here, too, many of the most successful programs are comprehensive in scope. They are designed to transform the broad social context in which children develop, providing enriched educational experiences as well as enhanced support services and outreach to parents. Indeed, many of them facilitate parental involvement in the school and in their children's learning process by, among other things, providing the families with badly needed health and medical services. For example, the Chicago Child-Parent Center has offered comprehensive services to economically disadvantaged children who were between the ages of 6 and 9 years. Children who participated in the program achieved higher scores in reading and math skills and were less likely to be retained in grade or receive special education services compared with those who did not.[21] Thus, even when children cannot be protected from early exposure to risk factors, steps can be taken to increase their resiliency and enhance the number of protective factors with which they are surrounded.[22]

As I noted, one of the core "War on Poverty" programs, Head Start, actually had a more significant impact on reducing future delinquent and criminal behavior in the adult lives of the children who attended than on subsequent educational attainment. Although the significant improvements in educational measures between children who attended Head Start preschools and others shrank over time—perhaps as a function of insurmountable public school deficiencies and other barriers they eventually faced—improvement in many important life outcomes remained stable. Some of the most reliable positive outcomes were with respect to the likelihood of engaging in future criminal behavior.[23] For example, the Perry Preschool children, who attended one of the most carefully studied preschools in the nation, were significantly less likely to have been arrested for either serious or nonserious crime. The boys went on to earn higher incomes and the girls were significantly less likely to use drugs.[24]

My point is that a host of successful programs have been in operation around the country—some for many years. They eschew individualistic, personal deficit models associated with the crime master narrative. Instead, each of them implements a contextual and community-based approach to address the long-term impact of exposure to risk factors and traumas and the effects of economic and race-based disadvantage. The knowledge about "what works"—early childhood enrichment programs, direct assistance for at-risk families, after-school programs—that has been gathered in largely localized programs needs to be shared and implemented on a widespread, coordinated, and systematic basis. It should be disseminated widely, both as part of a comprehensive program of preventive crime control as well as a strategy for advancing the cause of social justice more generally.[25]

As I noted in Chapter 4, the pernicious school-to-prison pipeline operates to increase minority student contact with the juvenile and adult criminal justice systems. A variety of approaches can be employed to eliminate it. Lizbet Simmons noted that "[w]hen teachers can send students to the principal's office and principals can send students home or have them arrested, there is a missing academic imperative."[26] That imperative needs to be reemphasized and recentered, especially in classrooms with predominately students of Color, where it has too often been subjugated to the goal of institutional control. Some past effective interventions have been as straightforward as training classroom teachers about their own implicit racial biases and the way that they promote discriminatory disciplinary practices.[27] Other reformers have used broader forms of social engagement to disrupt the pipeline,[28] while still others have initiated litigation to challenge overly punitive, discriminatory school practices directly in court.[29] This latter kind of systemic "impact" litigation is sometimes difficult to mount and the resulting remedies are challenging to enforce, but in the long run it may be the most effective way to address educational inequalities and directly dismantle the school-to-prison pipeline.[30]

Similarly, Chapter 4 also critically examined the role of that juvenile justice institutions often play in accelerating rather than redirecting persons on the pathway to delinquency and adult criminal behavior. Context-based models of crime control should drastically limit and, as much as possible, eliminate the practice placing children inside locked juvenile facilities that still too often resemble "prisons for kids." Out of the recognition that institutionalization has per se criminogenic effects, others have noted that, at the very least, "[i]ncarceration in secure facilities should be reserved only for a small number of chronic or violent offenders, with community-based dispositions used for all other[s]."[31] Of course, there is no reason to believe the even young persons who engage in "chronic or violent" criminal behavior will benefit from stays in conventional juvenile justice institutions as they are presently structured. If and when they are used at all, secure juvenile facilities must be radically redesigned to eliminate their retraumatizing effects, and even then exposure must be limited to the shortest amount of time possible, in those exceptionally rare instances in which it is deemed absolutely necessary. Indeed, there is a compelling social contextual argument to be made that the most troubled children need by far the *most* caring resources (when, in fact, they too often receive the least). They should be provided with this higher level of care in settings that are not only safe but also truly benign and supportive.

As psychologist Richard Redding argued decades ago: "Community-based programs can protect the community by providing close supervision and monitoring. These programs are about one-fourth to one-third less expensive than incarceration, and are much more effective in reducing recidivism."[32] The best of these programs teach children the consequences of their actions but also provide "the coping, life, and job skills needed to function appropriately in the community."[33] Moreover, because the nature of the environment to which young persons return is crucial to their long-term success, a comprehensive model of juvenile justice reform must include some kind of meaningful and continuing "after care" programs and enhanced family services that remain available to them long after release from juvenile justice system interventions.[34]

A contemporary movement in developmental psychology provides a useful perspective on these issues. It is strength- rather than deficit-based approach to addressing the traumatic experiences of marginalized children who have suffered systematic subordination, oppression, and exclusion in society. Although acknowledging the ways that these experiences can jeopardize the children's personal adjustment and academic and long-term success, it appropriately avoids characterizing them as "flawed."[35] Explicitly recognizing the ways in which marginalization is "*context-dependent* and largely determined by the historical, social, and cultural settings of a society"[36] allows researchers and practitioners to concentrate on ways of building on the children's already existing competencies (rather than assuming deficiencies), and advance programs of what they term "positive youth development."[37] This is a variation of what Laura Abrams described as an "ecological model" of juvenile justice that focuses on "key prevention alternatives, such as strengthening families, schools, and neighborhoods" because "engaging multiple systems is needed to address complex problems."[38]

There are other context-sensitive alternatives to the conventional model of crime control based on the crime master narrative. For example, what are termed "situational crime control" and "place-based prevention" approaches to crime prevention emphasize a variety of explicitly social contextual factors, including the ways in which the nature of the surrounding environment and structure of neighborhoods can affect criminal behavior.[39] Most situational crime control models are narrower than the framework I advocate here, largely because they focus more on eliminating opportunities for crimes to be committed and much less on addressing the social histories and contexts that create the needs or inclinations to commit those crimes. They ignore what Scott Briar and Irving Piliavin years ago described as "situationally induced motives to deviate."[40]

Thus, most forms of situational crime control privilege detection and deterrence over social justice-oriented approaches. They recommend modifying the social context in order to "harden it" by installing barriers, visibly increasing surveillance (e.g., cameras) and intensifying the presence of police and other so-called place-managers. Whether or not this approach displaces criminal behavior to other less well-fortified situations,[41] a more comprehensive form of contextual crime control would more explicitly address the underlying conditions that create the felt need to engage in criminal behavior. The one strictly situational form of crime control that I do believe is consistent with the broad contextual approach I have advanced (although it is often omitted from traditional discussions of situational crime control) is the need to modify social settings and interactions in ways that eliminate or greatly minimize the presence of firearms. Precisely because firearms can and do greatly amplify the magnitude and permanence of the consequences of interpersonal conflicts that can occur for any reason—including those that are fleeting, unintentional, or eminently resolvable—they constitute a characteristic or element of a situation that renders it more likely to be violent and increases the severity of whatever violence does transpire. For this reason, access to firearms should be effectively regulated and controlled in the name of situational crime prevention and control.[42]

A number of community-based programs include more psychologically informed attempts to identify neighborhood risk factors that can be addressed through early intervention that is designed to address and eliminate them. The most effective community-based violence prevention programs now recognize the social contextual origins of aggressive behavior and implement a range of approaches to directly reduce or eradicate them.[43] For example, as James Vigil wisely noted about effective ways to reduce gang-related behavior, "[b]ecause the seeds of the solutions to the gang problem are found in its root causes, there is always an opportunity to salvage many of the children who have been marginalized and left to the streets."[44]

The best of these programs reduce participation in neighborhood gangs by eschewing simplistic approaches based on the crime master narrative. The old and increasingly anachronistic models emphasized punitive suppression, mostly through the threat and reality of juvenile and adult incarceration. Instead, the new models are context-based, employing a more holistic perspective that provides young persons with attractive alternative opportunities in which to invest instead of gangs, and offer incentives for them to do so. In fact, there are a number of theory-based recommendations that acknowledge the value of "prevention efforts aimed at reducing the likelihood of gang membership" by finding "viable ways to increase the availability of prosocial opportunities for involvement in family and friend groups, schools, and neighborhood activities."[45] The programs include providing direct assistance to families that have been social and economically marginalized, implementing meaningful school reform to more effectively engage students and address their intellectual and other needs, building on and enhancing the strengths children and adolescents already have, and creating community partnerships that ensure broader access to meaningful employment and further educational opportunities. But these opportunities are only possible in communities that have the capacity to invest in and maintain them.

In a similar way, the most successful programs to address gang activity *inside* juvenile and adult correctional institutions also emphasize contextual rather than counterproductive individual punitive policies and practices. In many correctional systems, the single largest number of prisoners housed in solitary confinement—and virtually always those who spend the longest amounts of time there—are alleged gang members or affiliates. However, as Chantel Di Placido and her colleagues noted, because "[i]solated gang members are unlikely to receive any services or interventions that might reduce their risk to re-offend in the long term," and, perhaps even more problematically, because "such approaches could paradoxically enhance gang cohesiveness," a number prisons have decided to "change the context" by instituting less punitive and more program-oriented strategies of gang abatement.[46] One program reduced violent recidivism over a 2-year period by 20% (more than 3 times the percentage reduction for nongang members) as well as resulting in "significantly less major institutional misconduct such as fights and assaults."[47]

RESTRUCTURING COMMUNITIES TO FACILITATE REENTRY

I suggested in the last chapter that the time had come to drastically limit the use of conventional forms of imprisonment by radically reducing the number of persons incarcerated overall and to create alternative contexts and settings that more effectively address conflict and crime—ones that barely resemble the current prison form. However, there are a number of intermediate steps that need to be taken until these new approaches are properly devised and fully implemented.

We now know that even well-designed and conscientiously run in-prison rehabilitation programs are destined to fail if they ignore the role of the criminogenic social conditions that formerly incarcerated persons confront *after* their release from prison. That is, the social contextual perspective on crime causation underscores the way that powerful situational forces outside of prison can and typically do overwhelm whatever beneficial changes might have been brought about by effective institutional programming. The benefits that come about *inside*—as I say, even in the most humane and effectively run institutions—are of little long-term consequence if corresponding support is not provided in free-world settings on the *outside*.[48]

Rejecting the crime master narrative, which blames every postprison failure to successfully reintegrate on the "bad choices" made by persons who supposedly freely decide to reoffend, and instead substituting an awareness of the powerful influence that destructive social contexts have on criminal behavior makes the provision of postprison support services an absolutely essential component of meaningful criminal justice reform.[49] The challenges the formerly incarcerated face in the reintegration process are multifaceted, daunting, and largely structural in nature.[50] The assistance provided must be commensurate to help meet them.

For example, many formerly incarcerated persons enter prison with limited education and few marketable job skills. Even after long sentences, far too many leave prison without any those needs having been effectively addressed. This virtually ensures that they will confront even greater obstacles in the free-world. Because studies done over a period of many years have documented "a strong relationship between employment and recidivism,"[51] there is a substantial amount of support for the fact that providing employment services *after release* "can make an effective dent" in decreasing the likelihood that persons who have recently left prison will be enticed or feel compelled to commit crimes in the future.[52]

The barriers to gainful postprison employment are numerous and substantial, themselves enough to thwart successful reintegration. For example, Devah Prager and others have demonstrated the powerful stigma associated with having a criminal record and the way that knowing a job applicant has been in prison deters many potential employers from hiring them.[53] Meaningful criminal justice reform must directly and effectively overcome this barrier. It must move past simply providing access to what are admittedly important in-prison education and job training programs to implementing pre- and postrelease employment counseling, *and* job assistance and placement that facilitate establishing positive work histories and postprison employment successes.[54] Although there is thoughtful debate about exactly how best to address the issue of employer bias against the formerly incarcerated—either through some version of "ban the box" legislation that prohibits employers from inquiring at the time of application or some other way to prevent past criminal history from precluding future employment—removing this criminogenic barrier represents an important form of situational crime control.[55] Note that, in addition to obstacles to gainful employment, there are numerous other external contextual barriers to successful reentry. Many criminogenic influences are ones over which formerly incarcerated persons have little control (including scarce housing, a poor job market, lack of available health care, and the sometimes competing pull of criminal activity in the neighborhoods to which they return). This means that recidivism itself should be more correctly regarded as a social and structural, rather than individual, failure and addressed as such.

There is another important reentry issue that requires a social contextual solution. Specifically, even well-structured and properly implemented therapy and drug treatment programs in prison are likely to lower recidivism rates only if they are accompanied by well-designed aftercare programs in the community.[56] Thus, the same strong argument must be made for investing substantial resources in postprison mental health and drug treatment programs that change the contexts and situations that formerly incarcerated persons encounter outside of prison. This means that in-prison treatment represents no more than a first step in what should include longer-term community-based programming and access to meaningful transitional services after release.[57] Context-based mental health and drug and alcohol programs would not only provide persons with the tools and assistance to change behavior but also change the neighborhood contexts in which they live to facilitate their continued recovery, including treating drug use as more a public health than criminal justice issue.[58]

Moreover, as David Harding, Jeffrey Morenoff, and Jessica Wyse noted, we know that the relapse into substance abuse by formerly incarcerated persons is "often sparked by the challenges of reintegration as much as contributing to them." That is, they found that "[h]eavy drinking and returns to drug use often followed from stressful social relationships, and living arrangements, unstable housing, and struggles in the labor market."[59] In short, recognizing the important way that context matters means acknowledging the critical importance of the multiple contexts in which persons are immersed *after* their release from prison. Meaningful reentry programs would address these issues as well.

Finally, it is important to acknowledge that imprisonment itself entails a host of negative experiences and events that produce harmful psychological effects. Prisonization and the various survival strategies that are adopted in harsh and degrading correctional institutions represent habits of thinking and acting that can prove highly dysfunctional after release.[60] They may interfere with the ability of formerly incarcerated persons to navigate the radically different situations they later encounter in the freeworld and impair relationships at work and in their personal lives.

As long as we continue to confine people in institutional settings that remotely resemble the current prison form, where prisonization is routine and institutional trauma widespread, then a comprehensive, context-based strategy of crime control must include access to supportive "decompression," "step-down," or other kinds of transitional programs that directly address the negative after-effects of incarceration. Thus, in addition to providing education and job training, and opening up postprison employment opportunities, a context-based strategy of crime control would include access to trauma-informed counseling services in the communities to which formerly incarcerated persons return.

Moreover, as I suggested in the last chapter, the most effective way of reducing the negative overall effects of prisonization, prison trauma, and the challenges of reentry is to minimize the number of persons who are sent to prison in the first place. This means that the most effective strategies of crime prevention not only will require fundamental shifts in the nature of the prison experience and in the reentry process but also entail permanent, broader based structural reforms that extend well beyond prison itself. Thus, implicit in most of what I have said so far, the panoply of postrelease, community-based programs that are designed to train, educate, and employ formerly incarcerated persons must be combined with strategies to "rehabilitate" the very communities to which they return. Increased employment, educational opportunities, and decent housing and health care options are among the most effective crime control programs ever devised and must be recognized and implemented as such.

However futuristic and utopian these proposals may seem to some, they have much in common with ones made decades ago by Bernard Diamond, the influential forensic psychiatrist whose innovative thinking about broadening the scope of evidence and information used to assess criminal responsibility and culpability I touched on in the last chapter.[61] When the era of mass incarceration began to take shape in the 1970s, it was impossible to clearly foresee the runaway growth in the prison population that would eventually occur. Instead, Diamond envisioned a model of preventive crime control much like the one I am proposing here. As Diamond saw it, sensible crime control policies should be bounded by two overarching, commonsense principles: "What will insure the maximum rehabilitation potential of the individual prisoner, and what will provide the greatest protection to society against crime."[62]

All prisoners, Diamond thought, should be incarcerated under humane conditions for fixed terms that provided the public with a requisite amount of safety and protection. However, once a youthful or adult prisoner had served his time, Diamond thought he or she should be declared a "veteran of the war against crime," who, "like other veterans would be entitled to benefits for the purpose of making restitution for the damage done him by his involuntary institutionalization and to facilitate his restoration back into the community as a functioning citizen."[63]

These benefits would include a range of educational and vocational training opportunities, job placement services, and even, when called for, direct monetary compensation or support. Diamond argued that those formerly incarcerated persons who had continuing physical and mental health needs should receive whatever medical care, psychiatric treatment, and counseling services were necessary for them to readjust in the free world. He emphasized that the benefits provided to the prisoners needed to be "very real," rather than "hypocritical gestures," and emphasized that their long-term benefits would accrue not just to the prisoners but also to the larger society that they would be able to more successfully reenter and be more likely to remain. Under this model, "the recipient would be free from custody and punishment, living in his own community, and participating voluntarily."[64] Diamond was wise enough to recognize the radical implications of his proposal, but also practical enough to understand that the success of the program needed to be tied directly to crime reduction over the long run, and to the provision of equal or greater "restitutive benefits to the victims of crime."[65]

Diamond's proposals underscore the fact that there was a time in the nation's not-too-distant past when thoughtful scholars advocated broad-based, context-oriented approaches to crime prevention and control. Models of preventative crime control, like the one Diamond advocated, were beginning to emerge, focusing on social- and institutional- rather than exclusively individual-level criminal justice system responses.[66] They acknowledged the importance of reducing recidivism by addressing the inherently social contextual causes of criminal behavior and attacking criminogenic forces (e.g., child maltreatment, poverty, racial discord) directly in the community, and they focused on the reintegration rather than the degradation of persons who had committed crimes.

Although visionary, Diamond was not alone in calling for these kinds of alternative approaches. For example, the restorative justice practices that I discussed in the last chapter were pioneered decades ago by John Braithwaite, Stephen Mugford, and others to advance a reintegrative form of community-based justice. At the core of this approach is an understanding of the relationship between crime and the larger community in which it occurs, and the importance of recognizing the inherent humanity of persons who have transgressed and the need to ensure their subsequent reintegration.[67] The social contextual model of criminality I have advanced throughout this book is entirely consistent with these proposals, ones designed to implement new ways of reacting to crime that acknowledge, in Braithwaite and Mugford's words, "(a) how essentially good people have a pluralistic self that accounts for their occasional lapse into profane acts; and (b) that the profane act of a perpetrator occurs in a social context for which *many* actors may bear some shared responsibility."[68] Those "many actors" can be and often are enlisted in combining individual accountability with shared responsibility in ways that lead to interpersonal healing and community-level change.

I confess that, although I very much admire the social contextualist emphasis on reintegration in many restorative justice programs, I am not an advocate of the "shaming" component of at least some of these models. In my experience, the risk factors and traumas experienced by many persons who have violated the law have already created lifelong feelings of shame. The public enhancement of these psychic wounds often seems unnecessary, inhumane, and counterproductive. In fact, psychologist Shadd Maruna and others have shown the advantages of a much more positive "redemptive" approach in which prisoners are encouraged to create and maintain so-called redemption scripts. These scripts simultaneously acknowledge the prisoners' troubled pasts but also allow them to first envision and then to implement plans by which they can turn their lives around. Maruna is persuasive on the various ways in which such scripts facilitate the transition from prison to the freeworld. The process of positive, redemptive transformation is enhanced by social contexts that provide and promote opportunities to "give back" to the community and also ones that encourage community leaders, family members, and friends to participate in and acknowledge a "psychological turning point" in which the formerly incarcerated person's contributions and reconnection with the community are formalized in some way.[69]

In addition, the social contextual approach I have advanced in the preceding chapters would target probation and parole services for special attention, in large part because they are the explicitly community-based extensions of the existing criminal justice system, ones that operate directly inside free-world neighborhoods to which formerly incarcerated persons return.[70] Until restorative justice and other alternatives to incarceration are implemented on a much more widespread basis, probation and parole are likely to continue to play an important role in the administration of criminal justice. Not only are approximately 95% of the nation's over two million prisoners and jail inmates eventually released back into free society, but many of them will be placed under some form of continuing criminal justice supervision.[71] In fact, the number of persons on probation or parole greatly exceeds the number actually incarcerated—in 2015, for example, there were nearly 4 million persons on probation and another nearly 1 million on parole,[72] compared with a little more than 2 million in the nation's jails and prisons.[73]

In fact, in many ways the era of mass incarceration was also very much an "era of mass probation and parole" in which the "net" of correctional control was stretched over increasingly larger groups of people.[74] As mass incarceration gained momentum in the United States, and the size of probation and parole caseloads swelled as well, probation and parole supervision and assistance came increasingly from persons who were beleaguered and overworked (if, in fact, it came at all).[75] Probation departments during these years faced "a massive deterioration in supervision due to loss of staff and budget and a heavy increase of cases."[76] Even when the percentage of formerly incarcerated persons who left prison and were placed on parole began to decline—in part because of nationwide reductions in the use of discretionary parole—caseloads remained high.

Not surprisingly, perhaps, many probation officers and parole agents continued to rely on conventional law enforcement models of surveillance and control that were premised on the crime master narrative: persons under criminal justice system supervision who ostensibly failed to make the "right choices"—no matter how few viable alternatives they had been given—faced punitive consequences (typically, return to prison). As Mona Lynch reported, "the belief that the parolee is free and autonomous in his day-to-day choices appeared to be the first and foremost behavioral assumption that underlies parole's practical approach to managing parolees."[77] There was correspondingly little or no appreciation of the full range of unaddressed needs with which the formerly incarcerated routinely left prison or the nature and amount of postprison assistance that would be required to improve their chances for success.

Yet, exclusively individualistic approaches to probation and parole supervision that fail to address any of the contextual social and economic challenges that probationers and parolees confronted in the freeworld are self-limiting and counterproductive.[78] Close supervision and surveillance in the absence of effective services and meaningful support virtually ensures subsequent incarceration.[79] In fact, although the percentage has decreased somewhat in recent years, fully one quarter of persons sent to prison in 2014 were parolees who were returned to custody for technical violations alone.[80]

One solution to this counterproductive overreach might be to drastically reduce the use of probation and parole outright. However, in too many communities, especially ones that are underserved by nongovernmental organizations—if probation and parole agencies fail to provide probationers and parolees with access to essential services and necessary forms of assistance, then they are unlikely to get any at all. Thus, timely and well-advised calls to "reinvent" and "revitalize" these two arms of the criminal justice system must be heeded. They entail developing a "comprehensive and aspirational model for the future" designed to ensure that their decision-making is more reliable, flexible, and transparent.[81] At the same time, the research I have presented in the preceding chapters suggests that much more can be done.

For one, a significant change in the role of probation officers and parole agents is in order. Michelle Phelps recognized and lamented the fact that probationers "typically receive few of the kinds of supportive services that could help them overcome histories of trauma, addiction, unstable housing and homelessness, and underemployment." But she also understood that there was no obvious reason why these services could or should not be offered.[82] A context-oriented approach to preventive crime control would recognize that, along with persons released outright from prison, probationers and parolees are highly at-risk because of the criminogenic circumstances under which they are often forced to live, the economic challenges they face, and the shortage of effective community services, programs, and resources to which they have access. Under the new context-sensitive model, probation officers and parole agents should operate instead as "reentry specialists," functioning in what Jeremy Travis termed a "boundary spanner" role.[83] That is, they would become deeply involved in addressing their individual clients' needs as well as those of the larger community contexts in which their clients live. They could help to modify critical aspects of what Daniel Mears and his colleagues have called the "social ecology of recidivism"[84] by becoming more proactively involved in creating and improving opportunities to obtain employment, housing, education and vocational training, health care, and counseling and family-related services.[85]

There has already been much research and writing on the so-called "dual relationship" that probation officers and parole agents have with their clients and the benefits of shifting away from a traditional law enforcement to a more compassionate social worker role. Some authors have termed this newer role "caring" or "human service"–oriented supervision; others have analogized it to a "coaching" relationship.[86] The new role that I envision would move much more definitively in the direction social worker/problem solver and away from punitive overseer. It would require a fundamental shift in the way persons are educated and trained for these jobs, as well as changing their work environment to support and reward a more caring and service-oriented ethos.

The criminal justice system's role in creating and exacerbating criminogenic social contexts also must be addressed and eliminated. For example, the Bureau of Justice Statistics estimated that approximately half of all state and federal prisoners are living with their minor children at the time of their admission to prison.[87] The imprisonment of an adult family member increases the likelihood that children will become enmeshed in the juvenile justice system and, given its independent criminogenic effects, many will have a difficult time disentangling from it.[88] In light of what is now known about the developmental origins of much criminal behavior, minimizing the secondary harmful effects that incarceration can have on prisoners' families—especially their children—should become an explicit goal of our newly minted preventive crime control policies (i.e., limiting the use of incarceration in part to minimize its criminogenic consequences for future generations).

In what hopefully will become the increasingly rare cases in which some form of incarceration is deemed unavoidable, its secondary harmful effects on families can be directly acknowledged and proactively addressed. For example, a portion of state and federal correctional budgets could be allocated to provide direct social and human services to the families of persons who are incarcerated, in order to reduce its potentially harmful emotional, social, and economic effects on them and the larger community.[89] Thus, as soon as someone is sentenced to prison, an in-depth "needs assessment" might be conducted to evaluate its likely long-term impact on the family members who remain behind, to ensure that the needed services and resources are made available to them to mitigate the anticipated problems and lessen potential harms. This would minimize the likelihood that a cycle of crime and incarceration would be set in motion in families where children suffer as a result of parental imprisonment and, at the same time, an incarcerated parent's likelihood of postprison success would be improved. We know that the level of "family problems" that parolees confront once they are released is a potent predictor of parole outcomes (i.e., the greater the number of family problems, the higher their "parole maladjustment score" and the more likely parole violations are to occur). Alleviating these problems is an important form of preventive crime control.[90]

ERADICATING THE COLLATERAL CONSEQUENCES OF IMPRISONMENT

Social contextualism teaches us that structural and community-level reforms are essential in order to create a model of crime control that is fair, effective, and humane. These reforms will require that we acknowledge, address, and eliminate a special set of existing barriers to reentry—the numerous, burdensome, legally created and imposed "collateral consequences" of a criminal conviction.[91] Successful reentry is significantly undermined by the draconian prohibitions and restrictions that follow formerly incarcerated persons back into the community. They operate as social contextual barriers that can have significant criminogenic consequences, and there are a staggering number of them. In fact, the National Institute of Justice estimated that there are now some 44,000 collateral consequences, including various civil law sanctions, restrictions, and disqualifications, that can be applied to persons because of their criminal history.[92]

Collateral consequences can prevent or impede a person from participating in the political process (e.g., voting, serving on a jury, holding office), living in certain kinds of housing, furthering their education (because they may be prohibited from financial aid and college admission), and looking for and obtaining employment (because they can be prevented from obtaining a driver's license or other kinds of licenses or qualifying for certain kinds of jobs). As I noted in Chapter 5, these added burdens have been termed a "new civil death," because they so effectively marginalize formerly incarcerated persons, excluding them from accessing public benefits, spaces, and opportunities.[93]

The collateral consequences are not only counterproductive, but they also render postprison success nearly impossible because of the obstacles they interpose. A number of them also have far-reaching, counterintuitive, and perhaps unintended effects. For example, as Lynne Haney showed, child support laws are written and enforced in such a way that many incarcerated fathers have become hopelessly entangled "in feedback loops of disadvantage that complicated [their] social reintegration and put pressure on their familial networks, often to the breaking point."[94] Ironically, a significant portion of the mounting debt entails added obligations to the state, in the form of interest, "processing" and other fees charged by courts to enforce the support orders; even when the debts are repaid, children and custodial parents typically receive much-reduced amounts. Eventually, as child support obligations "spiraled into excessive debt," Haney found that formerly incarcerated fathers also faced a series of accumulated fines, wage withholdings, contempt citations, and arrest warrants that in some cases eventually led to parole revocations and reincarceration, as well as "all the ways guilt, anger, and regret made it hard for [them] to remain caring parents."[95]

Collectively, the extraordinary number of collateral consequences that burden formerly incarcerated persons both reflect and, in turn, are facilitated by the crime master narrative. Whatever else their alleged justifications, they are based on an unshakable assumption about the inherent badness of lawbreakers. The crime master narrative regards this badness as durable enough to justify further punishment (beyond imprisonment) and to warrant continuing restrictions and prolonged monitoring. The imposition of these onerous postprison prohibitions and obligations also proceeds oblivious to their significant and potentially disabling contextual implications—that is, the degree to which they erect barriers that make successful reentry and reintegration difficult if not impossible. Many of these collateral consequences, such as felon disenfranchisement, serve no ostensible purpose other than prolonging the punishment and stigma that persons who have broken the law endure. The social contextual perspective on criminal justice reform I have advanced in this book would eliminate many of them outright. Other collateral consequences, such as the enforcement of child support laws, have a legitimate underlying purpose whose implementation has gone horribly wrong; it requires a radical but careful overhaul that, as Lynne Haney noted, would benefit from "some advice from incarcerated fathers themselves," who are intimately involved with the complicated, daunting contingencies they face.[96] In any event, as Michael Pinard recommended, "the criminal justice system of the future" must eliminate or significantly modify these collateral social contextual barriers to reintegration so that formerly incarcerated persons can "mov[e] past their criminal records to lead productive post-punishment lives."[97]

SOCIAL RECONSTRUCTION AS PRIMARY PREVENTION

The criminal justice system operates to mask and obscure structural dysfunction in society at large. It does so by translating societal-level problems and the real costs of ignoring them into messages about personal failure and deficit. As I have argued throughout this book, the crime master narrative is at the core of that process, functioning as an integral part of the political alchemy by which social and economic injustices are reduced to individual-level pathologies. The imminent demise of the crime master narrative will help to decisively shift the focus of the nation's crime control agenda so that these larger issues can finally be acknowledged and addressed. Comprehensive, meaningful criminal justice reform requires a wholehearted commitment to primary prevention that, in turn, necessitates the creation of a fairer and more just society, including a host of broad-based socioeconomic and other reforms. The utopian scale of these proposed reforms is matched by the urgency of the need to achieve them.

Poverty Reduction as Crime Control

Fifty years ago, the Kerner Commission observed that there were "two Americas" divided along racial and economic lines. The Commission warned that these divisions would have long-term implications for future civil unrest.[98] President Johnson's War on Poverty was commenced in part because he understood that "[i]f poverty had its origin in circumstances too powerful for the individual to alter," then crime would be one way the poor would be forced to cope with their surrounding environment.[99] Five decades after the War on Poverty was prematurely ended, stark racial and economic divisions remain. In some ways, they have become much greater.[100] Racial and ethnic minorities are still marginalized and are still more likely than Whites to be consigned to precisely those sectors of American society where criminogenic influences and risk factors abound. These problematic structural realities continue to have profound implications for the fairness and effectiveness of our nation's criminal justice system.

During the past four decades, in which policies of mass incarceration and disproportionate minority confinement have plagued the criminal justice system, crime in the United States has remained primarily economically motivated. This fact becomes more apparent if the nature of criminal offense of "robbery" is reframed to more accurately reflect its underlying psychological motivation. Robbery represents one of the largest categories of what is currently classified as "violent crime,"[101] implying that it results from the manifestation of the allegedly inherent violent tendencies of those who engage in it. Yet this categorization obscures the underlying economic nature of the crime. In two thirds of all robberies, the victims suffer no physical harm.[102] This observation is not intended to minimize the fact that the emotional impact of robbery—any robbery—on its victims is likely to be substantial. Most robbery victims experience the crime as a traumatic encounter, whether or not they are actually physically injured. It is nonetheless important to understand what *motivates* the behavior. In fact, the overwhelming majority of persons who engage in robbery do so for the same reasons most property crimes are committed—to address material needs. Classifying robbery with other property crimes would underscore the powerful criminogenic role played by structural disadvantage in our society.

As Table 10.1 illustrates, since the start of the so-called war on drugs, drug-related offenses and property crime (including robbery) have accounted for between nearly one half to fully three quarters of all state prison commitments and over 90% of federal prison commitments. These statistics indirectly reflect something that we know from other sources of data—namely, the degree to which most people who break the law are "disadvantaged minorities,

TABLE 10.1. Percentage of Prison Commitments Attributable to Property Offenses, Robbery, Drug, and Public Order Offenses

Year	State prison	Federal prison
1991	67.8[a]	91.7[a]
1997	66.7[a]	94.2[a]
2013	46[b]	92.4[c]
2015	44.8[d]	91.8[e]

Note. [a]Data from McGuire and Pastore (2000). [b]Data from Carson (2015). Estimate based on prisoners serving sentences in excess of 1 year (statistic as of December 31, 2013). [c]Data from Carson (2014). Estimate based on prisoners serving sentences in excess of 1 year; statistic as of September 30, 2013. [d]Data from Carson (2018). Estimate based on most serious offense for prisoners serving sentences in excess of 1 year; statistic as of December 31, 2015. [e]Data from Carson and Anderson (2016). Estimate based on most serious offense for prisoners serving sentences in excess of 1 year; statistic as of September 30, 2015.

unemployed, uneducated, and poor, who have entered a 'revolving door' relationship with the police, courts, and correctional institutions." Because they are often "[r]eturning to crime-ridden environments, plagued by the stigma of incarceration, and often suffering from a general lack of social and family support, the cycle continues."[103]

Indeed, poverty is so inextricably bound to mass incarceration—at multiple levels and over time—it is inconceivable that the latter could ever be effectively addressed without making significant progress on the former.[104] Poverty is itself a risk factor for criminal behavior, contributing indirectly but substantially to mass incarceration. In addition, poverty and mass incarceration *jointly* contribute to the "reproduction of childhood disadvantage," which can increase the likelihood that children will engage in future criminal behavior.[105] These pernicious cycles can only be effectively broken by directly addressing poverty and economic inequality and the various related structural and contextual factors that jointly contribute to them and, in turn, to criminal behavior. Mercer Sullivan wisely noted some years ago that because of these inextricable interconnections, "[p]olicies to improve social control cannot be separated from policies to improve economic conditions."[106] The observation clearly still applies.

As I have argued throughout this book, a broad-based social contextual perspective on crime focuses explicitly on the role of traumatic social histories (many of which are rooted in disadvantage and marginality), the problematic nature of the institutional interventions that figure prominently in the lives of adolescents and adults who are "justice-involved," and the criminogenic immediate social circumstances in which crime often occurs. Social contextual solutions to these criminogenic forces require targeting them directly—including child maltreatment, institutional abuse, racial discrimination, and neighborhood disadvantage, as well as the crucial nexus between poverty and the increased likelihood that poor persons will be subjected to these other risks.

As detailed in Chapter 6, the effects of poverty are broad and deep, and affect a life course in multiple ways. A National Academy of Sciences committee recently put it this way: "A fundamental lesson from the social and the behavioral sciences is that the context of people's lives can affect their behavior in profound ways. Poverty itself is a powerful context because of its economic, physical, social, and psychological dimensions."[107] In some cases, those multiple dimensions have criminogenic long-term consequences. In fact, we know that persons who grow up poor are far more likely to end up in prison than those who do not, and that those who do go to prison tend to stay poor over the course of their lifetimes. Not only do persons who go to prison struggle to find gainful employment after imprisonment, but the great majority of them struggled long before they were incarcerated.

For example, Adam Looney and Nicholas Turner found that a little more than half of formerly incarcerated persons reported any income in the year following their release from prison, but also that fewer than half of all prisoners had any reported income in the three years that *preceded* their incarceration as well.[108] They were poor before they entered prison and stayed poor once they were released. Looney and Turner interpreted this fact "less as evidence that incarceration has little effect on employment but rather as an indication that the challenges ex-prisoners face in the labor market start well before the period of incarceration."[109] As I have repeatedly noted, poverty is the gateway risk factor that can trump all others and it must be effectively addressed as part of an overall strategy of context-based crime control.

Shifting budgetary priorities away from punitive criminal justice practices to social contextual programs of poverty reduction and other forms of crime prevention is more a political than economic challenge. This can be perhaps most clearly illustrated by the juxtaposition of so-called million dollar blocks and efforts made in various jurisdictions to implement what has been termed "justice reinvestment."[110] "Million dollar blocks" is the term that has been given to geographical concentrations of imprisonment, where the state spends a million or more dollars per year incarcerating the residents of single blocks throughout certain urban areas.[111] The implicit, powerful message of the visual depictions of locally "imprisoned communities"[112] is that such substantial sums could be more productively utilized or invested, for example, in programs of crime prevention that were fairer (i.e., had less disproportionate impact, typically on communities of Color), more effective (i.e., were preventive rather than reactive), and humane (i.e., did not incur the deep, broad, and long-lasting harms associated with imprisonment).

Attempts to redirect or "reinvest" the massive resources currently devoted to imprisonment have taken different forms, with varying degrees of overall commitment and success.[113] Efforts to promote justice reinvestment have occurred internationally and been labelled a criminal justice reform "movement."[114] From my perspective, however, neither the unbridled enthusiasm for nor the harsh criticism directed at justice reinvestment is entirely justified. Justice reinvestment is neither a *reason* to do criminal justice reform nor a *framework* that should guide its ultimate shape and direction. Instead, it is a useful mechanism to appropriate funds that would otherwise have gone into punitive policies (as illustrated with million dollar blocks) and a strategy for reallocating them to alternative programs and approaches that should be pursued for other reasons. I agree with commentators who argue that the simple notion that the criminal justice system can "do more (of the same) for less" does not advance a blueprint for a meaningful or lasting change.[115] There are clearly better and worse strategies for truly effective and transformational forms of justice reinvestment. Yet, the ease with which criminal justice and governmental constituencies have endorsed the reallocation of funds away from excessively punitive approaches that were once enthusiastically endorsed is telling. It suggests a long-overdue openness to change that can and should be harnessed.

Whether under the banner of justice reinvestment or some other label, at some point in the process of creating more effective strategies of crime control, reactive criminal justice policymaking must give way to proactive polices of social reconstruction that focus on economic development and making stable employment available to residents of communities where crime is concentrated. Here, too, there are theory-driven and data-based models on which to rely. For example, a National Academy of Sciences report recently developed several carefully constructed policy proposals to serve as a realistic "road map" for reducing childhood poverty in the United States by 50% over a period of 10 years.[116] The proposals included increasing tax credits for poorer workers and providing direct income supports as well as suggested modifications in a range of policies and programs designed to achieve substantial reductions in poverty rates. The report acknowledged that, although initially costly, there would be long-term economic benefits that would offset the immediate investment.[117] However, given what we now know about the relationship between childhood poverty and criminal behavior, the economic benefits from future crime prevented should serve as an especially important, additional justification for undertaking the task.[118] Indeed, notwithstanding the political challenges to initiating programs of large-scale poverty reduction, connecting this goal to current criminal justice reform efforts may help frame it as a more palatable and necessary undertaking.[119]

Whatever models of large-scale poverty reduction are ultimately implemented, they are essential to the goal of fundamental criminal justice reform. In this regard, finally decentering the crime master narrative, relinquishing the myth of completely free and autonomous choice-making, and ending the needless pathologizing of persons who engage in criminal behavior collectively underscore the need to develop and implement this and other more psychologically sophisticated programs of proactive crime prevention. As part of this process, communities that have suffered from what I described in Chapter 5 as widespread "neighborhood disadvantage" must be made more livable, vibrant, and cohesive, and their residents afforded meaningful opportunities to create sustainable futures for themselves. The most effective crime prevention comes in the form of opportunity enhancement—something brought about by introducing fundamental community-based change.

Creating an Effective Public Mental Health System

The United States has lacked a fully functioning public mental health system since at least the time of the deinstitutionalization or "decarceration" movement that commenced in the 1970s, when public mental hospitals were closed and the vague promise that an effective community mental health system would be created in their place was made but never kept.[120] This historical fact has resulted in a tragic anomaly: despite the fact that correctional institutions are uniquely ill-suited to address their needs, there are presently about 10 times more identified mentally ill persons in prisons and jails in the United States than in our nation's mental hospitals.[121] As currently structured and operated, the nation's jails and prisons are fraught with danger, dehumanization, and deprivation, and many are pervaded by high levels of fear, despair, and hostility. They are thus the very antithesis of the kind of safe, treatment-oriented milieus that are capable of engendering the openness, caring, and mutual concern that mentally ill persons require to stabilize and recover.[122]

The seriousness of the problems from which many mentally ill prisoners suffer cannot be overstated. They often have extensive trauma histories that include chronic poverty and deprivation, severe forms of emotional, physical, and sexual abuse, and abject neglect. Many have been hospitalized for mental health problems dating back to their early childhoods and have taken numerous psychotropic drugs over the course of their lifetimes. They frequently suffer from so-called co-occurring substance abuse disorders that complicate their response to what prison systems commonly use as their default (indeed, often their only) form of mental health "treatment"—more psychotropic medication.[123] Some mentally ill prisoners suffer from the aftereffects of having received substandard, abusive care by shoddy mental health practitioners long before they entered prison or during prior incarcerations; they are understandably wary and suspicious of even well-intentioned staff members.[124]

It is worth noting that the mentally ill could only be shunted in such large numbers into jails and prisons in a society blindly devoted to the crime master narrative, where even persons who are in the throes of severe psychological disorders are presumed to make free and autonomous choices and are punished as if they had. This is perhaps the most extreme illustration of our criminal justice system's unwavering allegiance to the free choice legal fiction and its willingness to sacrifice even a semblance of individualized justice in its name.

Moreover, once mentally ill persons enter prison, the same "free choice" fiction is applied: Despite the very high probability that their mental illness is exacerbated by the harsh conditions of jail and prison confinement to which they are exposed, the disciplinary infractions of mentally ill prisoners are sanctioned in essentially the same punitive ways as in every other case. In many jurisdictions, this results in a disproportionate number of mentally ill prisoners being relegated to draconian solitary confinement units where, not surprisingly, many of them deteriorate even further, often spiraling down into a cycles of misbehavior or self-harm that virtually ensure their long-term isolation. As I say, this could only be countenanced on the basis of a profoundly mistaken assumption that even the mentally ill are free to behave differently, no matter how disabling the effects of their past trauma or how powerful the destructive pressures generated by their present circumstances.

In fact, our nation's prison and mental health systems remain inextricably and problematically intertwined. As one commentator noted, "no discussion of community mental health in the United States is complete without consideration of the prevalence of mental illness within prisons and the policies that contribute to it."[125] At some point, however, the two systems must be clearly and definitively separated. Thus the wide-scale social reconstruction that must be undertaken in order to bring about real criminal justice reform and implement a new model of crime control will require the creation of a comprehensive community-based mental health care system that includes effective and accessible drug and alcohol treatment programs.[126]

Absent the investment of substantial resources to create and maintain a well-functioning mental health care system, persons who need to receive mental health treatment in dedicated, properly designed and conscientiously operated facilities will continue to be incarcerated in places that exacerbate their psychiatric conditions—sometimes irreparably—and subject them to extreme retraumatization of the sort that I discussed in Chapter 4. These inexcusable practices ensure that large numbers persons will leave prison virtually destined to return. Our current misguided policies have not only created a genuine humanitarian crisis but also represent a major impediment to effective crime control. Put in stark but candid terms: Unless and until the plight of mentally ill prisoners is adequately addressed, no truly meaningful criminal justice reform in the United States will be possible.

Pursuing Racial Justice in Law and Society

The magnitude of the racial injustices perpetrated by the American criminal justice system underscores the urgent need to provide a truly commensurate response. The brutal mistreatment of racial minorities in our nation's early history is in many ways its "original sin," one that, as many commentators have noted, has never been honestly confronted.[127] Nor has the criminal justice system's role in continuing to mask and facilitate it. Here as elsewhere, the crime master narrative has functioned to obscure the operation of racial oppression and deprivation by individualizing their consequences and blaming the victims for the predictable consequences of their victimization.

Sentencing models that systematically ignore the backgrounds, situations, and circumstances of persons who have engaged in criminal behavior inevitably lead to higher rates of incarceration among those persons and groups who are differentially exposed to social and economic ills that are related to crime. The failure to improve the life chances of persons who have experienced these criminogenic conditions and to instead intensify the rates of their criminal prosecution and incarceration—as occurred during the last several decades of mass incarceration in the United States—ultimately produces outcomes that are not only excessively punitive but unjust. It has led to an entrenched criminal justice system that continues to ignore what Dorothy Roberts described simply as "the injustice to individual human beings who are punished more harshly than they deserve."[128] In ways that I discussed in Chapter 7, and that remain painfully obvious to anyone close to the realities of prison life, much of that injustice is race-based.

Much of the racial injustice that continues to plague American society is tightly interconnected with economic inequality, and the impacts of both are clearly manifested in the criminal justice system. Social reconstruction in the name of crime control must include a vigorous plan to right the wrongs of the nation's racist past and remedy race-based inequities. Meaningful and comprehensive criminal justice reform cannot proceed without an aggressive strategy designed to remedy these inequities. Because the inequities themselves are part of the deep structure of the American economy, effective remedies will require massive investments in the form of the economic revitalization of the inner cities, enhanced educational and job training, and employment opportunities, and the rewriting of the New Jim Crow–era laws, policies, and practices that operate to preserve existing forms of racial apartheid. What Richard Rothstein correctly observed with respect to race-based housing segregation—that "[b]y failing to recognize that we now live with the severe, enduring effects of *de jure* segregation, we avoid confronting our constitutional obligation to reverse it"[129]—can be applied more broadly to many other areas of law and policy as well.

Unfortunately, many of the legal mechanisms available to pursue racial justice have been undermined by the existence of a number of doctrinal roadblocks, ones that are directly related to the kind of psychological individualism that animates the crime master narrative. Here, too, the law's unduly narrow, context-free model of behavior premises legal accountability entirely upon a showing of individual ill-will. This constrictive framework undermines efforts to effectively address injustices that are suffered as a result of the institutional and structural patterns and practices that inflict racial harm.[130] Indeed, legal doctrines that limit the definition of actionable harm done by police, legal decisionmakers, and prison staff exclusively to intentional wrongdoing on the part of individual actors, officers, or administrators parallel those that define and limit redress for racial discrimination in education, housing, and employment to only those cases in which it can be proven to be purposeful, intentional, and willful.[131]

The legal sleight of hand by which the powerful influence of historical, structural, contextual, and situational forces on human behavior is reduced to an inquiry into individual-level, intentional acts of wrongdoing prevents us from addressing broader forms of hurtful and harmful forms of racial injustice in meaningful and effective ways. As a result, "[t]he criminal justice/

prison complex disproportionately targets, captures and incarcerates persons of color" while police shootings of unarmed black victims continue to be "grimly commonplace,"[132] with few viable legal remedies available for redress. Here, too, the demise of the individualistic model of behavior on which the crime master narrative is based should eventually help in shifting attention onto the broader structural and institutional causes of discrimination and race-based disadvantage, including within the criminal justice system itself.

I concede that the ultimate resolution of these complex issues will be challenging. Yet, given the magnitude and longevity of the injustice, and the criminal justice system's complicity in it, all possible remedies must be acknowledged as worthy of serious and in-depth discussion, debate, and consideration. This is true no matter how unprecedented the proposals, or the number and nature of the legal barriers that have been erected against them,[133] and despite what many commentators have preemptively complained are their insurmountable pitfalls.[134] These potential remedies necessarily involve legal as well as social reforms and they are all important to consider and implement as appropriate. They include the radical reform of police training, practices, and accountability to significantly limit racial bias and mistreatment[135]; enacting and implementing meaningful "racial justice acts" to address racial discrimination in criminal justice decision-making[136]; explicitly acknowledging and legitimizing the potentially adverse effects of "biographical racism" on the lives of defendants of Color that may bear on their criminal defense[137]; implementing specialized sentencing rules, considerations, or limits to apply in cases involving defendants of Color[138]; the creation of so-called truth and reconciliation commissions[139]; and the provision of substantial reparations for the generations of racial injustice inflicted.[140] If we do nothing, or respond with more merely pallid, largely symbolic gestures,[141] the entire enterprise of criminal justice reform and the implementation of policies of effective, humane crime control will continue to be irreparably compromised.[142]

CONCLUSION

The research on the social historical and contextual causes of criminality that I have presented throughout this book represents a theoretically grounded and empirically well-documented argument for modifying and supplanting traditional crime control policies. We now know that the social contextual causes of crime are widespread, chronic, and entrenched. They take many and varied forms as risk factors and traumas, institutional malfeasance and mistreatment, and poverty- and race-based structural disadvantages that affect familial, interpersonal, and community relations. Understanding criminal behavior in broad contextual terms means taking into account the full range of social historical factors that shape and influence persons throughout their life course as well as the immediate situational circumstances and structurally created environments in which criminal behavior typically transpires.

Put simply, effective crime control must target criminogenic social contexts, structural inequality, and broad-based injustice instead of persisting with a myopic focus on individual lawbreakers to the exclusion of all else. Effectively addressing these criminogenic factors and forces will require the implementation of a panoply of proactive strategies of and investments in primary prevention that are multifaceted, in-depth, and sustained over the long-term. Sustained policies must be "durable," as Patrick Sharkey defined them, ones that recognize that multigenerational problems like the ones I have described throughout this book "cannot be addressed with point-in-time interventions or influxes of funding that fade away after a few years."[143] The social contextual model of crime does not require us to elevate one set of causes above others, and recognizes that many of these factors operate in tandem, with different force and effect over any given life course. But this new level of understanding underscores the urgent need to move past the anachronistic crime master narrative and to embrace a fundamentally different view of who commits crime and why.

Dorothy Roberts was surely correct in observing that facts "can only inform, not determine, normative judgments" and that, in the final analysis, sweeping criminal justice reforms like the ones I have proposed here "are a matter of political will, not empirical data."[144] And yet, amassing facts and drawing out their unavoidably broad and deep implications are essential first steps in this process. The preceding pages were intended to provide some of the intellectual underpinnings of a fundamental transformation of the criminal justice system's policies, practices, and settings. Data alone may not be enough, but no reform effort that ultimately leaves the crime master narrative firmly in place is likely to succeed for very long or accomplish very much.

NOTES

1. Christie, N. (1982). *Limits to pain*. Oxford, England: Robertson, p. 25.
2. Bazelon, D. (1976). The morality of the criminal law. *Southern California Law Review, 49,* 385–405, p. 405.
3. National Research Council. (2014). *The growth of incarceration in the United States: Exploring causes and consequences.* Washington, DC: National Academies Press. Most statistical analyses indicated that no more than about 25% of the drop in the crime rate was produced by the more than 200% increase in rates of imprisonment over the same time period. On this and related issues, the National Research Council reached three key conclusions: (a) "[m]ost studies estimate the crime reducing effect of incarceration to be small and some report that the size of the effect diminishes with the scale of imprisonment" (p. 155); (b) "the evidence base demonstrates that lengthy prison sentences are ineffective as a crime control measure" (p. 155); and (c) "although the body of credible evidence on the effect of the experience of imprisonment on recidivism is small, that evidence consistently points either to no effect or to an increase rather than a decrease in recidivism" (p. 156).
4. Hulsman, L. (1991). The abolitionist case: Alternative crime policies. *Israel Law Review, 25,* 681–709, p. 708. http://dx.doi.org/10.1017/S0021223700010694

5. As comprehensive and seemingly unprecedented as the basic reformulation of the crime master narrative that I have proposed may seem, it is important to recognize that it is already underway in some sectors of the criminal justice system. For example, there is increasing recognition among juvenile justice professionals that the narrow individualistic model of crime causation must be greatly expanded if prevention efforts are to succeed. Indeed, "[t]here's a growing awareness that you don't just change the kid or the parent or the schools, but you also need to look at neighborhood and community contexts as well." Preston Britner, quoted in DeAngelis, T. (2011, December). Better options for troubled teens. *APA Monitor, 42*, 69–73, p. 70. In addition, although not specifically focused on criminal justice reform, social justice-oriented psychologists have proposed a number of "preventive interventions" that are consistent with some of those advanced in this chapter. See, e.g., Kenny, M., Horne, M., Orpinas, P., & Reese, L. (Eds.). (2009). *Realizing social justice: The challenge of preventive interventions.* Washington, DC: American Psychological Association. http://dx.doi.org/10.1037/11870-000
6. See, e.g., Woodhead, M. (1988). When psychology informs public policy: The case of early childhood intervention. *American Psychologist, 43,* 443–454. Woodhead cautioned against simplistic applications of successful models of intervention and reminded scholars and policymakers of the important role that the broader contexts of family, community, and school play in bringing about positive outcomes. See also the exchange between Moncrieff Cochran and Burton Mindick concerning the difficulties encountered in moving social programs from the conceptualization to implementation stage. Cochran, M. (1988). Parental empowerment in family matters: Lessons learned from a research program. In D. R. Powell (Ed.), *Parent education as early childhood intervention: Emerging directions in theory, research and practice: Vol. 3. Annual advances in applied developmental psychology* (pp. 23–50). Westport, CT: Ablex; and Mindick, B. (1988). Lessons still to be learned in parent empowerment programs: A response to Cochran. In D. R. Powell (Ed.), *Parent education as early childhood intervention: Emerging directions in theory, research and practice: Vol. 3. Annual advances in applied developmental psychology* (pp. 51–65). Westport, CT: Ablex.
7. See, e.g., Borduin, C. (1999). Multisystemic treatment of criminality and violence in adolescents. *Journal of the American Academy of Child & Adolescent Psychiatry, 38,* 242–249. http://dx.doi.org/10.1097/00004583-199903000-00009; Borduin, C. M., Mann, B. J., Cone, L. T., Henggeler, S. W., Fucci, B. R., Blaske, D. M., & Williams, R. A. (1995). Multisystemic treatment of serious juvenile offenders: Long-term prevention of criminality and violence. *Journal of Consulting and Clinical Psychology, 63,* 569–578. http://dx.doi.org/10.1037/0022-006X.63.4.569; Henggeler, S. W., Cunningham, P. B., Pickrel, S. G., Schoenwald, S. K., & Brondino, M. J. (1996). Multisystemic therapy: An effective violence prevention approach for serious juvenile offenders. *Journal of Adolescence, 19,* 47–61. http://dx.doi.org/10.1006/jado.1996.0005
8. See, e.g., Yoshikawa, H. (1994). Prevention as cumulative protection: Effects of early family support and education on chronic delinquency and its risks. *Psychological Bulletin, 115,* 28–54. http://dx.doi.org/10.1037/0033-2909.115.1.28. Yoshikawa concluded that successful programs directed at children under the age of 5, who live in high-risk areas, last for at least 2 years and provide supportive help and education to parents and family. See also Yoshikawa, H. (1995). Long-term effects of early childhood programs on social outcomes and delinquency. *The Future of Children, 5,* 51–75. http://dx.doi.org/10.2307/1602367; and Zigler, E., Taussig, C., & Black, K. (1992). Early childhood intervention: A promising preventative for juvenile delinquency. *American Psychologist, 47,* 997–1006. http://dx.doi.org/10.1037/0003-066X.47.8.997

9. See, e.g., Zigler, Taussig, & Black (1992), Early childhood intervention: A promising preventative for juvenile delinquency. Indeed, as far back as the 1970s, practitioners warned of the "consequences of incompetent intervention" in abusive families, expressed concern that the punishment that was being imposed on families "in the guise of help" was doing more harm than good, and urged professionals to understand that many abusing parents were themselves "sad, deprived, needy human beings" who deserved to be provided with "compassionately proffer[ed] supports and services to aid them in their struggle." Newberger, E., & Bourne, R. (1978). The medicalization and legalization of child abuse. *American Journal of Orthopsychiatry, 48,* 593–607, p. 594. http://dx.doi.org/10.1111/j.1939-0025.1978.tb02564.x
10. Even the U.S. Department of Justice understands that the relationship between strengthening child protective services can help reduce rates of delinquency. The Justice Department promulgated this message in an Office of Juvenile Justice and Delinquency Prevention Bulletin widely disseminated to law enforcement, school, and social welfare agencies. See Wiebush, R., Freitag, R., & Baird, C. (2001, July). *Preventing delinquency through improved child protection services.* Juvenile Justice Bulletin. Washington, DC: Office of Juvenile Justice and Delinquency Prevention.
11. Campbell, K. A., Cook, L. J., LaFleur, B. J., & Keenan, H. T. (2010). Household, family, and child risk factors after an investigation for suspected child maltreatment: A missed opportunity for prevention. *Archives of Pediatrics & Adolescent Medicine, 164,* 943–949. http://dx.doi.org/10.1001/archpediatrics.2010.166
12. Stagner, M. W., & Lansing, J. (2009). Progress toward a prevention perspective. *The Future of Children, 19,* 19–38. http://dx.doi.org/10.1353/foc.0.0036
13. Pelton, L. (1987). Not for poverty alone: Foster care population trends in the twentieth century: Special issue on the history of social welfare. *Journal of Sociology and Social Welfare, 14,* 37–62.
14. Cusick, G., Havlicek, J., Courtney, M. (2012). Risk for arrest: The role of social bonds in protecting foster youth making the transition to adulthood. *American Journal of Orthopsychiatry, 82,* 19–31, p. 28. http://dx.doi.org/10.1111/j.1939-0025.2011.01136.x
15. Lee, J., Courtney, M., & Tajima, E. (2014). Extended foster care support during the transition to adulthood: Effect on the risk of arrest. *Children and Youth Services Review, 42,* 34–42, p. 36. http://dx.doi.org/10.1016/j.childyouth.2014.03.018
16. See, e.g., Freisthler, B., Wolf, J. P., Wiegmann, W., & Kepple, N. J. (2017). Drug use, the drug environment, and physical abuse and neglect. *Child Maltreatment, 22,* 245–255. http://dx.doi.org/10.1177/1077559517711042
17. Raney, C., Campbell, F., & Blair, C. (1998). Enhancing the life course for high-risk children: Results from the Abecedarian Project. In J. Crane (Ed.), *Social programs that work* (pp. 163–183). New York, NY: Russell Sage Foundation.
18. Much of this research and policy analysis was done by psychologist Edward Zigler. See, e.g., Zigler, E., & Styfco, S. (2001). Can early childhood intervention prevent delinquency? A real possibility. In A. Dohart & D. Stipek (Eds.), *Constructive and destructive behavior: Implications for family, school, and society* (pp. 231–248). Washington, DC: American Psychological Association; Zigler, E. F., & Styfco, S. (1996). Head Start and early childhood intervention: The changing course of social science and social policy. In E. F. Zigler, S. L. Kagan, & N. W. Hall (Eds.), *Children, families, and government: Preparing for the twenty-first century* (pp. 132–155). New York, NY: Cambridge University Press.
19. See, e.g., Reynolds, A. J., Temple, J. A., Robertson, D. L., & Mann, E. A. (2001). Long-term effects of an early childhood intervention on educational achievement and juvenile arrest: A 15-year follow-up of low-income children in public schools. *JAMA, 285,* 2339–2346. http://dx.doi.org/10.1001/jama.285.18.2339

20. Schweinhart, L., & Weikart, D. (1998). High/Scope Perry preschool program effects at age twenty-seven. In J. L. Crane (Ed.), *Social programs that work* (pp. 148–183). New York, NY: Russell Sage Foundation, p. 148 (emphasis added, reference deleted). See also a later, longer term follow-up that reported similar results: Schweinhart, L. J., Montie, J., Xiang, Z., Barnett, W. S., Belfield, C. R., & Nores, M. (2005). *The High/Scope Perry Preschool study through age 40: Summary, conclusions, and frequently asked questions.* Ypsilanti, MI: High/Scope Educational Research Foundation. Retrieved from http://nieer.org/wp-content/uploads/2014/09/specialsummary_rev2011_02_2.pdf
21. See Reynolds, A. (1998). The Chicago child-parent center and expansion program: A study of extended early childhood intervention. In J. L. Crane (Ed.), *Social programs that work* (pp. 110–147). New York, NY: Russell Sage Foundation; and Reynolds, Temple, Robertson, & Mann (2001), Long-term effects of an early childhood intervention on educational achievement and juvenile arrest.
22. See, e.g., Osofsky, J. D., & Thompson, M. D. (2000). Adaptive and maladaptive parenting: Perspectives on risk and protective factors. In J. P. Shonkoff & S. J. Meisels (Ed.), *Handbook of early childhood intervention* (2nd ed., pp. 54–75). New York, NY: Cambridge University Press; Werner, E. E. (2000). Protective factors and individual resilience. In J. Shonkoff & S. Meisels (Ed.), *Handbook of early childhood intervention* (2nd ed., pp. 115–132). New York, NY: Cambridge University Press.
23. See, e.g., Garces, E., Thomas, D., & Currie, J. (2002). Long-term effects of Head Start. *The American Economic Review, 92,* 999–1012. http://dx.doi.org/10.1257/00028280260344560
24. Heckman, J., Pinto, R., & Savelyev, P. (2013). Understanding the mechanisms through which an influential early childhood program boosted adult outcomes. *The American Economic Review, 103,* 2052–2086. http://dx.doi.org/10.1257/aer.103.6.2052
25. In addition to the ones I have reviewed in detail, there are many others. See, e.g., Campbell, F. A., Pungello, E. P., Kainz, K., Burchinal, M., Pan, Y., Wasik, B. H., . . . Ramey, C. T. (2012). Adult outcomes as a function of an early childhood educational program: An Abecedarian Project follow-up. *Developmental Psychology, 48,* 1033–1043. http://dx.doi.org/10.1037/a0026644; Campie, P., Petrosino, A., Fronius, T., & Read, N. (2017, April). *Community-based violence prevention study of the Safe and Successful Youth Initiative: An intervention to prevent urban gun violence.* Washington, DC American Institutes for Research. Retrieved from https://www.ncjrs.gov/pdffiles1/ojjdp/grants/250771.pdf; Cohen, M. A., & Piquero, A. R. (2008, March). *Costs and benefits of a targeted intervention program for youthful offenders: The YouthBuildUSA Offender project.* Retrieved from https://www.youthbuild.org/sites/default/files/TargetedInterventionProgramYouthfulOffenders.pdf; Dunworth, T., & Mills, G. (1999, June). National evaluation of weed and seed. *National Institute of Justice Research in Brief.* Washington, DC: Department of Justice, Office of Justice Programs, National Institute of Justice. http://dx.doi.org/10.1177/0887403414520699; Ericson, N. (2001, June). *Office of Justice Programs, Office of Juvenile Justice and Delinquency Prevention fact sheet: Healthy Families America.* Washington, DC: Department of Justice. Retrieved from https://www.ncjrs.gov/pdffiles1/ojjdp/fs200123.pdf; Gottfredson, D. C., Gerstenblith, S. A., Soule, D. A., Womer, S. C., & Lu, S. (2004). Do after school programs reduce delinquency? *Prevention Science, 5,* 253–266. http://dx.doi.org/10.1023/B:PREV.0000045359.41696.02; Greenwood, P., & Turner, S. (2009). An overview of prevention and intervention programs for juvenile offenders. *Victims and Offenders, 4,* 365–374. http://dx.doi.org/10.1080/15564880903227438; Lally, R. J., Mangione, P. L., & Honig, A. S. (1987, September). The Syracuse University family development research program: Long-range impact of an early intervention with low-income

children and their families. In D. R. Powell (Ed.), *Annual advances in applied developmental psychology. Parent education as early childhood intervention: Emerging directions in theory, research and practice. Annual advances in applied developmental psychology* (Vol. 3, pp. 79–104). Westport, CT: Ablex. Retrieved from https://files.eric.ed.gov/fulltext/ED293637.pdf

26. Simmons, L. (2017). *The prison school: Educational inequality and school discipline in the age of mass incarceration* (p. 149). Berkeley: University of California Press.
27. See, e.g., Bryan, N. (2017). White teachers' role in sustaining the school to prison pipeline. Recommendations for teacher education. *Urban Review, 49,* 326–345. http://dx.doi.org/10.1007/s11256-017-0416-y; Coggshal, J., Osher, D., & Colombi, G. (2013). Enhancing educators' capacity to stop the school-to-prison pipeline. *Family Court Review, 51,* 435–444. http://dx.doi.org/10.1111/fcre.12040; and Okonofua, J., Paunesku, D., & Walton, G. (2016). Brief intervention to encourage empathic discipline cuts suspension rates in half among adolescents. *Proceedings of the National Academy of Sciences of the United States of America, 113,* 5221–5226. http://dx.doi.org/10.1073/pnas.1523698113
28. See, e.g., Daly, B. P., Hildenbrand, A. K., Haney-Caron, E., Goldstein, E. S., Galloway, M., & DeMatteo, D. (2016). Disrupting the school-to-prison pipeline: Strategies to reduce the risk of school-based zero tolerance policies resulting in juvenile justice involvement. In K. Heilbrun, D. DeMatteo, & N. E. S. Goldstein (Eds.), *APA handbook of psychology and juvenile justice* (pp. 257–275). Washington, DC: American Psychological Association; Meiners, E. (2011). Ending the school-to-prison pipeline/building abolition futures. *Urban Review, 43,* 547–565; and Nance, J. (2016). Dismantling the school-to-prison pipeline: Tools for change. *Arizona State Law Review, 48,* 313–372.
29. Kim, C., Losen, D., & Hewitt, D. (2010). *The school-to-prison pipeline: Structuring legal reforms.* New York, NY: New York University Press.
30. See, e.g., Archer, D. (2009/2010). Introduction: Challenging the school-to-prison pipeline. *New York Law School Law Review, 54,* 867–872 (and articles contained the accompanying symposium issue); and Scully, J. (2016). Dismantling the school-to-prison pipeline: Strategies for a better future. *Arkansas Law Review, 68,* 959–1010.
31. Redding, R. (1997). Juveniles transferred to criminal court: Legal reform proposals based on social science research. *Utah Law Review, 3,* 709–763, p. 757.
32. Redding (1997), Juveniles transferred to criminal court, p. 759 (footnotes omitted). See also Barton, W., & Butts, J. (1990). Viable options: Intensive supervision programs for juvenile delinquents. *Crime and Delinquency, 36,* 238–256. http://dx.doi.org/10.1177/0011128790036002004
33. Redding (1997), Juveniles transferred to adult criminal court, p. 759.
34. See, e.g., Coates, R. (1981). Deinstitutionalization and the serious juvenile offender: Some policy considerations. *Crime and Delinquency, 27,* 477–486. http://dx.doi.org/10.1177/001112878102700403; Krisberg, B., Currie, E., Onek, D., & Wiebush, R. G. (1995). Graduated sanctions for serious, violent, and chronic juvenile offenders. In J. C. Howell, B. Krisberg, J. D. Hawkins, & J. J. Wilson (Eds.), *Serious, violent, and chronic offenders: A sourcebook* (pp. 142–170). Thousand Oaks, CA: Sage.
35. See, e.g., Causadias, J., Umana-Taylor, A., & Eccles, J. (Eds.). (2018). Special issue: New directions in developmental science with youth experiencing marginalization. *American Psychologist, 73,* 707–839. http://dx.doi.org/10.1037/amp0000336
36. Causadias, J., & Umaña-Taylor, A. (2018). Reframing marginalization and youth development: Introduction to the special issue. *American Psychologist, 73,* 707–712, p. 709 (emphasis in original). http://dx.doi.org/10.1037/amp0000336
37. Garcia-Coll, C., Lamberty, G., Jenkins, R., McAdoo, H., Crnic, K., Wasik, B., & Vasquez Garcia, H. (1996). An integrative model for the study of developmental

competencies in minority children. *Child Development, 67,* 1891–1914. http://dx.doi.org/10.2307/1131600; Gaylord-Harden, N., Barbarin, O., Tolan, P., & Murry, V. (2018). Understanding development of African American boys and young men: Moving from risks to positive youth development. *American Psychologist, 73,* 753–767. http://dx.doi.org/10.1037/amp0000300; Lerner, R. (2017). Commentary: Studying and testing the positive youth development model: A tale of two approaches. *Child Development, 88,* 1183–1185. http://dx.doi.org/10.1111/cdev.12875; and Tolan, P. (2016). Humanizing developmental science to promote positive development of young men of color. In L. Burton, D. Burton, S. McHale, V. King, & J. Van Hook (Eds.), *Boys and men in African American families, national symposium on family issues* (pp. 93–100). New York, NY: Springer.

38. Abrams, L. (2013). Juvenile justice at a crossroads: Science, evidence, and twenty-first century reform. *Social Service Review, 87,* 725–752, p. 744.
39. See, e.g., Brantingham, P., & Brantingham, P. (1990). Situational crime prevention in practice. *Canadian Journal of Criminology, 32,* 17–40; Clarke, R. (1980). "Situational" crime prevention: Theory and practice. *British Journal of Criminology, 20,* 136–147; Clarke, R. (Ed.). (2010). *Situational crime prevention: Successful case studies* (2nd ed.). Boulder, CO: Lynne Rienner; Clarke, R. (2009). Situational crime prevention: Theoretical background and current practice. In M. Krohn, A. Lizotte, & G. Hall (Eds.), *Handbook of crime and deviance* (pp. 259–276). New York, NY: Springer; and Weisburd, D., & Eck, J. (2018). *Unraveling the crime-place connection: New directions in theory and policy*. New York, NY: Routledge.
40. Briar, S., & Piliavin, I. (1965). Delinquency, situational inducements, and commitments to conformity. *Social Problems, 13,* 35–45, p. 36. http://dx.doi.org/10.1525/sp.1965.13.1.03a00030
41. See, e.g., Guerette, R., & Bowers, K. (2009). Assessing the extent of crime displacement and diffusion of benefits: A review of situational crime prevention evaluations. *Criminology, 47,* 1331–1368. http://dx.doi.org/10.1111/j.1745-9125.2009.00177.x
42. See the references cited in notes 71–75 in Chapter 5 for a more extended discussion of these issues.
43. Fagan, A., & Catalano, R. (2013). What works in youth violence prevention: A review of the literature. *Research on Social Work Practice, 23,* 141–156. http://dx.doi.org/10.1177/1049731512465899; Matjasko, J., Massetti, G., & Bacon, S. (2016). Implementing and evaluating comprehensive evidence-based approaches to youth violence prevention: Partnering to create communities where youth are safe from violence. *Journal of Primary Prevention, 37,* 109–119. http://dx.doi.org/10.1007/s10935-016-0422-y; McElhaney, S. J., & Effley, K. M. (1999). Community-based approaches to violence prevention. In T. P. Gullotta, & S. J. McElhaney (Eds.), *Violence in homes and communities: Prevention, intervention, and treatment* (pp. 269–299). Thousand Oaks, CA: Sage; and Morrel-Samuels, S., Bacallao, M., Brown, S., Bower, M., & Zimmerman, M. (2016). Community engagement in youth violence prevention: Crafting methods to context. *Journal of Primary Prevention, 37,* 189–207. http://dx.doi.org/10.1007/s10935-016-0428-5. See also early recommendations by psychologist Carl Clements, who argued that transforming the social context in which delinquency occurred—including examining aspects of neighborhoods, families, schools, and community practices that contributed to or exacerbated delinquency—was an essential component of an effective community-based program of intervention and prevention. Clements, C. (1988). Delinquency prevention and treatment: A community-centered perspective. *Criminal Justice & Behavior, 15,* 286–305. http://dx.doi.org/10.1177/0093854888015003003
44. Vigil, J. (2002). *A rainbow of gangs: Street cultures in the mega-city* (p. 175). Austin: University of Texas Press.

45. Bishop, A., Hill, K., Gilman, A., Howell, J., Catalano, R., & Hawkins, J. (2017). Developmental pathways of youth gang membership: A structural test of the social development model. *Journal of Crime and Justice, 40,* 275–296, p. 290.
46. Di Placido, C., Simon, T., Witte, T., Gu, D., & Wong, S. (2006). Treatment of gang members can reduce institutional misconduct. *Law and Human Behavior, 30,* 93–114, p. 94. http://dx.doi.org/10.1007/s10979-006-9003-6
47. Di Placido, Simon, Witte, Gu, & Wong (2006), Treatment of gang members can reduce institutional misconduct, p. 108.
48. Kassenbaum, G., Ward, D., & Wilner, D. (1971). *Prison treatment and parole survival—An empirical assessment.* New York, NY: John Wiley. Similarly, other researchers have concluded that individual-level psychological change does not necessarily ensure subsequent reductions in delinquency; psychologically-oriented treatment programs alone appear to have smaller than expected effects on juvenile recidivism. See Lipsey, M. (1995). What do we learn from 400 research studies on the effectiveness of treatment with juvenile delinquents? In J. McGuire (Ed.), *What works: Reducing reoffending* (pp. 63–78). New York, NY: John Wiley.
49. Even committed advocates of traditional prison treatment programs acknowledge that many prisoners "are disadvantaged minorities who return to crime-ridden environments carrying the stigma of incarceration, with inadequate education and employment histories as well as meager or nonexistent social support." Wexler, H., Williams, R., Early, K., & Trotman, C. (1996). Prison treatment for substance abusers: Stay'n out revisited. In K. Early (Ed.), *Drug treatment behind bars: Prison-based strategies for change* (pp. 101–108). Westport, CT: Praeger, p. 101. This fact underscores the importance of offering prisoners meaningful opportunities to acquire and develop marketable skills and ways to utilize those skills once they are released. Otherwise, the formerly incarcerated are likely to remain at the economic and social margins of society and whatever positive changes have been brought about by prison rehabilitation programs will rapidly erode.
50. For recent compelling accounts, see Harding, D., Morenoff, J., & Wyse, J. (2019). *On the outside: Prisoner reentry and reintegration.* Chicago, IL: University of Chicago Press; and Western, B. (2018). *Homeward: Life in the year after prison.* New York, NY: Russell Sage Foundation. http://dx.doi.org/10.7208/chicago/9780226607788.001.0001
51. Menon, R., Blakely, C., Carmichael, D., & Snow, D. (1995). Making a dent in recidivism rates: Impact of employment on minority ex-offenders. In G. Thomas (Ed.), *Race and ethnicity in America: Meeting the challenge in the 21st century* (pp. 279–293). Washington, DC: Taylor & Francis, pp. 290–291.
52. Menon, Blakely, Carmichael, & Snow (1995), Making a dent in recidivism rates, pp. 290–291.
53. See, e.g., Pager, D. (2007). *Marked: Race, crime, and finding work in a era of mass incarceration.* Chicago, IL: University of Chicago Press; Pager, D., & Quillian, L. (2005). Walking the talk: What employers say versus what they do. *American Sociological Review, 70,* 355–380. http://dx.doi.org/10.1177/000312240507000301
54. See Menon, Blakely, Carmichael, & Snow (1995), Making a dent in recidivism rates. On the importance of targeting job training programs for prisoners most likely to benefit from them, and on insuring that formerly incarcerated persons be given access to meaningful and reasonably well-paying jobs, see also Orsagh, T., & Witte, D. (1981). Economic status and crime: Implications for offender rehabilitation. *Journal of Criminal Law and Criminology, 72,* 1055–1071. http://dx.doi.org/10.2307/1143275
55. The issue is more complicated than it first seemed. Some empirical evaluations of the actual consequences of "ban the box" laws that prevented employers from learning about whether or not an applicant had a criminal record found that many of them simply assumed that African Americans did and discriminated on the basis of that assumption. For more in-depth discussions of whether and how this

particular reform can or should be implemented, see Doleac, J. L., & Hansen, B. (2016). *Does "ban the box" help or hurt low-skilled workers? Statistical discrimination and employment outcomes when criminal histories are hidden* (Working Paper No. 22469). Washington, DC: National Bureau of Economic Research, pp. 1–47. Retrieved from https://www.nber.org/papers/w22469; Flake, D. (2015). When any sentence is a life sentence: Employment discrimination against ex-offenders. *Washington University Law Review, 93,* 45–102; Gubernick, L. (2017). Erasing the mark of Cain: An empirical analysis of the effect of ban-the-box legislation on the employment outcomes of people of color with criminal record. *Fordham Urban Law Journal, 44,* 1153–1215; Weissert, E. (2016). Get out of jail free? Preventing employment discrimination against people with criminal records using ban the box laws. *University of Pennsylvania Law Review, 164,* 1529–1555. Whatever form they finally take, laws and policies must be implemented to eliminate barriers to postprison employment. As Dallan Flake put it, "[r]egardless of whether ban-the-box laws ultimately prove successful" or some better version of it or related reforms are implemented in their place, there is finally much broader recognition that formerly incarcerated persons need to be employed and that lawmakers need to "finally use the law to facilitate that effort." Flake, D. (2019). Do ban-the-box laws really work? *Iowa Law Review, 104,* 1079–1127, p. 1127.

56. Van Stelle, K., Mauser, E., & Moberg, D. (1994). Recidivism to the criminal justice system of substance-abusing offenders diverted into treatment. *Crime & Delinquency, 40,* 175–196. See also Leukefeld, C. (1985). The clinical connection: Drugs and crime. *International Journal of the Addictions, 20,* 1049–1064; Wilson, S., & Mandelbrote, B. (1978). The relationship between duration of treatment in a therapeutic community for abusers and subsequent criminality. *British Journal of Psychiatry, 132,* 487–491. For a discussion of the kinds of prison drug treatment programs that are effective in reducing future drug and alcohol use as well as the commission of drug-related crime, see Wald, H., Flaherty, M., & Pringle, J. (1999). Prevention in prisons. In R. Ammerman, R. Tarter, & P. Ott (Eds.), *Prevention and societal impact of drug and alcohol abuse* (pp. 369–381). Mahwah, NJ: Lawrence Erlbaum.
57. See, e.g., Cook, P., & Moore, M. (1993). Violence reduction through restrictions on alcohol availability. Special issue on alcohol, aggression, and injury. *Alcohol Health and Research World, 17,* 151–156.
58. See, e.g., Drucker, E., Anderson, K., Haemmig, R., Heimer, R, Small, D., Walley, A., . . . van Beek, I. (2016). Treating addictions: Harm reduction in clinical care and prevention. *Journal of Bioethical Inquiry, 13,* 239–249; and Stancliff, S., Phillips, B., Maghsoudi, N., & Joseph, H. (2015). Harm reduction: Front line public health. *Journal of Addictive Diseases, 34,* 206–219.
59. Harding, Morenoff, & Wyse (2019), *On the outside: Prisoner reentry and reintegration,* p. 217.
60. Haney, C. (2003). The psychological impact of incarceration: Implications for post-prison adjustment. In J. Travis & M. Waul (Eds.), *Prisoners once removed: The impact of incarceration and reentry on children, families, and communities* (pp. 33–66). Washington, DC: Urban Institute Press.
61. As I noted in the last chapter, Diamond was a noted scholar–practitioner whose expert testimony led to a number of important legal innovations.
62. Diamond, B. (1961). Criminal responsibility of the mentally ill. *Stanford Law Review, 14,* 59–86, p. 86.
63. Diamond, B. (1973). From *Durham* to *Brawner*: A futile journey. *Washington University Law Quarterly, 1973,* 109–125, pp. 121–122.
64. Diamond (1973), From *Durham* to *Brawner,* p. 122.
65. Diamond (1973), From *Durham* to *Brawner,* p. 122.

66. Elsewhere I have suggested that throughout the 1960s and into the early 1970s "there was increasingly widespread recognition that crime was in large part the product of social and economic inequality" and that it was "widely understood that no successful strategy of crime control could continue to focus only on the real or assumed problems of individual prisoners while simultaneously ignoring the larger structural forces that had influenced their behavior." Haney, C. (2010). Demonizing the "enemy": The role of "science" in declaring the "war on prisoners." *Connecticut Public Interest Law Journal, 9,* 185–242, p. 193. For evidence cited in support of this, see pp. 193–201.
67. Braithwaite, J., & Mugford, S. (1994). Conditions of successful reintegration ceremonies: Dealing with juvenile offenders. *British Journal of Criminology, 34,* 139–171, p. 140 (emphasis in original).
68. Braithwaite & Mugford (1994), Conditions of successful reintegration ceremonies, p. 146 (emphasis added).
69. Maruna, S. (2001). *Making good: How ex-convicts reform and rebuild their lives.* Washington, DC: American Psychological Association, p. 163. For a discussion of the potential and limitations of "reentry courts" that use the judicial process to manage the prisoner's return to the community, see Maruna, S., & LeBel, T. (2003). Welcome home? Examining the "reentry court" concept from a strength-based perspective. *Western Criminological Review 4,* 91–107. http://dx.doi.org/10.1037/10430-000
70. See, e.g., Lemert, E. (1993). Visions of social control: Probation considered. *Crime and Delinquency, 39,* 447–461. http://dx.doi.org/10.1177/0011128793039004003
71. In 2003, the Justice Department reported that 95% of prisoners would be released from prison at some point and, despite trends toward ending discretionary release from prison by parole boards, some 80% of persons released would be under parole supervision. Hughes, T., & Wilson, D. (2002). *Reentry trends in the United States: Inmates returning to the community after serving time in prison.* Washington, DC: Bureau of Justice Statistics.
72. The Bureau of Justice Statistics reported that, at the end of 2015, there were 3,789,800 persons on probation in the United States and 870,500 on parole. See Kaeble, D., & Bonczar, T. (2016, December). *Probation and parole in the United States, 2015* (NCJ 250230), pp. 1–25. Washington, DC: Department of Justice.
73. There were 2,172,800 persons incarcerated in jails and prisons during 2015. Kaeble, D., & Cowhig, M. (2018, April). *Correctional populations in the United States, 2016* (NCJ 251211), pp. 1–13. Washington, DC: Department of Justice.
74. See, e.g., Phelps, M. (2018). Ending mass probation: Sentencing, supervision, and revocation. *Future of Children, 28,* 125–146. She is certainly correct to argue that, as currently operated, "mass probation is one more example of the United States' uniquely punitive criminal justice system" (p. 126).
75. For example, a mid-1990s study of California probation departments indicated that they were relying increasingly on what were termed "banked" caseloads, a form of unsupervised probation with a statewide average ratio of 629 probationers per probation officer. Nieto, M. (1996). *The changing role of probation in California's criminal justice system* (CRB 96-006). Sacramento, CA: California Research Bureau.
76. Lemert (1993), Visions of social control: Probation considered, p. 447.
77. Lynch, M. (2000). Rehabilitation as rhetoric: The ideal of reformation in contemporary parole discourse and practices. *Punishment and Society, 2,* 40–65, p. 53. Indeed, agents saw the persons they supervised as "dispositionally flawed and responsible for [their] own improvement" (p. 40). Lynch also found that, at least in California, the parole agents she studied were reluctant to adopt Feeley and Simon's model of "new penology" and instead held tightly to a conventional view of themselves as "crime fighters" within the community. See Lynch, M. (1998).

Waste managers? The new penology, crime fighting, and parole agent identity. *Law & Society Review, 32,* 839–870. http://dx.doi.org/10.2307/827741

78. Compare, e.g., McMurray, H. (1993). High risk parolees in transition from institution to community life. *Journal of Offender Rehabilitation, 19,* 145–161, with Turner, S., & Petersilia, J. (1992). Focusing on high-risk parolees: An experiment to reduce commitments to the Texas Department of Corrections. *Journal of Research in Crime and Delinquency, 29,* 34–61.
79. Moreover, there are distinct racial differentials on probation and parole outcomes in which African American men fare worse than others. See, e.g., Steinmetz, K., & Henderson, H. (2016). Inequality on probation: An examination of differential probation outcomes. *Journal of Ethnicity in Criminal Justice, 14,* 1–20. http://dx.doi.org/10.1080/15377938.2015.1030527
80. Carson, E. (2015). *Prisoners in 2014* (NCJ 248955). Washington, DC: Bureau of Justice Statistics.
81. See, e.g., Rhine, E., Petersilia, J., & Reitz, K. (2017). The future of parole release. *Crime and Justice, 46,* 279–338. http://dx.doi.org/10.1086/688616
82. Phelps (2018), Ending mass probation: Sentencing, supervision, and revocation, p. 131.
83. Travis, J. (2005). *But they all come back: Facing the challenges of prisoner reentry.* Washington, DC: Urban Institute Press, pp. 243–244. Boundary spanners "attempt to understand human behavior in the context of systemic structures, operations, and barriers that exist within and between communities and prisons, seek to bridge communication, understanding, and service gaps and translate the workings of one entity into the language of another." Pettus, C., & Severson, M. (2006). Paving the way for effective reentry practice: The critical role and function of the boundary spanner. *Prison Journal, 86,* 206–229, p. 208.
84. Mears, D., Wang, X., Hay, C., & Bales, W. (2008). Social ecology and recidivism: Implications for prisoner reentry. *Criminology, 46,* 301–340. http://dx.doi.org/10.1111/j.1745-9125.2008.00111.x
85. See, e.g., Kennealy, P., Skeem, J., Manchalk, S., & Louden, J. (2012). Firm, fair, caring officer–offender relationships protect against supervision failure. *Law and Human Behavior, 36,* 496–505; Lovins, B., Cullen, F., Latessa, E., & Jonson, C. (2018). Probation officer as coach: Building a new professional identity. *Federal Probation, 82,* 13–19; Lowenkamp, C., Flores, A., Holsinger, A., Makarios, M., & Latessa, E. (2010). Intensive supervision programs: Does program philosophy and the principles of effective intervention matter? *Journal of Criminal Justice, 38,* 368–375; Romig, C., & Gruenke, C. (1994). Aiding the parolee adjustment process: A systemic perspective on assessment. *Contemporary Family Therapy: An International Journal, 16,* 301–314.
86. See, e.g., Kennealy, Skeem, Manchalk, & Louden (2012), Firm, fair, caring officer–offender relationships protect against supervision failure; Lovins, Cullen, Latessa, & Jonson (2018), Probation officer as coach: Building a new professional identity; Lowenkamp, Flores, Holsinger, Makarios, & Latessa (2010). Intensive supervision programs: Does program philosophy and the principles of effective intervention matter; Romig & Gruenke (1994), Aiding the parolee adjustment process: A systemic perspective on assessment.
87. U.S. Department of Justice, Bureau of Justice Statistics. (2000, August). *Incarcerated parents and their children* (Special Report, NCJ 182335). Washington, DC: Author.
88. See, e.g., Murray, J., & Farrington, D. (2008). The effects of parental imprisonment on children. *Crime & Justice, 37,* 133–206, pp. 186–187; and Wildman, C. (2009). Parental imprisonment, the prison boom, and childhood disadvantage. *Demography, 46,* 265–280.

89. For the discussions of some of the ways that families are impacted by incarceration and the kinds of psychological services they might be provided, see the articles in a special section of *Couple and Family Psychology: Research and Practice* devoted to these topics, including Arditti, J. (2016). A family stress-proximal process model for understanding the effects of parental incarceration on children and their families. *Couple and Family Psychology: Research and Practice, 5*, 65–88; Datchi, C., Barretti, L., & Thompson, C. (2016). Family services in adult detention centers: Systemic principles for prisoner reentry. *Couple and Family Psychology: Research and Practice, 5*, 89–104; Greenwood, P. (2016). Moving practice into theory: Bringing real-world considerations to a systemic perspective on incarceration. *Couple and Family Psychology: Research and Practice, 5*, 105–108; and Sexton, T. (2016). Incarceration as a family affair: Thinking beyond the individual. *Couple & Family Psychology, 5*, 61–64. http://dx.doi.org/10.1037/cfp0000058
90. Fendrich, M. (1991). Institutionalization and parole behavior: Assessing the influence of individual and family characteristics. *Journal of Community Psychology, 19*, 109–122. http://dx.doi.org/10.1002/1520-6629(199104)19:2<109::AID-JCOP2290190203>3.0.CO;2-6
91. In this context, "collateral consequences" can refer to the broad set of effects of imprisonment that extend beyond those directly impacting the persons incarcerated or, more specifically, to the special set of postconviction legal sanctions that are imposed on persons as a result of having a criminal record. Michelle Alexander deserves much credit for systematically categorizing and greatly increasing the visibility of the collateral consequences of conviction and imprisonment and, especially, for drawing attention to their impact on communities of Color. See Alexander, M. (2010). *The new Jim Crow: Mass incarceration in the age of colorblindness.* New York, NY: The New Press. In this section, I focus primarily on the added legal sanctions that are imposed as a result of a criminal conviction, especially ones imposed on formerly incarcerated persons after their release from prison.
92. See, e.g., Berson, S. (2013, September). Beyond the sentence: Understanding collateral consequences. *National Institute of Justice Journal, 272*, 24–29; Council of State Governments. (2018). *The National Inventory of Collateral Consequences of Conviction*. Retrieved from https://niccc.csgjusticecenter.org/about/; Malcolm, J. (2018). The problem with the proliferation of collateral consequences. *Federalist Society Review, 19*, 36–42; and Pinard, M. (2006). An integrated perspective on the collateral consequences of criminal convictions and reentry issues faced by formerly incarcerated individuals. *Boston University Law Review, 86*, 623–690.
93. Chin, G. (2012). The new civil death: Rethinking punishment in the era of mass incarceration. *University of Pennsylvania Law Review, 160*, 1789–1833.
94. Haney, L. (2018). Incarcerated fatherhood: The entanglements of child support debt and mass imprisonment. *American Journal of Sociology, 124*, 1–48, p. 39.
95. Haney (2018), Incarcerated fatherhood: The entanglements of child support debt and mass imprisonment, p. 40.
96. Haney (2018), Incarcerated fatherhood: The entanglements of child support debt and mass imprisonment, p. 41.
97. Pinard, M. (2010). Reflections and perspectives on reentry and collateral consequences. *Journal of Criminal Law and Criminology, 100*, 1213–1224, p. 1224. See also Jefferson-Jones, J. (2014). A second chance: Rebiography as "just compensation." *West Virginia Law Review, 117*, 203–230; Jones, D. (2015). When the fallout of criminal conviction goes too far: Challenging collateral consequences. *Stanford Journal of Civil Rights and Civil Liberties, 11*, 237–268; and Lee, E. (2010). The centerpiece to real reform? Political, legal, and social barriers to reentry in California. *Hastings Race and Poverty Law Journal, 7*, 243–260.

98. Kerner, O., & The National Advisory Commission. (1968). *Report of the U.S. National Advisory Commission on Civil Disorders*. Washington, DC: Government Printing Office.
99. Zarefsky, D. (1986). *President Johnson's War on Poverty: Rhetoric and history* (p. 39). Tuscaloosa: University of Alabama Press.
100. Harris, F., & Curtis, A. (Eds.). (2018). *Healing our divided society: Investing in America fifty years after the Kerner Report*. Philadelphia, PA: Temple University Press.
101. For example, the Bureau of Justice Statistics reported that, in 1992, more than a quarter of all state prison admissions were for "violent" offenses, with approximately 10.7% of those being for the crime of robbery. That year, robbery and burglary alone accounted for about one quarter of all prison admissions. If robbery had been counted as a property offense instead, then property, drug, and public order offenses would have accounted for over 80% of all state prison admissions that year. McGuire, K., & Pastore, A. (1995). *Sourcebook of Criminal Justice Statistics, 1994*. Washington, DC: Department of Justice, Bureau of Justice Statistics, p. 552.
102. Curtis, L. A. (Ed.). (1985). *American violence & public policy: An update of the National Commission on the Causes and Prevention of Violence* (p. 248). New Haven, CT: Yale University Press. See, also, Catalano, S. M. (2005). *Criminal victimization, 2005*. Washington, DC: Bureau of Justice Statistics.
103. Early, K. (1996). Introduction. In K. Early (Ed.), *Drug treatment behind bars: Prison-based strategies for change* (p. 3). Westport, CT: Praeger.
104. For example, the era of mass incarceration played a significant role in elevating levels of poverty. See, e.g., DeFina, R., & Hannon, L. (2013). The impact of mass incarceration on poverty. *Crime and Delinquency, 59*, 562–582. http://dx.doi.org/10.1177/0011128708328864
105. See, e.g., Sykes, B., & Pettit, B. (2014). Mass incarceration, family complexity, and the reproduction of childhood disadvantage. *Annals of the American Academy of Political and Social Science, 654*, 127–149, p. 127. http://dx.doi.org/10.1177/0002716214526345
106. Sullivan, M. (1989). *Getting paid: Youth crime and work in the inner city* (p. 252). Ithaca, NY: Cornell University Press.
107. National Academies of Sciences, Engineering, and Medicine. (2019). *A roadmap to reducing child poverty*. Washington, DC: Author, p. 193. http://dx.doi.org/10.17226/25246
108. Looney, A., & Turner, N. (2018, March 14). *Work and opportunity before and after incarceration*. Retrieved from https://www.brookings.edu/research/work-and-opportunity-before-and-after-incarceration/
109. Looney & Turner (2018, March 14), *Work and opportunity before and after incarceration*, p. 1.
110. Homel, R. (2014). Introduction: Justice reinvestment as a global phenomenon. *Victims & Offenders, 9*, 6–12. http://dx.doi.org/10.1080/15564886.2013.860937
111. See, e.g., Gonnerman, J. (2004, November 16). Million dollar blocks: The neighborhood costs of America's prison boom. *The Village Voice*; Kurgan, L. (2013). *Close up at a distance: Mapping, technology, & politics*. New York, NY: Zone Books; and Tucker, S., & Cadora, E. (2003). *Justice reinvestment*. New York, NY: Open Society. Similarly, see Kelly Lytle Hernandez's project on what she termed "Million Dollar Hoods" in the city of Los Angeles. She and her research team provide a mapping of the neighborhoods where the Los Angeles police and sheriff departments spent at least $6 million between the years of 2010–2015 devoted to incarcerating the persons who lived there. https://milliondollarhoods.org See, also: Hernandez, K. (2017). *City of inmates: Conquest, rebellion, and the rise of human caging in Los Angeles*. Durham, NC: North Carolina Press.

112. Clear, T. (2007). *Imprisoning communities: How mass incarceration makes disadvantaged neighborhoods worse*. New York, NY: Oxford University Press. http://dx.doi.org/10.1093/acprof:oso/9780195305791.001.0001
113. For example, some forms of reinvestment involve increased use of correctional programming. See Taxman, F., Pattavina, A., & Caudy, M. (2014). Justice reinvestment in the United States: An empirical assessment of the potential impact of increased correctional programming on recidivism. *Victims & Offenders, 9,* 50–75. http://dx.doi.org/10.1080/15564886.2013.860934. Others have implemented new strategies to reduce crime and delinquency by shifting resources away from the use of "secure facilities" to relying instead on community-based programs for youth. See, e.g., Schweitzer, M., Labrecque, R., M., & Smith, P. (2017). Reinvesting in the lives of youth: A targeted approach to reducing recidivism. *Criminal Justice Policy Review, 28,* 207–219. http://dx.doi.org/10.1177/0887403415579262. For a thoughtful overview, see Byrne, J. (2014). The future of justice reinvestment—Assessing the merits of individual and community change strategies. *Victims & Offenders, 9,* 1–5. http://dx.doi.org/10.1080/15564886.2013.860934
114. See, e.g., Homel (2014), Introduction: Justice reinvestment as a global phenomenon.
115. See, e.g., Aviram, H. (2015). *Cheap on crime: Recession-era politics and the transformation of punishment.* Berkeley: University of California Press; Cate, S., & HoSang, D. (2018). "The better way to fight crime": Why fiscal arguments do not restrain the carceral state. *Theoretical Criminology, 22,* 169–188. http://dx.doi.org/10.1177/1362480617690801; and Gottschalk, M. (2007). Dollars, sense, and penal reform: Social movements and the future of the carceral state. *Social Research, 74,* 669–694.
116. National Academies of Sciences, Engineering, and Medicine (2019), *A roadmap to reducing child poverty*.
117. The National Academy committee concluded that there were two "packages" of programs that were capable of meeting the goal of reducing childhood poverty 50% in 10 years, at an estimated cost of between $90–$111 billion per year. Alternative approaches that came close to but did not completely achieve the initial goal cost could be accomplished at considerably less. National Academies of Sciences, Engineering, and Medicine. (2019), *A roadmap to reducing child poverty,* pp. 191–194. However, measured against the aggregate cost of child poverty, estimated at $500 billion per year, investing in effective child poverty reduction has obvious compensating effects. See Holzer, J., Schanzenbach, D., Duncan, G., & Ludwig, J. (2008). The economic costs of childhood poverty in the United States. *Journal of Children and Poverty, 14,* 41–61. http://dx.doi.org/10.1080/10796120701871280. Indeed, addressing *childhood* poverty is an especially cost-effective public policy. Researchers have estimated that for every dollar spent on reducing childhood poverty, the nation saves approximately $7 in the overall economic costs of poverty (which includes increased health care costs and reduced lifetime earnings, in addition to crime-related costs). See McLaughlin, M., & Rank, M. (2018). Estimating the economic costs of childhood poverty in the United States. *Social Work Research, 42,* 73–83. http://dx.doi.org/10.1093/swr/svy007. In addition, for recent research on and policy analyses of the harmful, long-term effects of poverty and income inequality and the role that the discipline of psychology can play in addressing them, see articles in a special *American Psychologist* section edited by Heather Bullock, including: Crowley, M. Supplee, L., Scott, T., & Brooks-Gunn, J. (2019). The role of psychology in evidence-based policymaking: Mapping opportunities for strategic investment in poverty reduction. *American Psychologist, 74,* 685–697; Hostinar, C., & Miller, G. (2019). Protective factors for youth confronting economic hardship: Current challenges and future avenues in reslience research. *American Psychologist, 74,* 641–653; Reynolds, A., Ou, S.,

Mondi, C., & Giovanelli, A. (2019). Reducing poverty and inequality through preschool–third-grade prevention services. *American Psychologist, 74,* 653–672; and Thompson, M., & Dahling, J. (2019). Employment and poverty: Why work matters in understanding poverty. *American Psychologist, 74,* 673–684.

118. Although estimates of the economic costs of crime vary widely, largely as a function of the measures and methods employed, they are unquestionably substantial. The Government Accountability Office report acknowledged the extremely wide variations and potential sources of unreliability in the data, but reported estimates from researchers that ranged from $690 billion to $3.42 trillion annually. Government Accountability Office (2017, September). *Costs of crime: Experts report challenges estimating costs and suggest improvements to better inform policy decisions* (GAO-17-732). Report to Congressional Requesters. Washington, DC: Author. A recent study estimated the overall costs of incarceration alone (including costs to incarcerated persons, families, children, and communities as well as the direct costs of corrections) at $1 trillion annually. McLaughlin, M., Pettus-Davis, C., Brown, D., Veeh, C., & Renn, T. (2016). *The economic burden of incarceration in the United States* (Working Paper No. IJRD072016). Tallahassee, FL: Institute for Justice Research and Development.
119. Political commentators may have been correct when they argued several years ago that the combination of "budget crises at the national and state levels" and "the strong political power of conservative groups" meant that "a significant effort to reduce poverty or deal with the closely related issue of racial segregation is not in the political cards, at least for now." Ladd, H., & Fiske, E. (2011, December 12). Class matters. Why won't we admit it? *The New York Times,* p. A21. However, times have changed. There is no longer a pressing budget crisis, and even conservative groups are part of the coalition pressing for criminal justice reform. Moreover, there is research to suggest that the public would be willing to pay directly for programs that effectively reduced crime. For example, one study suggested that households would pay as much as $100 to $150 per year to reduce certain violent crimes in their community by 10%. See Cohen, M., Rust, R., Steen, S., & Tidd, S. (2004). Willingness-to-pay for crime control programs. *Criminology, 42,* 89–109. http://dx.doi.org/10.1111/j.1745-9125.2004.tb00514.x. In addition, when given the choice, participants in another study clearly preferred and were willing to pay for prevention and treatment over prison-based responses. See Cohen, M., Rust, R., & Steen, S. (2007). Prevention, crime control, or case? Public preferences towards criminal justice spending priorities. *Justice Quarterly, 23,* 317–335. http://dx.doi.org/10.1080/07418820600869103
120. I agree with Michael Perlin that the real failure of the deinstitutionalization movement was not that it closed what were often inhumane state mental hospitals, but that it failed to replace them with the promised community care. However, it is hard to argue that the mentally ill are currently better off, languishing in abusive prisons or homeless on urban streets. This is, of course, not a reason to repeat the sins of those past times. See Perlin, M. (2013). "Wisdom is thrown into jail": Using therapeutic jurisprudence to remediate the criminalization of persons with mental illness. *Michigan State University Journal of Medicine & Law, 17,* 343–371. For some of the story of how this happened and with what consequence, see Scull, A. (1977). *Decarceration: Community treatment and the deviant.* Englewood Cliffs, NJ: Prentice-Hall; Scull, A. (1990). Deinstitutionalization: Cycles of despair. Special issue: Challenging the therapeutic state: Critical perspectives on psychiatry and the mental health system. *Journal of Mind & Behavior, 11,* 301–311; and Smith, D., & Polloway, E. (1993). Patterns of deinstitutionalization and community placement: A dream deferred or lost? *Education and Training in Mental Retardation and Developmental Disabilities, 30,* 321–328.

121. Torrey, E., Zdanowicz, M., Kennard, A., Lamb, H., Eslinger, D., Biasotti, M., & Fuller, D. (2014). *The treatment of persons with mental illness in prisons and jails: A state survey*. Arlington, VA: Treatment Advocacy Center. Retrieved from http://tacreports.org/storage/documents/treatment-behind-bars/treatment-behind-bars.pdf
122. See, e.g., Fellner, J. (2006). A conundrum for corrections, a tragedy for prisoners: Prisons as facilities for the mentally ill. *Washington University Journal of Law & Policy, 22*, 135–144; Haney, C. (2017). "Madness" and penal confinement: Observations on mental illness and prison pain. *Punishment and Society, 19*, 310–326. http://dx.doi.org/10.1177/1462474517705389; Mulvey, E., & Schubert, C. (2017). Mentally ill individuals in jails and prisons. *Crime and Justice, 46*, 231–275. http://dx.doi.org/10.1086/688461; Roth, A. (2018). *Insane: America's criminal treatment of mental illness*. New York, NY: Basic Books; and Vitiello, M. (2010). Addressing the special problems of mentally ill prisoners: A small piece of the solution to our nation's prison crisis. *Denver Law Review, 88*, 57–71.
123. See, e.g., Peters, R. H., Wexler, H. K., & Lurigio, A. J. (2015). Co-occurring substance use and mental disorders in the criminal justice system: A new frontier of clinical practice and research. *Psychiatric Rehabilitation Journal, 38*, 1–6. http://dx.doi.org/10.1037/prj0000135
124. In addition to persons formally diagnosed as mentally ill, the nation's prisons and jails house large numbers of especially psychologically vulnerable persons—those who also share extensive trauma histories, have suffered severe forms of material or economic deprivation, or are affected by other background risk factors that have often gone unacknowledged and untreated. This diverse group, too, is of special concern because, like all of us, prisoners range along a continuum of psychological vulnerability, which sometimes manifests itself as diagnosable mental illness and sometimes not. Placing these persons in prison or jail exposes them to significant risk of harm. That harm entails the possibility of lasting psychological damage (which includes, but is not limited to, the development or exacerbation of mental illness).
125. See, e.g., Prins, S. J. (2014). Prevalence of mental illnesses in U.S. State prisons: A systematic review. *Psychiatric Services, 65*, 862–872. http://dx.doi.org/10.1176/appi.ps.201300166
126. The interconnectedness of mental health, substance abuse problems, and economic vulnerability that is directly related to arrest and incarceration is apparent. See, e.g., Gonzalez, J., Jetelina, K., Roberts, M., Reitzel, L., Kendzor, D., Walters, S., & Businelle, M. S. (2018). Criminal justice system involvement among homeless adults. *American Journal of Criminal Justice, 43*, 158–166. http://dx.doi.org/10.1007/s12103-017-9413-7. The creation of a fully functioning public mental health care system is essential to breaking that cycle.
127. Among many discussions of the dynamics by which the effects of this original sin have been repeatedly denied and then reinscribed by the criminal justice system, see, especially, Alexander (2010), *The new Jim Crow: Mass incarceration in the age of colorblindness*; and Muhammad, K. (2010). *The condemnation of Blackness: Race, crime, and the making of modern urban America*. Cambridge, MA: Harvard University Press.
128. Roberts, D. (2004). The social and moral cost of mass incarceration in African American communities. *Stanford Law Review, 56*, 1271–1304, p. 1303.
129. Rothstein, R. (2017). *Color of law: A forgotten history of how our government segregated America* (p. xi). New York, NY: W. W. Norton. See his Chapter 12, "Considering Fixes," for ways to approach changing the laws and policies that have operated to maintain housing segregation in the United States.
130. For a thoughtful discussion of how these legal narrowing principles obfuscate and erase the "systemic and serpentine" way that racism operates in the criminal justice system, see Murakawa, N., & Beckett, K. (2010). The penology of racial

innocence: The erasure of racism in the study and practice of punishment. *Law & Society Review, 44,* 695–730. http://dx.doi.org/10.1111/j.1540-5893.2010.00420.x

131. Compare Haney, C., & Hurtado, A. (1994). The jurisprudence of race and meritocracy: Standardized testing and "race-neutral" racism in the workplace. *Law and Human Behavior, 18,* 223–248. http://dx.doi.org/10.1007/BF01499586
132. Lawrence, M. A. (2018). Racial justice demands truth and reconciliation. *University of Pittsburgh Law Review, 80,* 69–134, p. 69.
133. See, e.g., Spann, G. (2004). The dark side of *Grutter. Constitutional Commentary, 21,* 221–250.
134. See, e.g., Posner, E., & Vermeule, A. (2003). Reparations for slavery and other historical injustices. *Columbia Law Review, 103,* 689–747. http://dx.doi.org/10.2307/1123721
135. These reforms should incorporate existing social psychological knowledge about the way that the nature of the police role and situational context in which they operate contributes to race-based abuses. See, e.g., Eberhardt, J. (2019). *Biased: Uncovering the hidden prejudice that shapes what we see, think, and do.* New York, NY: Viking; Henning, K. (2017). Boys to men, p. 78–86; Swencionis, J., & Goff, P. (2017). The psychological science of racial bias and policing. *Psychology, Public Policy, and Law, 23,* 398–409. http://dx.doi.org/10.1037/law0000130
136. Racial justice acts can take somewhat different forms. Most have been restricted to capital cases, although there is no obvious reason why they could not be applied more broadly. They essentially require a defendant to demonstrate that race was "a significant factor" in the decision-making process by which he or she was prosecuted, convicted, subjected to, or given the death penalty and, if successful, result in a prohibition to seek the death penalty and an already entered death verdict being vacated and a life without parole sentence imposed instead. See, e.g., Alexander, R. (2014). A model state racial justice act: Fighting racial bias without killing the death penalty. *George Mason University Civil Rights Law Journal, 24,* 113–157; Vidmar, N. (2012). The North Carolina Racial Justice Act: An essay on substantive and procedural fairness in death penalty litigation. *Iowa Law Review, 97,* 1969–1983.
137. For example, for an especially thoughtful discussion of the fact that "[t]he literature may indeed provide sufficient support for an infusion into the criminal law of information detailing the distressing, humiliating and cumulative impact of racism," see Nelson, C. (2003). Breaking the camel's back: A consideration of mitigatory criminal defenses and racism-related mental illness. *Michigan Journal of Race & Law, 9,* 77–147, p. 121.
138. As Dorothy Roberts pointed out, "Canadian law attempts to remedy high rates of incarceration among aboriginal people by requiring judges to take into account systemic racial injustice in their assessment of aboriginal offenders' individual deserts." Roberts (2004), The social and moral cost of mass incarceration in African American communities, p. 1304. For one example of explicitly racially sensitive judicial sentencing in the United States, see *United States v. Leviner,* 31 F. Supp. 2d 23 (D. Mass. 1998), in which federal judge Nancy Gertner decided not to consider a defendant's prior convictions when she downwardly departed from the federal Sentencing Guidelines (Guidelines), because she believed that the traffic offenses for which he had been previously convicted were the likely product of racial profiling. As partial justification for taking an approach that went beyond merely relying on "numbers on a grid" (p. 25), Judge Gertner cited "scholarly and popular literature [that] strongly suggests that there is racial disparity in the rates at which African Americans are stopped and prosecuted for traffic offenses" (p. 24).
139. See, e.g., Ensign, O. (2018). Speaking truth to power: An analysis of American truth-telling efforts vis-à-vis the South African Truth and Reconciliation Commission. *New York Review of Law and Social Change, 42,* 1–44; Ironwood, J.,

Alderman, D., & Barron, M. (2016). Addressing structural violence through US reconciliation: The case study of Greensboro, NC and Detroit, MI. *Political Geography, 52*, 57–64; and Lawrence (2018), Racial justice demands truth & reconciliation.

140. The legacy of racial injustice is manifested perhaps most starkly in the American criminal justice system, where the justification for reparations-based reform is thus greatest. See generally Balfour, L. (2014). Unthinking racial realism: A future for reparations? *Du Bois Review, 11*, 43–56; Bittker, B. (1979). *The case for Black reparations*. New York, NY: Random House; Brophy, A. (2006). Reconsidering reparations. *Indiana Law Journal, 81*, 811–849; Coates, T. (2014, June). *The case for reparations*. Retrieved from http://www.theatlantic.com/magazine/archive/2014/06/the-case-for-reparations/361631/; Dyson, M. (2017). *Tears we cannot stop*. London, England: St. Martin's Press; King, D., & Page, J. (2018). Towards transitional justice? Black reparations and the end of mass incarceration. *Ethnic and Racial Studies, 41*, 739–758; Spann (2004), The dark side of *Grutter*; Yamamoto, E., Serrano, S., & Rodriguez, M. (2003). American racial justice on trial—again: African American reparations, human rights, and the war on terror. *Michigan Law Review, 101*, 1269–1337.

141. Some of the most thoughtful and well-intentioned proposals to educate judges and jurors about their own implicit racial biases and to perhaps provide prophylactic jury instructions serve as useful intermediate remedies. See, e.g., Bennett, M., & Plaut, V. (2018). Looking criminal and the presumption of dangerousness: Afrocentric facial features and criminal justice. *U.C. Davis Law Review, 51*, 745–803. In my own view, however, they ultimately do not go nearly far enough.

142. For similar systemic proposals, and reminders of the shortcomings of the remedies for racial injustice that have been implemented to date, see Butler, P. (2016). The system is working the way it is supposed to: The limits of criminal justice reform. *Georgetown Law Review, 104*, 1419–1478; Fiss, O. (2003). *A way out: America's ghettos and the legacy of racism*. Princeton, NJ: Princeton University Press; Kleven, T. (2009). Systemic classism, systemic racism: Are social and racial justice achievable in the United States? *Connecticut Public Interest Law Journal, 8*, 207–253; Lempert, R. (2010). A personal odyssey toward a theme: Race and equality in the United States: 1948–2009. *Law and Society Review, 44*, 431–462; Wilson, W. (1987). *The truly disadvantaged: Race, the underclass, and public policy*. Chicago, IL: University of Chicago Press; and Yamamoto, Serrano, & Rodriguez (2003), American racial justice on trial—again.

143. Sharkey, P. (2018). *Uneasy peace: The great crime decline, the renewal of city life, and the next war on violence*. New York, NY: W. W. Norton, p. 183.

144. Roberts (2004), The social and moral cost of mass incarceration in African American communities, pp. 1300–1301.

Afterword

I began this book by describing the striking commonalities that I observed in the social histories of a group of prisoners on San Quentin's death row, persons whom I had interviewed about the lives they lived before being sentenced to death. It was decades ago when I made those first visits as a beginning psychology professor interested in crime and punishment. My involvement in death penalty cases grew significantly over the years, as trying to understand the roots of serious violent crime became a much larger part of my professional life. It led me to work in some capacity on well over a hundred such cases since then and facilitated countless more interviews with persons accused or convicted of capital crimes—just like the ones I had conducted in those early years before so much was understood about the social historical and contextual roots of criminal behavior.

Years working on capital cases also provided me with opportunities to interview many other persons intimately familiar with the defendants' lives—parents, siblings, friends, neighbors, teachers, mental health counselors, and criminal justice system employees—who shared invaluable personal knowledge about the often traumatic past experiences many of the defendants had undergone growing up. And it allowed me to pore through hundreds and sometimes thousands of pages of official documents from schools, hospitals, and other institutions that served as partial, yet contemporaneous chronicles of the path of each defendant's life.

http://dx.doi.org/10.1037/0000172-012
Criminality in Context: The Psychological Foundations of Criminal Justice Reform,
by C. Haney

Over the 40 years that have passed since that initial set of interviews at San Quentin, the tentative conclusions that I reached then have been repeatedly corroborated, so much so that, although each case and life are unique and impossible to know beforehand, it is possible to talk about a kind of "sociohistorical profile" that characterizes the life stories of most of the persons who have committed the most serious violent crimes in our society.[1] Over this same period, numerous other scholars and researchers extensively documented the powerful role played by traumatic childhood experiences and other social historical events, as well as the myriad ways that immediate situational or contextual factors contribute to criminal behavior. The psychological forces that influence, encourage, provoke, and provide opportunities for criminal behavior are generated inside the inequity-ridden social contexts in which much crime occurs rather than in the allegedly innate deficits or willfully faulty choice-making of its perpetrators. These insights have profoundly important implications for the future shape of a rational and just overall strategy of crime control.

Unfortunately, over that same 40-year period, the nation also lived through an unprecedented era of mass incarceration, one in which criminal defendants were stereotypically dehumanized, derogated, and demonized as never before. An especially vitriolic form of the crime master narrative helped to drive much of the process by which historically unheard of levels of incarceration were reached, and the United States became the world's unquestioned leader in the rate at which it imprisoned its citizens. Ironically, then, much of the psychological and criminological research reviewed in the preceding chapters—establishing a more enlightened and empirically valid understanding of criminal behavior—was conducted during the same "mean season" of corrections, the most aggressive and sustained "law and order" period in our nation's history. This historical accident helps to define the parameters of our present paradox and dilemma: how to close the enormous gap that exists between what we now know about crime and what we continue to do about it? Some way must be found to break through this irrational block against creating and implementing policies based on genuine knowledge, ones that are more humane, just, effective, and healing. Deconstructing the anachronistic crime master narrative and its related, harshly punitive doctrines is an important first step in this process.

I also spent a fair amount of time over these same years speaking with crime survivors and listening to and reading their testimony about the impact of crime in their lives and the contexts in which it occurred. I continue to believe that the greatest contribution that the criminal justice system can make to them is to not only provide a full panoply of services designed to facilitate their healing (something the present system too often fails to do) but also to devise more effective crime control policies and programs to ensure that there are fewer persons who experience this kind of trauma in the future. Applying insights into the social contextual nature of criminal behavior and implementing the kind of programs and policies of criminal justice reform

I have advocated throughout are not only compatible with but essential to these goals.

In fact, we may have finally arrived at a critical juncture in the history of American criminal justice system when the excesses of its recent past can be meaningfully discussed and effectively remedied. Many diverse and previously opposed political constituencies and interest groups seem aligned and ready to undertake exactly this task. Yet, as law professor Susan Herman has correctly noted, although the current movement to radically reform the criminal justice system in the United States has generated much enthusiasm and offers much promise, it remains "improvisational" and "undertheorized."[2] My goal in this book has been to contribute at least some of the empirical and theoretical grounding that is needed to bring about fundamental, lasting criminal justice reform on a scale that is commensurate in scope with the magnitude of injustices the current system has inflicted and the cruelty with which it has often operated. I believe that the terms of this debate must be fundamentally reframed around thinking differently about the causes of crime and the people who have committed it. Rather than merely limiting the degree to which the criminal justice system debases and dehumanizes persons who break the law, we can implement a new vision, exploring whether and how individuals, groups, and communities can be lifted up and empowered to break criminogenic cycles.

The use of a more nuanced and ultimately more valid model of social behavior should serve to moderate unequivocally all-or-nothing harsh judgments that our criminal justice system has become accustomed to making. We now know that exposure to damaging risk factors, traumatic events, and harsh circumstances can powerfully shape and direct a person's life course. Those trajectories are often determined by external forces and contingencies over which individuals have little or no control, especially in early developmental stages when the life-altering effects are greatest. In much the same way, people's capacity and willingness to strive to "do the right thing" also has an externally determined component that is unchosen. This should also serve as a humbling reminder that persons who have led law-abiding, successful lives may owe at least some of their achievements to good fortune as well as their noble or wise choices.

Precisely because the model that I have presented in the preceding chapters demonstrates the ways in which many persons who have broken the law have reacted to the legacies of past experiences over which they have had little or no control, it serves as the basis for an uncomfortable but overdue conversation about some of the moral limits of punishment. It forces us to ask how much pain a society can or should be authorized to inflict in response to individual wrongdoing, once it has relinquished the fiction of equally autonomous, unencumbered free choice. I have argued that this new knowledge creates an ethical obligation to explore alternatives that are more consistent with what is known about the social historical and contextual causes of crime.

To be sure, "mere" exposure to a single risk factor—even an especially potent one such as poverty or racism—or to several childhood risks or traumas—no matter how painful—does not necessarily, irreparably, or insurmountably predispose a child to a life of adult crime and violence. Instead, the model I have presented focuses on the nature and severity of the risks and traumas, the age and duration of the exposure, the additive combination and interactive effect of multiple risks, vulnerabilities, and protective factors that all combine over a life course. And, as I noted in an earlier chapter, it is important to acknowledge that there is virtually always a powerful situational component to criminal wrongdoing and violent encounters that helps determine whether, when, and how crime and aggression are manifested. Factors such as the availability of lethal weapons also play key roles in distinguishing deadly aggression from less tragic manifestations of anger and impulsivity.

As research and writing about capital cases have shown, the most serious forms of violent crimes are often committed by persons who are outliers on a continuum of exposure to multiple risk factors and traumas.[3] The extreme adaptations many have made to the cumulative trauma in their lives underscore the toll that experiencing so many destructive experiences can take, collectively precluding meaningful (let alone truly "free") choice and the opportunity to fully overcome the legacy of their troubled past. Multiple risk factors are typically required to produce deeply criminogenic life paths, and their effects are frequently amplified by the harmful influence of failing institutions that were supposed to ameliorate rather than exacerbate these problematic behaviors. And even that—the accumulated consequence of multiple risk factors—is often not enough. In addition, crime is often precipitated by an additional set of more immediate conditions, ranging from neighborhood disadvantage to mounting microaggressions in day-to-day interactions. Sadly, we now know that risk factors have the perverse capacity to both increase the probability that persons will be exposed to precipitating criminogenic conditions later in life and that, if and when they are, to limit or compromise their ability to extricate themselves or choose noncriminal alternatives.

It is also important to acknowledge something that is easily lost sight of in a book written primarily about the negative forces and problematic influences that can so drastically compromise a life course—namely, that all of us are much more than the sum total of the risk factors to which we have been exposed. Even the tragic social histories of the capital defendants whose lives I studied consisted of much more than stories of unmitigated failure and defeat. Virtually all of the protagonists at the center of these stories strove and fought back and struggled and resisted against ultimately insurmountable odds, however frequently unjust and undeserved those bad odds were. Like so many other criminal defendants, their lives were filled with just-missed opportunities, treatment plans that were carefully developed but then never followed, interventions that went awry or were prematurely discontinued, second chances that never quite materialized and, yes, sometimes ill-advised decisions to travel paths that seemed promising or even necessary at the time but that led to unanticipated tragic ends. The social histories of people who have engaged in serious criminal behavior are less stories of a lack of resilience or talent (both of which many of them possess in abundance) and more of a dearth of opportunities, little or no recognition of the things they had to offer, and few, if any, pathways with which to demonstrate and be rewarded for their positive qualities. They are also often stories of maturation and positive change much later in life, if and when they were given the chance to live under fundamentally different circumstances.

Civil rights attorney and criminal justice reformer Bryan Stevenson wisely observed that people should not be judged only by the worst things they have ever done in their lives.[4] Even in the cases of persons who have committed the worst transgressions, there is *always* much more to them, no matter the crime, that reminds us of the richness of the human condition, the complexity and the astonishing range of human capacities, and the potential for redemption. Much of this book has been intended to make a companion point—not only should people never be judged merely by the worst things they have ever done but also that even those "worst things" come with a history and context that help to explain them and should provide nuance to the way our society judges them.

I have tried to emphasize and make clear that the criminogenic traumas and the mistreatment to which disadvantaged children are disproportionately exposed are the consequences of social and economic deprivation, racial inequality, and other forms of structural dysfunction. They are not the products of having been "born bad," raised by parents who were themselves inherently defective and pathological, or suffering from alleged cultural deficits in the groups or communities from which they have come. Continuing to ignore the real source of these risks and traumas ensures that there will be young people in future generations who will grow up still hurting from the victimization inflicted upon them as children, many lacking any sense of their own value. Some of these children will be angry when they become young adults, some will be damaged by the destructive experiences to which they were subjected, and some will model and replicate this destructiveness in their own behavior. None of this means that they cannot overcome their past. The fact is that a great many of them do. But all too often they beat the odds despite what our society has done to them in the name of helping. And the sad truth is that some of them simply cannot overcome the life-altering effects of these awful earlier experiences without the caring assistance that we still too often fail to provide.

These new perspectives on human behavior underscore the wrongheadedness of our excessive dependence on imprisonment and reveal it to be a brutally anachronistic policy. Its continued overuse in the opening decades of the 21st century represents a failure of political courage, an unwillingness to confront the real causes of crime, and a shortage of humane concern by one segment of society for the plight of another—"other people's children" grown to adulthood. The massive expansion of the prison system left terribly destructive consequences in its wake, and criminal justice reformers now face the daunting task of repairing damaged communities and helping the persons most affected to heal. Of course, even a criminal justice system that operates with perfect fairness and complete efficiency can do little more than carefully pick up the pieces of social dysfunction and attempt to patch together the shattered lives of the social casualties produced by much larger forces that operate outside the system itself. This challenging fact of life—that genuine long-term crime reduction will require broad-based contextual and structural change—tests our commitment to a goal that has preoccupied citizens and politicians alike for generations. In short, we must decide whether we are more committed as a nation to justly and effectively addressing the real causes of crime and injustice or to preserving status quo views that misleadingly presume unencumbered free choice, focus narrowly on individual responsibility to the exclusion of all else, and continue to enforce the extremely punitive models of legal culpability that they imply.

I am genuinely hopeful that we have finally arrived at the moment in our nation's history when criminal justice programs and policies will no longer be premised on the anachronistic set of individualistic assumptions at the heart of the crime master narrative, especially in light of what is increasingly recognized as the flawed and outmoded psychology on which they are based. It seems reasonable to hope and even to expect that the gap between what we now know about the causes of crime and the outdated crime control policies we have continued to pursue will finally be narrowed and closed. If so, we can begin to create a system of not just criminal but social justice that is truly worthy of the name.

NOTES

1. See, e.g., Haney, C. (1997). Psychological secrecy and the death penalty: Observations on "the mere extinguishment of life." *Studies in Law, Politics, and Society, 16,* 3–69; and Haney, C. (2009). On mitigation as counter-narrative: A case study of the hidden context of prison violence. *University of Missouri-Kansas City Law Review, 77,* 911–946.
2. Herman, S. N. (2018). Getting there: On strategies for implementing criminal justice reform. *Berkeley Journal of Criminal Law, 23,* 32–72. http://dx.doi.org/10.15779/Z389882N0J
3. See, e.g., Haney, C. (1995). Social context of capital murder: Social histories and the logic of capital mitigation. *Santa Clara Law Review, 35,* 547–609; and Lisak, D., & Beszterczey, S. (2007). The cycle of violence: The life histories of 43 death row inmates. *Psychology of Men & Masculinities, 8,* 118–128. http://dx.doi.org/10.1037/1524-9220.8.2.118
4. Stevenson, B. (2014). *Just mercy: A story of justice and redemption.* New York, NY: Spiegel & Grau, p. 17.

INDEX

S

ABOUT THE AUTHOR

Craig Haney, JD, PhD, is one of the nation's most highly regarded psycholegal scholars and sought-after experts, whose research, writing, and testimony have helped to transform many aspects of the criminal justice system. Since serving as one of the principal researchers on the Stanford Prison Experiment while still in graduate school, Haney has been a distinguished researcher who, among other things, served on a National Academy of Sciences committee studying the causes and consequences of mass incarceration and been awarded a UC Presidential Chair. He has worked for decades at the front lines of the American criminal justice system—including serving as an invited witness before the U.S. Senate and having his research and testimony cited by the U.S. Supreme Court. He brings to bear the rare voice and perspective of someone who has not only mastered the theory and data of crime and punishment but also seen firsthand how the forces of social and economic injustice operate to produce crime in our society and how often the criminal justice system acts to worsen rather than alleviate these problems.